MW01152421

THE
MOA

For a free color catalog describing Gareth Stevens Publishing's list of high-quality
books and multimedia programs, call 1-800-542-2595 (USA) or 1-800-461-9120 (Canada).
Gareth Stevens Publishing's Fax: (414) 225-0377.
See our catalog, too, on the World Wide Web: http://gsinc.com

Library of Congress Cataloging-in-Publication Data

Green, Tamara, 1945-
    The moa / by Tamara Green ; illustrated by Tony Gibbons.
        p. cm. — (The extinct species collection)
    Includes index.
    Summary: Describes what is known of the history and habits
of the large extinct bird of New Zealand.
    ISBN 0-8368-1592-0 (lib. bdg.)
    1. Moas—Juvenile literature. [1. Moas. 2. Birds. 3. Extinct
animals.] I. Gibbons, Tony, ill. II. Title. III. Series.
QE872.D5G74   1996
568'.5—dc20   96-5178

First published in North America in 1996 by
Gareth Stevens Publishing
1555 North RiverCenter Drive, Suite 201
Milwaukee, Wisconsin 53212 USA

This U.S. edition © 1996 by Gareth Stevens, Inc. Created with original © 1995 by
Quartz Editorial Services, 112 Station Road, Edgware HA8 7AQ U.K.

Additional artwork by Clare Heronneau

U.S. editors: Barbara J. Behm, Mary Dykstra

Printed in Mexico

1 2 3 4 5 6 7 8 9 99 98 97 96

THE
MOA

Tamara Green
Illustrated by Tony Gibbons

Gareth Stevens Publishing
MILWAUKEE

Contents

Meet the moa

People today will never meet a **moa** because, unfortunately, this bird is extinct. Nevertheless, the **moa** remains one of the great curiosities of the animal kingdom.

The **moa** was an unusual-looking creature. But what have scientists been able to discover about its behavior? In which part of the world did it live? And could any of these birds actually have survived into fairly recent times?

In the 1870s, when the **moa** was thought to already be extinct, some fresh, mysterious, three-toed **moa**-like footprints were found. Did a few **moas** still exist, or were the prints from some other creature? Was someone playing a trick? Read on for facts about the **moa**, possibly the tallest of all birds ever to have lived on the planet.

Spectacular species

Does the **moa** pictured here look like any other creature? It resembles today's African ostrich, but the **moa** was much taller. Curiously, the **moa**'s remains have been found only on the islands that make up New Zealand.

Moas normally ranged in height from 3-10 feet (1-3 meters). Some were as tall as 12 feet (3.6 m). They could grow twice as tall as an average man! Their legs were long and slender, and their necks were very snake-like. Their pointed beaks curved downward.

Although **moas** looked like ostriches, which are fast runners, they were probably not very athletic. In fact, scientists believe **moas** moved very slowly due to their heavy leg bones.

The bones of an ostrich are light in weight, allowing the ostrich to move quickly. It's hardly surprising, then, that the **moa** — although a bird — could not fly. The **moa**'s bones weighed too much to permit easy movement.

In addition, and most unusual for birds, **moas** had no trace of wings.

The **moa**'s head was very small for its body size. According to descriptions passed down by the natives of New Zealand, the Maori people, some **moas** had brightly colored necks with a crest on their heads. Some remains — but not all — show areas in the skull where a crest may have grown.

Perhaps these crests were only features of certain types of **moas**, or of only males or females, since they did not appear on all the birds. The illustrations in this book feature some **moas** with crests and some without.

Moas were mainly herbivores. They usually ate plants but did eat some insects. Their strong claws must have been ideal for digging nutritional roots out of the soil. The **moa**'s sharp beak was also well suited for snapping at grubs, as well as for snipping off leaves and fresh plant shoots.

Owen's great discovery

A British natural history expert, Sir Richard Owen, was intrigued by the idea of a mysterious, large, flightless bird that inhabited only New Zealand.

He had been given a single fragment of bone in 1839 that seemed to be from a bird's leg. A man by the name of Dr. Rule, who was in possession of the bone, thought it came from a large eagle. But Owen thought otherwise. He was convinced that it belonged to a bird that could not fly. Unlike an eagle's leg bone, which is filled with air, this bone was solid.

Dr. Rule first offered the piece of bone to a museum for a modest price.

The staff at the museum, however, did not want it. They were not interested in something as ordinary as an eagle's bone. In the end, a private collector purchased the leg bone from Dr. Rule and donated it to the British Museum in London, England.

8

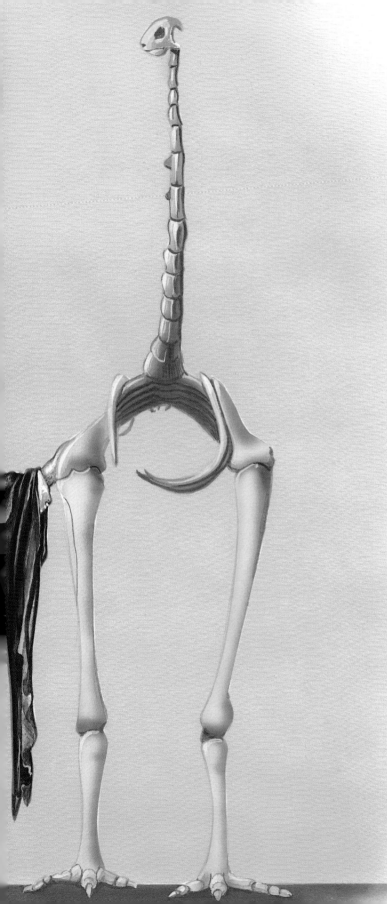

Much of the public thought Owen was a very odd man to reach his conclusion from such a small piece of bone. But soon, as further skeletal remains were brought to Britain from New Zealand, he was proved right.

Owen's discovery aroused a great deal of interest in the bird. People wondered if any surviving **moas** would ever be found. There were many tales of supposed sightings, but none produced evidence of a living **moa**. Before long, scientists were even squabbling over who had first identified the **moa**.

This illustration shows Owen standing next to a **moa** skeleton. The original piece of leg bone was only 6 inches (15 centimeters) long. Owen was quite a thorough detective to come to his conclusion from such a small clue!

Fathers of the moa

A New Zealand missionary and printer, the Reverend William Colenso, heard of Owen's discovery. He and two friends began their search of the landscape to find this strange bird. Colenso was the first to actually call the bird *moa*. He gave it this name because of the way the natives said the word *more* when they brought him more and more bones.

Determined to beat Owen in the search for further knowledge about the species, Colenso even went so far as to call himself "father of the **moa**."

Colenso sent his large collection of bones, like those shown here, to England for examination. But he was unlucky, for scientists there passed them on to Richard Owen for study.

Colenso was not the only one to take credit for **moa** discoveries. A traveling merchant, Joel Polack, also claimed to have discovered a great deal of information about the **moa**. Soon, there were others arguing about who had contributed most to the study of this large, extinct bird.

11

A last

In 1878, a newspaper called the *Otago Witness* told of the sighting of an extremely large and rather odd bird in a remote area of the district of Waiau, on the South Island of New Zealand.

According to the report, widely believed at the time, the huge, flightless bird was startled by a shepherd and his barking dog. At first, the bird began to run away. But it suddenly turned on the dog, which backed off. The strange bird then stood rooted to the spot for about ten minutes, bending its long neck up and down and from side to side. It looked like an angry swan in a defensive posture.

The report also stated that sizable footprints, seemingly those of a large bird, had frequently been found in the area. Was it possible that some **moas** had survived to the late 1800s in this remote area?

survivor?

Geographical mystery

New Zealand lies in the southern Pacific Ocean. This country consists of two main islands — North Island and South Island. The two are separated by a stretch of water called the Cook Strait, named after explorer Captain James Cook.

About 130 million years ago, the two main islands that now form New Zealand broke off from a much larger landmass, known as Gondwanaland. This was during the time of the dinosaurs, long before humans existed. At that time, New Zealand, as it is known today, was cut off by sea from the rest of the world.

So how did the **moa** get there?

New Zealand seems to be the only part of the globe where the **moa** lived. Could it be that these birds were already living there when the land split off and formed the two islands? This is a question that scientists have been unable to answer so far.

When explorers first reached the islands, they found mostly bird life. The only land mammals were small creatures like bats and rats. There were no large carnivores, such as lions, tigers, or wolves.

Some scientists wonder if, at one time, the **moa** could fly.

But because there were no large predators on the island, perhaps the **moa** did not need to fly to escape — and gradually lost the ability. Why **moas** were so common in New Zealand, and mammals were not,

also remains a mystery. **Moas** probably survived for a very long time, however, because they were not threatened by predators — that is, until humans arrived.

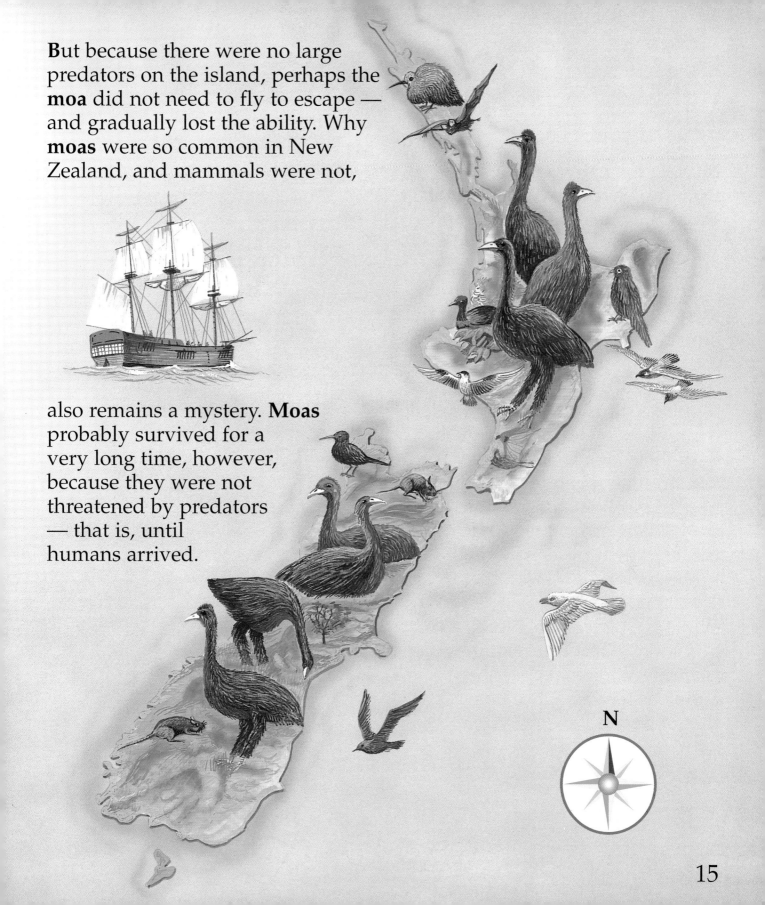

N

Tales about

Maoris, the natives of New Zealand, have a wealth of stories about the **moa**. In the nineteenth century, for example, they said **moas** were being captured by people. If the information is true, then **moas** did indeed live into the nineteenth century.

According to these accounts, the flightless birds would try to defend themselves by kicking furiously with their long legs. But they were not strong enough to survive the hunt. After being driven into pits, the birds were speared to death. It is said their nests were frequently robbed, too.

William Colenso, the New Zealand missionary, also heard strange Maori legends that described a **moa** as having a face like that of a man.

the moa

One story states that a particular **moa** survived on just air. It did not need food, and it lived in a cave on a mountainside.

This description, of course, sounds like pure fiction. But, bizarre myths are often woven around creatures that have become extinct.

There is also a legend that a **moa** greeted Captain Cook's ship *Endeavour* when it arrived at New Zealand in 1769, as shown here.

If so, the **moa** must have been quite startled by the sight of this huge ocean vessel. By all accounts, it quickly ran off before the crew had time to land.

Again, there is no real evidence to support this story. Probably only certain legends have some basis in fact.

17

Nesting

Not much is known about how the **moa** nested and cared for its young. Experts, however, have been able to make some intelligent guesses.

Scientists have found some intact **moa** eggs. They were about four times the size of an ordinary chicken egg, and up to 10 inches (25 cm) long. The shell was thin and pale greenish cream in color.

Unable to fly, **moas** must have nested on the ground. They probably looked for isolated places in which to nest. There, the nests would be safe from rats or lizards that were hungry for **moa** flesh or eggs.

Moas probably did not lay many eggs at a time. Like ostriches, **moas** may have scooped out a hole in the ground in which to lay their eggs. The male **moas** would bring food to the nesting females.

18

habits

Today's male ostriches have the job of incubating the eggs that have been laid by the female. Male and female **moas** may have shared parenting, too.

They, too, then paired off, mated, and produced eggs. During the

Once the **moa** eggs had hatched, the females probably fed the chicks for a while, until they were able to fend for themselves. The newborn **moas** — which were wingless and flightless — probably stayed close to their parents for quite a time.

time with their parents, the young would learn, by watching the adults, how to find food and defend themselves with their feet.

How the moa

No one is sure when or why the **moa** finally became extinct. A number of theories have been put forward by experts who have studied the remains of this bird. Together, these theories may explain why the moa disappeared from the face of the planet.

Some scientists think changes in the climate may have had a great part to play in the **moa**'s extinction. **Moas** may not have liked wet weather. They may also have preferred grasslands to the forests that developed due to an increase in rainfall.

was lost

Serious flooding after the last Ice Age may have reduced the **moa** population, as well.

New Zealand has a history of violent volcanic activity, too. Eruptions of boiling mud and cinders may have made the environment unsuitable at times for the **moa**.

Whole flocks of them may have been wiped out by the volcanic debris. It is also possible **moas** died of fright and shock.

But then came humans. By the time Polynesian invaders reached the shores of New Zealand centuries ago, the **moa** population had probably already severely declined. Nevertheless, there were probably enough **moas** surviving to provide these settlers — who were cannibals at the time — with meal after meal.

The Maoris, many scientists believe, probably hunted the **moa** to final extinction during the nineteenth century. They even coined the phrase, "we are lost as the **moa** is lost." They use the phrase during times of war and illness.

Moa data

There were several types of **moas** — perhaps more than twenty. The **slender moa**, for instance, was a particularly slim species, as its name suggests. Known in Latin as *Dinornistorosus* (<u>DINE</u>-OR-NIS-<u>TOR</u>-OH-SUS), it was large but by no means was the biggest of the **moas**.

The *Euryapteryx gravis* (<u>YURE</u>-EE-<u>APT</u>-ER-ICKS <u>GRAH</u>-VIS), or **burly lesser moa**, had a more rounded, wider beak than most others. It may have been the tallest and bulkiest of all. Bones from this **moa** have been widely found on both the North and South Islands of New Zealand. Scientists think it may have lived in flocks, unlike most **moas**. Other types of **moas** include the **heavy lesser moa**, the **robust green moa**, the **turkey-like lesser moa**, the **pygmy lesser moa**, and the **crane-like lesser moa**. Two types are shown *at left*. All were similar looking.

Good digestion

Scientists have found the remains of seeds, twigs, and grasses in the stomach region of a **moa** skeleton found on the South Island of New Zealand. In the stomach cavity, too, were a number of stones, known as *gastroliths*. These were swallowed by the birds to help grind food.

Small head, long neck

It is not hard to imagine how the **moa** used its long curving neck. Lengthy and *S*-shaped, its neck probably bent very easily. This type of neck would have been helpful for eating vegetation overhead as well as near the ground.

The **moa**'s head, meanwhile, was very small, suggesting the **moa** probably had a tiny brain.

Broad feet, long legs

As you have seen throughout this book, **moas** had wide feet at the end of remarkably long legs. In fact, it was a single piece of leg bone from a **moa** that first caught the attention of Sir Richard Owen in 1839.

Glossary

Cook, Captain James — the British sea captain (1728-1779) who was the first explorer to arrive in New Zealand and Australia.

Endeavour — the ship on which Captain James Cook made his first journey to the Pacific.

gastroliths — stones that some animals swallow to aid digestion.

Gondwanaland — the huge landmass from which Africa, South America, Australia, Antarctica, and India split off during the Jurassic Period — between 190 and 135 million years ago.

Maoris — the people who originally inhabited New Zealand.

New Zealand — the country in the southern Pacific Ocean that consists of two islands — North Island and South Island.

ostrich — the largest living bird of today's world. It has a long neck and does not fly. It lives in Africa, south of the Sahara Desert.

Polynesia — the name given to many of the islands of the central Pacific Ocean.

Index

The Billboard Book

ONE-HIT Wonders

WAYNE JANCIK

BILLBOARD BOOKS
An imprint of Watson-Guptill Publications/New York

To my wife Charlene
and my son Matthew,
for their love and support.

Edited by Fred Weiler
Assistant Editor: Stephen Kelly
Senior Editor: Tad Lathrop
Book Design: Bob Fillie
Jacket Illustration: Irving Freeman
Production Manager: Ellen Greene

First published 1990 by Billboard Books, an imprint of
Watson-Guptill Publications, a division of BPI Communications, Inc. 1515 Broadway, New York, NY 10036.

Library of Congress Cataloging-in-Publication Data
Jancik, Wayne.
    The Billboard book of one-hit wonders / by Wayne Jancik.
      p. cm.
    ISBN 0-8230-7530-3
    1. Musicians—Biography.   2. Popular music—United
States—History and criticism. I. Title.
ML394.J36   1990
782.42166'0922—dc20
[B]   90-884
                                       CIP
                                       MN

Manufactured in the United States of America
First Printing, 1990

1 2 3 4 5 6 7 8 9 / 95 94 93 92 91 90

Acknowledgments

This book was made possible by the many participants who gave me their time, their stories, their insights, written material, and photos. I am, of course, indebted to everyone I spoke with, but the following individuals were especially helpful: Carl Perkins, Frank Pizani of the Highlights, George Lanuis of the Crescendos, Johnny Otis, Frankie Ford, Phil Phillips, Bo Diddley, Dr. Walter Nadel of the Islanders, Jimmy Wisner (a.k.a. Kokomo), Sylvester Potts of the Contours, Johnny Thunder, Johnny Cymbal (a.k.a. Derek), P.F. Sloan, Roy Hensley of the Castaways, Bob Kuban, John McElrath of the Swingin' Medallions, Chip Taylor, Jim Post of Friend & Lover, René Ornalas (of René & René), Denny Craswell of the Castaways and Crow, Tommy James, Pepe Cardona of Alive and Kicking, Sammi Smith, Mike Brewer & Tom Shipley, Rupert Holmes, Dr. John, Dan McCafferty of Nazareth, Phil Lynott of Thin Lizzy, and T.C. Furlong of the Jump 'n the Saddle Band.

My thanks also to the band of rock and roll researchers who responded generously to my requests for their help. My good friend Bob Pruter, the R & B editor for *Goldmine* magazine, went well beyond the call of duty in tracking down countless articles and historical scraps. Skip Rose, a collector of nearly every rock and roll photo known to man, provided me with names, places, and rare photographs. Thanks to Ed Salamon, president of Uni-Star Communications, for his many leads and his enthusiasm; Peter Grendysa for his article clippings and feedback on the manuscript; Colin Escott for his input; Jerry Osborne, editor of *DISCoveries* and the creator of those priceless record-collecting guides; and Jeff Tamarkin, *Goldmine*'s rock editor.

The following books were invaluable for double-checking facts and offering details: Joel Whitburn's *Top Pop Singles 1955-1986* and *Top R & B Singles 1942-1988*; Fred Bronson's *The Billboard Book of Number One Hits*; Barry Lazell's *Rock Movers & Shakers*; Jon Pareles and Patti Romanowski's *The Rolling Stone Encyclopedia of Rock & Roll*; Richard Aquila's *That Old Time Rock & Roll*; and Terry Hounsome's *Rock Record*.

Thanks to the senior editor of Billboard Books, Tad Lathrop, whose guiding hand saved this project from oblivion; and thanks to associate editor Fred Weiler for his help in assembling all this information, shaping it, and reining in my "Wayne-isms."

I must not forget my dear friends, who have tolerated hours of my yapping about this project: Sam Mandel, Richard Schutz, Roy Thedford, Bill Kincaid, Elvis Paisley, and Commander Pickle. These behind-the-scenes movers were also of great help: Paul Mahinney, *Recorder* editor Phil Schwartz, Jeff Hubbard at Associated Booking, Jack Baker of the Busters, Aaron Mintz at radio WHAI, Jerry Granahan, Ken Keene, Bobby Poe of the Chartbusters, Fred Masotti, Jerry Schollenberger, Paul Grenyo, and William Menor.

Finally, a loving thanks to my wife, Charlene, and my son, Matt, who have endured my absent-mindedness, my late evenings at the Macintosh, and the house-cluttering results of my vinyl addiction. Thanks, honey.

Contents

Foreword

They called it top 40 radio: a set playlist of 40 top hits plus a few extras and "up-and-comers," selected by a radio station committee of disc jockeys, music directors, and program directors. Their selections were based on surveys of best-selling records in the trade papers, local record stores, and the committee's own evaluation of some of the hundreds of new singles that came in every week. If this sounds like an unnecessarily restrictive system—and a lot of people thought so at the time—the truth of the matter is something else.

Top 40 radio was nothing like the formatted radio of today. Listeners accustomed to tuning their radios to different stations for "modern rock," "album rock," "adult contemporary," "new age," "country," "dance," or "black" music would be amazed to find all of those styles on one top 40 station in the '50s and '60s. The mix of music played on radio, and consequently purchased in the stores, represented every breed of singer and song imaginable. If it sounded good, it got airplay, and somebody went out and bought it. And that's exactly why the people in this book are in this book.

Why do we have hit records? What makes a hit record? How is it possible for an artist to be so very popular, but only once? Lots of good questions, but not so many good answers. The stories of these One-Hit Wonders provide the clues, although the mystery remains. The rise of top 40 radio offered a chance for many new artists and record companies to make hits, and those times were the most exciting in popular music.

The years during and immediately following the Second World War saw the emergence of a new phenomenon, the independent record label. Often operating on shoestring budgets in makeshift studios, these feisty entrepreneurs could react quickly to fads and trends, and turn out the records the public wanted. More often than not, these were songs and singers the major labels never bothered with in the first place. Rhythm & blues, the forerunner of rock and roll, developed during this period and spread across the country on independent labels.

Country music, too, moved into the spotlight after years on the sidelines.

Independent labels rose and fell swiftly, since few of them could survive any downturn in the industry, however minor. When one went bankrupt, it seemed that two others would spring up to take its place. There was money to be made in records. People had money to spend, and they flocked to packed movie houses, filled ballrooms when the big bands came to town, and bought millions of records. All the "indies," as they were called, put out the latest, the newest, the most radical sounds and styles on records. This was especially satisfying to teenagers, who were looking for something different and, hopefully, for records that would annoy their parents. But first, they had to know it was out there to buy.

The playlist of a typical top 40 station in late 1957 shows a refreshing diversity. Listen long enough and you would hear the Everly Brothers, Mario Lanza, Faron Young, Count Basie with Joe Williams; instrumentals by Bill Doggett, Pete Fountain, Bill Justis, and Hugo Winterhalter; Marty Robbins, Frank Sinatra, Fats Domino, Perez Prado, Eydie Gorme, Gene Vincent, and polkateer Will Glahe. All of these artists appeared alongside the usual gang of superstars—Elvis, Buddy Holly, Pat Boone, Johnny Mathis, and Ricky Nelson. With a chance at getting airplay and a million-seller, hundreds of small labels were dragging pompadoured, pouty would-be teen idols, black vocal groups, dirt-farming guitar pluckers, calypso singers, screaming rockers, and anybody who had ever appeared on TV or in a film into the studio.

Hits in the 1950's and 1960's meant singles—magical three-minute jewels that said and did it all. Radio and jukebox operators didn't want anything longer, for obvious reasons. If an artist had a few good hits, an album would be released compiling those hits with some "B" sides and previously unreleased tracks. This method kept production costs down. Usually only one session of four tracks would be cut on an unknown artist. If the first single broke out in a big way, another would be issued, and the artist would be brought in for a follow-up session. Sessions were limited to three hours—none of this taking two or three years to cut an album—and after three hours, you began paying overtime to the musicians.

When success could be achieved with a three-minute 45, there were great incentives for new labels to enter the market. Costs were minimal, the risks small, and the potential rewards astronomical. The recording studio frequently consisted of nothing more than a production booth at a local radio station. One microphone was all you needed in the pre-stereo days, and a two-track mono tape recorder was the usual standard of "hi-fi" excellence. Finding the talent was easy, too—budding rock and roll bands and vocal groups filled the waiting rooms and halls of office buildings which often contained a dozen or more record companies.

A typical record company was usually a rented room with a desk and chairs, and a filing cabinet full of standard recording and publishing contracts. Since a large number of the new artists wrote their own songs, it was customary for those songs to be published by the record company through a subsidiary. The company operators knew full well that in the long run, the song copyrights would be worth much more than a hit record. This little business tidbit was not passed on to the teenaged singing hopefuls, and some of the biggest names in early rock and rhythm & blues signed away all rights to their songs for $25 or $50.

Recording contracts were unblushingly slanted in the company's favor, too. A 3 or 4 percent royalty was promised on 80 or 90 percent of the records sold at retail, after deducting all taxes and packaging costs (the other 10 to 20 percent went directly to the label owner). Just in case that wasn't enough margin for the company, the singer also found such incidentals as "promotion costs," arranging, services of a music copyist, musician's fees, and studio costs, all deducted from his share of royalties. Promotion covered a lot of ground, the biggest chunk being the freebies given to disc jockeys, distributors, and record stores as an incentive to push the record. Therefore, the artist was actually paying for his own promotion.

A solo artist could expect to get 2 cents for every single sold, or about $20,000 for a million-seller, from which all those other expenses would be deducted. Each member of a quartet would get only one-quarter of that amount. Of course, if the artist had a manager, he'd get his 10 percent or more off the top. Some managers took 25 percent; Colonel Tom Parker, the manager of Elvis Presley, got 50 percent. Since the singer was charged recording costs for all the tracks cut, whether or not they were ever used on a record, it becomes clear why so many hit-record stars of the past complain that they never received any money from their big records. The wiser young generation of today goes into a recording company accompanied by accountants and lawyers.

Once the papers were signed, studio time was reserved. Rehearsals were done on the artist's own time; the artist was expected to come in and start recording with a minimum of (costly) delays. Sometimes the original songs needed the attention of an arranger, but even if they didn't, the singer/songwriter might find the record company owner's name next to his own as a co-writer when the record came out. This creative credit might have been earned by nothing more than telling the artist to say "eee" instead of "ahh" during the second chorus. Owners of independent record companies who did this regularly hid behind a variety of pseudonyms; one simply spelled his name backwards, another had the strange habit of using only women's names. A lot of mothers found their maiden names on rock records, too.

However they did it, the record companies did it for the songwriting royalties. A penny or half-cent per record doesn't seem like much, but added to the publishing royalties, it all adds up, and it was not subject to the horrendous deductions imposed on the artist's share.

Once the labels were printed and the records pressed up, promotion and distribution would begin. The major disc jockeys and radio stations received promo copies, distributors were lined up (frequently by giving them as many as 10 free copies out of every 100 they ordered), and the distributors got the records into the stores, where the kid with the dollar was waiting to buy them. The artist paid for the free copies, made personal appearances at sock hops and concerts for little or no money, and anxiously watched the pages of *Billboard* to see if he had a hit.

Some of the most poignant recollections to come out of interviews with yesterday's record stars are their memories of having a top 40 hit on the charts, and hearing their record on jukeboxes and car radios all across the country, while receiving royalty statements showing 200,000 copies sold, and a bill for studio costs instead of a check. If the disk got real hot, the record company might even take out a full page ad in *Billboard* proclaiming "a million copies shipped!" to spur on interest in the song.

So, what's the point? That one chart record isn't going to make the singer rich, but it *will* send him off on tours to places he never dreamed of working, and where some real money can be made. The hit will even bring him back into the studio to cut a follow-up release. If the record is too big for the indie label to handle (as was the case for many of the singles in this book), the masters will be leased or sold to a bigger label. Sometimes the artist went along, sometimes not. The master sale or lease didn't bring any money directly to the artist, but it did wonders for the owner of the masters.

One major figure in today's music industry was missing back in those days: the producer. At the smaller companies, the owner himself or herself was standing at the board behind the engineer (unless he or she also did the engineering), directing the proceedings in the studio. Many influential producers got their start this way, finding it more lucrative to cut some tracks and then simply market them directly to bigger labels, rather than going through the hassles of promotion and distribution themselves. The concept of the independent producer originated in the top 40 era.

Few record companies, large or small, will carry a non-productive artist on their roster for long. If the hits don't come, the artist goes. Almost every artist in this book got at least a second or third chance to make another hit. Some were fortunate enough to continue making good-selling, although non-hit, records for several years, and that was enough to keep them on the major labels. The indpendents, without a large roster to keep the hits coming, couldn't afford this luxury.

To date, no one has yet figured out how to make a sure-fire hit record. Maybe it would be easier to analyze what makes a flop. Even though each of the artists in this book has a different reason for not coming up with a second super hit, there seem to be a few common underlying factors at work. Artists are quick to blame the record company for failing to promote their follow-up platter. It is true that a small company, perhaps finding another big hit with another singer on its roster, simply concentrates its limited resources on the sure thing. All of the costs from the first hit have been recovered, with a good profit, besides.

Sometimes the reason can be found in the song material done by the One-Hit Wonder. A hit song from a movie or TV show is fine, once. But the public seems to want somebody different or new to do the next movie or show tune it buys. Songs based on the latest real or contrived dance craze do well, but only Chubby Checker, America's dancemaster, seems to have been able to hit with more than one of those.

Likewise the novelty and comedy records. It seems to be impossible for one artist to succeed with a whole string of these (sorry, "Weird Al" Yankovic). Another pitfall is having the follow-up record sound too much like the one that hit the top of the charts, even though the industry slavishly follows trends and believes wholeheartedly in sound-a-likes. Finally, a hit based on current events is self-limiting, unless the artist wants to build a career singing the pages of *Time* magazine.

Then there's the talent issue. While some of the people in this book probably didn't deserve to have even that one hit, the fact is that thousands of people thought otherwise at the time, and there's no point in discussing musical tastes. On the other hand, many of these people deserved to have a whole lot more success than they got. They were as good as, or better than, some of the icons of the pop music world, and that's one of the unfortunate enigmas of an industry that has to cater to a fickle public.

If the talent was there, what happened? Sometimes the artist is just too generic. How many white or black singing groups do we need if they all sound alike? How many lounge crooners can compete with Johnny Mathis? Does that rock band sound significantly different from any others, or is it just their makeup and costumes? Some of these hit "artists" didn't even really exist—acts that were little more than studio concoctions or a computer's bad dream. And then there are the crossover hits, one-time appearances by superstars from other genres such as country or soul. It's not too hard to cross over once, but doing it again and again means changing your style into something pop-friendly. Some of the people who tried that succeeded, while others lost their original fans and failed in pop, too.

The mathematically-inclined will detect that there are fewer and fewer One-Hit Wonders every year. Since formatted radio isn't playing anything except records that fit the format, and music videos cost tens of thousands of dollars to produce, major record companies seem to be taking fewer chances on anything too different or new. Nonetheless, the popular music business—despite periods of creative retrenchment—remains as volatile and exciting as ever. Behind every low-risk rehash of yesteryear's hit formula lies an undiscovered new talent ready to unleash fresh sounds and unique ideas. Among them are those who, like this book's One-Hit Wonders, will leave an indelible imprint on popular culture and taste success—perhaps only once—in the rarefied air of the Hot 100's upper reaches.

—PETER A. GRENDYSA

Introduction

A One-Hit Wonder is any recording act that placed only one 45 RPM single on *Billboard*'s top 40 chart. What types of artists are One-Hit Wonders? As you leaf through the entries, you'll find all kinds of performers—vocal groups, duos, singer/songwriters, comedians, jazz bands, and even symphony orchestras. Some of these recording artists seemed to come from out of nowhere; others had been toiling in the music business for years before their monster moment.

Omitted from consideration as a One-Hit Wonder is any one-off pairing—most commonly, a duet featuring two solo artists, like Barbra Streisand and Donna Summer. In such cases, when the individuals did not come together with the intention of forming an enduring "act," their lone hit does not count. Also omitted are artists that have a one-time hit under a "cosmetic" name change. For example, Harvey & The Moonglows had only one top 40 hit; but as the Moonglows, two previous records made the top 40, so Harvey & The Moonglows would not be considered a One-Hit Wonder.

So who does that leave? All "studio groups"—that is, non-touring pseudo-groups made up of session musicians, usually assembled by songwriters or producers to meet some musical need. The Pipkins, Edison Lighthouse, and the Cowboy Church Sunday School are examples of this type of artist. Also included are artists who use two different personae but are actually one and the same individual or group. For example, although Johnny Cymbal and Derek are the same person, both acts are in this book, because two separate recording entities were presented to radio listeners and record-buyers. Similarly, the Jayhawks and the Marathons are virtually identical groups in terms of the members, but both were considered by radio programmers and the public as distinct acts.

All of our rich heritage of One-Hit Wonders is here between the covers—all, that is, except those artists who do not meet one of two criteria.

First, *The Billboard Book of One-Hit Wonders* confines itself to the "rock and roll era," here defined as beginning on January 1, 1955. Second, a grace or "lag" period of five years was allotted to One-Hit Wonders up through December 31, 1984—after all, these acts could have a second scoring any day now. An additional consideration: due to limitations of space, only those records that peaked in the top 20 of the top 40 are covered in detail. The other 400-plus One-Hit Wonders—those whose singles appeared in the lower half of the top 40 (i.e. charted at positions #21-40)—are listed on page 410, and may be the subject of a second volume.

Billboard first published its "Music Popularity Chart" on July 20, 1940, and thus began reporting the best-selling records in America week by week. But it was never that simple: before long, the "international newsweekly of music and home entertainment" was publishing a variety of charts such as "Best Sellers in Stores," "Most Played in Juke Boxes," "Most Played by Jockeys," and "Honor Roll of Hits." Although a "Top 100" appeared as early as November 12, 1955, pop historians assert that up until August 4, 1958, the true test of a record's popularity was the "Best Sellers in Stores" list, because it was based on actual retail sales. In *Top Pop Singles 1955-1986*, Joel Whitburn integrates these competing charts to generate one chart position. Throughout the early part of this book, you'll see references to the Top 100; consider this shorthand for the record's chart number according to Whitburn's system.

On August 4, 1958, *Billboard* debuted its "Hot 100" chart. Since that time, the Hot 100 has been acclaimed as the definitive source for the weekly ratings of the nation's most popular records, and is the basis of the top 40 chart—quite simply, the top 40 chart represents the top 40 records of the Hot 100 chart.

A few stylistic notes: Throughout the book, you'll notice next to almost every record title a notation like (**#14, 1967**). This means that the single reached the #14 position on the top 40 chart in 1967. Two other charts are referred to in this book. A position on the R & B (Rhythm & Blues) chart is indicated by (**—/#14, 1967**), meaning the record made #14 on the R & B chart. For the C & W (Country & Western) chart, (**—/—/#14, 1967**) means that the record made #14 on the C & W chart. The R & B listings have appeared under a variety of names over the years, from "Hot R & B Sides" through "Best-Selling Rhythm & Blues Singles" to "Hot Black Singles." The country chart has evolved from "Most Played C & W by Jockeys" through "Hot C & W Sides" to "Hot Country Singles." The "top pop albums chart" occasionally mentioned refers to a listing of the best-selling 200 albums, currently known as "Top Pop Albums."

If both sides of a single charted (i.e. made the Hot 100), the year is given only for the first side. A double-sided hit would be shown like so: **"Silhouettes" (#20, 1957) b/w "Daddy Cool" (#4).**

All One-Hit Wonders are cross-referenced within the text in small capital letters, e.g. THE DUBS. If this reference occurs twice within the same entry, it appears in small caps only for its first mention.

The name of the artist at the head of each entry is the name that appears on the record label itself. Thus, although you might be familiar with the act as Scandal, the entry reads **Scandal featuring Patty Smyth** because that is how the group is credited on the label. The name of the songwriter, as it also appears on the record label itself, is shown in parentheses.

The sources of much of the quoted material include books, magazines, and newsletters. For some quotations, however, you will see the construction ". . . recalled in an exclusive interview." This indicates that I interviewed the person or persons speaking.

Welcome to the wild and wacky world of One-Hit Wonders!

The

Joan Weber
LET ME GO LOVER
(Jenny Lou Carson, Al Hill)
Columbia 40366
No. 1 *January 1, 1955*

"Joan Weber had a five-and-dime voice," Mitch Miller told *Circular*'s Harvey Geller. "She sounded like every girl you ever heard singin' behind the counter in a five-and-dime store."

Joan Weber was born in 1936, raised in Paulsboro, New Jersey, and married to a young bandleader. She was pregnant in 1954 when she hit the streets of New York to audition. She stumbled upon Eddie Joy, the right man with the right ideas—a manager who brought her around to music publishers in the famed Brill Building.

"She was a wide-eyed, virginal, vulnerable, 105-pound waif," CHARLES RANDOLPH GREAN, Weber's discoverer, recalled. One day, Ginny Gibson, one of Grean's most-used demo singers, was unavailable; Weber was. "Joan did a credible job on this song 'Marionette,' but it was no Grammy winner." Grean took the tape around to various labels and found Mitch Miller of Columbia Records most interested—not in "Marionette," but in that five-and-dime voice.

The producers of the long-running CBS program "Studio One" were planning a drama about shady activities in the record industry and needed a torchy song to provide some musical counterpoint. They approached Miller, who in turn approached Hill & Range Songs. Arnold Shaw, then general manager of the music publishing house, offered Miller a tune that had bombed a year earlier for Georgie Shaw, "Let Me Go, Devil." When Miller turned it down, Shaw had a team of house writers under the pseudonym "Al Hill" rewrite the country ode, eliminating references to lust for that demon rum. "I wanted to cut ["Lover"] with a voice nobody knew, so the audience wouldn't be distracted from the story line," Miller recalled. Before Joan's baby was due, the 18-year-old lass was in front of a microphone and Jimmy Carroll's Orchestra.

The big day arrived for the excited songstress and mother-to-be. On November 15, 1954, Joan's song appeared and reappeared six times in the "Studio One" presentation. The response was immediate: within two weeks, her first recording had sold half a million copies. Reportedly, this was the first time a song shot overnight into the nation's hit parade solely by means of a lone television plug. Despite successive cover versions of this lover's dirge by the well-established Teresa Brewer, Patti Page, and Sunny Gale, Joan's version outdistanced all the others, rocketed to the top, and held down *Billboard*'s sacred number-one position for four weeks.

On the same Monday that "Let Me Go Lover" hit number one, Joan's first-born arrived prematurely. The following Sunday, she sang on "The Ed Sullivan Show." Within a month, she was co-starring with Jack Carter at the Copacabana, reportedly for $10,000 a week. "It May Sound Silly" and "Gone" were issued; neither single charted, despite the promotion as well as the extensive diction and vocal classes that she took.

Eighteen months after her dizzying ride to the top, Joan's record contract was terminated and her marriage ended. She performed in nameless bars in Philadelphia, worked as a clerk in a public library in New Jersey, and, according to rumors at the time, she was confined to a state mental hospital. "Let Me Go Lover" appeared on several anthology LPs, and in 1969, Columbia mailed Ms. Weber a sizeable royalty check. It was returned, the envelope stamped "address unknown."

Joan Weber died on May 13, 1981.

Penguins
EARTH ANGEL (WILL YOU BE MINE)
(Curtis Williams)
DooTone 348
No. 8 *February 5, 1955*

True, Toronto's Crew-Cuts did create a Caucasian cover version (#3, 1955) and steal much of the initial action on the Penguins' "Earth Angel." But by now, all is nearly forgiven, and sales of the original rendering may well have exceeded the 10,000,000 mark. Recorded in eight or nine takes, amid the bicycle pumps and scrapwood in someone's backyard garage, "Earth Angel" has become one of the most cherished of all rock and roll records. The tune is also reportedly the very first R & B record to ever crack the nation's top 10 pop chart.

Lead singer Cleveland "Cleve" Duncan (b. July 23, 1935) and tenor Dexter Tisby formed the Penguins with bass Curtis Williams and baritone Bruce Tate in 1954. After much rehearsal, the quartet approached Dootsie Williams, owner of DooTone/Dooto Records, to record a song that Curtis had written, "Earth Angel."

"It's comical," Duncan told *Bim Bam Boom*'s Steve Flam and Sal Mondrone. "We couldn't pick out a name. One of the fellows just happened to be smoking a pack of Kools and we got to kidding each other about the picture of 'Willie the Penguin' on it, and that's how we came by the name." Before "Earth Angel," DooTone issued a pair of Penguin tracks, "Ain't No News Today" b/w "When I Am Gone." "It was really a demonstration record for someone else," Duncan explained. "Dootsie had the rights on it and when we did it, it was a demo."

"After 'Earth Angel' was released—I imagine that we had gotten somewhere within the top ten, and the group became in need of a small advance on royalties—Dootsie denied the group. Dootsie would not advance us any money whatsoever . . . not even $50."

Discouraged and angered, the Penguins sought out the help of Buck Ram, manager of their friends, the Platters. Buck signed on as their representative and negotiated a record-ing contract with Mercury for the Penguins; as part of the agreement, the then-unsuccessful Platters were tossed into the deal. In the interim, Dootsie issued two follow-ups ("Ookey Ook" and "Baby Let's Make Some Love") which both flopped. Bruce Tate left the group after being involved in an auto accident in which he struck a pedestrian; his replacement was Teddy Harper.

Mercury/Wing eventually issued eight disks by the group, but not one of these 45s nudged the nation's notice. Atlantic shipped one single by the Penguins (a cover of KEN COPELAND's "Pledge of Love") that proved fairly successful on the R & B charts. Thereafter, the classic bird group returned to Dootsie's DooTone/Dooto. After one single, Curtis Williams left, to be replaced by Randolph Jones. Dootsie issued two more 45s and an EP. The group broke up in 1963. Months later, Frank Zappa managed to coax Cleve back into the studios and produced Zappa's "Memories Of El Monte" and later "Heavenly Angel," both credited to the Penguins, for Original Sound.

Cleve did a one-off single with the Radiants; Harper, Jones, and Tisby later toured with Cornell Gunter's Coasters. According to Duncan, all of the original members of the Penguins "have given up entertaining all together."

DeJohn Sisters

(MY BABY DON'T LOVE ME) NO MORE

(Julie DeJohn, Dux DeJohn, Leo J. DeJohn)
Epic 9085
No. 6   *February 12, 1955*

Dux and Julie DeGiovanni worked behind the counter at Sears, Roebuck & Co. in Chester, Pennsylvania. The girls had dreams of things you don't see everyday, and dreams of things you just can't buy at Sears, Roebuck. From their mid-teens onward, they would get together in their spare time and sing. Mom and Dad had a drycleaning shop; they hoped the girls would come to their senses and join the family business.

In the mid-'50s, the Four Aces were the hometown heroes, but when Decca Record scouts heard the Aces and took the boys off to stardom, the Ukrainian Club—which the foursome had been using as their base of operations—needed a new attraction. Dux (b. Jan. 21, 1933) and Julie (b. Mar. 18, 1931)

Johnny Ace

approached the club, and much to their surprise, they were offered a slot there. Their name went up in lights, and Chester had a new group to cheer about. Representatives from Epic Records came sniffing about in search of another Four Aces-type grouping, and decided to give the gals from Sears a chance.

"(My Baby Don't Love Me) No More" made the Chester girls big stuff for a while. The song—with hiccups and all—went top 10 nationally. But nothing the Pennsylvania kids ever tried for Okeh, Sunbeam, Columbia, Capitol, or United Artists Records even again went top 40. Hopefully, "No More" brought the girls some of those dreams money can't buy. And hopefully, Dux and Julie got to taste some of that good money, because after "No More," there was no more.

Johnny Ace

PLEDGING MY LOVE

(Ferdinard Washington, Don Robey)
Duke 136
No. 17   *March 19, 1955*

Johnny Ace killed himself with a gun while playing Russian Roulette one month before the release of what would become his lone pop hit. He's been called rock and roll's first fatality, by some; others whisper of Johnny being the victim of some sinister plot. But all have called his passing an extreme tragedy.

Here was a singer who could mix blues and ballads with a profound sadness and in a manner unheard of, before and since. James Mattis, his manager, struggling to define Ace's unique talent, told *Whiskey, Women And . . .*: "He had that funny voice surrounded by soft purple sounds. Ah, [like] Nat Cole. It wasn't a style . . . it was something natural."

Johnny had spent two short but solid years atop *Billboard*'s R & B listings, with "My Song" (—/#1, 1952), "Cross My Heart" (—/#3, 1953), "The Clock" (—/#1, 1953), "Saving My Love For You" (—/#2, 1954), "Please Forgive Me" (—/#6, 1954), and "Never Let Me Go" (—/#9, 1954). Everything he recorded charted, and his following, through largely black, was becoming massive. White radio was discovering the Platters and Fats Domino, and no doubt would soon find Ace to be equally accessible.

But all that changed on Christmas Eve of 1954 at Houston's Civic Auditorium. It was just before midnight, and Ace had just finished his performance. An audience of 2,000-plus was still jumping and jiving when Johnny went backstage to celebrate with his band. B.B. King, Willie Mae "Big Mama" Thornton, and possibly a dozen others were in his dressing room when Johnny pulled out his recently-purchased gun, put it to his right temple . . . and pulled the trigger, once.

St. Clair Ace (a.k.a. Buddy Ace), John's younger brother and fellow Duke Recording artist, believes that his sib was murdered. "I don't want to mention names," he told *The Chicago Sun Times'* Dave Hoekstra, "because the guy might not be dead, but one of [the musicians] who played in his band told me the murder wasn't like they said it was. Taxes had Don Robey [then-owner of Duke Records] tied up. I was told he was putting a lot of trips [for Ace] down for places that he never played."

John's sister, Norma Williams, now a secretary at a Memphis school, disputes this appraisal. "We thought about foul play until we talked to [Johnny's girlfriend]," Ms. Williams told Hoekstra. "She told us she was seated in Johnny's lap when he got the gun and she put her temple against his head. The bullet went in one side of his temple, but didn't come through.

"She told us they had been doing this on the road show. During intermission, they would go back in the dressing room and each person took turns with the gun. She didn't say how many people had pulled the trigger, but they certainly had been engaged in the game before it got to Johnny."

Johnny Ace was born John Marshall Alexander in Memphis on June 9, 1929. After completing some years at Booker T. Washington High, he enlisted in the Navy. During his absence, Johnny's mom had purchased a piano and after his discharge in 1947, he took a serious interest in the sounds that box could make. By 1949, he was playing well enough to win a slot with Adolph Duncan's band (a unit which evolved into the Beale Streeters, with sometime members that included Bobby "Blue" Bland, Earl Forrest, Roscoe Gordon, and B.B. King) and later, a job with B.B. King's group.

When B.B. hit paydirt and the road in 1951 with his "3 O'Clock Blues," Johnny auditioned for a position as a studio pianist at Memphis' radio WDIA. One of the executives at the station, David James Mattis, noticed the kid and his smooth style, and asked him to work as an accompanist on some sessions he had planned. Mattis had formed Duke Records largely to show off the talents of another WDIA staple, Roscoe Gordon, and his chauffeur,

Bobby "Blue" Bland.

During one session, Bland had difficulties getting his performance together, so Mattis asked John if he would like to try a take on the tune. The song was "My Song," the first record—and first R & B hit—for Johnny Ace, as he was now known (after the Four Aces). Two years of R & B chartings followed before his tragic end. Duke issued the phenomenally successful "Pledging My Love" and other disks after Ace's death, but only one further offering, "Anymore" (—/#7, 1955), fared well.

Cowboy Church Sunday School
OPEN UP YOUR HEART
(AND LET THE SUNSHINE IN)
(Stuart Hamblen)
Decca 29367
No. 8   *April 2, 1955*

"**S**tuart Hamblen had this record label called Voss," said music researcher and writer Robert L. Synder in an exclusive interview. "He recorded this group; actually they were never what you would call a show business act. In fact, there really was no group to it. 'Open Up Your Heart' was a solo record by this little girl named Carole Sue. She didn't get billing on the label, but she did on the sheet music. They were all probably some kids who attended the same church that Stu did, and he had this song and probably thought this girl had a good voice . . ." Decca leased the master and the Cowboy Church Sunday School had their mini-moment. A few other disks were printed, but nothing sold very well and peace returned to the valley.

Stuart Hamblen (b. Carl Hamblin, Oct. 20, 1908, Kellerville, Tex.) was a singing cowboy star who began recording in the late '20s for RCA. In 1928, he moved to Hollywood, where for the next two decades he made spot appearances in movies and performed on the radio—as Country Joe, and as a member of radio's first Western singing group, the Beverly Hillbillies. Later, he hosted such programs as "Covered Wagon Jubilee" and "King Cowboy and His Woolly West Review." Stu turned gospel singer in the late '40s, after evangelist Billy Graham inspired him at a tent meeting to give up his evil ways. He even ran for President on the Prohibition ticket in 1952.

Country fans probably remember Stu best for a tasty tune he wrote and recorded but didn't want released, "(I Won't Go Huntin' With You Jake) But I'll Go Chasin' Women" (—/—/#3, 1950). Having just become a born-again Christian, Hamblen asked Columbia Records not to issue the disk. Disregarding his heartfelt wishes, the company pressed thousands of copies. Its success was followed by Stu's renditions of three of his finest compositions: "(Remember Me) I'm The One Who Loves You" (—/—/#2, 1950), "It's No Secret (What God Can Do)" (—/—/#8, 1951), and "This Ole House" (—/—/#2, 1954).

Stu Hamblen died at age 81 on March 8, 1989, during surgery for a brain tumor.

Lenny Dee
PLANTATION BOOGIE
(Lenny Dee)
Decca 29360
No. 19   *May 4, 1955*

For years, Lenny Dee would amaze audiences with his organ playing, commanding his Hammond to flap like a bass fiddle, beat like a tom-tom, and strum like a banjo.

He was born in the '20s in Illinois, was raised in Florida, and took to making music early. When he was seven, Len started to study the piano and accordion. For fun, he'd pluck a banjo for his friends. After three years of service on an aircraft carrier, Dee took advantage of the G.I. Bill to enroll at the Music Conservatory of Chicago.

With his studies behind him, Lenny landed a series of bookings at hotels and nightclubs. After hearing Lenny at the Plantation Club in Nashville, Red Foley encouraged Decca Records to sign him to a recording contract. Dee remained a viable recording act, and stayed with the label for 20 years. Oddly enough, "Plantation Boogie," Dee's only charting record, would also be his very first recording. And *Dee-lightful!*, the album from which the "Boogie" was extracted, would become Lenny's largest-selling LP.

Caterina Valente
THE BREEZE AND I
(Al Stillman, Ernesto Lecuona, Tutti Carmarata)
Decca 29467
No. 8   *May 14, 1955*

Caterina (b. Jan. 14, 1931, Paris) was born into a world of entertainment. Her Italian mama Maria, billed as The Female Grock, was a famous clown; Daddy, a Spaniard, was an accordion virtuoso who went by the name of Di Zazzo. As her show-biz family toured about, Caterina learned to play guitar and to speak and sing fluently in English, French, German, Italian, Japanese, and Swedish.

In 1952, she married a German juggler named Eric Van Aro and became a circus singer. The following year, she auditioned and won the front spot in Kurt Edelhagen's band. Her second disk, "The Breeze And I," a Cuban song sung in German, became her prime pop moment in the States. No further recordings charted. She toured the U.S. and performed on "The Colgate Comedy Hour," but turned down the offer to appear in any American films. In 1964, she co-starred with Carol Burnett and Bob Newhart in the syndicated variety series "The Entertainers" (1964–1965).

While her visibility has diminished in this country, Caterina Valente remains well-known in Europe as a singer, dancer, and actress.

Sunnysiders
HEY, MR. BANJO
(Freddy Morgan, Norman Malkin)
Kapp 113
No. 12   *June 18, 1955*

Freddy Morgan (b. Nov. 7, 1910, New York City) was a banjo man and a member of Spike Jones & The City Slickers from 1947 to 1958. Morgan also fancied himself a songwriter, and penned tunes like "I Love You Fair Dinkum" and "Er War Ein Schoner Monsieur." In 1955, as an outlet for his compositional brainstorms, he formed the Sunnysiders with Norman Milkin, Jad Paul, and MARGIE RAYBURN. "Hey, Mr. Banjo" was reportedly the group's first recording, and was their only tangle with top 40 success.

For the next two years, Morgan picked his brain in search of that follow-up. Assisting him was his occasional collaborator, Norman Milkin, who would later marry the best-known member of the Sunnysiders, Margie Rayburn. Once the Sunnysiders' days were behind them, Margie would have solo success with "I'm Available," a sensuous Patti Page-like platter, and in 1962, Milkin would reappear on the charts as the writer and producer of JACK ROSS' "Cinderella."

The Sunnysiders continued to work that banjo motif with "Banjo Pickers Ball" and "The Lonesome Banjo (In The Pawn Shop Window)," but nothing further charted. Morgan did, however, write "Japanese Farewell Song (Sayonara)"—*not* the Irving Berlin number popularized by Eddie Fisher and used in the like-titled Marlon Brando flick (1957). Morgan died in 1970.

Eddie Barclay
THE BANDIT (O'CANGACEIRO)
(Alfredo Ricardo de Nascimento)
Tico 249
No. 18   *July 16, 1955*

Surprise, surprise! Not ten months after Percy Faith (#25, 1954), the Johnston Brothers (#26, 1954), and Tex Ritter (#30, 1954) raided the charts with their versions of this tune from a Mexican flick called *O'Cangaceiro* (1954), a young Parisian named Eddie Barclay was back like a bandit to snatch yet some more gold dust.

Eddie (b. Jan. 26, 1921, Paris) was schooled at the Ecole Massillon in Paris. He was a conductor, composer, record producer, and eventually the president of the French record label Compagnie Phonographique Francaise.

Priscilla Wright
THE MAN IN THE RAINCOAT
(Warwick Webster)
Unique 303
No. 16   *August 6, 1955*

Not many people have heard this ode to a shadowy being in shiny, squeaky, pitch-black plastic. While the title suggests a song about a flasher, the Wright reading is period-appropriate and quite innocuous.

At the time of her mini-moment, Cilla was only 14 and had a face full of braces. Her father was Don Wright, the leader of a choir in London, Ontario. Priscilla fooled around with dad's tape machine, leaving some rough vocal tracks. On a chance listen, Don Knight heard Priscilla's moody and broody singing—here was a young voice with the sting of a worldly Eartha Kitt. Wright excitedly raced about for weeks in search of the right vehicle for his daughter, sifting through more than 120 numbers before choosing "The Man In The Raincoat." Sparton Records released the disk in Canada; the Unique label picked up the platter's distribution, and "The Man In The Raincoat" successfully crossed the border.

Marion Marlowe, known for her "Whither Thou Goest" (#27, 1954), also worked up a version of this musical mystery. Marion was a "friend" on the popular boob-tube bonanza "Arthur Godfrey and His Friends." Her "Raincoat" waxing (#14, 1955) competed with Cilla's, and likewise placed in the nation's top 40.

Vinyl voyeurs note that Cilla was last captured, cloaked, and disseminated by 20th Century Fox Records in 1959.

Cliffie Stone
THE POPCORN SONG
(Bob Roublan)
Capitol 3131
No. 14   *August 20, 1955*

The son of banjo-plunkin' comedian Herman the Hermit, Clifford Gilpin Snyder was born in Burbank, California on March 1, 1917. One of country music's most versatile king-pins, Mr. Stone worked until the late '70s as a singer, composer, bandleader, bass player, recording artist, comedian, disk jockey, TV host, consultant for Capitol Records, and founder of the independent and still-pumping Grante label.

To the pop-music audience, "The Popcorn Song" (with a lead vocal by Bob Roubian) was a fluke hit, an old-timey cornball throwback, a one-off hillbilly novelty. Country folk knew Cliffie for his "Silver Stars, Purple Sage, Eyes Of Blue," "Peepin' Through The Keyhole," and "When My Blue Moon Turns Gold." Some of them probably knew of him as the co-author of such notables as "Divorce Me C.O.D.," "Steel Guitar Rag," and "So Round, So Firm, So Fully Packed." As a youth, Cliffie performed as a comedian and as a member of Ken Murray's Hollywood Blackouts, and once appeared in a sketch with fellow Blackout member and future singer-songwriter legend Gene Austin. He played bass in big bands with Anson Weeks and Freddie Slack, and worked for years on L.A. country radio stations as a disk jockey, MC, and performer.

In the late '40s, Cliffie aligned himself with the newly-formed Capitol Records as their country & western consultant, where he helped the careers of Tennessee Ernie Ford, Hank Thompson, Merle Travis, Tex Williams, and Jimmy Wakely. His '50s TV program "Hometown Jamboree" was a proving ground for artists like Billy Strange, Molly Bee, and JEANNE BLACK. A half-dozen albums and a good pile of singles were released over the years with Cliffie Stone's name on them, but "The Popcorn Song" was his lone crossover onto the Hot 100.

Chuck Miller

THE HOUSE OF BLUE LIGHTS
(Don Raye, Frank Slack)
Mercury 70627
No. 9   *August 27, 1955*

Chuck was a scat-singin' hepcat who played that eight-to-the-bar boogie woogie piano. He was born, bred, and based in California. Chuck played the lounge scene—and when the lights were low and the hour was late, he'd "blow piano." He'd take standards like "I Can't Give You Anything But Love" and alter them, syncopate them, drag them out. The result wasn't really jazz, but then it wasn't squeaky-clean pop, either. When rock and roll took hold, Miller sounded like he belonged with spit-curl Haley, duck-walkin' Berry, and all those pompadoured boys. His cover of Frank Slack's 1946 hit "The House of Blue Lights" found receptive ears, but "Hawk-Eye," a follow-up with the feel of a scotch-and-soda, seemed a bit antiquated.

After "Lights" went off the charts, Miller targeted his sounds to younger minds and bodies. "Bang Tang Ding Dong," "Bright Red Convertible," and "Cool It, Baby" approached rock and roll. His country cover of "The Auctioneer" charted at number 59 in 1956, and "Plaything," his cover of Nick Todd's hit, closed out Miller's recording career.

Prior to Chuck's momentary popularity with beatniks and teens, he had cut some collectible sides for Capitol Records. "Hopahula Boogie" is one to find, as is "Rogue River Valley."

Lillian Briggs

I WANT YOU TO BE MY BABY
(Jon Hendricks)
Epic 9115
No. 18   *October 1, 1955*

From the age of 12 on, Philly Lillie spent all her spare time messin' with the instruments:

the accordion, piano, violin, and, in high school, the trombone. Lill became so good on the trombone that she represented her school at a district festival. In her senior year, she joined the Swingettes, an all-girl boogie-woogie band. After graduation, she worked the window at a movie theater and continued making rounds with the Swingettes. When the group broke up, Lill formed her own orchestra, playing the Philadelphia night spots and appearing weekly on radio WAEB. By day, she drove a truck.

In April of 1954, Briggs, joining Joy Cayler and her All-Girl Orchestra, started singing. Alan Freed discovered her during her New York City singing debut at the Arcadia, "The Million Dollar Ballroom." Legend has it that Freed—attracted to Lill's vocal talents as well as her skin-tight silver- and gold-lamé dresses—helped Ms. Briggs get an audition with the folks at Epic Records. The boys there liked her, too, and waxed her in no time flat.

"I Want You To Be My Baby" was Lillian's first offering, and, unfortunately, her only hit recording. If not for Georgia Gibbs' competing rendition, "I Want You" might have wriggled its way into the top 10. The seasonal "Rock 'n' Rol-y Poly Santa Claus" failed to break any chart ground. Next up and quickly down was Lillian's cover of "Eddie My Love." Competing with the original version by THE TEEN QUEENS and covers by the Chordettes and the Fontane Sisters, Briggs' tasty take flopped. ABC-Paramount, Coral, and Sunbeam all tried their best to mold her into a choice chart item, but nothing worked.

For some years thereafter, Lillian Briggs continued working Alan Freed's many New York rock and roll shows. Perhaps, determined as she was, she is still out there somewhere, rockin' her stuff in an all-girl boogie-woogie bar band.

El Dorados

AT MY FRONT DOOR
(CRAZY LITTLE MAMA)
(J. Moore, E. Abner)
Vee-Jay 147
No. 17   *November 12, 1955*

The El Dorados were born and raised on Chicago's South Side. When Louis Bradley (tenor), Robert Glasper (bass), Jewel Jones (second tenor, baritone), James Maddox (baritone, bass), and Pirkle Lee Moses (lead vocals) met in 1952, all were attending Engel-wood High. Johnny Moore, the school custodian, became their manager. They sang in the streets and the pool halls as the Five Stars. By the time Vivian Carter of Vee-Jay Records heard them at a talent contest, the group was six in number—Glasper had left to join the Air Force, and Arthur Basset (tenor) and Richard Nickens (baritone, bass) had joined up—and was now named after their favorite set of wheels, the 1954 Cadillac El Dorado.

"Mostly we sang songs by the Dominos and the Orioles. We did 'White Christmas,''Bells of St. Mary's,''Don't Tell Her What Happened To Me' . . . things like that," Moses explained to *Record Collector's Monthly* writer Robert Pru-ter. "[Carter] was impressed not only with our singing, but also with our showmanship, so she signed us."

What little success did visit this now legend-ary group came with the release of their fourth 45, "At My Front Door." Once they had char-ted, the El Dorados became a hot property. "We went to the East Coast, the West Coast, and also the South—Nashville, Atlanta, all through there," Moses told Pruter. "And the Apollo. It was great, there was no other house in the country like that at the time. The Apollo was a theater that was renowned for talent, and for the discovery of talent, and it was thrilling to be a part of that."

The double-sided follow-up, "I'll Be Forever Loving You" b/w "I Began To Realize," should have done well on the nation's pop listings, but didn't. No other El Dorados 45 even made the Top 100, and by early 1957, all of the group's original members save Pirkle Lee Moses were gone.

The El Dorados reappeared in a number of different incarnations. Carter set up a new El Dorados with Moses (lead vocals), Doug Brown (second tenor), Johnny Carter (bass), Teddy Long (second tenor, baritone), and John McCall (first tenor). Brown, Carter, Long, and McCall had already recorded together—with Dee Clark singing lead—as the Kool Gents and the Delegates. "Lights Are Low" and "Boom Diddle Boom" bombed, so this edition of the El Dorados broke up. In 1958, Bradley, Jones, Maddox, and Marvin Smith recorded one single as the Four El Dorados and one as the Tempos. Johnny Carter assembled yet an-

The El Dorados

other El Dorados (Spencer Goulsby, Jr., Eugene Huff, Lee Toussaint, and Willie Williams) for the release of a few 45s on Paula in 1971. Meanwhile, Pirkle Lee reformed his group with Melvin Morrow and George Prayer, both former members of the Moroccos; their lone single for Torrid died an unkind death. (Pirkle had previously the Squires and Perk Lee.)

The El Dorados story has yet to see its conclusion. In 1978, Pirkle Lee and yet another edition of the El Dorados—Tony Charles, Billy Henderson, George Prayer, and Norman Palm, a one-time member of the Pastels—had a hard-to-find 45 issued on the Delano label. Richard Nickens of the original line-up has since rejoined the group.

Julie London

Bonnie Lou
DADDY-O
(Louis Innis, Charlie Gore, Buford Abner)
King 4835
No. 14 *December 3, 1955*

Bonnie was born Sally Carson on November 27, 1924, in Bloomington, Illinois. For more than 20 years, she was a favorite of country fans in the Midwest. Her big break came by chance when *Billboard*'s Bill Sachs and WLW-Cincinnati talent scout Bill McCluskey—en route to the 1944 International Showman's Convention in Chicago—overheard a salesman on the radio singing the praises of this little guitar-picking yodeler. McCluskey sought out Sally (then a regular on Kansas City's KMBC), gave her a listen, and hired her for his station's "Midwestern Hayride."

A decade later came Bonnie Lou's lone pop hit, "Daddy-O," a take-off on a hip phrase then in teen currency. The lyrics were, to youthful 1955 ears, thought to be "like the most, Dad." The arrangement was rock and roll Cincinnati-country style, meaning it included clarinet and accordion. The vocal featured Bonnie squealing in her best Teresa Brewer manner.

For years before and thereafter, Miss Lou had local chartings and some country hits. Bonnie Lou is still delighting fans with concert and nightclub appearances.

Julie London
CRY ME A RIVER
(Arthur Hamilton)
Liberty 55006
No. 9 *December 17, 1955*

Julie's (b. Sept. 26, 1926, Santa Rosa, Cal.) parents were vaudeville song-and-dance entertainers, Jack and Josephine Peck. Between gigs, the couple ran a photographic studio and shopped their tot around. At age three, Ms. Julie Peck made her radio debut singing "Falling In Love Again." School never agreed with Julie's sensibilities; by her 15th year, she was on her way up—and down—as an elevator operator in L.A. While working in a department store on Hollywood Boulevard, Alan Ladd's wife spotted the budding beauty and suggested that Julie attend a screen test for a bit part in something called *The Girl and the Gorilla.*

For the remainder of the decade, Ms. London appeared in a number of minor flicks like *Jungle Girl* (1944), *Nabonga* (1945), *A Night in Paradise* (1946), *The Red House* (1947), *Tap Roots* (1948), *Task Force* (1949), *Return of the Frontiersman* (1950), and *The Fat Man* (1951). All the while, she kept her $19-a-week job at the department store. In 1947, she married radio announcer Jack Webb. When Jack came up with "Dragnet," that boob-tube success, in 1950, Julie retired to raise two daughters, Lisa and Stacy. The marriage ended in divorce in 1953.

The following year, Julie met songwriter ("Route 66," "Baby, Baby All The Time") and jazz musician Bobby Troup. At a private party, Troup heard London's captivating crooning for the first time. He encouraged her singing endeavors and made arrangements with the newly-formed Liberty label that would culminate in the haunting "Cry Me A River" as well as scads of successful LPs: *Julie Is Her Name* (1955), *Lonely Girl* (1956), *Calendar Girl* (1956), *About the Blues* (1957), *The End of the World* (1963), and *The Wonderful World of Julie London* (1963).

During the '50s and early '60s, Julie made numerous appearances for such TV filler as the "Zane Grey Theatre" and "Adventures in Paradise," fleshing out the role of a dangerous blackjack queen in "Laramie." For five years in the '70s, Ms. London was a regular on "Emergency," a notable Saturday-night favorite. Interestingly enough, the series was produced by Jack Webb, her ex-husband, and co-starred Bobby Troup, her then-current mate.

Barry Gordon

NUTTIN' FOR CHRISTMAS
(Sid Tepper, Roy C. Bennett)
MGM 12092
No. 6   *December 31, 1955*

Barry Gordon was born in Brookline, Massachusetts, on December 21, 1948. At the age of three, he made his TV debut on Ted Mack's "Original Amateur Hour." In the '50s, he appeared on "The Jackie Gleason Show" and on Benny Goodman's and Francis Langford's musical variety program "Star Time." When the need arose at MGM Records to find a kid to sing the new Tepper & Bennett Christmas tune, seven-year-old Barry was chosen. "Nuttin' For Christmas" was rapidly covered by JOE WARD, Ricky Zahnd, Stan Freberg, Homer &

Jethro, and the Fontane Sisters, to name a few. Barry's platter would outchart them all, eventually selling more than 2,000,000 copies.

Barry's follow-up—"Rock Around Mother Goose" (#52, 1956)—would be his swan song from the music listings. Gordon continued recording throughout his adolescence and young adult years. In 1968, Barry even donned a Dylan look and sang folk-rock songs for the Dunhill label.

"Nuttin' For Christmas" opened a lot of doors for Barry. During the '50s and '60s, he appeared on "The Jack Benny Show," "The Danny Thomas Show," and "Alfred Hitchcock Presents." He won a Tony nomination for his role in the show *A Thousand Clowns* (1963) with Sandy Dennis and Jason Robards, also appearing in the movie. Gordon played an ad-agency salesman on "The Don Rickles Show" (1972), a soap-opera writer on "The New Dick Van Dyke Show" (1973–1974), and a social worker on "Fish" (1977–1978). When last spotted, Gordon was Archie's accountant on "Archie Bunker's Place" (1981–1983).

Joe Ward
NUTTIN' FOR CHRISTMAS
(Sid Tepper, Roy C. Bennett)
King 4854
No. 20   *December 31, 1955*

"**N**uttin' For Christmas" was absolutely the hottest Xmas tune of the year. Who can ever forget those endearing lines: "I'm gettin' nuttin' for Christmas/Mommy and daddy are mad." Every label in the land was out to find a kid to sing those words. Columbia had Ricky Zahnd. MGM had BARRY GORDON. Next to jump on the bandwagon was the Cincinnati-based King company. Syd Nathan had found a lad of a few years named Joe Ward. Joe's not singing anymore, or so it seems. His artsy rendering sold some copies and earned a place on *Billboard*'s top 40—but when the yule tree came down, Joe was out of a job and back in school.

Kit Carson
BAND OF GOLD
(Bob Musel, Jack Taylor)
Capitol 3283
No. 11   *January 7, 1956*

The real Kit Carson—American frontiersman and Union general—died in 1868. *This* Kit, a fair-haired female, was born and raised under the name Liza Morrow. In the '40s, she and Alan Dale were vocalists with George Paxton's big band. George's many platters for Guild, Major, and MGM never caught on. Discouraged, Paxton shut the show down late in the decade. He went on to arrange for Vaughn Monroe and Charlie Spivak, then formed the Coed label in 1958. Thanks to George's musical and business abilities, the Crests, the Duprees, and Adam Wade became hot recording artists. Alan Dale had a few big-selling duet disks in the early '50s, and in 1955 clicked twice with "Sweet And Gentle" (#10) and "Cherry Pink And Apple Blossom White" (#11), the latter from the Jane Russell-Jayne Mansfield film frolic *Underwater!* (1955).

Kit's recording career, however, proved to be less successful. Except for "Washing Machine Blues," a 1952 side for the King label, Carson's waxings went largely without notice. Capitol Records offered her a catchy number by Bob Musel and Jack Taylor—"Band Of Gold"—and although it did well, a cover version by Don Cherry out-distanced her effort. Musel and Taylor returned the following year with another *Billboard*-bound tune called "Earthbound." Kit didn't cover it, but Sammy Davis, Jr., did, and charted with it. By year's end, Carson was off the label and out of sight.

Bobby Scott
CHAIN GANG
(Sol Quasha, Herb Yakus)
ABC-Paramount 9658
No. 13   *February 18, 1956*

Bobby Scott was born on January 29, 1937, in Mount Pleasant, New York. He began his music study when still a youngster. In his teens, he played piano in dance bands, worked the Big Apple's jazz circuit, accompanied Louis Prima, and toured with the Gene Krupa Orchestra. In 1955, Bobby met with the cigar-chompin' big cats at ABC-Paramount, who politely gave him a listen and signed him to a contract. "Chain Gang" was an early release, and it clicked.

Further recordings did not sell as well, and Scott turned to arranging for Harry Belafonte, Bobby Darin, and Sarah Vaughn. He also took to songwriting, and hit paydirt when his incidental music for the Broadway play *A Taste of Honey* won a Grammy Award for "Best Instrumental Theme" in 1962. Three years later, Herb Alpert revived Scott's tune, and "A Taste Of Honey" won three more Grammy Awards: "Record of the Year," "Best Instrumental Performance–Non-Jazz," and "Best Instrumental Arrangement."

Bobby Scott's solo career continued through the '60s on MGM, Mercury, and Columbia. Scott has since worked as a music director for Dick Haymes and as a producer of sessions for Aretha Franklin and Marvin Gaye. As a songwriter, he penned hits like "A Natural Woman" for Aretha Franklin, "He Ain't Heavy, He's My Brother" for the Hollies, and "Where Are You Going?" for Jerry Butler. Scott also recorded with Chet Baker, Larry Elgart, and Quincy Jones, and has been credited with the discovery of both Bobby "Sunny" Hebb and Jesse Colin Young of THE YOUNGBLOODS.

Bonnie Sisters

CRY BABY
(Unknown)
Rainbow 328
No. 18 *March 3, 1956*

In the winter of 1955, three sisters checked out of Bellevue Hospital. The sisters—Sylvia, Jean, and Pat—were nurses at the facility who sang together on the side. Mickey "Guitar" Baker (later of MICKEY & SYLVIA) heard them and offered them a contract with Rainbow Records. The girls left their jobs. As the Bonnie Sisters, they issued a pop moaner, "Cry Baby," that remained in the top 40 for only three weeks. "Track That Cat" was the follow-up single. And weeks later, quite probably, Sylvia, Jean, and Pat were back at Bellevue.

Four Voices

LOVELY ONE
(Fred Weismantel)
Columbia 40643
No. 20 *March 17, 1956*

From somewhere in the U.S.A. came four voices. They were what was called, in their time, "sweet singers." The mid-'50s were hot on that tight four-part harmony. The Four Aces, Four Coins, Four Esquires, Four Preps, Four Lads . . . whenever one turned on the TV, there'd be men in clusters of four, short hair greased into place and mouths open.

Allan Chase (tenor), Frank Fosta (bass baritone), Sal Mayo (tenor), and Bill McBride (baritone) did their stuff for the "Arthur Godfrey's Talent Scouts" TV show and won top honors. Mitch Miller, A & R man over at Columbia Records, happened to hear their cheerful sounds, and in 1955 signed the guys to his label to make hits. But other than "Lovely One" and a nibble on "Dancing With My Shadow" (#50, 1958), the pre-fab foursome sidestepped stardom.

After five years of zips, Chase decided to move on and do some solo recordings, which fared poorly. Meanwhile, the three other voices cooled on ice. The wise thing was done in 1962 when the original guys got together again for Mr. Peacock Records and re-recorded their lone moment in the sun. It sounded good, but by this time, it was too late.

The Four Voices dispersed, each Voice returning to his respective hometown.

Blue Stars

LULLABYE OF BIRDLAND
(George Shearing)
Mercury 70742
No. 16 *March 24, 1956*

Blossom Dearie—yes, that's her real name—was the brains, if not the brawn, behind the short-lived Blue Stars. She was born on April 28, 1926, in East Durham, New York. In the '40s, she sang with the Penn State-Fred Waring group, Woody Herman's Blue Flames, and Alvino Rey's Blue Reys. In 1952, after some wearying gigs as a cocktail piano player, Dearie fled to Paris, where her solo singing career flourished.

Two years later, Dearie began thinking of forming an octet of French, jazzy vocalists. She dreamed up some musical arrangements, and with an eye to her earlier bands, she labeled the chirpy eightsome the Blue Stars. Their unusual scat rendition of George Shearing's "Lullabye Of Birdland"—sung in French and arranged by Michel Legrand—caught the responsive ear of French and American audiences alike. The follow-up, "Speak Low (Tout Bas)," plus other experimental excursions, fell flat saleswise. About this time, Blossom fell in love with Bobby Jaspar, a Belgian tenor saxophonist. Months later, the lovebirds took flight to New York, shelving the Blue Stars concept.

In the years since, when the whim strikes her, Dearie unpacks her baggage, hits the night spots, and sings in a soothing supper-club style.

Teddi King

MR. WONDERFUL
(Jerry Block, Larry Holoflener,
George Weiss)
RCA 6392
No. 18 *March 24, 1956*

For a jazz-influenced songstress, Teddi King did well commercially when she charted with "Mr. Wonderful," from the Broadway musical of the same name, followed by "Married I Can Always Be" (#75, 1956) and "Say It Isn't So" (#98, 1957). "I worked the big rooms and was on network TV, and the public became aware of my name," King told Whitney Balliett in *American Singers.* "But it wasn't me. I was doing pop pap, and I was in musical despair. I didn't have my lovely jazz music and the freedom it gives."

Teddi quickly walked away from the glare of the limelight. For much of the '60s, she worked the Playboy Club in New York City. In 1970, she was diagnosed as suffering from systemic lupus. Singing engagements diminished in number, and Ms. King died of the debilitating disease on November 18, 1977.

Teddi was born Theodora King in Boston on September 18, 1929. After graduating from high school, she joined the Tributary Theatre and eventually won RKO's Dinah Shore singalike contest. She briefly studied classical singing, as well as classical and jazz piano; she worked with bands led by Jack Edwards and George Graham. Her recording debut came in 1951 with the taping of a set by Nat Pierce's band. Before going solo, Teddi toured for two years and recorded with George Shearing. It was her solo appearances at Chicago's Mr. Kelly's and Philadelphia's Rendezvous that brought her to the attention of RCA and her subsequent "pop pap" recordings.

Months before Teddi's death, the Audiophile label issued two albums of what Ms. King referred to as "my lovely jazz music." Both *Lovers and Losers* and *Someone to Light Up Your Life* are still in print.

The Teen Queens

Teen Queens
EDDIE MY LOVE
(Aaron Collins, Maxwell Davis, Sam Ling)
RPM 453
No. 14 *March 31, 1956*

Aaron Collins and Maxwell Davis were sure they had a hit on their hands. Collins was a member of THE CADETS/Jacks (Modern/RPM/Flair's house group) and Davis was the label's arranger. Along with Willie Davis, Will "Dub" Jones, Lloyd McCraw, and Austin "Ted" Taylor, Collins and Davis—as the Jacks—had a hit in 1955 with a cover of the Feathers' "Why Don't You Write Me?" In just a few months, the very same group, recording as THE CADETS, would chart with their cover of THE JAYHAWKS' "Stranded In The Jungle." Now, however, Collins and Davis had an original, a catchy rock-aballad called "Eddie My Love," that they brought to Modern/RPM/Flair's Sam Bihari. Auditioning the tune were Aaron's sisters, Betty and Rose. Sam heard the number and rushed the girls into the Modern Studios in Culver City.

Despite the competition from "whitened" cover versions by both the Chordettes and the Fontane Sisters, Betty and Rose went top 40 with "Eddie My Love." Their follow-ups were arguably as high-quality as "Eddie"; their jump tunes, like "Rock Everybody," were especially pleasing. Nothing, however, charted, and not even a move to a major like RCA Victor helped gain the girls the further notice.

Carl Perkins
BLUE SUEDE SHOES
(Carl Perkins)
Sun 234
No. 2 *May 19, 1956*

Carl Perkins (b. Apr. 9, 1932) was born the son of a dirt-poor sharecropper in Tiptonville, Tennessee. His father, Buck, was crippled, and suffered from ill health after the removal of a lung. Times were tough; by age 11, Carl was helping his family pick cotton 14 hours a day. When the crops were good and Carl's parents could afford it, they would buy batteries for the radio, and Carl would listen closely.

"I started playing guitar when I was about six or seven," Carl recalled in an exclusive interview. "I always loved the sound of the guitar, and finally got me this old one from a black man named Uncle John, who lived on the same plantation that my family did. I used to go over and listen to him play a simple blues-type thing. I loved the way he pushed the strings. I'd practice up on Bill Monroe and Ernest Tubb's 'Walking The Floor Over You,' and I'd add Uncle John's blues licks. That's where my style came from."

In 1953, Carl formed his first band, the Perkins Brothers, with siblings Jay (rhythm guitar) and Clayton (bass fiddle), plus "Fluke" Holland on drums. Forced to leave school to support his family, Carl worked in a bakery, on a dairy farm, and in a battery factory—but all the while, the brothers kept practicing.

The group sent some homemade demo tapes around to various labels, including Sam Phillips' Sun Records. In December 1954, Phillips granted the guys a 10-minute listen, and immediately thereafter, a recording contract. "Movie Magg" b/w "Turn Around" (issued on Sun's Flip subsidiary) and its follow-up, "Gone, Gone, Gone" b/w "Let The Jukeboxes Keep On Playing," both sold only locally. Carl's next single, however, proved to be a winner.

"It was the easiest song I ever wrote. Elvis and Johnny [Cash] and myself were playing Parkins, Arkansas, when John said to me, 'Carl, you oughta write a song called "Blue Suede Shoes"' . . . [Cash] said, 'In the Army, guys would line up for chow in their combat boots and somebody'd always say, "Man, don't step on my suedes."' I thought about it, and about three weeks later, I was watching this couple jitterbug. I noticed that this cat had on suedes, and at one point, he says to her, 'Don't step on my suedes.' I knew what I was gonna say right then . . . I couldn't find any paper, so I took three potatoes out of a brown paper sack, and wrote 'Blue Suede Shoes' on that sack, exactly as it is today."

"Blue Suede Shoes," released on New Year's Day of 1956, sold over a million copies, and by March of that year, it was number one on the pop, R & B, *and* country charts. The same month, Elvis Presley recorded a hit version of the song. Carl was set to appear on "The Ed Sullivan Show" as the first rockabilly artist on national TV. But en route to the show, fate stepped in and dealt Perkins a cruel blow—he had a serious car accident that killed his manager, knocked him unconscious for three days, and laid him up with four broken ribs and a fractured right shoulder.

"They were gonna give me a gold record. Sam Phillips was already in New York . . . He

Carl Perkins

was gonna surprise me and announce to the world on 'The Ed Sullivan Show' that my record was number one on all three charts—something that rarely ever happened then.

"As a result of the wreck, I didn't get to make the show. I watched Elvis from my hospital bed do 'Blue Suede Shoes.' I've been asked many times how I felt about that. I always admired Elvis, I liked what he did. I knew he had the same feel for the music that I did; we loved the same type of things. And nobody was topping anybody . . . I *did* lay there thinking, 'what if?'—but Elvis had the looks on me. He was hittin' 'em with his sideburns, flashy clothes, and no ring on his finger; I was married, with three kids. There was no way of keepin' Elvis from being the man."

With most of his money gone to pay the hospital bills, Carl's career momentum stalled, and depressed at the loss of his brother—who had also been in the car accident and died of complications months later—Carl started drinking heavily. He appeared in one of the earliest rock and roll flicks (*Jamboree*, 1957), also writing and recording songs like "Boppin' The Blues" (#70, 1956), "Your True Love" (#67, 1957), "Pink Pedal Pushers" (#91, 1958), and "Pointed Toe Shoes" (#93, 1959). "Matchbox," "Honey Don't," and "Everybody's Trying To Be My Baby," three of his compositions, were recorded by the Beatles in one late-night session that Perkins attended in 1963; the tracks appeared on *The Beatles For Sale* (1964) (U.S. version: *Beatles '65*). Perkins also toured with Johnny Cash's traveling show from 1964 through 1976.

Perkins is still actively performing and recording today. He is acclaimed as one of rock and roll's surviving legends, and even as one of the originators of rockabilly. But Carl steadfastly refuses to take primary credit for this accomplishment.

"[Sam] Phillips, Elvis, and I didn't create rockabilly; it was just the white man's response to the black man's spiritualness. It was born in the South. People working those cotton fields as I did as a youngster would hear black people singing . . . There's a lot of cats that was doin' our things, and maybe better, that were never heard of—they're the ones that created rockabilly, the ones who never even got on record. We're just the lucky ones."

George Cates

MOONGLOW AND
THEME FROM "PICNIC"
(Will Hudson, Eddie De Lange, Irving Mills / Steve Allen, George W. Duning)
Coral 61618
No. 4 June 2, 1956

Both of these titles were taken from the Academy Award-winning film *Picnic* (1956). Based on a play by William Inge and directed by Joshua Logan, *Picnic* utilized a basketful of movie stars (such as William Holden, Kim Novak, Cliff Robertson, and Rosalind Russell) to tell the heart-warming story of a good-for-zip guy who appears in town one day to steal his best friend's damsel. MORRIS STOLOFF, musical director for the film, beat George to the top of the charts with his rendition of this medley. Both versions sold a million copies before the picnic was over.

George Cates was born on October 19, 1911, in New York City. Besides working as a com-

poser, conductor, and producer, Cates labored for years as a music director for Coral Records and later Dot Records. He did arrangements for the Andrews Sisters, Teresa Brewer, and Bing Crosby; he also served for 25 years as music director for Lawrence Welk's long-running TV show.

Months before his lone top 40 landing, Cates appeared on two other chart numbers: the mildly popular Champ Butler disk "Someone On My Mind" (#77, 1955) and Steve Allen's "Autumn Leaves" (#35, 1955). George Cates continued recording throughout the '70s, but only his immediate follow-up, "Where There's Life" (#75, 1956), made the Top 100.

Don Robertson

THE HAPPY WHISTLER
(Don Robertson)
Capitol 3391
No. 6 June 2, 1956

Donald Irwin Robertson (b. Dec. 5, 1922, Peking, China) has become known and respected in the industry as one of the best postwar C & W tunesmiths, and has been credited with creating the "country piano" or "Nashville piano" style largely popularized by Floyd Cramer. Yet Don never managed to have his own C & W hit, and were it not for "The Happy Whistler," the public-at-large might never have taken notice of the man.

Don's father was a distinguished physician who once headed the Department of Medicine at Peking Union Medical College. When Dr. Robertson was offered a position at the University of Chicago, the family moved there; Don was four years old, and began taking piano and composition lessons. The Robertson family summered in Birchwood Beach, Michigan, where Carl Sandburg, a family friend, lived. Carl's *American Songbag*, an anthology of almost 300 folk songs assembled during the poet's years of wandering the nation's farmlands, was published in 1927, and with Sandburg's aid, Don learned many of these tunes.

Don played in school bands, and by the age of 14 was playing piano in local dance bands. After dropping out of a pre-med program and studying at the Chicago Musical College, Robertson worked as a musical arranger for radio WGN. In 1955, he moved to L.A., where he landed a position as a rehearsal and demo keyboardist for Capitol Records.

"The Happy Whistler," Robertson's first solo

side, was a full-fledged fluke hit. The whistled instrumental, while not quite countrified and hardly mainstream pop, was a memorably melodic march just gorged with gaiety. The closest Don ever got to the Hot 100 again came with the release of "Born To Be With You" (1960) and "The Tennessee Waltz" (1961). The former, a one-off duet with BONNIE GUITAR, was recorded under the name of the Echoes.

As a C & W songwriter, Robertson has been phenomenally prosperous. Elvis recorded a dozen of his tunes, including "Anything That Is A Part Of You" (#31, 1962), "I'm Yours" (#11, 1965), "I Really Don't Want To Know" (#21, 1971), "They Remind Me Too Much Of You" (#53, 1963), and "There's Always Me" (#56, 1967). His songs have also been recorded by Eddie Arnold, the Chordettes, LORNE GREENE, Sonny James, HANK LOCKLIN, and Les Paul & Mary Ford.

When the Country Music Hall of Fame was opened in 1967, Don Robertson's name was in its Walkway of the Stars.

Morris Stoloff
MOONGLOW AND THEME FROM "PICNIC"
(Will Hudson, Eddie De Lange, Irving Mills / Steve Allen, George W. Duning)
Decca 29888
No. 2 *June 2, 1956*

Born on August 1, 1898, and raised in Philadelphia, Morris studied violin with Leopold Auer and Theodore Speiring. After a position as concertmaster of the Paramount Studio Orchestra, Stoloff in 1936 began his reign as composer-conductor and general music director for Columbia Pictures. His film scores for *Cover Girl* (1944), *The Jolson Story* (1946), and *Song Without End* (1960) won Academy

Awards. Stoloff's rendition of this medley of tunes from the film *Picnic* was the more successful of the two versions that charted, the other being by GEORGE CATES. In addition to composing the pop songs "A Song To Remember," "Dream Awhile With Me," and "Love Comes But Once In Awhile," Morris created the film scores to *The Eddie Duchin Story* (1956), *Gidget* (1959), *They Came To Condura* (1959), and *The Last Angry Man* (1974).

Morris Stoloff died on April 16, 1980, at the age of 82.

Cathy Carr
IVORY TOWER
(Jack Fulton, Lois Steele)
Fraternity 734
No. 2 *June 16, 1956*

Cathy Carr was born in the Bronx on June 28, 1938. From the age of six, she took extensive dance and singing lessons, and appeared on the locally popular "Horn & Hardart Children's Hour." After graduating from Christopher Columbus High School, she joined a U. S. O. troupe as a singer and dancer. On her return, Cathy

Cathy Carr

fronted the orchestras of Johnny Dee, Sammy Kaye, and Larry Fotine.

While touring with Fotine, she leveled with him: she wanted to be a single act, a songstress, a star. Recognizing Cathy's talent, Fotine offered to become her manager. Coral Records signed the bubbly blond to their roster in 1953. Nothing Carr recorded moved the nation—or the vinyl off the record-store shelves—until Cathy cut a cover of Otis Williams & The Charms' R & B hit "Ivory Tower." Cathy's sweetened and polished cover cut into the chart success of the Charms' version, but not by much; Williams and his group were already known to the ever-growing rock and roll audience for their big-time hits "Hearts of Stone" and "Ling Ting Tong."

For years, Cathy Carr continued recording pretty pop things in a Teresa Brewer/Patti Page vein, usually with a mini-touch of rock and roll piano or a youthful vocal-group backing. In 1959, her teen tune "First Anniversary" (#42) almost wormed its way into top 40-land. An album issued by Dot Records in 1966 was the last noted Carr waxing.

Rover Boys
GRADUATION DAY
(Joe Sherman)
ABC-Paramount 9700
No. 16 *June 23, 1956*

In 1950, Doug Wells (second tenor) moved from his birthplace in Southampton, England, to Toronto. With the voice of a cherub and an interest in money, Dougie quickly fashioned the idea of forming a pop group along the lines of his heroes, the Four Aces. He had already spotted Larry Amato (first tenor) at the United Music Center and Al Osten (bass) wiggling his vocal cords on a local TV program. Larry and Al thought Doug's idea was swell.

After some practice sessions, the Rovers three wandered to Long Island and a night spot called the Top Hat. Prior to the gig, the chaps enlisted a Brooklyn boy, Billy Albert (lead), to flesh out their sound. At the Top Hat, they sang *a cappella*. The people drank and danced to it. And one night in September 1954, a local disk jockey named Bill Silbert heard their vocalizing and rushed them to the studios of Coral Records to record their first single (and first flop), "Show Me."

At the Stage Coach Inn in Hackensack, New Jersey, the Rover Boys carried on and created such a din of delight that Sid Feller, an ABC-Paramount rep, signed them to the label. "Come To Me" moved but a few to buy a copy; "My Queen" stiffed in the stall. But "Graduation Day" made an appreciable mark on the charts, despite competition from a cover of the ballad by the more well-known Four Freshmen. The follow-up, "Little Did I Know," did little, although "From A School Ring To A Wedding Ring" later in 1956 made a brief chart appearance at number 79. RCA and United Artists each gave a mini-whirl on the Rovers, but nothing further ever cracked *Billboard*'s Top 100.

Jayhawks
STRANDED IN THE JUNGLE
(James Johnson, Ernest Smith)
Flash 109
No. 18 *July 28, 1956*

Carver Bunkum (bass), Carl Fisher (tenor), Dave Govan (baritone), and Jimmy Johnson (lead) met while serving time in their local L.A. high school, and soon became the jumpin', jivin' Jayhawks. With tunes in each head and the urge for bread, the guys drifted over one afternoon to the Flash Record Store on Vernon Avenue. The store's owner liked their vocal vibrations, in particular something called "Counting My Teardrops," and took the Jayhawks into a nearby garage/studio, where a half-dozen sides were recorded.

"Stranded In The Jungle," the group's second disk on the Flash label, was a big seller and burned its way into rock and roll history as one of the decade's finest R & B novelty numbers. Unfortunately for the fellows, a quickly-constructed but similar-sounding cover version by another local group, THE CADETS, surpassed the Jayhawks' original in record sales. Follow-ups like "Love Train" and the honkin' "Johnny's House Party" failed to catch much of a listen.

By 1960, Bunkum had left the group to be replaced by Don Bradley (bass) and Richard Owens (tenor), and the unit's name had changed. Feeling that they wanted to do more ballad material and that the "Jayhawks" name was typecasting them as a novelty act, the fellows decided to call themselves the Vibrations. As such, they would hit the top 40 with two rock and roll notables, neither of them ballads—"The Watusi" (#25, 1961) and "My Girl Sloopy" (#26, 1964), the original rendition

The Jayhawks

of the McCoys classic "Hang On Sloopy." In 1961, with an urge to go gimmicky again and an itch for some spending change, the same basic line-up did a one-off recording of "Peanut Butter" as THE MARATHONS.

Cadets

STRANDED IN THE JUNGLE
(James Johnson, Ernest Smith)
Modern 994
No. 15 *August 4, 1956*

They started in L. A. in 1954, with the intent of being a spiritual group. For a moment, they called themselves the Santa Monica Soul Seekers. Their main man and manager from Arkansas, baritone Lloyd McCraw, had a gospel-belting history dating back to the mid-'40s; he had sung with the Royal Four and the Dixie Hummingbirds. Soon after their formation, McCraw, lead vocalist Aaron Collins, second tenor Willie Davis, bass Will "Dub" Jones,

and first tenor Austin "Ted" Taylor shifted to secular singing. As the Jacks, they approached the Bihari brothers at Modern/RPM/Flair.

Joe Bihari was impressed with their abilities, and in April of 1955, he walked the group into Modern's studios in Culver City, California. Joe had heard and picked Nappy Brown's "Don't Be Angry" for the group to record. In an effort to capture some action on the tune, Bihari had McCraw and his music movers cover the tune as "The Cadets." "Angry" did not chart for the unit, but a cover of the Feathers' "Why Don't You Write Me?" (#82), released just weeks later under the "Jacks" name, did.

For the next year and a half, the public—and, more importantly, the nation's radio programmers—had no idea that the very same group was issuing disks under two different names. "Cadets" records were pressed on the Modern label; according to music researchers Donn Fileti and Marv Goldberg, these usually featured either Aaron Collins or "Dub" Jones on lead vocals. Smoothies and

19

jumpers by "The Jacks" were issued on RPM, and usually featured Willie Davis.

The Cadets/Jacks became Bihari's house band, cutting ballads, jump tunes, or calypsos. They accompanied other Modern acts such as Donna Hightower, Young Jessie, and possibly even Paul Anka. As "Kings of the Covers," they re-recorded happening disks by Elvis ("Heartbreak Hotel"), Peppermint Harris ("I Got Loaded"), JOHNNIE & JOE ("I'll Be Spinning"), the Marigolds ("Rollin' Stone"), the Willows ("Church Bells May Ring"), and, for their most publicly-known pinching, THE JAYHAWKS ("Stranded In The Jungle").

After "Stranded," not one of the group's fine records ever managed to regain a spot on the nation's pop or R & B listings. The "Jacks" name was shelved in mid-'56 when McCraw and Taylor left the group. Thomas "Pete" Fox and sometime member Prentice Moreland were brought in as their respective replacements. Shortly after, *Jumpin' with the Jacks*, one of the very first albums by an R & B group, was released. With this line-up, the Cadets continued on for another half-dozen singles and a highly sought-after album, *Rock and Rollin' with the Cadets*.

By 1958, the Modern Record Company complex was in financial difficulties. McCraw, Jones, and Collins formed their short-lived MJC label and issued one single as the Rocketeers. Minus Collins, the dwindling group (with George Hollis and Tommy Miller of the Flares) recorded as the Cadets for the Sherwood ("Lookin' For A Job") and Jan-Lar ("Car Crash") labels. In 1962, they cut two singles as the Thor-Ables for McCraw's own Titantic label.

Ted Taylor went on to solo success; before his death in an auto accident on November 22, 1987, a number of his hard-soul singles— "Stay Away From My Baby," "It's Too Late," and "Something Strange Is Goin' On In My House"—placed quite well on the R & B charts. "Dub" Jones joined the Coasters in 1958, remaining with the classic comedians until 1968. In 1961, Buck Ram, the Platters' producer and manager, asked Collins and Davis to write some tunes, and he eventually invited them to join his Flairs/Flares group. One interesting footnote: Aaron Collins' sisters, Betty and Rose, gained their own spot on the charts as THE TEEN QUEENS with the original take on "Eddie My Love."

The Cadets

Sanford Clark

THE FOOL
(Naomi Ford)
Dot 15481
No. 7 *September 22, 1956*

Sanford Clark (b. 1935, Tulsa, Okla.) certainly was a mystery man, then as now. Seldom was he seen, and almost never were his recordings given mass airings. He had a distinctive style that was engaging enough to rival that of BO DIDDLEY, Jerry Lee Lewis, and Elvis. Sounding as despondent as Johnny Cash in his blackest prime, Clark on record was encased in a sparse, echoey accompaniment of Sun-sounding rockabilly. "The Fool," his debut single, made the pop, R & B, and country charts all at once. His follow-ups were of equal or better quality. So what happened?

Even to click but once, all the necessary elements had to be present. Lee Hazlewood, a promising young DJ from Mannford, Oklahoma, had recently moved with Naomi Ford, his songwriting wife, to Phoenix and radio KTYL. Hazlewood, who had already tried marketing some rock and roll tracks while stationed in Tucson, Arizona, soon became friends with the leader of the Arizona Hayriders, guitarist Al Casey. It was Casey who had first heard Sanford Clark, and Casey introduced Clark to both Hazlewood and Naomi's mournful song.

The Hazlewoods, Casey, and Clark pooled their resources and bought some time at Floyd Ramsey's Audio Recording Studios in Phoenix (later known as the house that created all those twangy-guitar hits for Duane Eddy—a sometime accompanist on some of Clark's waxings). MCI Records was formed by these interested parties to issue "The Fool." The response was immediate and positive, and soon Dot Records had acquired the rights to distribute the record nationally.

Clark apparently did little to promote the nation-shakin' hit. "A Cheat" (#74, 1956) charted, but nothing further would ever again garner mainline pop, R & B, or country attention. By 1960, Sanford had joined the U.S. Air Force. On his return, he reportedly became a croupier, continuing to sing on the side. His subsequent performances were issued by the Dot, Jamie, 3-Trey, Project, Warner Bros., Ramco, and LHI labels. Only the latter company, owned by Hazlewood, released an LP, *Return of the Fool.*

Helmut Zacharias

**WHEN THE WHITE LILACS
BLOOM AGAIN**
(Fritz Rotter, Franz Doelle)
Decca 30039
No. 12 *September 22, 1956*

In the mid-'50s, German violinist Helmut Zacharias and his Magic Violins were quite popular in Europe. A representative from Decca Records brought some of Zach's zingers over to the U.S., and the label's Milt Gabler approved their stateside release. "China Boogie" shook no one, but Zach's "Lilacs" number, a tune written in 1928, played on the emotions of many post-teens. Leroy Holmes, Billy Vaughn, Lawrence Welk, and Florian Zabach all rushed their string men into the studios to record their own renditions. Helmut's hummer, however, was the hit.

Well into the '60s, additional singles, EPs, and LPs by Helmut Zacharias were sporadically issued by Philips, RCA, and Capitol.

Jane Powell

TRUE LOVE
(Cole Porter)
Verve 2018
No. 15 *October 27, 1956*

Jane Powell was born Suzanne Bruce in Portland, Oregon, on April 1, 1929. She performed on the radio from early childhood, and at the tender age of 15 made her film debut in *Song of the Open Road* (1944) with W. C. Fields, Edgar Bergen, and Charlie McCarthy. As a very innocent and sugary blue-eyed blond, Jane became an adolescent star in several light romances and movie musicals during the late '40s and early '50s. With a stiff whiff of purity, Jane moved through productions with teasing titles like *Rich, Young and Pretty* (1951), *The Girl Most Likely* (1957), and *The Female Animal* (1958). Her career reached a pinnacle with her lead role opposite Howard Keel in *Seven Brides for Seven Brothers* (1954).

In the musical *Royal Wedding* (1951), Jane Powell sang a ditty with Fred Astaire, "How Could You Believe Me When I Said I Loved You When You Know I've Been A Liar All My Life?" The duet, a pre-rock-and-roll-era hit, eventually sold a million copies. Over the years, other twosomes and solo settings were tried, but only a filler of a flip side would fill the bill and give Jane her lone hit as a solo artist.

Bing Crosby had lustfully sung "True Love" to Grace Kelly in what he later considered his favorite scene in his favorite movie, *High Society* (1954). While Jane's cover version of this Crosby tune, originally intended as the "B" side for a single, did not outsell the crown crooner's original, Miss Powell surprised many when her recording charted only paces behind Bing's. But storm clouds were gathering, rock and roll was on the horizon, and Jane, with her distinctively mellow and mature style, was never to place another record on *Billboard*'s Top 100.

Jane Powell occasionally appears at nightclubs, in summer stock, and in TV specials; she has vacationed on "The Love Boat" and at "Fantasy Island." None of her recordings are currently in print.

Eddie Cooley & The Dimples

PRISCILLA
(Eddie Cooley)
Royal Roost 621
No. 20 *November 24, 1956*

Eddie was a New York City songwriter. He is known for only one song, "Fever"—a tune that he co-wrote with Otis Blackwell and that was popularized by Little Willie John, Peggy Lee, and the McCoys. Cooley also concocted "Priscilla," and legend has it that he liked the song so much that he and three unnamed ladies (the Dimples) recorded the tune for Royal Roost Records. Judging from the sound of "Priscilla," it seems like Cooley might have been a true rarity: a black man with rockabilly roots.

Despite its chart status, "Priscilla" remains one of the least played of all hits from the '50s. And Cooley, whose name is difficult to locate in the annals of pop history, continues to live in obscurity.

Eddie Cooley made three more singles—"A Spark Met A Flame," "Hey You," and "Leona"—before his ride into the shadows.

Highlights

CITY OF ANGELS
(Nick Joven, Bev Dusham)
Bally 1016
No. 19 *November 24, 1956*

"When I was a kid, I played the accordion for a while," Frank Pizani, lead singer of the Highlights, recalled in an exclusive interview. "I also played the violin, till my dad broke it over my head—not on my head, but on the wall over my head. I was terrible."

While attending DePaul University as an education major, Frank met Frank Calzaretta. "He had a group with his brother Tony [tenor] and a couple of other guys [baritone Bill Melshimer and bass Jerry Oleski] that he called the Highlights. They'd do hops and high school dances. I knew a Frank McNulty and had done some demos for him. He had this song he wanted me to do called 'Jingle-lo,' with all kinds of complex parts. I told him, 'I know this group and together, I think we can do a good number on it.'

"So we went downstairs in the hallway of WGN Studios. There was this great echo-chamber-like sound, and with the help of Joe Scotti on piano, we did a take on the song right there in this hallway on Michigan Avenue. McNulty said it was great and took the tape around. He brought it to Bally Records, and they liked it and wanted to sign us up, immediately."

"City Of Angels," the group's first single for Bally, was a smash hit. But according to Pizani, success created problems with the rest of the Highlights. "They wanted to be their own group, not some back-up for me, so the fellows' parents got a lawyer and they took the name. Then they approached the label and me, and said that if I wanted to record with them, I'd have to work for them. I wasn't happy with this and left."

Bally had "To Be With You," with Frank singing lead, in the can, and issued it posthumously; it reached number 84 in 1957. Pizani was signed on as a solo act and charted with his debut, "Angry" (#70, 1957). "Indiana Style," the first and only Pizani-less Highlights record, appeared during the summer of 1957, but the record bombed and the group broke up. Pizani, meanwhile, went into the service.

"When I returned, Bally Records was gone. The other guys, well, they finished their schooling and college and got 9-to-5 jobs. Jerry, he's an insurance salesman. Billy is a high school coach. Tony works at Ditka's [a club owned by Chicago Bears coach Mike Ditka] as their entertainment director. His brother Tony is off doing business-type stuff somewhere."

Before his momentary retirement, Pizani had a few singles issued—for Afton, Warwick, and Carlton—then returned to college to complete his requirements for a teaching certificate. During the '60s and '70s, he taught in Chicago's grammar schools. Most recently, Frank has appeared in a number of Chicago-area TV commercials, worked as a comedian, and for some years was the vice president of Carl Bonedfede's Chi-Town Records. That label and Pizani's own Happyday label released a few Pizani obscurities like "Fighting Jane (Byrne)" and "I Love You Papa."

In the '80s, Pizani signed up with Ron Smith's Look-a-Likes agency as a Tony Bennett imitator. In that capacity, he briefly appeared in the Rick Springfield flick *Hard To Hold* (1984), crooning—you guessed it— "I Left My Heart In San Francisco."

Sonny Knight

CONFIDENTIAL
(Dorinda Morgan)
Dot 15507
No. 17 *November 24, 1956*

Joey C. Smith (b. 1934, Maywood, Ill.) was going to be an author, or a jazzman. Joey would practice some on Ma's piano and listen to Dizzy Gilespie on the jukebox. One story has him saved from an untimely death by Dinah Washington. He and a buddy had snuck into one of her band's practice sessions. Some older punks spotted the 12-year-old and flipped Joey over a balcony railing, when Dinah intervened and stopped his possible termination.

By the early '50s, Joey and his family were living in L.A. There he attended Belmont High and L.A. City College, wrote a novel that would be rejected, and played local theaters and talent shows with a drummer. "There was this one particular girl who used to come in and listen to me," Knight told *Goldmine*'s Randall C. Hill. "She suggested I get into recording, that I was as good as the folks who were getting airplay. So I looked in the L.A. phone book, starting, naturally, at the 'A' section. Aladdin was the first company I came upon."

Joey called the label's Eddie Mesner, who told him to come on down the next day for an audition. "[Mesner] heard me play, then he called in his wife. I played the same few songs for her. They left the room for 10 minutes, and the guy came back alone and asked me if I wanted a contract. So I signed a record contract and a manager's contract and was unknowingly in with the sharks."

From his first record on, except for a 1955 Cal-West single, Joey was "Sonny Knight."

"My cousin and I were working on a car. It was hot and we were drinking a lot of beer. We thought the name was a clever joke. I never thought that I'd have to live with it."

Aladdin issued "But Officer" and "Baby Come Back." When the royalties failed to appear, Sonny switched to Specialty Records. One release later, Specialty's Bumps Blackwell introduced him to the Morgans, Hite and Dorinda. They were songwriters and had a recording studio in their home. After a bit, Sonny and the Morgans worked up a song called "Confidential."

"I was disillusioned [by this point]," Knight recalled to liner-note writer Bill Millar. "I was working at a really bad club, A Bucket Of Blood on Central Avenue. They had the front door open, and I could see the funeral home where my mother was lying in state and that was traumatic. My mother never wanted me to be a musician and I thought I was letting her down . . . eventually, I thought, I don't have to spend the rest of my life doing this, and went into the studio."

The session Sonny debated attending produced his money-making moment. Unfortunately, two record companies, Viva and Dot, issued the track, and neither, according to Sonny, reported an accurate count on the number of disks sold. "The case was settled out of court, eventually . . . out of the whole thing, I got $2,100."

Sonny Knight currently lives in Hawaii. Finally an author, his book *The Day the Music Died* was published under his God-given name by Grove Press in 1981.

Sonny Knight

Joe Valino

GARDEN OF EDEN
(Dennise Haas Norwood)
Vik 0226
No. 12   *December 8, 1956*

Fossilized footprints of the man called Joe Valino are hard to come by in the world of pop music. Joey does a fine job of crooning this tune of apples and lust in a semi-operatic manner, complete with *Bolero*-like tensions and what years later would become known as an Orbisonian ending. Follow-ups like "In the Arms Of Love," "God's Little Acre," and the semi-autobiographical "Legend Of The Lost" failed to rekindle listener enthusiasm.

Valino continued working well into the '60s. His only album was issued by Debut in 1968.

Sil Austin

SLOW WALK
(Sil Austin)
Mercury 70963
No. 17   *December 22, 1956*

"Ping Pong," as Ella Fitzgerald has called Sylvester Austin (b. Sept. 17, 1929, Donellon, Fla.) was born to be a doctor, or so he thought. He took to playing the tenor saxophone when he was a little one. Only at his friends' insistence did 17-year-old Sil venture up to New York City to compete in a talent contest at the Apollo Theatre. Playing "Danny Boy," his favorite song, Sil won first prize and a two-week engagement at a local club—that gig matured into six months' work. Thereafter, he was in demand, playing sax with Roy Eldridge (1949), Cootie Williams (1949–1951), and Ray "Tiny" Bradshaw (1952–1954). The following year, Austin formed his own combo and recorded "Crossfire Part 1 & 2," along with some other obscure sides, for Jubilee Records.

In the summer of 1956, Sil was signed to the Mercury label. His finest singles, including the classic honky-tonk honker "Slow Walk," were cut in New York City with his usual assemblage of musicians: Mickey "Guitar" Baker (later one-half of MICKEY & SYLVIA), Clarence Collier (bass), Panama Francis (drums), Heywood Henry (baritone sax), Wallace Richardson (guitar), Maurice Simon (tenor sax), and George Stubbs (piano).

Touring in support of "Slow Walk," Sil was nearly killed when he lost control and flipped his car. Follow-up 45s continued to work the frenzied-sax terrain he shared with Big Jay McNeely, Red Prysock, and Clifford Scott, but only "Birthday Party" (#74, 1957) and his waxing of "Danny Boy" (#59, 1959) did well.

When last noted, Sil Austin was living in Florida. On occasion, Sil has been known to pick up his horn and honk for Sew City, Jerri, and, most recently, Shelby Singleton's SSS International label.

Vince Martin with The Tarriers

CINDY, OH CINDY
(Bob Baron, Burt Long)
Glory 247
No. 9   *December 22, 1956*

Critics reporting on Vince's few East Coast appearances at the South Boston or the Village Vanguard in the mid-to-late '50s noted that he was a "tall, personable," but "shy-appearing youngster." He was usually accompanied on two guitars and banjo by Alan Arkin, Bob Carey, and Erik Darling, THE TARRIERS. Midway through their act, Vince would come out and sing "Casey Jones," "So Long It's Been Good To Know You," and "Cindy, Oh Cindy," and then he'd walk off. Arkin, Carey, and Darling were also present on Vinnie's vinyl excursion. No one could have guessed it, but months later, the Tarriers would create their own momentous moment with "The Banana Boat Song." Although Martin and the Tarriers appeared on a few other 45s, nothing further clicked.

Vince continued to work at a low-profile music career well into the '70s. ABC-Paramount and Elektra issued a few singles; Elektra even shipped an LP in 1964. In 1973, during the height of the singer-songwriter epidemic, Capitol made a last-ditch effort to revive Martin's flagging popularity with an album entitled, logically enough, *Vince Martin*.

Ivory Joe Hunter

SINCE I MET YOU BABY
(Ivory Joe Hunter)
Atlantic 1111
No. 12   *December 29, 1956*

With a daddy preacher who played guitar, a mama who sang in a choir, a house full of instrument-abusing sibs, and a God-given name like Ivory, it was natural that Ivory Joe (b. Nov. 10, 1914, Kirbyville, Tex.) would take up the piano. He performed in school orchestras, sang in a church quartet, and after graduation, he and his combo played the bars from Galveston to Port Arthur. In the '40s, Joe and his jumpers held down a radio program on KFDM in Beaumont, Texas. With the outbreak of World War II, Hunter dropped the band and hoofed it to the West Coast, where he worked the L.A. and San Francisco clubs.

In 1945, Hunter formed the Ivory label and pressed up some copies of his first record, "Blues at Sunrise" b/w "You Taught Me To Love." Accompanying him on the disk were the soon-to-be-famous Three Blazers (Charles Brown, Johnny Moore, and Eddie Williams). The disk sold well and was picked up for distribution by Leon Rene's Exclusive label. The following year, Hunter formed Pacific Records and, using top-drawer sidemen like Pee Wee Crayton, Wardell Gray, and Eddie Taylor, dashed off a series of now impossible-to-find waxings: "Ivory Joe's Boogie," "Pretty Mama Blues," "She's A Killer," "Jumpin' At The Dew Drop," "Boogie In The Rain," and "Big Wig."

In the fall of '47, Ivory Joe was so hot that King Records signed him up for what would prove to be a string of top-selling "race" records: "Don't Fall In Love With Me" (—/#8, 1948), "What Did You Do To Me" (—/#9, 1948), "Waitin' In Vain" (—/#5, 1949), "Guess Who" (—/#2, 1949), "Landlord Blues" (—/#6, 1949), "Jealous Heart" (—/#2, 1949), and "I Quit My Pretty Mama" (—/#4, 1950).

Ivory's first session for MGM produced "I Almost Lost My Mind" (—/#1, 1950), which many critics consider to be Hunter's finest outing. Although it topped the R & B charts and sold over a million copies, Hunter's classic was not even listed on *Billboard*'s pop charts. Six years later, Hunter's hymn would become a million-seller all over again, this time for the up-and-coming Pat Boone.

With two singles that sounded very much like "Almost"—"Since I Met You Baby" and "Empty Arms" (#43, 1957) b/w "Love's A Hurting Game"—Ivory Joe finally had major crossover success. Yet while he continued to record fine bluesy ballads and gospel-tinged country disks for Dot, Goldisc, Capitol, Smash, VeeJay, Stax, and many other labels, Ivory Joe Hunter never made the pop or R & B listings after 1960.

In December 1973, Hunter began receiving treatment for lung cancer. He died in Memphis on November 8, 1974.

Tarriers

THE BANANA BOAT SONG
(Alan Arkin, Bob Carey, Erik Darling)
Glory 249
No. 4 *February 9, 1957*

When Erik Darling (b. Sept. 25, 1933, Baltimore) was growing up in Canandaigua, New York, Burl Ives was his hero. Oh, to be Burl and roam the countryside, free of all concerns! Appearing before people to sing and strum truth seemed a great way to make money. Erik found a loose guitar, learned the chords, and listened intently to Josh White, Pete Seeger, and Brownie McGhee. In 1953, Darling joined a group of 19 singers, dancers, and actors that had been organized by Mary Hunter for New York's Theatre Guild. For half a year, he performed one-nighters with the unit. Next, with buddies Alan Arkin (b. Mar. 26, 1934, Brooklyn) and Bob Carey, Erik formed his own unit of traveling, soothsaying performers, the Tarriers (originally called the Tunetellers).

Since 1953 and Perry Como's hit "Pa-paya Mama," artists like Burl Ives, Harry Belafonte, the Fontane Sisters, TERRY GILKYSON, and Steve Lawrence had been making the charts with calypsoesque Caribbean-styled tunes. Contributing to the blooming genre was the Tarriers' "The Banana Boat Song" and VINCE MARTIN's "Cindy, Oh Cindy." Reportedly, the musicians used on both releases were identical, only the names were changed to sell more records simultaneously. Neither Martin nor the Tarriers, however, ever again charted, and the "calypso explosion" of the '50s petered out as rapidly as it had puffed up.

Bob Carey remained with the Tarriers, recording with them well into the folk movement of the early '60s and the group's demise in 1964. Erik Darling stayed with the Tarriers for two years, then toured and recorded with the legendary Weavers. In 1963, Erik formed the Rooftop Singers with Bill Svanoe and one-time jazz singer Lynne Taylor.

From the mid-'70s on, Darling has concentrated on teaching music. Alan Arkin left the Tarriers in the late '50s to pursue a successful career on Broadway and in the movies, appearing as Sigmund Freud in *The Seven Percent*

The Tarriers,
with Alan Arkin
(center)

Solution, and as a lovable, bumbling luster in Neil Simon's *Last of the Red Hot Lovers*. He has twice been nominated for an Oscar.

Joy Layne
YOUR WILD HEART
(James Testa, Charles Sano)
Mercury 71038
No. 20   *February 23, 1957*

Joy Layne (b. late '30s, Chicago) seemed to be on the brink of a big-time career when "Your Wild Heart," her cover version of a single by THE PONI-TAILS, charted nicely. She had a searing range and the kind of one-two vocal punch that Brenda Lee was just about to unleash on "Dynamite" and "That's All You Got To Do."

Joy's dad was a construction worker but a household violinist and piano-picker as well. Mom was actively involved in local theater production and her little 15-year-old's future. One day, Joy's mother took her downtown to see Mercury A & R man Art Talmadge. "She was bouncy and bright-eyed and carried her mascot, this squeaky toy dog Brownie," Talmadge

recalled to *TV Radio Mirror*. Art already knew of this promising Poni-Tails platter, and after a quick audition, he had found the right singer to cover the wild number.

Lennie LaCour, a multi-indie label owner (Lucky Four, Magic Touch, 620), talent scout, and recording artist, was the last person to record any tunes on Joy, in 1961. As Lennie revealed in an exclusive interview, "Her mother was her manager, and she had certain things that she didn't want Joy doing, like traveling and promoting her records. And that was the end of her career.

"She looked and sounded to me like Sandy Duncan. Everytime I see or hear Sandy, I think of Joy Layne."

Mickey & Sylvia
LOVE IS STRANGE
(Ethel Smith)
Groove 0175
No. 11   *March 2, 1957*

In 1950, while attending Washington Irving High School, Sylvia Vanderpool (b. Mar. 6,

1936, New York City) was spotted by a scout and given the chance to record some sides with Hot Lips Page for Columbia Records. "Chocolate Candy Blues, "Pacifying," and "Sharp Little Sister" were worldly numbers for a 14-year-old to handle. While these now-collectible records were critically lauded, they flopped commercially, as did the 78s she cut as "Little Sylvia" for Savoy and Jubilee.

In 1954, while Ms. Vanderpool was in the studio recording for the Cat label, she met prolific session guitarist McHouston "Mickey" Baker. Mickey (b. Oct. 15, 1925, Louisville, Kent.) had been all over New York providing back-up licks for King, Okeh, and Savoy artists. Sylvia's Cat tracks failed to sell, and she approached Baker about guitar lessons. From this evolved the relationship that would produce a mammoth hit and sexually suggestive rock and roll classic—"Love Is Strange," their sixth disk as a duet.

Incredible singles like "There Ought To Be A Law" (#47, 1957) b/w "Dearest" (#85) and "Bewildered" (#57, 1958) followed—but their act was always viewed as a novelty, a throwa-way, and not one of this dynamite duo's disks ever captured a mass audience again.

In 1959, Mickey & Sylvia split. Baker signed on with Atlantic Records to cut jazzy items; Leiber & Stoller later teamed him with Kitty Noble for some obscure sides as Mickey & Kitty. Mickey and Sylvia soon patched up their "lover's spat" and returned to the studios to produce some songs for their King-distributed Willow label and for RCA. "Baby You're So Fine" (#52, 1961) b/w "Lovedrops" (#97) were not up to par, but they charted.

"That was Ike Turner playing on 'Baby You're So Fine' and on the follow-up 'He Gave Me Everything,'" Sylvia told *Blues & Soul's* Tony Cummings. "We returned the favor for Ike. In 1960, we'd recorded this song called 'It's Gonna Work Out Fine' but RCA didn't release it. So Tina Turner recorded it in 1961. I played lead guitar and Mickey did the spoken bits. It was a smash hit, of course . . . for Ike & Tina Turner."

In 1962, Mickey moved to Paris. Two years later, Sylvia married Joe Robinson and made some records as Sylvia Robbins for Sue and

Mickey & Sylvia

Jubilee. The couple set up the All Platinum Studios and a stable of record labels that eventually included Horoscope, Stang, Turbo, Vibration, and Sugar Hill. Sylvia went on to write several successful songs like "Love On A Two-Way Street" (a hit for the Moments in 1970 and Stacy Lattislaw in 1981), and to produce recordings for Linda Jones, the Moments, SHIRLEY & CO., the Sugarhill Gang, the Whatnauts, and Lonnie Youngblood.

Mickey has been playing sessions in France and elsewhere. He has recorded with the Coasters, Champion Jack Dupree, Willie Mabon, Sunnyland Slim, and TOMMY TUCKER. He has made nearly a dozen solo albums, and sporadically records duets with yet another "Sylvia," Monique Raucher. Baker is also well-known to guitar students worldwide for his guitar-instruction books.

SYLVIA, meanwhile, became a one-hit wonder in 1973 with her breathy solo recording of "Pillow Talk" (#3), which introduced her to a whole new generation of pop music fans.

All-American Light-Heavyweight Champion of the Military—he moved to San Francisco. A head-on car crash (in which Peter Morgan, brother of baseball's Joe Morgan, was killed) halted his career. Shortly after, McCracklin turned his attention to singing, blowin' harp, and poundin' piano blues in Bay-area bars. Jim had been messin' with music for years; he had cut a number of singles for Globe, Excelsior, Courtney, Cavatone, Downtown, Trilon, and Modern, all before 1950. Nothing made the pop or R & B charts until Jim, on a dare and in disgust, wrote "The Walk" and lowered himself to the level of rock and roll.

In the intervening years, Jimmy has written a couple of classic songs ("The Thrill Is Gone" and "Tramp") and recorded some fine R & B numbers, some of which crossed over to the pop charts: "Just Got to Know" (#64, 1962), "Every Night, Every Day" (#91, 1965), "Think" (#95, 1965), and "My Answer" (#92, 1966).

Jimmy McCracklin

THE WALK
(Jimmy McCracklin)
Checker 885
No. 7   *March 10, 1957*

Legend has it that bluesman Jimmy McCracklin was annoyed by the poor quality of rock and roll records, and threw together what he thought was a dog of a disk to prove that rock consumers had no taste. "The Walk" strolled off with hit honors; it's been decades since, and for whatever reason, Jimmy has never again accurately sized up or serviced the pop public's musical needs.

McCracklin was born James David Walker on a cotton plantation outside of Helena, Arkansas, on August 13, 1921. Jimmy's parents separated when he was young, and he moved with his mom to St. Louis, where he sang in the choir of his Baptist church. While still in his mid-teens, Jimmy and a cousin named John Henry Murrell hopped a train to fame, fortune, and California. Their goal was to find boxer Archie Moore and to convince him to teach them all he knew about the sport. Reportedly, they found Archie in San Diego, and he let the boys hang out with him for a while.

Jimmy was yearning to become a professional boxer. In the late '40s, after a tour of duty with the Navy—where he won the title of

Terry Gilkyson & The Easy Riders

MARIANNE
(Terry Gilkyson, Frank Miller, Richard Dehr)
Columbia 40817
No. 4   *April 6, 1957*

Hamilton Henry "Terry" Gilkyson (b. 1919, Phoenixville, Penn.) was born in a stone house near the Schuykill River. He attended the University of Pennsylvania as a music major until he grew bored with formal studies. During the summer of 1938, he traveled to Tucson, Arizona, to work on a ranch, hear genuine cowboy tunes, and learn how to play the guitar. He started singing in local watering holes, and sang folk songs over the Armed Forces Radio Service during the '40s. A decade later, Terry was humming and picking for Decca Records, recording numerous singles and a few LPs. Most notable among these waxings was a highly successful recording that Gilkyson cut with the Weavers, "On Top Of Old Smokey" (#2, 1951).

By 1954, Terry had tailored and tuned an accompanying unit which he dubbed the Easy Riders. With Richard "Rudy" Dehr and Frank Miller, they roamed about the land performing folk favorites. T. G. and his Riders almost had a hit with an under-relished weirdie called "Yermo's Nightmare, Yermo Red." The calypso-flavored "Marianne" did what "Yermo" had barely managed to do—garner Gilkyson and his group a genuine folk hit.

For some reason, Terry immediately had his name pulled off all subsequent releases by the Easy Riders, and at some fuzzy point left the group entirely. Before his departure, he wrote or co-wrote "The Cry Of The Wild Goose" for Frankie Laine (#1, 1950) and Tennessee Ernie Ford (#15, 1950); "Greenfields" for the Brothers Four (#2, 1960); "Love Is A Golden Ring" for Frankie Laine (#10, 1957); and "Memories Are Made Of This" for Dean Martin (#1, 1956) and Gale Storm (#5, 1956).

The Riders, meanwhile, carried on into the early '60s. Nothing further charted, but the group's everchanging composition did allow a number of later music-makers an apprenticeship. Jerry Yester, a former member of the New Christy Minstrels who would move on to work with the Lovin' Spoonful and the Association, was an Easy Rider for a brief time, as was Doug Myres of Bud & Travis.

Terry is still of this earth, living a life of anonymity in Mexico. His son Tony plays bass for the rock group X; his daughter Liza is a folk artist with a recent LP on Gold Coast Records.

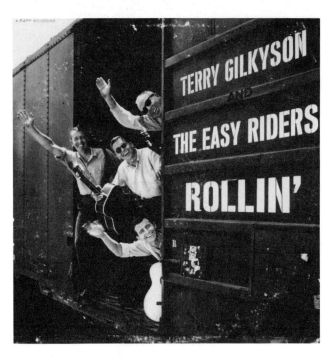

Jimmy Bowen with The Rhythm Orchids

I'M STICKIN' WITH YOU
(Jimmy Bowen, Buddy Knox)
Roulette 4001
No. 14   *April 27, 1957*

Jimmy Bowen (b. Nov. 30, 1937, Santa Rita, N.M.), Buddy Knox (b. July 20, 1933, Happy, Tex.), and Don Lanier met in 1954 or 1955. They were all attending West Texas State College on athletic scholarships. Don Lanier played lead guitar, Buddy played rhythm guitar, and Jimmy—as Buddy told Jean-Pierre Chapados in *New Kommotions*—was "the worst bass player I have ever heard." As the Rhythm Orchids, they gigged at school functions and local night spots. Once the world got a listen, the boys were pronounced co-creators, with Buddy Holly and his Crickets, of the "Tex-Mex Sound."

Drummer Dave Alldred was added, but would soon leave the fold to record with Gerry Granahan (a.k.a. Jerry Grant) as part of Dickie Doo & the Don'ts. Before his departure late in '57, the group ventured into Norman Petty's studios in Clovis, New Mexico, to record four

tunes. Two of these, "I'm Stickin' With You" and "Party Doll," were issued back-to-back on the Blue Moon label, and later, on the group's own Triple D label (named after radio KDDD in Dumas, Texas).

The response was so hot for "I'm Stickin' With You" b/w "Party Doll" that George Goldner, Phil Kahl, and Morris Levy reportedly formed Roulette Records just to distribute the Rhythm Orchids' record nationally. Seeing that airplay was evenly divided between the sides, and that each side featured a different lead singer, the Roulette bosses decided to split the disk in two, figuring that two hits would be better than one. "Party Doll" by Buddy Knox & The Rhythm Orchids eventually went to number one on the pop charts. "I'm Stickin' With You," with Bowen singing lead, was not quite as successful but still secured a spot in the top 40.

Buddy went on successfully clicking for a while with platters like "Rock Your Baby To Sleep" (#17, 1957), "Hula Love" (#9, 1957), "Somebody Touched Me" (#22, 1958), and "Lovey Dovey" (#25, 1961). Bowen's "Ever Lovin' Fingers" (#63, 1957), "Warm Up To Me Baby" (#57, 1957), and the maudlin "By The Light Of The Silvery Moon" (#50, 1958) did fairly well, and for a few years, occasional releases bearing his name appeared on Crest, Decca, Capehart, Reprise, and his own Amos label.

The Fifties

While with Roulette, Bowen worked at becoming a producer. In the early '60s, he filled this role for Crest and later, Chancellor. In 1963, Bowen was asked to join Reprise Records, where he produced such acts as Sammy Davis, Jr., Dean Martin, Jack Nitzsche, and Frank and Nancy Sinatra—not bad for a new kid on the block. Jim moved to Nashville in 1977 and produced numerous hit recordings for John Anderson, the Bellamy Brothers, Glen Campbell, Crystal Gayle, Merle Haggard, Reba McEntire, the Oak Ridge Boys, Waylon Jennings, JOHNNY LEE, Kenny Rogers, JOHN SCHNEIDER, George Strait, Mel Tillis, Conway Twitty, and Hank Williams, Jr.

Jim Bowen was president of MCA's Nashville division, then held an executive position with Warner Brothers Records. Currently, he is president of Capitol Records' Nashville operation.

Ken Copeland

PLEDGE OF LOVE
(R. Redd)
Imperial 5432
No. 12   *May 6, 1957*

The Mints were a local nightclub pleasure for the folks of Gainesville, Texas. Late in 1956, Joe M. Leonard, Jr., manager of radio KGAF and owner of the indie Lin label, approached Ken Copeland (b. 1937) and his group about cutting some tunes. Early the following year, "Busy Body Rock" was released (as by the Four Mints), but there was not much of a stir beyond the Gainesville area. "Pledge Of Love," however, was another story. Here was the type of song that was so innately appealing that almost any performer could have had a hit with it. When interest in the disk exceeded the ability of the lads at Lin to supply the stores with the side, a quick arrangement was made with Lew Chubb's Imperial label for national distribution. Speed was of the essence, for Mitchell Torok, Johnny Janis, accordionist Dick Contino, and a host of others were competing with nearly identical cover versions.

The initial pressings of "Pledge Of Love" credited the disk's artist as "The Mints." As time progressed and the disk rose in popularity, Copeland, the group's lead singer, was given sole billing. Despite the competing covers—each which cut deeply into the potential sales of the Mints original—the Copeland-crooned "Pledge" managed to reach the num-

ber 12 position. But in all the uproar, Ken never established himself with the pop public as *the* singer of "Pledge Of Love." Consequently, only three additional 45s by Copeland — "Teenage," "Someone To Love Me," and "Fanny Brown"—were issued before Copeland and his Mints returned to their local-level celebrity status.

Only years later, after Kenny had evolved into a "televangelist," would he freely admit that all of this earthly success had left him sick, broke, overweight, and depressed. "Motorcycles, airplanes, and rock music were my life," he wrote in a biographical sketch for the members of the Kenneth Copeland Ministries. Five years after "Pledge Of Love," Ken made his personal commitment to the teachings of Christ. In 1968, after attending Oral Roberts University, he and his wife Gloria formed their ministries in Fort Worth, Texas. Copeland's bio reports that he touches millions with his weekly and daily TV programs, TV specials, monthly magazine, teaching tapes, gospel recordings, and conventions.

Bonnie Guitar

DARK MOON
(Ned Miller)
Dot 15550
No. 6   *June 10, 1957*

She was born Bonnie Buchingham on March 25, 1924, in Seattle. Friends called her "Guitar" because she was so skilled with one. Starting in the early '50s, she led her own country band in L.A., and worked recording sessions. While her haunting take on "Dark Moon," a NED MILLER tune, would become her lone pop notable, she continued to rack up country hits into the early '80s.

In 1958, Ms. Guitar started her own record label, Dolphin—later called Dolton—and successfully signed on the sound-making services of the Fleetwoods, the Ventures, and DON ROBERTSON. With Robertson, Bonnie recorded some undercover disks in the early '60s like "Born To Be With You" as the Echoes. Dolton was later sold to Liberty, now part of the EMI empire.

Bonnie has recorded for numerous labels (Radio, Dot, Dolton, RCA, Jerden, Fabor, Paramount, Columbia, ABC, MCA, 4-Star) and has done country A & R work for Dot and Paramount Records. Several fine LPs (*Dark Moon*, 1957; *Two Worlds*, 1966) were issued through the '60s, though all of them are out of print.

Ms. Guitar currently records for Playback Records.

Marvin Rainwater

GONNA FIND ME A BLUEBIRD
(Marvin Rainwater)
MGM 12412
No. 18   *June 10, 1957*

Part Cherokee, with Rainwater as his mother's maiden name, Marvin Karlton Perry (b. July 25, 1925, Wichita, Kans.) took classical piano lessons as a child, until an accident in an auto-repair shop left him minus a right thumb. Perry kept writing songs, though. He took pre-veterinary courses at Washington State University in Walla Walla, then spent the next three years working with his father in an Oregon lumber camp. With the outbreak of World War II, he studied for two years as a pharmacist's mate. Whenever possible, Perry would bring out his guitar and sing to his peers.

On his return to civilian life, Marv worked as a tree surgeon and nearly got himself killed. "I was trying to write a song while cutting out the top of a tree," Rainwater told *Goldmine's* Bill Millar. "I'd cut it off before I woke up and realized what I was doing." While hanging by his safety belt, some 75 feet above a slab of solid concrete, Rainwater re-evaluated his career goals. "That's when I quit tree surgery."

Perry picked up his guitar and toured about "itty bitty clubs" in the Washington, D.C. area. A local studio owner named Ben Adelman heard something special in Marvin's rockabilly sound and recorded 50 of his songs. (Most of these have been issued without Rainwater's approval on budget labels like Spin-O-Rama, Crown, and Premier.) Red Foley heard one of Marv's reworked Hank Williams numbers, liked it, and offered him a spot on his "Ozark Jubilee" radio program. When Teresa Brewer and Justin Tubb covered Marv's self-penned "I Gotta Go Get My Baby" and outsold his own version, MGM president Frank Walker offered Rainwater a contract. "Gonna Find Me A Bluebird," his first single for MGM, was a hit—but it did not generate much moolah, so Marvin struggled through two years of die-hard country and hillbilly rock and roll.

Reminiscing with *Goldmine* in 1980, Marvin noted that some miscalculations and misfortunes tripped up his career. Rainwater would

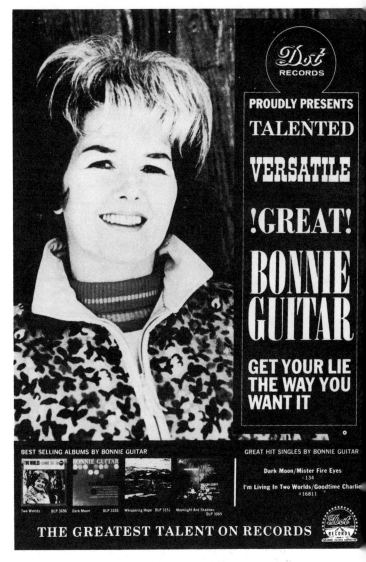

appear in a headband, buckskins, and full Indian garb, a publicity ploy that he now feels typecast him. In 1959, he developed some vocal problems. "I didn't know it then but I had calluses on my vocal cords and should have quit for months. Instead, we'd spend hours and hours in the studio without ever getting anything decent. I felt bad for Jim Vienneau, the producer, 'cause he was really patient. One day I followed him out and he was setting fire to a $20 bill. That gave me the message—he needed to spend his time with Connie Francis while MGM was burning money trying to cut a record on me."

Before having throat surgery, Marv persisted in trying to make records for Warwick

like teen tune with plenty of "la-la-las" and a deep-voiced male chorus.

Her debut disk, "Love Me Always," had appeared on the tiny Teen label in 1955 only to reappear and disappear under the Bernlo logo months later. Bob Marcucci, who would later discover Fabian and Frankie Avalon, was one of the few who noticed the disk; when he formed his Chancellor company (reportedly with help from Dick Clark) in 1957, Jodie was his first signing.

Although Sands' "Sayonara (Goodbye)" was featured in the rock and roll flick *Jamboree* (1957), this follow-up to "With All My Heart" flopped. After some minimal action with "Someday (You'll Want Me To Want You)" (#95, 1958), Sands was forever absent from the airwaves and the charts. Up through the early '60s, numerous sides were issued by the Signature, Thor, Paris, and ABC-Paramount labels.

Johnnie & Joe
OVER THE MOUNTAIN; ACROSS THE SEA
(Rex Garvin)
Chess 1654
No. 8 *July 22, 1957*

Zell Sanders was always itchin' to be an entertainer. It never happened, but Ms. Sanders did become a cult legend as the owner of the tiny J & S label and as a mentor to numerous aspiring talents.

"She'd written a couple of songs when she was a child, and she answered a couple of those ads in the papers saying 'send us your song and we'll get it published,'" Johnnie Louise Richardson, Zell's daughter and half of Johnnie & Joe, told *Goldmine*'s Aaron Fuchs. "That was it. She was dedicated. And she liked kids, too . . . [Later, when] she was working for the Police Athletic League in Harlem in the 23rd Precinct, she saw the talent, and it was just there on the street. 'Do you sing?' she'd ask them. 'Come on up to my house.' They all got to know her around as the lady that goes around grabbing groups."

One of those groups was the Hearts, which consisted of Hazel Cruchfield, Louise Harris, Joyce Weiss, and, at various times, Betty Harris and Baby Washington. In 1953, Sanders placed the girls with Baton Records. Disappointed with the productions and the royalty

and Brave. After his recovery, he cut even better disks for Wesco, United Artists, and Warner Bros., but none of these ever charted, and most died quiet deaths. British tours in the mid-'70s led to the release of British-only LPs for Philips (*Marvin Rainwater Gets Country Fever*, 1972) and Westwood (*Especially For You*, 1976). Throughout the '80s, Germany's Bear Family label repackaged some of Marvin's finest rockabilly efforts.

Rainwater is still alive and kicking. "I think rock and roll makes you look younger and stay younger. I'm certainly not gonna stop. I'll be doing it till I'm baldheaded and lose all my teeth."

Jodie Sands
WITH ALL MY HEART
(Bob Marcucci, Pete De Angelis)
Chancellor 1003
No. 15 *June 24, 1957*

Jodie Sands was a mainline pop vocalist from Philadelphia who sang in the tradition of Edie Gorme, Gisele MacKenzie, and Kay Starr. But unlike these other songstresses, Jodie could sound like a sweet but sexually-charged kid. Most of her songs had a seductive and slightly sassy Latin feel. Her solid seller was a cha-cha-

statements issued by the label, Zell formed her own label, J & S, the following year. She issued singles by Niecy Dizelle and the Machines, the Gospel Wonders, the Harptones, THE JAY-NETTES, the Plants, and the Pre-Teens.

"Rex [Garvin, a pianist/songwriter who lived next door] brought Joe Rivers up one night, and said 'Hey, Miss Sanders, this is Joe Rivers and we've been rehearsing some things,'" Richardson told Fuchs. "'We want you to listen because we want to do a thing together called 'Over the Mountain'.' So, she listened and listened, and said 'I think it needs a little something . . . I tell you what, Johnnie, you get over there and you sing with them.' I said, 'Oh no, do I have to?' So she gave me that look that distinguishes between mother and record manufacturer. So I knew I better get over there and join them.

"At first they didn't want to do it with me. But when we got into the studio and we all listened, I guess it all dawned on us, 'Hey, maybe we got something here.'"

Issued on J & S, the disk almost immediately started to take off. Chess Records had picked up national distribution on Johnnie & Joe's debut disk, "I'll Be Spinning" (—/#10, 1957), and did the same for the duo's only mammoth mover. In addition to some fine follow-ups shipped by J & S and Chess, and a re-charting of "Over The Mountain" (#89, 1960), numerous other Johnnie & Joe 45s appeared on ABC-Paramount, Blue Rock, Gone, Masterpiece, Omega, and Tuff.

Personal appearances were rare, and tensions developed between the duo. Johnnie formed Dice, her own short-lived label, and recorded the Avalons, the Clickettes, and the Premiers. In the '60s, she turned away from the biz to marry and to raise a family.

Ambient Sound resurrected the act in 1983. *Kingdom of Love*, their first and only LP, was issued, as was a single, the album's title track. Neither generated more than a cultish stir.

Johnnie Louise Richardson died on October 25, 1988.

Russ Hamilton

RAINBOW
(Russ Hamilton)
Kapp 184
No. 4 *September 16, 1957*

Years before the Beatles got together, Ronnie Hulme sailed out of Liverpool and into the ears and hearts of teenage America. It was only a brief cross-cultural fling, but Ronnie's "Rainbow" sold so darn well in the U.S. that he garnered a gold record (signifying sales of over 1,000,000 copies), becoming only the sixth British bloke to do so.

Russ Hamilton, as he was known in the States, was born in 1934 in Liverpool. After some education, he worked for seven years in the costing office of a metal box manufacturing company. For adventure, Russ joined the Royal Air Force and acquired some decorations for activities in the Korean War. On his return, it was back to the metal box manufacturing company. For more adventure, Russ started singing and strumming guitar at parties and clubs. In 1955, he secured the first of a succession of jobs as a "red coat" (sort of a singing waiter) at a summer camp. A scout from Britain's Oriole Records heard him sing while Russ was serving and cleaning at the Ocean Hotel in Brighton.

Russ sweetly and cheerfully sang of his wish to buy his little bird a rainbow, and, if he could scrape up enough, buy the moon itself. In England, teens weren't buying this ode—they wanted something with meat on it. Someone flipped the record over and found "We Will Make Love." To the surprise of many observers, the selection actually made it past the BBC censors, proof that Russ truly did sound like a lad who never had a lustful thought in his head.

All of his follow-up efforts, including "Tip Toe Thru' The Tulips," were given a pass by listeners in both the U.S. and Russ' homeland. By the time Hamilton got a good thrust on a tune, as in the thumping rockaballad "My Unbeatable Heart," his media moment had passed.

Bobbettes

MR. LEE
(Reather Dixon, Helen Gathers, Emma Ruth Pought, Jannie Pought, Laura Webb)
Atlantic 1144
No. 6 *September 23, 1957*

These eight youngsters were attending P.S. 109 at the corner of 99th Street and Second Avenue in Manhattan in 1955. They met in the glee club, became after-school playmates, and started singing together as the Harlem Queens. Two years later, they were discovered by James A. Dailey when he spotted them on Herb Sheldon's local TV show. Dailey liked their sound, but not that godawful name: "Sounded like some female motorcycle gang," he said. A sister of one of the girls had just named her baby Chantel Bobbette. Since there was already a "Chantels," the girls decided that they were going to be "The Bobbettes."

By the time Dailey took control of the group, there were five Bobbettes: baritone Reather Dixon (b. 1945), alto Helen Gathers (b. 1944), tenor Laura Webb (b. 1943) and the Pought sisters, alto Emma (b. 1944) and soprano Jannie (b. 1945). One of the tunes they had been toying with was this ditty about a fifth-grade teacher that they did not exactly dig. Dailey brought the girls and their "Mr. Lee" song to Atlantic Records. The response was a positive one, but the company insisted that some of the negative comments about this Mr. Lee fellow would have to be deleted.

To the surprise of all, "Mr. Lee" sold 2,000,000 copies. "We didn't consider ourselves famous or even talented," Reather Dixon told *Goldmine's* Jeff Tamarkin. "We were just singing. I think the record must have been out about six months before we said, 'Gee, we're on the radio and in the jukeboxes!'" For the next two years, Atlantic kept issuing new platters by the girls, but nothing clicked. When not busy touring or attending New York's Professional School for Children, they sang backup for the Five Keys, IVORY JOE HUNTER, Clyde McPlatter, and JOHNNY THUNDER.

A few singles for Triple-X in 1960 almost restored the Bobbettes' momentum. In rapid succession, they charted: "I Shot Mr. Lee" (#52), "Have Mercy Baby (#66) b/w "Dance With Me George" (#95), and "I Don't Like It Like That" (#72), their "answer" to CHRIS KENNER's "I Like It Like That."

Helen Gathers left the group in 1961, and the girls continued on as a quartet.

The Bobbettes have yet to retire.

"We have been singing together with the same four girls for 20 years," Ms. Dixon wrote years back in *Yesterday's Memories*. "And we will remain together for another 20, until we are old and gray, with one thing in our minds: that is to get one more gold record on the top."

The Bobbettes

Joe Bennett &
The Sparkletones

Joe Bennett &
The Sparkletones

BLACK SLACKS
(Joe Bennett, Irv Denton)
ABC-Paramount 9837
No. 17   *October 14, 1957*

History has finally granted rightful kingpin roles to BO DIDDLEY and CARL PERKINS; someday even Ronnie Hawkins will get a piece of the action. Unfortunately, Joe Bennett & The Sparkletones, one of the finest and raunchiest '50s rock bands, are hardly ever given a mention. Some may recall "Black Slacks," which an oldies DJ will occasionally spin, but beyond that, Joe and the boys are largely forgotten.

At the pinnacle of their popularity, Bennett and band ranged in age from 14 to 17. They were all strict churchgoing boys, born and raised in Spartanburg, South Carolina. Joe was reportedly the leader of the Church Youth Movement in his state. While other cats were meandering around the countryside boppin' mean licks, Joe and the fellows would drop everything come Sunday morn to attend a

showing at the closest House of the Lord. Bob Cox happened onto a Sparkletone scene, dug their cool sounds, became their manager, and secured them a contract with ABC.

"Black Slacks," their first release, sold well and long, remaining on the *Billboard* charts for more than four months. The tune sported teenage expressions like "cool breeze," "crazy little mama," "hep cat," "cool daddy-o," and "rarin' to go." Joe (vocals and lead guitar), Wayne Arthur (stand-up bass), Howie "Sparky" Childress (guitar), and Jimmy "Sticks" Denton (drums) appeared at an Alan Freed stage show and even made the scene on Ed Sullivan's "r-r-really big show." Their 1957 follow-up, also an ode to tuff teenwear called "Penny Loafers And Bobby Socks," did fairly well and logged in at number 42 on the Top 100—not a bad showing.

Nothing with the Sparkletone name upon it, however, ever charted again. After three tamer singles for ABC, the guys moved over to Paris Records for four fair-to-fine, mostly puffy-pop, records. Nothing was heard of the group until, in the belly of the folk-rock movement, the Sparkletones reappeared with one limp single, "Well Dressed Man."

Tune Weavers

HAPPY, HAPPY BIRTHDAY BABY
(Margo Sylvia, Gilbert Lopez)
Checker 872
No. 5 *October 28, 1957*

Frank Paul, a former bandleader and music director for off-Broadway shows, had acquired master recordings from the DuBonnett and Onyx record labels. By 1952, Frank was releasing some of these masters on a label he called Casa Grande, after his old Boston-based big band.

Nearby, Frank's brother-in-law ran a school that taught pattern-making for men's clothing. One of his students, Gilbert Lopez (b. July 4, 1934), had been singing with an *a cappella* group for about four months, so he pestered Frank to check out these "Tone Weavers," as they initially called themselves.

"I thought jeez . . . just another group," Frank recalled to *Goldmine*'s George Moonoogian. "So finally, one Sunday in October of '56, they were coming over to my brother-in-law's house in Medford, and I went over to hear them."

The group consisted of bass Johnnie Sylvia (b. Sept. 8, 1935), his wife and lead singer Margo (b. Apr. 4, 1936), plus tenor Lopez (Margo's brother) and Margo's cousin, obligato Charlotte Davis (b. Nov. 12, 1936). They played some tapes for Paul and sang some songs *a cappella*. When the Tone Weavers broke into a new tune that Margo and Gil had just written, "Happy, Happy Birthday Baby," Paul "jumped up and said, 'That's it! That's the one we're going to record!' I could then see its hit potential."

Contracts were drawn up, Paul became their manager, and on March 7, 1957, the renamed Tune Weavers were ushered into Boston's Ace Recording Studio to record two tracks, "Happy, Happy" and its eventual flip side, "Old Man River." Once the promo copies got around, it became apparent that "Happy, Happy Birthday Baby" could be a big, big hit, and Paul made arrangements with Phil Chess to have the disk distributed on Chess' Checker subsidiary.

The response was phenomenal: sales eventually totaled 2,000,000 copies. The Tune Weavers toured the nation, making stops at the Apollo Theatre, the Paramount Theatre (where they were part of an Alan Freed rock and roll show), and Dick Clark's "American Bandstand."

The following year, Charlotte dropped out of the group, and was replaced by William Morris, Jr. An album and some nifty follow-ups appeared. "I Remember Dear," "There Stands My Love," "Little Boy," and "I Hear The Mission Bells" all received zip in the way of airplay, and all bombed.

The group also experienced some major problems when it came to compensation. "I wrote 'Happy' . . . and Gil paid $6 to copyright the song," Margo complained. "[As of December 1988], neither my brother nor I have received any money as artists. Corruption and greed are the reasons I stopped singing."

Margo and John have since divorced. Margo reportedly pursued an on-and-off solo singing career. John worked as a therapist for a while at Boston State College. Gil went on to become a manager of an electrical plant. Charlotte has been a Boston housewife.

Rays

SILHOUETTES
(Frank Slay, Bob Crewe)
Cameo 117
No. 3 *November 4, 1957*

Stanley "Bob" Crewe had been a male model and a less-than-successful teen idol. At a party in Philadelphia in the mid-'50s, he met a pianist named Frank C. Slay, Jr. Frank worked for Cameo Records by day and the British Information Service by night. The two hit it off, and talked of making their way in the world of pop music. Soon after, they formed a songwriting partnership and set up a little label called XYZ.

One night while riding the rails into Philly, Bob caught sight of a silhouette of two lovers in a warm embrace; the image stuck. Crewe told Slay of the incident, and one evening while shuffling papers for the Brits, Frank wrote the story line. Crewe created the chorus and thought up the title.

First tenor Walter Ford (b. Sept. 5, 1931, Lexington, Kent.), baritone Harry James (b. 1932), second tenor Davey Jones (b. 1931), and lead vocalist Harold "Hal" Miller (b. Jan. 17, 1931) were the Brooklyn-based Rays. Hal and Davey had recorded with the Four Fellows, whose 1955 hit "Soldier Boy" had peaked at number four on the R & B charts.

When the Rays met the proprietors of XYZ, they had been together only a year or so. Chess had issued their "Tippity Top," but it had flopped. While doing his workaday chores at

Cameo, Slay overheard the group's audition for the label. Cameo turned them down on the spot, but legend has it that Frank chased after them and signed them up with XYZ.

"Silhouettes" b/w "Daddy Cool" was a double-sided smash. For the next two years, Crewe and Slay put forth a number of goodies on their own XYZ and Topix labels, and, through a leasing arrangement, Cameo. Eventually, the persistence paid off, and the Rays returned to the airwaves with "Mediterranean Moon" (#95, 1960) and its copy-cat sister tune, "Magic Moon (Clair De Lune)" (#49, 1961).

Thurston Harris

LITTLE BITTY PRETTY ONE
(Robert Byrd)
Aladdin 3398
No. 6 *November 11, 1957*

Thurston Theodore Harris (b. July 11, 1931, Indianapolis) began singing in church as a six-year-old member of the Canaan Crusaders. Years later, Thurston and brother William sang in the Indiana Wonders. After his return from military service, Harris started singing secular in a hometown joint named the Sunset Terrace. There, guitarman Jimmy Liggins—noted for his "Tear Drop Blues" (—/#7, 1948) and "Drunk" (—/#4, 1953)—caught Thurston's act. Liggins liked what he heard and hooked Harris up with his brother, Joe Liggins of "The Honeydripper" fame. "I toured with Joe around the Midwest for a while," Harris told *Goldmine*'s Jim Dawson, "and I came out West with him to Los Angeles. As soon as we got [t]here, the band broke up."

Once in L.A., Harris allegedly went around passing himself off as the lead vocalist on the Five Royals' "Help Me Somebody" (—/#1, 1953), bluffing his way onto Hunter Hancock's popular R & B radio show and into talent shows. While appearing at the Club Alimony, Harris and a rag-tag group soon called the Lamplighters (Matthew Nelson, Willie Blackwell, and Leon Hughes, the latter an original Coaster) were spotted by Al Frazier. Drawn to their wildness and Thurs' voice, Al landed a recording contract for the group with Federal. The label released 13 Lamplighters singles between 1953 and 1956. Nothing charted, but all of these churners are now highly sought-after disks.

On several occasions, Harris and the guys would have a falling-out. "[They] were too interested in wine, women and dope," reported *Now Dig This'* Pete Bowen. After one of their break-ups, Thurston returned to Indianapolis. Variations of the Harris-less Lamplighters recorded as the Tenderfoots, the Sharps (backing Duane Eddy on "Rebel-'Rouser"), and still later as the Rivingtons. The Lamps reunited on a few occasions with Harris, and "Little Bitty Pretty One" was the result of one of these gatherings.

Thurston was released from a mental hospital the night before he and his Sharps (Al Frazier, John "Sonny" Harris, Matthew Nelson, and Carl White) recorded their moment of truth, "Little Bitty Pretty One"—actually a cover version of a song originally done by BOBBY DAY. Apparently, as Frazier told Bowen, "Thurston [had] gotten drunk and broke somebody's windows or something, and instead of calling the police they called the hospital."

Thurston's follow-ups to "Pretty One" were as good, if not still better, than the hit, but sales were relatively paltry. "Do What You Did" (#57, 1958) and another Bobby Day cover, "Over And Over" (#96, 1958), charted, but "Be-Baba-Leba," "(I Got Loaded At) Smokey Joe's," "Runk Bunk," and other efforts slipped into obscurity without notice. Aladdin Records folded, and Thurston moved on to recording some one-off sides for Imperial, Dot, Cub, and Reprise. The last of these was issued in 1964.

Jim Dawson interviewed Harris for *Goldmine* and produced a limited-release Harris EP in 1984. He reported that during the interview, Harris did not say much about those years, but that it was plain that there were a few hospitals and jails along the way, as well as a drug habit that he eventually shook. Thurston lived for a while in Indianapolis, and most recently in Pomona, California, where he drove a bus for L.A. County's Rapid Transit District. Harris died of a heart attack in Pomona on April 14, 1990.

Shepherd Sisters

ALONE (WHY MUST I BE ALONE)
(M. Craft, S. Craft)
Lance 125
No. 18 *November 11, 1957*

Not so very long ago, four sisters from Middletown, Ohio—blonds all—sang their way across this country. Martha, Mary Lou,

Gayle, and Judy Shepherd performed at gatherings, niteries (as booze-houses were politely called at one time), and talent shows. Frequently, they would take top honors on the "Arthur Godfrey's Talent Scouts" TV show. Herbie Space noted their cheerful sound and invited the girls to fill a void in his band. A booking agent named Karl Taylor caught a glimpse of the act often referred to as the "La La Quartet" and put the sisters on a multinational U.S.O. tour.

On their return, a canny Morty Craft signed the Shepherd Sisters to Melba Records for a spunky but forgettable "Gone With The Wind." Craft next suited the quartet in his own number, "Alone (Why Must I Be Alone)," possibly the happiest heartacher to ever chart. The song, its arrangement, and those voices were so catchy that even those who noticed the girls' imprecise harmonies still liked it. The sisters worked the Nautilus Hotel in Miami, the Town and Country in New York, and the Barclay in Toronto. They were picked up by Mercury for a single or so—then in turn by MGM, Warwick,

and United Artists Records—but nothing sold very well.

Finally, in 1963, the act passed through a watershed of sorts when they met someone who knew just how to make the best of the Shepherd Sisters' distinctive vocalizations. It was Bob Crewe who produced the sisters at their finest. Their Atlantic release "The Greatest Lover" had the feel of an innocent Shelley Fabares record, and their 20th Century Fox single "Finders Keepers" jumped out as if rendered by the livid EXCITERS. "Don't Mention My Name" staked out the number 94 slot on the Hot 100 in 1963, but it was all too late. The Shepherd Sisters' time had passed.

Bill Justis

RAUNCHY
(Bill Justis, Sidney Manker)
Phillips 3519
No. 2 *December 16, 1957*

Little Billy (b. Oct. 14, 1926, Birmingham, Ala.) and his family moved to Memphis when he was five. His mom was a concert pianist; under her influence and prodding, Bill took to tooting on the sax. He formed his first dance band when he was 15. After gathering some post-grad credits, he worked as the music director at Tulane University in New Orleans, and did choral arrangements for Arizona University. He moved to Memphis and married in 1954. Quite soon thereafter, Justis realized that extra money was needed. He kept dropping in on Sam Phillips' Sun studios, hoping to interest the legendary record man with his abilities.

"Justis, man, he was the first hip-talkin' cat that I ever heard," recalled Phillips in an interview with *Mean Mountain Music* magazine. "He'd repeatedly come by the studio at 706 Union and play these little dangle deals, 'Two Step,' 'Soft Shoe,' 'Be-Bop' . . . I had never really took him seriously. I don't know why. I guess I thought he was a joke. I think everyone did. In my opinion, the guy's a genius. He's just been misdirected, all his life, until he cut 'Raunchy.'"

Phillips finally flagged and hired the cool dude with the honkin' sax to be his music director at Sun/Phillips. In that role, Bill arranged and led the studio bands for Elvis, Johnny Cash, Jerry Lee Lewis, and the rest. Legend has it that it was Justis who first labeled Lewis "The Killer." "Bill would be around the studio all the time," said Phillips, "and I'd say, 'Now Bill, you've got to get raunchy sounding! Darn if he and [guitarist] Sid Manker didn't write a song and instrumentally put it down to become the biggest instrumental that was ever cut and out in the '50s."

A number of follow-up 45s were issued, but only "College Man" (#42, 1958) made the grade. After a dispute in March of 1960 involving charges of insubordination, Justis left Sun Records to form his own short-lived label, Play Me. Not many did, and in the early '60s, Bill moved his services to RCA, and later to ABC-Paramount, Monument, Sound Stage, and Smash. Several LPs of increasing schmaltzy sounds appeared on Smash label. Both *Bill Justis Plays 12 Big Instrumental Hits* (1962) and *Bill Justis Plays 12 More Big Instrumental Hits* (1963) clicked, but with a more sedate audience.

Bill never got to right these later wrongs. The hip-talkin' honker died of a brief illness on July 15, 1982, at the age of 55.

Margie Rayburn

I'M AVAILABLE
(Dave Burgess)
Liberty 55102
No. 9   *December 16, 1957*

Margie, born in Madera, California, attended Hollywood High School. Later, she sang with Ray Anthony's Orchestra, toured with Gene Autry, worked the Frisco night clubs, and had some singles issued locally on Alma and S & G labels—all before she was discovered by Norman Milkin, her future husband. Norm occasionally collaborated with Freddy Morgan on material for THE SUNNYSIDERS. Morgan, a banjo picker with Spike Jones and the City Slickers from 1947 to 1958, had created the Sunnysiders as an outlet for his tunes. As a member of that group, Margie appeared on their lone hit, "Hey, Mr. Banjo." After the Sunnysiders tried more numbers with the banjo motif like "Banjo Pickers Ball" and "The Lonesome Banjo (In The Pawn Shop Window)," Margie went solo again.

"I'm Available" was sensuous, in a Patti Page-like manner. The tune was found by her hubby and was written by a young Dave Burgess, who a few years later would have a successful career as the leader of the Champs. Margie recorded a string of fine follow-ups— "Smoochin'," "Try Me," and "Here I Am." Most

of them were drenched in heavy echo and used multi-tracking to give her voice the same slinky and suggestive quality that "Available" had featured. But no subsequent efforts charted, and Margie last recorded in 1966.

Ernie Freeman

RAUNCHY
(Bill Justis, Sidney Manker)
Imperial 5474
No. 4   *December 30, 1957*

Ernie was right there at the dawn of rock and roll. Next time you check out the classic Bill Haley flick, *Rock Around the Clock* (1956), take notice of the unimposing piano man tinkling in the shadows way behind the Platters as they warble "Only You." That's Ernie Freeman, the man behind a pile of California-born hits.

A little Freeman was born the morn of August 16, 1922, in Cleveland. Ernie took to the keyboards early and studied music at the university level. After his return from the service at the start of the '50s, Freeman worked the clubs playing light jazz and accompanying the likes of Dorothy Dandridge and Dinah Washington. In 1956, songwriter and producer Jerry Leiber discovered Ernie and used him as the pianist and arranger for his one-off rock and roll ensemble, Scooby Doo. Imperial Records got wind of Ernie, and enlisted his services as A & R man and recording artist.

For the next half-dozen years, Freeman recorded nearly 30 oldfangled rockin' instrumentals. In 1957, Freeman covers of both Doc Bagby's "Dumplin's" (#75) and BILL JUSTIS' classic "Raunchy" charted, as did three later disks—"Indian Love Call" (#59, 1958), "Theme From 'The Dark At The Top Of The Stairs'," (#70, 1960), and a version of "The Twist" (#93, 1962). These instrumentals usually featured Plas Johnson (sax), Irv Ashby (guitar), and a contingent of sticky strings.

In 1960, Percy Faith turned solid gold with the release of his mushy "Theme From 'A Summer Place'." Freeman, in response, wrote, arranged, and produced an equally bathetic string-thing he called "Beautiful Obsession." Released under the name of "Sir Chauncey," Ernie's record sold well enough to chart (#89, 1960). Freeman and his usual session crew also hit pay dirt as "B. Bumble & the Stingers" when their recordings of "Bumble Boogie" (#21, 1961) and "Nut Rocker" (#23, 1962) made the big time. Over the next two decades, Ernie's keyboard sounds, his arrangements, and/or his producing skills were used by Sammy Davis, Jr., Connie Francis, Dean Martin, Gene McDaniels, Sandy Nelson, Simon & Garfunkel, and Frank Sinatra, to name but a few.

Late in the '70s, Ernie Freeman retired and moved to Hawaii. On May 16, 1981, Ernie died of a heart attack.

Hollywood Flames
BUZZ-BUZZ-BUZZ
(J. Gray, R. Byrd)
Ebb 119
No. 11   *January 27, 1958*

"The Flames originated in 1949, when we were all in our teens. We met at the Largo Theatre in Watts [in Los Angeles] at a talent show," Flames leader Bobby Byrd said in an article for *Yesterday's Memories*. "There were about 10-15 lead singers there, so the owner suggested that we get together to form several groups."

Byrd (bass) circulated and wound up with David Ford (tenor) and Willie Ray Rockwell (second tenor). After the show was over, the guys decided to remain together, and so the Flames were born. Curley Dinkins (baritone) was added, and the group started working the club scene. Success was definitely not an overnight operation: singles appeared on Selective, Specialty, Spin, Unique, and Recorded in Hollywood.

In 1953, Rockwell left to join the Lamplighters, and was replaced by Leon Hughes; Hughes left to sing with the Coasters, and was replaced in turn by ex-Platter Gaynell Hodge. That same year, the group signed with Aladdin; Dinkins left shortly thereafter, but only momentarily. *His* brief replacement was Curtis Williams (who moved on the following year to form THE PENGUINS and write "Earth Angel"). After Aladdin, the Flames recorded more golden greats for the Lucky, Swingtime, Decca, Hollywood, and Money labels. The various companies released the group's records under an array of names—the Flames, the 4 Flames, the Hollywood 4 Flames, the Hollywood Flames, the Eddtides, the Jets, the Satellites, and the Tangiers.

"We were very popular all over Los Angeles, but we just didn't have a hit record," Byrd wrote. Hodge left in 1957, and his shoes were filled by Earl Nelson. Earl would later record as half of the Bob & Earl team ("Harlem Shuffle"), and also charted in 1965 as JACKIE LEE. Like Hodge, Byrd also left the Flames in 1957, after waxing "Buzz-Buzz-Buzz."

"That was my song and Earl sang lead," Byrd explained. "I wrote and arranged it and the financing came from John Dolphin. He sold the song to Lee Rupe, who was the ex-wife of Specialty Records' Art Rupe, and the owner of Ebb Records.

"When the song became a hit, I found out I didn't have any publishing rights and only half the writer credit. Dolphin admitted he owed me $6,000, but he was killed before I could get any of it."

Less than a year later, Byrd, recording as BOBBY DAY, got his just due when his "Rockin' Robin" (#2) b/w "Over And Over" (#41) became a double-sided smash.

The Flames would continue for another ten years, with their line-up changing more rapidly than the seasons. Never again, despite flashes of high-quality music, would the group win its place on the pop charts.

Silhouettes
GET A JOB
(Silhouettes)
Ember 1029
No. 1   *February 24, 1958*

Rick Lewis (tenor) wrote "Get A Job" in the Army, while he was stationed in Germany. On his return to civilian activities in Philadelphia, he joined the Parakeets. In 1956, after the Turbans had cracked the top 40 with "When You Dance" (#33), Rick was offered a position as their road manager. He accepted, but after a few tours, he returned to singing, hooking up with the Gospel Tornadoes (baritone Earl Beal, bass Raymond Edwards, and lead Bill Horton). These sacred singers went secular, changed their name to "The Thunderbirds," and hammered out Rick's "Get A Job." While appearing at the Uptown Theatre, the Thunderbirds attracted the attention of DJ, producer, and owner of Junior Records, Kae Williams.

Williams really liked their ballad and intended "A" side, "I'm Lonely." In a wink, arrangements were made and the Thunderbirds were ushered into the Robinson Recording Laboratories at radio WIP. "Get A Job" was chosen as the flip side. Junior Records' arranger, Howard Biggs, came up with the "sha na na na" hook, and Edwards worked up the "yip, yip, yip, yip, yip, yip, yip, yip, boom, boom, boom, boom, boom" bit. Rollie McGill was brought in to honk sax, and someone dreamed up the group's new name, probably derived from the RAYS hit "Silhouettes."

"Get A Job" sold over a million copies, and still sells thousands every year. It was one of the first R & B singles to cross over into the pop/rock world and to simultaneously top both charts. Eventually, it became one of the most played and most memorable rock and roll recordings of all time.

While their fleeting fame lasted, the Silhouettes played the Apollo, toured with Sam Cooke and Clyde McPlatter, and made extensive Alan Freed and Dick Clark Caravan tours. Both the Tempos and the Heartbeats would record "answer records" to "Get A Job." The Miracles' very first disk was "Got A Job."

All of the follow-ups were fine efforts, but all failed. "Headin' For The Poorhouse" was an uptempo reworking of the job theme. "Bing Bong" was divinely inane. "I Sold My Heart To The Junkman" was a classic and their finest ever. While the Silhouettes faded, Patti LaBelle & The Blue-Belles would establish themselves with their frantic rendition of "Junkman" in 1962.

After the release of "Rent Man" in 1962, Horton and Edwards left the group, and were replaced by Cornelius Brown and John Wilson. Later that year, with the aid of Jerry Ragavoy (producer of Garnet Mimms and the Majors) and VAN MCCOY, the revamped Silhouettes recorded a single each on the Grand and the Imperial labels. Sales were poor, and the group called it quits in 1968 after the release (on the Goodway label) of their only album, *The Original and New Silhouettes—'58/'68 Get a Job.*

In the late '60s, Bill Horton recorded some sides with the Dawns and also had a few solo singles issued. Since 1980, the Silhouettes, with all four original members, have been making occasional reunion appearances at rock and roll revival shows.

Crescendos
OH JULIE
(Kenneth R. Moffit, Noel Ball)
Nasco 6005
No. 5 *March 3, 1958*

"**O**ur situation was like a lot of acts back then— a bunch of naive school kids being taken under

The Crescendos

the wing by individuals who took most of the profits," former Crescendo George Lanuis, lead singer on the group's million-seller and currently a Nashville realtor, recalled in an exclusive interview. "["Oh Julie"] is still in print, and we haven't gotten a royalty check since 1963."

The Crescendos were five in number— Lanuis, Tommy Fortner, Kenneth Brigham, Jimmy Hall, and Lanuis' cousin Jim. They formed the group while attending Cumberland High in Nashville. In 1957, they started doing talent shows; Nashville DJ Noel Ball discovered them, brought them to the Nasco label, and gave them "Oh Julie" to record. The group heavily promoted the record on a package tour with the Everly Brothers, Brenda Lee, Sam Cooke, and LaVern Baker. All told, the Crescendos were together for only a year.

"We were just out of high school and on the road for nine months, straight. And that will burn you out really quick. Three of the boys went to college, two of us got married—all that makes it hard to get together. We were burnt, and we had a bad taste in our mouths on how things had been handled. The rest of our records ["School Girl" b/w "Crazy Hop," "Young And In Love" b/w "Rainy Days," and "Strange Love" b/w "Let's Take A Walk"] probably didn't sell well 'cause we'd had it, and had stopped traveling and promoting."

Lanuis is currently a realtor; Brigham is a doctor; Fortner is an architect/builder; Jim Lanuis is an accountant; and Jimmy Hall has been working for years at Ford Motors.

Eddie Platt

TEQUILA
(Chuck Rio)
ABC-Paramount 9899
No. 20   *March 31, 1958*

Near zip is known about this Cleveland sax man. He did blow horn and he did have a band that played local clubs and dances. When the Champs' "Tequila" heated up, Eddie and his guys burned rubber to a nearby recording studio to cop a cover. Eddie and the boys collected enough action on their instrumental version to hold down the number 20 position for a week. Their follow-up was another cover—this time of "Cha-Hua-Hua" by the Pets. It didn't chart. No further releases were ever to bear the name of Eddie Platt, and never again was his name heard over the airwaves of this great nation.

John Zacherle

DINNER WITH DRAC—PART 1
(Jon Sheldon, Harry Land)
Cameo 130
No. 6   *March 31, 1958*

A review of his early years would make Mr. John Zacherle (b. Sept. 26, 1918, Philadelphia) look like a highly unlikely candidate for the status of great ghouldom. The gentleman who came to be known as "The Cool Ghoul" earned a bachelor's degree from the University of Pennsylvania in English literature. During World War II, he served in the Army, eventually working his way to the rank of major. On his return, however, John reportedly looked about for what he considered a more relaxed

profession, something with bite and depth, something intelligent, yet emotive. Yes, why not become an actor?

For years, he worked in local stock companies. "Action in the Afternoon" was a sudsy TV Western, broadcast daily over Philly's WCAU. For the role of an undertaker, John donned spats and a long black frock, and his dark performances left an impression. When Universal issued for TV consumption *Dracula* (1931), *Frankenstein* (1931), *The Werewolf* (1956), and a mess of lesser-known horror flicks, TV producers created the "horror host" to make these films more palatable to the boob-tube bunch. When WCAU launched "Shock Theatre," someone at Channel 10 recalled Zach's hack-'n'-pack role in "Action in the Afternoon." John became Roland, the program's blood-drinking midnight MC.

The response was immediate. Ratings soared, Zacherle fan clubs were formed, personal appearances were demanded, and none of this madness was lost on the offspring of Cameo Records president Bernie Lowe. Bernie stayed up with his kids one weekend night and caught a glimpse of "The Cool Ghoul." The next day, Lowe approached Zach and offered him a shot at rock and roll stardom. A session was arranged. Staff writers created some gruesome lyrical lines, while Dave Appel and his Applejacks (formerly known for hits like "Mexican Hat Dance" and "Rocka-Conga") provided the legitimate rock accompaniment. "Dinner With Drac," a honkin' but flagrantly distasteful dish which featured a Dracula imitation from Zach, received enough airplay to plant this ghoul and his goons firmly in the upper reaches of the pop charts.

John moved his hobgoblin hosting to New York City and WABC. He fronted "American Bandstand"'s Halloween party in 1958, and for years thereafter. In 1963, when "Bandstand" shifted to Saturdays only, Zach moved to WOR-TV to host a run of RKO horrors and whodunits. After "Dinner With Drac," several more singles ("Eighty-Two Tombstones," "I Was A Teenage Caveman," "Hury Bury Baby," "Hello Dolly") and eventually a few LPs (*Spook Along with Zacherle*, 1960; *Monster Mash*, 1962; *Scary Tales*, 1963) were packed and pushed, but nothing much in the way of attention was given to most of these artifacts.

Zacherle is still with us, though. Numerous format and channel changes have transpired ("Creature Features," "Zacherle's Disco-Teen"), but the now-70-plus Zach is still going strong.

Laurie London

HE'S GOT THE WHOLE WORLD IN HIS HANDS

(Traditional)
Capitol 3891
No. 1 *April 14, 1958*

A lad (not a lass) named Laurie London was born in London on January 19, 1944. When a wee one of 13, Laurie, with a high-pitched voice and no musical training, came to the forefront of pop consciousness when he auditioned for "London's Radio Show" and was given the opportunity to record a Geoff Love adaptation of an old gospel song. While the recording sold moderately well in his homeland, Laurie's tune, with a flash of fluke, resided in the coveted top spot on the Top 100 for four weeks.

Whether it was Laurie's timing or the infectious feel the recording created that made London's big moment happen, we will never know. Neither Laurie nor his label had any idea what made this number so successful. Laurie went on to make a few more recordings for his label, and still more for Roulette Records, but nothing the little shaver ever recorded, even after his voice changed, came near to making *Billboard*'s charts.

Ronald & Ruby

LOLLIPOP

(Beverly Ross, Julius Dixon)
RCA Victor 7174
No. 20 *April 14, 1958*

In January 1958, young Beverly Ross, along with a black singing partner of 13 or 14 named Lee Morris, approached her manager, song plugger Arnold Shaw (who later wrote a number of books about rock history). They performed a catchy song Beverly had penned with Julius Dixon. Shaw flipped for the tune, called "Lollipop," and rushed Ronald and Ruby, as the duo would be called, into Associated Recording Studios. A demo was cut and packed within an hour. Before Shaw could have Lee's parents sign a recording contract for the underage lad, Archie Bleyer at Cadence Records had his Chordettes cover the song. The Chordettes were on a trail of hits ("Eddie My Love," "Born To Be With You"), and their version of "Lollipop" stole much of the sales and charting action from Beverly and her sidekick.

"Lollipop" was not Ross' first shot at success. Born in 1939, the daughter of a New Jersey chicken farmer, she moved with her family to New York City while she was in her teens. Beverly wrote a number of songs for Bill Haley & His Comets, including "Dim, Dim The Lights." Shaw, who became her manager in the mid-'50s, convinced Columbia Records head (and prominent rock-hater) Mitch Miller to record some tunes that his client had penned.

Despite his scorn for rock and roll, Miller let Ross cut "Stop Laughing At Me" b/w "Headlights," using full and hip rock accompaniment, but after generating some initial sparks, the platter sputtered.

Over the years, Beverly Ross Has had substantial success as a songwriter, since artists like Lesley Gore ("Judy's Turn to Cry"), the Earls ("Remember When"), and Roy Orbison ("Candy Man") recorded her material. Currently, she owns her own recording studio and is involved in composing for the theater.

Huey "Piano" Smith & The Clowns

DON'T YOU JUST KNOW IT

(Huey "Piano" Smith, Johnny Vincent)
Ace 545
No. 9 *April 14, 1958*

For many years now, Huey Smith, renowned New Orleans piano man, has been content with working his garden. Now a Jehovah's Witness and a strict Bible reader, Huey has long been embittered by the bad deals, the mistakes, and the way his best material has been stolen from him.

He was born in the city's Garden District on January 26, 1934. Uncle played the piano, and Huey would imitate him. "I used to play till the neighbors used to bang on the walls for me knock it off," Huey told *Goldmine*'s Almost Slim. "When I was seven or eight, I began makin' songs up like 'Robertson Street Boogie.' My father used to give me money to take lessons every week. But I didn't go! I kept the money, and learned from my sister, who took lessons from the lady next door."

When he was 15, Huey met Eddie "Guitar Slim" Jones. "I had been fooling around with a friend of mine, Roosevelt Nettles, who played drums. One night I was coming home from Cohen [High School] and stopped over at Roosevelt's and there was this guy there with a guitar. He was dressed in purple and yellow pants, a lime green shirt and a straw hat! Roosevelt said, 'He sounds just like Gatemouth Brown.' It was Guitar Slim."

Smith made a living recording with Guitar Slim ("The Things That I Used To Do"), Earl King ("Those Lonely Lonely Nights"), Little Richard ("Tutti Frutti"), Lloyd Price, and Smiley Lewis ("I Hear You Knockin'"). Ace Records released the first 45 under Huey's name—"Little Liza Jane"—when the core idea for Smith's earliest solo hit came.

"I was always trying to pick up catchy lines, and Chuck Berry had this line, 'I got rockin' pneumonia, sittin' down at a rhythm review,' and Roy Brown had some line about 'young man rhythm.' So I started thinkin' about opposite lines like, 'kissin' a girl that too tall.' We came up with 'Rockin' Pneumonia And The Boogie Woogie Flu' [—/#5, 1957] that night in the studio."

Bobby Marchan (who was working as a female impersonator when he met Huey) sang lead on this New Orleans classic, and joined Smith to form the Clowns. The idea was that Marchan would handle lead vocals, and Smith would write the tunes, play piano, and arrange. The line-up was liquid, but present during the band's heyday were Marchan, James Booker, Curly Moore (lead singer for most post-1959 recordings), Roosevelt Nettles, ROBERT PARKER, and even Jessie Hill.

"Don't You Just Know It," Huey's next single, was a huge pop success. Gerri Hall, ex-Clown and later one of Ray Charles' Raelettes, told John Broven in *Rhythm & Blues* that the tune's title came from an expression that Rudy Ray Moore, the Clowns' driver, was accustomed to saying. The Clowns hit the road in support of the disk, leaving a number called "Sea Cruise" behind in the can.

"In my mind, ["Sea Cruise"] was the one that was gonna throw me over the hump," Huey recalled. "But Johnny [Vincent] and FRANKIE FORD'S manager Joe Caronna, liked it also. So Johnny came to me and said, 'Let Frankie do this.' I said, 'No way!' But Johnny said there was nothing I could do about it. It was coming out on Frankie."

The track was issued under Frankie Ford's name, with Frankie singing lead. Huey was livid. "I never got any royalties from Johnny. He kept sayin', 'It's comin', it's comin'.'"

When his contract ran out, Huey was gone, and so were the chartings. He continued recording for Imperial, Teem, Spinett, Instant, Constellation, and White Cliffs. Many times, his disks would appear under other names like

Shindig Smith, Snuffy Smith, the Hueys, the Pitter Pats, and the Soul Shakers.

Smith worked where he could, even returning to the Ace label in the early '60s. Once he had recovered from a serious drinking problem, he turned to religion, working as a janitor in a drugstore and eventually turning to gardening. He has vowed never to perform again.

Monotones
BOOK OF LOVE
(Warren Davis, George Malone, Charles Patrick)
Argo 5290
No. 5 *April 21, 1958*

They were buddies living in the same housing project in Newark, New Jersey. They sang four-part harmony but were six in number; they called themselves the Monotones because, as one of the group told *Goldmine's* Jeff Tamarkin, "the word means 'one tone' and we were so close, like one." Warren Davis, George Malone, Charles Patrick, Frank Smith, and the Ryanes brothers—John and Warren—started putting an act together in 1955. They had already done some singing together as part of their church choir—the same choir that included Cissy Houston, Dionne Warwick, and some of THE SWEET INSPIRATIONS.

In 1956, the Monotones were polished enough to appear on Ted Mack's "Amateur Hour": they won the first week, singing the Cadillacs' "Zoom," but lost the following week. Soon after, Charles' brother James joined the Kodaks, and this group's successful appearances at the Apollo spurred the Monotones to think more seriously of their careers. One day, as the group recalled to Tamarkin, "Charles heard [this] commercial ["You'll wonder where the yellow went/When you brush your teeth with Pepsodent"] on the radio . . . He went home and got George and Warren and forged the song out of it."

They made a demo and took it around to all the labels in the area. Bea Casalin at Hull Records was impressed, and quickly arranged to get the group into Bell Sound Studios in New York City. "Book Of Love" was initially released in December of 1957 on Mascot, a subsidiary of Hull Records. Within weeks, the response was too much for the little label to handle, and Argo Records picked up the disk for national distribution. The Monotones, meanwhile, were out having a ball on an extended tour with Bobby Darin and Frankie Lymon & The Teenagers.

No one gave a thought to putting a follow-up record together. By the time word came from the group's label to hustle home and record something, it was already May. The initial plan was for "Legend Of Sleepy Hollow," written by Charles and his brother James, to be the next release; a few more months, however, were needed to get the eerie classic together. In the meantime, the label issued "Tom Foolery," but it failed to chart. Eventually, "Legend" was released, but by then, the group had lost its momentum. Only three more singles appeared before the group quietly disbanded. Members went off to marriages, the military, and regular jobs.

The Monotones still perform at oldies shows. The group has the same line-up as the day it was born, except for the Ryanes brothers—both John (d. May 30, 1972) and Warren have since died.

Art & Dotty Todd
CHANSON D'AMOUR
(SONG OF LOVE)
(Wayne Shanklin)
Era 1064
No. 6 *May 5, 1958*

Arthur (b. Mar. 11, 1920) and Dotty (b. June 22, 1923) were born and raised in Elizabeth, New Jersey. It wasn't until a chance encounter in Providence, Rhode Island, in 1941 that they met and learned of their mutual interest in making music. At the time, Art was playing guitar and banjo and studying music at Syracuse University; Dot had studied the piano, and was attending a business college. Before year's end, Art and Dot shared the same last name, and before decade's end, the twosome were performing together at clubs and hotels. RCA Victor issued some of their duets, which had sold well in Europe but which stiffed in the States.

Art then happened on to what he thought was a neat number by Wayne Shanklin, "Chanson d'Amour." Possibly with the successful sounds of Les Paul and Mary Ford in mind, Art and Dotty shaped and recorded their mellow shuffle. Era Records gave it a spin, and the husband-and-wife act had their one and only crash into the nation's top 10. Radio programs for ABC and CBS followed. For years, the

couple recorded Shanklin tunes and their own creations, but nowhere was that follow-up hit to be found.

When last spotted, the Todds were performing as a lounge act in the Las Vegas area. An album by Art, *I Love The Banjo*, is still in print on the GNP label.

Voxpoppers
WISHING FOR YOUR LOVE
(Sampson Horton)
Mercury 71282
No. 18 *May 5, 1958*

Officials at the Mercury label have confessed a complete ignorance of this one-charting act. But because the Voxpoppers' one-off EP had a picture sleeve, we can surmise that they were self-contained—playing guitar, bass, sax, accordion, and drums—and that they were five in number. The group from New York City cut guitar- and sax-dominated instrumentals like "Guitar Stroll" and "Stroll Roll," and sang group-harmony rockaballads like "Wishing For Your Love."

Presumably, the Voxpoppers' vinyl voyage began with a little-noted number called "A Love To Last A Lifetime." The tiny Poplar label issued the disk, backed with "Come Back Little Girl," just months before the group signed with Amp-3. "Wishing For Your Love" was their initial offering for the label. The response immediately moved Mercury to seek national distribution for the disk. Yet despite the group's striking success with "Wishing," only one further 45 ("Ping Pong Baby") and that rare EP appeared. A few years later, the Voxpoppers did manage to convince Morty Craft at Warwick Records to release two now hard-to-find smoothies, "Helen Isn't Tellin'" and "In The Heart Of Hearts."

Renato Carosone
TORERO
(Renato Carosone)
Capitol 71080
No. 18 *June 2, 1958*

Nothing is known of Mr. Carosone.

Moments after Renato's sole intrusion into the U.S. charts, Julius LaRosa's cover version of this Mexican-sounding instrumental en-

Valerie Carr

Valerie's first offering for Roulette was "You're The Greatest." Billy Scott happened to cover the tune at the same time, and his rendering (#73, 1958) overshadowed Valerie's. Next out of the hatch was "When The Boys Talk About The Girls," a teen-dipped tune that was to be Valerie's primo moment. Its pimple lyrics and clinky piano was enough to classify the disk as a rock and roll record.

Unfortunately for Valerie's career, much of her future work was packaged as lush-stringed, sophisticated, and adult. She never managed to click saleswise with the square market, and ended up losing forever her adolescent admirers.

tered the *Billboard* listings (#21, 1958). "Torero" would be Renato's only contender and the last of the seven chartings for LaRosa, the Italian crooner familiar to TV viewers from his appearances on the popular program "Arthur Godfrey and His Friends."

Valerie Carr
WHEN THE BOYS TALK ABOUT THE GIRLS
(Bob Merrill)
Roulette 4066
No. 19   *June 9, 1958*

Valerie was born in New York in 1936. A publicity pud from her label referred to her as a "normal girl" living "a normal school girl's life." She attended the High School of Performing Arts and diligently studied to be a classical pianist. In her late teens, the lush lark decided to test her wings and flew to Boston, where she continued her musical studies at the Berklee School of Music. She studied voice with Lee Daniels and began singing at local nightclubs.

In 1956 or thereabouts, Valerie returned to New York to cut demo recordings for a music publisher. One number, "So Goes My Love," was brought to the attention of Roulette A & R men Hugo Peretti and Luigi Creatore. Hugo and Luigi signed her on the spot.

Ed Townsend
FOR YOUR LOVE
(Ed Townsend)
Capitol 3926
No. 13   *June 9, 1958*

Anyone who has ever heard Ed Townsend sing must have asked himself at least once, "What happened?" With his very first release and only hit, "For Your Love," Ed made it known that he was one of the finest ballad singers alive. How could such a talented individual have missed out on major stardom?

Townsend was born on April 16, 1929, in Fayetteville, Tennessee, a hamlet outside of Memphis. Dad was a Methodist minister, and from early on, Ed was thoroughly involved in church affairs. He served as president of his church's youth council, and at 17, was elected leader of the International American Methodist Episcopal Youth Council. He majored in education at Wilberforce University, and graduated from Arkansas State College. After teaching in a backwoods school for a year, Ed put in two years in Korea in the Marine Corps. It was while entertaining military buddies that he was discovered by Horace Heidt, who enlisted Ed to join his traveling minstrels.

On his return to the States, Ed was offered the opportunity to host a local TV program in Los Angeles. In his spare time, he had been composing tunes that Nat "King" Cole, Etta James, Gogi Grant, and Bull Moose Jackson were recording. Ed approached Joe Zerga at Capitol Records with a demo of "For Your Love." Zerga realized that Ed Townsend was no vocal fluff, and had him record the tune.

To this day, "For Your Love" is a gospely golden great, a non-moldie oldie which should

46

have created a mammoth career for Ed Townsend. The follow-up, "When I Grow Too Old To Dream"—an old Glenn Gray hit from the '30s—was an equally fine recording. In 1958, the disk worked its way slowly up the bottom of the Hot 100, peaked at number 59 then disappeared, along with a sizeable portion of Townsend's career. Over the years, Ed continued releasing records. "Stay With Me" and "Dreamworld" on Warner Bros. were two winners by any pop-esthetical standard. Mysteriously, neither they nor anything else sold very well.

As a writer and/or producer, Ed Townsend has created gold for the Main Ingredients, the Impressions, the Shirelles, Chuck Jackson, Maxine Brown, Theola Kilgore (Ed's wife), and Jimmy Holiday Townsend also wrote and pro duced Dee Dee Warwick's Grammy nominee "Foolish Fool," and Marvin Gaye's classic "Let's Get It On."

Sheb Wooley

PURPLE PEOPLE EATER
(Sheb Wooley)
MGM 12651
No. 1 *June 9, 1958*

Sheb's been around, done it all, and in some parts, he's more well-known than his inclusion in this book might suggest. This Wooley critter has been a DJ, songwriter, music publisher, bandleader, scriptwriter, comedian, and TV and movie actor. And, of course, a singer—with numerous C & W chartings under not one, but two different names and personae.

He was born Shelby F. Wooley, part Cherokee, on a farm 12 miles outside of Erick, Oklahoma, on April 10, 1921. Shelby and his three brothers got on good with horses. In his teen years, he got to be something of a local rodeo star. Somewhere in this timeframe, Sheb talked his pa into trading in his shotgun for a tattered guitar.

Sheb Wooley

Wooley practiced on the thing and formed his first band, the Plainview Melody Boys, while still attending high school.

Sheb worked as a welder in California, but soon discovered music-making to be the more satisfying. He and the Boys toured and did some radio programs. After World War II, Sheb set out on his own for Nashville with a sack of homemade tunes under his arm. "I spent about a year there," Wooley told *Now Dig This*. "I was pretty much starving. Eventually everybody heard my songs. Everybody seemed to like them. Ernest Tubb encouraged me and Eddie Arnold let me mow his lawn!" Soon, music folk like Jimmy Dean, Hank Snow, and others were recording his songs.

Wooley had some sides issued by Bullet and Bluebonnet, and in 1948, he started his long residency at MGM Records. One of his first efforts, "Peepin' Through The Keyhole, Watchin' Jole Blon," was a local hit in the late '40s. The idea for his biggie, "Purple People Eater," came from a throwaway joke that DON ROBERTSON told him. As Wooley told *Goldmine*'s Larry Stidom, "[Robertson] said his son came home from school and asked him, 'Daddy, what has one eye, one horn, flies and eats people?' When he said he didn't know, his son told him, 'A one-eyed, one-horned people eater'; and I just took it from there."

"People Eater" made use of the speeded-up recording technique popularized by David Seville's "Witch Doctor," and later, by the squeaky Chipmunks. The record eventually sold more than 3,000,000 copies, and started a whole merchandising rampage. Kids and kooks alike wanted People Eater T-shirts, hats, horns, and even ice cream. But reportedly, when Wooley first approached MGM with the "Purple People" piece, they were less than enthusiastic about it. Sheb himself, after auditioning a number of tunes, even told the label's decision-makers, "It's nothing you wanna hear . . . it's the bottom of the barrel."

Other than a semi-serious chart-topping C & W hit, "That's My Pa" (#51, 1962), pop fans didn't seem to want to hear Wooley singing anything but silly ditties. While Sheb has had numerous other chartings, most of these— "Hello Walls No. 2," "Almost Persuaded No. 2," and "Harper Valley P.T.A. No. 2"—were parodies created under the guise of an inebriated character Wooley called Ben Colder.

Describing the creation of "Ben Colder," Sheb told *Goldmine*: "It was 1963, I think, and MGM was holding a song for me called 'Don't Go Near The Indians.' I didn't get into town to record it, though . . . Rex Allen [did] and it was

a smash. I told [MGM] I'd do one called 'Son, Don't Go Near The Eskimos,' and the name 'Ben Colder' seemed to go with the title."

Wooley has also worked wonders in Hollywood, appearing in nearly 50 flicks, such as *Rocky Mountain* (1950) with Errol Flynn, *Distant Drums* (1952) with Gary Cooper, *Giant* (1956) with James Dean, and *Rio Bravo* (1959) with John Wayne. His most notable movie role was that of whiskey-drinking killer Ben Miller in *High Noon* (1951). But Sheb Wooley is probably best remembered for his four-and-a-half year stay opposite Clint Eastwood as "Pete Nolan" on TV's Western series "Rawhide."

Wooley, who lives in the Nashville suburb of Old Hickory Lane, is still working, writing scripts, and singing his silly, but occasionally serious, songs. "I'm not retiring. No way. I'm having too much fun."

Gino & Gina

(IT'S BEEN A LONG LONG TIME) PRETTY BABY
(Artie Zwirn)
Mercury 71283
No. 20   *June 23, 1958*

They were no Sonny & Cher. In fact, were it not for the fluke flight of their one tame tune, Gino (b. Aristedes) and Gina (b. Irene) Giosasi, the brother-and-sister team from Brooklyn, might only be known today for their tangential relationship to the hit "Sorry (I Ran All the Way Home)." Gino Giosasi and Artie Zwirn, Gino & Gina's manager, wrote the song for THE IMPALAS and hooked the youngsters up with MGM's Cub subsidiary.

The two G's had a few more 45s issued by Mercury and (in 1961) by Brunswick. Gino, possibly in 1960 or so, tried for a solo bid with something called "Hand Clappin' Time." If the siblings had kept "Sorry" for themselves, it is possible that their faded names could have been absent from this book.

Jan & Arnie

JENNIE LEE
(Jan Berry, Arnie Ginsburg)
Arwin 108
No. 8   *June 30, 1958*

Jan Berry (b. Apr. 3, 1941, Los Angeles) and Arnie Ginsburg (b. early '40s) were members of the Barons, an informal all-male club based at L.A.'s University High—the same school that spawned the Beach Boys' Bruce Johnston, Sandy Nelson, and Phil Spector. One night, for kicks, the fellows trekked down to the New Follies Theatre at Fifth and Main. It seems that the feature of the evening was an overly-endowed stripper named Jennie "The Bazoom Girl" Lee. Arnie and Jan were especially impressed. All the way home, they gestured and sang freely of the miss' mammoth mammaries.

"I was the predominant writer on that piece," Arnie told *Time Barrier Express'* Stuart Hersh. "I had the melody, and I think about two thirds of the words, before going up to [Jan's] house and working out the rest." The boys were determined not to let their feelings go unexpressed. To create an echoey shower-room effect, two tape players were set up in Berry's garage. "The track was actually recorded there in the garage on an old sort of out-of-tune piano; [the other parts] were over-dubbed in one of the recording studios in Hollywood." Musicians on the disk include ERNIE FREEMAN (piano), Rene Hall (guitar), and Jackie Kelso (sax).

A couple of Berry's buddies, the then-unknown duo of Lou Adler and Herb Alpert, successfully managed to get the dub placed on the Arwin label, reportedly then owned by Doris Day. All parties were surprised when the 45, with Arnie beating a cardboard box and singing nearly indecipherable lyrics, penetrated the nation's sacred top 10.

But, according to Arnie, "I began to get disenchanted very quickly with entertainment . . . with the business and with the people. It didn't seem worth it . . . It wasn't enough fun. Jan was a difficult person to deal with, and the people in the industry were not very 'neat.' They didn't seem very stable . . . And it's hard to be an entertainer, a really hard thing."

Despite the tensions and Arnie's disenchantment, the duo did manage to tape enough for two more singles before their break-up: "Gas Money" (#81, 1958) b/w "Bonnie Lou" and "I Love Linda" b/w "The Beat That Can't Be Beat."

Arnie had one waxing issued by Arvin as by the Rituals ("Girl From Zanzibar" b/w "Guitarro") before leaving the music business for a career in commercial art and graphic design. Jan Berry found Dean Torrence, and with the help of the Beach Boys, Jan and Dean created almost the entire cross-fertilized genre of surfing/hot rod music.

Jan & Arnie

Jody Reynolds
ENDLESS SLEEP
(Jody Reynolds, Delores Nance)
Demon 1507
No. 5 *June 30, 1958*

John Wesley Adams encouraged his young nephew Jody (b. Dec. 3, 1938, Denver) to take a poke or two at the family guitar while he was growing up in Mountain View, Oklahoma. Jody formed the Storms in 1952 with drummer Eddie Firth, guitarist Billy Ray, and bassist Noel Sutte, to play hops and bar-room stops. When not gigging or boxing, Reynolds worked as a cotton picker, an insurance salesman, a miner, and a mortician's assistant.

After the boys had rocked and reeled their way through the Western states for some years, a couple named Herb and Liz Montei, who had good ears and record-biz connections, encouraged Jody and his Storms to journey to L.A. and audition for Joe Green at the newly-established Demon label. Green was duly impressed and rushed Reynolds—plus session players Al Casey (guitar), Howard Roberts (guitar), Ray Martinez (drums), and Irv Ashby (bass)—into Gold Star Studios to record some tracks. "Endless Sleep," a number Jody had been working on with George Brown (who wrote under the pseudonym "Delores Nance"), was the first of three tunes taped that day. Only 20 minutes were needed to lay out "Endless."

The dusty disk is now a golden great, one of the finest of the "Death Rock" ditties to gather a mass audience (others include MARK DINNING's "Teen Angel" and Ray Peterson's "Tell Laura I Love Her"). Aside from the immediate follow-up, "Fire Of Love" (#66, 1958), none of Reynolds' half-dozen other Demon disks charted. Jody and his Storms persisted and blew through the '60s, disbursing singles for such labels as Sundown, Emmy, Smash, Brent, and Pulsar. Jody even duetted with a then-unknown Bobbie "Ode To Billy Joe" Gentry on one Titan single.

Reportedly, Jody Reynolds lives in Yuma, Arizona, where for a time he owned a guitar shop. He has shelved rock and roll in favor of "prospecting or building houses," according to *New Kommotion*'s Adam Komorowsky. His only solo LP appeared on Tru-Gems in 1978.

Danleers

ONE SUMMER NIGHT
(Danny Webb)
Mercury 71322
No. 7 *July 28, 1958*

Fresh out of the confines of a Brooklyn high school, good buddies Jimmy Weston (lead singer) and Johnny Lee (first tenor) were full to the brim with teen dreams of singing and success. In order to put together a hot-shot vocal group, they enlisted three of their mutual friends: Willie Ephriam (second tenor), Roosevelt Mays (bass), and Nat McCune (baritone). They practiced up a mite and approached Danny Webb; someone had fingered him as being the one in the know about making records (and making money). Danny groomed them, gave them a name (a variant on his own), and secured the Danleers their first recording contract with Bill Lasley's Amp-3 label.

For their first waxing, Webb supplied them with a jumper, "Wheelin' And A-Dealin'," plus what was to become one of summer radio's perennial classics, "One Summer Night." "Summer" was such a scorcher that Mercury Records picked up the Danleers' recording contract from Amp-3. Mercury was the big time, and in 1958, "One Summer Night" was one of the most thermal make-out tunes to be heard on rock and roll radio.

Unfortunately for Jim, John, and the rest, none of the other fine sounds they pressed in vinyl ever sold as well. "I Really Love You" was loosed, followed by "A Picture Of You" and "I Can't Sleep"—but nothing sold well enough to even make *Billboard*'s "Bubbling Under The Hot 100" chart.

After four stiffs, Mercury Records passed on issuing any more records by the group. Discouraged, the Danleers dispersed, but Jimmy Westin proclaimed that he was not ready to let the "Danleers" name die. Webb brought in members of another group he was managing, the Webtones, to fill in for the departed Danleers, and Epic Records gave the "new" Danleers a two-single spin. Record sales were as cool as a Klondike bar, and Epic politely showed the group the door.

Well into the mid-'60s, the Everest, Smash, and Le-Mans record labels gave the fluctuating mix of original members, Webtones, and fill-ins a shot at recording what culminated in a pile of fine doo-wop numbers. Good records all, they just didn't sell.

Jimmy Weston still fronts the Danleers, and the group still appears at local and revival concerts.

Johnny Otis Show

WILLIE AND THE HAND JIVE
(Johnny Otis)
Capitol 3966
No. 9 *August 4, 1958*

Often referred to as "The Godfather of Rhythm & Blues," Johnny Otis (b. John Veliotes, Dec. 28, 1921, Vallejo, Cal.) has worked in almost every realm of pop music—as arranger, publisher, musician (drums, vibraphone, piano), songwriter, DJ, producer, TV variety-show host, talent scout, record-company owner, and founder/frontman of the first "Rock 'n' Roll Caravan of Stars." His R & B revues gave artists like Hank Ballard, Etta James, Esther Phillips, and Jackie Wilson their first breaks. Johnny has also been a painter, sculptor, actor, politician, newspaper columnist, and, for more than a decade now, a preacher.

Otis had his first hit in 1946 with "Harlem Nocturne," a huge seller that, mysteriously, never charted nationally, pop or R & B. In 1950, nine of his recordings made *Billboard*'s R & B charts: "Double Crossing Blues" (—/ #1), "Mistrustin' Blues" (—/#1) b/w "Mersey"

(—/#3), "Cry Baby" (—/#6), "Cupid's Boogie" (—/#1), "Deceivin' Blues" (—/#4), "Dreamin' Blues" (—/#8), and "Wedding Boogie" (—/#6) b/w "Faraway Blues" (—/#6).

"I only had one pop hit," explained Johnny in an exclusive interview, "because in those days . . . there was a well-defined black show business, and the general pop/white-oriented market. My stuff was blues- and jazz-oriented, and my audience was black . . . It wasn't until the mid-'50s that the music began crossing over to the pop charts. So back in the early days, I must have had 30 hits that I wrote or that one of my singers sang, but they were all called 'rhythm and blues' hits."

When Johnny signed with Capitol Records in 1957, they wanted him to create music that was "more tolerable to the white audience." He responded with "Willie And The Hand Jive," a pop monster sporting the now-classic "shave-and-a-haircut, two-bits" beat. Johnny insisted that he had *not* lifted this bit from BO DIDDLEY.

"I was down South, after I'd had a few hit records, and saw a chain gang. Its a traumatic experience, seeing men in chains, under the shotgun, in the hot sun. Workin' on the rail-road, they'd be called 'gandy dancers,' and their long metal hammers would go 'chung-y chung-y chung-chung, chung-chung' . . . The next time I heard that beat, it was on a hit called 'Hambone' [Red Saunders & His Orchestra, 1952]. All that pre-dates me and Bo.

"One day Bo was at my house—we both raised chickens and ducks, and I was giving him some—when he said to me, 'Motherf***er, what are you doin' takin' my song?' He said it half-jokingly. I said to him, 'You ever heard "Hambone"?' And he said, 'Shhh!'"

There has recently been some talk of a major TV production company reviving Johnny's traveling revue as a weekly program. "The word is, I'm the Lawrence Welk of black music."

Domenico Modugno
VOLARE (NEL BLU DIPINTO DI BLU)
(Franco Migliacci, Domenico Modugno)
Decca 30677
No. 1 *August 18, 1958*

Franco Migliacci, a bunkie of Domenico Modugno, was inspired by the divine light of creation one day while peering at the back panel on a pack of cigarettes. At that instant, Franco had the idea to create a dream-like song about a man with hands painted blue who flies through "blue painted in blue." Yes, it was quite an idea for a song, or so thought his buddy; Domenico drummed up the music, and together, they got the words just right.

The duo entered "Volare" in Italy's annual San Remo Festival of Music, where the flying blue man's tale was selected the best of the batch. Most Americans didn't know a hink about what this fellow was singing; some listeners figured that it must have something to do with love or a romp in the hay, because Domenico sure sounded happy. When the dust had settled, "Volare" had sold millions of copies and had won Grammys for "Best Male Vocal Performance," "Song of the Year," and "Record of the Year."

Domenico Modugno was born on January 9, 1928, in Polignano a Mare, Italy. While no more than a tyke, Domenico ran away from home with 2,000 lire in his pocket to search out fame and fortune. He worked as a waiter and a factory worker, served a stint in his county's military, and enrolled in Rome's Experimental Movie Center, where one of his fellow students was a then-unknown Sophia Loren. Domenico won small parts in Italian flicks, wrote some tunes, made radio appearances, and played Athos in a European TV takeoff on the Three Musketeers.

On three other occasions, Modugno won top honors at the San Remo Festival of Music. None of his vocal efforts, however, ever again successfully managed to cross the oceans. Not even his "Nuda," a sensitive song of a spiritual lad's lusty wish to embrace a naked damsel, sold very well. Try as he might to reconnect with his Muse while staring at a cigarette pack, Franco was never again to capture the magical touch of that flying blue man.

Elegants

LITTLE STAR
(Arthur Venosa, Vito Picone)
Apt 25005
No. 1 *August 25, 1958*

They were young, talented, and hungry. They met on the streets of Staten Island, New York, and found their name on the label of a whiskey bottle ("Schenley's, The Whiskey of Elegance"). After years of hard work, they successfully molded themselves into the group that created that smooth, unforgettable variation on Mozart's "Twinkle, Twinkle, Little Star." And still talented, hungry, and not so young, they would disappear. Like THE SILHOUETTES, THE HOLLYWOOD ARGYLES, and THE SINGING NUN, the Elegants have the dubious distinction of hitting the number-one niche on the pop charts, then dropping out of sight entirely.

In the mid-'50s, as the Crescents, lead singer Vito Picone (b. March 17, 1940), baritone Carman Romano (b. Aug. 17, 1939), Ronnie Jones, and Patti Croccitto worked up a style and a repertoire impressive enough to convince Club Records to record and release one of Vito's compositions, "Darling Come Home." The record sold well locally, but since the group's average age barely broke 15, the Crescents were hardly able to tour behind "Darling Come Home" and generate any action. Pat soon left the unit to record as Pat Cordel, eventually working as a June Taylor Dancer and, still later, as a daredevil skydiver. Ronnie vanished in 1956; Vito and Carman searched about for replacements.

Bass singer James Moschella (b. May 10, 1938), second tenor Frank Tardogono, (b. Sept. 18, 1941), and first tenor Arthur Venosa (b. Sept. 3, 1939) joined up, and by early 1958, the Elegants were set. One of their songs, "Little Star," had been knockin' 'em dead at hops and talent shows, so the group auditioned the tune at a number of labels. Bea Casalin at Hull Records liked what she heard, signed them, and told them to start the song with that "Where are you, little star?" hook. Once the disk began its meteoric ascent, Apt, ABC-Paramount's new subsidiary, picked up the waxing for national distribution.

With "Star" atop the charts, the Elegants toured with Bobby Freeman, Jack Scott, and Dion & The Belmonts. For some now-forgotten reason, the group had no follow-up issued for nearly 18 months. By the time "Goodnight" was finally shipped, the Elegants were yesterday's news. "True Love Affair" and the half-dozen 45s that followed were quite good, but almost no one ever got the chance to hear them.

Vito went on to record some solo singles and became a car salesman. When last noted, Art was a construction worker, Carmen was a hairdresser, Jimmy was a bus driver, and Frankie was working for New York's Department of Sanitation.

Several times over the past few years, Vito has reassembled a vocal group, called them the Elegants, and played the "oldies" circuit.

Poni-Tails

BORN TOO LATE
(Fred Tobias, Charles Strouse)
ABC-Paramount 9934
No. 7   *September 15, 1958*

Toni Cistone (lead vocals), Karen Topinka (low harmony), and LaVerne Novak (high harmony) began singing together at Brush High School in Lyndhurst, Ohio. Discovered while performing at a benefit, they were introduced to a music publisher named Tom Illius. The girls showed him "Que La Bozena," a song that they had written; Tom liked the tune and the girls' voices. He offered to become their manager and to hawk their song around town.

Soon after, parental pressure forced Karen to quit the group; Patti McCabe replaced her. Point Records, a subsidiary of RKO Pictures, recorded the Poni-Tails singing "Que La Bozena" and another innocent number, "Your Wild Heart." The latter, the "A" side, was nearly a hit, but a young Chicago voice named JOY LAYNE beat the Poni-Tails to the punch with a successful cover version of the song.

After "Can I Be Sure" slipped from sight, Illius managed to interest Don Costa at ABC-Paramount in recording the girls. "Just My Luck To Be Fifteen" stiffed, but "Born Too Late" did as well as the trio of teens could have hoped. They appeared on "American Bandstand." They received fan mail and some spending money. And although their platter about an older boy has yet to be certified as a million-seller, "Born Too Late" is a rock and roll classic, a "girl group goldie," and a 'round-the-world turntable favorite.

For the next two years, the Tails tried their best to recapture that magic. Despite its suggestive title, "Seven Minutes In Heaven" (#85, 1958) was innocuous. "I'll Be Seeing You" (#87, 1959) was a rockaballad which went down well at hops as a "ladies choice" number. Both charted, but that was about it for their recording success.

Toni, Patti, and LaVerne never wrote any more songs. The authors of their classic waxing did, however. Tobias wrote "Good Timin'" (a hit for Jimmy Jones) and "One of Us" (a hit for Patti Page); Strouse wrote the music for *Bye Bye Birdie* and "Those Were The Days,"

Recorded by THE PONI-TAILS on ABC Paramount
BORN TOO LATE
Lyric by FRED TOBIAS   Music by CHARLES STROUSE

PRICE 95¢ IN U.S.A.

MANSION MUSIC Corporation
Sole Selling Agent
Edward B. MARKS MUSIC Corporation

The Poni-Tails

the theme for TV's "All in the Family."

"The three years were fun," Toni told *Goldmine*'s Carlo Wolff, "but I just wanted to get out of the record business and get back to normal living." Each Poni-Tail married and settled down. Toni (Cistone) Costabile works at a high school in Shaker Heights, Ohio. LaVerne (Novak) Glavic is a grandmother five times over, lives in Menor, Ohio, and works for a real estate agent. Patti (McCabe) Barnes died of cancer on January 17, 1989.

Quin-Tones

DOWN THE AISLE OF LOVE
(Quin-Tones)
Hunt 321
No. 18   *September 15, 1958*

While his name never dangled on many a lip, Doc Bagby was a fairly successful organist and bandleader. More importantly, he was a man with a knack for finding and shaping potential hitmakers. For a brief spell in the late '50s, Doc set up the Red Top label in Philadelphia with Irv Nahan and Marvin Schwartz. During his stay with the label, he recorded the Students, the Sharmeers, Tony & The Twilights (later billed as Anthony & The Sophomores), a group assembled by Curtis Mayfield called the Kingsmen, and the Ivy Tones.

The most successful and short-lived of all the Red Top recording acts was the Quin-Tones. Roberta Hayman and her back-ups— Phyllis Carr, Eunice Cristi, Caroline "Cissy" Holmes, Ronnie Scott, and lone male Kenny Sexton—hailed from York, Pennsylvania. While particulars on their individual lives are lacking, what is known is that Bagby caught an earful of the group singing their self-penned "drag" (a slow number for dancing, or a "ladies' choice"). Doc liked what he heard, and bagged the group on the spot. "Aisle," their first record, sold so well and so fast that Bagby enlisted the aid of Dick Clark's Hunt label to issue the winner on a national scale.

"There'll Be No Sorrow" and "Oh Heavenly Father" were issued each in turn, but sales were minuscule. No further recordings by the Quin-Tones are known to exist. Recording at nearly the same time for Gee, Park, and later Chess Records was another group calling themselves the Quintones. To distinguish themselves from the Quin-Tones, this other unit did not use a hyphen in the group name.

In the fall of 1986, Roberta, Phyllis, and Cissy re-formed the Quin-Tones.

Shields

YOU CHEATED
(Don Brunch)
Dot 15805
No. 12   *October 6, 1958*

The circumstances behind the Shields' "You Cheated" is, according to *Yesterday's Memories'* Dave Hinckley, "one of the most tangled stories ever to surround a hit record."

Most simply put, the Shields never existed. George Matola, the big cheese at Tender Records, heard this great little number by the Slades called "You Cheated." Matola reportedly had his good buddy Jessie Belvin toss together a one-shot group to do a quickie cover

on the Slades' original. Everyone agrees that the lead vocalist on the track is Frankie Ervin. Frankie has identified the other Shields as Belvin (falsetto), Buzzy Smith (baritone), Johnny "Guitar" Watson (bass), and Mel Williams (second tenor). To complicate matters, Watson denies being involved. And to untidy the affair further, performers like Tony Allan, Buster Wilson, and Charles Wright (later leader of the Watts 103rd Street Rhythm Band) claim to have been among the voices taped that night.

The Shields' cover version of "You Cheated" cheated the Slades out of most of the chart action; the Slades' original rendition (#42, 1958) never even broke into the top 40. To promote the hit disk, something calling itself the Shields had to tour. The label hastily rounded up three guys to hit the road with Frankie Ervin.

For a follow-up, Nat "King" Cole's "Nature Boy" was dressed up and dished out. Ervin was reportedly present on this session, but beyond that, things get quite fuzzy. Hinckley has suggested that Belvin, Wright, "Pookie" Wooten, and James Monroe Warren might also perform on "Nature Boy." The voices on the Shields' third and last Dot release, "Fare Thee Well, My Love," could have been supplied by Belvin, Wright, Warren, Johnny White, and maybe even Chuck Jackson. As for "You'll Be Coming Home Soon"—released on Transcontinental and later Falcon Records—Tony Allan, a member of the various touring editions of the Shields, claims that he was on this recording with Tommy Youngblood, Charles Patterson, and David Cobb.

Regardless of who appeared on which record, none of these follow-ups to "You Cheated" sold more than a dribble. Collectors and pop historians may someday straighten out this cluttered pile of educated conjecture.

Bobby Day

ROCKIN' ROBIN
(Jimmie Thomas)
Class 229
No. 2   *October 13, 1958*

Bobby Day—born Robert Byrd on July 1, 1932—moved from Fort Worth, Texas, to Los Angeles in 1947. He would have only been 15 then, but claimed, in an interview with Jeff Tamarkin in *Goldmine*, that he came to town on a college scholarship. "In mathematics and music, I got straight A's and one B, but I don't talk about that B."

School was out for good once Bobby, David Ford, Willie Ray Rockwell, and Curley Dinkins formed THE HOLLYWOOD FLAMES. The Flames recorded a slew of singles on labels like Selective, Specialty, Spin, Unique, and Recorded In Hollywood. Before they would finally click in a big way with Byrd's "Buzz-Buzz-Buzz," members would come and go, as would the names under which they recorded—the Flames, the 4 Flames, the Hollywood 4 Flames, the Hollywood Flames, the Eddtides, the Jets, the Satellites, and the Tangiers. Byrd left the group in 1957.

"Little Bitty Pretty One," penned by Bobby, was not his first record as a solo act; he had recorded as Bobby Byrd as far back as 1955. Nor was "Little Bitty" his first 45 as Bobby Day—months earlier, Chess had released his "Come Seven" under that name. But "Little Bitty Pretty One" was a single that looked like it would be a solid hit. Unfortunately, competitors at the neighboring Aladdin label had THURSTON HARRIS cover Day's dazzler, and while Bobby's original reading did make the pop listings (#57, 1957), it was hardly the smash it could have been.

After a few forgettable follow-ups, Bobby came across the song of his life. "I was in tight with Leon Rene [a.k.a. Jimmie Thomas]," he told Tamarkin. "He called one night and told me about this tune he had and he thought we should do. So actually, 'Rockin' Robin' was his song, but we sort of had a little deal on this song. We used my group, which had been called the Hollywood Flames but was now called the Satellites. I told them how to sing the song. We were only recording on a one- or two-track in those days, so we couldn't make mistakes."

They didn't, and both sides charted. But in hindsight, perhaps it would have been better to have issued the "B" side, "Over And Over" (#41, 1958), separately. Day's next three singles, all released in 1959, did make the Hot 100, but only barely—"The Bluebird, The Buzzard, The Oriole" (#54), "That's All I Want" (#98), and "Gotta New Girl" (#82).

Bobby Day continued to record throughout the '70s, but nothing further ever ventured onto the listings. Day soon joined forces with Hollywood Flame Earl Nelson as half of Bob & Earl. The act had hits with "Don't Ever Leave Me" (#85, 1962) and the original "Harlem Shuffle" (#44, 1964); by 1964, Bobby Relf, a.k.a. JACKIE LEE, had replaced Day.

Bobby formed his own label, Birdland, and kept plugging away under various guises, as "Baby Face" Byrd, the Birds, the Birdies, the

rockin' robin
with BOBBY DAY

Daybirds, and the Sounds. His compositions, as recorded by other acts, were quite successful. "Little Bitty Pretty One" was a hit for Thurston Harris (#6, 1957), Frankie Lymon (#58, 1960), Clyde McPhatter (#25, 1962), and the Jackson 5 (#13, 1972); "Over And Over" was a hit for Thurston Harris (#96, 1958) and the Dave Clark Five (#1, 1965); and "Rockin' Robin" was a hit for THE RIVIERAS (#96, 1964) and Michael Jackson (#2, 1972).

And where has Bobby been all these years? After his own records failed to chart, he moved to Australia and New Zealand, remaining there for a lengthy spell.

Bobby Day is currently living in Florida, and is reportedly writing songs once again.

Earl Grant

THE END
(Sid Jacobson, Jimmy Krondes)
Decca 30719
No. 7   *October 13, 1958*

Rock and rollers never gave more than a passing notice to Earl. Countless parents in the early '60s described Earl's style to their teenagers as "relaxing." A word like that was the kiss of death to any self-respecting hepcat, and boppers and rockers just couldn't understand. Man, it didn't have no beat; it wasn't blues, and it wasn't jazz, either. Nonetheless, Earl sold piles of plastic by tinkling the ivories and crooning, in a Nat "King" Cole style, all those standards only Mom and Dad could appreciate.

Born in Oklahoma City on January 20, 1933, little Earl took to playing the organ even before he set foot in kindergarten. When not touching the keys, Earl was blowing trumpet or pounding on drums. Earl's dad was a Baptist minister, and while still a mere tyke, the little one would perform at his pop's church services.

Earl went on to study at the Kansas City Conservatory of Music, the New Rochelle Conservatory, the University of Southern California, and Chicago's DePaul University. Thereafter, Earl became a music teacher. During World War II, while stationed as a soldier at Fort Bliss, Texas, he started his career as a singing organist in nearby nightclubs, signing with Decca Records in 1958.

"The End" was his first release and his only top 40 hit. Five more singles did make the Hot 100, and two of Grant's albums sold well enough to place on the top pop albums chart. Earl was heavily heard on the "beautiful music" stations, showed up often on *Billboard*'s easy-listening chart, and appeared in several motion pictures such as *Tender is the Night* (1962), *Imitation of Life* (1959), and *Tokyo Night* (1959). While Earl's big moment on the charts may have passed by the late '60s, Decca Records never slowed down the flow of new releases. And bubbly Earl never cut back on his TV and nightclub appearances.

After a performance at the La Fiesta Club in Juarez, Mexico, on June 10, 1970, Earl Grant was killed in an automobile crash near Lordsburg, New Mexico.

Robin Luke

SUSIE DARLIN'
(Robin Luke)
Dot 15781
No. 5   *October 13, 1958*

Robin (b. Mar. 19, 1942, Los Angeles) started playing guitar when he was only eight years old; within just as many years, he had written a sackful of songs, including a nifty number about his sister Susie. Starting in 1957, Robin co-starred on a local TV program with Kimo McVay. Not long after, someone in the biz brought the boy to the attention of Bobby Bertram, owner of International Records.

Bertram didn't care too much for "Susie Darlin'," but was impressed instead with the 16-year-old's "Living's Loving You." Both tunes, recorded in a small studio in Honolulu, Robin's hometown at the time, received a lot of Hawaiian airplay. Luckily for Luke, Art and Dorothy Freeman, distributors for the stateside Dot label, were honeymooning in Waikiki when they happened to hear Robin's record on the radio.

Dot Records acquired the distribution rights from International, and Robin Luke had a hit. Although Luke and Bertram didn't give up the follow-up effort for years, almost no one in the U.S. even knows that the poor chap made another recording. His "A" sides included "Chicka, Chicka Honey," "Strollin' Blues," "Five Minutes More," "Make Me A Dreamer," "Bad Boy," "Everlovin'," "Poor Little Rich Boy," and a duet with Roberta Shore, "Foggin' Up The Windows."

When most recently spotted, Robin Luke was a college professor in Norfolk, Virginia.

Royaltones

POOR BOY
(Mel Mitchell, David R. Sanderson)
Jubilee 5338
No. 17   *December 1, 1958*

"Poor Boy" started out as a soft number along the likes of another Mel Mitchell song, "The Petticoats Of Portugal." There was no way Mel could have expected that these Royaltone upstarts would rock the daylights out of his "Poor Boy." But they did, and on the basis of their performance, it is hard to deny that the Royaltones were one of the best instrumental acts in rock and roll.

Despite their ability, no Royaltones album has ever been released. Their dozen singles are long out-of-print. And next to no one knows much of anything about who they were or how on Earth they got so good.

The four Royaltones were from Dearborn, Michigan. George (Katsakis) Kaye was their screamin' sax man; the futuristic guitar cries were by Karl Kay; the Popoff brothers, Greg and Mike, played drums and piano, respectively. They played dances, and surely must have driven their audiences into a frenzy. Someone with clout spotted the group and brought them to the attention of Jerry Blaine at Jubilee Records. History has yet to tell whether or not such a perfect pounder as "Poor Boy" was the Royaltones' first release.

The honkin' disk found a niche on the nation's radios, but follow-ups were another story.

After the double-sided classic "Seesaw" b/w "Little Bo," Kaye, Kay, and the Popoff brothers had "Flamingo Express" (#82, 1961), possibly their finest piece of musical madness, issued on George Goldner's Goldisc label. Goldner continued to release other Royaltone records despite their dismal sales. "Holy Smoke," "Lonely World," and "Yea Yea" appeared as late as the mid-'60s, long after the nation stopped hungering for sax-powered instrumentals.

Teddy Bears
TO KNOW HIM IS TO LOVE HIM
(Phil Spector)
Dore 503
No. 1   *December 1, 1958*

When Phil Spector (b. Dec. 26, 1940, New York City) was nine, his father committed suicide. Engraved on the tombstone were the words: TO KNOW HIM IS TO LOVE HIM. Mrs. Spector picked up the pieces and moved with the family to L.A.'s Fairfax area. In his early teen years, Phil performed on acoustic guitar in talent shows and organized the Sleepwalkers, his first tentative group. He wrote bits of songs and studiously observed the goings-on at the Gold Star Studios on Vine Street in Hollywood.

Once he was ready to record, Phil formed the Teddy Bears—himself, Marshall Leib, Harvey Goldstein, and Annette Kleinbard (who later changed her name to Carol Connors). Leib and Kleinbard had frequented Phil's practice sessions in his girlfriend's garage, and it would be this quartet that would provide our pop heritage with one of its best-loved rockaballads.

"They'd been searching for a name left and right and couldn't come up with one," Goldstein (who soon left the group and became an accountant) told Mark Ribowsky in *He's a Rebel*. "Elvis' 'Teddy Bear' was a big hit at the time, so I casually mentioned at one of our bull sessions that we ought to name ourselves the Teddy Bears."

The Teddy Bears, with Phil Spector (right)

A demo of Spector's "Don't You Worry, My Little Pet" was cut at Gold Star and presented to the owners of Era/Dore Records, Lew Bedell and Herb Newman, who signed the group. "Don't You Worry" needed a "B" side, though. Tacked onto the remaining minutes of a two-hour session that was supposed to produce something called "Wonderful Loveable You" was a hollow and haunting number Phil had written especially for Annette's voice. In two takes, "To Know Him Is To Love Him" was done.

"To Know Him Is To Love Him" soared up the charts, and almost immediately, wrangling of all sorts broke loose. Phil allowed his sister Shirley, to everyone's displeasure, to become the group's manager. Spector and the label heads disagreed on just what the Teddy Bears' follow-up should be, so the group quickly moved to Imperial. Arrangements were made to cut an album—a rare occurrence in these early days of rock and roll—and issue "Oh Why" (#90, 1959) b/w "I Don't Need You Anymore" (#98), the tunes that Era/Dore had refused to release as the Bears' next 45.

The *The Teddy Bears Sing!* LP sold poorly. A Spector instrumental issued as by Phil Harvey called "Bumbershoot" b/w "Willy Boy" also flopped. Two further Teddy Bears singles ("If You Only Knew" and "Don't Go Away"), plus "Wonderful Loveable You" on Dore, barely scratched the bottom of the nation's charts.

In September 1960, Annette Kleinbard was seriously injured when her MG convertible tumbled down a mountainside. Four facial operations were required to reconstruct her features. When hospital visits were allowed, Phil reportedly never appeared.

As Carol Connors, Annette has become a top songwriter. She wrote or co-wrote VICKI LAWRENCE's "The Night The Lights Went Out In Georgia," Billy Preston and Syreeta's "With You I'm Born Again," the Rip Chords' "Hey Little Cobra," BILL CONTI's "Gonna Fly Now" from *Rocky* (1976), and movie themes for *Falling in Love* (1980), *Sophie's Choice* (1982), and *Mr. Mom* (1983). Her music for *Rocky III* (1982) was nominated for two Academy Awards and a Grammy. Ms. Kleinbard has had a number of noncharting 45s issued sporadically under various names like Annette Bard, the Bompers, Carol Connors, and (with producer/songwriter Steve Barri) the Storytellers.

Marshall Leib formed the Marsh label, sang with the touring line-up of THE HOLLYWOOD ARGYLES, played second guitar on a number of Duane Eddy sides, and produced such acts as the Everly Brothers and Timi Yuro. Leib was the music supervisor for such movies as *Macon County Line* (1974), *Ode to Billy Joe* (1976), and *Take This Job and Shove It* (1981).

Phil Spector? Well, that's a whole other story . . .

Billy Grammer

GOTTA TRAVEL ON
(Paul Clayton)
Monument 400
No. 4   *January 12, 1959*

Billy was one of 13 kids clamoring for attention. Born on a 40-acre farm in Benton, Illinois, on August 28, 1925, he was surrounded by stringed instruments and raised by a daddy who was a fiddle-playing coalminer. Pop spotted his son's musical abilities early and taught him what he knew. Bill, fascinated by the sounds and realizing that making music could possibly make him some money, soon picked up on playing the guitar, mandolin, and banjo.

Before serving in the Army, Bill played dances and local events; on his return from duty, he secured a spot on "Radio Ranch" (a program on WARL in Arlington, Virginia) and performed as a trusty sideman to country singers like Grandpa Jones, T. Texas Tyler, Clyde Moody, and honky-tonker Hawkshaw Hawkins. In 1955, Bill became a regular on Jimmy Dean's daily TV show out of Washington, D.C. Two years later, "The Jimmy Dean Show" was picked up for national broadcast, and Billy was offered a contract with Monument Records.

"Gotta Travel On," a song based on a 19th-century British tune that had been adapted by the Weavers, hit the jackpot. The record was to become Billy's only major crossover record. The follow-up, however, did not do too badly— "Bonaparte's Retreat" (#50, 1959) and its flip side, "The Kissing Tree" (#60), both received extensive pop airplay, and both tunes charted on *Billboard*'s Hot 100.

Throughout the '60s, Grammer had minor hits on the country charts such as the curious "Ballad Of John Dillinger," "Jesus Is A Soul Man," and "I Wanna Go Home" (the latter was covered by Bobby Bare as the pop and country monster hit "Detroit City"). All during this time, Grammer served as one of the busiest accompanists and session guitarists in Nashville.

Billy Grammer still tours and performs at the Grand Ole Opry. He most recently recorded with Stoneway Records in the mid-'70s. Billy is also the originator and manufacturer of the Grammer flat-top guitar.

Bill Parsons

THE ALL AMERICAN BOY

(Bill Parsons, Orville Lunsford)
Fraternity 835
No. 2   *February 2, 1959*

Bobby Bare was born on April 7, 1935, in Ironton, Ohio. His family was musical, and he grew up pickin' and singin'. Money was tight, however, and Bobby's mother died when he was five years old. He went to work on a farm, and later in a clothing factory. Bob joined a country band that worked the night spots in Springfield. When he was 18, he picked up and moved to California, where, in 1956, he was discovered by the boys at Capitol Records. After three singles failed to spark much interest, the same folks turned him out.

When Bobby got his draft notice, he had to trek back to Ohio for his induction. There he met an old singing buddy named Bill Parsons (b. Sept. 8, 1934, Crossville, Tenn.), who was just getting out the service and wanted to cut a record. Since Bare had some time to kill, he and Bill wandered over to Cincinnati, where they bought some studio time and proceeded to knock out songs.

"We spent almost all of the three hours working on [Bill's] 'Rubber Dolly' thing, and we had at the most maybe twenty or thirty minutes," Bare told Bob Shannon and John Javna in *Behind the Hits*. "So I grabbed my guitar and said, 'Let me put this other song down before I forget it.'" The "other song" was a talkin' blues called "The All American Boy" that Bobby (alias "Orville Lunsford") and Bill proceeded to write together. The tune was a parody of Elvis' rise to fame and subsequent military conscription.

The recordings were sold to Fraternity Records; at this point, the label was erroneously informed that Bill Parsons was the singer on all the tunes. Months later, Bobby—at Fort Knox for his basic training—was shocked to hear his "All American Boy" on the radio. Even more of a jolt was the DJ's announcement that the record was by a new kid named Bill Parsons! By the time the error had been revealed, Bobby's baby was high atop the charts.

Fraternity issued one more Bare record as by "Bill Parsons," "Educated Rock And Roll." When Bobby was discharged, he returned to Fraternity, where he had a series of superb singles issued under his God-given name. A number of his country and pop records charted in the '60s and early '70s, most notably "Shame On Me" (#23, 1962), "Detroit City" (#16, 1963), "500 Miles Away From Home" (#10, 1963), and "Miller's Cave" (#33, 1964).

The real Bill Parsons was given the chance by Starday Records in 1960 to show his stuff. A couple of singles were issued—"Guitar Blues," and something called "Hot Rod Volkswagen." Nothing sold very well, and Bill returned to the quiet life in Wellston, Ohio.

Reg Owen

MANHATTAN SPIRITUAL

(Billy Maxted)
Palette 5005
No. 10   *February 9, 1959*

Eric Danlaney, Joe Loss, Jack Parnell, Ken Mackintosh, Ronnie Scott, and Reg Owen (b. Feb. 1928)—what do these English folk all have in common? All of them are big-name bandleaders in their native nation, yet almost total unknowns in the U.S. Unlike his associates, however, Reg Owen did miraculously manage to crack the stateside charts with his reworking of composer Billy "Satin Doll" Maxted's spirited "Manhattan Spiritual." For the next few years, Palette Records issued his swinging, brass-blowin' disks, but nothing more caught the record-buying public's ear.

Jesse Lee Turner

THE LITTLE SPACE GIRL

(Jesse Lee Turner)
Carlton 496
No. 20   *February 9, 1959*

Almost nothing is known about Jesse Lee. Born in the late '30s in Bowling, Texas, he had an Elvis-like quiver in his voice. "Teen-Age Misery" b/w "That's My Girl," his first waxing for Fraternity, sold miserably. The ducktailed kid next brought forth a tale about a sexually-charged, alien beauty with "four arms, the better to hold you/Three lips, the better to kiss you"—sung in an Alvin Chipmunk-like voice.

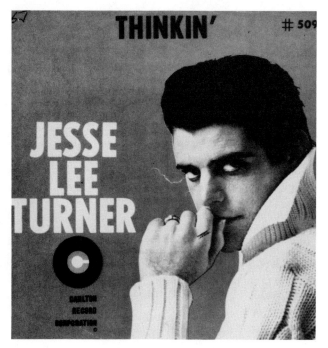

THINKIN'   # 509

JESSE LEE TURNER

CARLTON
RECORD
CORPORATION

Like many a novelty number, it was cute the first time around but irritating after a few listens.

Jesse's immediate follow-up looked like two competing "A" sides, but both "Thinkin'" and "Baby Please Don't Tease" were slightly less than top-of-the-charts material. It was clear, however, that Jesse Lee did have some innate rockabilly ability; all the Texan needed was direction and some decent songs. His next outing, "Do I Worry (Yes I Do)" on the Top Rank label, was possibly his finest outing ever, but the record stiffed. Turner was persuaded by the lads at the Sudden label to record an embarrassing turkey about mismatched "Elopers."

Moments before the arrival of the Beatles and the British Invasion, J. L. Turner reappeared, one last time, with two obscurities for GNP, "The Voice Changing Song" and "The Ballad of Billy Sol Estes."

Chris Barber's Jazz Band
PETITE FLEUR (LITTLE FLOWER)
(Sidney Bechet)
Laurie 3022
No. 5 *March 2, 1959*

Chris Barber (b. April 17, 1930, Welwyn Garden City, England) took up the trombone when

a mere lad. Later, becoming quite proficient on the bass trumpet and the string bass, he attended the Guildhall School of Music. After a stay in Cy Laurie's band, and an attempt at forming his own group, Chris joined Ken Colyer's band. In 1954, luck smiled upon him when Colyer reportedly "fired" the whole outfit and Barber took over.

With a repertoire that ranged from jug-band tunes to folk-blues to Duke Ellington numbers, Barber set up small units within his band to work up presentations of these various styles. One of these subgroups included Lonnie Donegan strumming guitar, Barber on bass, and a bloke beating a washboard. The resulting music, dubbed "skiffle," was a pleasantly crude blend of well-aged American folk, blues, and rock and roll. Barber's group cut an album in 1954, and two of these skiffle numbers were on it.

In response to the huge interest in skiffle, British Decca issued "Rock Island Line" and "John Henry" as a single, and with Lonnie's name prominent. Donegan up and left Barber's group to become the most consistent hitmaker in Britain in '50s. The simple arrangements and primitive musicianship required for playing skiffle encouraged thousands of young Brits to do likewise. Strongly influenced by skiffle-mania were four lads named John, Paul, George, and Ringo.

Yet despite his influence on British popular music, Barber himself never charted much, not even in his homeland; "Petite Fleur" was one of only three such entries. While patching together a third LP, Chris got the notion to include a clarinet number. "I told Monty Sunshine [the group's clarinetist] to go away and think of something to do, and he came back the next day with Sidney Bechet's 'Petite Fleur'," Barber explained to Sheila Tracy in *Who's Who in Pop Music in Great Britain*. "That album was released in 1957. Two years later, I hear we are number one in the German charts. 'With what?' I asked. 'We haven't got a single out.'"

Once the band's sound had been supplanted by those of the Beatles, the Stones, and others, Chris re-fashioned the group into the Barber Jazz & Blues Band. An electric rhythm section was brought in that at times included Tony Ashton (later of Ashton, Gardner & Dyke), Pete York (later of the Spencer Davis Group), and, for a tour in the '80s, DR. JOHN.

Barber and the boys are still active. Teaching at Leeds Music College, Chris has also been working on his 6-volume autobiography, to be published by the Black Lion Press.

The Bell Notes

Bell Notes

I'VE HAD IT
(Carl Bonura, Raymond Ceroni)
Time 1004
No. 6 *March 9, 1959*

Back in the late '50s, Alan Fredericks was a rock and roll DJ on New York City's WADO. Like all good record-spinners, Al made appearances at teen dances. The Bell Notes were popular rockers with a sound that was slightly ahead of their time. "They were a local band from East Meadow who had worked with me at record hops," Fredericks told *Record Collectors Monthly*'s Don Mennie. "I took them to a Manhattan studio, produced this record ["I've Had It"], and sold it to Bob Shad, who had just started Time Records. It was a great success."

For their short spell together, the Bell Notes consisted of Carl Bonura (lead vocals, sax), John Casey (drums), Ray Ceroni (lead vocals, guitar), Lenny Giamblavo (bass), and Pete Kane (piano). With success momentarily theirs, they appeared on Alan Freed's TV show and toured with Frankie Avalon and Bobby

Darin. Time Records rush-released a now hard-to-find EP and four high-quality 45s: "Old Spanish Town" (#76) b/w "She Went That-A-Way," "That's Right," "You're A Big Girl Now," and "No Dice."

In 1960, Fredericks brought the Bell Notes to Larry Utall's Madison label. After their cover version of Paul Chapman's "Shortnin' Bread" (#96, 1960), and the unnoticed "Friendly Star," the Bell Notes vanished.

Thomas Wayne

TRAGEDY
(Gerald Nelson, Fred Burch)
Fernwood 109
No. 5 *March 23, 1959*

Thomas Wayne Perkins was born in Battsville, Mississippi, on July 22, 1940. His older brother was Luther Perkins, Johnny Cash's guitarist. While attending Elvis' alma mater, Humes High School, Perkins formed a group with three girls called the De-Lons. Together, they worked up some numbers and approached Scotty Moore, Elvis' guitar man. Moore, who was a part-owner of the Memphis-based Fern-wood label, swiftly produced some De-Lons sides: "You're The One That Done It," released nationally by Mercury Records, bombed.

Meanwhile, in Paducah, Kentucky, Gerald Nelson and his Escorts were tying down a take on something called "Tragedy." Early in 1958, Nelson and a buddy named Fred Burch dashed off this sad, sad ode of love lost. Tom Perkins and the fellows at the Fernwood label heard the Escorts' disk and dreamed up a cover version.

After Thomas appeared on "American Bandstand," his rendition of "Tragedy" rocketed to the top of the charts, and even became a hit later on for the Fleetwoods (#10, 1961). But the similar-sounding follow-up ("Eternally") and numerous other offerings failed to solidify Wayne's career. In the late '60s, he took a behind-the-scenes position with Audio Recorders in Nashville. Like brother Luther, he met his life's end at a young age—on August 15, 1971, Wayne was killed in a head-on car crash near Memphis, Tennessee. He was 31.

Frankie Ford

SEA CRUISE
(Huey Smith, Frankie Ford)
Ace 554
No. 14 *April 6, 1959*

Frankie Guzzo (b. Aug. 4, 1939, Gretna, La.) started early. "I was in about third grade, singing in the backyard one day," he recalled in an exclusive interview, "when the lady that lived in back of us said, 'He sounds better than the kids on the radio. You ought to see about getting him lessons.'" His mother did, and before long, Frankie was winning talent contests, appearing on Ted Mack's "Amateur Hour," and performing locally with Carmen Miranda, Ted Lewis, and Sophie Tucker.

In 1958, Johnny Vincent approached Frankie, who was then fronting a group called the Syncopators, about recording for Vincent's label, Ace Records. The first single, waxed at New Orleans' legendary Cosimo Studios, was "Cheatin' Woman." While Frankie was on the road promoting the disk, HUEY "PIANO" SMITH & THE CLOWNS were recording "Sea Cruise," the follow-up to their hit, "Don't You Just Know It." Once Frankie returned, the producers decided to try him singing lead on "Sea Cruise."

"I went into the studio, not knowin' the song. I still have a piece of paper that Huey had written the words on for me, misspellings and

all. My manager and the owner of the label said, 'Huey, you don't need a release now. Let's put it out on Frankie.'" Despite Smith's protests, the producers took the Clowns' original tracks, erased Bobby Marchan's lead vocal, and replaced it with Frankie's. Ace released "Sea Cruise," featuring the instrumental backing of Huey Smith & The Clowns, under Frankie's name.

Frankie did sing a few more rock and roll numbers—like "Roberta" and "Alimony" (#97, 1959)—before veering toward a more easy-listening vocal style. "I was trained to be a crooner. I was getting a bit older, and the trend then seemed to be going that way—Bobby Darin and Bobby Rydell were going in that direction—so I recorded 'Time After Time' [#75, 1960] and 'Chinatown,' stuff like that. I looked old enough, and I could start working at the nightclubs, which was a lot better than those rock and roll road tours."

After five singles and some questionable royalty statements, Frankie and his manager, Joe Caronna, left Ace to form Spinet Records. With Huey "Piano" Smith, ROBERT PARKER, and Frankie's second cousin, Mac Rebennack (a. k. a. DR. JOHN), Frankie, still under contract to Ace, recorded some obscure New Orleans favorites as Morgus & The Three Ghouls ("Morgus The Magnificent"), the Cheerleaders ("Chinese Bandits"), and Frank & Mac ("True Love").

"Ace was getting so diversified, and they weren't taking care of their artists. Imperial gave me front money [reportedly $10,000] to go with them, and I took Huey with me." Frankie's first Imperial single, "You Talk Too Much" (#87, 1960), actually made more money than "Sea Cruise" ever would. JOE JONES had recorded "You Talk Too Much" for Roulette Records, then had turned around and done the same for Ric Records. When the version of the song on Ric began to take off, Roulette realized that they had the record, too; the labels slapped injunctions on each other. "My producer, Dave Batholomew, called and said, 'Can you sound like Joe Jones?' I said, 'Yeah, sure.' With the exception of one guy, we used the very same musicians that Joe had used. His was a turntable hit, but I sold a million on it."

Frankie's career was moving along nicely until that dreaded piece of mail arrived—he was drafted. "When I got back to the States in '65, it was all changed; the studio had moved. And sessions, there used to be one or more a day, now there was zip; nothing was happening."

But Frankie was determined to keep working, and played a number of clubs in New Orleans for years. In the '70s and thereafter, he recorded some hard-to-locate sides for the White Cliffs, Doubloon, Paula, Cinnamon, ABC, Briarmeade, and SYC labels.

Rod Bernard
THIS SHOULD GO ON FOREVER
(Bernard Jolivette, Jay Miller)
Argo 5327
No. 20 *April 13, 1959*

In the mid-'50s, Rod Bernard (b. Aug. 12, 1940, Opelousas, La.) was a DJ on KSLO in Opelousas, Louisiana. "Hot Rod," as his station called him, used to catch Guitar Gable and his singer King Karl (Bernard Jolivette) playing a number called "This Should Go On Forever" at their club dates. Karl had been announcing for a long spell that the swamp-pop song was set to be their very next disk.

"It really hit me as being one helluva song," Bernard told *Goldmine*'s Bill Milner, "and whenever I saw Karl, I'd ask him when it was coming out. He kept saying, 'Well, it's comin',' but it never did. Eventually, I went to his home and asked him if I could record it, and he taught me how to sing it."

Rod had started on radio one warm Saturday morn in 1950, when Dezauche's Red Bird Sweet Potatoes sponsored a talent search. Thereafter, Rod and his guitar would show up every Saturday to pick a quarter-hour's worth of Hank Williams songs and Cajun items. During his high school days in Winnie, Texas, he fronted a band that played tunes by local legends Bobby Charles, Johnnie Allan, and T. K. Hulin. In 1957, Jake Graffagnino, owner of Winnie's music store, recorded a couple of sides on Bernard ("Set Me Free" and "Linda Gail") for his tiny Carl label. All this was a preamble to "Hot Rod"'s pop peak.

With King Karl's blessings, a promise from Floyd Soileau that he would issue "This Should Go On Forever" track on his newly-formed JIN label, and his band in tow, Rod went into the studio. Legend has it that it took so many efforts to get an acceptable take on the tune that Bernard developed a nosebleed, and that for the last few takes (including the one eventually etched in vinyl), he was singing through a towel.

"Maybe that was the key," quipped Bernard to John Broven in *South to Louisiana*. "Maybe I should have kept singing with a towel around my face." Maybe—though Rod claims the offer was a good one—he should not have switched to the big-time Mercury label and started recording in Nashville. "Mercury had so many people like Brook Benton, Dinah Washington, and the Platters doing exceptionally well they didn't need to spend money on me," Bernard explained to Milner.

After a string of sleepers on Mercury—including "One More Chance" (#74, 1959)—Rod enlisted in the Marine Corps. Since 1970, Bernard has lived in Lafayette, Louisiana, writing and producing commercials for KLFY-TV, occasionally releasing singles up until 1978. (Some of his Hall/Hallway sides featured the guitar and sax work of a young Johnny and Edgar Winter.) Five albums have been issued on such home-state labels as JIN, La Louisianne, and Crazy Cajun.

Dodie Stevens
PINK SHOE LACES
(Mickie Grant)
Crystalette 724
No. 3 *April 13, 1959*

"He wears tan shoes and pink shoe laces/And a big Panama with a purple hat band"—Geraldine Ann Pasquale (b. Feb. 17, 1947, Chicago) was a mere miss of 11 when she first sang that song. "I really didn't like the song at all," Geri Stevens (as she is now known) explained to *Goldmine*'s Wayne Jones. "I thought it was dumb. I was really into rock and roll. Since I didn't have anything to lose by doing it, I just went ahead and recorded it, kept my fingers crossed and it was a hit."

Geraldine's folks had moved to California when she was three. A few years later, Geraldine was performing at U.S.O. functions, at veterans' hospitals, and on local television. "I was more or less discovered on one of these local television programs at the age of 11 [actually 9 or 10]. That's when the president of Crystalette Records happened to see the show and called backstage to talk to my mom and dad. He wanted to know if I was available to do records. Of course, I was. So, he said he would . . . search for material and when the right thing came along, he would give me a call. We didn't hear from this man for about a year and a half."

"Pink Shoe Laces" was "the right thing" and her very first recording. "I was dubbed Dodie

Dodie Stevens

Stevens . . . and I didn't like it! Didn't like the song, didn't like the name. But it was all quite a success for me." Three non-charting LPs (*Dodie Stevens*, 1959; *Over the Rainbow*, 1960; *Pink Shoe Laces*, 1963) were shipped. A few follow-ups 45s made the pop listings from 1959 through 1961—"Yes-Sir-ee" b/w "The Five Pennies," "No," and "Yes, I'm Lonesome Tonight"—but the record game had pretty much run its course before Geri was out of her teen years.

Geri appeared in several films—*Hound Dog Man* (1959), with Stuart Whitmark and Fabian, *Convicts Four* (1962), with Vincent Price and Ben Gazzara, and *Alakazam The Great* (1961), with Frankie Avalon. The latter was a full-length animated feature for which Geri did the voice of a monkey.

"I gave it up. I was 16 when I got married. After about three years of a very active career, I was just through with it . . . I moved to Missouri, lived on a farm, and I had a baby when I was nineteen. Very shortly after her birth, I started feeling as though I wanted to do more. Being a housewife wasn't making it, and when I became a mother, I realized that wasn't making it, either."

Geri's marriage ended, and in 1968, Stevens resumed her singing career. After voice lessons and much daily practice, Geri contacted her old manager, who arranged for her to be one of the two female voices in Sergio Mendes & Brasil '66. She went on to work some rock and roll revival shows, sing on numerous sessions, and tour as a back-up singer for acts like Mac Davis.

Travis & Bob

TELL HIM NO
(Travis Pritchett)
Sandy 1017
No. 8 *April 27, 1959*

Travis Pritchett and Bobby Weaver were born in 1939 and raised in and around Jackson, Alabama. In the late '50s, they began strummin' and a-singin' at haunts throughout the South. In Mobile, they persuaded the big boys at Sandy Records to let them have a shot at the brass ring with a tune that Travis had a-pluckin' away at his innards. The song had this catchy little chorus that kept pleading, "Tell 'em no, oh, oh, oh/Tell 'em no, oh, oh, oh." On the recorded version, Bob and his buddy sound like a rough version of Everly Brothers.

Since the Everly Brothers sound was hot back in 1959, Travis and Bob looked and sounded like they were headed for the big time. Dot Records picked up national distribution for "Tell Him No," then released "Oh Yeah," "Wake Up And Cry," and "Little Bitty Johnny" in rapid succession. Only the latter number did much of anything when for one week, it occupied the number 114 slot on *Billboard*'s "Bubbling Under The Hot 100" chart. Two other labels, Big Top and then Mercury, gave the duo further opportunities to score another hit, but nothing ever charted again. In 1959, Dean and Marc (Mathis) had a hit on the Bullseye label with their cover version of "Tell Him No" (#42).

The whereabouts of troubadours Travis and Bob are not known. Why they failed to solidify their hit status can only be guessed. The fellows' harmonizing was not as tight as the Everlys'; their overall sound was very country and not too teen-oriented. Still, "Tell Him No" was so appealing that even if it had steel guitars and fiddles on it, any semi-literate and youthful duo with a name like "Cliff & Jed" could have cracked the pop charts with it.

Virtues

GUITAR BOOGIE SHUFFLE
(Arthur Smith)
Hunt 228
No. 5 *April 27, 1959*

Good timing was not one of the Virtues' virtues. Created by Frank Virtuoso in 1946,

nearly a decade before the official birth of rock and roll, the band waited 13 years for their first record and only hit, "Guitar Boogie Shuffle." By the time their classic cut was on the charts, the golden age of instrumentals (created in large part by acts like Johnny & The Hurricanes, Duane Eddy, and the Bill Black Combo) was just about to peak—and so was the band's career.

Frank Virtue (né Virtuoso) was born and raised in South Philadelphia. In 1945, he enlisted in the Navy. With his musical background—he started studying violin at age nine—he played in the Regular Navy Dance Band stationed at Bainbridge, Maryland. A year later, Frank was discharged from the Navy to care for his father, who was suffering from cancer.

At this point, Virtue decided to form a group (at first called the Virtuoso Trio) modeled on Nat "King" Cole's trio. Within months of their formation, Frank, Jimmy Bruno (who remained with the group throughout its 16-year career), and two others recorded "Limehouse Blues" and "Bye Bye Blues." Neither song was ever released. For the next 12 years, the unit stayed close to home, playing club dates and performing on local radio and TV programs.

In 1958, Frank remembered a tune that his former Navy buddy Arthur Smith had created. As he explained to *Goldmine*'s Robert Dalley, "I had heard [Smith's] guitar boogie and liked it. I went one step further and made a rock record of it by using a different jazz ad-lib in between the boogie theme and adding a shuffle rock beat to it. To this day, people tell me that the song was different enough that we should have had the original copyright to the song, but I felt as a friend I should give Arthur the writer's credit."

Released in early 1959, "Guitar Boogie Shuffle" shot to *Billboard*'s number five position. Eventually, 2,000,000 copies were sold, but Frank (bass) and crew—Jimmy Bruno (guitar), Dave Raplin (vocal), John Renner (sax), and Joe Vespe (drums)—could never quite top that number, despite fine efforts like "Flippin' In," their follow-up. With each successive record, the Virtues sounded more and more dated, almost pre-rock, as if they were unearthing and releasing material recorded back in the early '50s.

In 1962, the year the band split up, the Virtues tried with some success to update their boogie with a twist beat. "Guitar Boogie Shuffle Twist" (#96) lasted a week on the charts before vanishing. Since then, Frank Virtue has recorded under various names—

the Frank Virtue Orchestra & Chorus, the Frank Virtue Combo, and the Frank Virtue Quintet. Frank also produced "That's Life" for Gabriel & The Angels (#51, 1962), "Who Stole The Keeshka" for the Matys Brothers (#55, 1963), and "Hey There Lonely Girl" for EDDIE HOLMAN (#2, 1970).

Tommy Dee
THREE STARS
(Tommy Dee)
Crest 1057
No. 11 *May 4, 1959*

The music died, we've been told, at 1:50 AM on February 2, 1959. The small airplane carrying Buddy Holly, the Big Bopper, and Ritchie Valens crashed that morn. Numerous records were rush-released to commemorate rock and roll's loss; Tommy Donaldson's spoken-word tribute was the most successful of them all.

Tommy (b. July 7, 1937, Vicker, Va.) was a record-rider at KFXM in San Bernardino that fateful day. Raised in Boston, he had worked his virgin flight over the airwaves at KCLS in Flagstaff, Arizona. A short stint at KOFA in Yuma followed. It was during Tommy's first week on the Bernardino airwaves that Ritchie, Buddy, and the Bopper passed on to rock and roll heaven. Within days, Dee had conceived of his idea for a talkie-tribute and cut a demo. He approached the Crest label and recorded the disk with Carol Kay & The Teen-Aires.

None of Dee's numerous follow-ups to his monster moment—"The Chair," "Merry Christmas, Mary," "There's A Star-Spangled Banner Waving Somewhere," "The Ballad Of The Drag Race," and "A Little Dog Cried"—received national notice. Tommy even tried his hand (or mouth) at singing like Johnny Cash, but the result was less than successful. In the '70s, Dee returned to the pop landscape with a non-charting country classic, "Welfare Cadillac." Years later, Mr. Dee nearly pulled off a Hot 100 hit with an item called "Here Is My Love" (1981). Ah yes, persistence does count.

Meanwhile, Carol Kay, now Carol Kaye, moved on to a successful career as a West Coast session guitarist and bassist. Her credits include studio work with the Beach Boys, Ray Charles, Joe Cocker, the Four Tops, the Monkees, Harry Nilsson, Sonny & Cher, the Supremes, the Temptations, and Stevie Wonder. Carol even made a brief appearance on Frank Zappa's landmark *Freak Out* album.

Her plucking sounds can be heard daily in the themes and musical backdrops of syndicated TV programs like "Hawaii Five-O," "Hogan's Heroes," "Ironside," "M*A*S*H," and "Mission Impossible." Her movie-soundtrack credits include *Airport* (1970), *Butch Cassidy and the Sundance Kid* (1969), *In Cold Blood* (1967), *The Pawnbroker* (1965), and *Valley of the Dolls* (1967). Carol Kaye has authored 11 music-method books, and currently runs Gwyn Publishing in Monterey, California.

Edd Byrnes
KOOKIE, KOOKIE
(LEND ME YOUR COMB)
(Irving Taylor)
Warner Brothers 5047
No. 4 *May 11, 1959*

Born in New York City on July 30, 1933, with the unhip moniker of Edward Breitenberger, Edd made the scene, like, weekly, on this tip-top TV trip, "77 Sunset Strip." As Gerald Lloyd Kookson III, the dad would lay wheels flat, perpendicular, and nowheres square at Dino's, a grease and bug-juice palace. You dig? Kookie was a skizzard with a comb, and had a thing for his hair and females with grooves to ride. Chicks were flippin' their wigs, saying that he was the utmost—like, dreamsville. Then, in 1963, the bubble burst—TV viewers were weary of Edd and "kookie-isms" like "piling up some Z's" (sleeping) and "a dark seven" (a depressing week).

Byrnes has admitted to being a reformed alcoholic. In 1988, while dedicating a drug and rehabilitation clinic in Maryland, he told a reporter for UPI: "It was hard to admit I had a problem when I still had money, property, prestige. How can I have a problem when I'm driving my new Mercedes, and it's paid for, and I have a house in Malibu?" Byrnes kicked the habit in 1983.

Edd had five good years with "77 Sunset Strip," but found it hard to shake his hip "Kookie" image once the series had been mothballed. He played some secondary roles in B-grade flicks (*The Secret Invasion*, 1964; *Beach Ball*, 1965) and moved to Europe, where he acted in spaghetti Westerns like *Winchester per un Massacro* (1967) and *Ammazzo e Torno* (1967). He guested on TV shows like "The Hardy Boys" and "Police Woman," also appearing in *Wicked Wicked* (1973), *Star-*

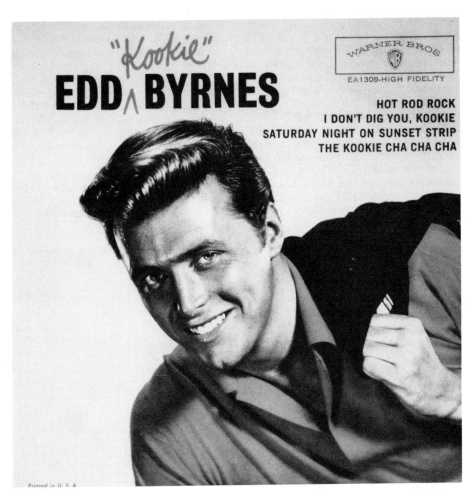

dust (1975), and, with Frankie, Annette, and CONNIE STEVENS, *Back to the Beach* (1988).

Only four 45s, an EP, and one album were ever recorded by Byrnes. Aside from "Kookie, Kookie," which featured a duet with Connie Stevens, only the immediate follow-up—"Like I Love You," billed as by Edd Byrnes and Friend (actually JOANIE SOMMERS)—managed to chart nationally (#42, 1959).

Impalas

SORRY (I RAN ALL THE WAY HOME)
(Artie Zwirn, Harry Giosasi)
Cub 9022
No. 2 *May 11, 1959*

"Well, the true story is there were three guys," Joe "Speedo" Frazier (b. Sept. 5, 1943)

told *Goldmine*'s Wayne Jones. "Richie Wagner, Lenny Renda and Tony Carlucci. [They] all used to meet at a candy store in Canarsie [a section in Brooklyn]. They were trying to get it together without much success. I was living in the same neighborhood and I used to listen to them. One night, I offered to help them out."

Speedo was added to the Impalas line-up pronto, so that the group now had a black lead vocalist with three white back-up singers. The time was ripe for their big break. They were singing on the street corner one night when Artie Zwirn and Aristedes Giosasi ("Gino" of the GINO & GINA act) happened by, liked what they heard, and invited the Impalas to their house to pick some material to do.

Artie and Harry offered the group a tune called "Sorry (I Ran All The Way Home)." The Impalas worked out an arrangement and brought the number to Alan Freed, who in turn set them up to audition for MGM Records. "Sorry," their debut disk on MGM's Cub subsidiary, ran all over the charts, sold a million-plus copies, and is currently one of the most requested rock and roll dusties on "Golden Oldies" radio stations, at high school reunions, and at nostalgia night spots.

Four more singles and a one-off LP were issued on Cub. Only "Oh What A Fool" (#86, 1959) was given the slightest exposure. "Basically, I feel it was poor management on the part of the record company," recalled Frazier. "Our second release, 'Oh What A Fool', had 100,000 advance sales. We were in Chicago at the time, and received a telegram congratulating us that it looked like we had a second major hit . . . instead of the record company getting

behind the record as they did with "Sorry". . . they figured 'Fool' would carry by itself. So, they just left it out there, and unfortunately it didn't carry itself."

After a final single for 20th Century in 1961, the Impalas hit the pavement. Lenny Renda went on to become a New York City police officer. Richard Wagner married his childhood sweetheart and moved to New Mexico, where he is a lineman with a telephone company. Tony Carlucci, according to Frazier, "simply disappeared."

In 1980, "Speedo" Frazier resurrected the Impalas as a touring act. The current line-up includes John Monforte, Rick Shaw, and Randy Silver.

The Fiestas

Frank Pourcel's French Fiddles

ONLY YOU
(Buck Ram, Ande Rand)
Capitol 4165
No. 9 *June 1, 1959*

The Platters were the most popular vocal group of the '50s; with Tony Williams up front, they soared. Who can ever forget "The Great Pretender," "My Prayer," and "Only You"? Buck Ram discovered the group, managed them, and penned the lyrics to some of the Platters' great ones, including "Only You."

Nearly five years later, Frank Pourcel (b. Jan. 1, 1915, Marseilles, France) stripped off the words to "Only You," and with a houseful of fiddles and a touch of some clinky rock and roll piano, brought Buck's ballad back as a lush instrumental. Record sales are reported to have reached 15,000,000 worldwide.

Frank studied at the Paris Conservatory. Thereafter, he arranged, composed, and led his string orchestra through piles of recordings. His disks have been available in the States for more than three decades, yet aside from his Platters platter, Pourcel is a virtual unknown. Not one of his middle-of-the-road albums has made *Billboard*'s top pop albums chart. He currently records for EMI-America; his most recent release is *In A Nostalgic Mood*.

Fiestas

SO FINE
(Johnny Otis)
Old Town 1062
No. 11 *June 15, 1959*

Sam and Hy Weiss operated their Old Town label out of a cloakroom in New York's old Triboro Theatre, on 125th Street and Third Avenue. One day, Hy overheard some guys singin' and horsin' around, and thereby discovered the Fiestas. "I heard them singing in the toilet next to my office," Weiss told liner-note writer Dan Nooger. "It cost me $40 to record 'So Fine,' that's all."

Another story has it that lead vocalist Tommy Bullock, tenor Eddie Morris, baritone Sam Ingalls, and bass Preston Lane—who had grown up together in Newark and had been singing together for about a year—went to Jim Gribble's hometown studios to cut a demo. Gribble was impressed, and it was Gribble who supposedly brought the resulting disk to the attention of Hy Weiss.

Whichever of these two versions is the true story, Hy did realize that this bunch of rhythm makers had something special. "[They] were really a soul group, not a doo-wop group. They stood by themselves. There's a big difference between R & B and doo-wop, just like there's a big difference between doo-wop and rock and roll." The Fiestas' sound was gritty and delightfully crude, but their rough edges were possibly too much for '60s radio.

Weiss released many years' worth of capable follow-ups, trying to establish his group. But only "Broken Heart" (#85, 1962) managed to hold down a position on either the pop or R & B charts. After the Fiestas parted company with the Old Town label in 1965, Tom left the group to record a few solo sides, as well as duets with Cleveland Horne as Tommy & Cleve. Randy Stewart, who later managed the Gypsies/Flirtations, joined the group.

The "Fiestas" name was kept alive through the '70s, with sporadic singles issued by Vigor, Respect, RCA, and Chimneyville.

Preston Epps

BONGO ROCK
(Preston Epps, Arthur Egnoian)
Original Sound 4
No. 14 *June 29, 1959*

While stationed in Okinawa during the Korean War, Preston (b. 1931, Oakland, Cal.) learned how to play the bongos. He soon became adept at other percussive instruments as well. On his return from duty, he worked as a waiter, club manager, and gas-station attendant. At night, Preston would venture into the coffeehouses that dotted Hollywood. While playing in one of these pads, Epps was spotted by Art Laboe, a DJ on L.A.'s KPOP and the new owner of Original Sound Records.

"Bongo Rock" would be the first hit for Laboe's label. With the very next Original Sound release, Laboe would score again with another percussionist, Sandy Nelson, and the classic "Teen Beat" (#4, 1959). As for Preston, try as he did, he could not craft another chart-shaker. The first of his two LPs (*Bongo, Bongo, Bongo*, 1960; *Bongola*, 1961) did well—and his initial follow-up, "Bongo, Bongo, Bongo" (#78, 1960), did make the listings—

but Preston began losing momentum. "Bongo In The Congo," "Bongo Rocket," "Bongo Boogie," "Flamenco Bongo," "Mr. Bongo" . . . the public just lost interest. Not even Epps' last offering, "Bongo Rock '65," could garner enough sales to justify a continued career.

Many years later, Canadian producer Michael Viner put together a studio assemblage called the Incredible Bongo Band and returned Preston's pounder to the charts (#73, 1973).

In the early '70s, Preston toured and recorded with JOHNNY OTIS.

Mystics
HUSHABYE
(Doc Pomus, Mort Shuman)
Laurie 3028
No. 20 *June 29, 1959*

They grew up within blocks of each other and attended the same school in the Bensonhurst section of Brooklyn. For a brief time, bass Al Contrera (b. Jan. 8, 1940), baritone Albee Cracolici (b. Apr. 29, 1936), lead singer Phil Cracolici (b. Sept. 17, 1937), first tenor Bob Ferrante (b. 1936), and second tenor George Galfo (b. 1940) were street-corner singers, the Mystics—a name they literally drew out of a hat.

"We first went out and auditioned for a lot of record companies and didn't get anywhere," Contrera told *Goldmine* writer Wayne Jones. "So we figured we needed a demo record. We went up to the Broadway Recording Studio at 1650 Broadway and while we were doing this demo, Jim Gribble happened to be there." Gribble was then managing the Classics, THE FIESTAS, the Passions, and a young singer/ songwriter named Paul Simon. (Paul sang

Preston Epps

back-up on "To Think Again Of You," the "B" side of the Mystics' third single.) "Jim heard us, liked us, signed us, and introduced us to Laurie Records."

Laurie's founder, Gene Schwartz, commissioned the songwriting team of Doc Pomus and Mort Shuman to come up with something teenage for the group. "A couple of weeks later they came up with 'A Teenager In Love,'" said Contrera. "Laurie Records thought the song was so great they decided instead to give it to Dion & The Belmonts . . . they were established." Doc and Mort were asked if they could hammer out something else for the Mystics. "So they went home and the very next day, we got a call that they had another song for us to do, which was 'Hushabye.'"

"Hushabye," the Mystics' first record, was a huge hit. "Don't Take The Stars," the follow-up, charted, but not too well (#98, 1959). Even worse, the next four 45s failed to capture any attention. A cover version of the Harptones' "Sunday Kind Of Love" would be the Mystics' last release for Laurie. "After that," Contrera noted, "we decided we had to get jobs."

All of the original Mystics except George Galfo found down-to-earth employment as engineers. Al Contrera, Albee Cracolici, and Phil Cracolici still perform under the name that they drew out of a hat decades ago. A comeback album and doo-wop delight called *Crazy for You* appeared on the Ambient Sound label in 1983.

Falcons
YOU'RE SO FINE
(Willie Schofield, Lance Finnie, Robert West)
Unart 2013
No. 17   *July 13, 1959*

Eddie Floyd (b. June 25, 1935, Montgomery, Ala.) was black, Bob Manardo was white. They met in 1955 while working together in a jewelry shop in Detroit. After learning of each others interest in what was then called "race music," they talked of forming a vocal group and began practicing together after work. Eddie (lead vocals) suggested they include a friend of his named Arnett Robinson (second tenor). Bob (first tenor) recommended Tom Shetler (baritone). Completing the line-up was a street singer, Willie Schofield (bass). Luckily for the Falcons—a timely "bird" name that

Arnett had proposed—Eddie's uncle, Robert West, owned and operated a number of Detroit record labels (Contour, Kudo, Flick, LuPine, and Silhouette). After a quick listen, West offered to manage the group.

West got the group some club dates, plus a one-off release on Mercury Records in 1956. When Bob Manardo was drafted and Tom Shetler enlisted, two former members of the Fabulous Four—Lance Finnie (first tenor) and Four Top Levi Stubbs' brother Joe (lead vocals)—joined the Falcons. A month later, Arnett Robinson left and was replaced by Bonny Mack Rice (baritone), a former member of the 5 Scalders.

After a few highly-collectible false starts were issued, the gospel-gritty "You're So Fine," with a one-of-a-kind lead vocal by Stubbs, was let loose upon the world. Stubbs only remained with the group through 1960; his replacement, brought in by Schofield, was a young Wilson Pickett (b. Mar. 18, 1941, Prattville, Ala.). With "Wicked Pickett" front and center, the group entered the pop charts for the last time. "I Found A Love" (#75, 1962) was possibly the Falcons' greatest number, but only a moderate pop-chart mover.

Willie Schofield was drafted. Floyd and Pickett were not always available, and finally, early in 1963, the group scattered. In an effort to keep the name alive and the money flowing, West, according to *Whiskey, Women And . . .*'s Marv Goldberg, took a group variously called the Ramblers or the Fabulous Playboys—comprising Johnny Alvin, James Gibson, Frank Holt, and Carlis "Sonny" Monroe—and renamed them the Falcons. This second unit carried on through the late '60s.

Stonewall Jackson
WATERLOO
(John D. Loudermilk, Marijohn Wilkin)
Columbia 41393
No. 4   *July 13, 1959*

Stonewall Jackson was born in a railroad shack outside Tabor City, North Carolina, on November 6, 1932. His daddy, who named him after his great-grandfather (the famous Confederate general), died when Stonie was but two. Conditions were rough, with money hard to come by. Jackson played on an improvised, hand-me-down string box until 1949, when as a Navy submarine man, he got the chance to touch a real guitar. During these years, he wrote and performed songs that he would record many moons later.

From 1954 to 1956, Stonie worked hard as a farmer and logger, saving up to go to Nashville and become a country star. Without any arrangements or recommendations, Stonewall drove his logging truck to the doors of the Grand Ole Opry, where he somehow wrangled an audition with Judge George D. Hay, the founder of the institution. The somber judge signed him on the spot, and Jackson made his first appearance on the Opry that night, November 3, 1956. The chances of managing such a move without a hit record, then as now, were next to nil. Two years later, Stonewall would have that hit.

Once he played the Grand Ole Opry, doors of opportunity opened, including those at Columbia Records. "Life Goes On," his first single, charted top 10 on the C & W charts. The follow-up, "Waterloo," was a monster crossover hit, the most momentous recording of his entire career. Three more singles made *Billboard*'s Hot 100, and a few more charted big on the country listings. Twenty years ago, the hits stopped, but not Stonewall.

Things begin, things end. "Every puppy has his day," Stonewall sang, "Everyone must pay." How true, how true. And "Everyone must meet his Waterloo."

**Stonewall
Jackson**

Jerry Keller
HERE COMES SUMMER
(Jerry Keller)
Kapp 277
No. 14 *August 17, 1959*

Jerry Keller was born in Fort Smith, Arkansas, on June 20, 1937. When he was seven, he and the family moved to Tulsa, Oklahoma, where he became a member of the Tulsa Boy Singers, a choral group that toured the Midwest. In high school, he formed a secular quartet called the Lads of Note. Singing solo, Jerry won a talent contest organized by Horace Heidt (discoverer of ED TOWNSEND), and he fronted Jack Dalton's Orchestra for a while.

In 1956, Jerry moved to the city of glitz and garbage, New York. While dreaming of fame and fortune, he worked as a clerk for an oil company; he also studied singing, cut demos when he could, and appeared occasionally on local TV shows. But it was a Sunday meeting with Pat Boone on the steps of a church that opened that big door to secular stardom. Pat gave Jerry a list of individuals that might be able to help him. One of them, Marty Mills, was to be Keller's manager and his connection to Kapp Records.

Jerry's self-penned "Here Comes Summer" was apparently the 22-year-old's first waxing. For years afterward, whenever summertime was approaching, Jerry's joyous single would ride the turntables. None of Keller's subsequent outings ever received much airplay; without hits, he was forced to move from Capitol to Coral to Reprise to RCA before chucking his career.

No Jerry Keller recordings are currently in print. Keller did continue penning tunes, though: his "Turn-Down Day" was a sizeable hit for the Cyrkle in 1966, and his "Almost There" appeared in the 1964 flick *I'd Rather Be Rich* (a version by Andy Williams reached number 67 the same year). Keller made film appearances in *You Light Up My Life* (1977) and *If Ever I See You Again* (1978).

Phil Phillips with The Twilights
SEA OF LOVE
(George Khoury, Phil Baptiste)
Mercury 71465
No. 2 *August 24, 1959*

Phil Phillips

Nineteen fifty-eight was a long year for John Baptiste, a frustrated guitar-playing bellhop. By day, he would move the luggage at the Chateau Charles in Lake Charles, Louisiana; by night, he would try to move a young girl named Verdie Mae.

"She'd not always be a lover and I had my guitar, so I went and wrote this song, 'Sea Of Love,'" reported Baptiste in an exclusive interview. "You see, she really didn't believe in me. But I felt if I could sing about it, a sea of love, you know, where it's quiet and peaceful, I could really show her how much I loved her and cared for her."

One day the gas-meter reader, making his usual housecall, overheard John practicing his ode of oceanic love. "He's the one that impressed on me that I really had something. He said, 'You're walking around with a million dollars in your hand. All you got to do is do something about it.'"

The meter man told John about George Khoury, a local record producer who had worked on Cookie & The Cupcakes' "Matilda"

(#47, 1959). Khoury liked what he heard in John, and immediately brought him to Eddie Shuler's small Goldband Recording Studio. "We went in there, and I sung the song over and over again. We went back the next night, and the next, and over and over again we went on that tune, until we were sure that we got the cut on it."

John got some friends together and taught them how to sing the tune's haunting and seductive backing vocals. Shuler brought in a number of musicians, searching for the just-right sound which he eventually extracted from the Cupcakes. For reasons related to his interest in hypnosis, Khoury suggested that John make double use of his middle name, Phillip. By June 1959, John was "Phil Phillips," and "Sea Of Love" was selling so well on Khoury's independent label that the record was leased to Mercury for national distribution. Within weeks, this eerie swamp tune was number two in the nation.

One-time gospel singer and bellhop Baptiste was never again to have another hit. Four more singles were released, but despite Clyde Otis' lush production—and back-up vocals by Brook Benton and the Jordanaires on several of these numbers—not one of them even came close to returning "Phil" to the charts.

Phillips never married Verdie Mae, the girl for whom he wrote "Sea Of Love." "No, no, I sure didn't," he explained. "I married the right one, though, yes indeed. But ooh, it's a good thing I didn't marry that Verdie." He never got his hands on that million dollars. "I'm waitin' by the mail box, yet. I never did get my money. The only thing I did get off that record as an artist was $6,800."

Currently, John is a weekend DJ at KJEF in Jennings, Louisiana, and the producer of the Fire Ants' cover version of his one hit. The Fire Ants are Rabbi, Shapina, Israel, Manedalisha, and Ethopia Baptiste—five of his children.

In 1982, Del Shannon remade "Sea Of Love" and charted at number 33; in 1984, the Honeydrippers—a one-off group consisting of Robert Plant, Jimmy Page, Jeff Beck, and Nile Rodgers—reached number three with their rendition.

Ivo Robic

MORGEN
(Paul Moesser)
Laurie 3033
No. 13   *September 21, 1959*

Floyd Robinson

The only Ivo in all of pop-rock history was born near Zagreb, Yugoslavia, in 1927. With plans of becoming a music teacher, Ivo Robic (pronounced *Eevo Robish*) studied the bass, clarinet, flute, piano, and saxophone at the local music conservatory. In 1948, he tried out for a dance orchestra as vocalist and was given the chance to begin making records. Great numbers of recordings, possibly 50 to 100 releases, were issued in his homeland before Ivo—who sings in English, French, German, Italian, and Spanish—had his one big moment on the U.S. charts. As a matter of fact, by the time "Morgen" came out, Ivo was one of Yugoslavia's top entertainers.

To those top 40 radio listeners who didn't speak German, "Morgen" sounded like a bizarre love chant. With all the robust flair of a Swiss mountain climber, Ivo longingly implored "Morgen, Morgen" to do something we never knew. The title, however, is not a man's name, but the German word for "morning."

Ivo's next romp and last *Billboard* hit, "The Happy Muleteer" (#58, 1960), is probably just as innocent a ditty. After a few more singles, Ivo returned to being solely a homeland hero.

Floyd Robinson

MAKIN' LOVE
(Floyd Robinson)
RCA 7529
No. 20   *September 28, 1959*

Floyd, born in 1938 and raised in the Nashville area, knew in his pea-pickin' heart that he was gonna grow up to be a music-makin' man. Before puberty set in, Floyd and his boys had a group called the Eagle Rangers. They would work the pre-teen hops, parties, and local radio programs. While in high school, Robinson and his Rangers had regular radio programs broadcast on Nashville's WLAC and WSM. When school days were through, Floyd made money and a name for himself providing back-up for touring country artists.

Floyd wrote tunes on the side and tried his best to have somebody to record them. JESSE LEE TURNER cut a rendition of Robinson's silly extraterrestrial love lyric, "The Little Space Girl" (#20, 1959). The gigantic sales success of such loony tunes as Betty Johnson's "Little Blue Man," David Seville's "Witch Doctor," and SHEB WOOLEY's "Purple People Eater" had created a nutty-novelty craze, so RCA ordered their scouts to find "The Little Space Girl"'s

creator. Asked if he had any funny songs, Floyd sang "My Girl," a darling dinky about a strange boy and his emotionally-damaged girlfriend. Chet Atkins and the big boys at RCA liked it, waxed it, and put something called "Makin' Love" on the "B" side. Someone discovered that the "B" side was better, and Floyd made the charts for his first and only time.

A self-titled album and many more teen-oriented 45s were issued. Some were quite interesting, like the Everly Brothers-influenced "Why Can't It Go On" and the hillbilly/surfer tune "Sidewalk Surfboard," but nothing sold too well. Not being one to quit easily, Floyd worked as an engineer on Duane Eddy sessions and continued to record novelty singles well into the '60s for Jamie, Dot, Groove, and United Artists.

Nina Simone

I LOVES YOU, PORGY
(DuBose Heyward, Ira Gershwin, George Gershwin)
Bethlehem 11021
No. 18   *October 5, 1959*

She's a talented, bluesy woman with jazz influences, known the world over; a political activist, a pianist, a composer, a voice with a wallop. Yet Nina Simone has only made the nation's top 40 once . . . and that was 30 years ago.

She was born Eunice Kathleen Waymon, on February 21, 1933, in Tryon, South Carolina. Her parents were Methodist ministers, and she was surrounded by seven other sibs, all musical. She attended the Curtis Institute of Music in Philadelphia and the Juilliard School of Music in New York, starting her career as a piano accompanist. Her interpretation of "I Loves You, Porgy" from *Porgy and Bess* was one of her first recordings.

Ms. Simone has appeared at countless festivals, halls, and nightclubs, and has charted on numerous occasions on both the pop/rock and R & B listings. Her best-known singles include "Nobody Knows You When You're Down And Out" (#93, 1960), "Trouble In Mind" (#92, 1962), "Do What You Gotta Do" (#83, 1968), and "To Be Young, Gifted And Black" (#76, 1970). Many of her jazz LPs have crossed over to the top pop albums listings: *Nina at Newport* (1961), *Nina Simone in Concert* (1964), *I Put A Spell On You* (1965), and *Pastel Blues* (1965). Ms. Simone now only records sporadically.

Bo Diddley

SAY MAN
(Ellas McDaniel)
Checker 931
No. 20 *October 26, 1959*

Bo Diddley, the legendary "Black Gladiator," was born Ellas Bates in McComb, Mississippi, on December 30, 1928. He was raised by his mother, a hardcore Baptist, and her cousin, Gussie McDaniel, who actually adopted him and gave him the "McDaniel" surname. The family moved to Chicago in 1935, where Bo started his musical training under the close watch of O. W. Frederick, music director of the Ebenezer Baptist Church. Frederick taught him violin; Bo's fellow pupil grew up to be jazz violinist Leroy Jenkins.

"I used to play all this funny music like Tchaikovsky," Bo confessed in an exclusive interview. "I wanted to play some jazz and get down, and everybody else is playing 'Drink To Me Only With Thine Eyes'! I found out later that I couldn't play blues. I could *not* play like Muddy Waters—I wanted to, but I just couldn't. I was cut out to be what I am, Bo Diddley."

At some point in the early '40s, Ellas picked up a cheap guitar and his nickname. He worked as an elevator operator, made circuit boards, drove a truck, and fought several bouts as a semi-pro boxer. All the while, Diddley and his band, the Langley Avenue Jive Cats (later named the Hipsters), played dives with names like the Sawdust Trail and Castle Rock; they also played street corners and passed the hat around. "We had a washboard and a guitar, and I was the man with the guitar. Roosevelt Jackson played the washtub, and Jerome Green [d. early '60s, "probably from alcohol"] shook the maracas, though he could play some tuba, too."

After a failed audition at VeeJay Records, Bo tried Chicago's Chess/Checker label. "I just walked in there one day and asked [Phil and Leonard Chess] if they was makin' records. They told me, 'Yeah, what do you want?' I said, 'I wanna make a record.' They listened and liked this song, 'Uncle John' . . . They had me change the words, and that became my first record—'Bo Diddley' [—/#1, 1955] b/w 'I'm A Man' [—/#1].'"

Bo acquired an early rock and roll mystique, with his pounding, hypnotic beat, a menacing onstage presence, a slew of odd-shaped guitars, and an all-black outfit complete with Stetson hat and oversized turquoise ring. He had a string of R & B hits like "Diddley, Daddy" (—/#11, 1955) b/w "Pretty Thing" (—/#4, 1955) and "I'm Sorry" (—/#17, 1959) before crossing over to the pop charts with "Crackin' Up" (#62, 1959).

"Say Man," his follow-up to "Crackin' Up," was an accident of sorts. As Bo explained in an article in *Record Review*, Leonard Chess and the recording engineer "had a tape recorder on, caught me and Jerome in the studio, clowning . . . pieced it together, took all the dirt out of it, and came up with 'Say Man.'"

Although he recorded a number of albums for the Chess brothers in the following years, only one of them (*Bo Diddley*, 1962) would find a large audience. He had three more pop hits: "Road Runner" (#75, 1960), "You Can't Judge A Book By The Cover (#48, 1962), and "Ooh Baby" (#88, 1967). Despite a brief cameo appearance as a pawnbroker in the movie *Trading Places* (1983), Bo kept a low profile throughout the '70s and '80s. But he was highly visible across the nation in 1990 with his TV ads for Nike sneakers, and reappeared in the record racks with an album on Triple X, *Breakin' Through The B.S.*

"Nah, I ain't retirin'. I still got people out there looking for Bo Diddley. And I'm gonna go back to the roots with my next stuff, and get that '50s sound. I'm back up into the future."

Mormon Tabernacle Choir

BATTLE HYMN OF THE REPUBLIC
(Julia Ward Howe, William Steffe)
Columbia 41459
No. 13 *October 26, 1959*

The Mormons have often been nicknamed "The Singing Saints," and vocal rejoicing has been a part of their religious practice since the formation of the Church of the Latter-Day Saints by Joseph Smith in 1830. The forerunner of the Salt Lake Mormon Tabernacle Choir, as it is officially known, was established on August 22, 1947, less than two weeks after Brigham Young and his hardy followers began setting up their base in Utah's Valley of the Great Salt Lake. Two years later, John Perry became the choir's first regular director.

Richard P. Condie (b. 1898, Springville, Utah), a graduate of the New England Conservatory of Music and a young tenor in many traveling opera-company productions, worked as the assistant conductor of the choir for 20 years before becoming the choir's 11th conductor in 1957, at the age of 59. The group had toured and recorded on numerous occasions: for one recording session, in 1910, the Columbia Phonograph Company used two mammoth horns, coupled directly to the recording needle and wax disk, to capture the rejoicing.

Condie had certain ideas about just how the choir should sound. He had grown up listening to Italian immigrants singing the romantic old songs, and wanted a sound like that for the choir. Many have since credited Condie with creating the "Tabernacle Choir sound."

In 1958, Condie and his 300-plus voices, with the full support of Eugene Ormandy and the Philadelphia Orchestra, recorded one of the most memorable—and one of the strangest—entries on the charts, the "Battle Hymn Of The Republic." Their rendition of this "oldie" from 1862 earned them a Grammy as "Best Performance by a Vocal Group."

The Mormon Tabernacle Choir has appeared on many TV programs, including "The Ed Sullivan Show"; an intercontinental satellite broadcast from Mt. Rushmore (1962); and NBC's coverage of the Statue of Liberty Centennial. More than 150 albums have been issued, and four of them—*The Lord's Prayer* (1959), *The Spirit of Christmas* (1959), *Songs of the North & South 1861–1865* (1961), and *The Lord's Prayer, Volume II* (1963)—made *Billboard*'s top pop albums chart.

Wink Martindale

DECK OF CARDS
(T. Texas Tyler)
Dot 15968
No. 7 *November 2, 1959*

Winston Conrad was born on December 4, 1934, in Bells, Tennessee. As early as 16 years of age, Wink, as he became known to his school chums, began making money with his mouth—first as a radio announcer, then as host of Los Angeles' "Teenage Dance Party" on KHJ-TV, in 1959. That year, Dot Records chief Randy Wood spotted the young lad's face, heard that Wink voice, and placed him in a recording studio to recite his way into pop history.

"Deck Of Cards," a remake of T. Texas Tyler's 1948 spoken-word tale of a lonely soldier's peculiar relationship with a pack of cards, was not Wink's first effort at singing (or talking) his way onto the charts. In 1954, Martindale had waxed a few sides for OJ Recordings. Nothing much happened with those, or with Wink's follow-ups to "Deck." Only "Black Land Farmer" (#85, 1961), a cover version of Frankie Miller's C & W hit, made the Hot 100.

While Wink's voice is no longer heard on pop radio, gobs of daytime television viewers have seen him on TV since 1978 as the host of the syndicated game show "Tic Tac Dough." In the fall of 1989, Martindale shifted to the Fox Network to host another game show, "Last Word."

Islanders

THE ENCHANTED SEA
(Frank Metis, Randy Starr)
Mayflower 16
No. 15 *November 16, 1959*

The Islanders were Frank Metis (keyboards, accordion) and New York dentist Dr. Warren Nadel (guitar, whistles). The good doctor was no stranger to top 40-land: as Randy Starr, he had scored a hit in 1957 with "After School" (#32). Years later, he wrote tunes for Elvis' fluffy films ("Kissin' Cousins," "Almost In Love").

"The Islanders were a studio-only orchestra," Dr. Nadel (b. July 2, 1930, Bronx) explained in an exclusive interview. "When I got out of the service, I was about to open my practice, but I decided to go on a boat cruise first. The two strangers that were assigned to the state room I had booked were Frank Metis and, as it happened, Eddie Layton. Eddie [currently the New York Yankees' organist] was then a name recording artist with Mercury Records."

While cruising the seas, the threesome talked music, and Metis (b. Aug. 8, 1925) and Nadel came up with some ideas for exotic instrumentals in the style of Martin Denny's chart-busting "Quiet Village." "The Enchanted Sea" would be the Islanders' lone hit for the Mayflower label, and their only find of buried treasure. An impossible-to-find album, and follow-up 45s with teasing names like "Forbidden Island" and "Blue Rain," sank from sight in shallow waters.

Frank Metis went on to become an arranger, and did charts for George Shearing and Dave Brubeck. Dr. Warren Nadel's dental practice is still thriving in Manhattan.

Rock-A-Teens

WOO-HOO
(G. D. McGraw)
Roulette 4192
No. 16 *November 23, 1959*

Not much is known about these once-rockin'
teenagers: Bill Cook, Paul Evans, Vic Mizell,
Eddie Robinson, Bill Smith, and Bobby "Boo"
Walker were from Virginia. They convinced
the management of the tiny Doran record label
to let them tape and release a couple of songs
allegedly written by one "G.D. McGraw." A
vocal number called "Untrue" was coupled
with "Woo-Hoo," a wailing instrumental with
one of rock's first mid-tune drum solos. This
wild teen concoction featured searing guitar
and sax work, topped off with a contagiously
yodel-like "woo-hoo, woo-hoo" melodic line.

Once "Woo-Hoo" started receiving some
positive notice, Morris Levy at Roulette acquired the rights to the disk's national distribution. An album was hastily assembled and released; sales were minimal, but the LP is now
a highly sought-after item. Only one other
Rock-A-Teens 45 is known to exist—the
"Woo-Hoo"-styled "Twangy."

Only one member of these purveyors of
rock and roll primitivism has been sighted on
the musical landscape. Bill formed the Bill
Smith Combo and had a few more well-tailored
instrumentals like "Raunchy" released on
Chess in the early '60s.

Ernie Fields

IN THE MOOD
(Joe Garland, Andy Razaf)
Rendezvous 110
No. 4 *December 14, 1959*

Ernie had been tilling the fields for years and
years before rock and roll discovered him. He
was 54 years of age when his bottom-heavy
revamping of Glenn Miller's "In The Mood"
found teen approval and bounced into the nation's charts.

Ernie Fields (b. Aug. 26, 1905, Nacogdoches, Tex.) was a pianist, trombonist, bandleader, and arranger. By the '30s, he was
rooted in Tulsa and locally known for a band he
fronted. Beginning in the late '30s, he recorded for Vocalion, Frisco, Regal, Bullet,
Gotham, and Combo. Moving to Los Angeles

in the mid-'50s, he found a comfortable if low-
profile niche as an arranger for West Coast pop
and rock sessions.

When Ron Pierce and Gordon Wolf formed
the Rendezvous label in 1958, they enlisted
Ernie to come up with some ideas for releases.
"In the Mood," reportedly utilizing well-known
sessioneers Rene Hall, Plas Johnson, and Earl
Palmer, was the first of what would be a series
of rockin'-good readings on big-band moldies
like "Chattanooga Choo Choo," "12th Street
Rag," "Charleston," "Castle Rock," "String Of
Pearls," and "Hucklebuck."

Around this same time, Rendezvous Records struck it rich with "B. Bumble & The
Stingers," a studio band comprising some of
same session men as those on the Ernie Fields
recordings. The Stingers are best remembered for stabs at the "classics" like Rimsky-
Korsakov's "Flight Of The Bumble Bee" (issued as the "Bumble Boogie," #21, 1961) and
Tchaikovsky's "Nutcracker" (issued as the
"Nut Rocker," #23, 1962). Reportedly, Fields
was involved to varying degrees with a few of
the Bumble/Stingers sides.

The Nutty Squirrels

UH! OH! PART 2
(Sascha Burland, Don Elliott)
Hanover 4540
No. 14 *December 28, 1959*

The Nutty Squirrels were the creation of Don
Elliott and Sascha Burland. Working their
"squirrels" like David Seville did his Chipmunks, Don and Sascha speeded up their scat-
like voices to sound like the chatterings of
some hip little creatures.

Don Elliot (b. Oct. 21, 1926, Somerville,
N.J.) has been active on the jazz scene since
the '50s. He has played mellophone, trumpet,
and vibes with Benny Goodman, Buddy Rich,
George Shearing, and Teddy Wilson. Elliot has
his own 16-track recording studio, where he
wrote and produced numerous radio and TV
commercials during the '60s. He has composed for, and played in, Broadway shows like
A Thurber Carnival, The Happiest Man Alive,
and *The Beast in Me*; he has also supplied
soundtracks to such films as *The Getaway*
(1972), *In the Heat of the Night* (1967), and *The
Pawnbroker* (1965).

In the '50s, Alexander "Sascha" Burland (b.
Oct. 25, 1927) began producing, writing, and
working for TV and radio jingle sessions. Sas-

cha was the creator of the theme song for "What's My Line?".

In 1959, the pair came up with the idea of having chipmunk-like characters singing jazzy scat numbers. Steve Allen and Bob Thiele had just formed Hanover-Signature Records, and were pleased pink to give it a try. "Uh! Oh!" was a hit, but a novelty hit at most, which meant that follow-ups like "Zowie" failed to excite record-buyers.

Despite successful records by the Nutty Squirrels, Ray Bryant, Bill Evans, and Jack Kerouac, Allen and Thiele shut down Hanover-Signature in 1960. With the help of Columbia and RCA, Don and Sascha continued to work their nutty turf for another four years. None of these efforts fared well, and eventually the two returned to their previous endeavors.

The

Sixties

Larry Hall

SANDY
(Terry Fell)
Strand 25007
No. 15 *January 4, 1960*

Lawrence Hall was born June 30, 1941, in Cincinnati. With the completion of school and the encouragement of friends, Larry recorded two songs for the tiny Hot label; "Sandy" was "A" side. His lusting moans for this dream queen would be all the known world would ever hear of Mr. Hall.

It was a great teen tune, and Larry sang it like he was smirking and twitching. The New York-based Strand label picked up distribution for the disk and acquired Hall's contract. Record number two was an early and forgettable Burt Bacharach item called "A Girl Like You." Unfortunately, by this point, someone had reached the boy, smoothed out his rough edges, and cleaned him up; he sung this cha-cha like a Frankie Avalon.

For the next few years, Strand Records

Larry Hall

spared no expense with Larry, bringing in Al Caiola and Jimmy Haskell to produce. The label secured hit songwriters like Billy Page (who would later create "The In Crowd") and the team of Aaron Schroeder and Wally Gold, who had written "A Big Hunk Of Love" and "Good Luck Charm" for Elvis, "Because They're Young" for Duane Eddy, and "Fools Hall Of Fame" for Pat Boone. It was all for naught; after a few more dingies for Gold Leaf, Larry checked out of the business and into the great hall of rock and roll obscurities.

A year after "Sandy" charted, the tune's songwriter, Terry Fell, returned to the nation's playlist when BOBBY EDWARDS' "You're The Reason" (#11), which Fell co-wrote, became a country-rock hit.

Mark Dinning

TEEN ANGEL
(Jean Surrey, Red Surrey)
MGM 12845
No. 1 *February 8, 1960*

"I was born on August 17, 1933 on a farm near Drury, Oklahoma," Mark Dinning told *Record Exchanger*'s Bob Kinder. "Patti Page was once a babysitter for my sisters. She got her name from the Page Milk Company there. My singing sisters were once known as the McDerring Sisters, because of the McCormick-Derring Tractor Company. It's odd how some of these people got their show business names."

Mark was born the last in a line of nine— five girls, four boys. His dad and his uncles were either ministers or evangelist singers. In the early '40s, three of his sisters were taken by brother Wade to the "Barn Dance Show" on radio KFH in Chicago. Ginger, Jean, and Louise soon dropped their tractor moniker in favor of their surname. As "The Dinning Sisters," they became quite popular with such disks as "My Adobe Hacienda" (#9, 1947), "I Wonder Who's Kissing Her Now" (#12, 1947), and "Buttons And Bows" (#5, 1948).

Meanwhile, little Mark milked cows and won first prize with his turkeys at a local 4-H show. His father had given him an electric guitar when he was 17, but this last of the Dinnings was determined to stay with what he knew best, farming. All that changed, however, once Mark and his guitar were assigned to an isolated military outpost in the Mojave Desert. "I was in the USO Club in Barstow, California, when I heard my first rock and roll record, 'Rock Around The Clock,' by Bill Haley & The Comets. I was 21 at the time, and when I got my discharge at 23, I decided to make music my career."

His successful sisters introduced Mark to star-makers like Wesley Rose and Mitch Miller. By 1957, Mark was a recording artist with MGM—but, for three years, an unsuccessful one. His sister Jean, and her hubby, Red Surrey, had worked up a song they were sure was just right for the kid. The idea for "Teen Angel" had come to Jean via a magazine article by a DJ who argued that not *all* teens were dirty delinquents. According to Dinning, the article read: "I hear all the people putting down the teenagers of today: how rough and tumble they are, undisciplined, and how they're all a bunch of little devils. From my own experience, I happen to know quite a few teen angels." That last phrase stuck with Jean, who awoke one night from a nightmare to scribble down the lines to this classic death dirge.

"I didn't even think it was going to be a hit," Mark recalled. "They banned it in England because they considered it 'too bloody awful.' It was kind of a silly song, really; a girl going back for the ring and all that. It was a far-out, left-field teenage folk song that sold 3,500,000 copies."

Follow-ups were another story. The next few releases did receive airplay and charted — "A Star Is Born (A Love Has Died) (#68, 1960), "The Lovin' Touch" (#84, 1960), and "Top 40, News, Weather And Sports" (#81, 1961)—but eventually the records stopped, and the dust settled on Mark Dinning's career.

From 1962 through 1970, Mark moved through the South playing lounges as a solo act, or in the company of his brother Ace. He began drinking heavily in the late '60s. "The Beatles really took us out. It was a blow to my ego and my wallet . . . Groups were in and singles were out."

After appearing in a club in Jefferson City, Missouri on March 21, 1986, Mark returned home, where he died of a heart attack.

Spencer Ross

TRACY'S THEME
(Robert Ascher)
Columbia 41532
No. 13   *February 22, 1960*

In the late '40s, Spencer Ross wrote arrangements for Gordon Jenkins and his orchestra, then arranged and led orchestral ensembles for both Bigtop and Columbia Records throughout the '50s and early '60s. One of Ross' sporadically-issued singles caught fire in the winter of 1959. "Tracy's Theme"—limned by the silky sax of Jimmy Abato, an instructor at the Juilliard School of Music—had been the theme to a TV special called "The Philadelphia Story."

Before returning to his behind-the-scenes duties, Ross featured Abato on an album's worth of material, and on a pair of plush but long-forgotten follow-ups—"Theme For A Lonely Evening" and "Song For A Summer Night."

Little Dippers

FOREVER
(Buddy Killen)
University 210
No. 9   *March 28, 1960*

She was talented and ambitious, but no one could have guessed that Anita Kerr would become involved in possibly half of all the records that came out of Nashville in the '50s and '60s.

She was born Anita Jean Grob on October 31, 1927, in Memphis. For 11 years, beginning at the age of four, she took piano lessons. While still in elementary school, she arranged songs for her church and formed the secular-singing Grilli Sisters to perform on her mother's radio programs on WREC. By age 14, she was a staff pianist at the Memphis station, and after graduation, she moved to Nashville to search out fame and fortune.

Anita made ends meet for several years by playing piano in local night spots. In 1949, she formed her first professional group with Dottie Dillard (alto), Louis Nunley (baritone), and Gil Wright (tenor). The Anita Kerr Singers/Quartet made radio appearances, and soon found that elusive cloud with the silver lining—studio back-up work.

For the next 10 to 15 years, the Anita Kerr Singers sang on piles of disks recorded in Nashville. To list all of their credits would be an encyclopedic task, but (to mention a sprinkling of acts) the Kerr Singers have accompanied Eddie Arnold, Chet Atkins, Brook Benton, the Browns, Perry Como, Floyd Cramer, Jimmie Davis, Skeeter Davis, Red Foley, Connie Francis, LORNE GREENE, Brenda Lee, Roy Orbison, and Jim Reeves.

Beginning in 1951, Kerr's groupings had the

The Sixties

first of their very own disks issued by Decca Records. Over the next two decades, stacks of wax were shipped on several major labels. Surprisingly, none of these ever found positions on *Billboard*'s C & W singles charts. Kerr did check into the pop charts as Anita & The So-And-So's with "Joey Baby" (#91, 1962). For her Little Dippers, the singers, according to Joel Whitburn's *Top Pop Singles 1955-1986*, were actually Delores Dinning, Emily Gilmore, Darrell McCall, and Hurshel Wigintin.

Anita scored the Kate Jackson film *Limbo* (1972) and did well with a couple of albums in the late '60s (*The Anita Kerr Singers Reflect on the Hits of Burt Bacharach & Hal David* and *Velvet Voices and Bold Brass*). She also composed the music—with words and narration supplied by Rod McKuen—to seven LPs by the San Sebastion Strings & Singers.

The Little Dippers

Connie Stevens
SIXTEEN REASONS
(Bill and Doree Post)
Warner Bros. 5137
No. 3   *May 2, 1960*

She was born Concetta Ann Ingolia, in Brooklyn, on August 8, 1938. After dollin' up Monroe-style, platinum hair and all, and winning several talent contests, Concetta made a name change and a number of brief TV appearances ("The Bob Cummings Show," "Sugarfoot"). She also played innocent roles in teen flicks like *Young and Dangerous* (1957), *Rock-a-Bye-Baby* (1958), and *The Party Crashers* (1958).

While under contract to Warner Bros. Studios, Connie was chosen to appear opposite "77 Sunset Strip" star EDD BYRNES on "Kookie, Kookie (Lend Me Your Comb)," his much-ballyhooed debut as a rock and roll "singer." Like the TV series itself, "Kookie" Byrnes' vinyl venture was a winner.

Hoping to score again, "77 Sunset Strip"'s executive producer and other studio operatives quickly developed a TV series called "Hawaiian Eye"—according to Mike Bego of *Modern Screen*, an "island version of '77.'" Connie played Cricket Blake opposite two ever-vigilant and virile detectives, Lopaka (Robert Conrad) and Steele (Anthony Eisle). When not singing at the Hawaiian Village Hotel, Stevens would sashay about as a table-to-table photographer and snoop.

"Hawaiian Eye" ran from 1959 to 1963, and was a boob-tube hit. Like Edd Byrnes, Stevens was offered a shot at making a pop record. "Sixteen Reasons" was not bad for her label debut—unlike the insipid "Why Can't He Care For Me," a limited-release single she cut for ABC-Paramount in 1958. Four more 45s made the listings—"Too Young To Go Steady" (#71, 1960), "Why'd You Wanna Make Me Cry" (#52, 1962), "Mr. Songwriter" (#43, 1962), and "Now That You've Gone" (#53, 1965)—but by mid-decade, Ms. Stevens' recording career was almost history.

Connie has voyaged frequently on "The Love Boat," worked regularly on TV, and appeared in a number of movies: *Parrish* (1961), *Susan Slade* (1961), *Palm Springs Weekend* (1963), *Two on a Guillotine* (1965), *Never Too Late* (1965), *Way Way Out* (1966), *The Grissom Gang* (1971), *The Sex Symbol* (1974), *Scorchy* (1976), and *Back to the Beach* (1987).

Sixteen years later, Penny Marshall and

Cindy Williams—recording as those lovable brewery bimbos, LaVerne & Shirley—recharted (#65, 1976) with their tender reading of Ms. Stevens' golden glory.

Billy Bland
LET THE LITTLE GIRL DANCE
(Spencer, Glover)
Old Town 1076
No. 7 *May 16, 1960*

Big Billy Bland is still around cooking up edibles. No longer actively performing, Billy now runs his own soul-food kitchen in New York City, dishing out fried chicken, black-eyed peas, and candied yams. A glance at the fine fellow's discography reveals the presence even then of a fowl fascination—"The Chicken Hop," "Momma Stole The Chicken," "Chicken In The Basket."

Bill Bland was born the youngest of 19, on April 5, 1932, in Wilmington, North Carolina. The Bland family was religious, and from early on, Bill was encouraged to sing his soul out. While still a student, he managed to cut the now-collectible "Mairzy Doats" for a small hometown label.

Bland moved to New York at age 15, and quickly plugged in to the nightclub scene. He was performing at the Baby Grand when Edna McGriff discovered him. Edna, who had charted with "Heavenly Father" in 1952, took him around town and got him booked at the Apollo Theatre and with the Lionel Hampton Band.

For two years, Billy was part of the 4 Bees, which had a string of failed singles on the Imperial label. After the unit buzzed off, he came to the attention of Hy Weiss, owner of the Old Town label. Hy thought well enough of Billy Bland to weather five years of only mildly successful singles, but in 1960, Bland made good on Weiss' expectations with the feeble but teen-targeted "Let The Little Girl Dance." While several of Bland's follow-up singles were more soulfully substantive, and three disks did chart on *Billboard*'s Hot 100 through 1961, nary a one ever again cracked the top 40.

Jeanne Black
HE'LL HAVE TO STAY
(J. & A. Alison, Charles Grean)
Capitol 4368
No. 4 *May 30, 1960*

Billy Bland

Jeanne was born Gloria Jeanne on October 25, 1937, in Mount Baldy, California. Her singing ability was discovered while on a trip in the family car—her harmonizing with sister Janie in the back seat didn't sound bad at all. The girls were brought to the attention of CLIFFIE STONE, bandleader and executive at Capitol Records. Jeanne made many appearances on Cliffie's local TV program, "Hometown Jamboree," and eventually was given the chance to record an answer record to Jim Reeves' colossal C & W crossover hit, "He'll Have To Go."

An *answer record* takes the recognizable central idea or melody from what is usually a hit recording and places it in the heart and soul of a "new" song. The operating idea is that if the public liked it a whole bunch the first time and they still look a mite hungry, well then, they just may eat up the second offering, too. It doesn't always work: answer records to Buchanan & Goodman's "The Flying Saucer" and Ray Peterson's "Tell Laura I Love Her" stiffed as badly as if the record labels had issued Ubangi tribal recordings.

Reaching the number four position, "He'll

Have To Stay" was about as successful an answer record as has ever been made. An interesting new twist was added to the answer-record tradition when some mush-mouthed individual named Brumley Plunket came up with a response to Jeanne's number entitled "He'd Better Go."

Jeanne's visual presence was low-key, and she sang in a pop-country style that was just beginning to be dubbed "The Nashville Sound." This style was not "real" country & western music as the old folks knew it, but it wasn't rock and roll, either. Despite the protests of traditionalists, the Nashville country-pop blend did continue to pick up a following and grow in popularity.

Jeanne's career, however, just seemed to fade away. After "Lisa" (#43, 1960), Jeanne was rushed into the studio in the initial burst of heat generated by Elvis Presley's "Are You Lonesome To-night?" An answer record, "Oh, How I Miss You Tonight," was concocted, but the public wasn't buying this time, or ever again.

Ron Holden

LOVE YOU SO
(Ron Holden)
Donna 1315
No. 7   *June 13, 1960*

When Ron Holden (b. Aug. 7, 1939, Seattle) was 18 years old and en route to a stay in jail, he met the man who saved him from musical oblivion. Officer Larry Nelson had just finished fingerprinting Ron when he heard Holden's doo-wop echoing off the jailhouse walls. Nelson told Ron that he was about to quit the force, that he was thinking of doing something in the music field, and that Ron should look him up when he got out.

Holden and his Thunderbirds had been playing a teen sock hop that night. During a break, the guys in the band had taken a ride with a half-pint of I. W. Harper and what Holden described to *Goldmine* writer Steve Propes as "one of them funny little cigarettes." When the police pulled them over, Ron was the only one over 18.

Once free as a bird, Holden made plans to stop over at Officer Nelson's house. Nelson had decided to cut some tracks on Ron, and when Ron arrived at Nelson's home, there were microphones, a tape recorder, and a marching band waiting in the living room. For 20 hours,

Holden and the kids in the band struggled to nail down what was to become Ron's big moment, "Love You So." To complicate matters, there was a barking dog in the house.

With the "perfect" take in the can, Nelson set up Nite Owl Records and pressed some copies. The disk started to take off locally, and Ron and Larry met with Ritchie Valens' discoverer, Bob Keane of Donna/Del-Fi Records. Keane, as Holden told *Goldmine*, "had a briefcase full of contracts, a big green cigar, and a pocketful of money. He said, 'We're gonna make this record a hit—now.' We said, 'Hey, now you're talkin', that's what we want."

Unfortunately, Holden's subsequent recordings for the Donna label made use of studio pros like Rene Hall, Plas Johnson, Earl Palmer, and the Blossoms—musicians who could never play, as Holden put it, "a little bit out of tune," like that marching band had done on "Love You So." Ron moved about cutting singles for Eldo, Rampart, Challenge, VMC, and Now. He even got the opportunity to record a one-off single (as half of Rosie & Ron) with Rosalie Hamlin of ROSIE & THE ORIGINALS, but nothing further charted.

Ron Holden was last spotted working as an MC at Art Laboe's Oldies But Goodies club from 1972 to 1977.

Dante & The Evergreens

ALLEY-OOP
(Dallas Frazier)
Madison 130
No. 15   *July 4, 1960*

Dante & The Evergreens' cover version of a number originally done by THE HOLLYWOOD ARGYLES was the most sanitized of the three chartings of the tune (the least successful version was by the Dyna-sores). Production was handled by Herb Alpert and Lou Adler, who were just starting their careers in the music business.

Lead vocalist Dante Drowty (b. Sept. 8, 1941) had met the rest of the Evergreens while attending high school. Dante, first tenor Tony Moon (b. Sept. 21, 1941), bass Frankie Rosenthal (b. Nov. 12, 1941), and second tenor Bill Young (b. May 25, 1942), were all born and bred in Los Angeles. When they got their sound down, they approached Herb and Lou, two struggling producers, with "Alley-Oop."

Equally fine or better 45s followed "Alley-Oop" in 1960—"Time Machine" (#73) and

"What Are You Doing New Year's Eve?" b/w "Yeah Baby" stirred some interest. Despite the response, the group seems to have broken up by the end of their one good year, with one LP issued by the Madison label.

For the next few years, Dante continued to record at a feverish pace, cutting singles for Imperial, Mercury, Decca, and Tide. Some of these featured his own name, and some were credited to "Dante & His Friends." In 1966, Dante Drowty returned to Herb Alpert and A & M Records to wax his final outing, a cover version of the Cadillacs' "Speedo."

Fendermen
MULE SKINNER BLUES
(Jimmie Rodgers)
Soma 1137
No. 5 *July 11, 1960*

Phil Humphrey and Jim Sundquist were both born in rural Wisconsin on the same day, November 26, 1937. Phil's hometown was Niagara, and Jim came from Stoughton. In 1957, they met at University of Wisconsin in Milwaukee. Two years later, when they transferred to the main campus in Madison, they were both accomplished guitarists. In the back of William Dreger's record store in Middleton, Wisconsin, they taped their sparse but driving rendition of "Mule Skinner Blues."

Jimmie Rodgers, the "Singing Brakeman," had cracked the country charts with his original version in 1931. The tune, a bodacious boast about handling a mule, featured the Fendermen's delirious whooping and their crackling guitars. The record rocked, and no one seemed to question just why these boys were so whipped up about a mule.

After a short and successful stay on the Cuca label, Phil and Jim's raucous record was acquired for national distribution by Amos Heilicher's Soma company. Sales were phenomenal—within weeks, the public seemed wild about mules. The Fendermen, with Johnny Howard on drums, toured as an opening act for Johnny Cash and Johnny Horton. There were appearances on "American Bandstand" and even at the Grand Ole Opry.

A second and third single were released, but nothing further charted. After a failed 45 for Dab Records, Phil and Jim went their separate ways. Phil surfaced for a moment as a member of the inconspicuous Barbara Lee and the Kountry Kats.

Hollywood Argyles
ALLEY-OOP
(Dallas Frazier)
Lute 5905
No. 1 *July 11, 1960*

Skip & Flip's cha-cha, "It Was I" had hit number 11 in 1959, and "Cherry Pie" had matched that position in 1960. But with their chart days apparently behind them, the "Flip" half of the team —Gary Paxton—moved out of his place in Arizona and headed for Hollywood. When he arrived there, it was 2:00 AM, and legend has it that the first gas station he stopped at was manned by Dallas Frazier. Dal's musical day had not come just yet—his songs "Mohair

Sam" and "Elvira" were still to be conceived. He did tell Gary, though, that he was going to make it as a songwriter, and Paxton promised to look him up the next time he needed a tune.

Once settled in Hollywood, Paxton met Al Kavlin (head of the Lute label), formed a music publishing company with Kim Fowley, and called on Frazier for a hit tune. Dallas came up with the tale of a cartoon caveman from way back named "Alley-Oop." As Sandy Nelson told Charlie Gillett in *The Sound of the City*, everyone present was sloshed on the day of the recording. The band (Ted Marsh, Bobby Rey, Deary Weaver, Gary Webb, and Ted Winters) was divinely sloppy, and "Flip" was so zonked that some soul had to hold him upright and aim him at the mike.

Paxton's first 45 on Lute was "You're Ruining My Gladness"; the label credits read "Gary Paxton." "Alley-Oop" was likewise to be a solo single, until someone advised Paxton that he and "Skip" (Clyde Battin, an old University of Arizona buddy) were still under contract to Brent Records. To avoid any legal hassles, Gary created the "Argyle" moniker. Why *Hollywood Argyles*? The recording studio was located at the corner of Hollywood Boulevard and Argyle Street.

An album, now nearly extinct, was released. It sold poorly, as did the group's remaining follow-ups (if you can locate it in a used lot, test-drive the Argyles' "Grumble"). Paxton formed a few record labels like Paxley and Garpax. The latter issued Bobby "Boris" Pickett's "Monster Mash." Skip Battin went on to play bass for the Byrds, the Flying Burrito Brothers, and the New Riders of the Purple Sage.

In more recent years, Paxton became a born-again Christian, issued some theological tunes, and wound up romantically linked to Tammy Bakker.

Hank Locklin

PLEASE HELP ME, I'M FALLING
(Don Robertson, Hal Blair)
RCA 7692
No. 8   *August 1, 1960*

Hank, who was born Lawrence Locklin in McLellan, Florida, on February 15, 1918, was like a lot of pickers. When just a wee one, he learned the ways of the guitar and hit the talent contests. He also picked a lot of cotton, and

during the Depression, he worked road projects for the government's Works Progress Administration. In the meantime, Hank played at clubs, barnyard parties, wherever he could.

In the late '40s, Decca and then 4-Star Records enlisted Hank to cut some country sides. His first Decca disk in 1949, "The Same Sweet Girl," proved a C & W winner. A few others made the country charts, and Hank secured a regular slot on the "Louisiana Hayride" radio show. His popularity increased, and RCA signed Locklin to a long-term recording contract. Hank's "Geisha Girl" and self-penned "Send Me The Pillow You Dream On" charted big on the country listings and crossed over into the lower reaches of *Billboard*'s Hot 100. But no one could have expected that his pure-country rendition of DON ROBERTSON'S "Please Help Me, I'm Fallin'" would crash into the top 10.

Because his follow-up singles were too conventionally country to garner airplay on the mainstream pop stations, none of Hank's successive releases did well on the pop charts. Country fans treated him much better, though not too many of his 45s ever climbed into the upper reaches of the C & W charts.

In the mid-'60s, Hank returned to live in his hometown of McLellan, where he was elected mayor in short course. Hank still lives on his ramblin' Singin' L Ranch and occasionally ventures forth to sing some of his country tunes for the Plantation or Country Artist labels.

Garry Miles

LOOK FOR A STAR
(Tony Hatch)
Liberty 55261
No. 16   *August 1, 1960*

James E. Cason, a.k.a. Garry Miles (b. Nov. 27, 1939, Nashville), began his career playing guitar in the Casuals, Brenda Lee's back-up band. In the late '50s, along with Hugh Jarrett and Richard Williams, he organized a vocal group called the Statues. Liberty Records signed the fellows, and issued their smooth teen take on a Tony Bennett winner, "Blue Velvet." This debut disk charted (#84, 1960), but not until after the label had convinced Cason to record "Look For A Star," a tune extracted from the British horror flick *Circus of Horrors* (1960). Dean Hawley and someone named Garry *Mills* also did charting versions of the same song.

After his moment of glory, Jimmy "Buzz" Cason had a few more 45s issued as Garry Miles ("Dream Girl" and "Love At First Sight"); before breaking up, the Statues had at least one other single issued, "Jeannie With The Light Brown Hair." Buzz, as he now preferred to be known, produced some disks for the Crickets, set up a publishing company with Bobby ("A Taste Of Honey") Russell, and built the Creative Workshop Recording Studio in Nashville.

Recording as Buzz Cason, Jimmy cut a number of fine 45s through the '60s and the '70s on the Elf, Caprice, DJM, Mega, Monument, Warner Bros., and Capricorn labels. Buzz also recorded on the Amy label as part of Buzz & Bucky ("Bucky" was John Wilkin, founder and leader of Ronny & The Daytonas; together, they wrote "Sandy" for Ronny & The Daytonas). He also sang back-up for Jimmy Buffett, John Denver, Elvis, and Kenny Rogers. Alone—or in collaboration with such artists as Mac Gayden, Freddy Weller, Dan Penn, Bobby Russell, and Leon Russell—Cason has created such tunes as "Everlasting Love," "Popsicle," and "Fantasy Island."

Safaris

IMAGE OF A GIRL
(Richard Clasky, Marv Rosenberg)
Eldo 101
No. 6 *August 1, 1960*

Sheldon Briar is now a criminal attorney. Richard Clasky runs his own market research firm. Marv Rosenberg is Dr. Rosenberg, a psychologist with a hospital insurance company. The Safaris' former lead voice, Jim Stephens, is a sales manager at a bottled-water company. They are still friends, and they still sing together.

In the late '50s, Marv and Rich met at a party and quickly discovered that each had plans to become a rock and roll songwriter. Neither one of them wrote or read music, but in a wink they had penned something called "Touch Of Love." To flesh out the front of the group and warble the female sections of the tune, they rounded up Sandy Weisman.

The threesome grabbed the name "The Enchanters" and hawked their song to Orbit Records. Saleswise, "Touch" didn't manage more than a twiddle. Sheldon Briar was added, and the gang relabeled themselves the Dories. With their new tune, "I Love Him So," they

convinced producers Herb Alpert and Lou Adler to let them have another crack at the charts. Both "I Love Him So" and "A Lover's Prayer"—issued as by the Angels on the Tawny label—stiffed as well.

Sandy married and took flight from the group, so Jim Stephens was brought in to sing lead. A local DJ introduced the group to the owner of Eldo Records. The first record on Eldo was "Image Of A Girl," a doo-wop number with its origins in a spat between Marv and his girlfriend.

Marv's girlfriend, upset by his overinvolvement with music and underinvolvement with her, had asked Marv to choose between his music and her, then stormed angrily out of the room. Marv, thoroughly depressed, had flopped down on the girl's bed and thought to himself, "Why can't there be a girl to really love me for *me*?"

"Well, she had this really loud clock in her room, and there was a drip coming from the bathroom. That formed the beginning of the song. The rest just came to me . . . I wrote the whole thing in about five minutes." In two takes, with Bobby Rey pounding on two ends of a wooden block to create that clocklike sound, "Image Of A Girl," an atmospheric rock and roll moment, was created.

On the road to promote "Image," the Safaris encountered riots, terrible tours, and hotel rooms with roaches. Worst of all, they reportedly received little in the way of remuneration for their colossal hit. After recording the follow-up, "Girl With A Story In Her Eyes," Rich, Marv, and Sheldon left the group to acquire some college education. One further Safaris single and a couple of Jim Stephens solo singles appeared, but nothing sold well enough to chart. Late in 1961, and then again in 1963, the original Safaris came together to record two singles as the Suddens, but neither of these records caused much of a stir.

What became of that girlfriend that inspired Marv to create his classic number? "A month after the record hit, she called me and said, 'My mother and I are moving—would you be interested in buying the bed you wrote that song on?'"

Demensions

OVER THE RAINBOW
(Harold Arlen, E.Y. Harburg)
Mohawk 116
No. 16 *September 5, 1960*

Lenny Dell (b. 1944) and Howie Margolin (b. 1943) sang together in the Bronx High School choral group. Early in 1960, Len and Howie approached classmate Marisa Martelli (b. 1944) about joining them in a pop group. Some-one introduced the kids to the older and more experienced Phil Del Giudice (b. 1938). The Demensions were now complete. Lenny's father, a professional musician, helped shape their sound, and when the time was right, brought them to Irving Spice at Mohawk Records.

Dreamy vocal-group remakes were hot in 1960. Early in the year, Dion & The Belmonts had clicked with Hal Kemp's 1937 hit "Where Or When," and that spring, the Skyliners scored with their version of the Bing Crosby oldie from 1936, "Pennies From Heaven." "Over The Rainbow," first sung by Judy Garland in *The Wizard of Oz*, was a top 10 hit for her in 1939—as were cover versions by Larry Clinton, Bob Crosby, and Glenn Miller—yet no one had touched the tune since then. With a slight rock and roll arrangement by Seymour Barab, Mohawk Records presented what would be the Demensions' lone note in the annals of pop history.

Other rockaballad remakes of oldie standards were soon dished up: "Zing Went The Strings Of My Heart," "As Time Goes By," and "You'll Never Know." However, the only Demensions' follow-up to make the Hot 100 was their retake on Billy Eckstine's "My Foolish Heart" (#95, 1963). The Demensions' lone album was issued, but by this point, Marisa was ready to quit the group; Phil and Howie had already departed. At some point in the mid-'60s, Lenny Dell shelved the group name forever.

Ivy Three
YOGI
(Louis Stallman, Sid Jacobson, Charles Koppelman)
Shell 723
No. 8 *September 19, 1960*

The Ivy Three consisted of three students from Adelphi College in Garden City, New York. Hula hoops were hot, goldfish-gulping and Volkswagen-jamming were hip. When not

The Ivy Three

engaged in such extracurricular activities or cramming for tests, Artie (Berkowitz) Kaye, Charlie (Koppelman) Cane, and Don Rubin would lift a glass or two and harmonize. Friends encouraged them, and one warm day, the trio walked into Shell Records at 1697 Broadway in Manhattan.

Shell Records had started with a dentist's bankroll and a street-smart songwriting team. Lou Stallman and/or Sid Jacobson had penned hits like "Treasure Of Love" for Clyde McPhatter, "Round And Round" for Perry Como, and "Don't Pity Me" for Dion & The Belmonts. The day that the Ivy Three came in, Lou and Sid were constructing a novelty number based on the cartoon character Yogi Bear, then appearing on TV's "The Huckleberry Hound Show." Charlie kicked in his two cents, and the tune was done.

"Hush Little Baby," the non-novelty follow-up, was a flop. A few more silly singles like "Nine Out Of Ten" and "Bagoo" were issued, but it was too little, too late. Artie went off into the exciting world of insurance sales. Charlie and Don formed Koppelman-Rubin Productions and worked with the Critters, Tim Hardin, and Gary Lewis. In 1972, Lou Stallman, plus co-producer Bobby Succer and an assemblage of studio players, scored a pop hit as Think with "Once You Understand."

Jimmy Charles
A MILLION TO ONE
(Phil Medley)
Promo 1002
No. 5 *September 26, 1960*

Jimmy Charles was born in Paterson, New Jersey, in 1942. As a pre-teen, he sang in church and at civic affairs. When 16, he entered a talent contest at the famed Apollo Theatre and won—not once, but for four straight weeks. Jimmy's uncle was impressed with the kid's abilities and took him to Phil Medley, a songwriter, producer, arranger, and sometime recording artist.

Phil had a slow teen tune called "A Million To One" that he was looking to get waxed. He had Jimmy cut a demo, and presented it to Bill Lashley, the main cheese at Promo Records. Lashley signed Hughes to cut the dirge, with a group called the Revellettes on back-up vocals, for his tiny label.

With odds something akin to a million to one, Charles' first outing on the Promo label

rose to the top of the charts. The follow-up, "The Age Of Love," charted fairly well at number 47, but none of the angst-ridden ballad-belter's successive sides garnered more than a minor audience. In 1961, when he released "Just Whistle For Me," no one did.

Larry Verne
MR. CUSTER
(Fred Darian, Al DeLory, Joseph Van Winkle)
Era 3024
No. 1 *October 10, 1960*

"I really wasn't serious about nothin'," Larry Verne told *Record Digest* writer Bill Cappello. "I had all kinds of jobs; truck driver, bartender, TV stuff as a stunt man." When Verne (b. Feb. 8, 1936, Minneapolis) was discovered, he was a photographer's assistant. "[Al DeLory and Fred Darian] had an office in the same building as the photo studio where I worked. In fact, their office was right across the hall, so I got to know them at the time they were writing 'Mr. Custer' . . . They invited me to the recording studio where they were going to make a dub of the song. When we got there, they said, 'Okay, Larry, you go in the booth and do it.' That's how it happened."

As anyone who has heard Verne's spoof on Custer at Little Big Horn will attest, the disk is a slice of off-the-wall, dark humor. Yet nothing else Larry fooled with ever stood a chance of competing. "I had eight singles in addition to an album. There was 'Abdul's Party,' 'The Speck,' and so many non-descript records that we did . . . 'The Porcupine Patrol,' 'Running Through The Forest,' and 'Charlie At Bat.' They were just sessions that we did, some released and some not."

When the records stopped in 1963, what became of Larry Verne?

"Since then I've been doing something I like much better—I'm working in motion pictures now, as a construction foreman and assistant set director."

Bob Luman
LET'S THINK ABOUT LIVING
(Boudleaux Bryant)
Warner Bros. 5172
No. 7 *October 24, 1960*

Bob Luman's dad—fiddle player, guitarist, and harmonica-honker extraordinare—taught his boy (b. April 15, 1937, Nacogdoches, Tex.) to play country tunes. Bob was slightly interested, but liked baseball more. In high school, he also fronted a country band, singing his heart out like Webb Pierce and Lefty Frizzell. In his junior year, he tried out for the Pittsburgh Pirates. Whether he was picked up or passed on depends on whom you listen to, but either way, Luman never showed up at minor league camp.

Bob, you see, had seen Elvis and was quite impressed. "Man, I didn't believe it," Luman recalled to Paul Hemphill in *The Nashville Sound.* "This cat came out in red pants and a green coat . . . [and] started moving his hips real slow like he had a thing for his guitar. He made chills run up my back."

That was it for baseball and country music. Bob and his band switched to playing rock and roll, and in senior year, they won a talent contest sponsored by the Texas Future Farmers of America. In 1955, Imperial Records issued three classics—"Red Cadillac And A Black Moustache," "Red Hot," and "Make Up Your Mind Baby." Capitol followed up with "Svengali," then Warner Bros. rush-released "Class Of '59" b/w "My Baby Walks All Over Me" plus "Dreamy Doll." All of these disks were teenage dynamite, and represent Luman at the pinnacle of his form as a rockabilly artist—but none of them charted.

For the next record, Luman and the label leaders opted for a change of pace, and toned down the rock and roll energy. "Let's Think

The Paradons

About Living" was a punchy protest piece: "Let's forget about the lyin' and the cryin'/The shootin' and the dyin'/And the fellow with the switchblade knife." None of Bob's immediate follow-ups, not even similar-sounding songs, charted pop or country. In August 1964, he became a regular member of the Grand Ole Opry. He toured and toured, eventually clicking with 39 singles on *Billboard*'s C & W listings, five of them in the top 10.

In 1976, Bob was hospitalized for nearly six months for an operation on a blocked artery. After his release, Johnny Cash brought him back into a recording studio and produced Bob's penultimate LP for Epic, *Alive and Well*.

Bob Luman died on December 27, 1978, in Nashville. He was 41.

Paradons

DIAMONDS AND PEARLS
(West Tyler)
Milestone 2003
No. 18   *October 24, 1960*

Milestone Records was set up by Werly Fairburn, a one-time Louisiana rockabilly contender, and Madelon Baker, a model who was groomed by General Mills in 1956 to be the next Betty Crocker. Neither one of them wound up fulfilling their career dreams, but they did record some interesting California vocal groups. Fairburn was planning to record C & W tunes when he stumbled onto a Bakersfield high school group called the Paradons. In January 1960, Fairburn led Billy Myers, William Powers, Chuck Weldon, and lead singer West Tyler into the Audio Arts Recording Studio in Hollywood. They cut "Diamonds And Pearls" and the flip side in a flash.

"Diamonds And Pearls" had all the secret ingredients necessary to become a national top 40 hit, and it sparkles to this day. Unfortunately for the excited Paradons and the little record label, nobody was able to get that secret stuff out of them ever again—"Bells Ring" didn't, and "I Had A Dream" was an apparition with no happy ending.

A quick switch was made over to the big-time Warner Bros. label, but after only one sour release, "Take All Of Me," the Paradons vaporized. Nothing further is known of the group or its members. Madelon Baker, however, later formed the Audio Arts label and discovered the Incredibles and Jimmy Webb.

Joe Jones

YOU TALK TOO MUCH
(Joe Jones, Reggie Hall)
Roulette 4304
No. 3   *November 14, 1960*

"Joe had a big mouth—just like his song," DR. JOHN told *Blues & Soul* writer John Broven. "He talked his way into deals, and talked his way out just as quick. He had big ideas, and although Joe got his feet in the door, he had no talent to stay there."

Born on August 12, 1926 in New Orleans, Joe Jones attended the Corpus Christi Catholic and Booker Washington High Schools. He was drafted in 1942, and claims to have been the first black petty officer in the Navy; "handled mines, depth charges, that sort of thing," he explained to Broven. Joe played piano in the U.S. Navy Band, and on his return to civilian life, he formed his own group, the Atomic Rebops.

When Roy Brown came to New Orleans in 1948 to record his "Good Rockin' Tonight," he used a good portion of Jones' band. Next in town was B.B. King. "He told me he needed a piano player right away, so I played for him in New Orleans and I became his pianist, also his valet. I was driving and playing, then I became his assistant bandleader and was tuning his guitar up every night . . . I was writing the charts."

B.B. and Joe separated in 1954, and Capitol Records issued Joe's first single, "Adam Bit The Apple" b/w "Will Call." Three years would pass before his second single, "When Your Hair Has Turned To Silver" b/w "You Done Me Wrong," came and went. In between, Joe's band toured or did studio work for Ruth Brown, Jerry Butler, Dee Clark, and Shirley & Lee.

Things started to heat up when Sylvia Vanderpool of MICKEY & SYLVIA (and later, SYLVIA) fame, met Joe. "Sylvia was so impressed [with me] that when her date in New Orleans was over she flew back to record me on 'Every Night About Eight,' which she cut herself on her own money. She sang duet with me on another song, 'A Tisket, A Tasket' and she got me a deal with Roulette, then she was going to represent me as my manager."

The next recording session, produced by Harold Battiste, would yield "You Talk Too Much," or was it the next three sessions? Some confusion still exists. It seems that while under contract to Roulette, Joe recorded the

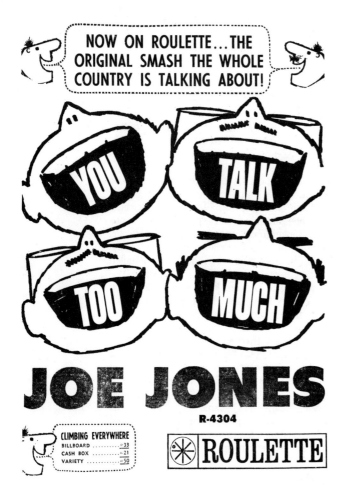
bly for Alvin Robinson ("Something You Got") and the Dixie Cups ("Chapel Of Love").

Maurice Williams & The Zodiacs

STAY
(Maurice Williams)
Herald 552
No. 1 *November 21, 1960*

Maurice Williams (b. Apr. 26, 1938, Lancaster, S.C.) started his singing career in a gospel group called the Junior Harmonizers. It was there that he met Zodiac-to-be Earl Gainey (tenor, guitar); both were students at Lancaster's Barr Street High School. Willie Jones (baritone), William Massey (tenor, baritone, trumpet), and Norman Wade (bass), also Barr Street students, soon joined Earl and Maurice in a secular group, the Royal Charmers (named after the Five Royals and the Charms). The Royal Charmers won a talent contest in 1955, and a Saturday morning hometown radio show gave them exposure and a growing audience.

After numerous successful nightclub gigs, public parties, and a tour throughout the South, the Royal Charmers—with the addition of drummers Mac Badskins and Bob Robertson, seven in number—headed to Nashville to record for Ernie Young's Excello label. "Sweetheart Please Don't Go" b/w "Little Darlin'," credited to the Gladiolas, appeared in 1957; "Little Darlin'" went to number 41, but a cover version by the Diamonds was even more successful (#2, 1957). Excello released three more 45s by the Gladiolas—"Run Run Little Joe," "Hey, Little Girl," and "Shoop Shoop"—but not one nudged a notice.

When the group left Excello, Ernie Young insisted that he owned the "Gladiolas" name, and forbade the group to use it from that point onward. Harry Goins, the act's visionary and manager, was sitting in an auto-repair shop reading a newspaper when he spotted an ad for a deluxe foreign car called a Zodiac. "That's it! That's our new name!" Goins is reported to have exclaimed. Under this monicker, Maurice and his group (minus Badskins and Robertson) briefly recorded for the Cole and Selwyn labels. Massey and Wade left, and the group dissolved.

Maurice rebounded with a new and improved Zodiacs —Wiley Bennett (tenor), He-

tune for them, and that they rejected it, filing it in their vaults. Believing that the tune would be a sure hit, Joe recorded the same number for Ric Records and possibly Flame Records.

Ric Records chief Joe Ruffino gave Jones $600 to hit the road and promote the disk. It all paid off—"You Talk Too Much" was a huge hit, in spite of the stiff competition provided by FRANKIE FORD's cover version (#87, 1960). But heated discussions developed between Ric and Roulette Records as to just who owned the rights to the master recording. Roulette secured the rights, so Ruffino rushed home to cut an answer record, "I Don't Talk Too Much," with the very same band and Martha Nelson's voice. It failed to fly, as did the few Joe Jones 45s that followed: "One Big Mouth," "California Sun" (#89, 1961)—which THE RIVIERAS covered and took to number 5 in 1964—and a dance number called "The Big Mule."

Joe Jones moved on to production work for Red Bird Records in the mid-'60s, most nota-

nry Gaston (tenor), Albert Hill (bass guitar), Little Willie Morrow (drums), and Charles Thomas (baritone). After two singles on the Soma label, Maurice approached Al Silver at Herald about an exciting little tune.

Silver liked "Stay," which would become the shortest number-one disk in pop history, but he told the group to sing it flat. "He said we were singing it too good," Williams recently told *Rolling Stone*'s Parke Puterbaugh. "Man, we had cut this thing I don't know how many times, tryin' to get it right for him. When he said, 'Sing it flat,' that just pissed everyone off. I said, 'We couldn't care less how it comes out.' "

The outcome is history. Over the years, numerous other artists have had hits with their own readings of "Stay," among them the Hollies (1963), the Four Seasons (#16, 1964), Jackson Browne (#20, 1978), and Rufus & Chaka Khan (—/#3, 1978). Williams and the Zodiacs followed up with two singles that made the Hot 100—"I Remember" (#86, 1961) and "Come Along" (#83, 1961). Curiously enough, while the group's 1961 release of "May I" has been certified by the RIAA as a million-seller, the disk never appeared on either the pop/rock or R & B listings.

Despite an ever-shifting line-up over the years, Williams has never shut down the Zodiacs. When the times started a-changin', the Zodiacs did, too. According to Maurice, "we got Beatle wigs and had us a Beatle act! And when the hard rock came in, we started singin' hard rock, to keep workin'."

Maurice has outlived it all. His sides have appeared on Atlantic, Scepter, Sphere Sound, Vee Jay, Deesu, Sea-Horn, 440/Plus, Veep, and his own R & M label. Maurice is currently living in Charlotte, North Carolina, awaiting the release of a greatest-hits album he recorded for Ripete.

Lolita

SAILOR
(Werner Scharfenberger, Fini Busch)
Kapp 349
No. 5 *December 19, 1960*

Lolita Ditta was born in St. Poelten, Austria, about 40 miles outside of Vienna. Until getting a chance airing over Radio Linz, Ditta was a children's nurse who sang mostly in her church choir on Sundays. The response to her radio debut was such that TV appearances, films,

and the chance to make records were offered to her. One of the petite fraulein's first vinyl efforts was "Sailor."

A copy of the husky-voiced nurse's recording landed on the desk of the president of Kapp Records, Dave Kapp. Sensing something, Kapp released the record in the U.S. Despite its German lyrics, and with only a breathy monologue over one chorus in English, "Sailor" sold well enough to become the very first record sung in German by a female to reach *Billboard*'s top 10.

Despite the higher probability back in the '50s of having a hit with a song in a foreign tongue, outlanders like Rocco Granta, IVO ROBIC, and KYU SAKAMOTO never managed to explore the reaches of the top 40 more than once. And holding to the tradition, Lolita's "Sailor" was her lone top 40 success.

Rosie & The Originals

ANGEL BABY
(David Ponci)
Highland 1011
No. 5 *January 23, 1961*

We don't know what she looked like, but from the sound of that high-pitched voice on "Angel Baby," Rosalie Hamlin was probably as thin as a barber's pole, with a 16-inch waist, two-inch-long eyelashes, and a stiff beehive hairdo up to there. Here was a sad, bad girl who just needed a boy, a beer, and the submarine races, and everything would be all right.

Rosie was born and raised in Alaska, until her family moved to San Diego when she was a teenager. She had taught herself how to play the piano; with dreams of being a singer, she auditioned at age 14 for songwriter and guitarist David Ponci and his band, the Originals. The Originals consisted of drummer Carl von Goodat, saxophonist Tony Gomez, and guitarist Noah Tafolla. Rosie and the boys rehearsed a few numbers, then approached Highland Records about recording some of their material.

Rosie had scribbled the words to the unit's first and penultimate single as a poem in her notebook, then crafted a melody based on the chord changes to "Heart And Soul." She sings "Angel Baby" in one of the skimpiest voices to ever grace the *Billboard* charts (she had a cold that day), with the Originals pounding a sparse and primitive backdrop. At moments, the drummer seems to forget what track he's playing on, the record is flawed with flubs, and the sound quality of the recording is poor—but "Angel Baby" is undoubtedly one of rock and roll's greatest moments.

Within weeks of the platter's success, the group disbanded; Rosie stormed out because Highland Records had credited Dave Ponci as "Angel Baby"'s writer. The follow-up, "Angel From Above," went unnoticed by radio programmers and the public. Jackie Wilson, however, did take notice, and introduced Rosie to his manager, Nat Taranapol. Nat got Rosie a recording contract with one of the big-time labels, Brunswick Records. But the Originals were not part of the deal, and they apparently vanished from the face of this planet.

In place of the crudities the Originals had supplied were the lush strings and flubless instrumentation of the Dick Jacobs Orchestra. Two of Rosie's self-penned tunes, engulfed in the finest sounds money could buy, were issued; both failed miserably. An album appeared, but sales were minor-league.

"The band on that album [*Lonely Blue Nights*] kind of swallowed me up," Rosie admitted to *Sh-Boom*. "They wanted to duplicate that 'Angel Baby' sound, but they were too professional. The saxophonist tried to get that off-key sound, and it sounded terrible—like he was *trying* to play off-key. Plus, the company didn't push the album. I think it was a tax write-off or something."

Two further solo singles were issued, but record-buyers' interest was apparently elsewhere, so Brunswick set the girl free.

Rosie and Originals guitarist Noah Tafolla married and raised a family. After they divorced in 1984, Rosie began appearing at oldies shows in her hometown, San Bernardino. Ms. Hamlin has since acquired the rights to "Angel Baby," and is currently performing with a group called the L.A. Rhythm Section.

Capris
THERE'S A MOON OUT TONIGHT
(Al Striano, Joe Luccisano, Al Gentile)
Old Town 1094
No. 3 *February 27, 1961*

"I had just started to learn harmony," Mike Mincelli, first tenor (b. 1941) told *Record Exchanger*'s Art Turco and Bob Galgano. "I went over to a friend's house [that of John Cassessa,

bass (b. 1941)] one day. There was a song out then called 'Bermuda Shorts' by the Del Roys. I wanted this guy to sing the bass part and he couldn't do it. Finally, he got it down and I decided we would keep him. The other guys were picked up one by one. It took over a year."

By 1958, all the pieces had fallen in place—the line-up was complete with Mincelli, Cassessa, second tenor Vinny Narcardo (b.1941), baritone Frank Reina (b.1940), and lead singer Nick Santo (b. Nick Santamaria, 1941). All were from Queens, and in a shot at class, they named themselves after the Isle of Capri. Their big break came when some independent producers dropped by to hear the guys rehearsing. "There's A Moon Out Tonight" was recorded at the Bell Tone Studios and finished in an hour. "We did ["Moon"] in three takes and they took the first one, it came out the best."

"There's A Moon Out Tonight" has a strange ending, technically known as a voice overlay: each Capri chants the tune's title in turn, but slows it down a little each time. After nearly three decades, this is still one of the most memorable endings in rock history. "I don't think it was intentional," Mincelli recalled. "It was one of the mistakes—there were a lot of mistakes on that record."

Planet Records picked up the rights to the release, but the disk bombed. By 1959, the Capris were no more. Nick joined the Army, and the others went their separate ways.

What happened next was pure serendipity. In 1961, the owners of the Lost Nite label bought the "Moon" master for a few hundred dollars and reissued it. Murry the K, a big-time Big Apple jock, began riding the record like it had a satin saddle. Within six months, "There's A Moon Out Tonight" was such a smash that Lost Nite could no longer handle distribution, so Old Town Records provided the platter with national availability.

Although "There's A Moon Out Tonight" has yet to be certified as a million-seller, the Capris' musical monster still sells worldwide. The band regrouped to record four more singles, three of which charted: "Where I Fell In Love" (#74, 1961), "Girl In My Dreams" (#92, 1961), and their last waxing, "Limbo" (#99, 1962).

The Capris split up again in 1962. There have been various reunions over the years. In 1981, Mincelli, Reina, and Santo reunited with Tommy Ferrara (formerly of the Del Satins) and Tony Danno (formerly of the Emotions) to record an excellent '80s doo-wop treat for the Ambient Sound label.

Buzz Clifford

BABY SITTIN' BOOGIE
(Johnny Parker)
Columbia 41876
No. 6 *March 13, 1961*

Buzz was born Reese Francis Clifford III, on October 8, 1942, in Berwyn, Illinois. Buzz was hot on Westerns and singing cowboys. Mom and Dad bought him a guitar, and the boy would stroll around the house pickin', grinnin', and makin' up the words to his own cowpoke tunes. As a high school senior, Buzz entered an amateur contest at the Morris County Fair in New Jersey, and clobbered the competition. Soon after, Columbia Records approached him to cut some recordings. The first, "Hello Mr. Moonlight," lived and died without notice. But his novelty number—complete with goo-goo sounds from the producer's kid—took off.

Buzz's tot tune was so catchy that it charted across-the-boards: pop/rock, C & W, and R & B. The follow-up, "Three Little Fishes," was another cutesy number, but neither this nor any further 45s would click. In the mid-'60s, while producing disks for ABC-Paramount and Apt, Clifford recorded some self-penned folk-rock sides for RCA. As the decade came to a close, he had a fine hippie-headed LP issued by Dot titled *See Your Way Clear.*

Jorgen Ingmann & His Guitar

APACHE
(Jerry Lordan)
Atco 6184
No. 2 *April 3, 1961*

Jorgen Ingmann-Pedersen was born on April 26, 1925, in Copenhagen, Denmark. He took violin lessons, then acquired his first guitar at age 18. Two years later, he was playing jazz guitar in the style of Charlie Christian with his own quintet. Svend Asmussen, a noted homeland violinist, got wind of Ingmann and enlisted him in his band, where he remained for the next dozen years. In 1953, Jorgen got his first chance to create some solo singles. With Birthe Buch or Grethe Clemmensen (later Mrs. Ingmann), he also tried his hand with a sound modeled on the then-popular Les Paul-Mary Ford records.

In 1959, Jorgen's manager, Metronome Rec-

Jorgen Ingmann
Apache

ord Company head BENT FABRIC, arranged for the stateside Atlantic label to issue disks by Danish talent. Songwriter Jerry Lordan had a catchy tune for which he could dream up no lyrics. British instrumentalist Bert Weedon cut the first side on "Apache"; it drew little attention. The legendary Shadows worked up a rough and beat-bottom rendition that eventually outsold all versions worldwide, but that failed to chart in the U.S.

"Apache" was intended as the "B" side of Ingmann's self-penned "Echo Boogie," a number that he believed would establish him in America. His version of "Apache" featured guitar riffs that sounded like arrows whizzing by. When Fabric called in March 1961 to tell him that "Apache" was a hit, Jorgen could only respond with disbelief.

Jorgen Ingmann never toured the U.S. Promotion for his future releases, he charged, were minimal, and other than his initial follow-up, "Anna" (#54, 1961), nothing further sold well. Over the years, Jorgen has had sporadic homeland hits with "Drinamarch" and "Toy Balloons"; in 1963, he and his wife won the Eurovision Song Contest with their "I Love You."

In the mid-'60s, Ingmann became a head producer with Metronome Records. Gradually, he withdrew from public appearances due to bad nerves and alcohol problems.

Kokomo
ASIA MINOR
(Jimmy Wisner)
Felsted 8612
No. 8   *April 17, 1961*

Jimmy Wisner (b. Dec. 8, 1931, Philadelphia) was classically trained on piano at the Philadelphia Academy, where he studied under Romeo Cascaremi and the conductor of the Philadelphia Orchestra, Henry Smith. By 1959, the Temple University graduate had formed the Jimmy Wisner Trio with Chick Kinney on drums and Ace Tsome on bass. The combo played local clubs and accompanied Mel Torme and Carmen McCrae. Their first album, *Blues For Harvey*, was released by the London Record subsidiary Felsted Records.

Jimmy had an idea for something new—sort of a rock-and-roll-meets-the-masters, but he didn't know what the heck you'd call it. He only knew what kind of sound he wanted to make.

"We bought this upright piano for $50," Jim recalled in an exclusive interview, "and painted the hammers with shellac to give it a sound between that of a tack piano and that of a hard harpsichord. We had only four string players, so to make it sound fuller, we overdubbed them. I played this melody that I loved from the Grieg Piano Concerto." The rocked-up Grieg number was in the key of A minor; when someone at the session called out, "What key's is it in?", the reply was "Asia Minor."

Wisner and company were turned down by 10 or 11 record labels, so they put the disk out themselves. A few weeks after Jim formed Future Records with a local record distributor and the record's engineer, "Asia Minor" became something of a local sensation. Only a few weeks more, and Kokomo was a national item with a top 10 hit.

"I put 'Kokomo' on the record label as a pseudonym because it was basically a rock and roll record, and I was a jazz man. I didn't want to tarnish my position in the community, but ironically, the jazz guys I knew really liked it the best." No photos were ever published of Kokomo, no interviews were ever granted with this reclusive character, and no performances were ever held in support of "Asia Minor" or the "Kokomo" name. An album and two further singles appeared before Jimmy shelved the Kokomo concept. The Jimmy Wisner Trio's second album, *Apperception*, was issued in 1962.

But Kokomo was just the beginning for Wisner, who continued in the music business as an arranger/producer for many a pop record. He worked with Len Barry on "1-2-3," the Cowsills on "The Rain, The Park & Other Things," and with Spanky & Our Gang on "Lazy Day" and "Sunday Will Never Be The Same." Jimmy also co-wrote "Somewhere" for the Tymes and the Searchers classic "Don't Throw Your Love Away." In addition to doing jingles and commercials, Wisner is currently producing the Florida rock band Rising Tide.

Cathy Jean & The Roommates
PLEASE LOVE ME FOREVER
(Malone, Blanchard)
Valmor 007
No. 12   *April 24, 1961*

Steve Susskind (lead vocals, baritone) and Bob Minsky (bass) were in the same homeroom at Russell Sage High in Forest Hills, Queens. After discovering a mutual interest in singing, the duo competed in a talent contest at Forest Hills High, and came in second place—Paul Simon and Art Garfunkel, calling themselves Tom and Jerry, came in first. By 1959, Steve and Bob had formed the Roommates, with second tenor Felix Alvarez and first tenor Jack Carlson. After much practicing, they spent $75 at the Associated Studios to make a demo of the Five Keys' classic "The Glory Of Love." They hawked the number around to all the small labels they could locate, but no one was interested.

One night, while honing their skills in an apartment-building lobby, the Roommates were overheard by Gene and Jody Malis, owners of the new Valmor label. The Malises became the group's managers and brought the guys down to Bill Lashley's Promo label. Lashley, who was momentarily hot with a one-off item by JIMMY CHARLES, released the Roommates' reworking of Kitty Wells' "Making Believe," but the single stiffed.

Noting the success that Kathy Young and the Innocents were having with their "A Thousand Stars," Jody Malis got the idea to package the Roommates with her new "discovery," Cathy Jean (b. Sept. 8, 1945, Brooklyn). Cathy had already recorded a version of "Please Love Me Forever"; Jody rounded up the Roommates and had them overdub a harmonized background onto the track. According to *Story Untold* writer Paul Heller, "The group was not enthused in taking a 'back seat' on somebody else's record. After hearing the playback, the group begged [the Malises] not to release it."

The disk *was* released on Valmor, and "Please Love Me Forever" became a rock-aballad biggie. To reward the Roommates for their involvement in the well-received record, the Malises gave the group a free three-hour session at the Regent Sound Studio. They laid down and packaged some of their finest stuff ever that day: "Band Of Gold," "Glory Of Love," and "My Foolish Heart." Unfortunately, none of their reworked standards—other than their take on "Glory Of Love" (#49, 1961)—garnered much notice. Neither did any of Cathy Jean's follow-ups.

In 1962, Valmor Records shut down. The Malises, still functioning as the group's managers, connected the Roommates to labels like Cameo, Philips, and Canadian-American. Cover versions of "Gee" and "Sunday Kind Of Love" were waxed and shipped, but no one was buying. Cathy, likewise, had another whirl at it, but her few 45s for Philips failed to fly.

Cathy married and quit the music business. Her kids are now grown, and Cathy's back. As Catherine Jean Ruiz, she currently fronts a new version of the Roommates and hosts a Saturday-morning radio show on WNYG in Long Island, New York.

Echoes

BABY BLUE
(Sam Guilino, Val Lagueux)
Seg-Way 103
No. 12   *May 1, 1961*

Harry Doyle (b. 1943), Tommy Duffy (b. 1944), and Tom Morrissey (b. 1943) were some Brooklyn boys who liked to hang out and harmonize. They were calling themselves the Laurels when a friend of Duffy, Johnny Power, turned them on to "Baby Blue," a tune that two

music teachers from Hicksville, Long Island had handed him. Power's own group, the Jokers, passed on the song to record their own "Do-Re-Mi Rock" for Harvard Records.

Meanwhile, the Laurels changed their name to the already overused "Echoes" name. With funds from their own pockets, the guys cut a demo of "Baby Blue"—a slow, *a cappella* rendition. They brought the track to Jack Gold at Paris Records. Gold, who had formerly worked on recordings by the Tempos and JOE BENNETT & THE SPARKLETONES, liked the group's gentle sound and that baby-talkin' tune. He took the tape back into the studio to add instrumental backing and speed up the tempo. To release the disk, he formed the SRG label (named after his newly-born son, Steven Richard Gold).

The initial response to "Baby Blue"—which the group misspells in the song as "Babby Blue"—was promising. A slightly larger independent label, Seg-Way Records, picked up the group's contract and the rights to the recording, and the Echoes had their first and only moment. A number of fine follow-ups were issued, but nothing else nudged the nation—not "Gee, Oh Gee," not their cover of Ersel Hickey's "Bluebirds Over The Mountain," not their moving remake of Brook Benton's "A Million Miles From Nowhere."

When last noted, in the mid-'70s, Tommy was still working with a new edition of the Echoes; Tom and Harry had a group called The Red Hook.

Ernie K-Doe

MOTHER-IN-LAW
(Allen Toussaint)
Minit 623
No. 1   *May 22, 1961*

He's still a wild man, that Ernie K-Doe. Often dressed in iridescent apparel and huge gold rings, he'll jump about like a banshee during his unsettling sets, flippin' and trippin' and rippin' perfectly new suits. Even with an audience of 15 or less, Ernie K has been known to let loose. "I don't like to brag," he told Almost Slim, author of *Walking to New Orleans*, "but I still believe I can out-perform any man in show business. Ernie K-Doe can stop any show at the drop of a hat."

"Mother-in-Law" is possibly the finest record to ever emerge from the bubbling New Orleans scene of the early '60s, and Ernie

The
Sixties

Ernie K-Doe

Orleans in 1954, K-Doe and his Blue Diamonds began playing neighborhood clubs and bars. Savoy Records' Lee Magid spotted the act at the Tijuana Club and set up a session for them: only one single ("Honey Love" b/w "No Money") was released, though Specialty ("Do Baby Do") and Ember ("Tuff Enough") also issued some K-Doe sides.

Minit Records was set up in 1960; Ernie's manager, Larry McKinley, was part-owner of the operation. "Mother-in-Law" was Ernie's third single for the fledgling label. For the next couple of years, his 45s filed onto the charts— "Te-Ta-Te-Ta-Ta" (#53, 1961), "I Cried My Last Tear" (#69, 1961) b/w "A Certain Girl" (#71), and "Popeye Joe" (#99, 1962). Even the ones that didn't sell well were solidly-crafted, and are now highly collectible efforts. Eventually, his releases became fewer and farther between.

"Oh, Ernie K-Doe slipped up," Ernie admitted to Almost Slim. "But I have to believe that I'm going to the top. The only thing I know is singing and dancing. Ernie K-Doe is going back to the top. That's all there is to it."

Beginning in 1982, Ernie has been spotted occasionally hosting an R & B radio program on New Orleans' WWOZ. In mid-'89 a compilation cassette, *New Orleans: A Musical Gumbo*, was released; produced by "Half a Head" Batiste, the work includes three new K-Doe sides.

performed it with conviction. "'Mother-in-Law' wasn't a hard song to sing," he told Dave Hoekstra of the *Chicago Tribune*, "because my mother-in-law was staying in my house. I was married 19 years, and it was 19 years of pure sorrow. When I sang, 'Satan should be her name,' I meant that . . . Oooh, she was a lowdown."

The way Ernie remembers it, he literally found "Mother-in-Law" in an overstuffed garbage can: "Allen [Toussaint] had wrote it and thrown it away . . . I saw it in the garbage can and pulled it out. I looked at the words and said, 'Hey man, this is good. I want to do it.'" Others, like the tune's creator, have disputed Ernie's tale.

He was born Ernest Kador, Jr., on February 22, 1936, in New Orleans, the ninth of eleven offspring. His dad was a Baptist minister. For unreported reasons, Ernie's aunt on his mom's side raised him, and religiously so. He sang in his father's New Home Baptist Church, and toured with gospel groups while still an adolescent.

When he was 17, Ernie moved to Chicago, where he recorded his first solo and secular sides for United Records (none of the four cuts have been officially released). Back in New

Shep & The Limelites
DADDY'S HOME
(James Sheppard, William Miller)
Hull 740
No. 2 *May 29, 1961*

The Heartbeats (initially called the Hearts), Jim "Shep" Shepherd's first group, evolved from the friendship of four students at Woodrow Wilson High: second tenor Robbie Adams, first tenor Andrew Crump, bass Wally Roker, and baritone Vernon Seavers. It was 1953, and like many of the countless quartets working the New York City landscape, the Hearts would sing on street corners, in echoey school hallways, and in johns. One night, while the guys were rehearsing at Vern's house, someone tipped them off to some guy singing in St. Albans Park who was too good to be true. The group dashed to the park, where they found Shep. The five tried out a few numbers right there in the park. "Everyone blew their mind," is how Crump later described the occasion to *Big Town Review*'s Jeff Beckman.

By way of their neighbor, saxophonist Illinois Jacquet, Shep and the Hearts hooked up with Gotham/Network Records, an independent Philly label, and recorded "Tormented" b/w "After Everybody's Gone." Since a girl group had already beaten them out on the use of the "Hearts" name, they rechristened themselves the Heatbeat Quartet. The printer goofed, and the record label read: "The Heartbeats."

A frequent visitor to Vernon's neighborhood was Bea Casalin, a bookkeeper at Herald Records. Bea was preparing to leave Herald and start up her own label, Hull Records, so the Heartbeats did some recording for her in a Brooklyn basement: "Crazy For You," "Hurry Home Baby," "People Are Talking," and the classic "A Thousand Miles Away" (#53, 1957; #96, 1960). With the success of the latter platter, Bea sold the Heartbeats' contract to George Goldner's Rama label. Despite some truly great recordings and the broader audience assured by their new affiliation, only one other Heartbeats 45 made the charts—"Everybody's Somebody's Fool" (#78, 1957).

The Heartbeats began having internal problems. According to Roker, the group promised away too much of a percentage on their action; Shep was becoming intolerably bossy and drinking heavily, and musical differences arose. The end came in 1960, when Shep passed out at the microphone in Philadelphia. The Heartbeats disbanded. Albert went on to become a psychologist. Rob is currently a teacher, Vernon is an electrical engineer, and Wally is working in the music business.

Two years later, Shep formed Shep & The Limelites with two former members of the Videos, Charles Baskerville (second tenor) and Clarence Bassett (first tenor). After two disks on Apt ("Too Young To Wed" and "I'm So Lonely"), Shep and the new crew found their slot in pop history with an answer record to the earlier Heartbeats number. "I felt, since 'A Thousand Miles Away' was a hit," Bassett told *Big Town Review*'s Mike Rascio, "why not write a song, relating to the guys coming home from the service 'A Thousand Miles Away'? You know, 'Daddy's Home.'"

After the record peaked in the nation's top 10, Shep became unmanageable. "[Shep] felt he didn't have to make the gigs anymore," Bassett recalled. "He was just too hard to get along with, so me and Charles gave it up."

The Limelites broke up, but the Hull label continued to issue 45s up through 1965. Five of

these made the Hot 100 listings. Charles joined the Players; Clarence joined the post-prime Flamingos' line-up, and later sang with the Creative Funks.

Jim Sheppard was found dead in his car on the Long Island Expressway, on January 24, 1970—he had been beaten and robbed.

Faron Young

HELLO WALLS
(Willie Nelson)
Capitol 4533
No. 12   *May 29, 1961*

Nora Jo Catlett of Clarksville, West Virginia, was six years old that day in September 1972. Nora stood in front of the stage at the Nathan Goff Armory, waiting for some country-music celebrity to add yet another autograph to her collection. Faron Young, self-proclaimed "Singing Sheriff," was performing onstage when he spotted little Nora. Several times did Faron ask her to join him on stage, and several times did Nora refuse. Faron reportedly muttered a few choice words, walked offstage, grabbed little Nora, lifted her skirt, and spanked her repeatedly!

There ain't much old Faron Young ain't done. As one of the top 10 all-time charting artists in country music, he's had dang near 100 singles on *Billboard*'s C & W charts; 42 have placed in the top 10. With more than 60 albums to his name, Young has sold roughly 30,000,000 records.

"I've been around so long," Young told Joe Edwards of the *Associated Press*, "that when I tell people I'm 56 years old, they laugh and say, 'And how many more?' The best thing is to say you're 75 and then they say, 'You look good for your age.'"

Faron (b. Feb. 25, 1932, Shreveport, La.) spent most of his early years on a dirt farm outside of Shreveport. He got his first guitar in grade school and spent hours figuring out how to play it, with a herd of cattle as his audience. At Fair Park High, he formed his first band to play school dances and local fairs. He attended Centenary College, until his growing popularity as a singer encouraged the young man to re-evaluate his career goals.

While Faron was working as a shirt salesman for Sears, Roebuck & Co., some of his songs reached Webb Pierce. Webb didn't care much for the tunes, but took Young on the road to perform as a fill-in. Soon "The Singing Sheriff" was asked to join the "Louisiana Hayride" radio show (1951), to sign with Capitol Records, and, in 1952, to perform at the Grand Ole Opry. The country hits came almost immediately—a half-dozen crossed over onto the pop listings. Not one to till but one field, Faron even branched out into films, music publishing, and recording.

Faron has led a rough-and-tumble outlaw lifestyle. He shot up some light fixtures in a Nashville bar; his wife divorced him on the grounds of physical abuse; and on one occasion, he allegedly threatened his wife and 16-year-old daughter with a loaded pistol, which he repeatedly fired into the kitchen ceiling.

As for that child-spanking episode, Young was arrested while leaving the county, on charges of assault and battery. The case has long since been settled; Nora's family received $3,400 in damages.

Cleftones

HEART AND SOUL
(Frank Loesser, Hoagy Carmichael)
Gee 1064
No. 18 *June 19, 1961*

In 1955, lead singer Herbie Cox (b. May 6, 1939), bass Warren Corbin (b. 1939), first tenor Charlie James (b. 1940), baritone William McClain (b. 1938), and second tenor Berman Patterson (b. 1938) were students at Jamaica High School in Queens. They all started working for a student who was running for school president. "The idea of his campaign was to have singing slogans," Cox explained to *Bim Bam Boom*'s Bob Galgano. "The guys started singing in school and after the elections we just decided to stay together [calling ourselves the Silvertones]. After our smash success in the school election, we started doing gigs around the community."

David Ralnick, a schoolmate, approached the guys as a pseudo-manager, assuring them that his father and some friends had connections in the music business. Ralnick arranged recording auditions for the group. One of these was with George Goldner, the founder of legendary labels like End, Gee, Gone, Rama, and Roulette. Goldner rushed the Cleftones into the Master-Tone Studios. "You Baby You" (#78, 1956), their first offering, clicked, especially in local doo-wop circles. "Little Girl Of Mine" (#57, 1956) did likewise. "Can't We Be Sweethearts," "String Around My Heart," and

"Why Do You Do Me Like You Do," though quality outings, did not chart nationally.

"We went into a slump," Cox recalled. "[The company wanted] a production line of hits. They made no attempt to feed the artists new material. They made the next record almost exactly like your last record, [and] the public lost interest. We didn't realize what was happening."

Five years of persistence paid off, though. The Cleftones—now comprising Cox, Corbin, James, Gene Pearson (baritone), and Pat Span (second tenor)—had their most successful recording effort in 1961 with "Heart And Soul." Two subsequent singles made *Billboard*'s Hot 100—"For Sentimental Reasons" (#60, 1961) and "Lover Come Back To Me" (#95, 1962)—but that was it for one of the era's finest vocal groups. Only a few more 45s were pressed.

After a final single issued on Ware in 1964 ("He's Forgotten You" b/w "Right From The Git Go"), the Cleftones lapsed into a period of inactivity. "We did stop performing for a couple of years, but we stayed together always as songwriters and maintained a very close relationship, personally," Cox told *Goldmine*'s Wayne Jones. "We've always been very good friends and still are."

Gene and Berman now work in law enforcement offices; Charlie works for IBM; and Herbie is a computer programmer.

Marathons

PEANUT BUTTER
(Barnum, Cooper, Smith, Goldsmith)
Arvee 5027
No. 20 *June 19, 1961*

As the Vibrations, Don Bradley (bass), Carl Fisher (second tenor), Dave Govan (baritone), Jimmy Johnson (lead) and Richard Owens (first tenor) were hot stuff and in heavy demand in early 1961. Their delightful dance disk on the Checker label, "The Watusi," was a top 40 item (#25). As THE JAYHAWKS, almost the identical line-up had made the nation's charts in 1956 with the original rendition of "Stranded In The Jungle."

Arranger/producer/tunesmith H.B. Barnum (or possibly another hungry rep at the Hollywood-based Arvee label) offered the Vibrations some sideline cash if they would moonlight their way through a sticky novelty number called "Peanut Butter." Neither Barnum nor any of the vinyl pushers at Arvee

The Marathons

expected "Butter" to spread its appealing way through thousands of American households, but it did.

However, since the Vibrations were under contract to Checker at the time, the success of "Peanut Butter" prompted the label to file a law suit against Arvee, and the Chess-Checker-Argo organization won the right to issue the single under its own logo. Arvee Records secured the rights to the "Marathons" name, and soon after released a highly-collectible LP and a follow-up single about an overly endowed vixen who should have known better than to wear a "Tight Sweater." (As a tasty tidbit of trivia, the "Sweater" songsmith was SONNY BONO.) This number did not sell well, and reportedly no Vibrations voices were present on this or any successive Marathon offerings.

Little Caesar & The Romans
THOSE OLDIES BUT GOODIES
(REMIND ME OF YOU)
(Paul Politti, Nick Curinga)
Del-Fi 4158
No. 9 *June 26, 1961*

David Caesar Johnson (b. June 16, 1934, Chicago) began singing in church at a young age. After high school, "Little Caesar" joined the Air Force. While doing his time in Alaska, he formed the Northern Crusaders, a gospel group. Back in civilian life, Caesar sang with the Ivory-Tones.

In 1958, Caesar moved to Los Angeles and recorded with the Cubans—Early Harris,

**Little Caesar &
The Romans**

Johnny O'Simmons, Leroy Sanders, and a fellow remembered now only as Curtis. (Strangely enough, not one of these fellows was Cuban.) Johnson's next group, the Upfronts, featured Johnson, Harris, Sanders, and Bobby Relf (of later Bob & Earl fame). The Upfronts cut two singles for Lummtone Records—"It Took Time" and "Too Late To Turn Around"—but neither one made any serious moves on the charts.

Caesar soon met a young tunesmith named Paul Politti, who had a tune in hand called "Those Oldies But Goodies." Bob Keene at Del-Fi/Donna Records wanted Johnson's group to do the number. Little Caesar & The Romans—Johnson, Harris, Sanders, ex-Cuban Johnny O'Simmons, and Carl Burnette—labored in the studio for six weeks. "Del-Fi didn't want the typical black sound," Johnson explained to *Goldmine's* Rick Gagnon and Dave Gnerre. "They were looking for a white sound to reach the crossover audience."

"Oldies But Goodies" clicked, and is now considered an early rock classic. Little Caesar & The Romans toured with Jackie Wilson, Gary U.S. Bonds, and the Vibrations. "Here were five black dudes all dressed up in toga and sandals, wearing wreaths on their heads!" Caesar told *Goldmine.* "It was a good gimmick, but we hated it at the time. Not only did we hate the togas, we hated the song, too!"

Weeks later, they were back in the studio to cut an answer to the Olympics' "(Baby) Hully Gully" called "Hully Gully Again" (#54, 1961). This would be their last hit. Their third disk, "Memories Of Those Oldies But Goodies," looked like it was going to take off, but Johnson claims that the group and Keene were involved in a "financial dispute," and that Keene failed to adequately promote the record. Before Little Caesar *et al* disbanded, Del-Fi issued two more singles ("Ten Commandments Of Love" and "Yoyo Yo Yoyo") and an LP entitled *Memories of Those Oldies But Goodies* (1962).

Caesar sang solo at various L.A. nightspots throughout the '60s and early '70s, and reformed the Romans in 1975. For a six-month period in 1978, Rickie Lee Jones was even a member. "She could sing black, white, any style you wanted," Johnson recalled. The lineup has evolved considerably over the years, and as of 1988 included Johnson, Nathaniel Johnson (no relation), Laurie Ratcliff, and Larry Tate.

Arthur Lyman

YELLOW BIRD
(Norman Luboff, Marilyn Keith,
Alan Bergman)
Hi Fi 5024
No. 4 *July 24, 1961*

Arthur Lyman (vibraphone, piano, guitar, drums) was born in 1934 on the island of Kauai, Hawaii. After his father lost his eyesight in an accident, the family moved to the island of Oahu and settled in Makiki, a section of Honolulu. Following years of messing around with the marimbas and whatever instruments he could get his hands on, Lyman joined a downtown juice-bar jazz band. In the early '50s, Art worked with a group that would eventually become his primary competitor—the Martin Denny Trio.

Denny and his boys, with their bag of percussive toys and jungle calls, preceded Art in creating "exotic mood music." Denny would also precede his protege on the stateside charts: in 1959, a Martin Denny Trio instrumental, "Quiet Village," exploded, creating popular interest in the romantic and magical sounds of the rain forests.

By this time, Art—accompanied by Harold Chang (boobams, cocktail drums, ankle spurs, ass' jaw, bongo, conga, samba, xylophone), John Kramer (bass, bamboo flute, ukelele), Allen Soares (piano, celeste), plus nearly 50 instruments—was ready to roll. The group was holding down a gig in the Shell Bar at Henry J. Kaiser's Hawaiian Village Hotel when Lewis Amiel at Hi Fi Records approached them about recording some of their titillating tunes.

"Taboo," the title of Arthur Lyman's debut album and single (#55, 1959), clicked. While the Caribbean-flavored "Yellow Bird" was Lyman's sole excursion into the wilds of top 40-land, Art and his sound explorers continued to perform and sell albums well into the '80s.

Chris Kenner

I LIKE IT LIKE THAT, PART 1
(Chris Kenner, Fats Domino)
Instant 3229
No. 2 *July 31, 1961*

According to Chris Kenner's booker, Percy Stovall, Kenner was not too professional a performer. "He couldn't sing, he couldn't dance, he dressed raggedy—he just stood there," Stovall told Almost Slim in *I Hear You Knockin'*. "He would get so drunk he would forget the words to his song; they used to throw bottles at him." Despite problems of this sort, Kenner created some rock and roll perennials, cutting and canning some of the finest recorded examples of the New Orleans sound.

Chris was born *Christ*mas Day 1929, in *Kenner*, a suburb of New Orleans. He worked as a longshoreman and sang in a number of gospel groups, including the Harmonizing Four. In the '50s, Chris switched over to rhythm & blues. His first disk, "Grandma's House" b/w "Don't Pin That Charge On Me" — released on Baton Records in 1955—bombed. A few years later, the producer for Imperial Records, Dave Bartholomew, let Kenner have another crack at it. "Sick And Tired" (—/#13, 1957) turned out to be a big seller in New Orleans.

Kenner only made one other record with Imperial because label owner Lew Chudd didn't think he had much of a future. But the following year, Fats Domino covered "Sick And Tired" (#22, 1958) and sold a million copies. After a single for Ponchartrain ("You Can't Beat Uncle Sam" b/w "Don't Make No Noise") and one for Ron ("Life Is A Struggle" b/w "Rocket To The Moon"), Kenner had his moment.

" 'Like It Like That' was a slang gimmick," Kenner told John Broven in *Rhythm & Blues in New Orleans*. "It was a good title and I tried to put a story to it. I worked on it a little while and got it together, you know. We didn't think it would be a hit record . . . I had it on tape at Allen Toussaint's house, and one day [Instant Records'] Joe Banashak stopped by. He played him some old tapes, and that particular song Banashak liked." THE BOBBETTES, the Dave Clark Five, and Loggins & Messina liked it like that, too: each group charted with cover versions of Kenner's smash.

Chris received a Grammy nomination for "I Like It Like That," appeared on "American Bandstand," and toured with the Coasters, Gladys Knight & The Pips, and Jackie Wilson. He continued to wax solid efforts like "Something You Got," a much-covered disk, and in 1963 recorded his career crowner, the original version of "Land Of A Thousand Dances" (#77, 1963). Although most pop fans associate the tune with Wilson Pickett (#6, 1966), "Land" was also a hit for Cannibal & The Headhunters (#30, 1965), Thee [*sic*] Midnighters (#67, 1965), THE ELECTRIC INDIAN (#95, 1969), and the J. Geils Band (#60, 1983).

As Kenner explained to Boven, the song "actually came from a spiritual, 'Children Go Where I Send You,' and I turned it around. It was inspired by the dance tunes going around." Nowhere on the record does Kenner say anything about a "land of a thousand dances." But upon listening to the original master tape, *Goldmine*'s Almost Slim noted a ten-second introduction, snipped from the track at the last minute, that had Kenner calling out: "I'm gonna take you, baby/I'm gonna take you to a place/The name of the place is the Land of a Thousand Dances."

Chris' career came to a halt in 1968 when he was sent to the Louisiana State Penitentiary for statutory rape of a minor. On his release four years later, $20,000 in accumulated royalties was there for him. Almost Slim wrote that "in true Chris Kenner style, the money was exhausted within a month." Hep' Me Records issued two further singles, "You Can Run But You Can't Slip Away" and "We Belong Together."

Chris Kenner was found dead from heart failure in his rooming house on January 28, 1976—he was 46.

Curtis Lee

PRETTY LITTLE ANGEL EYES
(Tommy Boyce, Curtis Lee)
Dunes 2007
No. 7 *August 7, 1961*

Curtis Lee (b. Oct. 28, 1941, Yuma, Ariz.) was a vegetable picker. Blue-eyed and blond, he sounded on his best days a mite like Bobby Rydell (on other days, he could sound more like Fabian singing flat). In 1960, Ray Peterson, the teen crooner noted for that masterful piece of "death rock," "Tell Laura I Love Her," happened to catch one of Lee's sets at a Yuma nightspot. Curtis was hot that night, and Peterson liked what he heard enough to tip off Stan Shulman, owner of the Dunes label. Despite Lee's poor track record on the Warrior and Hot labels, Shulman rushed the kid into the studios to cut a cover on KEN COPELAND'S "Pledge Of Love." Like Lee's earlier sides, this tune nose-dived, as did another single, "D In Love."

In 1961, the production and songwriting team of Leiber & Stoller recommended to Shulman the dial-twiddling skills of an up-and-coming producer named Phil Spector. Up to this point in his career, Spector was known

only for being a former member of THE TEDDY BEARS. Phil produced Ray Peterson's "Corinna, Corinna" for Dunes, then turned his attention to the hit-less Curtis Lee.

Curtis had some tunes that he and an L.A. singer/songwriter named Tommy Boyce had dashed off. Spector listened to the rough outlines of the song and arranged to record "Pretty Little Angel Eyes" and some other numbers at the Mira Sound Studios. Brought in to provide that catchy doo-woppin' background were the Halos, a recording act just an instant away from their own success with "Nag" (#25, 1961). "We came in and [Spector] gave us the lyric sheets and told us to do what we felt," Arthur Cryer of the Halos told Mark Ribowsky, author of *He's A Rebel*. "We stole all those 'bomps' and 'ha-ha-has' from the Spaniels and Cleftones."

"Angel Eyes" was a magnificent piece of rock and roll, as was the Spector-produced follow-up, "Under The Moon Of Love" (#46, 1961). Soon afterward, Spector and Dunes Records parted company. Try as he did with C & W tunes, Del Shannon-like numbers, and fine material provided by Otis Blackwell and the team of Gary Geld and Peter Udell, Curtis Lee never again managed to get that "right" sound.

Curtis still lives in Yuma, and works in the construction business.

Mar-Keys

LAST NIGHT
(Mar-Keys)
Satellite 107
No. 3 *August 7, 1961*

The Mar-Keys started out in 1957 as the Royal Spades. They all attended Messick High in Memphis, and all liked that funky black sound. Initially, the group consisted of Charles "Packy" Axton (tenor sax), Steve Cropper (guitar), Donald "Duck" Dunn (bass), Charlie Freeman (guitar), Terry Johnson (drums), and occasionally Jerry Lee "Smoochie" Smith (piano).

Estelle Axton and her brother, Jim Stewart—both bankers by day—had just set up a small makeshift recording studio in Brunswick, Tennessee. When the two ventured into the realm of record-making, they decided to name their label after those huge, thorny-looking golf balls that Cape Canaveral was blasting into space. Unfortunately, one immediate result of the success of Satellite's

The Mar-Keys

"Last Night" was the threat of legal action by a similarly-named California company, so Jim and Estelle quickly renamed their label "Stax Records" (*St*ewart + *Ax*ton).

The first few Satellite singles failed to lift off. Meanwhile, the Royal Spades—who in various configurations appeared on some of these early efforts—tightened up their chops playing sock hops, bars, and other venues, practicing every weekend in the primitive Stax studios in East Memphis. They backed up early Stax hitmakers like Rufus Thomas and his daughter Carla. But it was "Last Night," a deceptively simple, blues-riffin' instrumental worked up by those studio musicians, that established the trademark Stax sound—a sound that in its day was as unique, and nearly as influential, as Detroit's Motown sound.

"When we put it out, it exploded like nothing had ever exploded before," Estelle Axton told Peter Guralnick in *Sweet Soul Music*. "I'm telling you, I sold over two thousand of it one by one over the counter [of Satellite's record store]. They certified a million on it eventually . . . I was so proud of it. I've never been so proud of a record in my life."

The tune reportedly evolved over a six-month period, and went through so many changes that the actual line-up of personnel present on the disk is in dispute. Guralnick has theorized that present for *the* session were probably Curtis Green (drums), Bob McGee (bass), "Smoochie" Smith, and a horn line-up comprising Packy, Gilbert Caples (tenor sax), and Floyd Newman (baritone sax). Yet it was the ever-evolving Royal Spades—Axton, Cropper, Dunn, Smith, and Johnson, plus Wayne Jackson (trumpet) and Don Nix (baritone sax)—who would tour and record as "The Mar-Keys."

Before the name was scrapped in the early '70s, several albums appeared, as did singles like "Morning After" (#60, 1961), "Pop-Eye Stroll" (#94, 1962), and "Philly Dog" (#89, 1966). Despite the act's success, internal frictions appeared almost immediately. Even by the end of 1960, Steve and Duck were off to join Booker T. Jones and Al Jackson, Jr. in the label's second classic back-up unit, Booker T. & The MGs. By 1965, Packy was fronting the

Packers, a studio act that charted with a Mar-Keys knock-off called "Hole in the Wall" (#43, 1965). Nix went on to produce artists like Jeff Beck, Delaney & Bonnie, Albert King, Freddie King, and John Mayall.

Both Packy Axton and Charlie Freeman have since passed away.

Ann-Margret

I JUST DON'T UNDERSTAND
(Wilkin, Westberry)
RCA Victor 7894
No. 17   *September 11, 1961*

Considering her "sex kitten" image, one would have expected Ann-Margret on vinyl to come on like gangbusters, penetrate the charts, and leave American teens smouldering in her wake. RCA Victor certainly expected it, dishing her up as a curvaceous female Elvis who was going to make the label *mucho dinero*. On her early recordings, they garbed her in the

Ann-Margret

dark soulfulness of Willie Dixon and Lincoln Chase, and subjected her to the teen vibrations of Gerry Goffin and Carole King.

Ann-Margret's lone top 40 hit, "I Just Don't Understand," sported a mournful harmonica and possibly the earliest example of fuzz-tone guitar ever to be heard on the airwaves. It was a slinky, teasing number, and the follow-up, "It Do Me So Good" (#97, 1961), was no dog, either. Adolescent listeners could easily imagine little Annie on a zebra skin, gyrating and pleading, "Close your lovin' arms around me, it do me so good." So much for a recording career: two fine rock and roll platters, and Ann-Margret was off to Hollywood, never to return to the charts again.

She was born Ann-Margret Olsson, the only child of an electrician, on April 28, 1941, in Valsjobyn, Sweden. At the age of five, she was brought to the U.S. and raised in various towns in Illinois. After a year attending Northwestern University and a well-noted spot on Ted Mack's "Amateur Hour," Miss Olsson joined a combo and began making appearances at nightclubs.

In 1961, at the peak of her chart success, Ann was making her screen debut as Bette Davis' daughter in Frank Capra's *A Pocketful of Miracles*. Following in rapid succession were *Bye, Bye Birdie* (1963), the Elvis flick *Viva Las Vegas* (1964), and *Kitten With A Whip* (1964). She was nominated for an Oscar for both *Carnal Knowledge* (1971) and *Tommy* (1975). She still sizzles, sings, and dances—she just doesn't do it on vinyl anymore.

Dreamlovers

WHEN WE GET MARRIED
(Don Hogan)
Heritage 102
No. 10   *September 18, 1961*

Tommy Ricks (lead), Cleveland Hammock (second tenor), Morris Gardner (baritone), and Cliff (first tenor) and Ray Dunn (bass) had been sharing a common dream since they met in 1956 on the streets of Philadelphia. For years, they frequented the sidewalks, doo-wopping and working gigs wherever they could. In 1960, V-Tone Records gave them a double shot at success with the release of "Annabelle Lee" followed by "May I Kiss The Bride." Both disks stiffed, but Parkway Records signed up the dreamers to provide backup for the Chubby Checker recording session that

would culminate in "The Twist."

Obviously, "The Twist" secured money and a successful career for Chubby—yet the Dreamlovers were awarded neither royalties nor credit for their role in the blockbuster. They were, however, quickly offered further jobs as background vocalists. Some funds did find their way into the pockets of group members, but eventually, making "ooh ooh" and "wop wop" sounds behind acts who got all the billing and the bread began to dispirit the fellows one and all.

Jerry Ross and Murry Wecht were forming their own label, Heritage, and offered the Dreamlovers the chance to stand front and center with their very own release. "When We Get Married," composed by former member Don Hogan, was the label's first release and the group's one moment in the sun. With a quiet, simple styling reminiscent of Shep & The Limelites, "When We Get Married" was a doo-wop lover's delight. So were the follow-ups, "Welcome Home" and "Zoom, Zoom, Zoom," but neither of these sold well.

The Dreamlovers charted in 1962 with their next one, "If I Should Lose You" (#62), but this was their last Hot 100 appearance. Fine-fine wop-wop recordings were made for Swan, Cameo, and even big-time labels like Columbia, Mercury, and Warner Bros., but doo-wop was on its way out. Younger ears wanted Detroit soul, not street-corner harmonies. The fellows tried to adapt with numbers like "The Bad Times Make The Good," but the public wasn't buying it.

The current whereabouts of the group and its members are not known.

Jarmels

A LITTLE BIT OF SOAP
(Jarmels)
Laurie 3098
No. 12   *September 18, 1961*

Nathaniel Buff, Paul Burnett, Earl Christian, Tommy Eldridge, and Ray Smith were all from Richmond, Virginia, and had been crossing paths for years. They attended the same church; they sang in the same glee club in school. They eventually became good friends, and decided to pull themselves together into a legitimate singing group. As for the group name, they lifted that from a street sign in Harlem.

Jim Gribble, manager of the Passions and

THE MYSTICS, happened onto the group, liked their material, and pointed them toward Gene Schwartz at Laurie Records. Although Laurie was well-known as a doo-wop label, their artists were usually Italian (e.g. the Belmonts, the Del Satins), not black. Still, six singles in all were issued, all of them with a racially integrated feel to them.

The Jarmels hit paydirt with "A Little Bit Of Soap." It cracked the top 10, but nothing else the fellows ever waxed even brushed the Hot 100. "Soap" was loaded with magic, and over the years, Garnet Mimms, Paul Davis, Nigel Olsson, and THE EXCITERS all charted with cover versions of the Jarmels' original.

The Jarmels apparently disbanded when their recording contract with Laurie Records ended in 1963. No further records were ever released under their name.

Barry Mann

WHO PUT THE BOMP
(IN THE BOMP, BOMP, BOMP)
(Barry Mann, Gerry Goffin)
ABC-Paramount 10237
No. 7   *September 25, 1961*

Barry Mann's name is usually whispered with a reverence accorded very few. To mention

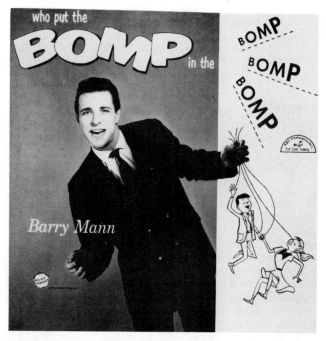

Mann and not Cynthia Weil, his wife and songwriting partner of nearly 30 years, is next to impossible. Together, Mann and Weil composed some of the greatest rock and roll hits of all time. The list is long, and most are commonly known to even casual pop fans: "Blame It On The Bossa Nova," "Here You Come Again," "I Love How You Love Me," "Kicks," "Looking Through The Eyes Of Love," "On Broadway," "Shapes Of Things To Come," "Sometimes When We Touch," "(You're My) Soul And Inspiration," "We Gotta Get Out Of This Place," and "You've Lost That Lovin' Feelin'."

He was born Barry Iberman, in Brooklyn, on February 9, 1939. In grammar school, Barry was introduced to a ukelele. He learned a few chords, but only a few—to this day, Barry maintains that he can barely read or write music. By age 12, Barry was pickin' and peckin' his way through pop songs that he would hear on the radio. With time and practice, he began writing his own little tunes.

After a year of architectural studies at Pratt Institute, Mann went to work for George Paxton's music-publishing firm. The Diamonds had a hit with Barry's "She Say (Oom, Dooby, Doom)," Steve Lawrence scored with "Footsteps," and Barry moved on to Aldon Music, headed by Al Nevins and Don Kirshner.

"I was with them almost a year when I went to play a song for Teddy Randazzo, and I saw this girl who was writing with Teddy," Mann recalled to Joe Smith in *Off the Record*. "I presumed she was his girlfriend." She wasn't; it was Cynthia Weil, an aspiring actress/dancer/singer/songwriter. Mann and Weil married in 1961, and became an up-and-coming songwriting team.

That year, Kirshner convinced Barry to record some of his own songs. An unforgettable novelty record, "Who Put The Bomp" was Barry's third try. "I think a lot of people didn't get it," Mann told *Goldmine*'s Jeff Tamarkin. "They bought it because they dug the groove . . . it was a piece of the times, a put-on of all the doo-wop records."

Barry has charted a few times over the years, most recently with "The Princess And The Punk" (#78, 1976). His releases are sporadic, and range wildly in quality. If you get the offer, give a listen to his "Young Electric Psychedelic Hippy Flippy."

In 1987, Barry and Cynthia won the "Best Song of the Year" Grammy for "Somewhere Out There," featured in the animated film *An American Tail* (1986).

Jose Jimenez
THE ASTRONAUT (PARTS 1 & 2)
(Bill Dana)
Kapp 409
No. 19 *October 2, 1961*

Jose was born in the fertile mind of Bill Dana in the cold winter of 1959. In a fit of creativity, Dana, the head writer for TV's "The Steve Allen Show," dreamed up this goodhearted Hispanic character who was to be the teacher in a one-off sketch involving a school for department-store Santas. The skit was so well-received that "Jose" became a regular on Allen's show. Nightclub appearances, five fine-selling comedy albums, a hit single, and a spin-off TV turkey whizzed by like a fast-moving freight train.

Bill was born William Szathmary on October 5, 1924, in Quincy, Massachusetts. He graduated from Emerson College in 1950, and for the next few years performed as a stand-up comic in local watering holes and houses of laughter. Bill appeared in bit roles on TV programs with Imogene Coco and Martha Raye, and began writing gags for Don Adams. From 1956 to 1960, Dana was a behind-the-scenes writer for Steve Allen. After the Jose Jimenez character took on a life of its own, Bill cut some sides as Jose for the Kapp label. "The Astronaut," an "interview" with Jose, would be Dana's only top 40 single, but all five of Jose's LPs sold well enough to place on *Billboard*'s top pop albums chart.

In the early '60s, Jose made regular appearances on "The Danny Thomas Show," and, for a season and a half, Bill's character had his own program on NBC. But with the rise of ethnic sensitivities in the late '60s, pressures were placed on Dana to put a stop to his characterization; some viewers looked on Jose's naiveté as a racial put-down. In 1970, Dana "murdered" Jose, and a mock funeral was held in Los Angeles.

While lying low during much of the '70s, Bill returned to public view in the short-lived TV series "No Soap, Radio" (1982) and "Zorro and Son" (1983).

Bob Moore
MEXICO
(Boudleaux Bryant)
Monument 446
No. 7 *October 2, 1961*

Bob Moore was born in the heart of country & western music, in Nashville, Tennessee, on November 30, 1932. As if answering a calling from the holy soil itself, Bob took to playing the bass fiddle, and after years of practice found himself laying down that bass foundation on countless C & W tours and recordings. As an accompanist, Bob toured the land with a young and wild Elvis Presley, country folkie Red Foley, and teen queens Connie Francis and Brenda Lee.

In 1959, Monument Records mainman Fred Foster noticed Moore's ability to take charge in the studio yet fit in well with almost any sound, and hired him to be the label's music director. Roy Orbison had just joined the Monument label, and it was Bob who created the plush and throbbing orchestral ambience of every one of those "Big O" soap operettas. Foster liked what he heard, and decided to cut Moore loose to see what the kid could do as a solo act.

After a mildly successful initial release, "(Theme From) 'My Three Sons,'" Moore recorded an instrumental by Boudleaux Bryant called "Mexico." In sound, Moore's lone top 40 hit anticipated by a full year the style that would keep Herb Alpert's Tijuana Brass all over the charts for years to come.

Throughout the remainder of the decade, Moore, on Monument and later Hickory, tried to keep up his momentum, with little success. An album entitled *Mexico and Other Great Hits* did sell well, but only on the strength of his big pop moment.

For a session man who played with rock and rollers like Elvis and Jerry Lee Lewis, Bob had a brassy yet tame sound on his solo sides. But listen to Jerry Lee Lewis' "What Did I Say?"— the pounding bass on that number reveals another, more primal side of Bob Moore. *This* is the Bob Moore found on records by CARL PERKINS, J.J. Cale, Moby Grape, Pearls Before Swine, Harvey Mandel, Kenny Rogers, Don McLean, and post-Righteous-Brothers Bill Medley. Bob Dylan also made use of Moore's talents on the *Dylan* (1970) and *Self-Portrait* (1973) albums.

Troy Shondell

THIS TIME
(Chip Moman)
Liberty 55353
No. 6 *October 23, 1961*

Troy Shondell was born on May 14, 1944, in Fort Wayne, Indiana. For years, he worked hard, learning how to play the guitar, organ, drums, sax, and trumpet. In 1958, Little Anthony & The Imperials recorded one of his songs. Two years later, Troy and some of his music buddies rented a hometown recording studio to tape Chip Moman's tear-jerking rock-aballad, "This Time." Friends told Troy that he had a hit on his hands—if he could only get the world to hear it.

After a few rejections, the 17-year-old formed his own Gold Crest label and had copies of "This Time" pressed. Gaye Records also issued a few hundred highly sought-after replicas. When the disk was played on the radio, the local response was such that Liberty Records immediately picked up Troy's swamp-rock classic and released it nationally.

In the fall, Shondell entered the Valparaiso University as a music major. For years thereafter, he struggled to keep a music career going. Both sides of his follow-up, "Tears From An Angel" (#77, 1962) b/w "Island In The Sky" (#92), charted; ironically, these tunes seem rather lame in comparison to some of his later, but less successful 45s. Phil Spector produced "Na-Ne-No," a dynamite disk which featured a wall of echoey voices and the squeak of a doggy toy, but record-buyers passed on it. Troy's "Little Miss Tease," a shaky Elvis knock-off, was likewise a solid but overlooked effort.

In the late '60s, Shondell moved to Nashville and made some country disks for TRX and Bright Star. He became a songwriter for the publishing house of Acuff-Rose, and worked for ASCAP in the '70s. He never stopped recording, though: the Shondell name; in various spellings, appeared on 14 different record labels. In 1981, Troy had a 45 issued on the tiny Telesonic label.

Troy only went to the top only once, but his impact on aspiring rockers was apparently significant. A young Detroit guitarist named Tommy James named his "Hanky Panky" group the Shondells; Jim Peterik, later of the Ides of March, did the same with his first Chicago group; and when ROD BERNARD and rockabilly legend Warren Storm teamed up to recorded for the La Louisianne label, they called themselves the Shondells.

Bobby Edwards

YOU'RE THE REASON
(Bobby Edwards, Mildred Imes,
Fred Henley, Terry Fell)
Crest 1075
No. 11 *November 20, 1961*

Not much is known about Robert Moncrief (b. Anniston, Ala.). Reportedly, he was a member of the Four Young Men, a group of Alabamans with teen tunes like "You've Been Torturing Me" and "Sweetheart Of Senior High." Between 1961 and 1963, the Four Young Men had some sides issued in rapid succession on Dore, Crest, and Delta. Bobby Edwards revived Tex Ritter's "Jealous Heart" in 1959 on Bluebonnet; the same record was reissued on the Manco label in 1962.

Bobby's "You're The Reason," with the Four Young Men in accompaniment, appeared in the fall of 1961. It was a choppy but melodically appealing country moaner. Cover versions that year by Joe South and HANK LOCKLIN shaved some of the chart momentum off Bobby's biggie, but his version still made the top 10 on the C & W charts. Capitol Records invited the boy over to their stable, and dished up an incredibly derivative follow-up, "What's The Reason" (#71, 1962)—Bob's last pop placement.

Though Edwards continued recording throughout the late '60s, country-music listeners probably last noted his existence in 1963 with "Don't Pretend."

Barbara George

I KNOW (YOU DON'T LOVE ME NO MORE)

(Barbara George)
A.F.O. 302
No. 3 *January 27, 1962*

Barbara (b. Aug. 16, 1942, New Orleans) was 19 when she was discovered by New Orleans recording artist Jessie Hill of "Ooh Poo Pah Doo" (#28, 1960) fame. When Hill spotted her talent, Barbara had only been working the street scene for a few months; her musical background was the Church. At an audition for Harold Battiste, head of A.F.O. (All For One) Records, Barb sang "I Know (You Don't Love Me No More)," a tune she had penned based on "Just A Closer Walk With Thee." Reportedly, Battiste was not too impressed with Ms. George's abilities, nor with the song. But Battiste badly needed material for his new label, so he reluctantly gave the go-ahead to record "I Know." Once it became apparent that George's catchy groove could become a national monster, Juggy Murray at Sue Records picked up the platter's distribution.

An album and only one further single by George appeared on the All For One label. Money, you see, had entered the picture. As Battiste told John Broven in *Rhythm & Blues in New Orleans*, Juggy Murray lured her to the Sue label with a fancy car and new clothes— and although Battiste urged Barbara to resist these temptations, "fatherly advice is no good when you're fighting Cadillacs and money." Barbara signed with Sue Records and cut a few more singles, but nothing sold very well. Shortly after the label switch, George abandoned her singing career to pursue other activities.

In 1980, Barb made a brief comeback attempt with a few 45s issued on the Hep' Me label. She currently resides in Raceland, Louisiana.

Bruce Channel

HEY! BABY

(Bruce Channel, Margaret Cobb)
Smash 1731
No. 1 *March 10, 1962*

Deep into the late '60s, Bruce managed to tour here and abroad on the strength of "Hey! Baby." Flashing a healthy sense of humor, Channel would often open for the Beach Boys or other big-time acts with the wisecrack, "And now, I'd like to do a medley of my hit."

Channel was born in Jacksonville, Texas, on November 28, 1940. Most of his youth was spent in nearby Grapevine, where his parents worked in a tomato-packing warehouse. Bruce's brothers played guitar; his father played the harmonica. A cousin showed him how to form a few guitar chords, and by his 15th year, Channel had his own country band. They played youth centers, local bars, and barns, even working the legendary "Louisiana Hayride" radio show for six months.

"I wrote 'Hey! Baby' about 1959, with a good friend, Margaret Cobb," Channel recalled to Frank McNutty in *We Wanna Boogie*. "I had played the song in the clubs, although at the time [of the recording] I put more of an R & B feel to it. Somehow over the years, the song evolved." Originally taped in Fort Worth as a demo for producer/promoter Major Bill Smith, "Hey! Baby" featured DELBERT McCLINTON on harmonica. Delbert's wailing accompaniment came from his band's local back-up work behind blues artists like Jimmy Reed.

Several more Channel singles charted— "Number One Man" (#52, 1962), "Come On Baby" (#98, 1962), "Going Back To Louisiana" (#89, 1964), and "Mr. Bus Driver" (#90, 1967)—and Bruce did manage to make a good living with his music for a few years. But he never could locate that next big clicker.

Channel did, however, indirectly influence the next generation of rock and rollers when he toured England late in 1962 with McClinton. While Bruce was handling an interview, his harmonica man was backstage at the Castle in New Brighton, near Liverpool. McClinton got to talking with John Lennon, one-quarter of the opening act, the then-little-known Beatles. John was impressed with Delbert's harmonica style, and asked him if he'd show him how he did that "Hey! Baby" solo. A year later, John would play a similar harmonica break on the Fab Four's "Love Me Do."

For the time being, Bruce Channel is off the road. In the late '70s, he worked in Nashville as a staff songwriter with a music publisher.

"It amazes me," Channel remarked to *Goldmine*. "People still come up to me and say, 'I was in Pango-Pango' or wherever 'and heard "Hey! Baby."' And it amazes me that people would hear that record after so long. It's like the song never really died. It just keeps coming back."

Kenny Ball & His Jazzmen
MIDNIGHT IN MOSCOW
(Kenny Ball, Jan Burgers)
Kapp 442
No. 2 *March 17, 1962*

Nineteen sixty-two was the year a batch of non-rock-and-roll instrumentals paraded themselves all over the top 40. Herb Alpert and his Tijuana Brass let loose with their mournful tribute to a "Lonely Bull," a clarinetist named MR. ACKER BILK snoozed us with "Stranger On The Shore"—and Kenny Ball and his band of trad-jazzmen gave us a reworking of a Russian tune originally called "Padmeskoveeye Vietchera."

To radio listeners in the U.S., this Russian number, with a banjo and horns all over it, seemed to come from out of, like, nowhere. In Kenny's merry ole England, jazz was then becoming immensely popular. Fans were split between the modernists, who were attuned to the stateside hard bop and "cool jazz," and the traditionalists, who emulated the sounds of Dixieland and King Oliver. Ball and his boys represented the latter approach. Before British youth fell under the sway of American blues, R & B, and free-form jazz, Ball's tradmen would rack up 14 hit singles on the British pop charts.

Kenneth Daniel Ball was born May 22, 1931, in Ilford, Essex. After working at an advertising agency, and a brief stint as a salesman, Ball decided on a career as a professional musician. Before forming his own unit in late 1958, Kenny blew trumpet and harmonica with bands led by Sid Phillips, Eric Delaney, and Terry Lightfoot. The "King of the Skiffle," Lonnie Donegan, chanced on Ball's band in 1961 and set up an audition for the guys with Pye Records. While their first release, "Teddy Bear's Picnic," stiffed, the band's next 14 records all charted.

For a few years, Britain was a ga-ga about the trad-jazz of Ball and his two main competitors, CHRIS BARBER'S JAZZ BAND and Mr. Acker Bilk. In the U.S., only Ball's fourth single, "Midnight In Moscow," broke the top 40 barrier. Kenny had a way with dressing up nearly any tune in that New Orleans idiom, yet while his instrumental versions of "March Of The Siamese Children" and "The Green Leaves Of Summer" did make the Hot 100, American pop fans were, for the most part, unaccustomed to the sounds of trad-jazz—their attention was focused elsewhere.

New Orleans offered Kenny Ball honorary citizenship in 1963, and in so accepting, Kenny became the first British jazzman so honored. When last noted, Kenny and some configuration of his Jazzmen were still playing on British TV, radio, and in the clubs.

Billy Joe & The Checkmates
PERCOLATOR (TWIST)
(Lou Bideu, Ernie Freeman)
Dore 620
No. 10 *March 17, 1962*

Louis Bideu was born on March 21, 1919, in El Paso, Texas. He attended Santa Barbara State College for four years, then worked nightclubs and TV as a comedian. For a time in 1954, calling himself Lew Bedell, he fronted "The Lew Bedell Show" on WOR in New York. The following year, he entered the music field working for a publisher, Meadowlark Music. In the early '60s, Louis redubbed himself Billy Joe Hunter and hooked up with noted West Coast composer/keyboardist/producer ERNIE FREEMAN. With a roomful of sessioneers, and the help of a xylophone, the pair created a catchy tune that sounded like the rhythmic pulsations of a perking coffee pot.

For the next half-decade, Billy Joe tried to reproduce the appealing innocence of that debut disk. But a string of singles—"Rocky's Theme," "One More Cup," "Nashville West," "Claire de Looney," and "Voyage To The Bottom Of The Sea"—all sold poorly.

Corsairs
SMOKY PLACES
(Abner Spector)
Tuff 1808
No. 12 *March 17, 1962*

The Corsairs were three brothers and a cousin from La Grange, North Carolina, that grew up and attended the same schools together. They were Jay "Bird" (b. July 14, 1942), James "Little Skeet" (b. Dec. 1, 1940), and Mose "King Moe" Uzzell (b. Sept. 13, 1939), plus cousin George Wooten (b. Jan. 16, 1940). They started singing together as members of the school glee club, performing at local gatherings and talent shows. Calling themselves the Gleems, they eventually made tracks to Newark, New

Jersey, to audition for the record companies in and around the New York area.

One night early in 1961, the Gleems were playing in a smoky Newark nightclub. Abner Spector, a producer and big wheel at Tuff Records, was in the audience. Abner liked what he heard, and told the group that he wanted to record them as the Corsairs. The rest, as they say, is history—but very sketchy history.

"Smoky Places," the Corsairs' second release, was a top-of-the-line neo-doo-wop goodie. Quality vocal-group numbers like this one were becoming increasingly scarce on the airwaves. (True, there were groups like the Classics and the Earls, but their days on the radio—and the charts—were numbered.) The Corsairs' follow-up, "I'll Take You Home," hit number 68 in 1962, and the singles kept rolling out: "Dancing Shadows," "On The Spanish Side," and "At The Stroke Of Midnight." But regardless of who was credited on the disk as lead singer—"King Moe," Jay "Bird," or "Little Skeet"—not one of these well-arranged platters charted.

With time, the group's members did some weeding and seeding. Larry McNeil was added in 1965, the last year the group was known to exist. Just what happened to the Corsairs after this point is not known.

Don & Juan

Don & Juan
WHAT'S YOUR NAME
(Claude Johnson)
Big Top 3079
No. 7 *March 17, 1962*

Claude Johnson, Roland Trone, Estelle Williams, and Fred Jones were high school buddies from Brooklyn who got together and cut what should have been a big hit record. In the spring of 1959, they were the Genies, and "Who's That Knocking," a fine number that promised to be their proverbial moment in the sun, inexplicably stalled at the number 71 slot on the Hot 100. Shad Records shed them like a hound with fleas, and subsequent outings for Hollywood Records and Warwick Records were unsuccessful.

Three years later, Claude and Roland were both working as house painters in an apartment building, singing as they slapped paint. A tenant with a refined ear told a friend, agent Peter Paul, about the duo, and once again, it looked like Claude and Roland would have a shot at musical careers. Paul piqued Big Top

Records' interest, and one of the earliest tunes laid out in the recording studio was this number Claude had been developing.

"It was common back then," Claude Johnson told *Chicago Sun-Times* writer Dave Hoekstra, "for everybody to ask 'What's your name?' And there was a girl I used to see in a grocery store that I wanted to meet. Finally, I told her I had seen her all the time and wanted to know, 'What's your name?' The idea just stuck with me."

This time, Roland ("Don") and Claude ("Juan") saw their record rocket into the ozone. "Magic Wand," the follow-up, peaked at number 91 in 1962, and that was it, even though 18 Don & Juan singles were released before the twosome called it quits in 1967.

Roland Trone died in 1982. Claude Johnson, 53, is back on the road again, touring with a new "Don"—Alexander Faison, formerly a member of the Genies.

Sensations
LET ME IN
(Yvonne Baker)
Argo 5405
No. 4   *March 17, 1962*

The Sensations formed as the Cavaliers in Philadelphia in 1954. Lead singer Yvonne Mills and bass Alphonso Howell were half of the initial group. Before success was to be so kind as to let them in, nearly a decade would have to pass. Meanwhile, only months into the group's career, Atco Records sized up the appeal of the Cavaliers' female-lead doo-wop approach, and signed them to a multi-disk contract. Executives at the label considered the three guys and the coy-voiced gal something of a sensation, and changed the unit's name accordingly. Of the Sensations' many releases, "Yes Sir, That's My Baby" and "Please Mr. Disk Jockey" nearly caught a national audience. But after three years of Atco releases, Yvonne Mills settled down to being Mrs. Yvonne Baker, housewife and mother, and the Sensations disbanded.

Doo-wop started making an amazing resurgence in 1961; ethereal harmonies were popping up everywhere. Pointing to the success of groups like the Edsels, the Stereos, and the Marcels, Alphonso Howell urged Yvonne to join him in re-forming the Sensations. She acquiesced, and Alphonso picked Kae Williams, a local DJ, to manage and record

the new group. Filling out the ranks were baritone Sam Armstrong, a one-time voice with THE RAYS, and tenor Richard Curtain, an original member of the Hide-a-ways.

The Sensations' initial effort was the uptempo "Music, Music, Music" (#54, 1961). With "Let Me In" and its contagious, nonsensical hook—"We-oop, we-oop, ooo-we-oop-we-ooo"—the group struck gold. "That's My Desire," credited to Yvonne Baker & The Sensations, charted (#69, 1962), but later releases did not. The group's moment of glory had come and gone (although Bonnie Raitt did include a cover version of "Let Me In" on her 1973 album *Takin' My Time*).

Various gatherings of Sensations continued on, recording for Junior and later Tollie Records. Yvonne Baker attempted a solo career.

Ketty Lester
LOVE LETTERS
(Edward Heyman, Victor Young)
Ers 3068
No. 5   *April 14, 1962*

Ketty was born Revoyda Frierson, on August 16, 1934, in Hope, Arkansas. Papa was a poor farmer, and Ketty was one of 15 siblings. After winning a scholarship, she moved to California to attend San Francisco City College as a nursing major. She sang in church and in the school choir, acting on the side in summer-stock productions. While performing at the Purple Onion, Ketty met country singer/comedienne Dorothy Shay. Dorothy, "The Park Avenue Hillbilly," had made the country charts in 1951 with "Feudin' and Fightin'," and helped make some record-business connections for Lester.

Four Preps alumnus (and later STANDELLS producer) Ed Cobb and Lincoln Mayorga were eager to record Ketty. Cobb tracked down just the right tune for her—"I'm A Fool To Want You"—and someone dug up Dick Haynes' 1945 hit, "Love Letters," for a flip side. "We recorded in a room over a garage," Ketty recalled to *DISCoveries'* Jon E. Johnson. "The piano, bass, drums, and guitar were all we had space for in the main room, and I had a little . . . well, it was like a toilet. I was forced to sing it in the toilet."

"I'm A Fool To Want You" b/w the sensuous-sounding "Love Letters" was released by Era Records. Once "Love Letters" proved to be a hit, an LP (*Ketty Lester*, 1962) was shipped by the independent, as were a pair of charting follow-ups, "You Can't Lie To A Liar" (#90, 1962) and "This Land Is Your Land" (#97, 1962). RCA released a few LPs and a number of singles, but nothing further attracted much of an audience. Elvis covered "Love Letters" in 1966, and took it to number 19. Before a momentary retirement to care for her son and her husband (who had suffered two heart attacks), Ketty cut some unsuccessful disks for the Tower and Pete labels.

Ketty had continued acting after college. In 1963, she even won an Off-Broadway Theatre Award for her role in the revival of *A Cabin in the Sky*. The producers of the TV show "Julia" noticed Ketty in an L.A. production of *A Raisin in the Sun* and offered her the lead role in the series that eventually starred Diahann Carroll. Numerous TV appearances on episodes of "The FBI," "Laugh-In," "Love American Style," "Marcus Welby, M.D.," and "Sanford and Son" followed. She co-starred in films like *Blacula* (1972), *The Terminal Man* (1974), and *The Prisoner of Second Avenue* (1975); was a cast member on the soaps "Days of Our Lives" and "Rituals"; and was a regular for four years on "Little House on the Prairie."

Mega Records approached Ketty about returning to the recording studio in 1985. "[They] actually wanted me to sing pop, but I said I wanted to make an album of Christian music. With the experiences that I've had . . . it could have only been the will of God that I have been able to help my husband the way I have. So when [Mega] asked me if I would record again, I told [them] no, unless I could do at least the first one for Jesus." The label agreed and issued *I Saw Him* in 1985.

Larry Finnegan

DEAR ONE
(Larry Finnegan, Vincent Finnegan)
Old Town 1113
No. 11 *April 21, 1962*

Johnny Lawrence Finneran was born in 1939 in New York City. With his brother Vinnie he studied and played guitar, piano, and drums, then made several radio and TV appearances. At Notre Dame College, he played a few dances, wrote songs, and listened to Del Shannon records.

In 1961, instead of cracking the books in his senior year at Notre Dame, John worked with Vinnie on a song derived from the familiar "Dear John letter" format. Once all the words

had fallen into place and the melody felt just right, John recorded a demo, and walked the track into the offices of Hy Weiss' Old Town Records. Weiss waited not, and signed the boy on the spot. "Dear One" was issued in November 1961, with John's last name altered to "Finnegan." The response was incredible, as the up-tempo and country-flavored tune worked its way up the nation's pop charts.

Finnegan's follow-up flopped, as did a fine country number produced by Billy Mure called "Pick Up The Pieces." In 1964, John returned to the tried and true with "Dear One, Part Two": in the sequel, our hero gets the unfaithful hussy back. No one seemed to care, or even notice. Even Finnegan's tribute to Ringo Starr called "The Other Ringo" (based structurally on LORNE GREENE's "Ringo") failed to stir more than a few grains of interest.

In 1966, Finnegan moved to Stockholm to set up his own independent record label, Svensk-American.

Jack Ross

CINDERELLA
(J. Ross, E. Nemeth)
Dot 16333
No. 16 *April 28, 1962*

Nearly a year before Herb Alpert recorded "The Lonely Bull" and got hip to the commercial potential of Americanizing sounds from south of the border, Jack Ross cut and released "Happy Jose (Ching Ching)" (#57, 1962). Dot Records picked up the novelty instrumental for national distribution from the small Ramal label, and Jack almost had a top 40 hit on his hands.

"Cinderella," the follow-up to "Happy Jose," was an entirely different affair—a comedy record. Ross, in this case, played a beatnik storyteller; in his hands, the familiar fairy tale was transformed into a jive-talkin', pig-Latin string of titillating innuendos. Both disks were produced by Norman Malkin. The husband of MARGIE RAYBURN and founder of THE SUNNYSIDERS, Malkin wrote most of the selections for Ross' few recordings. Dot issued Ross' solitary album later in 1962.

Jack Ross (b. 1917) had been a trumpeter and orchestra leader throughout the big band era; he performed for 15 years at the Mark Hopkins Hotel in San Francisco, and later, at the Sahara Tahoe. Jack Ross died on December 16, 1982.

Ernie Maresca

SHOUT! SHOUT!
(KNOCK YOURSELF OUT)
(Ernie Maresca, Thomas F. Bogdany)
Seville 117
No. 6 *May 19, 1962*

Ernie Maresca wrote or co-wrote God knows how many hits. He gave "Runaround Sue," "The Wanderer," "Lovers Who Wonder," and "Donna The Prima Donna" to Dion; "No One Knows," "A Lover's Prayer," and "Come On Little Angel" to the Belmonts; "Runaround" to the Regents; "Whenever A Teenager Cries" to Reparata & The Delrons; "Hey Jean, Hey Dean" to Dean & Jean; "Child Of Clay" to Jimmie Rodgers; and piles of other enjoyables to the Del-Satins, the Five Discs, and Nino & The Ebbtides.

"I'm originally from the Bronx," Maresca told *Goldmine*'s Wayne Jones. "Dion lived on the next block. The Regents lived up the street. My block was Garden Street and 182nd Street. I grew up with guys like Guy Vallari of the Regents, so we used to all sing and start groups. I had cut a demo record on 'No One Knows' . . . Dion heard the demo and liked it, so he brought it down to Gene Schwartz at Laurie Records. That's how I got into it. That became the next record [for Dion & The Belmonts] after their 'I Wonder Why.'"

Ernie's chance to step out front and do his own thing happened as a direct result of the phenomenal success of "Runaround Sue," which Maresca co-wrote with Dion. Ernie admitted to *Goldmine* that he never liked the song, and never thought it would be a smash.

"In all honesty, we wrote 'Runaround Sue' around [Gary U.S. Bonds'] 'A Quarter To Three,' which was a big hit then. Laurie, at the time, was handling the distribution of the record. It's incredible: 'Sue' was more like a riff song, you know, with 'hep hep, bum de diddle it' . . . and it's not really a story."

Ernie wrote "Shout! Shout!" with a friend named Tom Bedagny. "I went around trying to get people to hear ["Shout! Shout!"] because I wasn't working exclusively for Laurie at the time. I took it to Seville, which was just a tiny outfit . . . they had me re-record it."

It takes not a critic's ear to hear echoes of "Runaround Sue" or "Quarter To Three" in Maresca's "Shout! Shout!" Released on Seville and distributed by London Records, the disk sold well and went top 10. Follow-ups were something else altogether. "Mary Jane (You're A Pain In The Brain)" bombed, as did successive disks issued under names like Artie Chicago, the Desires, Foreign Intrigue, and the Hubcaps.

Ernie Maresca is still active with Robert Schwartz and the rest of the staff at Laurie Records, packaging seemingly endless compilations of that golden stuff from long ago.

Mr. Acker Bilk

STRANGER ON THE SHORE
(Acker Bilk)
Atco 6217
No. 1 *May 26, 1962*

Mother was a church organist; Father was a Methodist preacher. And son Bernard Stanley Bilk (b. Jan. 28, 1929, Somerset, Avon, England) was serving three months in a brig in Egypt for sleeping on guard duty when he first discovered his love for the clarinet. "Acker" (slang for "buddy" or "mate") was just 18 then, and started playing to while away the sweltering evenings. After his army discharge, Bilk labored in a tobacco factory in Bristol, then worked as a builder's laborer and a blacksmith. The job was tough and dirty; a musician's life, he soon realized, might be a mite less demanding.

After a stay with Ken Colyer's jazz band, Acker formed his own Paramount Jazz Band in 1958. Two years later, Denis Preston, an independent producer, spotted Bilk, his ever-present bowler hat, and that trad-jazz band of his. Prior to his monster moment, Bilk and the band almost connected with their quiet, bluesy number, "Summer Set." Two years and a few more near-hits later, "Stranger On The Shore" appeared.

"Stranger" was a tame instrumental, not a rock and roll record, and its staggering chart success took everyone in popdom by surprise. "Stranger" remained on the British listings for a whopping 55 weeks, eventually selling 4,000,000 copies. Acker also had the distinction of preceding the Beatles and the British Invasion acts as the first British artist to ever hit number one on *Billboard*'s pop charts.

Acker Bilk remains an active musician. In addition to touring extensively, he has appeared in two Royal Command Performances (1978 and 1981) and fronts his own British radio program, "Acker's 'Alf 'Our," on BBC's Radio 2.

Ronnie & The Hi-Lites

I WISH THAT WE WERE MARRIED
(Marian Weiss)
Joy 260
No. 16   *May 26, 1962*

In the early '60s, Stanley Brown (baritone), Sonny Caldwell (first tenor), Kenny Overby (bass), and John Witney (second tenor) were the Cascades, a Jersey City street-corner group in need of a lead singer. Their frontman had just been drafted, and without a replacement, the Cascades were sure to wash away. Witney, the group's organizer, happened to hear Ronnie Goodson singing in a class play at his school, P.S. 14. Before the day was out, Witney convinced the 12-year-old's parents to let Ronnie try out for their vocal group. Ronnie quickly fit in with the sounds the Cascades were making.

Mike Amato, the Duprees' original lead singer, told Witney about Hal and Marian Weiss, some music buffs who might be able to help the group make its mark. Marian had written some songs that publishers and record companies had turned aside, and was sure that she could tailor-make something hot for the Cascades. "I Wish That We Were Married" was her first offering, and it was a doozy.

A demo of the Cascades doing "I Wish That We Were Married" was taped and shopped around to various labels. ABC-Paramount Records passed on it, and so did Atlantic, but the ears over at Joy Records heard something in the demo, and quickly struck up a deal with the Weisses, Ronnie, and the group, now re-dubbed the Hi-Lites.

"I Wish That We Were Married" tore up the charts. Ronnie & The Hi-Lites hit the ceiling of pop success with appearances on "American Bandstand," shows at the Apollo Theatre, and tours with the Crystals and the Ronettes. Ronnie was even Little Eva's boyfriend for a time!

The Sixties

Ronnie & The Hi-Lites

The Sixties

Not all stories of riches and fame end sadly or rapidly, but this particular one does. Weiss, in an interview with *Harmony Tymes* writer Joe T. Sicurella, complained that Joy Records issued the wrong follow-up single: instead of "Send My Love," the label should have released the group's "natural" follow-up, something utilizing that marriage theme (namely, "What A Pretty Bride You'll Make"). The latter platter has yet to be released, while "Send My Love" stiffed.

A lawsuit between the Hi-Lites and Joy Records developed over a dispute as to just how many copies of "I Wish" were pressed. The Weisses set up their own label, Win Records, and issued several more Ronnie & The Hi-Lites singles—but nothing the group ever again recorded charted on the Hot 100.

One by one, the guys graduated from high school, separated, and sought out other careers. Sonny Caldwell became a computer programmer. John Witney is now a diesel mechanic. Ronnie Goodson died in his sleep on November 4, 1980.

Joe Henderson

SNAP YOUR FINGERS
(Grady Martin, Alex Zanetis)
Todd 1072
No. 8 *July 7, 1962*

Joe Henderson (not to be confused with the jazz saxophonist of the same name) was born in Como, Mississippi, around 1938. Shortly after, he and his family moved to Gary, Indiana, where Joe remained until he went off on his own to Nashville in 1958. Henderson's roots were in the Baptist Church, and over the next few years he performed with various gospel groups like the Fairfield Four.

In the early '60s, Henderson came to the attention of the disk dealers at Todd Records. Some initial waxings, such as the silky-smooth "Baby Don't Leave Me," sounded fine to those ears that managed a listen, but all of Joe's Todd sides failed to click—until "Snap Your Fingers."

"Snap Your Fingers", a catchy, hook-laden number with an uncanny Brook Benton sound, became Henderson's lone chart-shaker. A now-collectible album was released, and for the next two years, the Todd label issued a little pile of soulful sides. "Big Love" (#74, 1962), "The Search Is Over" (#94, 1962), and others were slick yet sincerely soulful. Apparently, these

disks also sounded a little too much like the then-popular and well-established Brook Benton.

In 1964, the prestigious Kapp label, then Ric Records, gave Henderson a try at the charts, but he fared no better with these outings. Joe Henderson passed away in a Nashville hotel in 1966 at the age of 36.

Emilio Pericoli

AL DI LA
(Guilio Rapetti, Carlo Donida)
Warner Bros. 5259
No. 6 *July 7, 1962*

When first sung by Betty Curtis, "Al Di La" became the 1961 winner of Italy's San Remo Song Festival. Over the next few years, more than 50 different run-throughs of the catchy tune would be recorded. Connie Francis (#90, 1963) and the Ray Charles Singers (#29, 1964) would both chart in the States with their renditions, but it was Emilio Pericoli's virile version that sold more than a million copies.

Pericoli was born in Cesenatico, Italy, in 1928. As a young man, Emilio trained to be an accountant. While at school, though, his appearances in local plays led others to encourage Emilio to study singing and acting. Although it was not until 1960 that he made his professional singing debut, Emilio had by that time secured some guest spots on Italian TV.

Fleeting international fame came when Pericoli was approached to croon "Al Di La" in *Rome Adventure* (1962), a Troy Donahue/Suzanne Pleshette flick. Emilio continued to crank out the corn, but never again was he to have his way with American hearts and charts.

Claude King

WOLVERTON MOUNTAIN
(Merle Kilgore, Claude King)
Columbia 42352
No. 6 *July 21, 1962*

Claude is known to rural and urban folk alike for his tall tale of a dude's determination to possess a gal with "lips sweeter than honey" whom he's never met. Clifton Clowers, a mean mountain man "mighty handy with the gun and knife," has his daughter in storage on Wolverton Mountain, and there ain't no one gonna get her. The outcome of Claude and Clifton's confrontation is not revealed in the song's lyrics. "Wolverton Mountain" did typecast Claude as a "saga singer," but for the brief time that sagas were selling, King was the monarch of the mound.

Claude was born on February 5, 1933 in Shreveport, Louisiana. Before school bells were ringing for little Claude, his family moved to a farm in the wilds of Louisiana. When 12, he bought his first guitar for 50 cents from a neighbor. He picked at the thing, but it was sports that was young Claude's passion. He attended the University of Idaho on a baseball scholarship, but unfortunately, an arm injury snuffed his baseball dreams.

Upon his return to Shreveport, Claude turned to pickin' and singin' at local watering holes and on radio shows. Appearances on the "Louisiana Hayride" radio program led to unsuccessful recordings for the Gotham, Specialty, Dee Jay, and Pacemaker labels. At the behest of country star Johnny Horton, Columbia Records offered Claude a contract, and with his first release, "Big River, Big Man" (#82, 1961), King won a position on both the pop and country charts. The follow-up, "The Comancheros" (#71, 1961), did likewise. But with "Wolverton Mountain," a tune co-written with Merle Kilgore about a real man and real place in Arkansas, Claude King hit paydirt.

Pop-wise, Claude only had one more story-song in him—"The Burning Of Atlanta" (#53, 1962)—and his reign on the C & W charts throughout the '60s had its downs and ups, but mostly the latter. During the '70s, though, his career began to stall. After six albums and a healthy run of C & W chartings, Claude and Columbia parted company.

Claude King continues singing to this day of Clifton Clowers, and occasionally records country tunes. He has also turned up in obscure flicks like *Swamp Girl* and *Year of the Wahoo*.

Joanie Sommers

JOHNNY GET ANGRY
(Hal David, Sherman Edwards)
Warner Bros. 5275
No. 7 *July 21, 1962*

One of Ms. Sommers' LPs called her "The Voice of the Sixties." An overstatement, yes; but Joanie was the "Pepsi Girl," singing "Now it's Pepsi for those who think young" and

"Come alive! You're in the Pepsi Generation." As *Goldmine*'s Frank Wright observed, she also sang, on "One Boy" (#54, 1960): "One boy to laugh with, to joke with/Have a *Coke* with . . ."

Born on February 24, 1941, in Buffalo, New York, Joanie moved with her parents to Southern California in 1954. Soon after, she began singing with her high school dance band and later, with groups at the Santa Monica City College. Talent scouts for the newly-formed Warner Bros. label spotted her and signed her to a contract in 1959. Her first assignment was to replace CONNIE STEVENS singing opposite "77 Sunset Strip" celebrity EDD BYRNES. She appeared on a couple of "77 Sunset Strip" episodes, and added a breathy break to "I Dig You Kookie" on Edd's 1959 debut LP, *Kookie* (her name was misspelled on the record label as "Jeanie Sommers").

After "One Boy" (#54, 1960) and a number of non-charters, Joanie scored with "Johnny Get Angry." Who can ever forget those classic lines: "Johnny get angry/Johnny get mad/Gave me the biggest lecture I ever had/I want a brave man/I want a caveman"? They don't make 'em like that anymore, and though Joanie tried hard with 45s like "Where The Boys Get Together," "Bobby's Hobbies," "Little Girl Bad," and "Big Man," she never managed to top her earlier record.

Joanie played opposite teen idol Rick Nelson in ABC-TV's "Stage 67" production of *On the*

Flip Side, then retired to turn her attention to raising a family. Nevertheless, oddball 45s like "Trains And Boats And Planes" (1967), "Tell Him" (1968), "The Great Divide" (1968), and "Peppermint Choo Choo" (1977) were sighted well into the '70s.

Her career is not yet buzzin', but Joanie Sommers has since returned to the entertainment biz.

Don Gardner & Dee Dee Ford

I NEED YOUR LOVING
(Don Gardner, Bobby Robinson)
Fire 508
No. 20   *July 28, 1962*

Donald Gardner was born and raised in Philadelphia. In 1952, with his school days behind him, Don and some neighborhood souls formed the Sonotones and cut some now-collectible disks for the Gotham and Bruce labels; sales, however, were zip. The Sonotones broke up, and for the next few years, Don and a quartet of musicians worked the Philly bars. Gardner had some solo sides issued on Bruce, Deluxe, Kaiser, and Val-ue.

During the '60s, the definition of a "commercial" R & B sound began to shift. Musical forms like the blues and doo-wop were fading in popularity; Ike & Tina Turner's hot and sweaty sound was selling a lot of records. In 1961, a keyboardist named Dee Dee Ford met Gardner, and together they taped a gutsy duet of "Glory Of Love" for New York's KC Records. (The label sat on the sides until the duo's "I Need Your Loving" took off and stimulated the need for more gospel-influenced shouters.) For a handful of months—starting with "I Need Your Loving"—Don and Dee Dee had their sassy screams and screeches featured on AM radio. White boys and girls jumped all about. "Glory Of Love" (#75, 1962) charted later in the year, as did Don and Dee Dee's official follow-up to "I Need Your Loving," "Don't You Worry" (#66).

Internal discord was not apparent—if the two were fussin', no one seemed to notice. By year's end, however, Don and Dee Dee separated. Before an unsuccessful one-off reunion in 1966, they each issued a few solo singles. Don did resurface briefly in 1973 on the R & B charts with a tune called "Forever," a duet with Jeanette "Baby" Washington.

Barbara Lynn

YOU'RE GONNA LOSE A GOOD THING
(Barbara Lynn Ozen)
Jamie 1220
No. 8   *August 11, 1962*

Huey Meaux, legendary record man, has been deeply involved in shaping the careers of swamp-pop artists like Joe Barry, Freddie Fender, Roy Head, Jivin' Gene, the Sir Douglas Quintet . . . and Barbara Lynn.

Fresh out of the Army, Huey worked as a DJ—he'd mix a little 7-Up and bourbon, say whatever, and play Cajun music, or dang near anything else. He had some difficulties keeping the job, and his brother talked him into attending barber school. Huey opened a barber shop in Winnie, Texas, but continued to dabble in pop music.

"I got a tape from a guy in Beaumont," Meaux recalled to *Goldmine*'s Colin Escott. "It had been recorded over. This guy wanted to sell me an act by the name of T-Baby Green. In between the T-Baby cuts was this girl they had recorded over. It was knocking me o-u-t. It was reaching at the roots of my heart. I just wanted to meet that voice. I had a guy named Big Sambo recording for me. I played him the tape and said, 'Who's this?' He said, 'That's Barbara Lynn. If you want her, I'll get her.'

"So I keep cutting hair, and he came back around 6:30 with Barbara Lynn. She was about 15 or 16 [19, actually], I guess, and she limped a little because she had one leg longer than the other. I said, 'Barbara, if you'll pay the expenses for you and your mother, I'll meet you in New Orleans at Cosimo's studio. I'll pay for the musicians and the tape.' She went for it, and we recorded 'You'll Lose A Good Thing.'"

Goldmine's Almost Slim has reported a different version of these events. It seems that a late-night DJ named "Bon Ton" Garlow had a home studio for neighborhood kids to jam in. One of these participating youngsters was a left-handed guitar player named Barbara Lynn Ozen (b. Jan. 16, 1942, Beaumont, Tex). As Garlow told Hannush: "I made a tape of her and took it to Huey Meaux. Huey listened to the tape and said, 'She's coming along, but I don't think she's strong enough yet' . . . The next time she was playing, I convinced Huey to come out and watch her lead a band. I picked Huey up and carried him to the Ten Acre Club outside of Beaumont. That's when he decided to sign Barbara Lynn."

Take your choice. Either way, Meaux recorded Lynn's "You're Gonna Lose A Good Thing," which Barbara had originally written as a simple poem when she was jilted at sweet 16. Six months after the session, studio boss Cosimo Matassa placed the disk with Harry Finfer's Philly-based Jamie label. While Barbara did have further local success, and did manage to chart with a steady stream of treats well into the '70s, the bluesy "Good Thing" would be her only top 40 entry.

Claudine Clark

PARTY LIGHTS
(Claudine Clark)
Chancellor 1113
No. 5 *September 1, 1962*

Born to a non-musical family in Macon, Georgia, on April 26, 1941, little Claudine, from early on, took a liking to producing musical sounds. Her parents encouraged her, giving her guitar and organ lessons. After completing high school, she won a musical scholarship to Coombs College in Philadelphia, where she eventually received a B.S. degree in Music Composition.

While out on the dusty trail attempting to sell her wares, Claudine sang on a television program in Wilmington, Delaware. The TV spot was seen by Herald Records executive Al Silver, who offered Claudine the opportunity to record a couple of her tunes. "Angel Of Happiness" bombed, as did her second effort for the Gotham label. Bob Marcucci's Philadelphia-based Chancellor label gave the lass her third crack at bat with "Disappointed" b/w "Party Lights."

"Disappointed," the intended "A" side, was a Marcucci-Faith composition with a plush Jerry Ragavoy arrangement; it sounded almost like Carla Thomas doing Brenda Lee's "I'm Sorry." But "Disappointed" didn't have a hit feel to it, so some DJ flipped the record to find this spontaneous, teen-alienation radiator, "Party Lights." Never again would Claudine implore and grovel like she did in this raunchy rocker. "I wanna, I wanna, I wanna," Clark moans, but "Momma just won't let me make the scene." Meanwhile, through her window, Claudine can see her friends next door partying it up, twistin', mashin', doin' the bop, and lawd knows what else.

The follow-up to "Party Lights" was a distasteful ditty called "Walkin' Through The Cemetery," complete with Claudine making creature sounds during the instrumental break. Months later, the powers that be decided to return Clark to her successful party theme. This time, in "Walk Me Home From The Party," Mama *does* let the poor girl go to that party and, of course, Claudine *does* find the right guy.

Sales were poor on both of these disks, so Clark next appeared on Swan Records under the billing "Joy Dawn"; her lone single under that monicker quickly sank from sight. Two records each were issued on the TCF and Jamie labels, but not many ears ever got to hear these, and Clark disappeared from public view. According to some reports, Claudine was off in the wilds writing a rock and roll operetta, or poetry, or plays.

When last heard from, Claudine Clark was in disguise as Sherry Pye. Her only release for Match Records: "Gimme A Break."

Springfields

SILVER THREADS AND
GOLDEN NEEDLES
(Dick Reynolds, Jack Rhodes)
Philips 40038
No. 20 *September 22, 1962*

Mary (b. April 16, 1939) and Dion (b. July 2, 1934) O'Brien—a.k.a. Dusty and Tom Springfield—grew up in Hampstead, London, singing with their parents in a rec room equipped with microphones and amplifiers. Dion worked as a bank teller, a stockbroker, and an interpreter for the military. Mary, educated in British convents in High Wycombe and Ealing, worked as a clerk in a record store, a salesgirl in a department store, and even took jobs selling dustbins and toy trains. In the late '50s, Dion started folksinging with an ex-wine tester and adman named Tim Feild. Dusty, as Mary now called herself, was soon invited to join Dion and Tim in a Peter, Paul & Mary–type group.

The trio's name surfaced while they were practicing one warm *spring* day in an open *field*. In 1961, the Springfields auditioned for Philips Records and secured a recording contract. Nearly a half-dozen of their singles rambled over the British charts before the Beatles even set foot in the States.

"Silver Threads And Golden Needles" was an updated and electrified rendition of an early Wanda Jackson country hit. But before it

The
Sixties

peaked on the U.S. charts, Feild had left and was replaced by Mike Hurst. The group's initial stateside LP, 1962's *Silver Threads and Golden Needles*, sold well, and their follow-up single, "Dear Hearts And Gentle People," hit number 95 the same year. British mags like *Melody Maker* and *New Music Express* rated them the country's number-one vocal group for 1961 and 1962. Despite all the attention, the Springfields splintered in September 1963, after a performance at the London Palladium.

Mike Hurst went on to manage a folk club, work as a DJ, and produce some recordings, most notably Cat Stevens' early sides for the Deram label. Tom Springfield has been working as an arranger, has made some orchestral recordings, and wrote several hits for the Seekers. Dusty, the most successful ex-Springfield, launched her solo career in the fall of 1963. "I Only Want To Be With You" (#12,

1964), was the first in a best-selling line of ultra-fine lusties—"Wishin' And Hopin'" (#6, 1964), "You Don't Have To Say You Love Me" (#4, 1966), "The Look Of Love" (#22, 1967), and onward through the '60s.

Dusty's singles stopped charting in 1970, and she kept a low profile throughout the '70s. However, she was recently back in the public eye collaborating with the Pet Shop Boys on their 1988 single "What Have I Done To Deserve This?"

Bent Fabric
ALLEY CAT
(Jack Harlen, Frank Bjorn)
Atco 6226
No. 7 *September 29, 1962*

The Springfields

Nineteen sixty-two was a goofy year. Two girls in Indiana standing two feet apart set some obscure record by tossing an ice cube back and forth 4,477 times before it melted. Some character baked up a 25,000-pound cake for the Seattle Fair. And a batch of instrumentals pervaded the airwaves of top 40 stations. KENNY BALL and his band of jazzmen gave us "Midnight In Moscow." A trumpeter named Herb Alpert scored his first of a string of hits, a tune about a "Lonely Bull." A clarinetist named MR. ACKER BILK presented us with "Stranger On The Shore." And a Danish piano man named Bent Fabricius-Bjerre picked out a memorable melody called "Alley Cat."

Bent was born in Copenhagen on December 7, 1924, to a mom and dad who apparently knew just how to raise a multi-talented lad. In the wink of an eye, Bent was a musician and a teenage bandleader. Under his direction, Bent's boys made some of what are claimed to be Denmark's first jazz recordings. In 1950, Bjerre became head of Metronome Records. He played a mean piano, and for a while was the host of the Saturday-night Danish TV program "Around a Piano." In addition to working as A & R man for Metronome, he composed tunes under the pseudonym "Frank Bjorn."

"Alley Cat," a Bent creation, was a very innocent-sounding number. Its catchy melody moved over a lethargic bass pattern and faint percussion—the type of arrangement Bent would use on most of his stateside records. His *Alley Cat* album made *Billboard*'s top pop albums chart; strangely enough, the title track won a Grammy for "Best Rock and Roll Record" in 1962. Only one other Bent Fabric single, an instrumental entitled "Chicken Feed" (#63, 1963), appeared on the Hot 100.

Frank Ifield

I REMEMBER YOU
(Johnny Mercer, Victor Schertzinger)
Vee-Jay 457
No. 5 *October 13, 1962*

"When I was 13, I worked with a fantastic old fellow called Big Chief Little Wolf, who taught me all the intricacies of show business in the old-fashioned manner," Ifield told Sheila Tracy, author of *Who's Who in Popular Music in Great Britain*. Frank (b. Nov. 30, 1937, Coventry, England) was a "spruker," a "roll over roll over," or what we in the Far West might call a "come-on man." His earliest of jobs, in other

Frank Ifield

words, was to get people to lay their money down for traveling tent shows and circuses.

Frank's dad was an inventor and design engineer, and although the family was originally from England, most of Frank's youth was spent in Australia. It was in Sydney that he made his debut as a singer in 1950 at the Hornsby Pacific Theatre. Within a year, Frankie was making TV appearances and had recorded his first single, "Did You See My Daddy Over There?" More than 40 other disks were to follow over the next half-decade or so. By the end of his teen years, Frank Ifield was reported to be the hottest vocal item in Tasmania, New Zealand, and Australia.

Seeking to broaden his realm of influence, Ifield moved back to England in 1959, where under the tutelage of Norrie Paramor, he was quickly signed to Columbia Records. His countrified cover version of Carl Dobkins, Jr.'s "Lucky Devil" established him in 1960. For the next six years, Frank could do little wrong: 15 singles charted in England. Three of these 45s—"I Remember You," "Lovesick Blues," and "The Wayward Wind"—topped the British listings; according to *New Music Express*, this was a first in British pop history. The only one of the trilogy to click in the States was "I Remember You," a remake of the Jimmy Dorsey hit from the Dorothy Lamour/Helen O'Connell flick *The Fleet Is In* (1942). Before being mothballed, Ifield's disk became the first record to sell a million copies in the U.K. alone.

Frank's stateside impact vanished as rapidly as the changing of the seasons. Although he did manage to place three other singles on the Hot 100 and four more on the C & W charts, not one could re-spark the nation's interest. Meanwhile, Ifield toured the remainder of the world, playing concerts and cabarets.

Frank is still very much a viable voice in England, where he was voted the "Best British Male Vocalist of the Year" for both 1981 and 1982 at the International Country Music Awards at Wembley.

Contours

DO YOU LOVE ME
(Berry Gordy, Jr.)
Gordy 7005
No. 3 *October 20, 1962*

Dirty Dancing, the silver-screen sensation of 1988, returned the Contours' name and "Do You Love Me" to the nation's top 10. It had been

years and years since the group's last biggie, but in their prime—from 1962 to 1967—the Contours racked up a series of well-tooled Motown hits.

The original group took shape in Detroit during the late '50s. Joe Billingslea (b. Nov. 14, 1937, Hamtramck, Mich.) and Billy Gordon, the Contours' lead singer, recorded as the Majestics for the Contour label ("Hard Times" b/w "Teenage Gossip"). Hubert Johnson, Billy Hogg, and Sylvester Potts jumped in, and the Majestics became the Contours. In 1960, with the help of Jackie Wilson—Hubert's cousin— the guys secured a recording contract with Motown.

After three singles for Motown, Berry moved the fivesome over to his new Gordy label. "Do You Love Me" was the first smash for Gordy, and the Contours' *Do You Love Me* LP was the first album ever released by the label. Yet ironically, "Do You Love Me" was not even originally intended for the group.

"We were in rehearsing a song [with new Contour Hugh Davis], 'It Must Be Love,'" Potts recalled in an exclusive interview. "Berry was standing at the bottom of the stairs just watchin' us go through this song, and he interrupts us and says, 'Hey, I got a tune that I was supposed to do on the Temptations, but they're late, so I'm gonna try it on you guys.' It was 'Do You Love Me.'"

Every record released thereafter save one ("You Get Ugly," 1963) made either *Billboard's* pop or R & B charts: "Don't Let Her Be Your Baby" (#64, 1963), "Can You Do It" (#41, 1964), "Can You Jerk Like Me" (#47, 1965), "First I Look At The Purse" (#57, 1965), "Just A Little Misunderstanding" (#85, 1966), and "It's So Hard Being A Loser" (#79, 1967). According to Potts, there are 25 or 30 more tracks in the can; some of them were released in England only, where a second Contours LP was issued.

Lead vocalist Gordon was the first to leave, due to drug problems. In 1964, Billingslea, Johnson, and Potts left, though Potts later returned. Filling in were such new Contours as Council Gaye, Jerry Green, former FALCONS member Joe Stubbs (brother to the Four Tops' Levi Stubbs), and Dennis Edwards. The group officially disbanded in 1967 as their final hit, "It's So Hard Being A Loser" (#79), dropped off the charts. Edwards joined the Temptations as a replacement for David Ruffin.

In 1970, Billingslea and Potts revived the group name, and both have been with touring versions of the act ever since.

Billy Hoggs is now a minister; Hugh Davis is

reportedly working as a songwriter. Hubert Johnson died by his own hand on July 11, 1981.

Mike Clifford

CLOSE TO CATHY
(Bob Goodman, Earl Shuman)
United Artists 489
No. 12   *November 3, 1962*

Not too much is known about Mike Clifford. According to company bios, Mike (b. Nov. 6, 1943, Los Angeles) came from a musical family. By the age of 16, he was greased up, suited, and crooning in nightclubs. Helen Noga, Johnny Mathis' manager, happened to hear Mike's singing and decided to manage him; she also introduced him to Mathis' label, Columbia. Mike's first few singles for Columbia were not bad; the Paul Anka-supervised "Uh Huh" actually had raw and youthful energy. His odes to girls like "Cathy" and "Joanna," though, were rather puffy, and not nearly as appealing to die-hard rock and rollers.

While "What To Do With Laurie" (#68, 1963) and "One Boy Too Late" (#96, 1963) did chart, the road got rougher for Mike. He made more records for Cameo, Sidewalk, America International, and Air Records. In the '70s, Mike played the role of Teen Angel in the Broadway production of *Grease*.

Kris Jensen

TORTURE
(John D. Loudermilk)
Hickory 1173
No. 20   *November 3, 1962*

Kris Jensen was on his way to perform on Buddy Dean's TV program in Baltimore. He had what he felt was the hottest record of his career in his hands—"Big As I Can Dream," a song penned by Bob Montgomery, one-time singing and recording partner of Buddy Holly. "En route to the TV studio, we heard a bulletin on the radio that President Kennedy was shot in Dallas," Jenson told *Goldmine*. "By the time we got to the station, the Buddy Dean show was cancelled for the day in order to cover the assassination. That was the last anyone heard of the record."

Kris was born Peter Jensen on April 4, 1942, in New Haven. As a little shaver, Pete was wild about the singing cowboys, Gene Autry and Roy Rogers. At age 16, he met Denise Norwood, a songwriter who had made good a couple of years earlier with JOE VALINO's rendition of her tune, "The Garden Of Eden." For three years, they worked together, with Jensen recording Norwood's compositions in her home studio. Colpix Records released his "Bonnie Baby" in 1959, and Leader, then Kapp, issued a few singles each—but nothing much happened.

When Nashville music publisher Wesley Rose heard a demo album that Norwood was shopping around to various labels, he hooked Kris up with Hickory Records. Kris' first release on Hickory, "Torture," was a smash. The hypnotic tune had a slow, humping rhythm and a pleading Presleyesque vocal. For some reason, DJ Alan Freed was supposed to choose which cut would be the follow-up; Jensen insisted, to no avail, on his favorite disk, "Big As I Can Dream."

All of Jensen's later releases stiffed. White Whale released the good-timey "Good Pop Music" in the late '60s; A & M gave Kris his final outing in 1970 with a pre-JANIS JOPLIN cover of "Me And Bobby McGee."

Of all the teen idols that peopled the pop landscape before the arrival of the Beatles, Kris Jensen is considered one of the best. Tracking down his Hickory singles, or his (lone and highly collectible) *Torture* album, is not a bad idea.

Jimmy McGriff

I GOT A WOMAN, PART 1
(Ray Charles)
Sue 770
No. 20   *November 24, 1962*

Although James Harrell McGriff (b. Apr. 3, 1936, Philadelphia) was born into a musical family—his father was a pianist, his grandfather was a trombonist, and his brother played bass and drums—Jimmy wanted to be a policeman when he grew up. After studying at the Pennsylvania Institute of Criminology, McGriff joined the Philadelphia police force.

It was not until McGriff heard jazz organist Jimmy Smith playing a Hammond B-2 organ at a jam session that he began to reconsider his life's work. He had already toyed with the sax, violin, piano, and bass, playing the latter in a number of hometown bands (including the Sonotones, a group led by Don Gardner of DON

GARDNER & DEE DEE FORD.) Smith, who lived nearby in Norristown, offered to help McGriff with his organ playing.

In 1962, Juggy Murray signed McGriff to his New York-based Sue label. Jimmy's instrumental reading of Ray Charles' "I Got A Woman" clicked with jazz, rock, and R & B fans alike. His style was jazzy, but danceable, and he continued to rack up Hot 100 chartings through the '60s with tunes like "All About My Girl" (#50, 1963) b/w "M.G. Blues" (#95), "The Last Minute, Part 1" (#99, 1963), "Kiko (#79, 1964), and "The Worm" (#97, 1968).

McGriff continues playing jazz organ to this day. As he has explained to Leonard Feather in the *Encyclopedia of Jazz*: "What I play isn't really jazz . . . it's sort of in between. Just old-time swing with a jazz effect."

Marcie Blane
BOBBY'S GIRL
(Henry Hoffman, Gary Klein)
Seville 120
No. 3   *December 1, 1962*

Marcie was no women's libber—all the poor little girl wanted to be in her whole darn life was "Bobby's Girl." Marcie, who was born on May 21, 1944 in Brooklyn, had just completed her home-economics classes and graduated from high school in June 1962. When Marv Holtzman, an A & R man from Seville Records, approached her about singing "Bobby's Girl," Marcie replied, "Sure." Teen girls could easily identify with Marcie's simple and stated wants, and bought up stacks of copies of "Bobby's Girl."

For the next few years, Marcie Blane continued to mine similar ground with "Little Miss Fool," "What Does A Girl Do?", and "Why Can't I Get A Guy?" They were all delightfully sweet but blatantly sexist singles. Male record collectors still play her demure disks, dreaming of her balloon-like bouffant and cherishing her singular sentiments.

By 1965, Marcie's name had disappeared from the record racks.

"[The music business] was impossible for me to deal with," Ms. Blane told *Goldmine*'s Bob Shannon and Jeff Tamarkin in 1989. "Everything changed. I felt very isolated and very lonely and I decided not to continue. I couldn't. It was too difficult. I didn't feel comfortable in front of a lot of people, with everyone making a fuss. I didn't have the sense of myself I needed. It's taken all these years to be able to enjoy what there was."

Marcie Blane is currently married with two children and working as an education director at an arts theater in New York.

The Routers

Routers

LET'S GO (PONY)
(L. Duncan, R. Duncan)
Warner Bros. 5283
No. 19 *December 22, 1962*

At some point in the early '60s, there really was a legitimate group called the Routers, inspired by Dick Dale, "Father of Surfing Music." Mike Gordon has told record researcher Skip Rose that the original Routers consisted of Gordon, Lynn Frazier, Al Kait, Bill Moody, and some fellow he could only recall as Neil. Yet once this West Coast band hooked up with producer Joe Saraceno and Warner Bros., it seems that the Routers' line-up became markedly nebulous.

"Let's Go" (with the subtitle of "Pony") was a natural for the act's first 45, considering that a dance called the Pony was then something of a sensation. To capitalize on the enthusiastic response the disk received, the Routers' first LP, and the only one to sell in respectable quantities, was issued (*Let's Go with the Routers*, 1963). Even at this earliest of points in the Routers' flash flight to fame, many pop historians suspect that most of the group's members did not actually play on the Routers' records. Those who most likely did so were L.A. studio pros like Hal Blaine, Rene Hall, Plas Johnson, Sid Sharp, and Scott Engel.

Further 45s and eventually more LPs were shipped by Warner Bros.; only "Sting Ray" (#50, 1963) managed to do well. In 1966, Jan Davis, a guitarist and regional charter with a biting instrumental called "The Fugitive," teamed up with the remnants of the Routers for a few RCA singles like "The Time Tunnel." And after a brief and largely undistributed outing on Mercury in 1973, the "Routers" name was boxed and buried.

Tornadoes

TELSTAR
(Joe Meek)
London 9561
No. 1 *December 22, 1962*

As a recording engineer, Joe Meek (b. 1933, Gloucester, England) did sessions for CHRIS BARBER'S JAZZ BAND, SHIRLEY BASSEY, Petula Clark, Lonnie Donegan, and Frankie Vaughan. Meek also wrote songs, and when one in par-

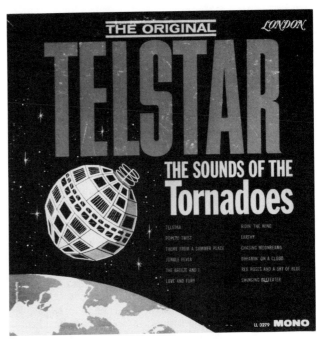

ticular was recorded by Tommy Steele, he took his royalties and opened his own studio and record label (Triumph) in North London.

To equip the studio with back-up musicians for recording sessions, Joe ran an ad in a London trade paper early in 1962. Five players responded and were chosen: guitarist George Bellamy (b. Oct. 8, 1941, Sunderland, England), bassist Heinz Burt (b. July 25, 1942, Hargin, Germany), keyboardist Roger Lavern (b. Roger Jackson, Nov. 11, 1938, Kidderminster, England), plus two former members of the Pirates—violinist/guitarist Alan Caddy (b. Feb. 2, 1940, London) and drummer Clem Cattini (b. Aug. 28, 1939, London).

Meek rehearsed the guys, tightened up their sound, and issued an unsuccessful debut 45, "Love And Fury." In 1962, when the U.S. launched the world's first communications satellite, Telstar, Joe was inspired to compose a commemorative instrumental featuring futuristic sound effects. The Tornadoes were on tour with Billy Fury, and Meek called them home. Legend has it that he managed to teach and tape the tune within 90 minutes.

British Decca acquired the rights, and London Records released "Telstar" in the States. The response was astounding. In a matter of weeks, the Tornadoes managed to do what no British group had ever done before—have a number-one hit in the U.S. The disk sold over 5,000,000 copies worldwide. Numerous follow-ups were duly shipped, but only "Ride The Wind" (#57, 1963) charted, and while three more 45s clicked in the U.K., by year's end, the game was pretty much played out.

Burt was the first to leave, for a semi-successful solo singing career. Next went Bellamy, then Caddy, then Lavern. In 1965, Cattini, the last original Tornado, quit. Meek persisted and carried on the group's name with a completely new line-up, but with no further success. On February 3, 1966—eight years to the day after the death of Buddy Holly—he took his own life, with a shotgun.

As Bellamy complained to Fred Dellar, author of *Where Did You Go To, My Lovely?*: "Though ["Telstar"] made a fortune, somewhere in the link between Decca, Joe Meek, and ourselves, the money seemed to disappear. Certainly Decca paid all the royalties, there's no doubt about that. But we received very little—and when Joe Meek died, he was penniless. So you figure it out."

Bellamy recorded some solo singles for EMI, worked for a British publishing house, did studio sessions, and in 1971 formed his own SRT label. In 1975, he reassembled all the original Tornadoes except Caddy for one last effort as the New Tornadoes. Their remake of "Telstar" passed largely without notice.

Lavern now lives in Mexico, where he works in advertising. Cattini lives in North London and is a top-flight studio drummer. Burt lives in Southampton, where he has worked as a baker and a potato delivery man.

Exciters

TELL HIM
(Bert Russell)
United Artists 544
No. 4   *January 19, 1963*

Herb Rooney was born in 1941 and raised in New York City. Hankering for a better life, Herb and some of his buddies tried for years to get a break for their vocal group, the Continentals. Luck, however, was not on their side, and the group dispersed. With the Masters, Rooney got to record for Bingo Records, but sales were slow.

In 1962, Herb met the Masterettes, three singing, swinging high school juniors from Queens. Rooney thought that the girls— Brenda Reid, Carol Johnson, and Lillian Walker—had a really hot sound, and brought them in to see the renowned production team

of Jerry Leiber and Mike Stoller. The duo concurred with Herb's assessment, and told Herb to stick around and sing bottom for the group, now re-dubbed the Exciters.

Before the year was out, the girls were out of school and the foursome's "Tell Him" was chuggin' up the charts. Five more Exciters singles would place on the Hot 100: "He's Got The Power" (#57, 1963), "Get Him" (#76, 1963), the original version of the Manfred Mann hit "Do-Wah-Diddy (#78, 1964), "I Want You To Be My Baby" (#96, 1965), and a cover version of THE JARMELS' "A Little Bit Of Soap" (#58, 1966).

The Exciters performed in Europe and the Caribbean, toured with Wilson Pickett, and opened for the Beatles. But after 1966, the media excitement died down to a dribble. Reid and Rooney continued to carry on whoopin' and hollerin', but in the '70s, Johnson and Walker quietly walked away from the Exciters, and were replaced by Skip McPhee and Ronnie Pace (both formerly of Mother Night). Tours of England brought the group a following on the Northern soul circuit and a minor U.K. hit with "Reaching For The Beat" in 1975. Releases continued through the '70s on Elephant Y, Fargo, H & L, 20th Century, and Tomorrow.

When last spotted, the act had dropped to a spirited twosome billed as Brenda & Herb.

Johnny Thunder

LOOP DE LOOP
(Teddy Vann, Joe Dong)
Diamond 129
No. 4   *February 9, 1963*

"**L**ike most everybody, I got my start in church and singing in high school," Johnny Thunder (b. Gil Hamilton, Aug. 15, 1941, Leesburg, Fla.) said in an exclusive interview. "My friends got me into this. They told me I was good." Because there wasn't much of a recording scene down in Florida at the time, Johnny headed up north to pursue a musical career. He went to New York to join the Drifters as their lead singer—Ben E. King was preparing to leave the group—staying with the Drifters for a few months.

A few singles appeared under the Gil Hamilton name for Fury and Capitol; the latter even issued the original take on "Tell Him," which would be a biggie for THE EXCITERS months later. To make ends meet, Johnny did uncredited back-up vocals on various recording sessions. Then he met Teddy Vann and recorded "Loop De Loop."

"Teddy was a character. He was like a black Marlon Brando. We met by accident . . . I just happened to be singing in the chorus, doing my back-up bit, trying to stay alive. Teddy liked me, and we did this 'Don't Be Ashamed.' We thought this was a good record, but we needed something to make the record symmetrical, so we threw together 'Loop De Loop.'

"We just made it all up as we went along, me and Teddy and his brother-in-law, Joey Dong. I was playing the drums, and they were feeding me words on scraps of paper. I just read what they handed me . . . We all knew it was just a piece of garbage—all, that is, but Teddy. He said, 'You guys are crazy, it's a hit.'"

Thereafter, Thunder found himself in the grips of that entertainment-industry evil, typecasting. "[That record] typecast me, boy did it ever. I met BO DIDDLEY and he said, 'I never seen nobody make a million dollars on nursery rhymes.' It's funny, but I wound up doing a lot of that simple stuff, like 'Ring Around The Rosey' [a.k.a. "The Rosey Dance," 1963] and 'Everybody Do The Sloppy' [#67, 1965]."

Johnny continued making disks throughout the '60s for Diamond, Calla, and United Artists. Johnny Thunder is still actively performing, and working on a compilation LP.

Ned Miller
FROM A JACK TO A KING
(Ned Miller)
Fabor 114
No. 6 *February 16, 1963*

Most would have bet that it was not in the cards for Ned Miller. His voice was rough, sad, and old-timey, even to country ears. His "From A Jack To A King" had been recorded in 1957, and had sold poorly when released by Dot Records that year. Who could have figured that nine years later, this very same flop would be reissued and sell more than 2,000,000 copies?

Ned was born Henry Miller in Rains, Utah, on April 12, 1925, and raised in Salt Lake City. His mother taught him how to play guitar, and by his teenage years, he was writing songs. Ned served three years in the Marines, and on his return, he studied two years under the G.I. Bill to become a pipefitter.

A pipefitter Ned may have remained, had BONNIE GUITAR not taken one of his tunes,

"Dark Moon," to the top 10 in 1957. Dot Records, Bonnie's label, was interested in just who this Ned Miller might be, and recorded his "From A Jack To A King." It bombed, and Ned returned to writing songs and pipefitting.

In 1962, Fabor Robinson, the owner of Fabor Records (where Ned had recorded the "Jack" track), decided to give the Dot disk another spin, and reissued the very same recording on his own label. To the surprise of all parties involved, even Robinson, the record sold its way into the top 10.

Nothing that Ned ever recorded could match the success of his eerie incantation. In 1964, "Do What You Do Do Well" reached number 52 on the Hot 100, but Miller's big-name days were over. Ned tried throughout the remainder of the '60s to attain renown in the country field, but to little avail.

Ned Miller's current activities and whereabouts are not known. A lone album did appear on Plantation Records in 1981.

Joe Harnell
FLY ME TO THE MOON-BOSSA NOVA
(Bart Howard)
Kapp 497
No. 14 *February 23, 1963*

Born in the Bronx on August 2, 1924, Joe Harnell studied at the Trinity College of Music in London and at Tanglewood, where for four years he studied under Leonard Bernstein, Aaron Copland, and Darius Milhaud. Once his education was complete, he became the conductor and arranger for Pearl Bailey, Marlene Dietrich, ROBERT GOULET, Peggy Lee, Anthony Newley, and Frank Sinatra. In addition to writing some piano preludes, chamber works, and art songs, Joe became the music director for many television programs, including "The Bionic Woman," "Cliffhangers," "The Incredible Hulk," and "The Mike Douglas Show." Recording for Columbia, Epic, Jubilee, Kapp, and Motown Records, Harnell has had more than a dozen albums issued.

The bossa nova—a sound, a style, and a dance—became a hot item in the winter of 1962. Following the release of Stan Getz & Astrud Gilberto's "The Girl From Ipanema," and preceding Eydie Gorme's "Blame It On The Bossa Nova" by a week or two, was Joe Harnell's instrumental, "Fly Me To The Moon-Bossa Nova." The tune eventually charted five times. Harnell's follow-up, "Diane," pulled into

Jan Bradley

the Hot 100 at number 97 position for a week before vanishing from the land of pop culture.

Given Joe Harnell's musical background, he probably didn't mind being a one-hit wonder. After all, there were still all those TV shows to score, all those easy-listening albums to create, and all those Tin Pan Alley singers to conduct and arrange.

Jan Bradley
MAMA DIDN'T LIE
(Curtis Mayfield)
Chess 1845
No. 14 *March 9, 1963*

When she was about four years of age, Addie Bradley (b. July 6, 1943, Byhalia, Miss.) and her family moved to Robbins, a suburb of Chicago. Early on, her mother and father noticed she had a talent for singing. In 1961, Don Talty, manager of R & B guitarist Phil Upchurch and owner of Formal Records, discovered Jan at a high school talent show. He had to wait two years, until Jan graduated, to get her parents' consent to become her manager and launch her recording career.

Through Upchurch, Talty got the Impressions' Curtis Mayfield to write some songs for her. "We Girls," Jan's debut disk and a Mayfield composition, sold well in Chicago, and garnered heavy airplay in the Midwest. There was something special to Jan's soft soul sound. "Sometimes as a singer it's not how well you sing," Mayfield told *Goldmine*'s Bob Pruter, "it's just that innocence or that certain something about the artist that makes a song appealing. Jan had that innocence in her voice."

After a few unsuccessful 45s, Jan recorded Mayfield's "Mama Didn't Lie," her big moment in top 40-land. Perhaps if Mayfield had come up with more material for Jan to do, her career could have picked up some momentum. But as Bradley told *Goldmine*, Mayfield and Chess Records parted ways over a dispute concerning publishing rights.

Aside from the minor success of "I'm Over You" (#93, 1965), Jan Bradley was thenceforth absent from the nation's pop charts. Talty produced a dozen more singles for Chess and for the small Adanti, Doylen, and Spectra Sound labels. But despite some fine Bradley-penned songs, guitar licks by Upchurch, and the occasional production wizardry of Billy Davis, nothing further clicked.

In 1970, Jan Bradley called it quits. She

married, raised a family, returned to school, and earned an MA degree. She is now known as Janice Johnson, social worker.

Cascades

RHYTHM OF THE RAIN
(John Gummoe)
Valiant 6026
No. 3 *March 9, 1963*

The Cascades were a self-contained band from San Diego, California. John Gummoe, the unit's spokesperson, lead vocalist/guitarist, and writer of their tip-top tune, met pianist Eddie Snyder and the three Daves—bassist Stevens, saxophonist Wilson, and drummer Zabo—in the late '50s. By 1962, the group had developed a solid reputation for supplying smooth sounds for parties and dances. One night, while the guys were working their magic at a club called the Peppermint Stick, an executive from Valiant Records happened to catch their act. In late 1962, the label ushered Gummoe and the Cascades into Hollywood's Gold Star Studios to lay down "Second Chance" for their first 45. The platter stiffed, but "Rhythm Of The Rain" rocked the pop and R & B (#7) charts.

The follow-up, "Shy Girl" (#91, 1963) b/w "The Last Leaf" (#60), proved to be a double-sided hit, with airplay split between the two tunes. The Cascades switched to RCA and issued "For Your Sweet Love" (#86, 1963). Although the latter 45, and subsequent Cascades cuts, were solid efforts, the group probably sounded dated (and, with Beatlemania in full force, much too American) to record-buyers. By 1969, only Dave Wilson remained from the original line-up.

Rockin' Rebels

WILD WEEKEND
(Phil Todaro, Tommy Shannon)
Swan 4125
No. 8 *March 9, 1963*

The story of the Rockin' Rebels is a rather convoluted one. During the late '50s and pre-Beatle '60s, Phil Todaro was a record producer, and Tommy Shannon was a DJ on Buffalo's WKBW with a night-time spot called "The Wild Weekend Show." "Wild Weekend,"

originally recorded by the Russ Hallet Trio, was the show's theme song. Apparently, Shannon hired a local band to re-cut his radio theme and placed the number with the Mar-Lee label in 1959.

Copies of "Wild Weekend" were pressed and shipped, and the disk sold fairly well. The players, including Jimmy and Mickey Kipper, Paul Balon, and Tom Gorman, were credited on the label as "The Rebels." (They later recorded two singles on Mar-Lee as the Buffalo Rebels.) Late in 1962, some East Coast stations picked up on "Wild Weekend" and rode the record like it was a new release, so the Swan label reissued the original Rebels record as by the Rockin' Rebels. The disk dented the nation's top 10, and an album was needed to meet the public's craving for Rebel-rockin' instrumentals. Unknown musicians were rushed into Swan's studios to cover classics like "Whole Lotta Shakin' Going On," "Tequila," and "Telstar."

The tale gets even cloudier: the Rockin' Rebels' follow-up and only other Hot 100 hit was a number called "Rockin' Crickets" (#87, 1963). The record was identical to an earlier release—also titled "Rockin' Crickets" (#57, 1959)—by a band called the Hot-Toddys. The Hot-Toddys consisted of Terry Gibson (lead vocals), Vaughn Jonah (guitar), Garry Kelba (drums), Johnny "T-Bone" Little (bass), and Bill Pernell (sax). What was going on here? Shannon and Todaro had not only owned the Shan-Todd label that originally issued the Hot-Toddys' "Rockin' Crickets," but had also retained the rights to future uses of the master. This is how a 1959 Hot-Toddys record could be re-released by the Rockin' Rebels.

Three more Rebels singles are known to have been issued. The whereabouts and further activities of the members of this elusive group are not known.

Bill Pursell

OUR WINTER LOVE
(J. Cowell)
Columbia 42619
No. 9 *March 30, 1963*

Bill was born in Oakland and raised in Tulare, California. He learned to read music and play the piano before the age of five. After high school, he attended the Peabody Conservatory of Music in Baltimore on a composition fellowship. During World War II, Bill worked

Bill Pursell

for three years as the official arranger for the Air Force Band in Washington, D.C. Once the war was over, Bill attended the Eastman School of Music in Rochester, where he received B.A. and M.A. degrees and won the first Edward B. Benjamin Award in composition. Bill, wife, and three little ones moved to a hillside house in Tennessee, where for years thereafter, he performed with the Nashville Symphony Orchestra and taught at Nashville's Vanderbilt University.

In 1962, Columbia Records signed Bill to a contract and sent him into the studio—with Grady Martin directing and BILL JUSTIS in the role of music arranger—to cut an album that would contain Pursell's haunting instrumental, "Our Winter Love." Never to chart again, Bill Pursell did not just vanish, however. Piles of singles and albums for the Dot, Epic, and Alton labels were issued. Bill continued teaching, as well as playing sessions behind Nashville's country pickers.

Johnny Cymbal

MR. BASS MAN
(Johnny Cymbal)
Kapp 503
No. 16 *April 13, 1963*

Johnny Cymbal was born in Ochiltree, Scotland, on February 3, 1945. His musical career began shortly after his family moved to Canada in 1952.

"I was about 13 or so when I saw this band in the town square," Johnny recalled in an exclusive interview. "Only then did I get the idea of singing. The next week, there I was up there with them, singing 'My Bucket's Got A Hole In It.' That was my first song; after that, I learned how to play guitar by watching this country show on TV."

Cymbal's clan relocated to Cleveland, and in 1960, MGM Records signed Johnny to a two-year contract. "The Water Is Red," his second release, was a tearjerker in the mucky mode of MARK DINNING's "Teen Angel." In Cymbal's tall tale, the girl of our dreams is eaten by a hungry shark. The record stirred some scattered radio action and some stomachs as well. Singles later, Cymbal again almost had a hit with the Bobby Vee-ish "Bachelor Man."

A switch to Kapp Records, and Johnny finally hit his stride with "Mr. Bass Man." With its doo-woppish sound, the tune was an uptempo paean to that dwindling breed, the "bottom man," or the singer who took the low harmony in a vocal group.

Cymbal moved to Don Costa's DCP label, then to the Columbia, Musicor, and Amaret labels. Nothing more charted, so he shifted his attention to writing ("Mary In The Morning," a hit for Al Martino), producing, and recording as a studio-only act. In the latter capacity, he recorded as Milk, DEREK, Taurus, and (with Peggy Clinger) Cymbal & Klinger.

Johnny Cymbal has continued to do production work (for David Cassidy, the Partridge Family, and Gene Pitney), occasionally reappearing, as he did in 1984, with a new single or two. He has lived in Nashville since 1980, writing country tunes that have been waxed by the Burrito Brothers ("I'm Drinkin' Canada Dry"), the Wright Brothers ("Fire In The Sky"), Glen Campbell, and Eddie Arnold.

Chantays

PIPELINE
(Bob Spickard, Brian Carman)
Dot 16440
No. 4 *May 4, 1963*

With only eight months of musical experience, Bob Spickard and Brian Carman created

"Pipeline," possibly the best surfing song ever, and one of only two surfing instruments to ever reach *Billboard*'s top 10.

Spickard (lead guitar) and Warren Waters (bass) were high school buddies. In the summer of 1961, they decided to learn how to play some instruments and become a surfin' band. In short order, fellow Santa Ana High School students Brian Carman (guitar), Bob Marshall (piano), and Bob Welch (drums) were enlisted.

"Pipeline" started out as a tough little dual-guitar idea that Spickard and Carman originally called "Liberty's Whip" and later "44 Magnum." But after seeing a surf flick about the notorious Hawaiian Pipeline, they named their tune "Pipeline." While playing a dance at the Big Bear, the Chantays were discovered by DJ Jack Sands, who offered to be their manager and get them a recording contract.

A few sides were cut at the Pal Recording Studio in Cucamonga, and Sands hawked the sounds around to the L.A. labels. No one nibbled except Bill and Jack Wenzel's Downey Record Company. The dinky label was buzzing with the mild surfin' success of the Rumblers' "Boss," and the Wenzels hoped that in securing the Chantays, they might continue their winning streak.

Within weeks of its release, "Pipeline" was a national hit and, as with the Rumblers disks, Dot Records stepped in to provide national distribution. An album was churned out, potential singles were cut and canned, but trouble was brewing. Promotion and touring by the group was limited, since the members were all full-time high school students. The guys fired Sands on the grounds that he was skimming too much off the top of the Chantays' earnings. Follow-up singles were issued—"Monsoon," "Space Probe," "Only If You Care"—but nothing charted or even appeared on *Billboard*'s "Bubbling Under the Hot 100" chart. After a three-month tour of Hawaii in the summer of 1964, the Chantays called it quits.

Bob Spickard joined his father-in-law's industrial equipment business. When last spotted, he was the president of the L & A Products Company. Brian Carman was last seen working at a musical instrument store in Anaheim, California. Bob Welch now works in a clothing store in Los Angeles. Spickard, Carman, and Welch still perform together on occasion as the Catalina Good Time Band. Rob Marshall plays part-time in a C & W band and is a schoolteacher in the Chico area of California. Warren Waters is reportedly a successful real estate broker.

Rocky Fellers
KILLER JOE
(Russell, Elgin, Medley)
Scepter 1246
No. 16   *May 18, 1963*

Frank "Killer Joe" Piro was the dancer who taught high society how to do everything from the Frug to the Watusi. They called him "Killer Joe" because he could outlast anyone on the dance floor. For decades, the little guy did his stuff on both the big stage and the little screen. Mostly what he did was make the Manhattan rounds, hopping and bopping at all the glitzy parties and clubs. The Duke and Duchess of Windsor, and dance-floor damsel Luci Baines Johnson, were among his countless students.

Poppa Feller (b. 1924) had a house full of

sons and daughters, born and raised in Manila, the Philippines. His boys—Eddie (b. 1955), Albert (b. 1953), Tony (b. 1947), and Junior (b. 1945)—were musically inclined, and, beginning in 1959, they formed a group. Pop and his rockin' and rollin' Rocky Fellers made periodic stops in the States, appearing on "The Ed Sullivan Show" and other variety programs.

Nothing much happened with the Rocky Fellers' first sides for the Parkway label. But in 1963, the group recorded a little tribute tune to this peerless, pirouetting Piro. "Killer Joe" sold well; it was, however, a novelty number, much like the band itself. Once its newness turned stale, the Fellers and their disks faded from view.

"Killer Joe" Piro, however, danced on. Dorian Gray had nothing on Frank. Reportedly, he danced until he died on February 5, 1988.

Dartells

HOT PASTRAMI
(Doug Phillips)
Dot 16453
No. 11 *May 25, 1963*

With their first serving, the Dartells cut the mustard. Fried, boiled and sauteed, "Hot Pastrami" was an enjoyably sloppy hit. Doug Phillips, leader of this group from Oxnard, California, claimed credit for writing this tune. But "Hot Pastrami" is actually a knock-off of an earlier number—"Mashed Potatoes," recorded in 1960 by Nat Kendricks, then James Brown's drummer.

The California kids were between 18 and 20 when their coach and manager, Tom Ayres, plucked them from out of the teen-scene clubs to audition for Buddy Jack at Arlen Records. Phillips (bass, vocals), Dick Burns (guitar), Gary Peeler (drums), Rich Peil (sax), Randy Ray (organ), and Corky Wilkie (sax) whipped up a batch of the stuff they were successfully serving up at the night spots. Most of these tunes were instrumentals in the tradition of the MAR-KEYS and Booker T. & The MGs.

Arlen Records decided to give the fellows a try, and wham, "Hot Pastrami." Dot Records picked up the national distribution when the "Pastrami" got hot, but nothing the band ever recorded thereafter got more than lukewarm. "Dance, Everybody Dance," the follow-up, checked into the charts at number 99 for a week, and then rightfully scurried for obscurity. A cover version of the Beau Marks' "Clap

Your Hands" interested almost no one, and the Dartells disbanded.

Doug Phillips formed another group in the late '60s called the New Concepts, and had singles issued on ABC-Paramount and Atco. In 1971, while fronting Cottonwood, Phillips and his band released *Camaraderie*, a hard-rockin' album for ABC. It is not known what became of the other members of the Dartells. There is some indication that a portion of the group remained intact to record several stray singles as a group called Rain.

Bill Anderson

STILL
(Bill Anderson)
Decca 31458
No. 8 *June 8, 1963*

"Whispering Bill," as he became known for his talkie singing style, was born James Anderson on November 1, 1937, in Columbia, South Carolina. In high school in Commerce, Georgia, Bill wrote songs, ran his own band, won talent contests, and worked as a DJ. He attended the University of Georgia's School of Journalism, all the while singing, writing, and winning contests. After graduation, Anderson became a sportswriter for the *DeKalb New Era* and a correspondent to the *Atlanta Constitution*.

In 1958, RAY PRICE recorded one of Bill's tunes, "City Lights," which went top 10 on the country charts. Bill was given the chance to make some recordings for Decca Records; first out of the barn was "That's What It's Like To Be Lonesome." Throughout most of the '60s, Bill's voice or the results of his pen were hardly ever off the C & W charts. His duets with Jan Howard, and with Mary Lou Turner, also found a sizeable country audience. ROY CLARK, Roy Drusky, Merle Haggard, Jim Reeves, Connie Smith, Porter Wagoner, and Kitty Wells all had hits with Bill's tunes.

The Country Music Association named Anderson "Top Songwriter of the Year" from 1963 to 1965, "Top Male Vocalist of the Year" in 1963, and the creator of the "Record of the Year" ("Still") in 1963. Four other country hits by Anderson crossed over to the Hot 100 charts from 1962 through 1978. Bill also found the time to make appearances in minor movies like *Forty Acre Feud, Las Vegas Hillbillies, Country Music on Broadway*, and *The Road to Nashville*.

Bill Anderson is currently recording for his

own Whispering label, though his singles don't make the country charts like they did some decades back. Bill presently spends most of energy acting in soap operas and hosting various syndicated game shows like "Mr. and Mrs." and "Fandango." His autobiography, *Whispering Bill*, was published in 1989.

Kyu Sakamoto

SUKIYAKI
(Hachidai Nakamura, Rokusuke Ei)
Capitol 4945
No. 1 *June 15, 1963*

Kyu Sakamoto

The crash of a Japan Airlines 747 near Tokyo on August 12, 1985 claimed 520 lives, including that of Kyu Sakamoto. Kyu was one of only three Japanese artists (the other two are Pink Lady and the Yellow Magic Orchestra) to ever chart on *Billboard*'s Hot 100. "Sukiyaki" was the only record of the bunch to reach number one, and the only Hot 100 hit sung entirely in Japanese.

"Sukiyaki" was a tear-jerker that had absolutely nothing to do with the Japanese taste treat. No, this was a tale of misery and desolation, as the translated lyrics indicate: "Sadness hides in the shadow of the stars/Sadness lurks in the shadow of the moon/I look up when I walk so the tears won't fall . . . "

Kyu was born in 1941 in the industrial city of Kawasaki, the ninth child of a Tokyo restaurateur. In his teen years, he sang in jazz clubs, and was discovered by Toshiba Records in 1959 while fronting a group called the Paradise Kings. Kyu scored 15 homeland hits, made appearances in 10 movies, and was a regular on several radio and TV programs—all before recording "Sukiyaki" and the follow-up, "China Nights (Shina No Yori)" (#58, 1963).

Sakamoto's top 40 moment was largely due to Louis Benjamin, then the head of England's Pye Records. While visiting Japan on business, Benjamin heard Kyu's ode and brought it home for his new artist, jazzman KENNY BALL, to record. The lyrics were dumped. Figuring that no one in the world would touch a tune with a title like "Ue O Muite Aruko" ("I Look Up When I Walk"), Benjamin decided to name the record after one of his favorite culinary delights. Ball's version eventually made the British top 10. Meanwhile, in the States, Richard Osborne, a DJ at KORD in Pasco, Washington, started playing and replaying Kyu's original rendition. The response was better than favorable, and the rest is history.

Before the sun set on Sakamoto's stateside success, his first and last LP—*Sukiyaki and Other Japanese Hits*, 1963—was packaged and pushed. Although satiation would set in all too soon, record-buyers snapped it up like chop suey.

Tom Glazer & The Do-Re-Mi Children's Chorus
ON TOP OF SPAGHETTI
(Tom Glazer)
Kapp 526
No. 14 *July 6, 1963*

Seeing that young Tom (b. Sept. 3, 1914, Philadelphia) took an interest in music, Mrs. Glazer encouraged him to sing in choirs and learn the basics on a number of instruments. After three years at New York's City College, Tom managed to earn a living playing tuba or string bass in jazz and military bands. By the

Rolf Harris

'40s, Glazer turned to singing folk tales for children. From 1945 to 1947, he fronted "Tom Glazer's Music Box," a radio program over the ABC network. Later in the decade, he made singing or acting appearances on radio shows such as "Listening Post," "Theatre Guild on the Air," "True Story," and "We the People." He narrated *Sweet Land of Liberty* and wrote the score for the movie *A Face in the Crowd* (1957).

From 1953 through 1967, Glazer recorded sing-a-long and folkie-flavored disks, his releases for the Young People's record label reportedly selling in the hundreds of thousands. While most who recall his name associate Tom with his parody of Burl Ives' "On Top Of Old Smokey" (#10, 1952), Glazer has also had success as a songwriter, usually as a lyricist. He was involved in the co-creation of "Melody Of Love" for Billy Vaughn (#2, 1955), the Four Aces (#3, 1955), and David Carroll (#8, 1955); "More" for KAI WINDING (#8, 1963) and Vic Dana (#42, 1963); "Old Soldiers Never Die" for Vaughn Monroe (#7, 1951); "Pussy Cat" for the Ames Brothers (#17, 1958); "Skokiaan" for Ralph Marterie (#3, 1954) and the Four Lads (#7, 1954); and "Till We Two Are One" for Georgie Shaw (#7, 1954).

Rolf Harris
TIE ME KANGAROO DOWN, SPORT
(Rolf Harris)
Epic 9596
No. 3 *July 13, 1963*

Rolf (b. Mar. 30, 1930, Perth, Australia) was full of talent and eager to gain fame and fortune. At the age of 22, he moved to England and became a TV cartoonist and storyteller. He sculpted, painted, sang, and pounded musical instruments. In 1956, London's Royal Academy of Art held an exhibition of his art works.

Whenever he felt homesick, Rolf would visit the Down Under Club. It was there that he began singing his strange songs and "wobbling" in public. "Wobbling" is shaking a warped Masonite board to produce bizarre rhythmic sounds. It was in large measure this strange sound that sold the world on Rolf's kookie "Kangaroo" number. In England, where the tune was a hit three years before its stateside embrace, the nutty need for record-buyers to create that sound at home became such that Masonite shipped out 55,000 warped boards.

Rolf's notoriety has rolled right along in England and Australia, where a number of his fractured follow-ups have charted. His 1969 reworking of the 1903 song "Two Little Boys" was reportedly the biggest-selling disk in the U.K. that year. In the late '60s, Harris had his own BBC-TV series, "Hey Presto, It's Rolf," and his own wildlife TV series, "Survival." In 1968, he received a royal accolade when he was awarded a medal from the Order of the British Empire, an honor he again received in 1977.

Doris Troy
JUST ONE LOOK
(Doris Payne, Gregory Carroll)
Atlantic 2188
No. 10 *July 27, 1963*

Born on January 6, 1937, Doris Payne was raised in the heart of New York City and soul of Mount Calvary Church, where her daddy was the preacher. From childhood on, she sang in the church choir and became the lead in various offshoot church groups. In the '50s, she worked as an usherette at the famed Apollo Theatre, joined a jazzy trio called the Halos, recorded as the "Dee" half of a short-lived Shirley & Lee–ish Jay & Dee, and dashed off tunes in her spare time.

One of Doris' numbers, "How About That," made its way through the channels and was spotted by Dee Clark, who charted (#33, 1960) with his recording of it. Jackie Wilson and Chuck Jackson recorded some of her creations; Jackson and Solomon Burke sought her out to sing back-up for their recording sessions. James Brown, after hearing her at a local nightclub, took an interest in Doris and walked her in to Atlantic Records.

"Just One Look" was Doris' very first single. The record was solid in sound, with a gospel edge and just a touch of teen—catchy, powerful, and somehow hard to forget. The Hollies covered "Just One Look" and drove it deep into the British top 10. Yet Troy's original did not even chart in the U.K., and her follow-up, "What'cha Gonna Do About It," did poorly here and only skirted England's charts.

Nothing more ever charted. Doris switched labels, first to Calla, then to Capitol Records. In 1969, she moved her body and soul to England to record some singles and an album for the Beatles' Apple label. *Doris Troy* featured a high-powered line-up of guest musicians; Doris co-wrote some of the songs with

George Harrison, Ringo Starr, and Steven Stills. In 1973, she won an immortality of sorts when she and Clare Torry sang back-up on Pink Floyd's *Dark Side of the Moon*.

Doris Troy still resides in London, still sings, still writes songs, still occasionally records tunes for British-only release—and still awaits that next and long-deserved hit.

Classics
TILL THEN
(G. Woods, S. Marcus, E. Seiler)
Musicnote 1116
No. 20 *August 3, 1963*

Second tenor Johnny Gambale (b. Feb. 4, 1942), lead vocalist Emil Stucchio (b. Apr. 9, 1944), bass Jamie Troy (b. Nov. 22, 1942), and first tenor Tony Victor (b. Apr. 11, 1943) all lived on Garfield Place in Brooklyn. They met on the streets, messed around on the streets, harmonized on the streets, and echoed in the hallways and johns. By 1958, they were singing at hops and on shows in and around their turf. They were the Perennials, but Sammy Sardi, the comedian and MC at the Club Illusion, couldn't pronounce their name, so he announced them as "The Classics" instead.

Louie Rotundo, a friend of the group and member of the Passions, suggested the guys audition for the Passions' manager, Jim Gribble. After a listen, Jim was singing their praises to Roger Sherman of the dinky Dart label. Sherman signed the Classics up, and rushed them into the Bell Sound Studios on 56th Street, where they recorded three singles. "Cinderella" sold fairly well regionally, but "Angel Angela" and "Life Is But A Dream" (sold to Mercury Records) stiffed.

The Classics hooked up with Andy Leonetti, the manager of the Paragons, who was about to set up his own little label. "Till Then," a cover of the Mills Brothers' 1944 hit, was the Classics' first release for Musicnote. Success was short-lived, but sweet: the Garfield Park boys got to tour the country and stand on the same stage with the Dubs, the Shells, and the Flamingos.

The follow-up, "P.S. I Love You," sold poorly. "The record didn't get much airplay," Emil Stucchio explained in an interview with *Bim Bam Boom* writer Steve Flam. "It was late 1963 and early 1964, and our style of music was going downhill. The English sound was in. The public didn't want to hear ballads." Two more

The
Sixties

singles were shipped, but failed to even smudge the lowest reaches of the charts.

Emil Stucchio has since become a transit policeman; John Gambale is a commercial artist; Jamie Troy has worked in the scrap-iron business; and Tony Victor had a seat on the New York Stock Exchange.

Surfaris
WIPE OUT
(Ron Wilson, James Fuller, Robert Berryhill, Patrick Connolly)
Dot 16479
No. 2 *August 10, 1963*

Rhythm guitarist Bob Berryhill (b. 1947), lead guitarist Jim Fuller (b. 1947), bassist Pat Connolly (b. 1947), drummer Ron Wilson (b. 1945), and saxophonist Jim Pash (b. 1949) were looking for practice space when they found Dale Smallin. Dale, who had a small recording studio, became the Surfaris' manager and, with the help of parental funds, arranged a four-hour recording session at the Pal Studios in Cucamonga. "Surfer Joe" (#62, 1963) was to be the single; "Wipe Out" (originally called "Stiletto") was to be a flip side, so not much thought or time went into doing it.

Gimmicks at the beginning of tunes were, as always, a big thing. Someone simulated the sound of a crashing surfboard by breaking a wooden shingle, Smallin's "witch laugh" was

added, Wilson worked up some drum breaks, and "Wipe Out" was cut and dried in two takes. Smallin pressed 100 copies of the disk on his own DFS label.

"Surfer Joe" b/w "Wipe Out" came to the attention of Richard Delvy, the bass player with another surf group, the well-established Challengers. Smallin gave Delvy the go-ahead to manufacture some copies of the disk using his Princess label. One of Delvy's pressings found its way to Dot Records, which issued the group's platter nationwide (note: the version of "Wipe Out" on the DFS label is a full 10 seconds longer than the Dot version).

While "Wipe Out" was to become one of the best-selling debut singles ever and one of the most cherished of all oldies, all was not well, and there were soon lawsuits a-plenty. There were fishy goings-on in connection with the group's first and only LP for Dot, *Wipe Out*—the only Surfaris cuts on the album were "Surfer Joe" and "Wipe Out," but all the other tracks had Delvy's Challengers playing on them! The result was that the Challengers, and not the Surfaris, received performance royalties from the best-selling album. Delvy also managed to swipe publishing rights without the group's permission. To top it all off, a group from L.A. brought suit against the fellows charging that *they* had the exclusive rights to the "Surfaris" name.

Once all the legal problems were ironed out, the group recorded some fine surf sounds for Decca. While only one other single made the Hot 100—"Point Panic" (#49, 1963)—the

The Surfaris

Surfaris churned out one high-quality single after another as well as five LPs. By the time the group formally signed with Dot Records in 1966 for the issuance of their last two singles, Berryhill, Connolly, and Fuller were gone.

The Surfaris have re-formed on many occasions. In 1976, Berryhill, Fuller, and Pash recorded a greatest-hits album for K-Tel. In the spring of 1989, Fuller, Pash, and Wilson toured the nation, but Fuller had to leave the tour when he broke an arm. Ron Wilson—who once set a record for drumming endurance by playing non-stop for 104½ hours, and who reportedly spent much of his life in poverty in Dutch Flats, California—died in May 1989 of a brain aneurysm.

Berryhill, a born-again Christian, has played with Christian groups and currently works as an instructor at an educational-opportunities center. Fuller was part of California groups like World War III and US, and was even a member of the Seeds for a time. Pash (who was not present at the "Wipe Out" session) is a born-again Christian as well; he is also the inventor and manufacturer of the Gitsitar.

Randy & The Rainbows

DENISE
(Neil Levenson)
Rust 5059
No. 10 *August 24, 1963*

Initially the Safuto brothers, Dominick (lead) and Frank (first tenor), along with cousin Eddie Scalla and Rosalie Calindo, were "The Dialtones." Later, while attending classes at Grover Cleveland High, the Safuto brothers, Dominick and Frank met the Zero brothers, Mike (baritone) and Sal (second tenor), and their singing buddy Ken Arcipowski (bass). The latter three had been singing around the neighborhood as the Encores. With the addition of the Safutos, the fivesome from the Maspeth section of Queens became Junior & The Counts. After six months of practice, they secured Fran Carrarie as their manager. Fran was friends with Neil Levenson, an aspiring songwriter who gave Randy (Dominick) & The Rainbows one of his tunes—"Denise"— and hooked them up with the Rust label.

The rest is history—and unfortunately for vocal-group fans, so was the group. Try as they did, Randy & The Rainbows could never again equal the phenomenal success of their debut single. "The follow-up was 'Why Do Kids Grow Up?'," Dominick told *Goldmine's* Jeff Tamarkin. "That would've been a big hit, perhaps as big as 'Denise,' had John F. Kennedy not been shot. The record was out a week when he got shot. The whole record industry died and everything was pulled off the radio. By the time it was over, the record was forgotten, we were forgotten."

Dom, the Zero brothers, and the rest of the Rainbows remained active and continued to record sporadically for the Rust, Mike, and B.T. Puppy labels through 1967. Thereafter, to secure a recording contract, they were compelled to disguise their identities. The Safutos, with Mike Zero and Vinny Corella, had a pair of platters released as Triangle for Paramount (1972) and a pair issued as Madison Street for Millenium (1978).

An interesting footnote: in 1978, the group Blondie had its first British chart success with "Denis," a remake of "Denise."

With the formation of Ambient Sound Records in 1982, Randy & The Rainbows returned to the recording studios. *C'Mon Let's Go, Remember,* and *Joy Ride,* the latter a fine compilation album on the Crystal Ball label, have since been released and are still in print.

Kai Winding

MORE
(R. Ortolani, N. Oliviero)
Verve 10295
No. 8 *August 24, 1963*

Winding blew into the States in 1934. Born on May 5, 1922 and raised in Aarhus, Denmark, Kai taught himself how to play the trombone during high school. At 18, Kai joined Shorty Allen's band. Throughout the '40s, Winding worked the big-band scene, playing and recording with Benny Goodman and Stan Kenton. During the '50s, he appeared at Broadway jazz clubs and formed various units with tip-top trombonist J.J. Johnson. Kai was in his artistic prime, winning various jazz polls, traveling the world, and producing records.

In 1962, Kai Winding was appointed musical director of the Playboy Club in New York City. Around this time, he started messing with mixing electronic instruments and more traditional ones. His *More* and *Mondo Cane #2* albums sold well; the title track from the former LP was Kai's lone pop hit. The tune was the theme from *Mondo Cane* (1963), an Italian

documentary about some of the shocking peculiarities of Man. The beat and sound of "More" were just right for those young listeners still hungry for something that would remind them of THE TORNADOES' "Telstar."

Kai Winding died on May 6, 1983.

Inez Foxx

MOCKINGBIRD
(Charlie & Inez Foxx)
Symbol 919
No. 7 *September 7, 1963*

Inez (b. Sept. 9, 1942, Greensboro, N.C.) and brother Charlie (b. Oct. 23, 1939) began making music together when both were students at Dudley High. Legend has it that Inez and Charlie (plus his three-string guitar) approached Sue/Symbol label head Juggy Murphy in a Broadway restaurant and played him a

nursery-rhyme novelty they had written called "Mockingbird." Juggy listened and liked what he heard, and by May 1963, the sound of that "Mockingbird" could be heard around the world. The sibling duo sounded much like Ike & Tina Turner—another one of Juggy's successful acts—but despite the vocal interplay between brother and sister, the label credited the disk to only "Inez Foxx."

Before the Sue/Symbol outfit folded, more Inez Foxx 45s were released: "Hi Diddle Diddle" (#98, 1963), "Ask Me" (#91, 1964), and "Hurt By Love" (#54, 1964). After their fifth single, Charlie was finally given equal billing on their releases and his own short shot at solo success ("Mulberry Bush" as by Chuck Johnson failed to chart). A change to the Musicor/Dynamo chain prolonged the duo's career with their R & B audience.

Inez and Charlie's final pop charting—"(1-2-3-4-5-6-7) Count the Days" (#76)—appeared on Dynamo in the opening months of 1968. At their new label, Luther Dixon became their producer, occasional co-writer, and eventually, Inez's spouse. A few more Foxx singles made the R & B listings before Inez called it quits in 1974—the same year that James Taylor and Carly Simon's cover version of "Mockingbird" went to the number-five slot on the pop charts. Charlie had "retired" from the act in 1969.

According to a report by Bob Grossweiner in *Goldmine*, Inez and Charlie have "no interest" in ever returning to the world of rock and soul.

Jaynetts

SALLY, GO 'ROUND THE ROSES
(Zell Sanders, Lona Stevens)
Tuff 369
No. 2   *September 28, 1963*

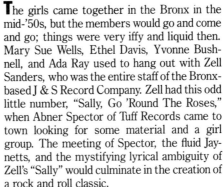

The girls came together in the Bronx in the mid-'50s, but the members would go and come and go; things were very iffy and liquid then. Mary Sue Wells, Ethel Davis, Yvonne Bushnell, and Ada Ray used to hang out with Zell Sanders, who was the entire staff of the Bronx-based J & S Record Company. Zell had this odd little number, "Sally, Go 'Round The Roses," when Abner Spector of Tuff Records came to town looking for some material and a girl group. The meeting of Spector, the fluid Jaynetts, and the mystifying lyrical ambiguity of Zell's "Sally" would culminate in the creation of a rock and roll classic.

Abner had been involved with acts like THE TUNE WEAVERS and THE CORSAIRS. In an interview with *Goldmine* writer Aaron Fuchs, Johnnie Richardson (of JOHNNY & JOE fame) described the "Sally" recording sessions and Abner's tendency to go a bit over the top in the studio. "He took them in the studio on a Friday and they didn't get out of there until the next week. And he used everybody on that track. Anybody [including Buddy Miles and pianist Artie Butler] that came in the studio that week he would put them on. Originally, I think he had about 20 voices on that 'Sally.'"

The cost of that project alone, Richardson figures, was over $60,000—an unheard-of amount of money to spend on recording a pop single in 1963.

"Sally, Go 'Round The Roses" is a timeless

The Jaynetts

wonder of a song, featuring an odd, hypnotic rhythm and soft voices seductively rising and falling. The lyrics seem to portray Sally in an alluring field of roses, catching an eyeful of her lover with another. But differing interpretations abound. Some listeners read the roses and the hushed throbbing of the music as expressions of a young woman's troubled acceptance of homosexuality. Others think that the song is about a religious experience, or possibly a mental breakdown. Still others remember "Sally" as nothing more than a silly nursery rhyme.

Zell and Abner are gone now, so we'll never know what it all meant, or even if "Sally"'s creators knew what it all meant. Abner never was able to concoct a follow-up with just the right ingredients. "Snowman, Snowman, Sweet Potato Nose" and "Keep An Eye On Her," produced in a Phil Spector-influenced style, yielded unsuccessful results. Some grouping of Jaynetts continued on with "Chicken, Chicken Crane Or Crow" and "Who Stole The Cookie From The Cookie Jar?", both for Zell's J & S label. According to Richardson, Vernell Hill was also a recording member of the Jaynetts, and the lead vocalist on the "Chicken, Chicken" flip side, "Winky Dink," is none other than Baby Washington.

Raindrops

THE KIND OF BOY YOU CAN'T FORGET

(Jeff Barry, Ellie Greenwich)
Jubilee 5455
No. 17   *September 28, 1963*

Jeff Barry (b. Apr. 3, 1938) and Ellie Greenwich (b. Oct. 23, 1940) met in 1960. Barry had just penned "Tell Laura I Love Her" (#7, 1960) for Ray Peterson, and was a songwriter with E.B. Marks. Greenwich was a singer with one RCA single to her credit ("Silly Isn't It" b/w "Cha Cha Charming," as by Ellie Gaye) and a student at Hofstra University. As their relationship grew, Jeff included Ellie in his activities, paying her $15 a session to record some demos on his songs.

When she graduated from college in 1961, Ellie auditioned for a staff writing position with the production team of Leiber & Stoller. They hired her as a writer for Trio Music at $100 a week. Jeff was also with Trio, and together, Barry and Greenwich went on to compose some of the finest moments in rock and roll: "Be My Baby," "Chapel Of Love," "Da Doo Ron Ron," "Do Wah Diddy Diddy," "Hanky Panky," "I Can Hear Music," "Leader Of The Pack," "The Look Of Love," and "River Deep, Mountain High."

The sale of most of these tunes involved the creation of a demonstration record. At times, the demo sounded good enough for an interested record company to issue as finished product. Such was the case with the Raindrops—the group was actually Ellie and Jeff doing all the voices.

"We did this demo for a group called THE SENSATIONS," Ellie told Charlotte Grieg in *Will You Still Love Me Tomorrow.* "It was a song called 'What A Guy', which we thought would be great for them. We made the demo, and the publishers said, 'This could be a record.' I said, 'What do you mean? There is no group.' But there had to be a group. So we released it as a record by 'The Raindrops' [after a record that Ellie loved, Dee Clark's "Raindrops"]. Back then, a lot of labels put out 'dummy groups.' We'd throw a few people together and have them go out and lip-synch the record. There really wasn't a 'Raindrops.' "

Group or not, the Raindrops scored with "The Kind Of Boy You Can't Forget" as well as a string of others—"That Boy John" (#64, 1964), a cover version of the Monotones' "Book Of Love" (#62, 1964), and "One More Tear" (#97, 1964). "What A Guy," that song that the Sensations had turned down, went to number 41 in 1963. When the chartings stopped, the name was shelved.

"Jeff and I lasted as a writing team about as long as we lasted as a married team—a little less than five years," Ellie explained to Joe Smith in *Off the Record.* "We tried to write together right after we split up, but it was awful. We couldn't sit and write 'Baby, I love you' with divorce papers sitting right next to us."

When the songs stopped, Ellie tried to establish herself as a solo singer. A couple of LPs (*Ellie Greenwich Composes, Produces, and Sings,* 1968; *Let it Be Written, Let it Be Sung,* 1973) and some singles were issued. Thereafter, she turned to writing and singing jingles. Clarence Clemons and Ellen Foley have recorded her newer tunes, and she occasionally appears on record as a back-up vocalist, as she has done for Blondie, Deborah Harry, and Cyndi Lauper. In the mid-'80s, Ms. Greenwich was the subject of an off-Broadway production, *Leader of the Pack.*

Ran-Dells

MARTIAN HOP
(John Spirt,
Robert Lawrence Rappaport,
Steve Rappaport)
Chairman 4403
No. 16   *September 28, 1963*

The Ran-Dells, from Villas, New Jersey, were actually the Rappaport brothers, Bob and John (both b. 1943), and their cousin John Spirt (b. 1949). They are known to have only recorded three singles: "Martian Hop," "Sound Of The Sun," and "Beyond The Stars." Their much-overlooked and underplayed "Martian" novelty number featured a bass line that thudded like a flat tire under an ethereal falsetto. The tune told of the dynamic dancing abilities of hip Martians.

What became of Spirt and the brothers after their one-off chart success is not known.

Little Johnny Taylor

PART TIME LOVE
(Clay Hammond)
Galaxy 722
No. 19   *October 5, 1963*

Johnny Young was born February 11, 1943, in Memphis. While still knee-high, Little John was asked to join the renowned Mighty Clouds of Joy. At 17, after a brief stay in the Stars of Bethel gospel group, John moved to Los Angeles to take up the secular life of a blues singer and harmonica player.

Little Johnny Taylor, as he renamed himself, worked the bars and let word of his music get around town. Scouts from the Berkeley-based Fantasy/Galaxy label offered him a contract. "You'll Never Need Another Favor" and "Part Time Love" were two of his earliest waxings for Galaxy. While pop listeners would get to hear little more by him—and would often confuse him with the more prominent Johnnie Taylor, of "Who's Making Love" and "Disco Lady" fame—Taylor, with his distinctive dry-voiced style, has maintained a loyal R & B following through the years. More than a half-dozen of his sides have made the black charts.

Little Johnny is still active, still recording for Ronn Records, and most definitely still a contender for a second crossover hit.

Sunny & The Sunglows

TALK TO ME
(Joe Seneca)
Tear Drop 3014
No. 11   *October 26, 1963*

Sunny Ozuna (lead vocals) and the rest of the Sunglows—Gilbert Fernandez, Alfred Luna, Tony Tostado, and the Villanueva brothers (Jesse, Oscar, and Ray)—met while attending the Burbank Vocational School in San Antonio, Texas. When they formed their act in 1959, they were Chicano rockers, but each member brought a unique musical influence to the total sound. Within the Sunglows were strong interests in the blues, country, Tex-Mex, mariachi, up-tempo polkas, and the swamp-pop leanings of Joe Barry, ROD BERNARD, and Jivin' Gene.

In 1962, the group formed the Sunglow label, which had limited distribution. A positive response to the Sunglows' eclectic offerings came with "Golly Gee," possibly their initial single. For a time, Okeh picked up the disk for national dispersal. The following year, producer Huey "Crazy Cajun" Meaux had Sunny and crew cover "Talk To Me," a ramblin' rockaballad first popularized by Little Willie John. The cut was swampy, pleasantly sloppy, and right on the groove.

"Rags To Riches" (#45, 1963) and "Out Of Sight-Out Of Mind" (#71, 1964) were similarly styled romps, and fairly successful ones at that. These platters appeared under the name "Sunny & The Sunliners," in order to distinguish the group's pop releases from the polka instrumentals that they were concurrently issuing under the "Sunny & The Sunglows" banner. One of these pop singles, "Peanuts," would reach number 64 in 1965.

Factions of the group, using a variety of names, continued to record for Disco Grande, Key Loc, and RPM. For a short period of time, the original unit also recorded as Los Stardusters.

Los Indios Tabajaras

MARIA ELENA
(Lorenzo Barcelata)
RCA 8216
No. 6   *November 16, 1963*

Surely one of the most unpredictable hits and strangest stories to arrive in the land of rock

The Sixties

and roll is this tale of two Brazilian Indians named Natalicio and Antenor Lima. These brothers, born the sons of a Tabajaras Indian chieftain in the far-out jungles of Ceara, were said to have found a guitar laying about in the wild. The boys touched the strings and felt their bodies fill with a mighty, mighty magic.

They trained themselves in the ways of this strange instrument, and traveled 1,200 miles to Rio de Janeiro to play their tribal folk songs for patrons and alcohol drinkers. A man calling himself an agent detected their presence, sized up their potential, and shipped them to Mexico to become schooled in the ways of Bach, Beethoven, and Latin American soul. The Lima brothers, who speak five languages in addition to their native Tupi, gave concerts in South America and began to pick up a following. RCA Records signed these keepers of the guitars to a contract, reasoning that the Lima brothers' tunes would sell well in their homeland. To everyone's surprise, someone at RCA ordered "Maria Elena," a remake of the 1941 Jimmy Dorsey hit, released in the U.S.

Most astonishing about this disk is neither the level of musicianship nor its melody, but the ability of two dudes with no electric guitars, drums, bass, yells, overdubbing, feedback, or echo chambers to secure a stateside hit.

The current whereabouts of Los Indios Tabajaras are not known.

One of Los Indios Tabajaras with unidentified woman (from "Maria Elena" sheet music)

The Village
Stompers

Village Stompers

WASHINGTON SQUARE
(Bob Goldstein, David Shire)
Epic 9617
No. 2 *November 23, 1963*

The Village Stompers were Dick Brady, Ralph Casale, Don Coates, Frank Hubbell, Mitchell May, Joe Muranyi, Al McManus, and Lenny Pogan—an eight-man band of Dixieland dusters. One was a music teacher by day, two had college degrees in music, and collectively, they claimed to have worked with almost every notable Dixieland jazz group of the period. Recording as Frank Hubbell & The Hubcaps, one subset of the Stompers had "Broken Date" issued on the Topix label.

The Stompers were Big Apple–based and got their new name from gigging in the Greenwich Village area. "Washington Square," their first single, was named after the large park smack-dab in the middle of the Village. Two of the next batch of 45s—"From Russia With Love" (#81, 1964) and "Fiddler On The Roof" (#97, 1964)—charted, and the unit's first LP, *Washington Square* (1963), sold well. Despite

the lack of further success, the Village Stompers continued to record for the Epic label through 1967.

The Singing Nun

DOMINIQUE
(Soeur Sourire)
Philips 40152
No. 1 *December 7, 1963*

In the spring of 1963, Sister Luc-Gabrielle (b. Janine Deckers, 1933) and a chorus of four other nuns from a convent in Fichermont, Belgium, recorded a dozen or so original tunes at the Philips studios in Brussels. Deckers' songs had been winners at youth retreats held at the monastery, and the order's elders wanted Philips Records to record and press up several hundred copies for the convent's own use. Bigwigs at the label, delighted with the simple, uplifting creations the good sister was offering, decided to test-market some of her recordings in Europe. An album released as by Soeur Sourire ("Sister Smile") sold well, so that *The Singing Nun* and a single,

147

"Dominique"—Deckers' tribute to the founder of the Dominican order—were issued in the States.

The response was unbelievable. Both the album and single rocketed to the top of the charts and stayed there for weeks. The sister with the smile in her voice appeared on "The Ed Sullivan Show," and more singles were released—but interest in the Sister's plaintive sound waned as quickly as it had waxed. *The Singing Nun*, a 1966 Debbie Reynolds flick, bombed. The following year, Sister Luc-Gabrielle left the convent. She attempted to continue her singing career, and, to the dismay of many church brethren, she recorded a poorly received pro–birth-control tune, "Glory Be To God For The Golden Pill."

Janine Deckers and her companion of ten years, Annie Pecher, committed suicide in Belgium in 1985. The two women reportedly downed a massive amount of barbiturates with alcohol. Both had been in despair after a center for autistic children that they had founded was closed due to a lack of funds. The Belgian government had also been hounding Miss Deckers for a large sum of back taxes.

Robin Ward

WONDERFUL SUMMER
(Gil Garfield, Perry Botkin, Jr.)
Dot 16530
No. 14 *December 14, 1963*

Robin was born Jackie Ward in Nebraska in the early 1940s; the family soon after moved to Los Angeles. As a young girl, Jackie loved to sing. She went to school and did all those things people do when they are growing up. The pattern continued: she married, settled down, and started raising a family, but still she dreamed of making a niche for herself as a singer. Jackie recorded some demos, and the tiny Songs Unlimited label released "Lover's Lullabye." Dot Records took an interest and issued a single of hers called "Top 40 Blues" (credited to Robin). Both disks were poor sellers.

In the heart of the winter, Dot released her Lesley Gore–like "Wonderful Summer." With the onset of spring, the label—with crossed fingers and pretzel logic—issued the similar-sounding "Winter's Here." No one bought the humor, and "Here" went nowhere. After a few more sides, Ward's career dimmed.

Caravelles

YOU DON'T HAVE TO BE
A BABY TO CRY
(Merrill, Shand)
Smash 1852
No. 3 *December 21, 1963*

In the early '60s, Andrea Simpson (b. 1946) and Lois Wilkinson (b. 1944) worked for a brokerage firm in London, their hometown. At office parties, after the rug had been rolled back and some folks had had a few, the girls would sing a few breathy numbers. Many a fellow employee thought the misses had the makings of stardom and encouraged them. Thereafter, Andrea and Lois spent many an afterhour rehearsing and tightening up their tunes.

Late in 1963, the duo made a demo of something called "You Don't Have To Be A Baby To Cry" and brought it to the blokes at B.P.R. Records. The label lads liked the girls' wholesome style, and signed them up. With an eye to the sky, the young ladies named themselves after the Caravelle, a famous French airliner. Just weeks before the stateside Beatle Invasion, "You Don't Have To Be A Baby" landed on the nation's charts. Similar-sounding singles followed in the jet stream, but nothing nudged the masses to buy these Caravelle waxings.

With the failure of their folk-rockin' "Hey Mama, You've Been On My Mind," Lois Wilkinson left the duo for a solo career as Lois Lane and married bandleader Johnny Arthey. Against all odds, Andrea Simpson and a series of replacements have carried the "Caravelles" name into the '80s, but none of their sporadically-released recordings have charted here or abroad.

The Secrets

THE BOY NEXT DOOR
(Johnny Madara, David White)
Philips 40146
No. 18 *December 23, 1963*

Josie Allen, Kragen Ray, Pat Miller, and Carole Raymont met in their Cleveland high school. During the early '60s, they performed as the Secrets at parties and school hops. An area manager named Redda Robbins heard them, and offered to take the girls under her wing. Robbins coached them, dressed them, and lined up some professional bookings in local clubs. At one of these, a talent scout for Philips, the Mercury Records subsidiary, heard the Secrets. Smash, another Mercury subsidiary, was having success with a girl group called the Angels, and with the intent of shaping a similar act, the Philips scout signed the teen queens to a recording contract.

Aside from their "My Boyfriend's Back" sound-alike, "The Boy Next Door," the details of the Secrets' career remain shrouded in mystery. Three more Philips singles—all breathy and bouncy, and all produced by the team of Johnny Mardra and David White—appeared. (Later in the '60s, Mardra and White would be members of the Spokesmen, whose "Dawn Of Correction" was a right-wing reply to BARRY McGUIRE's "Eve Of Destruction.") Before the Secrets became nary a whisper, a few more singles followed on DCP and Omen. Among these is their supreme effort—an obscure Diana Ross rouser called "I Feel The Thrill Coming On."

Joey Powers

MIDNIGHT MARY
(Artie Wayne, Ben Raleigh)
Amy 892
No. 10 *January 4, 1964*

Joey Powers was born in 1939 in Perry Como's hometown of Canonsburg, Pennsylvania. Apparently, the Powerses knew the Comos, for when Joey turned 20, Perry opened some doors and secured for Joey a job as producer of NBC-TV's "John Hill's Exercise Show." After a brief stint there, Joey taught wrestling at Ohio State University. At some point, Powers must have opened his mouth and sung a song or two, since RCA Victor signed him to a recording contract in 1962. A few promising teen idol-type disks were issued, but nothing—not even a number by Hal David and Burt Bacharach, "Don't Envy Me"—sold very well.

Early in 1963, Joe met aspiring singer/ songwriter/producer Artie Wayne. Artie had teamed up with Ben Raleigh (writer of "Wonderful! Wonderful!" and "Dungaree Doll") for a dirty little number called "Midnight Mary." Al Massler at Amy Records heard some preliminary demos and agreed to issue the tune. Of course, no one knew that Beatlemania was about to wipe out every single American teen idol with short hair.

"Mary" connected, but all of Joey's follow-up

singles were swept away by the Fab Four's music. Before Artie Wayne joined Powers in the sea of oblivion, Liberty Records let him cut a single that asked: "Where Does A Rock And Roll Singer Go?" Ben Raleigh went on to write "Love Is A Hurtin' Thing" and "Dead End Street" (both hits for Lou Rawls) as well as "Blue Winter" (a hit for Connie Francis).

Tams

WHAT KIND OF FOOL
(DO YOU THINK I AM)
(Ray Whitley)
ABC-Paramount 10502
No. 9 *February 22, 1964*

The Tams were Floyd Ashton (b. Aug. 15, 1933), Horace Key (b. Apr. 13, 1934), Bob Smith (b. Mar. 18, 1936) and the Pope brothers, Charlie (b. Aug. 7, 1936) and Joe (b. Nov. 6, 1933). In the late '40s, while still high school students in Atlanta, they came together to form a singing act; colored tam-o-shanter hats were all they could afford in the way of stage outfits, ergo their name.

The Tams rehearsed and played local clubs for more than a decade before they approached Lowery Music, the hub of music publishing and recording in Atlanta. Attracted to Joe's gravel-throated lead vocals and the unit's tight harmonies, Lowery assigned Joe South to produce them and provide them with songs. The collaboration continued for most of the Tams' recording career. "Untie Me," their very first release, appeared on the Arlen label and made both the pop and R & B charts. ABC-Paramount Records took notice of the Tams, and picked up their contract from Arlen.

At this point, the group's only personnel change took place when Ashton stepped aside for Albert Cottle, Jr. "What Kind Of Fool" was the next single, and the Tams' lone top 40 hit. Five more singles placed on the Hot 100 through 1968, and even more disks made the R & B charts. Not all one-off hitmakers return penniless to the cauldron of obscurity— persistence had paid off for the fellows from Georgia.

While the Tams never made the pop charts in the '70s, they continued to record fine releases on a consistent basis for 1-2-3, Capitol, and Dunhill. To the surprise of many, including the Tams themselves, Dunhill's re-release of "Hey Girl, Don't Bother Me" from 1964 earned them a number-one hit on the British charts in the summer of 1971. The group has retreated from the bright spotlights of pop idolatry, but every so often, the Tams reappear with a new single or two on some small independent label.

Rivieras

CALIFORNIA SUN
(Henry Glover)
Riviera 1401
No. 5 *February 29, 1964*

Bill Dobslaw (lead vocals, keyboards) was an "old man" of 21 but knowledgeable in the ways of the rock and roll world. He knew Ral Donner, and this impressed Doug Gean (bass), Marty Fortson (vocals, guitar), Otto Nuss (organ) Joe Pennell (guitar), and Paul Dennert (drums)—all high-schoolers from South Bend, Indiana. They formed the Playmates to play some hot rock and roll at sock hops, get the chicks, and make enough bread to buy a machine like that 1963 Buick Riviera.

"We started doing 'California Sun' pretty early," Otto Nuss told *Kicks* writer Miriam Linna. "It was always a favorite right from the beginning. The original song [recorded by JOE JONES] is slow. We turned it into a fast song with heavy guitar, organ, and drums. We did a lot of rock and roll hits then—Jerry Lee Lewis stuff, Elvis, Little Richard—but we'd do them our way, always red hot and fast."

In July 1963, Dobslaw, as the Playmates' manager, booked an hour of session time in Chicago's Columbia Recording Studios. In three takes, the guys had "California Sun" in the can. Also cut at the session was "Played On," the intended "A" side. Only a thousand copies were pressed, and one of these found its way into the hands of a DJ named Art Roberts. Art liked the "California Sun" side, and rode the tune repeatedly on the airwaves.

After just three days of airplay, U.S.A., a small independent Chicago label, picked up national distribution on the Playmates' first waxing. ("Played On" was mysteriously pulled off the disk, so part of the group returned to

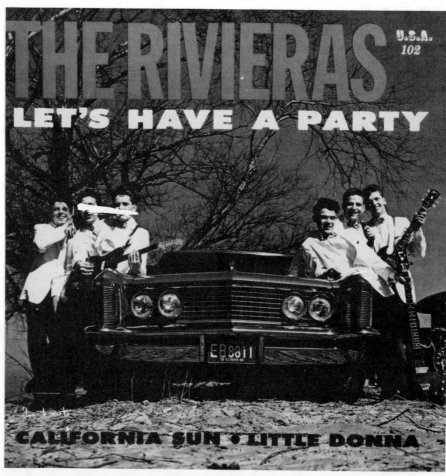

the studio to tape an instrumental dedicated to their label's owner, Howard Bedno: "H.B. Goose Step.") "We decided to name ourselves after the Buick Riviera," Marty Fortson explained. "It was the perfect name, being that the Riviera was hailed far and wide as the car of 1963."

Before Dobslaw even got the deal with U.S.A. for distribution, Joe and Marty had enlisted in the Marines. As Marty recalled, "I was in 'Nam getting shot at, and I heard the record. I thought, 'Oh man, you blew it.'" "California Sun" rocketed into the top 10.

"California Sun" sold like hotcakes, but the follow-up, "Little Donna" (#93, 1964) b/w "Let's Have A Party" (#99), barely cracked the Hot 100. Under parental pressure, a good chunk of the Rivieras dropped out of the group to clean up their educational act. That left Dobslaw, Gean, and various replacements to carry on with that crude but distinctive Midwestern surf-'n'-party sound.

A cover of BOBBY DAY's "Rockin' Robin" held down the number-96 slot for a week in 1964, but later issuances did not do as well. Dobslaw struggled to keep the "Rivieras" name alive and a functional group together. Two singles— "Somebody New" and "Never Felt The Pain"—even appeared under the "Rivieras" name without one original group member playing on them. Finally, in June 1965—slightly more than two years after the Playmates had come together—Dobslaw and the returning Otto Naus shut the group down.

"It just wasn't there at all," Naus said. "We just didn't have that sound we use to have, the sound I wanted—the Rivieras sound."

Pyramids
PENETRATION
(Steve Leonard)
Best 13002
No. 18 March 14, 1964

They had bald heads and were known as "the crazies of the surf scene." In the heat of the Beatle Invasion, the British press ran stories and referred to them as "America's answer to the Beatles." They were not to be, but the Pyramids did make an important contribution to the handful of never-ending summer classics annually activated by rock-radio programmers.

Willie Glover was a shy, poor, North Carolina-raised youth who moved to Long Beach, California, in the summer of 1961. Will would bring his guitar to school, keep to himself, and practice. Fellow Long Beach Poly High student Skip Mercer approached Will, struck up a friendship, and suggested they form a group. After some shuffling of members, the line-up was set and the name was chosen. In addition to Mercer (lead guitar) and Glover (rhythm guitar), the Pyramids were Steve Leonard (bass), Ron McMullen (drums), and Tom Pittman (sax).

John Hodge approached the group, offering to manage the Pyramids as well as record them. With borrowed money, he hustled the guys into the Garrison Studios in Long Beach and cut two sides. Issued on Best Records, "The Pyramid Stomp" sold only a handful: airplay had been zip, and distribution was nil.

The Pyramids returned to playing school dances and record hops. Steve Leonard created a take-off on "Pipeline," an instrumental smash by THE CHANTAYS. The Pyramids recorded "Penetration"—originally entitled "Eyeballs"—as a "B" side to the otherwise forgettable "Here Comes Marsha." This time, Hodge managed to secure local airplay and national distribution with London Records. With an eye to a marketable gimmick, he convinced the guys to shave their heads, and invited the press to take snapshots. "Penetration" pierced the nation's top 20.

The band was hotter than the noon-day sun. Stuffed in a station wagon with primitive sound equipment, the baldies moved about making TV appearances on "American Bandstand," "Hullabaloo," and "The Lloyd Thaxton Show"; they even snuck in a bit part in Frankie and Annette's third flick, *Bikini Beach* (1964).

Ironically, the Pyramids never received a penny for their chart-mounting moment in the sun. Glover, Leonard, and McMullen, in an interview with *Kicks* writer Robert Dalley, charged that their trusted manager, John Hodge, had gathered up all the money for himself and lost it all in bad investments. Disgust and discord set in, and even though a few more highly collectible singles were issued, the Pyramids rapidly crumbled.

Tommy Tucker
HIGH HEEL SNEAKERS
(Robert Higginbotham)
Checker 1067
No. 11 March 21, 1964

Tucker was born Robert Higginbotham in Springfield, Ohio on March 5, 1933. He acquired his "Tommy Tucker" name while sitting on the bench during a high school football game. Some friend affectionately yelled at him, "Little Tommy Tucker's a real motherf***er." Robert thought the phrase was catchy enough to make a memorable monicker.

As "T. Tucker," he joined his first band, the Bob Woods Orchestra, in the late '40s, playing clarinet and boogie-woogie piano. The band worked the clubs in Columbus, Dayton, and Springfield. They were also called upon to back up name acts like Big Maybelle, Billie Holiday, Little Willie John, and one harp-player that would greatly influence Tommy Tucker—Jimmy Reed.

In 1955, Tucker formed the Dusters, a doo-wop quintet, with James Crosby, Dave Johnson, Clarence LaVille (from the old Bob Woods

Tommy Tucker

band), and Yonnie Peoples. Things looked hot when ARC Records re-dubbed them the Cavaliers, recorded them, and issued a single, "Ivory Tower." Soon after, Hudson Records brought the Cavaliers into the King Studios to cut "Please Don't Leave Me To Cry." When both 45s failed to sell, the group disbanded. Tommy moved to Dayton, where for the next few years he worked a regular gig at the Harris Bar on 5th Street.

Johnny Smith, Tucker's manager, got the Hi, Atco, and Sunbeam labels to each record and release one Tucker single, but all three disks— "Miller's Cave," "Rock And Roll Machine" (as by Tee Tucker), and "My Blue Heaven"—fared poorly. However, once he met Herb Abramson (owner of the A-1 Studios and the Blaze, Festival, and Triumph labels), Tommy was set to score. With Jimmy Reed in mind, he took to the studios and cut a demo on "High Heel Sneakers," accompanied by Dean Young on guitar, Brenda Lee Jones on bass, and Johnny Williams on drums. Instead of asking Reed to record a polished version of the tune, Abramson, acting as Tommy's manager and producer, had Chess Records' Checker subsidiary issue the rough demo as a finished track.

The response was overwhelming and, unfortunately, unduplicable. After "Long Tall Shorty" (#90, 1964), "Alimony," and further sides stiffed, Tommy returned to school. In the late '60s, he received a liberal-arts degree from the Thomas Edison College in New Jersey. He briefly returned to Chess for a few singles, and did a pre-Sinatra version of "That's Life" for Abramson's Festival label.

Tommy Tucker died of poisoning on January 22, 1982. Reports vary as to the precise cause of his death.

Irma Thomas
WISH SOMEONE WOULD CARE
(Irma Thomas)
Imperial 66013
No. 17 *May 16, 1964*

Irma Thomas was born Irma Lee in Ponchatoula, Louisiana, on February 18, 1941. Her parents moved to New Orleans when she was a baby. They lived in a rooming house behind the Bell Hotel. "That's where I really got interested in music," Irma told Almost Slim, author of *I Hear You Knockin'*. "The lounge in the motel had a jukebox, and I'd sneak off and listen to it every chance I'd get. I'd hear Clyde

McPlatter and the Drifters, Joe Liggins, Lowell Fulsom, and Annie Laurie. My favorite record then was 'Ida Red' by Percy Mayfield."

Irma received her singing training on Sundays at the Home Mission Baptist Church. Her sixth-grade teacher entered her in a talent contest at the Carver Theatre, and she won first place singing Nat "King" Cole's "Pretend." But all was to stop when Irma became pregnant—a pregnant 14-year-old was not looked upon too highly in those days, and Irma felt like an outcast. She washed dishes for 50 cents an hour; her first marriage ended. It was during her second marriage and the creation of two more children that Thomas started singing with bandleader Tommy Ridgely at New Orleans' Pimlico Club.

Ridgely hooked Irma up with Ron Records owner Joe Ruffino, who was immediately interested in recording her on something called "Don't Mess With My Man." "Don't Mess" (—/#22, 1960) was a solid-selling first outing. After a fine follow-up, "A Good Man," failed to fly, Thomas moved to Minit Records for some of her grittiest efforts ever—"Cry On," "It's Too Soon To Know," "It's Raining," and "Ruler Of My Heart" (the latter was reworked by Otis Redding into "Pain In My Heart"). The Minit label had a family feeling to it: New Orleans artists like ERNIE K-DOE, Jessie Hill, AARON NEVILLE, and Benny Spellman would often drop by and sing back-up on Irma's sessions.

In 1964, Minit was acquired by Imperial, a subsidiary of Liberty Records. "Wish Someone Would Care" was Irma's first single under this arrangement. In 1984, "Break-A-Way," the disk's flip side, would regally resurface as a hit for TRACEY ULLMAN. Three other Thomas 45s on Imperial—"Anyone Who Knows What Love Is (Will Understand)" (#52, 1964), "Times Have Changed" (#98, 1964), and "He's My Guy" (#63, 1964)—made both the pop and R & B listings in 1964. A debut LP was packed and pushed, and Irma hit the road to tour behind her platters.

Irma's name may be familiar to rock and roll fans for another reason. The Rolling Stones took notice of Irma's soulful sounds, and quickly covered her unsuccessful follow-up to "Wish Someone Would Care"—"Time Is On My Side." The Stones' version was their first top 10 disk (#6, 1964), although Irma was less than flattered.

"The Rolling Stones version was worse [than mine]," Irma declared to the *Chicago Sun Times'* Don McLeese. "I mean we won't say similar in their case—it was worse. En-

glish groups were on the rise at the time, and whether it was good, bad or indifferent, they were English. It was beside the point whether or not they could sing." Irma told Bob Shannon and John Javna in *Behind the Hits* that with the success of the Stones' rendition, "I stopped doing it. I really liked that song, and I put my heart and soul into it. Then along comes this English group that half-sings it, and gets a million-seller."

Despite the creation of some high-quality product for the Chess, Roker, Fungus, RCA, and Maison de Soul labels, Irma never managed to replicate the success of "Wish Someone Would Care," though she did crack the R & B charts in 1968 with a cover of Otis Redding's "Good To Me" (—/#42). Irma Thomas has been active on the New Orleans club scene and the blues circuit ever since. Neighbors and faithful fans call her "The Soul Queen of New Orleans," and insist that she sounds every bit as good now as she did then. During the '80s, Rounder Records issued several LPs of new material.

Danny Williams
WHITE ON WHITE
(L. Crane, B. Ross)
United Artists 685
No. 9 *May 16, 1964*

Throughout the pre-Beatle '60s, South African-born Danny Williams functioned as England's cloned answer to Johnny Mathis. From his very first Mathis-molded smoothie in 1961, "We'll Never Be This Young Again," through his chart-topping rendition of "Moon River" and his top 10 tune, "Wonderful World Of The Young," Danny could do little wrong with British audiences.

Williams, who was born in Port Elizabeth, South Africa on January 7, 1942, had been singing professionally since his 13th year. While he was touring London with an African-based show called "The Golden City Dixies," record producer Norman Newell heard Dan's calming, crooning voice. Newell secured Danny a recording contract with the HMV label, and in 1960, Williams and his family moved to London.

A pile of singles were issued before Williams managed to connect with an American audience. "White On White," a variation (possibly unintentional) on Bobby Vinton's "Blue On Blue" tale, was Danny's only stateside hit. His follow-up, "A Little Toy Balloon" (#84, 1964), made the Hot 100, but none of his successive releases did. Strangely, neither single was a hit with his homeland, where well into the '70s, he continued to work cabarets and concerts.

Danny Williams graced the British charts one last time in 1977 with "Dancing Easy," a re-worked commercial jingle for a martini mix. He still continues to tour when the whim and the want are present. More recently, Danny has been breaking things up in his new career as a black-belt karate instructor.

Reflections

(JUST LIKE) ROMEO & JULIET

(B. Hamilton, F. Gorman)
Golden World 9
No. 6 *May 30, 1964*

Phil "Parrot" Castrodale (b. Apr. 2, 1942, Detroit), Ray "Razor" Steinberg (b. Oct. 29, 1942, Washington, Penn.), Tony "Spaghetti" Micale (b. Aug. 23, 1942, Bronx), Danny Bennie (b. Mar. 13, 1940, Johnston, Scotland), and Johnny Dean (b. 1942, Detroit) were the Detroit-based reflections, so named after Parrot caught the hot-shot reflection the group cast in the mirror of their rehearsal hall. Parrot, Razor, Spaghetti, and the rest were working record hops, school dances, and other social functions in 1963 when they were discovered by producer Jan Hutchens.

Hutchens liked the fellows' old-time doo-wop approach—they had a vocal style that was nearly extinct by this point in pop history—and lined up a recording session for the guys with the teeny-weeny Tigre label. The Reflections' first release, a cover of the Five Satins' "In The Still Of The Nite," charted in some Midwestern markets, including Chicago. Noting this response to the guys' throw-back sound, the Golden World label signed the group to a multi-record contract.

With their next release, "(Just Like) Romeo & Juliet," the Reflections secured their one and only sizeable hit. Yet ironically, the group never even took the tune seriously.

"When I first heard [the song], I hated it," Tony Micale told *Goldmine*'s Stu Fink. "We thought it was a real bubblegum song, the words in it and all. So we would practice it every day to the point where we would mimic it. And by mimicking the song, we put in all the falsetto stuff. We did that as a joke, as a kind of payback: if they wanted to make it stupid, we'd really make it stupid."

The follow-up to "(Just Like) Romeo & Juliet," "Like Columbus Did," held down the number 96 slot on the Hot 100 for a week. "Poor Man's Son" also charted (#55, 1965), but six further Golden World releases stiffed. The problem: the group was now typecast by record-buyers, who expected the Reflections to replicate the sound of their big hit. "They wanted us to do that falsetto on most everything we did after that. We hated it and we couldn't get any madder at a company than we were."

In 1966, the group switched to the ABC label for one rehash of their big moment ("Like Adam & Eve") and one effort at updating their sound ("The Long Cigarette"). The times were wrong or the approach wasn't right: nothing was coming together right for Spaghetti, Razor, Parrot, and the gang. In a last-ditch maneuver, the guys changed their name to the High and the Mighty—but their only single under their new identity, "Escape From Cuba," sputtered.

The Reflections carried on for years, playing college dates and clubs. Currently, Micale and Dean are playing in a Detroit-area band called the Larados.

Premiers

FARMER JOHN

(Terry Harris)
Warner Bros. 5443
No. 19 *August 1, 1964*

Very few Latino rock and roll bands, in the days before Santana, managed to successfully steal even a slight serving of the nation's auditory attention. Among the few such acts were the Blendells, the Midnighters, Cannibal & The Headhunters, and the Premiers.

The Premiers—George Delgado (guitar), Johnny Perez (drums), Larry Perez (guitar), Phil Ruiz (sax), Joe Urzua (sax), and Frank Zuniga (bass)—were East L.A.'ers through and through. Since they were building up a reputation on the Southern California circuit as a knock-out band, producers Billy Cardenas and Eddie Davis made a special effort to check out their paces at the Rainbow Gardens in Pomona. Cardenas and Davis were impressed, and approached the guys about making some recordings. "Farmer John," a cover version of an old Don & Dewey number, was the first side issued on the local Faro label.

The unruly crowd sounds in the background give the impression that "Farmer John" was a live recording; the label even claims that the number was taped "live at The Rhythm Room in Fullerton, California." In actuality, Cardenas and Davis brought the band and a pile of friends into an old studio on Melrose Avenue. The friends were duly inebriated and instructed to whoop it up as if they were at a wild party (this bit of trickery became an increasingly common way to simulate the excitement of a live performance on record). When sales on "Farmer John" ballooned beyond the Hispanic community, Warner Bros. picked up the 45 for national distribution.

"Annie Oakley," the follow-up, flopped, and was the only other Premiers disk to receive national distribution. Thereafter, a few years' worth of now-hard-to-find, similar-sounding singles were issued on Faro. The band reportedly carried on working the Southern California circuit for much of the '60s.

Jelly Beans
I WANNA LOVE HIM SO BAD
(Jeff Barry, Ellie Greenwich)
Red Bird 10003
No. 9 *August 8, 1964*

The Jelly Beans

The Jelly Beans were four gals and a guy from Jersey City. Alma Brewer, Diane Taylor, sisters Elyse and Maxine Herbert, and Charlie Thomas were just high schoolers when they were discovered by manager-to-be Bill Downs. Bill knew producer Steve Venet, who brought the group to Red Bird Records. At Red Bird, the legendary songwriting team of Jeff Barry and Ellie Greenwich were assigned the task of making the quintet into hit-paraders. "I Wanna Love Him So Bad" was the Jelly Beans' first release.

The girl-group sound was still hot. With Charlie's bass floppin' like a flat tire, and the girlies cheerfully chirpin' along, their disk sold close to a million copies. "Baby Be Mine" (#51, 1964), also penned by Barry and Greenwich, didn't do too badly, either. Things looked good for the Jelly Beans. There was talk of releasing an album, and some tracks were recorded; however, no LP and or subsequent singles ever appeared on Red Bird Records.

The following year, a lone 45 utilizing the group's logo was issued on the Eskee label.

Jimmy Hughes
STEAL AWAY
(Jimmy Hughes)
Fame 6401
No. 17 *August 15, 1964*

Not everyone who has a hit, becomes a star, and makes some money wants to remain in the limelight. "I enjoyed performing, but I missed my family," Jimmy told Peter Guralnick in *Sweet Soul Music.* "When I quit, I didn't miss it one bit." After eight years of singing, recording, touring, and touring yet some more, Jimmy walked away from the entertainment game. What he has been doing to make a living since is not known, but most likely, he still sings Sundays in his church choir.

Jimmy Hughes was born in Florence, Alabama. From early on, he sang of God and His glory. By the age of eight, he was the lead singer in his choir. For years, he sang in various gospel groups, most notably the Singing Clouds, a group that often made local radio appearances. In 1962, while Hughes was working at the Robbins Rubber Company plant in nearby Leighton, a friend convinced him to drop by Rick Hall's Wilson Dam studio and audition on some sinful secular songs.

Hall, who had just produced Arthur Alexander's "You Better Move On" (#24, 1962),

taped several of Hughes' tunes and soon managed to lease "I'm Qualified" to the Philly-based Jamie/Guyden vinyl-pushers. Hall had the gut feeling that Jimmy could have a hit with "Steal Away," a dank, adulterous piece of business that Jimmy had written. After several labels declined to release the track, Hall decided to set up his own label, Fame.

Hall was right on the money—"Steal Away" was to become a solid Southern-soul single. "Try Me" (#65, 1964), "Neighbor, Neighbor" (#65, 1966), and "Why Not Tonight" (#90, 1967) all climbed high on the pop charts. Still other singles clicked with the R & B audiences. But by the end of the '60s, Jimmy Hughes was burnt out on the whole scene, and walked away from it all, never to return.

Jumpin' Gene Simmons
HAUNTED HOUSE
(R. Geddins)
Hi 2076
No. 11 *August 26, 1964*

"One day, I guess it was about 1954, I was visiting a cousin of Elvis Presley's," Simmons (b. 1933, Tupelo, Miss.) recalled to Randy McNutt in *We Wanna Boogie.* "I didn't know who Elvis was at the time, but somebody said he played the guitar, so I handed him one and he just smiled. He said, 'I only play for myself.' Personally, I thought the guy looked weird. Greased-back hair, tight pants, all that. Yeah, this guy was hipper than we country boys."

Weeks later, Elvis linked up with Sun Records, and Gene, not one to be left shakin' in the cold, asked the Pelvis to put in some good words for Jumpin' Gene at Sun Records. Sun issued one Simmons single, "Drinkin' Wine," but it went down the drain. With kind words, the guys at the label snuffed out Gene's hopes of having any more yellow-labeled Sun releases bearing his name. Fortunately, a good buddy and fellow one-off Sun recording artist, Ray Harris, got Gene a spot singing with the big-time Bill Black Combo. Hi Records, Black's label, issued a pile of sides with Jumpin' Gene's name on them, but nothing moved an inch.

Gene crossed paths with the man who would later become "Sam The Sham," Domingo Samudio. Dom had been doing a well-received Johnny Fuller R & B horror called "Haunted House" as part of his club set. Hi Records asked Gene to bring Samudio into the studio to wax the number, but Domingo re-

HAUNTED HOUSE • ROCK AROUND THE CLOCK • TEEN-AGE LOVE • THE GREEN DOOR
JUST A LITTLE BIT • (I'M) COMIN' DOWN WITH LOVE • BONY MORONIE • DON'T LET GO
SLIPPIN' AND SLIDING • HOTEL HAPPINESS • YOU CAN HAVE HER • NO HELP WANTED

Hi
RECORDS

jumpin'
GENE
SIMMONS

HL 12018   HL 12018 **MONO**

fused, for some reasons now lost in the cracks of pop history. Hi was hot for the thing, so Gene offered to step in and record the contagiously inane tune.

Even though the British Invasion was in full force, Gene's Memphis ditty soaked up airplay time and creamed the charts. Follow-ups like "The Dodo" (#83, 1964), "The Batman," and "Keep The Meat In The Pan" did little to establish any momentum, however, and as the years rolled on, numerous 45s with Simmons' name on them sat around radio stations unplayed.

Gene was not deterred—well into the '70s, the lad from Tupelo continued finding record companies willing to give him one more shot. Nearly a dozen labels issued Jumpin' Gene records. Some sold to country listeners; some were high-quality but sold poorly anyway; and some just plain stiffed.

In the '80s Gene Simmons moved to Nashville, and currently works in music publishing.

Jackie Ross

SELFISH ONE
(McKinley, Smith)
Chess 1903
No. 11 *September 5, 1964*

When she was three, Jackie (b. Jan. 30, 1946, St. Louis) began her singing career on Mom and Dad's radio show. Her parents were preachers and ran a church. "All of the big gospel singers at the time who would come to St. Louis, they would appear on the broadcast," Ross told *Goldmine*'s Robert Pruter. "I've been knowing Sam Cooke ever since I was just a little thing. Not only him but all the big groups. We knew them pretty well, because they would visit my parents' house for big dinners and everything."

Cooke and the family were especially close, and when Jackie's dad died in 1954, Sam encouraged the family to move to Chicago, where he could keep an eye on them. In 1962, Cooke, who had taken notice of Ross' singing abilities, won her mother's permission to record her for his Sar label.

"After the record, Sam wanted to take me out to California. But as much as my mother loved him, she said, 'No, I'm sorry, I can't let you take my 15-year-old child and continue to raise her out there.'" Her single, "Hard Time," failed to sell.

After winning a talent contest at the Trianon Ballroom, Jackie began touring with Syl Johnson's band. She was discovered at one engagement by Bill Doc Lee, a DJ on a gospel station owned by Leonard Chess of Chess Records. "Selfish One," Jackie's debut disk for Chess, was her only major charting on either the pop or R & B listings. Surely, her powerful "We Can Do It" and her cover of Evie Sands' "Take Me For A Little While" should have established her. Early in 1966, Ross left the Chess label after a royalty dispute.

"It was a big let-down for me after what they told me 'Selfish One' did *not* do. If I had all my old papers, I could quote you a figure—but the amount of money I had gotten from it, it was just ridiculous."

After a couple of singles each for Brunswick, Mercury, and Jerry Butler's Fountain label, Ms. Ross found a half-dozen other labels to issue occasional singles with her name on them, but none of these attracted much attention.

Joe Hinton

FUNNY (HOW TIME SLIPS AWAY)
(Willie Nelson)
Back Beat 541
No. 13   *October 10, 1964*

Not much is known about Joe Hinton. He was born some time in 1929 and he died on August 13, 1968, in a Boston hospital of "natural causes." In between those two poles in life's continuum, Joe sang his guts out.

It was while singing with the Spirit of Memphis gospel group that Joe was discovered by Don Robey of the Duke and Peacock record labels. Robey persuaded Joe to sing of other things than Jesus. His first half-dozen singles elicited little response from pop audiences, but Robey had faith that something very real and urgent lived inside of Joe. More disks were waxed and shipped; "You Know It Ain't Right" (#88) and "Better To Give Than Receive"

(#89) grazed *Billboard*'s Hot 100 in 1963.

Next out of the gate was "Funny (How Time Slips Away)," a Willie Nelson country/soul song that Jimmy Elledge had charted with two years earlier (#22, 1962). "Funny" should have made Joe more accessible to the mainstream pop/rock radio listeners, but it didn't.

Gale Garnett

WE'LL SING IN THE SUNSHINE
(Gale Garnett)
RCA 8388
No. 4   *October 17, 1964*

Gale was born on July 17, 1942, in Auckland, New Zealand. Dad was a carnival pitchman and a music-hall entertainer; consequently, the family moved around a lot. They landed in the U.S. when Gale was nine, moved about some more, and eventually settled in New York City. Dad encouraged her to find her place in the sun. By age 12, Gale was onstage, acting.

When her father died, Gale left home to set up her own place on the Lower East Side. In between bit parts, Garnett worked as a waitress and janitor. In her late teens, she got a role in a touring company of *The Drunkard*. Over the next few years, she made 60 acting appearances on TV episodes of "Bonanza," "Hawaiian Eye," and "77 Sunset Strip." She also acted in stage productions of *Guys and Dolls*, *Threepenny Opera*, and *Show Boat*.

In her meager spare time, the exhausted youth wrote poetry and folk songs. Only three months before Gale walked into RCA Records with a pile of her compositions, she had made her singing debut in a Los Angeles coffeehouse. Label execs found her gravel-throated voice and material to be unique, and gave the go-ahead to record an album's worth of folkie things. "We'll Sing In the Sunshine" was the first single issued, and it was a winner. Garnett's feminist decree of eternal personal independence won a Grammy Award as "Best Folk Recording of the Year." But other than the immediate follow-up, "Lovin' Place" (#54, 1965), no other Garnett platters sold well.

It is not known what became of Gale Garnett. When her sun last shone, it was late in the '60s. Gale was backed by the Gentle Reign, an electric wall of hair, beads, and 12-string guitars. Two odd albums of acid-laced hippie happenings were unleashed by Columbia Records. Gale was definitely "far out" by this time.

Hondells

LITTLE HONDA

(Brian Wilson)
Mercury 72324
No. 9   *October 31, 1964*

Gary Usher is the number-one unsung hero of the subgenre of rock and roll known as surf/hot rod music. Just as Brian Wilson and the Beach Boys were preparing to lay down the entire foundation for this California sound, Gary's uncle introduced him to Brian Wilson. Within days of their meeting, Usher and Wilson created "The Lonely Sea," which later appeared as a track on the Beach Boys' *Surfin U.S.A.* album. Over the years, Gary and Brian would co-write "In My Room," "We'll Run Away," and numerous others. Usher's solo surfer projects, released under his own name, all crashed on the shore.

Usher then picked up on the idea of fabricating groups by bringing together a clutch of musical friends in the recording studio to lay down his tunes as he saw fit. The finished product could then be sold off to various interested record companies and credited to whatever performers the label wished. Usher and his recording pack included (at various times) Chuck Girard, Joe Kelly, Richie Podolor, Ritchie Burns, Jan Berry, Glen Campbell, Bruce Johnston, Terry Melcher, and Brian Wilson. This aggregate of friends were thus the Four Speeds (with the lead vocals being handled by Dennis Wilson), the Super Stocks, the Wheelmen, the Revells, the Knights, the Ghouls, the Silly Surfers . . . and the Hondells.

With the immediate success of "Little Honda," the pressure was on to put together a touring version of the Hondells to take the hit on the road. Ritchie Burns, who was on the actual recording as a background singer, was enlisted to front a "Hondells." As the Hondells' first album was about to be released, a group still did not exist—for the photo on the LP's cover, Ritchie, who was working days as a bank teller, had three other tellers at his bank pose for the photos.

The Hondells were much more successful than anyone had imagined. There were tours, "The Dick Clark Show," "Shindig," and movies like *Ski Party* (1965), *Beach Blanket Bingo* (1965), and *Beach Ball* (1965). More singles were issued, including "My Buddy Seat" (#87, 1965) and "Younger Girl" (#52, 1966), the latter a cover of the Lovin' Spoonful hit.

By the seventh single, the touring company had rehearsed sufficiently to enter the recording studio. Randy Thomas, with folk-rock leanings, had sung lead on "Younger Girl," and did likewise on their last Mercury release, "Cheryl's Going Home." Usher and Burns took the "Hondells" name over to Columbia, and later to Amos Records, where a few more 45s were released. By then, however, the summer sun had set on the surf/hot rod sound, and the group's efforts at folk-rock were generally unconvincing. In 1970, Gary Usher packed up the "Hondells" name placed it into cold storage.

Lorne Greene

RINGO

(Don Robertson, Hal Blair)
RCA 8444
No. 1   *November 7, 1964*

Born in Canada on February 12, 1915, Lorne had his first brush with music when 10 years old. His mother compelled him to study the violin, but a softball fall requiring many stitches soon spared little Lorne's family from the experience of further violin screeches.

It was an actor Greene wanted to be. He studied drama at Queen's University and won a fellowship to an acting school in New York City. In 1940, Lorne became a radio announcer for the Canadian Broadcasting Company, replacing Charles Jennings (father of ABC news anchor Peter Jennings). After a stint in the Canadian Army during World War II, Lorne returned to broadcasting and formed the Academy of Radio Arts.

To help radio announcers keep track of the time remaining in their programs, Lorne invented a stopwatch that counted backwards. While attempting to sell the gadget to an NBC executive, Greene crossed paths with television producer Fletcher Markle, who cast Lorne in the first of many stage and screen productions. Between 1954 and 1958, Lorne made 12 movies. After a guest appearance on "Wagon Train," he was offered what soon became his most famous role—Ben Cartwright, in NBC's "Bonanza" series.

After the runaway success of a "Bonanza" Christmas album—featuring all the Cartwrights doing their stuff—RCA herded Lorne, Dan Blocker, Michael Landon, and Pernell Roberts back into the studio. For one of the ditties, Greene was handed a six-verse poem about some sheriff who saves the life of a gunfighter named Johnny Ringo. The record label apparently didn't know what it had until a Texas DJ started to play the life out of that "Ringo" cut.

For a full-grown Canadian cowpoke to have a number-one hit with a talkie-style country song is hard to believe, but Lorne Greene did it. (Of course, the fact that the tune's title was also the name of one of the members of the Fab Four did not exactly hurt record sales.) Lorne recorded seven albums and many more singles, but he charted only one more time, with a religious talkie titled "The Man" (#72, 1965).

In 1973, after "Bonanza" went to rest in TV Boot Hill, Lorne starred in two other series, "Griff" and "Battlestar Galactica." On September 11, 1987, just prior to filming the resurrected "Bonanza" series, Lorne Greene died of respiratory failure from pneumonia in Santa Monica, California.

A NEW HIT SINGLE BY THAT "RINGO" MAN

LORNE GREENE SINGS "THE MAN"

#8490 c/w "POP GOES THE HAMMER" RCA VICTOR

Coming in February – New Lorne Greene Album "The Man" LPM/LSP-3302   The most trusted name in sound

Nashville Teens

TOBACCO ROAD
(John D. Loudermilk)
London 9889
No. 14 *November 7, 1964*

Not one of these underrated artifacts from the British Invasion had even set foot in Nashville—they were all from Weybridge, Surrey—nor was any one a teen at the time. And in no way were these root-rockers playing C & W. They were darn good, though, at their special blend of good old rhythm 'n' blues.

The Nashville Teens convened in 1962 when Ramon "Ray" Phillips (vocals, bass, harmonica) and Arthur Sharp (vocals), members of two local rival groups, decided to join their musical juices. Michael Dunford (guitar), Roger Groom (drums), John Hawkes (keyboards), and Pete Shannon (bass) completed the original line-up. The unit spent most of 1963 in Hamburg, Germany—at the now legendary Star Club—backing Jerry Lee Lewis for several months. When they returned to England, BO DIDDLEY recruited them for his European tour. Mickey Most—a singer with Bo's opening act, the Minutemen—convinced the teens that he was something of a producer and that he could get them on a label.

Most took the Teens into the studio as part of a one-off deal to record "Tobacco Road," a tune that Sharp had heard while working in a record shop. By this point, Dunford and Groom had left, so the group consisted of Phillips (b. Jan. 16, 1944, Tiger Bay, Wales), Sharp (b. May 26, 1941, Woking), Hawkes (b. May 9, 1940, Bournemouth), and Shannon (b. Aug. 23, 1941, Antrim, Northern Ireland), plus two new members—guitarist John Allen (b. Apr. 23, 1945, Albans) and drummer Barry Jenkins (b. Dec. 22, 1944, Leicester).

"Tobacco Road" was a major chart invader on both sides of the Atlantic. Unfortunately, for their follow-up, the Nashville Teens chose to remake another (and much less appealing) John D. Loudermilk tune—"Google Eye," a folkie tale about an unfortunate trout. The disk went nowhere in the States. The group made a few minor movie appearances (*Be My Guest*, 1965; *Gonks Go Beat*, 1965; *Pop Gear*, 1965), but visa restrictions limited the Teens to a tour of only New York State. Further singles—and there were a few peculiar ones over the next year or two—failed to capitalize on the group's talents. At this point, the Teens' tale becomes fuzzy to both fans and pop historians.

The Nashville
Teens

By 1966, members started their flight. Jenkins joined the Animals. Hawkins left to work with Spooky Tooth, the Strawbs, and Renaissance. Dunford went on to record with Renaissance. Sharp left in 1972 for a desk job alongside Don Arden at Jet Records. By the early '70s, only Ray Phillips remained from the original line-up; when last spotted in the mid-'80s, he was fronting a new edition of the Nashville Teens.

J. Frank Wilson & The Cavaliers

LAST KISS
(Wayne Cochran)
Josie 923
No. 2 *November 7, 1964*

"Last Kiss" was one of those short love stories about a guy, a girl, and a car crash. The tune, based in part on a true incident, was written by blue-eyed soul singer Wayne Cochran. Wayne, whose own vocal performances never cracked the Hot 100, was a wandering Georgia boy who had been screaming his guts out for years in an effort to bring home the bacon. In the early '60s, he lived in a $20-a-month shack on Route 1941. It was a main drag, so over the years he witnessed many a gory car accident. One night

in '64, three couples in a Chevy Impala were killed after crashing into a flatbed truck. With this tragedy as his inspiration, Cochran penned the tune.

Gala Records took an interest in Cochran's dirge and offered him a chance to record it. Locally, sales of the disk were promising enough for Syd Nathan to sign Cochran to the King label. Another rendering of the ode was waxed, but, according to Cochran, Nathan did not like the teen-death tune and failed to adequately promote the single.

In the early '60s, J. Frank Wilson (b. Dec. 11, 1941, Lufkin, Tex.), a former enlisted man in the Air Force, was fronting the Cavaliers (Gene Croyle, Jerry Graham, Phil Trunzo, and Bobby Woods) at proms and dances in San Angelo, Texas. An independent producer named Sonley Roush heard J. Frank and his gallant crew in 1964, and was attracted to their crude, rough sound. Roush convinced his partner at Accurate Sound to cut two of the band's tunes—one of these was a cover of Cochran's "Last Kiss." Roush then persuaded Tamara Records and LeCam Records to issue the record, with the New York-based Josie label picking up national distribution.

That year, in addition to the Texans' successful debut album and their top 10 tune, a cover of Dorsey Burnette's 1960 hit "Hey Little One" charted at number 85. Over the years, a number of other disks with J. Frank's name on them have appeared on the April, Charay, LeCam, and Sully labels. In 1971, an LP appeared on Dill Pickle; in 1974, a re-release of "Last Kiss" made number 92.

Honeycombs

HAVE I THE RIGHT?
(Howard Blaikley)
Interphon 7707
No. 5 *November 14, 1964*

Annie "Honey" Lantree (b. Aug. 28, 1943, Hayes, Middlesex, England) was a hairdresser and a drummer. In 1962, she worked at a small salon in Edgeware, North London, under the supervision of former skiffle guitarist Martin Murray (b. Oct. 7, 1941, London). Marty still took a whack at his axe every now and then, and despite the pleasure of doing numbers on heads full of hair, he still had an itch to form a group and play beat music.

To that end, Marty ran an ad in a music paper, which was promptly answered by guitarist/keyboardist Alan Ward (b. Dec. 12, 1945, Nottingham). Friends introduced Marty

to lead vocalist/pianist/guitarist Denis d'Ell (b. Denis Dalziel, Oct. 10, 1943, London), and Honey recommended her brother John (b. Aug. 20, 1940, Newbury, Berkshire) for the slot of bass player. The line-up was set, and a name was chosen: "The Sherabons."

By mid-'63, the group was garnering favorable notices at the local pubs. Songwriters Howard Blaikley and Ken Howard offered to manage the band and hooked them up with independent producer Joe Meek. Joe had worked wonders with Mike Berry, Lonnie Donegan, Johnny Kidd & The Pirates, and especially THE TORNADOES. Soon the Honeycombs (a monicker created from Annie's nickname plus Honey and Marty's occupation as "combers"), were stompin' near the top of charts with their debut disk, Blaikley's "Have I The Right?"

The only stateside LP (*Here Are the Honeycombs*, 1965) sold well, and follow-up 45s were quite appealing. (Oddly enough, the album's liner notes misidentified the Honeycombs as "The Sherations.") However, someone shipped the group off on a tour of France, Australia, and New Zealand. Because they were away from their home turf for so long, the Combs

The Honeycombs

failed to chart with their next batch of singles. On the group's return, Murray, having injured himself by falling off a stage, dropped out and was replaced by Peter Pye.

On February 3, 1967, Joe Meek, the Honeycombs' producer and guiding force, fatally shot himself in the head. No further records were issued by the group. Denis d'Ell departed for a lackluster solo career.

The Honeycombs' managers and songwriters, Blaikley and Howard, went on to create a string of sounds for the Herd and the British quintet of Dave Dee, Dozy, Beaky, Mick & Tich. They are currently working as in-house composers of theme music for the PBS series "Masterpiece Theatre."

Robert Goulet

MY LOVE, FORGIVE ME
(AMORE, SCUSAMI)
(V. Pallavicini, S. Lee, B. Mescoil)
Columbia 43131
No. 16   *January 2, 1965*

Robert was born Stanley Applebaum on November 26, 1933, in Lawrence, Massachusetts, and raised in Edmonton, Canada. He sang in church choirs and with local orchestras before winning a scholarship to the opera school of the Royal Conservatory of Music in Toronto. There he studied acting and singing, making many theater and TV appearances. In 1954, he came to New York City to try his luck at Broadway, but nothing panned out, so for four months he sold stationery in Gimbel's department store. Returning to Canada, he won a leading role in the CBC's production of *Little Women*. Numerous other theatrical productions followed.

Stanley's transformation into "Robert Goulet" occurred when he was cast as Sir Lancelot—opposite Richard Burton and Julie Andrews—in the Broadway production of *Camelot*. Columbia Records offered the saccharine singer a contract, and for years Goulet's easy-listening LPs graced *Billboard*'s top pop albums chart.

Before "My Love, Forgive Me," Robert did manage to chart with a recording of "What Kind Of Fool Am I?" (#89, 1962); his follow-up to "My Love," "Summer Sounds" (#58, 1965), also made the Hot 100. He continues to appear on TV variety programs, and in musical productions like *Brigadoon, Carousel,* and *Kiss Me Kate.*

Julie Rogers

THE WEDDING
(Joaquin Prieto, Fred Jay)
Mercury 72332
No. 10   *January 2, 1965*

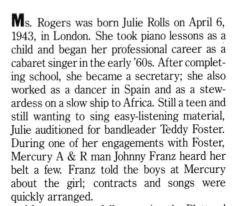

Ms. Rogers was born Julie Rolls on April 6, 1943, in London. She took piano lessons as a child and began her professional career as a cabaret singer in the early '60s. After completing school, she became a secretary; she also worked as a dancer in Spain and as a stewardess on a slow ship to Africa. Still a teen and still wanting to sing easy-listening material, Julie auditioned for bandleader Teddy Foster. During one of her engagements with Foster, Mercury A & R man Johnny Franz heard her belt a few. Franz told the boys at Mercury about the girl; contracts and songs were quickly arranged.

After unsuccessfully covering the Platters' "It's Magic," Rogers waxed "The Wedding," an Argentine tune that had made two earlier chart appearances—for the Chordettes (#91, 1956) and for June Valli (#43, 1959). June's rendition, however, became a perennial. For years thereafter, whenever young lovers tied the knot, some wedding guest would inevitably beseech the reception band to play the sugary strains of this song. By the time the recording had aged but 10 years, sales had totaled 7,000,000 copies worldwide.

Julie Rogers continued exploring that queasy (and decidedly unhip) easy-listening terrain. "Like A Child" (#67, 1965) and her "Hawaiian Wedding Song" sold fairly well in the U.K. After an LP and a few more stateside singles, Rogers' name, but not "The Wedding," faded away into oblivion.

Detergents

LEADER OF THE LAUNDROMAT
(Paul Vance, Lee Pockriss)
Roulette 4590
No. 19   *January 9, 1965*

Paul Vance and Lee Pockriss had been writing pop songs together for years. In the late '50s, they penned "Catch A Falling Star" (Perry Como), "What Is Love?" (The Playmates), and "Itsy Bitsy Teenie Weenie Yellow Polkadot Bikini" (Brian Hyland). Columbia Records let them make a stack of silly singles as Lee &

The Detergents

Paul. Only "The Chick," their nutty number of 1959 about a beatnik chicken and his electric guitar, ever earned a notch on the Hot 100.

Ron Dante (b. Aug. 22, 1945, Staten Island, N.Y.) was working for Don Kirshner's Aldon Music, recording demos for staff songwriters like Burt Bacharach, Carole King, Neil Sedaka, and Vance & Pockriss. In 1964, the latter duo worked up a parody of the Shangri-Las' chart-topping "Leader Of The Pack." Dante and a couple of Brooklyn boys—Danny Jordan (Vance's nephew) and Tommy Wynn—were recruited to cut a quickie demo on this "Pack" parody. A few minor changes were made, sound effects were added, and Morris Levy at Roulette Records issued the demo as by "The Detergents."

The response was immediate and favorable. Dante toured with the group for a few months, but eventually was replaced by Phil Patrick and Danny Jordan's cousin, Tony Favio. A half-dozen follow-ups were issued, of which only a James Bond-inspired novelty number, "Double-O-Seven" (#89, 1965), was mildly successful. Before they disbanded, the Detergents appeared with Nick Adams and Rose Marie in Morey Amsterdam's flaky flick, *Don't Worry, I'll Think of a Title* (1966).

Danny, who had recorded clean teen tunes for the Climax, Leader, and Smash labels, returned to his staff songwriter position at Columbia's Screen Gems, and later produced HOT BUTTER's 1972 hit, "Popcorn." Dante, plus session singer Toni Wine, became the voices for

the Archies (of "Sugar Sugar" fame); Dante was also, in multi-tracked form, all the voices in THE CUFF LINKS. In the '70s, Ron worked as a session singer for Melissa Manchester and Valerie Simpson; did numerous commercial jingles; and formed a lengthy personal and professional relationship with Barry Manilow.

Larks
THE JERK
(Don Julian)
Money 106
No. 7 *January 16, 1965*

The Larks—or the Meadowlarks, as they were first called—were an L.A. unit formed in 1953 by Don Julian (lead vocals, tenor), who tapped the vocal talents of his fellow high-school choirmates. The original crew included Ronald Barrett (tenor), Earl Jones (baritone, bass), and a later member of THE PENGUINS, Randy Jones (bass). Cornell Gunter, of the Flairs and later the Coasters, took an interest in the guys and introduced them to the Bihari brothers at Modern/RPM. A few singles were waxed and shipped, but nothing caught on. Barrett dropped out of the group.

While daydreaming in a warm bath, Julian wrote a nifty number called "Heaven And Paradise." With Earl, Randy, and a new tenor, Glen Reagan, Don approached Dootsie Williams, owner of the DooTone/Dooto label. In a flash, Dootsie knew the group had put together a doo-woppin' classic. "Heaven And Paradise," "Always And Always," and a number of other disks were issued. Members came and went; Don and his gang recorded for a while as the Medallions, backing up Vernon Green.

A decade passed. Don Julian had managed to have some further singles released under various names, but none of them sold very well. Then Don happened onto a new dance in his sister's front room. "I went over to my sister's; the kids were dancing to Martha & The Vandellas' 'Dancin' In The Street,'" Julian recalled to Goldmine's Steve Propes. "I said, 'Hey, what's that you're doing?' One of the kids said, 'The Jerk.' I asked her what it was and she said, 'If you don't know how to do it, come on, I'll teach you.'"

Don dashed home, wrote up some lyrics, and reassembled his Larks/Meadowlarks. (At this point, the "Meadowlarks" name was used to refer to the vocal group's back-up musicians; "The Larks" referred to the singers themselves.) The Larks now consisted of Julian plus two L.A. lads, Charles Morrison and Ted Waters.

Once "The Jerk" appeared on the Money label and started climbing the charts, all the majors rushed in to stomp out their own Jerk tunes and hopefully grab a piece of the action. Before the dust had settled, Bob & Earl ("Everybody Jerk"), THE CAPITOLS ("Cool Jerk"), Clyde & The Blues Jays ("The Big Jerk"), THE CONTOURS ("Can You Jerk Like Me"), the Dukays ("The Jerk"), the Miracles ("Come On And Do The Jerk"), and a mess of other acts had worn the craze out. There seemed no need for Don and his duo to keep jerking: it had all been said and done. Consequently, the Larks' follow-ups, "Soul Jerk" and "Mickey's East Coast Jerk," sold poorly.

Alvin Cash & The Crawlers

TWINE TIME
(Andre Williams, Verlie Rice)
Mar-V-Lus 6002
No. 14 *February 20, 1965*

Alvin Cash and his eight brothers and sisters attended Sumner High in St. Louis; fellow classmates included Luther Ingram, Billy Davis (later of the Fifth Dimension), and Annie Mae Bullocks—a.k.a. Tina Turner. "I used to sit behind Tina and kick my knee in her butt all the time," Cash confessed to *Chicago Sun-Times* writer Dave Hoekstra. "She'd turn around and say 'Alvin Cash, would you cut that out!'"

Around 1960, Alvin (b. Alvin Welch, Feb. 15, 1939, St. Louis) formed a song-and-dance act with three of his brothers, Arthur, George, and Robert, then aged eight to ten. "I danced pretty good in school," Cash told *Goldmine's* Robert Pruter, "and I wanted us to be the world's greatest dance act—tap, soft-shoe, flash, all of it." As the Crawlers, they did their stuff in town and across the river in East St. Louis. In 1963, Alvin trekked to Chicago to see if his act could cut a record.

Andre Williams (who had scored an R & B hit in 1957 with "Bacon Fat") was a producer and talent scout for a small label. Williams had caught the brothers' bit, and approached Cash about yelling some lines on a new dance disk he was planning called "The Twine." Cash came in with the Nightlighters, a band he was touring with at the time. This back-up unit subsequently changed its name to the Crawlers, and later, to the Registers.

"Twine Time" was a pleasantly crude instrumental with an unstoppably funky groove; sales of the disk came close to a million. Flush with solo success, Cash shelved his brothers' dance act and continued to cash in on dance disks: "The Barracuda" (#59, 1965), "The Penguin," "The Philly Freeze" (#49, 1966), "Alvin's Boo-Ga-Loo" (#74, 1966), "The Boston Monkey," "The Charge," "The Creep," and "Keep On Dancing" (#68, 1968). Alvin even recorded a few Muhammad Ali tributes: "Doin' The Ali Shuffle" and "Ali—Part 1 & 2."

The years have passed, but Alvin is still dancin'. Over the years, he has had bit-part appearances in 1978's *The Buddy Holly Story* (as a member of the Five Satins) and in a number of black action flicks like *Black Jack* and *Peetie Wheatstraw, the Devil's Son-in-Law*. Obscure disks with titles like "You Shot Me Through The Grease" and "Funky Washing Machine" still find their way into a handful of record stores.

Alvin Cash currently lives above a pool hall in Chicago, and works as the head of promotion for Triple T Records.

Ad Libs

THE BOY FROM NEW YORK CITY
(John Taylor)
Blue Cat 102
No. 8 *February 27, 1965*

The Boy from New York City

Words and Music by JOHN TAYLOR

Recorded by
THE AD LIBS on Blue Cat Records
TRIO MUSIC CO., INC.

75¢

Keys 3

04348

The Ad Libs

J.T. Taylor was born and raised in Morristown, New Jersey, and later attended the Bordertown Military College. During the '30s and '40s, J.T. played clubs, bars, and music houses, sitting in with the band that supplied the sounds for Martin Block's "Make Believe Ballroom" radio program. In the '50s, J.T. moved to Jersey's Hudson County and started teaching. One night late in the decade, a streetcorner group of doo-woppers caught his ear—the Creators, consisting of Johnny "Angel" Allen, Danny Austin, Chris Coles, Hughie Harris, and Jimmy Wright.

J.T. offered the guys some advice, gave them some songs, and took them down to the dudes at Diamond Disks. Diamond cut a few tunes and leased the tracks to the tiny T-Kay label. "I'll Never Do It Again" sold very little, but Philips Records waxed two more Creators singles. These collectible disks also made a poor showing.

One warm day, while sipping wine and thinking about a woman, J.T. got this notion for

a number to be called "The Boy From New York City." Taylor rounded up the Creators, now known as the Ad Libs, and had them record a demo of the song. Hughie and Danny were the only original Creators left; filling in the vocal gaps were Norm Donegan, Dave Watts, and Mary Ann Thomas.

A club owner brought the demo to the renowned production team of Leiber & Stoller, who signed the group to their new Blue Cat label. Taylor's tune hit the spot, but the Ad Libs 45s that followed—fine efforts like "He Ain't No Angel" and "I'm Just A Down Home Girl"— never matched the ample appeal of "The Boy From New York City."

As the '70s drew to a close, J.T. Taylor and the Ad Libs were still working hard at locating another hit. In 1981, Manhattan Transfer took a remake of "The Boy From New York City" into *Billboard*'s top 10; two years later, a new Ad Libs single, "Spring and Summer," appeared on the group-owned Passion label.

Jewel Akens
THE BIRDS AND THE BEES
(Barry Stuart)
Era 3141
No. 3 *March 20, 1965*

Jewel Akens was born in Texas in 1940. His mother had had her heart set on getting a daughter; Jewel was to be her name. Ma didn't get a daughter, but the babe got the name just the same. By age 11, Jewel was singing in church, and a few years later, after his family had moved to Los Angeles, he and his friend Eddie Daniels formed a group called the Four Dots.

Someone introduced the Four Dots to Jerry Capehart, Eddie Cochran's manager and songwriter. The group cut a single for Freedom Records in 1959; Akens and Daniels, recording as Jewel & Eddie, taped several sides for Capehart's Silver and Capehart labels. Rumors persist to this day that Eddie Cochran's guitar can be heard on these collectible singles. For the Imperial label in 1961, Jewel, probably Eddie, and possibly some reconstituted Dots— collectively calling themselves the Astro-Jets—recorded one of doo-wop's most durable double-sided delights, "Boom A Lay" b/w "Hide And Seek."

Lew Bidell and Herb Newman had formed Era Records in Hollywood in 1955. Herb wrote hit tunes for his artists under *noms de plume* like Steven Howard and Barry Stuart. Gogi Grant clicked in 1956 with Herb's "The Wayward Wind," and the Castells did likewise in 1962 with his "So This Is Love." In 1965, Jewel Akens found his moment in the sun when Herb handed him a funky little sing-song, "The Birds And The Bees."

Word was that the tune's writer, Barry Stuart, was a 12-year-old boy, and that the song was about his first encounter with lust. The lyrics were adolescent, all right, but that thrusting rhythm was definitely post-pimples. "Georgie Porgie" (#68, 1965), Jewel's immediate follow-up, charted only moderately, and Akens searched well into the '70s for the next gem that might resurrect his career. Most notable were his polished remakes of hits by Arthur Alexander ("You Better Move On") and THURSTON HARRIS ("Little Bitty Pretty One"). In 1973, Jewel co-produced the critically-acclaimed *Super Taylors*, a duet album of Southern soul by Ted and LITTLE JOHNNY TAYLOR. Two years later, American International Artists issued Akens' cover version of Sam & Dave's "When Something Is Wrong With My Baby."

Shirley Bassey

GOLDFINGER
(Leslie Bricusse, Anthony Newley, John Barry)
United Artists 790
No. 8   *March 27, 1965*

Life was not easy for young Shirley Bassey. She was born the youngest of seven on January 8, 1937, in Tiger's Bay, a working-class section of Cardiff, Wales. When Shirley was two, her dad died. Listening to the tunes on the radio, she taught herself how to sing and dreamed of being a star on the stage. In her teens, to help her family get by, Shirley worked in an enamel factory; all the while, friends would coax her into singing at parties and push her to audition for show-biz parts.

Shirley's first professional gig came with her assignment to a chorus line in a touring British show, *Memories of Al Jolson*. After her appearance in the 1956 revue of *Such is Life*, Bassey was signed to a Philips recording contract. Early the following year, "Banana Boat Song," a cover of the stateside Harry Belafonte hit, became the first of more than two dozen British Isle hits.

While "Goldfinger," the stirring theme from

the third James Bond thriller, was Shirley's lone top 40 hit on these shores, a few follow-up 45s did make the Hot 100, including a full-bodied version of the Beatles' "Something" (#55, 1970) and yet another Bond theme, "Diamonds Are Forever" (#57, 1972). A bountiful bunch of Bassey LPs are still in print, and Shirley is still a top-draw attraction in the theaters and nightclubs of Europe.

Sounds Orchestral

CAST YOUR FATE TO THE WIND
(Vince Guaraldi, Frank Werber)
Parkway 942
No. 10   *May 8, 1965*

British producer John Schroeder had been noticing with dismay that teens were just not appreciating the sounds of big orchestras with Sousa horns and glockenspiels. This rock and roll music, it seemed, was raucous and lacking in hummable melody. Schroeder's ambition was to rectify the situation by creating what he described, in the liner notes to Sounds Orchestral's only album, as "a better music . . . nearer to the understanding of the younger generation, keeping within commercial boundaries and retaining a teenage, yet adult appeal."

To shape such music, Schroeder enlisted pianist Johnny Pearson—BBC producer, radio personality, and arranger for the likes of Cilla Black, Connie Francis, and SHIRLEY BASSEY. Schroeder brought in drummer Kenny Clare and not one, but three bass players—Pete McGurk, Frank Clark, and Tony Reeves. The band laid down a sound bottom that teen ears would like, but that adult ones could tolerate.

"Cast Your Fate To The Wind," a cover version of the Vince Guaraldi Trio's instrumental jazz hit of 1963, was Sound Orchestral's first effort at tailoring a "better music" for teens. To the surprise of many, the disk took off, eventually cracking the top 10. The follow-up, "Canadian Sunset," appeared in the summer of 1965, and scraped onto the Hot 100 at number 76.

Glenn Yarbrough

BABY THE RAIN MUST FALL
(Ernie Shelton, Elmer Bernstein)
RCA Victor 8498
No. 12   *May 22, 1965*

The Limeliters were quite successful in their day. From 1959 to 1963, all 10 of this folk trio's LPs made healthy inroads onto *Billboard*'s top pop albums chart. The group played all the big New York nightspots like the Village Vanguard, Mr. Kelley's, and the hungry i. They appeared with Shelly Berman, Mort Sahl, and George Shearing. While only "A Dollar Down" made the pop charts (#60, 1960), the Limeliters were one of the hottest campus and concert acts of the entire hootenanny/folk revival period. Burn-out and the British Invasion ended all that.

Lou Gottlieb, Alex Hassilev, and Glenn Yarbrough parted company in 1964. Al and Lou continued on as the Limeliters for a spell, with Ernie Shelton filling in for Glenn. Months later, Yarbrough had his big moment with a Shelton number picked as the theme for the Steve McQueen/Lee Remick flick *Baby the Rain Must Fall* (1964).

Ten more Yarbrough albums followed—but

Horst Jankowski

his only other Hot 100 item came in 1965 with the folk-rockish "It's Gonna Be Fine" (#54). Glenn, you see, was big, bulky, and balding, and did not look like your hip and happening hoodoo. RCA packaged him as a lawn-tending family man: no problem there, only during the '60s this image began waning in fashionability. Change was a-blowin' in the wind.

Glenn Yarbrough (b. Jan. 12, 1930, Milwaukee) began his musical career at the age of eight, as a featured vocalist at Grace Church in upper Manhattan. His soaring soprano won him a scholarship to the St. Paul School in Baltimore. In his late teens, wanderlust struck, so he hiked around Canada and Mexico before settling down with ancient philosophy texts at St. John's College and, later, the New School for Social Research.

For post-Socratic fun, Glenn sang folk songs. His discovery in the mid-'50s by the owner of Chicago's Gate of Horn quickly led to a career on the coffeehouse circuit. For a while, Yarbrough and Alex Hassilev (b. July 11, 1932, Paris), an aspiring actor, owned their own coffeehouse in Colorado Springs called the Limelite. While the two were playing together at the Cosmo Alley Club in L.A., Lou Gottlieb (b. 1923, Los Angeles)—sometime arranger for the Kingston Trio and a former member of the Gateway Singers—appeared. The three formed the Limeliters.

As of the late '80s, a reconstituted Limeliters has been touring and recording albums for GNP Crescendo and Folk Era Records. Glenn is the only original member involved; the others now include Lou Gottlieb's son Tony and Mike Settle, formerly of the First Edition.

Horst Jankowski

A WALK IN THE BLACK FOREST
(Horst Jankowski)
Mercury 72425
No. 12   *July 10, 1965*

Horst Jankowski was born on January 30, 1936, in Berlin. He attended the Berlin Conservatory of Music, where he studied the contrabass, tenor saxophone, trumpet, and piano. At 16, he met the popular European singer/dancer CATERINA VALENTE, who engaged him for a two-year tour of Africa, France, and Spain. On his return, he did some arranging and composing for the German orchestra of Erwin Leha.

With his own jazz combo, Horst started

performing on the Berlin nightclub circuit, and from 1957 on, a number of various German polls voted Horst the top jazz pianist in Germany. In 1960, he worked as a free-lance orchestra director for such acts as Miles Davis, Ella Fitzgerald, Benny Goodman, Gerry Mulligan, and Oscar Peterson. He also began experimenting with various combinations of conventional instruments and the human voice, much as RAY CONNIFF was doing in the States.

With the Beatles, the Stones, the Dave Clark Five, the Byrds, the Yardbirds, and Dylan all in their prime—and all over the charts, airwaves, and teen mags—it seems quite incredible that this German jazzman could muscle his way onto the pop charts with a melodic piano-voice-orchestra thing originally called "Eine Schwarzwaldfahrt." Horst pulled it off, however, and the LP featuring Horst's hit aria even made the top pop albums chart in the U.S.

Another easy-listening lulu, "Simpel Gimpel" (#91, 1965), appeared on the Hot 100 for a week; several more albums, and many more singles, flowed forth. The saccharine jazz-pop of Horst Jankowski is occasionally heard even to this day on "Beautiful Music" radio stations across the land.

Ian Whitcomb & Bluesville

YOU TURN ME ON (TURN ON SONG)
(Ian Whitcomb)
Tower 134
No. 8 *July 17, 1965*

Ian Whitcomb (b. July 10, 1941, Woking, Surrey) acquired an unsavory reputation for punching out people, like that cop who called him "punk" and that one-legged bloke who called him "lady." He was even arrested in Jacksonville, Florida, for inciting the audience to "knock down the police" and have a good time. This Britisher washed ashore with the Beatle Invasion, yet he preferred Jerry Lee Lewis and Little Richard to the Fab Four and couldn't care less about the Stones, either. Bred in an upper-class setting, Ian was attending Dublin's Trinity College when a record of his that he didn't even like became a national novelty.

Throughout his younger years in exclusive boarding schools, Whitcomb listened avidly to rock and roll, this "devil music" from the States. Not only that, but he practiced piano-bangin' those very Satanic songs. During the summer of 1963, 22-year-old Ian took a trip to Seattle to visit a cousin. Once there, he tested his facility on the ivories in several coffeehouses around town. The following year he returned, this time in search of an American record company.

After hearing a crude demo, Jerry Dennson—owner of the Jerden label responsible for the Sonics, the Kingsmen ("Louie Louie"), and some early sides by Paul Revere & The Raiders—signed Ian up. First out of the stall was "This Sporting Life," which Capitol's Tower subsidiary soon picked up for national distribution. It was a mini-sized charter (#100, 1965), not bad for a starter. But no one, least of all Ian, could have predicted what would come next.

"I was visiting this lady in Seattle," Whitcomb recalled to *Goldmine's* Bill Guarneri. "I was at her house romancing her with my British accent . . . We were sort of doing heavy petting, when she suddenly said, 'Ian, your accent is turning me on.' I'd never heard this phrase used this way before. I thought it was very graphic and started using it in songs."

At first, Whitcomb used the catchy line in his Jerry Lee Lewis-styled rendition of "Memphis." Noting the positive audience response, he slowly developed the expression into a whole number. "No Tears For Johnny," a Dylanesque protest song against the Vietnam War, was slated as his follow-up single to "This Sporting Life." At the end of the recording session, there was time to spare, so Ian recorded "You Turn Me On." Tower picked that number as the "A" side, much to Ian's disgust: "I was just depressed, really depressed. I thought it was junk."

Nonetheless, rock and rollers coast-to-coast bought piles of Ian's "junk." He appeared on TV shows like "Shindig" and "American Bandstand," and toured with the Beatles, the Stones, and other British Invasion acts. On one of these package tours, Whitcomb slugged a program director—leading, he alleges, to his being blacklisted, with all of his later singles banned from airplay by the station and its affiliates. Despite numerous follow-ups, including "N-E-R-V-O-U-S!" (#59, 1965), Ian also seemed pegged as a novelty act; one "turn on" tune was all well and good, but one such record was all that American record-buyers needed.

His days of stardom are well behind him, but Ian Whitcomb is still a very busy man. He now lives in California and has issued nearly a dozen LPs, most of them featuring eccentric ragtime romps like "They're Parking Camels Where the Taxis Used to Be," "Charlie's a Cripple (You Know)," and "Yaaka Hula Hickey Dula." He has worked as a DJ on Pasadena's KROQ, written a few books (most notably *After the Ball*), scored a Las Vegas revue (*Doo Dah Daze*), composed music for the movie *Bugs Bunny, Superstar*, and scripted the PBS TV special "Tin Pan Alley."

Barry McGuire
EVE OF DESTRUCTION
(Philip F. Sloan, Steve Barri)
Dunhill 4009
No. 1 *September 25, 1965*

As songwriters for Lou Adler's Trousdale Music, P. F. Sloan and Steve Barri had cranked out piles of surfin' songs (and what Sloan would later refer to as "formula stuff") for Jan & Dean, the Rip Chords, and their own pseudo-groups—the Fantastic Baggies, the Lifeguards, the Rally Packs, the Street Cleaners, The Rincon Surfside Band, and Willie & The Wheels. All that changed in 1965, when Adler, hoping to influence Sloan's writing, handed him an early Bob Dylan album.

"After I heard that LP, I started writing by myself again," Sloan recalled in an exclusive interview. "The first songs that I wrote outside the partnership [with Barri], I wrote in one night—'Eve Of Destruction,' 'Take Me For

What I'm Worth,' 'The Sins Of The Family,' and 'This Mornin'.'"

"I went up [to Trousdale Music] and played them 'Eve Of Destruction' and the rest and they didn't like the songs. They thought they were awful—you know, 'that's not hit material, forget it.' Then one afternoon, Barry McGuire came to see them for material. He was a big star at the time. They played him all the hip things of the day that they had, Sloan-Barri formula stuff. I was sittin' alone in the corner, watchin' the business go down. [McGuire] came over, saw this depressed young kid playing guitar by himself, and said, 'What's the matter? You got any songs to play me?' I played 'Eve Of Destruction,' and boom! 'That's the one,' he said. He hugged me and said, 'You're what I've been looking for.'"

As for Barry McGuire, he was born in Oklahoma on October 15, 1935. He and Barry Kane recorded an album and single for the tiny Horizon label, but it was McGuire's role in the formation of Randy Sparks' New Christy Minstrels that brought the gravel-throated folkie his first notice. Barry wrote and sang lead on "Green, Green" (#14, 1963), the group's biggest hit. The same year, the Kingston Trio successfully recorded Barry's "Greenback Dollar" (#21, 1963). By 1965, Barry was ready to strike out on his own, and "Eve Of Destruction" would be his first solo single.

Adler had Sloan and Barri tape McGuire's rough vocal over the instrumental backing track, for Barry to use as a guide in creating the final version. But one radio station got hold of the unfinished record and began playing it; when "Eve Of Destruction" was released, it was the rough mix that Sloan and Barri had slapped together late at night.

According to Sloan, a number of radio stations banned the disk. "The record company had never seen anything like it. They were actually happy. When every major market refused to play it, that's when the label decided to really push it. I hear some DJ in Ohio or somewhere in the Midwest played 'Eve Of Destruction' every hour on the hour. It was number one there in, like, no time. That's what broke it nationally."

Barry's *Eve of Destruction* LP (1965) sold well, though only two of his subsequent singles—"Child Of Our Times" (#72, 1965) and "Cloudy Summer Afternoon (Raindrops)" (#62, 1966)—ever made the listings. McGuire made a few movie appearances, joined the Broadway production of *Hair*, and toured for a while with a spiritual group called The Agape Force. He is now a born-again Christian living in Waco, Texas, and recording gospel music sporadically for specialty labels like Myrrh and Word.

Phil "Faith" Sloan (alone or in partnership with Steve Barri) went on to create an enormous number of hit songs for Herman's Hermits, Jan & Dean, the Turtles, Johnny Rivers, and the Grass Roots. Before a reclusive phase in the mid-'70s, P.F. recorded his own versions of "Eve Of Destruction," "This Is What I Was Made For," and some of his other tunes. These appeared as now-collectible singles, and on four hard-to-find albums (*Songs of our Time*, *12 More Times*, *Measure of Pleasure*, and *Raised on Records*).

Sonny

LAUGH AT ME
(Sonny Bono)
Atco 6369
No. 10   *September 25, 1965*

They met in November 1962, in a little coffee shop on Hollywood Boulevard in L.A. Sixteen-year-old Cherilyn Sarkisian was just sitting with some friends, goofing off. Sonny, a promo man for Philles Records, was married and had a daughter. Their meeting that night would change their lives, and the couple would quickly move on to influence folk-rock as well as countercultural fashions like hippie wear and long hair.

Salvatore Phillip Bono was born in Detroit, on February 16, 1935, the youngest of three. Mama called him "Sonny," and the name struck. His family moved to Inglewood, California when he was seven years old. When he was 16, Sonny quit school to become a clerk in a grocery store. Within a few years, he was married to Donna Rankin and the father of Christy. Late at night, he would practice at the piano, scribble lyrics, and dream of pop stardom. He worked as a waiter, assembly-line worker, butcher's assistant, and truck driver.

Bono started out assisting Harold Battiste, the A & R man at Specialty Records. "His personality was contagious," Battiste told J. Randy Taraborrelli, author of *Cher*. "Sonny had style; man, the cat had boundless energy and ambition . . . There were dozens and dozens of cats in Los Angeles like Sonny, most of whom never made it big, most of whom ended up back at the grocery store baggin' food for old ladies. Not this guy."

Before long, Sonny was songwriting ("Koko

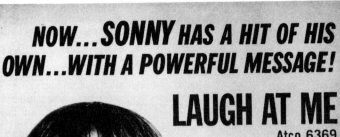

Joe," "She Said Yeah," and "Tight Sweater" for THE MARATHONS) and producing for Specialty; "Wearing Black," Bono's first solo effort, was issued by the label as by Don Christy late in 1959. By then, Sonny had left Specialty to buy into/become involved with/set up small labels like Fidelity, Go, Name, Rush, and Sawmi. He issued singles as Christy or Ronny Sommers.

Late in 1962—after co-writing the classic "Needles And Pins" with Jack Nitzsche—Bono was hired by Phil Spector to be a promo man, A & R rep, and sometime percussionist for his Philles label. Sonny's lanky new girlfriend was soon doing sessions, as a back-up singer. Bob B. Sox & The Bluejeans, the Crystals, Darlene Love, the Ronettes . . . what legendary acts and tracks Spector was recording, and what a sound! Spector became Sonny's idol, and he learned a lot about producing from watching Spector at work in the studio.

With "I Got You, Babe," written and produced by Sonny, Sonny & Cher became an overnight sensation in 1965. Their golden disks, on close inspection, feature a suspiciously Spector-like "Wall of Sound" technique. Sonny only recorded a few more solo sides after his semi-serious, partially-autobiographical "Laugh At Me" charted (interestingly enough, Mott the Hoople covered the tune on their debut album). There was "The Revolution Kind," "Pammie's On A Bummer," "Misty Roses," and one LP.

The bubble burst, as all bubbles must. Sonny still appears in commercials, in "B" flicks (in particular, 1988's *Hairspray*), and on reruns of "Fantasy Island" and "The Love Boat." In 1988, Sonny was elected mayor of Palm Springs, California.

Castaways
LIAR, LIAR
(James J. Donna)
Soma 1433
No. 12 *October 23, 1965*

The nucleus of the Castaways—guitarist Roy Hensley, drummer Dennis Craswell (later to join CROW), and bassist Dick Roby—attended junior high school together in Richfield, Minnesota. The guys all had musical training and played in the school band. Picking up guitarist Bob Folschow and keyboardist Jim Donna, the group recorded "Liar, Liar"—just so they could play the clubs around town.

"We couldn't get into any of the main rooms in town—it was sewed up," Craswell recalled in an exclusive interview with the group. "Everybody else, it seemed, had a record on the

The Castaways

radio. We approached Soma and they signed us to a one-record contract. It's funny, but once 'Liar, Liar' took off, we never got to play any of those rooms we had made the record for—we were too busy traveling the country.

"Now a regular label understands that you've got to have more product, but they had us on the road touring and doing TV and then, when it was too late, they say, 'Hey, you guys need another record.' We didn't know what was supposed to be done. 'Liar, Liar' was number 13 in *Billboard*, and we didn't even have a record contract. We could've signed with anybody, but we didn't know any better. We were only, like, 15 years old."

Soma had quickly shipped one other disk, "Goodbye Baby," but then, nothing. It looked like the label had, indeed, cast them away. Finally, after more than a year, the group was signed to Dunwich Productions and the Fontana label. Two non-charting 45s—"Walking In Different Circles" and "What Kind Of Face"—were issued by Fontana, but both bombed.

After that, the Castaways formed their own label, Tansy Records, named after the leaves that supposedly bring mummies back to life. They released a number of singles on that label like "Peace Of Mind" and "Hit the Road Jack."

"The Castaways have been together in one form or another ever since," Hensley explained. "People have left for periods, and for a few years the group was out on the West Coast playing places like Trader Nick's. Occasionally, we'd tour, and then *Good Morning Vietnam* [which included "Liar, Liar" on the soundtrack] came out. All of a sudden, agents were calling from all across the country. We appeared in Chicago with the Mamas & The Papas, and did some shows with Brian Hyland and Del Shannon. We've done some session jobs and played under different names. Currently, we're working on getting an album released and shopping around for a label.

"It's all new stuff—but we're ready this time."

Gentrys

KEEP ON DANCING
(Allen A. Jones, Willie David Young)
MGM 13379
No. 4   *October 30, 1965*

Formed in Memphis in 1963, the Gentrys—Larry Raspberry (guitar), Larry Wall

(drums), Bruce Bowles (vocals), Bobby Fisher (sax, piano, guitar), Jimmy Hart (vocals), Jimmy Johnson (trumpet, organ), and Pat Neal (bass)—started out playing school functions and sock hops. They came in third place in the Mid-South Fair Talent Competition, appeared on Ted Mack's "Amateur Hour," and won top honors at the Memphis Battle of the Bands.

In 1964, producer Chips Moman signed the group to his Youngstown label. The Gentrys taped an Everly Brothers-style number called "Sometimes" backed with a cover version of an obscure R & B item called "Keep On Dancing." When the latter disk showed some sparks, Moman contacted MGM's Jim Vienneau, who picked up the waxing for national release.

Like many one-shot top 40 moments, "Keep On Dancing" was a fluke hit, orginally intended as a throwaway "B" side. A group called the Avantis—three black guys who modeled themselves after the Isley Brothers, and who had toured with, and befriended, the Gentrys—had recorded the original version of "Keep On Dancing" on the Argo label. Because the song was conceived as filler material, the group cut the tune in 35 minutes; Raspberry did not even practice the number before the session.

"We were young kids and not great musicians," Raspberry explained to *Goldmine*'s Randle Hill. "We didn't know anything about tuning drums or even tuning guitars or how to make things really sound good . . . Chips wanted us to be competitive with the musicians being recorded in Nashville, and yet here he was with kids 17 years old who couldn't play worth a darn."

"Spread It On Thick" (#50, 1966) and "Everyday I Have The Blues" (#77, 1966) both charted, but the Gentrys were starting to lose momentum. Fisher and Johnson were gone by this point; Larry Butler was brought in from Nashville to play organ. Three singles appeared on MGM, three more on Bell, before what remained of the Gentrys broke up in 1970.

Hart, singing lead with a completely new line-up—Dave Beaver (keyboards), Mike Gardner (drums), Steve Speer (bass), and Jimmy Tarbutton (guitar)—revived the group's name for three chartings on Sun: "Why Should I Cry" (#61, 1970), "Cinnamon Girl" (#52, 1970), and "Wild World" (#97, 1971). This version of the Gentrys also recorded for Capitol and Stax.

Jimmy Hart is now a successful wrestling manager with the World Wrestling Federation (his new nickname: "Mouth of the

South"). Bruce Bowles is a sales rep at a Memphis radio station. Bobby Fisher is a civil engineer with the city of Memphis. Jimmy Johnson is a physician. Pat Neal works for the railroad and moonlights with local country bands. Larry Wall is a promo man with Columbia/Epic Records. Raspberry formed a hard-rock band called Alamo that recorded one self-titled LP for Atlantic in 1970; he has since fronted the High-Steppers and recorded four LPs with them to date.

Jonathan King
EVERYONE'S GONE TO THE MOON
(Jonathan King)
Parrot 9774
No. 17 *Nov. 6, 1965*

Kenneth King (b. Dec. 6, 1944, London) was right and proper when he was a lad. He was educated at London's Charterhouse School and went on a tour about the globe. He was attending Trinity College in Cambridge as an English Lit major when he came upon this scruffy bunch of beat musicians called the Bumblies. It was through the Bumblies that King met some execs at British Decca Records—in particular, a Mr. Ken Jones, who encouraged the youth to try his hand at writing some hip songs. One of the first of these was the hodge-podgy "Everyone's Gone To The Moon." At the time, everyone liked it, but no one seemed to really understand it. Nonetheless, King's thing became a worldwide hit, and can now be heard ad nauseam on oldies radio stations.

King was never a great rock and roll singer, but then again, he never claimed that he was. After the success of "Everyone's Gone," King issued further flakies, charting in the States with only one other single, "Where The Sun Has Never Shone" (#97, 1966). But more importantly, this upright lad became the assistant to Sir Edward Lewis, head of Decca's London office. At Decca, and later at his own U.K. Records label, King discovered and produced acts like the Bay City Rollers, Genesis, Hedgehoppers Anonymous, the Kursaal Flyers, and 10cc, to name but a few.

Jonathan also has the distinction of appearing on the British charts under more guises than any other bloke in all of popdom. In addition to eight further homeland chartings under the "Jonathan King" moniker, King had hits under pseudonyms like Father Abraphart and The Smurps ("Lick a Smurp for Christmas"),

Bubblerock ("Satisfaction"), 53rd and 3rd ("Chick-A-Boom"), 100 Ton and a Feather ("It Only Takes A Minute"), Sakharin (a heavy-metal version of "Sugar Sugar"), Shag ("Loop Di Love"), Sound 9418 ("In the Mood"), The Weathermen ("It's The Same Old Song"), and possibly untold others. Other less successful King personae include Nemo, the Piglets, Robin Jack, Saccharine, and St. Cecilia.

From 1979 through 1980, King hosted a radio talk show over New York's WMCA. He has written *Bible Two*, an anti-drug novel; hosted "Entertainment USA" and "A King in America" for the BBC; made regular appearances on "Top of the Pops"; and continues to work as an independent producer and recording artist.

Murmaids
POPSICLES AND ICICLES
(David Gates)
Chattahoochee 628
No. 10 *November 27, 1965*

Carol (b. 1948) and Terry (b. 1946) Fischer were sisters, and Sally Gordon (b. 1946) was a neighbor and a mutual friend. For a brief moment, they were the Murmaids from L.A. Daddy Fischer was a music arranger and director; Mama Fischer was the family's guiding light. Before the girls took off for college in the fall of 1963, Mrs. Fischer brought the teenage singers to the offices of Chattahoochee Record boss Ruth Conte.

Kim Fowley (a self-acknowledgedly bizarre and cultish personality who frequently pops up in accounts of '60s rock and roll) was then Chattahoochee's in-house producer. Fowley had recently been handed a tune from the pen of future Bread frontman David Gates. The ditty was silly and sweet, an obvious vehicle for a wholesome trio like the Murmaids.

Once they had recorded "Popsicles And Icicles," the girls packed their bags and headed for college. But the disk became a huge success, and the label tried to extract more winners from the lasses. Apparently, Chattahoochee issued an unsuccessful single or two before the group splintered. As Murmaid members swam off toward a sea of obscurity, Cathy Brasher and possibly Yvonne Vaughn (who would each later attempt solo careers) were called in to be the Murmaids (of '66). Their folk-rockish "Go Away" was not a bad effort, but after that one release on Liberty Records in 1968, the group did just that.

The Murmaids

Silkie
YOU'VE GOT TO HIDE
YOUR LOVE AWAY
(John Lennon, Paul McCartney)
Fontana 1525
No. 10 *November 27, 1965*

England's Silvia Tatler (lead vocals) and her mates—Ivor Aylesbury (guitar), Kev Cunningham (bass) and Mike Ramsden (guitar)— were specialists in traditional folk music and fellow students at Hull University. They met during the summer of 1963, and within two years, generated enough of a club reputation that Beatle-man Brian Epstein sought them out, signed them up for management, and connected them with Fontana Records.

Silkie's debut single, "Blood Red River," sold poorly. For their second disk, Epstein got John Lennon, Paul McCartney, and George Harrison to accompany and produce "You've Got To Hide Your Love Away," a remake of the Beatlesong from the *Help!* soundtrack. The three Beatles never again tangled with Silkie, and Silkie consequently never again received much of a hearing. For a while, the group toured England, but visa problems prevented them from playing throughout the U.S. They released an album and two more 45s, one of which was "Born To Be With You" (a remake of the Chordettes' 1956 number). Although "Born To Be With You" had all the markings of mini-hit, it wasn't, and Silkie eventually unraveled.

"Little" Jimmy Dickens
MAY THE BIRD OF PARADISE
FLY UP YOUR NOSE
(N. Merritt)
Columbia 43388
No. 15 *December 4, 1965*

Nineteen sixty-five was the 50th anniversary of the first nude scene ever in a motion picture (Annette Kellerman in *Daughter of the Gods*). The same precious year, someone set a world record by baking a loaf of bread that weighed 20 pounds and measured 20'5". Disposable paper dresses were being sold in cans for two bucks. And a 4'11" old-timey country singer with a Stetson and glittery stuff all over his duds treated radio listeners to such lyrical significa as "May an elephant caress you with his toes/ May your wife be plagued with runners in her hose."

"May The Bird Of Paradise Fly Up Your Nose" was the pinnacle of Jimmy Dickens' career. It would be his last major C & W hit and his only appearance on *Billboard*'s Hot 100. In 1982, the little guy with the tall hat was voted into the Country Music Hall of Fame.

Jimmy was born the youngest of 13 in Bolt, West Virginia, on December 19, 1925. After a stay at the University of West Virginia, Jim started hawking his vocal talents. While doing a radio spot for WKNX in Saginaw, Michigan, Dickens met Roy Acuff, who liked the kid's chops and offered him a guest spot on the Grand Ole Opry. The Opry outing opened doors for Jimmy, who was quickly signed to a contract with Columbia Records. Country top-

pers like "Out Behind The Barn," "A-Sleeping At The Foot Of The Bed," "Hillbilly Fever," and "Take An Old Cold Tater And Wait" followed.

While not as active as he used to be, "Little" Jimmy Dickens still performs and waxes his wares occasionally.

Wonder Who?
DON'T THINK TWICE
(Bob Dylan)
Philips 40324
No. 12   *December 25, 1965*

Pop fans did not have to wonder long: the sound on the record was so distinctive that recognition was nearly instantaneous. Call them Tubular Tinsel, the Barbies, the Sewer Rat Stinkers . . . no name alone could disguise one of the biggest pop groups of the '60s.

Little Jimmy Dickens

By 1966, the Four Seasons had reached the apex of their musical success. They had sold more than 50,000,000 records; nearly everything the Seasons released at this time would chart, and usually quite well. The group was saturating the radio with hit after hit. Thus was born The Wonder Who?, a bogus group fabricated as a drain for excess Four Seasons recordings.

Frankie Valli and the others had originally cut "Don't Think Twice" as part of a tribute album to Bob Dylan. The LP never materialized, and Frankie never could get his lead vocal just right. But the number was appealing in an oddball way, so the powers that be at the Philips label saw fit to issue it. To avoid competing with themselves and denting the sales action on other Seasons sides, another name had to be concocted. There was already the Who, the You Know Who Group, and the Guess Who, so why not a Wonder Who?

To the surprise of many, including the Seasons themselves, "Don't Think Twice" nearly cracked the top 10. Two more records were issued by Philips under the "Wonder Who?" name—"On The Good Ship Lollipop" (#87, 1966) b/w "You're Nobody Till Somebody Loves You" (#96, 1966), and "Lonesome Road" (#89, 1967). To further confuse fans, record collectors, and radio programmers, VeeJay (the Seasons' previous label) did a mini-issuance of the Seasons' "Peanuts" as by the Wonder Who?.

Barry Young
ONE HAS MY NAME (THE OTHER HAS MY HEART)
(Eddie Dean, Dearest Dean, Hal Blair)
Dot 16756
No. 13   *January 1, 1966*

Barry was a Dean Martin impersonator and a darn good one. Unless DJs made special efforts to stress that this was not the "lush one," listeners would probably assume that "One Has My Name" was yet another musical monster from Dean Martin, who was making a momentous return to the charts. Unfortunately for Young, the scam got old fast. None of his follow-ups for the Dot, Columbia, or Hooks Brothers labels measured more than zip on the popularity polls.

"One Has My Name" was a much-covered country number that went back more than four decades—it was a hit for cowpoke star Eddie

Dean (also the tune's co-writer) in 1948, for Jimmy "The Melody Kid" Wakely the same year, and for Jerry Lee Lewis in 1969.

Statler Brothers
FLOWERS ON THE WALL
(Lewis DeWitt)
Columbia 43315
No. 4   *January 8, 1966*

These boys are neither Statlers nor brothers, but they *are* the undisputed kings of country group harmony. The Statlers won the Country Music Association's "Group of the Year" award for every year between 1972 and 1977, and again in 1979 and 1980. More than 60 of their singles have made *Billboard*'s C & W charts, and a dozen of their LPs have made contact with the top pop albums listings. Their 1975 "Best of" compilation has reportedly sold more than 2,000,000 copies, and is still in print. Since 1971, the Statler Brothers have been throwing an Old-Fashioned Fourth of July Celebration in Staunton, Virginia, that draws more than 60,000 people, making it the largest annual country-music festival in the world.

Bass singer Harold W. Reid (b. Aug. 31, 1939, Augusta County, Va.), tenor Lew C. DeWitt (b. March 8, 1938, Roanoke County), and baritone Philip E. Balsley (b. Aug. 8, 1939, Augusta County) started singing together in 1955 at the Lyndhurst Methodist Church in Staunton. They were gospel groovers with a unique sound and they knew it, but in 1958, they went their separate ways. Two years later, they reorganized, adding a lead singer—Harold's younger brother Donald (b. June 5, 1945, Staunton).

Their big break came in 1963, when the group met Johnny Cash backstage at Watermelon Park in Berryville, Virginia. Cash eventually added the boys to his traveling show and soon introduced them to the bigwigs at Columbia. Figuring the "Man in Black" knew whereof he boasted, Columbia signed the singing act, which had switched over to secular music. For nearly two years, their vinyl issuances vanished without much notice. Columbia was about to cut the Statlers loose when Cash snuck them in on one of his recording sessions to cut "Flowers On The Wall." This nonsense number about languishing love, an early slice of psychedelia, won two Grammys—the Statlers were voted "Best New Country Group," and their smash won

"Best Contemporary Performance by a Country Group."

"I really shouldn't be saying this to a professional journalist," Harold once admitted to *Country Music*'s Patrick Carr, "but we just ain't got no hook. We're patriotism and nostalgia and Mom and apple pie, and that's it. What more can you say? We're the Bland Brothers."

Where did the "Statler Brothers" name come from, anyway? As Harold told Rick Marschall in *The Encyclopedia of Country and Western Music*, "We could just as easily have become the Kleenex Brothers." You see, when holed up in a shabby hotel and in need of a new name, one of the brothers happened to notice a box of Statler facial tissues.

The Statler Brothers' line-up has remained the same for all these years, except for the departure of Lew DeWitt in 1982 for reasons of ill health. His replacement was Jimmy Fortune.

Knickerbockers

LIES
(Buddy Randell, Beau Charles)
Challenge 59321
No. 20   *January 22, 1966*

The Castle Kings were born in Bergenfield, New Jersey, in the summer of the British Invasion. In various configurations, Beau (guitar) and Johnny Charles (bass), Buddy Randell (sax, vocals), and Jimmy Walker (drums, vocals) had been making music for years. Buddy had been an original member of the Royal Teens and co-wrote their smash, "Short Shorts." In mid-'65, the Castle Kings were enlisted by singer/songwriter/producer Jerry Fuller to back up some of the cats he was recording. Jerry, who liked their professionalism and clean-cut appearance, got the guys a contract with Gene Autry's Challenge label. They changed their name to the Knickerbockers, after one of their favorite hometown streets.

Their initial singles, "Bite, Bite Barracuda" and "Jerktown," did not sell very well. Neither did an oddball and now highly-collectible debut album, *Sing and Sync-Along with Lloyd: Lloyd Thaxton Presents the Knickerbockers*. The LP made use of a gimmick called Trick Track: when you put the stylus in the grooves, any one of five different cuts could be heard. For example, the listener might hear "Hully Gully," "It's Not Unusual," or the Knickers' fine rendi-

tion of "I Wanna Hold Your Hand." Cute idea, but what if you wanted to hear the fellows bounce about with the "Hully Gully" and nothing else? Odds were that the record's owner would have to stick that disk several times before he could get the right tune at the right time.

"Lies," the third Knickerbockers 45, was filled with so much energy (and sounded so much like the Beatles) that it could not be denied hit status. Their follow-ups, "One Track Mind" (#46, 1966) and "High On Love" (#94, 1966), did so-so. Because of their proficiency in mimicking the rock-radio sounds of the day, the Knickerbockers became regulars on Dick Clark's "Where the Action Is." More than a half-dozen singles were issued in succession, but not one of them even flirted with the charts.

The Knickerbockers disbanded in the late '60s. Both Buddy Randell and Jimmy Walker pursued unsuccessful solo careers; Jimmy replaced Bill Medley for a brief spell in the post-prime Righteous Brothers. In 1971, Buddy sang lead on an obscure one-shot 45 by a group called Blowtorch. "Come And Get It" was the tune—almost no one did.

Jackie Lee

THE DUCK
(Earl Nelson, Jr.)
Mirwood 5502
No. 14   *January 22, 1966*

Jackie Lee was born Earl Lee Nelson, Jr., on September 8, 1928, in Lake Charles, Louisiana. He was raised in California, where he sang in his church's choir. On and off again, from 1957 until their demise in 1967, Earl sang with THE HOLLYWOOD FLAMES. That was Earl up front, singing lead on their "Buzz-Buzz-Buzz" b/w "Crazy." That was Earl, recording rock-bottom soul singles with Bobby Relf as half of Bob & Earl, featured on "Harlem Shuffle" (#44, 1964). And that was Earl singing back-up on BOBBY DAY's "Rockin' Robin" b/w "Over And Over" as a member of Day's Satellites.

Jackie Lee—not to be confused with the Philly-based Jackie Lee who charted in 1959 with "Happy Vacation"—was just one of many names that Earl has recorded under; other aliases were Earl Cosby and Earl Nelson & The Pelicans. In the '70s, Earl recorded an album for Warner Bros. under the guidance of his old buddy Barry White. For this effort, Barry dubbed Nelson "Jay Dee." A single pulled from that one and only Jay Dee album became an R & B hit, "Strange Funky Games And Things" (—/#88, 1974).

Explaining his one-off dance hit as Jackie Lee, Nelson told *Soul* magazine: "I didn't create the dance. I saw kids doing it and I wrote the song. Some people at Mirwood Records liked it and said, 'Great, we'll put the name "Jackie Lee" on it.'"

Earl has continued to record under various guises, making the R & B listings twice more as Jackie Lee with "African Boo-Ga-Loo" (—/#43, 1968) and "The Chicken" (—/#47, 1970).

Mike Douglas
THE MEN IN MY LITTLE GIRL'S LIFE
(Eddie Dean, Mary Candy, Gloria Shayne)
Epic 9876
No. 6   *February 5, 1966*

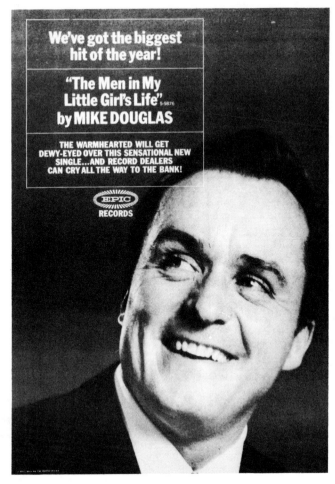

For a while, Mike was the hottest host on daytime television. According to *TV Guide*, his impact was such that "dishes go unwashed and shirts remain unironed when Mike Douglas comes on." In 1967, his syndicated program was piped over nearly 200 channels and viewed by close to 6,000,000 glassy-eyed housewives. That year, he won an Emmy Award for "Outstanding Daytime Performance."

Douglas was born Michael Dowd, Jr. in Chicago, on August 11, 1925. Mom encouraged him to open his mouth and let that voice out, which he did at all the family gatherings. In his teen years, he became a singing master of ceremonies aboard a cruise ship which bobbed about Chicago's shoreline. After his involvement in World War II and a spell at Oklahoma City College, Mike's big break happened. For five years, beginning in the mid-'40s, he got the chance to sing with Kay Kyser and his Kollege of Musical Knowledge, on radio, record, and TV. Mike even sang lead on Kyser's number-one hit, "Ole Buttermilk Sky" (1946).

In 1950, Kyser called it quits, and Mike's career floundered for a period. In 1961, he started up the Cleveland-based TV program that would eventually capture the hearts of daytime viewers everywhere; four years later, Epic Records signed Mike up to create mood music for his millions. "The Men In My Little Girl's Life" was one such mellow moment, and his lone top 40 hit.

In 1980, Douglas' production company shelved Mike in favor of John Davidson, whose youthful appeal was expected to draw in an even larger audience. Mike continued as the program's producer until its demise in 1982.

T-Bones
NO MATTER WHAT SHAPE (YOUR STOMACH'S IN)
(Sascha Burland)
Liberty 55836
No. 3   *February 5, 1966*

Liberty Records was quite hot with the surfing/hot rod sounds of Jan & Dean, and moved quickly to churn out similar products by groups like the Eliminators, the Zip-Codes, and the T-Bones. Nothing charted, but apparently the T-Bones were successful enough to be allowed to wax not one, but three drag-race LPs—*Boss Drag* (1964), *Boss Drag at the Beach* (1964), and *Doin' the Jerk* (1965).

By the time album number four was out the door, the T-Bones consisted of Danny Robert Hamilton (b. Spokane, Wash.) on guitar, Joe Frank Carollo (b. Leland, Miss.) on bass and drums, and Tommy Clark Reynolds (b. New York City) on drums and steel drums. Hamilton had worked sessions for Chad & Jeremy, Jerry Lee Lewis, the Marketts, Johnny Rivers, Ronny & The Daytonas, and the Ventures. Carollo had been playing bass and drums since his early teens, and had majored in music at Mississippi's Delta State College and Los Angeles City College. Reynolds had made and played steel drums in Bermuda.

The T-Bones' fourth LP (*No Matter What Shape*, 1966) was produced by Joe Saraceno—who handled similar duties for the Markettes, THE ROUTERS, the Sunshine Company, and the Ventures—and featured a contagious number created by Sascha Burland (half of THE NUTTY SQUIRRELS) for an Alka Seltzer commercial. Hoping to cash in on the cover-a-jingle craze, the T-Bone organization did their best with Chiquita Banana and Nabisco ditties; only the latter disk, "Sippin' And Chippin'" (#62, 1966), placed on the pop charts.

After two more LPs, Dan, Joe, and Tommy shelved the "T-Bones" name to become Hamilton, Joe Frank & Reynolds. The trio scored hits like "Don't Pull Your Love" (#4, 1971), "Fallin' In Love" (#1, 1975), and "Winners And Losers" (#21, 1976). They remained a viable force in pop music for much of the '70s.

Reynolds had also been a member of a group called Shango, and left Hamilton, Joe Frank & Reynolds in 1972. He is currently a minister in Texas.

David & Jonathan
MICHELLE
(John Lennon, Paul McCartney)
Capitol 5563
No. 18 *February 12, 1966*

"**D**avid" was Roger Greenaway (b. Aug. 23, 1942, Southmead, England); "Jonathan" was Roger Cook (b. Aug. 19, 1940, Bristol, England). Both dropped out of school at the age of 15 and worked their ways through the world of everyday jobs. In 1965, the Rogers began songwriting together as fellow members of a Bristol group called the Kestrels. One of their

David & Jonathan

tunes, "You've Got Your Troubles," was a hit for the Fortunes, and soon Petula Clark, Freddie & The Dreamers, and other artists were approaching the duo for songs.

Beatles producer George Martin heard one of the team's demos and offered to record them in the style of pop duos like Chad & Jeremy and Peter & Gordon. "Michelle" was David & Jonathan's initial release, and their only stateside charting. British fans responded even more warmly to the duo's follow-up, "Lovers Of The World Unite," but after that, even in their homeland, all future recordings failed to spark much interest.

By mid-'68, Cook and Greenaway had shelved the "David & Jonathan" *nom de plume* to concentrate on composing, jingle-writing, and session work. In addition to creating another biggie for the Fortunes ("Here Comes That Rainy Day Feeling Again") and hits for both the New Seekers ("I'd Like to Teach the World To Sing") and the Hollies ("Long Cool Woman"), Cook and Greenaway wrote the tunes that eventually made one-hit wonders out of WHISTLING JACK SMITH ("I Was Kaiser Bill's Batman"), EDISON LIGHTHOUSE ("Love Grows"), WHITE PLAINS ("My Baby Loves Lovin'"), and CAROL DOUGLAS ("Doctor's Orders"). In 1971, the British Songwriters Guild voted Cook and Greenaway "Songwriters of the Year."

When the itch to secure still more moneys entered their collective noodles, Cook and Greenaway wrote or performed commercials for Allied Carpets, British Gas, Typhoo, and Woodpecker Cider. They helped write "I'd Like To Teach The World To Sing (In Perfect Harmony)"—a hit for the New Seekers as well as THE HILLSIDE SINGERS—and reportedly dreamed up the entire "It's the Real Thing" ad campaign for Coca-Cola.

A studio group called Blue Mink gelled into a decade-long rock and roll ride for Roger Cook and co-vocalist Madeline Bell. In 1970, Blue Mink's "Melting Pot," an ode to racial harmony, nearly topped the British charts, yet neither Blue Mink nor any of Cook's solo outings managed to find much of an audience in the States. Roger Greenaway, meanwhile, has recorded with Edison Lighthouse, THE PIPKINS, White Plains, and a sprinkling of other lesser known pseudo-groups.

In the mid-'70s, Cook and Greenaway parted company. Cook has since moved to Nashville, where he continues to dash off songs. In 1983, Greenaway was appointed chairman of the British Performing Rights Society, and has since cut down on his composing.

Bob Kuban & The In-Men
THE CHEATER
(John Mike Krenski)
Musicland 20001
No. 12 *March 12, 1966*

The lyrics to "The Cheater," Bob Kuban & The In-Men's big hit, prefigured ironically in the fate of lead singer "Sir" Walter Scott, who met an untimely end at the hands of his wife and her lover.

"We were putting together the In-Men again," Bob Kuban recalled in an exclusive interview. "This was 1983. We had formed the band in 1964, and the 20th anniversary was coming up. Wally was excited about the idea . . . He'd been on the road a long time, and was planning on being home for the Christmas holidays. He left his home in his jogging suit and running shoes to get a battery for his car, and nobody ever saw him again—he just vanished, two days after Christmas . . . Three and a half years later, in April of '87, they found his body stuffed in a cistern."

The assistant prosecuting attorney for the case determined that Wally Scott (real name: Walter Notheis) had been tied up and shot in the back execution-style, and Scott's wife and her lover were indicted for murder. The two are still awaiting trial on homicide charges.

In 1963, when Kuban (b. Aug. 1940, St. Louis) and Scott first met, Bob was a high-school teacher who played drums for weekend wedding gigs, and Wally was lead singer in a group called the Pacemakers. Bob recruited Wally for a band he was putting together that included Pat Hixon (trumpet), Greg Hoeltzel (keyboards), Mike Krenski (bass), Ray Schulte (guitar), Harry Simon (tenor sax), and Skip Weisser (trombone). Almost immediately, Norman Weinstoer had the Bobby Kuban Band record for his Norman label, but neither "I Don't Want To Know" nor "Jerkin' Time" charted.

A friend of Weinstoer, Mel Freedman, heard the band and "The Cheater" (which, in its original form, was written in the first person, as "Look out for me, I'm the cheater"). Freedman had some connections in New York with Bell/Amy Records, and promised the group that if they went with him and his Musicland Records, they would get some national distribution. "The Cheater" was the first Bob Kuban & The In-Men single released under this arrangement.

Two albums and two 45s—"The Teaser"

(#70) and "Drive My Car" (#93)—appeared in 1966. Scott, Hoeltzel, Krenski, and Schulte spun off and recorded as the Guise. Kuban recruited replacements, and cut two further singles on the Musicland label—"Harlem Shuffle" and "The Batman Theme." In 1970, one final disk appeared on Reprise, "Soul Man" b/w "Hard To Handle." The Guise never got off the ground, so after an attempted solo career, Scott returned to the band for a brief period.

Kuban currently leads a band under his own name. But where are the In-Men of "The Cheater" fame now? "Greg's a dentist; Harry's a schoolteacher; Pat's a computer programmer; Skip's out in Vegas and has been working as a bartender; and Mike's been working with McDonald Aircraft. We're all still in contact with each other."

In 1975, The Bob Kuban Brass recorded an album entitled *Get Ready for Some Rock & Soul* for Norman Records. In the late '80s, the same label issued two 45s—"Everybody's Gonna Have A Party" and "Triple Shot Of Rhythm & Blues."

Bob Lind

ELUSIVE BUTTERFLY
(Bob Lind)
World Pacific 77808
No. 5   *March 12, 1966*

" 'Elusive Butterfly' came after I was up all night," Bob Lind told *Hit Parader*. "It was originally five verses, but I only got two recorded on the record. It was started when the sun was coming up, and I finished it about ten that morning."

Robert Lind was born on November 25, 1942, in Baltimore. His stepfather was in the Air Force, so the family moved around a lot. In his late teens, Bob enrolled in the theater-arts program at Western State College in Gunnison, Colorado. After three years of study, he dropped out, took his guitar, and moved to Denver, where he worked the folk clubs. Bob made a demo tape of some of his poetic pieces; Bert Brock at Liberty Records heard Lind's hypnotic hymns and signed the folk-rocker to World Pacific, a Liberty subsidiary.

Nearly every tune that would eventually account for Lind's cult status—"Elusive Butterfly," "Truly Julie Blues," "Mister Zero," and "Cheryl's Goin' Home"—was recorded at that first session, for Lind's first LP, *Don't Be Concerned*. Jack Nitzsche was producing, with

Leon Russell on piano. "Butterfly," Bob's first release, not only became an international hit, but brought the frail and frozen imagery of his songs to the attention of artists like Cher, Adam Faith, Marianne Faithfull, Noel Harrison, Bobby Sherman, Nancy Sinatra, the Turtles, and the Yardbirds. Within months, all had recorded versions of Lind's compositions. Both sides of Bob's follow-up single, "Truly Julie Blues" (#65, 1966) b/w "Remember The Rain" (#64), charted. Surely, great things were in store.

Lind recorded another high-quality and similarly-styled LP, *Photographs of Feeling* (1966), but it never made the top pop albums listings. None of Lind's successive 45s fared well, either. To make matters worse, Verve/ Folkways got hold of some old tapes of inferior material from Lind's Denver days, and (without permission, apparently) issued it in album form as *The Elusive Bob Lind*.

The last known musical effort from Lind appeared in 1971, when a single, "She Can Get Along," and an LP on Capitol, *Since There Were Circles*, surfaced.

Lind then went off into the deserts of New Mexico to retire. In the 80's, *Goldmine* researcher Steve Eng reported that all was well: Bob was writing short stories, plays, and even a novel (*East of the Holyland*). Eng noted that one of Lind's plays, *The Sculpture*, had won the California Motion Picture Council's "Bronze Halo" award.

Deon Jackson

LOVE MAKES THE WORLD GO ROUND
(Deon Jackson)
Carla 2526
No. 11   *March 19, 1966*

"I would cringe every time the song came on the radio," Deon Jackson told *Goldmine* writer Bill Dahl. "I'd think, 'God, I don't like that.' And I wrote it, too. I just don't like that song." The distasteful song? Deon's big musical moment, "Love Makes The World Go Around."

Deon Jackson was born on January 26, 1946, in Ann Arbor, Michigan. As a child, he studied clarinet and drums, and while a high school student, he formed a vocal group. In 1962, producer and publisher Ollie McLaughlin caught Jackson and his group singing their hearts out at a school concert. Ollie became Deon's manager, and in the mid-'60s he recorded two singles on Jackson that were issued on Atlantic Records—both bombed. Jackson, meanwhile, had dashed off that hated number and, unhappy with the results, had tossed it aside.

Eventually, Deon did record a demo of "Love Makes The World Go Round" and sent it off to his manager. The song that would bring Jackson his mighty minute on the charts sat around for another year until Ollie released it. Once available to the public, "Love Makes The World Go Round" sold like no one would have believed. While "Love Takes A Long Time Growing" (#77, 1966) and "Ooh Baby" (#65, 1967) were respectable follow-up efforts, everything else Jackson released for the remainder of the decade sank unceremoniously from view.

Deon Jackson turned away from the record biz, and for much of the early '70s tickled the keyboards in New York City night spots like Nathan's and Matt Snell's. Thereafter, Deon moved his base of operations to Chicago, where for the past 15 years he has touched the ivories to Nat "King" Cole, Johnny Mathis, and Frank Sinatra tunes. People in the know still ask Jackson to play "Love." "It kinda gets to me to do it," Jackson sighed. "But I do it."

Robert Parker

BAREFOOTIN'
(Robert Parker)
Nola 721
No. 7 *June 18, 1966*

Robert Parker (b. Oct. 14, 1930, Crescent City, La.) is remembered for one disk, one dance, one slim slice of time. But in addition to his mid-'60s hoofer hit, Parker packed more than 20 years with other musical quests.

In the '40s and '50s, Parker and his sax ran the house band at the Tijuana Club in New Orleans, backing performers like Ray Charles, Guitar Slim, CHRIS KENNER, and Little Richard. For several years, Parker was a member of Professor Longhair's Blue Scholars, and appeared on their celebrated "Mardi Gras In New Orleans" single. As a session saxophonist, he appeared on disks by New Orleans artists like Jimmy Clanton, ERNIE K-DOE, Fats Domino, FRANKIE FORD, IRMA THOMAS, and HUEY "PIANO" SMITH. Parker was also a member of Huey Smith's Clowns for a few of their peak years.

In the '60s, Robert was touring with Eddie Bo and Percy Stovall. "We worked a show in

A Great Performance
DEON JACKSON
A Great Song
OOH BABY
Carla 2537
Produced by Ollie McLaughlin
A Hit Record!

Distributed by ATCO

Tuskeegee, Alabama, where all the kids piled their shoes in the corner to dance," Parker told *Goldmine*'s Almost Slim. "We joked about it in the band and thought it might be a good gimmick for a tune." Once he had sketched out the tune, Parker brought the ditty to Wardell Quezergue, an arranger for Nola Records. When the foot-floppin' 45 took flight, Robert left his job as an orderly at Charity Hospital.

At one Apollo Theatre appearance, Parker, prodded by the MC, pulled off his shoes for his performance. "I went on stage and the crowd went nuts," Parker recalled. "I started doing that every night and it worked great."

Nola Records released an album of attractive New Orleans numbers. Follow-up singles were crafted to zero in on the barefoot theme—there was "Happy Feet," then "Tip Toe" (#83, 1967)—but it was all over quickly. Nola filed for

183

bankruptcy. Parker later recorded unsuccessfully for the Island and Silver Fox labels.

In the '80s, the folks at Spic 'n' Span made use of "Barefootin'" in one of their TV ad campaigns; Pete Townshend included a cover version of the tune on a live album in 1986. Robert Parker still makes occasional appearances at festivals and oldies shows.

Shades Of Blue

OH HOW HAPPY
(Charles Hatcher)
Impact 1007
No. 12 *June 25, 1966*

For years, the Shades of Blue have been shrouded in mystery. Recently, in an interview with *Soul Survivor*'s Richard Pack, Edwin Starr described his discovery of the group. Starr (real name: Charles Hatcher) had several major pop and R & B hits in the late '60s and early '70s: "Agent Double-O Soul" (#21/8, 1965), "Twenty-Five Miles" (#6/6, 1969), "War" (#1/3, 1970), and "Stop The War Now" (#26/5, 1971).

"I wrote 'Oh How Happy' while in the service in Germany [1960-62]. Golden World had one white act on its books at the time—THE REFLECTIONS. I told Ed Wingate [the record label's owner] that we needed another white act on the label, and that I was going to put one together . . . So I found this group of Italian-Americans and took them to Golden World to see Ed, who said, 'Get that group out of here! I don't want no more white groups!' So instead, I gave the record to a good friend of mine, Harry Balk, and his Impact label. It was a monster."

Who exactly were these "Shades of Blue"? Starr seemed unable to recall.

Before the shadows of abstruseness covered their young faces, the Shades of Blue charted with "Lonely Summer" (#72, 1966) and "Happiness" (#78, 1966).

Capitols

COOL JERK
(Donald Storball)
Karen 1524
No. 7 *July 2, 1966*

Each of the guys had been singing for as long as they could remember. In 1962, lead vocalist/drummer Samuel George, guitarist Donald

The Shades of Blue

184

The Swingin'
Medallions

Storball, and three others got their act together and presented Detroit producer Ollie McLaughlin with a number called "Dog And Cat." McLaughlin liked the ditty, and cut it for his Karen label. It flopped, and the Capitols returned to their workaday worlds. Four years later, George, Storball, and a new Capitol—pianist Richard McDougall—returned to McLaughlin's little label with an up-tempo dance number called "Cool Jerk." Again, Ollie liked what he heard and cut the track for his label. Like never before and never since, the Capitols danced into the nation's top 10.

The group returned to McLaughlin's offices on many more occasions with fast numbers and dance disks like the "Afro Twist" and the "Patty Cake," but America wasn't buying it. While tracks from their lone album indicate that the Capitols were quite capable of fine ballads as well as get-down bluesy bits, the group got pegged as an upbeat rug-cuttin' group. McLaughlin believed in the Capitols—only after eight failed singles did the guys and Ollie call it quits.

Donald Storball is currently a Detroit policeman. Richard McDougall's whereabouts and activities are unknown. Samuel George died in an "altercation" on March 17, 1982.

Swingin' Medallions
DOUBLE SHOT (OF MY BABY'S LOVE)
(Don Smith, Cyril E. Vetter)
Smash 2033
No. 17 *July 2, 1966*

"**W**e had recorded the song several times," explained Medallions leader John McElrath in an exclusive interview. "We tried all different arrangements and tempos, but it wasn't going anywhere. We decided to pick up and go to another studio, Arthur Smith's. We said, 'Look, let's set this up just like we're live, playing on stage.' We called in the roadies, our friends, and people from off the streets to make noise with us, to party with us; people we didn't even know. It worked: we did 'Double Shot' in one take. The song was originally recorded in Columbia, South Carolina, in the early '50s, by Dick Holler & The Holidays; it was a cult number, a beach number."

The Swingin' Medallions were first formed in 1962 when McElrath, a folkie attending 96 High in the tiny town of 96, South Carolina, met Carroll Bledsoe, a fellow folkie with a

185

hootenanny trio at nearby Greenwood High. A year later, Joe Morris, a native 96er, was added to the fold. By the mid-'60s, the Medallions line-up was in place: John McElrath (keyboards), Jimbo Doares (guitar), Carroll Bledsoe (trumpet), Charles Webber (trumpet), Brent Forston (keyboards, sax, flute), Steven Caldwell (sax), James Perkins (bass), and Joe Morris (drums).

Dave Roddy, the DJ at Birmingham's WSGN who broke "Double Shot" locally, suggested that the group add the "Swingin'" prefix to their monicker. Just before the release of "Double Shot," Dot Records issued the group's poor-selling debut single, "I Wanna Be Your Guy."

Follow-ups to the "Double" disk were hard to launch. "'She Drives Me Out Of My Mind' [#71, 1966] charted real good. And we did real well with our remake of BRUCE CHANNEL's 'Hey! Baby.' But we had to go back to college or we'd be drafted, so we couldn't devote ourselves to the music as much as we wanted to."

By 1970, the band started falling apart, as the guys began getting married and drifting away. McElrath started up his own studio in Greenwood, South Carolina; Brent Forston and Steven Caldwell had already split from the group in 1967 to record as the Pieces of Eight for A & M. Some labels bearing the "Pieces of Eight" name also tagged the group as "The Original Swingin' Medallions."

McElrath has kept the "Swingin' Medallions" name active—"We actually played more in 1989 than we did in all of the '60s." An album is planned for release in 1990. McElrath is the only original Swingin' Medallion touring under that name, but each year, from 1983 onward, all of the original members reunite for a one-off concert in Atlanta.

According to McElrath, Jimbo is currently an accountant; Carroll is a sales representative for Zenith; Charlie is a captain with the South Carolina Law Enforcement Department; Brent is a lawyer; Steve is the president of a computer firm; James is with Eastern Airlines; and Joe is an executive with the Sonoco Paper Company.

The Standells

Standells

DIRTY WATER
(Ed Cobb)
Tower 185
No. 11 *July 9, 1966*

The Standells, formed in Los Angeles in the early '60s, reportedly chose their name because they would stand around a lot in their agent's office waiting for work. Before they struck gold, the Standells practiced their craft long and hard. More than a half-dozen trial disks were issued on Linda, MGM, Vee Jay, and Liberty. The latter label even issued a now-rare LP, *The Standells Live at PJ's*.

By 1966, when the group came under the directive influence of producer, writer, and one-time Four Preps member Ed Cobb, their much fluctuating line-up had solidified. It was drummer Dick Dodd (former Mousekateer and one-time member of the Bel-Airs), bassist Gary Lane, keyboardist Lawrence Tamblyn (brother of actor Russ Tamblyn), and guitarist Tony Valentino that went into that little garage studio to record "Dirty Water."

"I wrote the song when I was in Boston," Cobb told *Blitz*'s Mike McDowell. "I was with a girl. We were walking along the Saint James River and two guys tried to mug us, but they ran away. So when I got back to the hotel, I wrote [the] song . . . I originally had another guitar lick intended for 'Dirty Water,' but the guitar player couldn't play it. So, I had to devise a simpler one.

"The group hated the record so much that they refused to do it! So they just fluffed through it every time. Every week I got a phone call from Tony saying 'Hey Eddie! My friends still don't like the song! I told you it was a turkey!' Nine months later it was a smash."

Larry's memories of the events are different. "We recorded it in Armin Steiner's little studio up in a garage," Tamblyn told *Goldmine*'s Robyn Flans. "'Dirty Water' was just an idea, more or less, with lyrics that Ed Cobb brought to us and said 'See what you can do.' Tony came up with the beginning riff, and we all kind of put our ideas into it. All that chanting that Dick does [at the beginning]—'I'm gonna tell you a story/I'm gonna tell you about my town'—Dick made up on the spot."

This seminal garage band was extinct within two years of the release of "Dirty Water." On the band's first tour in support of the release, Gary Lane left the group and the world of pop music to become a plumber, and

was replaced by Dick Burke. The response to the Standells' immediate follow-ups, "Sometimes Good Guys Don't Wear White" (#43, 1966) and "Why Pick On Me" (#54, 1966) was quite good. But by the release of "Can't Help But Love You" (#78) in the fall of 1967, the Standells were in disarray. "They had all these rhythm and blues musicians in there, horn players and string players," Tamblyn told *Goldmine*. "Ed Cobb said, 'This is the Standells; you aren't the Standells.'"

Dodd remained with Cobb and the Tower label for a solo album, *The Evolution of Dick Dodd*, and a few failed singles. Despite threats from Cobb, Tamblyn and Valentino—along with a young Lowell George, later of Little Feat—continued for a brief period to perform live as the Standells. In the mid-'80s, Tamblyn and Valentino formed their own indie label, Telco. Despite a few Standells reunions in 1986, the creators of "Dirty Water," one of rock and roll's raunchiest perennials, are together no more.

Syndicate Of Sound

LITTLE GIRL
(Bob Gonzalez, Don Baskin)
Bell 640
No. 8 *July 9, 1966*

Bassist Bob Gonzalez, keyboardist/guitarist John Sharkey (b. June 8, 1946, Los Angeles), lead singer/saxophonist Don Baskin (b. Oct. 9, 1946, Honolulu), lead guitarist Larry Roy, and drummer John Duckworth (b. Nov. 18, 1946, Springfield, Mo.). were the San Jose-based Syndicate of Sound. At the San Mateo Teenage World's Fair, this aggregate of guys showed up to play in the Fair's "Battle of the Bands." Bob, John, and the others won first prize—free recording time with Del-Fi Records.

A Syndicate single entitled "Tell The World" was issued in small quantities by Del-Fi, and illegally reissued on the Scarlet label. Garrie Thompson, who would later become the guys' manager, wanted to hook them up with Hush Records, and asked the group if they had any more original material on hand.

As Sharkey told *RPM*'s Don Rogers, "We didn't have very much, but we had gotten wind of the Leaves' 'Hey Joe.' They were said to be the latest and greatest. We were already into the Byrds and that kind of stuff, so we just made something up. We didn't even have the words till the day we went in to record. Well, we had some words, but lost them and made up some new ones."

Divinely sloppy, and created on the spot, "Little Girl" had a raw garage/punk sound. For a follow-up, the Syndicate of Sound, now with Jim Sawyers (guitar) filling in for Roy, dreamed up "Rumours" (#55, 1966), a much smoother number. Two more Bell releases rang no bells. Capitol Records tried the group on for size for a lone single, and Buddah Records issued two Syndicate sides. The first of these, "Brown Paper Bag" (#73, 1970), did mildly well. But the joyfully crude group sound of "Little Girl" could not be coaxed again from the group, and worse still, internal problems started to beset the Syndicate. John Duckworth got drafted, then Sharkey left the group.

The Syndicate of Sound kept playing concerts and club dates into the early '70s, but no further records were issued after the Buddah releases in 1970. John Sharkey is currently teaching music for a living, and reports having recorded a few solo albums. John Duckworth left the military and refurbishes homes. Don Basker was spotted in the mid-'80s playing bars with a C & W band. Bob Gonzalez manages a furniture store. And here and there, Jimmy Sawyers still plays rock and roll.

Ray Conniff

SOMEWHERE, MY LOVE
(P.F. Webster, M. Jarre)
Columbia 43626
No. 9 *August 13, 1966*

A creator of his own highly distinctive mood music, and one of the founding fathers of the whole genre of easy-listening music, Ray Conniff was born in Attleboro, Massachusetts, on November 6, 1916. Music was everywhere in the Conniff household: Ray's mother was a piano player, and his father was the leader and trombonist of the local Attleboro Jewelry City Band.

Under his dad's instruction, Ray quickly learned how to work the trombone, and while still in high school, he formed his own band. He soon became mesmerized by the different nuances and moods he could conjure simply by determining which instrument in his group would play what, when it would play, and against what type of backdrop. Excited about these possibilities, Ray sent away for a mail-order arranging course and taught himself the basics.

Graduating in 1934, Ray moved to Boston and played with a number of bands, then studied at Juilliard. While serving in the military during World War II as an arranger with the Armed Forces Radio Service, he worked with Meredith Wilson and Walter Schumann.

After years of analyzing pop music, Ray felt confident that he had discovered the secret of just what it takes to make a hit record. In 1953, he approached Columbia Records exec Mitch Miller with his brilliant idea; Miller played along. Conniff dreamed up an arrangement for big-band vocalist Don Cherry, whose career was in a downslide. Ray's arrangement of "Band Of Gold" pole-vaulted Cherry to the top of the heap once again.

Miller rewarded Ray with a position at Columbia as an arranger, conductor, and recording artist. Conniff's first album, 'S Wonderful, was a heavy hitter, and eventually sold more than 500,000 copies. Over the next decade, 27 albums with the Conniff name became full-blown successes. Apparently, Ray and his Ray Conniff Sound—which utilized "slap that mule" percussion and a skillful blend of instruments and voices—could do no wrong. Throughout the '60s, it was hard to listen to a "Beautiful Music" or "mood music" radio station for an hour without hearing that signature sound at least once.

As an arranger for others, Conniff produced an impressive array of smashes for Frankie Laine, Johnny Mathis, Guy Mitchell, Marty Robbins, and Johnny Ray. During the summer of 1966, Conniff grafted his unique sound onto a theme from *Doctor Zhivago*, "Somewhere, My Love." Ray had charted on the Hot 100 three times earlier, and would do so once more during his career, but the eerie theme would be his only top 40 hit.

Throughout the '70s, Ray Conniff remained active with Columbia Records. Many of his albums have never gone out of print and are still available.

Napoleon XIV

THEY'RE COMING TO TAKE ME AWAY, HA-HAAA!
(Jerry Samuels)
Warner Bros. 5831
No. 3 *August 13, 1966*

Jerry Samuels had a seemingly normal background and upbringing. He was born in 1938 in New York City. He became a recording engineer at the Associated Studios, writing songs on the side. One of his compositions, "The Shelter Of My Arms," became a huge hit for Sammy Davis, Jr. (#17, 1964).

Two years later, however, Jerry was of a different bent of mind. With the nub of a nutty number in his craw, Samuels booked himself an hour and a half of studio time. He brought in a drum, a tambourine, and this idea for a "tune" called "They're Coming To Take Me Away." Jerry beat his instruments and recited the composition with an ever-increasing feverishness. It was an odd song (as anyone who has ever heard it can attest), a bizarre novelty bit about a man who suffers an emotional setback when his beloved pooch leaves him.

George Lee, an executive at Warner Bros., heard Jerry's waxing and issued it immediately. Because the platter poked fun at the mentally ill, the negative response to it was substantial: within days, most radio stations pulled it from their playlists. The sales response, however, was strong—in less than a week, 500,000 copies had been purchased. "Take Me Away, Ha-Haaa!" became the fastest-selling record in Warner's history—and the only top 40 single to feature the same song recorded backwards on the flip side!

In support of his new career, Jerry formed a rock and roll band and performed in a mask as Napoleon XIV. Warner issued an LP full of like-minded ditties: "I Live In A Split-Level Head," "Marching Off To Bedlam," "I'm In Love With My Little Red Tricycle." The latter was released as Nap's follow-up. Both the single and the album were soon discontinued.

In 1973, Napoleon XIV's re-released rendition of "They're Coming To Take Me Away, Ha-Haaa!" returned to the charts (#87). Over the years, there have been reports of other Napoleon XIV sides being released. These reports, much like the alleged barroom sightings of the masked *mashugena* man, remain unconfirmed.

Tommy McLain

SWEET DREAMS
(Don Gibson)
MSL 197
No. 15 *August 20, 1966*

In the mid-'60s, Tommy McLain played bass with Clint West and the Fabulous Boogie Kings, a hot band known throughout South Lousiana. Floyd Soileau, the big cheese at Jin

Records, had been cutting regionally successful tracks on some configurations of the band ever since the label's inception in 1958. Clint and some of the guys had laid out numbers like "Jail Bird" and "Take A Ride" as Bob & The Veltones.

McLain, striking out on his own, cut a swamp-pop rendition of Don Gibson's country classic, "Sweet Dreams." He had a few hundred copies pressed, and tried to persuade local record stores to stock his disk. The proprietor of the Modern Record Shop in Alexandria, Louisiana, was soon reporting to Soileau that McLain's vanity pressing was selling quite well. When Floyd realized that McLain was in Clint West's band, which was already under contract to the Jin label, he had Tommy re-record "Sweet Dreams" for his Jin label, and used the uncredited Boogie Kings as back-up.

Soileau had a gut feeling that there was something wrong with McClain's rendering, according to John Broven's *South to Lousiana*, so he shelved the disk for several months. McLain pestered him about the release date until he finally issued the lopsided, slip-slidin' "Sweet Dreams." When soaring sales of the 45 outstripped Jin's ability to manufacture and distribute, arrangements were made with Jamie Records to create MSL. The new Jamie-distributed company would be owned by Soileau, Harold Lipsuis, and Huey P. Meaux.

Tommy McLain failed to find a successful follow-up. Covers of Ray Charles' "Sticks And Stones," Bobby Charles' "Before I Grow Too Old," and the Righteous Brothers' "Try To Find Another Man" only fared well regionally.

McLain is still active in the Texas and Louisiana regions with his band Mule Train. An album and a few singles appeared on the Starflite label in 1979.

Los Bravos

BLACK IS BLACK
(Tony Hayes, Steve Wadey)
Press 60002
No. 4 *October 1, 1966*

As Mike & The Runaways, Mike Kogel (b. Apr. 25, 1945, Berlin), Miguel Vicens Danus (b. June 21, 1944, Palma de Mallona, Spain), Manolo "Manuel" Fernandez (b. Sept. 29, 1943, Seville, Spain), Pablo "Gomez" Samllehi (b. Nov. 5, 1943, Barcelona), and Antonio Martinez (b. Oct. 3, 1945, Madrid) had a heap of success in Spain. Some observers claim they were the numero-uno groupo in their homeland. One of the representatives at Decca's branch office in Spain sent some copies of the group's recordings to England. There, Decca's Ivor Raymonde—a producer who had worked wonders for Dave Berry, Billy Fury, Dusty Springfield, Marty Wilde, and others—detected a Motown-ish British Invasion sound in the grooves. Raymonde flew to Madrid with a pile of British songs. After hearing Mike & The Runaways' magical rendition of "Black Is Black" (a tune penned by two blokes from the village of Hoo, England), Ivor invited the group to join him in London for a recording session.

"Black Is Black" was their first release as Los Bravos. In support of this disk, Antonio "the comedian" (guitar), Manuel "the quiet one" (organ), Miguel "the matador from Mallorca" (bass), Pablo "a gas-looking guy"

(drums), and Mike "no nickname" (lead vocals, guitar) toured feverishly. Despite their considerable talent and effort, their follow-ups were not successful. "I Don't Know" charted in the U.K., but only "Going Nowhere" (#91, 1966) and "Bring A Little Lovin'" (#51, 1968) made the listings in the U.S.

Hoping to start something of a "Spanish Invasion," Spanish groups with names like Los Brincos and Los Canarios shipped their Anglicized offerings over here, all to little avail. Mike "no nickname" Kogel did return to the charts for a brief moment in 1972 as Mike Kennedy with an album and a single, "Louisiana" (#62).

Count Five

PSYCHOTIC REACTION
(Kenn Ellner, Roy Chaney, Craig Atkinson, Sean Byrne, John Michalski)
Double Shot 104
No. 5 *October 15, 1966*

A psychedelic garage band, Count Five was the best in the San Jose area—and "Psychotic Reaction" was the best mind-altering mess of music they ever conceived.

Kenn Ellner (b. 1948), the leader, vocalist, harmonica man, and tambourine player, was from Brooklyn. Craig "Butch" Atkinson (b. 1947) was originally from Springfield, Missouri, and played drums. Sean Byrne (b. 1947) was born in Dublin and played rhythm guitar. Roy Chaney (b. 1948) was the bass player and a native of Indianapolis. Johnny "Mouse" Michalski (b. 1949), the lead guitarist, hailed from Cleveland. "Mouse" was still in high school, but the others met while attending college in San Jose.

For 18 months, they toured around playing their trebly Stones and Yardbirds music. They often appeared in Dracula gear at teen clubs and hops. A DJ named Brian Lord met them at one of these gigs, and alerted Irwin Zucker at the new Double Shot label of their existence. At an audition for Zucker, Count Five performed "Psychotic Reaction." Recognizing a hit, Zucker waxed and shipped the song. The reaction was immediate, and a pile of follow-ups were issued—but, as usually happens, not one of the disks approached the quality of Count Five's initial outing.

Once the band was counted out, Byrne returned to Ireland to continue his rock and roll career. In 1973, he surfaced as part of Public

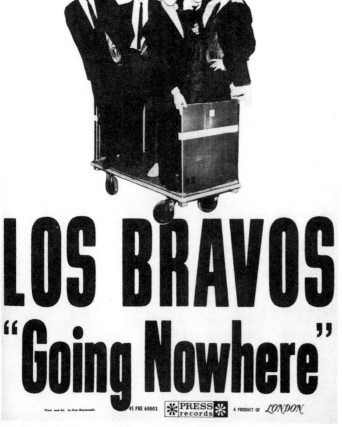

Another ride to the top!

LOS BRAVOS
"Going Nowhere"

Prod. and dir. by Ivor Raymonde   45 PRE 60003   ✳PRESS✳ records   A PRODUCT OF *LONDON*

Count Five

Foot The Roman; their critically underrated album was only issued in England. Five years later, Byrne, as a member of Legover, recorded an equally obscure LP, *Wait Till Nighttime*, for the Smack label.

New Vaudeville Band
WINCHESTER CATHEDRAL
(Geoff Stephens)
Fontana 1562
No. 1 *December 3, 1966*

Geoff Stephens (b. Oct. 1, 1934, New Southgate, England) taught French, English, and religion. In his spare time, he would spin 78s and search junk shops for those high-speed acetate jewels from the '20s and '30s. After dashing off mini-skits for the BBC and a brief twirl in the world of advertising, Geoff went to work for a London music publishing firm.

There, in his own cubicle, he dreamed up successful songs for British acts like the Applejacks and Dave Berry. One day, while staring at a photo of Winchester Cathedral on the wall, Geoff was inspired to scribble an unforgettable melody. Still in the heat of passion, Stephens organized a recording session, and with a megaphone to his mouth, crooned the tale of a poor lad whose girlie had left him heartbroken beneath that Gothic structure.

"Winchester Cathedral" quickly became an international item, and even won a Grammy for "Best Rock and Roll Record" in 1966. A Geoff-less debut album went top five and sold a million copies. Since a New Vaudeville Band did not actually exist, and since Stephens had no desire to tour singing and dancing this tune, a vaudevillian unit had to be built swiftly from scratch. Alan Klein, who liked to call himself "Tristram, seventh Earl of Cricketwood," was recruited to work the megaphone. At the core of the new construction was drummer Henry Harrison (b. June 6, 1943, Watford) and what

The Music Machine

had once been an R & B group called Cops 'n' Robbers. On keyboards was Stan Heywood (b. Aug. 23, 1947, Dagenham); on French horn, saxophone and trombone, Robert "Pops" Kerr (b. Feb. 14, 1943, London); on bass, Neil Korner (b. Oct. 6, 1942, Ashford); on trombone, Hugh "Shuggy" Watts (b. July 25, 1941, Watford); and on guitar, Mick Wilsher (b. Dec. 21, 1945, Sutton).

The immediate follow-up, "Peek-A-Boo" (#72, 1967), charted in the U.S.; a few others did likewise on their native turf. Nothing further was to save this pseudo-group from their impending stateside obscurity. Their descent, however, was slowed by a year's stay at the Aladdin Hotel in Las Vegas. In the '70s, after a three-year tour of Canada, the not-so-new Vaudeville Band returned to England and the cabaret circuit.

Remnants of the band, fronted by Henry Harrison, still romp through the oldies. Geoff Stephens still writes songs, penning hits for THE FLYING MACHINE ("Smile A Little Smile For Me") and CAROL DOUGLAS ("Doctor's Orders"). In 1972, Wayne Newton garnered his last hit with Stephens' "Daddy Don't You Walk So Fast."

Music Machine

TALK TALK
(Thomas Sean Bonniwell)
Original Sound 61
No. 15   Jan. 14, 1967

Sean Bonniwell (b. 1940, San Jose, Cal.) was the founding father and leader of the Music Machine, one of the most loved—if least played—garage bands of the '60s. Sean, now a born-again Christian, is quietly living in Lindsay, California, where he and his wife run a small engraving shop. His income from those masterful Music Machine sides totaled $7,000; his songwriter's royalties are less than $100. To free himself from a contract with Warner Bros., Sean sold off the group's name and the rights to all of the group's recordings to producer Brian Ross—for the paltry sum of one dollar!

Sean's mother was a ballerina; his father was a military man and a trumpet player. Sean started his own music career in a folk trio, the Noblemen, and learned how to play guitar. After a stint with the Wayfarers (and three albums for RCA), Sean gathered together drummer Ron Edgar and former GALE GARNETT bassist Keith Olsen to create a Beatle-influenced band, the Ragamuffins.

After several months of practice, the Ragamuffins evolved into the well-oiled Music Machine, five strong: Bonniwell, Edgar, Olsen, Mark Landon (guitar), and Doug Rhodes (keyboards). For their concert appearances, each member dyed his hair black, dressed in an all-black outfit, and mysteriously wore one black glove. "I wanted to make a statement that was rebellious, but not for the sake of rebellion," Bonniwell explained to *Goldmine's* Jeff Tamarkin. "It was for the sake of a unified image."

While the Music Machine was playing a

bowling alley, producer Brian Ross discovered the act. He plunked down $150 to tape demos on "Talk Talk" and "Come On In," quite a bargain in those days. Art Laboe at Original Sound offered to issue some sides, the first of which was "Talk Talk." "I wrote the song in about 20 minutes while I was waiting for my girlfriend to get ready," Bonniwell revealed. "I just sat down with the guitar and wrote it. All the good ones happen like that. I wrote it in '65, so it laid around for a year."

The Music Machine began dismantling itself even as the single was mounting the charts. Sean was at loggerheads with Laboe about which record to issue as the follow-up to "Talk Talk"; Bonniwell wanted to put out "Hey Joe," which no one had recorded yet. In addition, the group was growing resentful of Bonniwell's bossy ways. They recorded the (*Turn On) The Music Machine* LP (1967) in one intense 10-hour session, but the strain was beginning to show.

A few more 45s trickled into circulation, and one even charted—"The People In Me" (#66, 1967). Bonniwell secured a contract with a big label, Warner Bros., but no Machine men stuck around long enough to enter a studio again. He renamed the group Bonniwell Music Machine and used session players for several singles and a sole LP, *Bonniwell Music Machine* (1967).

During the '70s, Bonniwell dropped out of the music scene and tuned in to a variety of psychedelic experiences. "I made a practice of getting out of my body," he told *Rolling Stone*'s David Fricke. "I became very good at it." During his more grounded moments, Sean hosted an astrology radio program ("The Sun Sign Report") in Charleston, South Carolina; wrote a movie and music review column for *The Charleston*; trained Arabian horses; and made a brief appearance in the flick *Swamp Thing* (1982).

Keith Olsen has become the most visibly successful ex-Machine member. As a producer, Keith has worked with the Babys, Russ Ballard, Kim Carnes, Fleetwood Mac, Foreigner, the Grateful Dead, Heart, and Santana.

Aaron (b. 1941, New Orleans) and his brothers— Art (b. 1938), Charles (b. 1939), and Cyril (b. 1949)—have been in the music biz for nearly three decades. In the mid-'50s, as the Hawketts, Aaron, Art, and Charles recorded "Your Time's Up" and the perennial hometown favorite, "Mardi Gras Mambo." By 1960, Art was in the Navy, and Aaron was on his own, touring about in support of an R & B hit waxed with Allen Toussaint on the Minit label, "Over You."

More than half a decade would pass before Aaron would find his magic moment. "Tell It Like It Is," his debut single for the Par-Lo label, was an entrancingly blues-drenched ballad with a hip black expression of the day for its title. The record reportedly sold 40,000 copies in New Orleans during the first week of its release, but the Par-Lo label began having problems.

"This was the first thing that [the label's owners] tried in the production field and it was a smash," Art Neville explained to John Broven in *Walking to New Orleans*. "But business-wise, nobody was really up on what to do; consequently, the thing just folded up on them."

Aaron Neville

Aaron Neville
TELL IT LIKE IT IS
(Lee Diamond, George Davis)
Par-Lo 101
No. 2 *January 28, 1967*

Before Par-Lo collapsed, Neville's "She Took You For A Ride" (#92, 1967) made a respectable showing on the pop listings. Aaron continued on, recording sides for the Safari, Instant, and Bell labels, while brother Art formed the Meters, a house band (à la Booker T. & The MGs) that played sessions behind a number of seminal New Orleans artists. In 1975, the brothers backed up their uncle George "Big Chief Jolly" Landry in the Wild Tchoupitoulas, a tribe of Mardi Gras Indians.

With the disbanding of Art's Meters in 1977, the brothers decided to stick together as The Neville Brothers. After all, why break up? "When we play together the music just flows," Charles Neville told the *Chicago Tribune*'s Chris Heim. "We don't really have to make arrangements or work things out minutely. It's perfect. That's because of our spiritual connection."

The Neville Brothers recorded several albums—*The Neville Brothers* (1978), *Fiyo on the Bayou* (1981), *Neville-ization* (1984), and *Uptown* (1987)—before hitting their commercial stride with *Yellow Moon* (1989). With the issuance of *If My Ancestors Could See Me Now*, Aaron's son, Ivan Neville, also continues the family heritage. And Aaron himself was recently back in the public eye, garnering a Grammy in 1990 for "Don't Know Much," a duet with Linda Ronstadt.

Senator Bobby

WILD THING
(Chip Taylor)
Parkway 127
No. 20   *February 4, 1967*

Finally, the full story on Senator Bobby, rock and roll's Robert F. Kennedy impersonator. What follows are extracts from an exclusive interview with the man behind this bizarre version of "Wild Thing," Chip Taylor. Mr. Taylor (né James Voigt) is a country-rock singer and the songwriter responsible for classics like "Angel Of The Morning," "I Can't Let Go"— and "Wild Thing."

"My brother Jon [Voigt, the actor] had gone to school with Dennis Wholey. This one day, Dennis and I met on a bus; it was the fall of 1966. We were just kidding around when he started telling me about this guy he knew [Bill Minkin] who did all these impersonations— Chet Huntley, the Lone Ranger, Murray the K. Without thinking, I just said, 'Well, why

don't we bring him in the studio and just fool around, and do 'Wild Thing' as if it was Senator Everett McKinley Dirksen [who had recorded a spoken-word tribute to "Gallant Men" in 1966]?

"I went into the Mirasound Studios. I had this demo track, the original demo track that the Troggs had sent me, doing 'Wild Thing.' We had the guitar on this one channel, and we used that channel with a vocal overdub by this guy, Bill Minkin. We had Bill do one side imitating Robert Kennedy, and the other, doing Everett Dirksen.

"When the single took off, we just went back in with Minkin and a bunch that Dennis had assembled, called the Hardly Worthit Players [Wholey, Steve Baron, and Carol Morley], and did this straight-ahead comedy LP [*The Hardly Worthit Report*, 1967] as a follow-up. 'Wild Thing' surprised us all, and so we went and did one other single, 'Mellow Yellow' [#99, 1967; a "duet" as by Senator Bobby & Senator McKinley], but that was it."

Minkin has moved on to public relations firms and ad agencies, where he has created industrial videos for such firms as McGraw-Hill and Nabisco. Bill has also written comedic material for Sandy Baron and Dave Astor, and during the '60s made stand-up appearances at night spots like New York's Scene.

Baron has written TV scripts as well as pop and folk songs for publishers like April/Blackwood and Wild Indigo. Steve was a folk-singer and played at New York's Bitter End and Gaslight Cafe. More recently, Taylor reports, he has worked as an independent televison producer in Nashville.

Morley was active in the '60s, playing the theater scene in Newport, Rhode Island and Provincetown, Massachusetts. Carol also did TV commercials for Cascade Soap and Rival Dog Food.

Wholey was a TV talk-show host (WNDT) and DJ (WBAI-FM) in Baltimore. Dennis also emceed a late-'60s quiz show ("The Generation Gap," 1969) and functioned as a radio director for the NBC Radio Network. He is currently the host of a PBS late-night talk show.

Blues Magoos

(WE AIN'T GOT) NOTHIN' YET
(Ronald Gilbert, Ralph Scala,
Michael Esposito)
Mercury 72622
No. 5   *February 11, 1967*

The Blues Magoos, New York City's first psychedelic experience, took shape in 1964 around the core of lead singer/guitarist Peppy Castro (b. Emil Thielhelm, June 16, 1949), bassist Ronnie Gilbert (b. Apr. 25, 1946), and Ralph Scala (b. Dec. 12, 1947). In 1964, guitarist Mike Esposito (b. 1943, Delaware) and drummer Geoff Daking (b. 1947, Delaware) joined up, and the group started playing in Greenwich Village. Before the Magoos (originally spelled "B-l-o-o-s Magoos") developed a marketable persona, they waxed a few rare and righteous singles for Verve/Folkways ("People With No Faces" b/w "So I'm Wrong And You're Right") and Ganim ("Who Do You Love").

By the time their second 45 for Mercury was out, the Blues Magoos had gone psychedelic. These boys were literally wired: whenever they performed, their outfits would flash on and off. As Castro told *Goldmine*'s Lydia Sherwood, "Our concept really started after we had played the Night Owl for a while. People began freaking out and turning on. In those

early days of drugs, when people were really expanding, we were more conceptual, more psychedelic."

The Blues Magoos' first album, *Psychedelic Lollipop* (1966), was certainly "conceptual": the cover featured Peppy and his mind-bent bandmates in multicolored threads, superimposed on a far-out background of swirly goo. They opened the LP with their anthem, "(We Ain't Got) Nothin' Yet"; weirded out with an extended rave-up on "Tobacco Road"; and eerily sang that "*Love Seems Doomed.*" Their second LP, *Electric Comic Book* (1967), included an electric comic-book insert, the moving "*Albert Common Is Dead,*" and their follow-up single to "Nothin' Yet"—"Pipe Dreams" (#60, 1967) b/w "There's A Chance We Can Make It" (#81). *Basic Blues Magoos* (1968) sported a cover version of the Move's "I Can Hear the Grass Grow" plus a number called "Subliminal Sonic Laxative."

"By our third album, we had leased a house in the Bronx on University Avenue, and we did home recording," Peppy recalled. "Our music

room was done in black light and strobe. The cops would come over because people would complain that there were strange flashing lights. We literally had the police walk in the house and wham, we'd hit the strobes, and they'd go for their guns! . . . We were stoned all the time then."

The Blues Magoos drifted apart, and in 1969, Peppy and an entirely new Magoo constituency signed with ABC-Paramount for two albums. Castro then departed to act in the Broadway production of *Hair*. After a year there, he and two other cast members, Billy and Bobby Alessi, formed a pop unit called Barnabye Bye. Two LPs later, Peppy was part of the short-lived Polydor recording act Wiggy Bits. Finally, in 1981, Peppy Castro—with Doug Katsaros and Dennis Feldman—returned to the playlists and the top 40 charts as a group called Balance, with "Breaking Away" (#22, 1981).

Bob Crewe Generation
MUSIC TO WATCH GIRLS BY
(Tony Velona, Sid Ramin)
DynoVoice 229
No. 15 *February 11, 1967*

"Music To Watch Girls By" was born as jingle music for a mid-'60s Diet Pepsi ad campaign. Studio veteran Bob Crewe, best known for his production and songwriting work with the Four Seasons, thought the tune was catchy enough to record as a pop single for general release. He swiftly assembled a studioful of session musicians to play seven brass instruments, three saxes, three guitars, a piano, drums, tympani, and a xylophone as the Bob Crewe Generation.

Although none of the Generation's subsequent musical musings approached the popularity of "Music To Watch Girls By," Crewe's crew did do well with their *Music to Watch Girls By* (1967) LP and a follow-up single entitled "Birds Of Britain" (#89, 1967). More than a decade would pass before Bob bounced back with "Street Talk" (#56, 1976), issued under the acronym B.C.G.

Bob was born Stanley Robert Crewe on November 12, 1937, in Newark. During the '50s, Crewe moved to Detroit, then to Philadelphia, recording numerous puffy/teen-idol sides for the BBC, Jubilee, Spotlight, Vik, U.T., Warwick, and ABC-Paramount labels. Some of his later efforts were quite solid; "Sweetie Pie"

and "The Whiffenpoof Song" (#96, 1960) almost connected.

In Philadelphia, Crewe took up painting, modeled for magazine ads, and dabbled in interior decorating. In 1953, he struck up a friendship with a piano-playing Texan named Frank Slay, Jr. Together, Crewe and Slay wrote and arranged songs, set up the XYZ label, and did some independent production work. One of their earliest successes was the double-sided 1957 smash "Silhouettes" b/w "Daddy Cool" by THE RAYS. Before parting ways in the early '60s, the team of Crewe and Slay worked on disks by Billie & Lillie, Freddie Cannon, and Dickie Doo & The Don'ts, to name but a few.

Bob Crewe is best known to rock and roll fans for his instrumental role in shaping the phenomenal career of the Four Seasons. From the group's release of "Bermuda" in 1961, through 1967, Bob produced all of their recordings. With one of the Seasons, Bob Gaudio, Crewe also co-wrote many of the group's most memorable musical moments—"Big Girls Don't Cry," "Let's Hang On," "Rag Doll," and "Walk Like A Man."

Crewe has since formed music publishing companies, record labels (Crewe, DynoVoice), and produced or written for such artists as the Eleventh Hour, Lesley Gore, the Highwaymen, Ben E. King, LaBelle, Oliver, Diane Renay, Mitch Ryder & The Detroit Wheels, Norma Tanega, Disco Tex & The Sexolettes, and Frankie Valli.

Spyder Turner
STAND BY ME
(Ben E. King, Elmo Glick)
MGM 13617
No. 12 *February 11, 1967*

What a memorable song! Most people, if asked who had a hit with "Stand By Me," would respond with the name of Ben E. King, who recorded the original rendition of the song (#4, 1961; #9, 1986). Others might mention cover versions by John Lennon (#20, 1975) and country singer Mickey Gilley (#22, 1980). Poor Spyder; no one but a hardcore record buff would know that Spyder Turner's novelty working of this classic was also a chart-shaker. And worse yet, Spyder didn't even like the record.

"It was never intended to be used as a record," Spyder told *Blues & Soul*. It was only an audition tape of Turner doing impressions of how Jackie Wilson, David Ruffin, Billy Stewart, Smokey Robinson, and Chuck Jackson might have handled the song. "[MGM Records] felt it was good enough. I didn't agree. I didn't like it, but I wanted a [record] deal, so I went on ahead and did a 'B' side for them." Spyder's nutty number sped up the charts like nothing he would ever again create.

Spyder was born Dwight Turner in Beckley, West Virginia, in 1947. After some years of moving about, his family settled in Detroit. In his teen years, Dwight sang in glee clubs and in various doo-wop groups. By the mid-'60s, he and his eight-piece band, the Nonchalants, were working the watering holes around town. After the band split up, Annie Gellen—host of "Swing Time," a TV show out of Lansing, Michigan—arranged for Spy to submit the above-mentioned audition tape to MGM Records.

Turner's immediate follow-up, "I Can't Make It Anymore," scraped by at number 95 in 1967, but further releases fared poorly. For the next decade, Turner worked primarily behind the scenes, managing acts and trying to write songs. When Rose Royce successfully recorded his "Do Your Dance" (#39, 1977), Spyder approached Whitfield, the group's label, about letting him have one more crack at stardom. However, none of his numerous efforts in the late '70s and '80s (for both Whitfield and Polydor) have done well.

"Cannonball" Adderley

MERCY, MERCY, MERCY
(Joe Zawinul)
Capitol 5798
No. 11   *February 25, 1967*

Julian "Cannonball" Adderley—one of the few jazz musicians to appear with regularity on the pop charts—was born in Tampa, Florida, on September 15, 1928. Because he had such a huge appetite, his friends nicknamed him "Cannibal," later corrupted to "Cannonball." While still in high school, the alto saxophonist formed his first jazz combo. After graduation, he became a band director at Dillard High for two years, served in the military, led a few Army bands, and gigged with Oscar Pettiford. In the late '50s, he began attracting critical attention for his work with Miles Davis and John Coltrane.

Cannonball and his brother Nat formed their own funky unit in 1956. At various times, pianists such as Barry Harris, Victor Feldman, Bobby Timmons, and Joe Zawinul (a founding member of Weather Report) passed through the band. Multi-instrumentalist Yusef Lateef and flutist Charles Lloyd also played with Cannonball's group. Present at the "Mercy" sessions were Nat Adderley (cornet), Joe Zawinul (piano), Sam Jones (bass), and Louis Hayes (drums).

Seldom does a jazzman manage to attract a large pop audience with his recordings, but Cannonball's soulful sounds made the Hot 100 listings five times in all, from 1961 through 1970. His instrumentals were rooted in jazz, but always had an engagingly bluesy backbeat.

Cannonball Adderley died on August 8, 1975, in Gary, Indiana. He was only 45 when he suffered a massive stroke.

Casinos

THEN YOU CAN TELL ME GOODBYE
(J. D. Loudermilk)
Fraternity 977
No. 6   *March 11, 1967*

The Casinos consisted of Gene and Glen Hughes plus their buddies—Pete Bolton, Joe Patterson, and Ray White. The year was 1958. They were still in their teens, still in high school, and still neat and clean-cut. Gene, Glen, and the guys sang wherever they could, at dances and school functions. In 1964, they recorded two unsuccessful singles for the tiny Terry label—"Gee Whiz," a take on the Carla Thomas classic, and "Too Good To Be True." Harry Carlson of the Cincinnati-based Fraternity label liked their sounds and gave them another chance. A cover of "Moon River" sank from sight; others also fizzled. The Beatle-esque "Right There Beside You" had the group shakin' their crewcuts. It was a solid effort, but like all previous ones, the single stiffed.

In the mid-'60s, the Casinos swelled to nine in number by adding Bob Armstrong, Bill Hawkins, Tom Mathews, and Mickey Denton to the line-up. (Denton had almost made the big time in the early '60s, recording as a teen idol for Big Top, Amy, and World Artists.) By 1967, Mickey and the others were cutting a song that Gene had heard Johnny Nash sing. "Then You Can Tell Me Goodbye" was a musical throw-back, but it also sounded collegiate and choral, like something the Association would do.

Nonetheless, the record became a smash.

Things looked bright as the morning sun for the squeaky-clean crew from Cincinnati. Critic Earl Wilson congratulated the guys on their "normal look," and Gene let all know that he did not allow no long hair and no tight pants on his Casino crew. Follow-up 45s appeared on an assortment of labels well into the '70s, but with the exception of "It's All Over Now" (#65, 1967)—penned by Don Everly—not a one gained much of a notice.

Gene Hughes lives in Nashville and still performs. The "Casinos" name is alive; personnel changes have been numerous over the years.

Buffalo Springfield
FOR WHAT IT'S WORTH
(Stephen Stills)
Atco 6559
No. 7   *March 25, 1967*

These seminal folk-rockers were originally known as the Herd, until someone spotted, on the back of a parked steamroller, the name "Buffalo Springfield." The initial inspiration for the band seems to have come from guitarist Steve Stills (b. Jan. 3, 1945, Dallas), a member of the New York-based Au Go Go Singers. With the latter group's break-up, Stills headed for L.A. Once there, he phoned a fellow ex-Go Go, Richie Furay (b. May 9, 1944, Dayton, Ohio), asking him to come out and play rhythm guitar for a new group he was thinking of forming.

Legend has it that Stills and Furay, while stuck in a traffic jam, spotted a hearse with Canadian license plates. On closer inspection, Stills identified the driver as guitarist Neil Young (b. Nov. 12, 1945, Toronto), a folkie whom Stills had met in Canada. In Young's

company was a fellow Canadian, bassist Bruce Palmer. Now all that the new group needed was a drummer. Enter Dewey Martin (b. Sept. 30, 1952, Chesterville, Canada).

Buffalo Springfield became the house band at L.A.'s Whiskey A Go-Go, where they were soon spotted by Sonny & Cher's managers, Charlie Green and Brian Stone. Green and Stone secured a recording contract for the guys with Atco, a division of Atlantic Records. Although it was a fine track, not many people picked up on the group's debut single, "Nowadays Clancy Can't Even Sing."

The follow-up was a Stills number inspired by riots on Sunset Strip following some student protests. "For What It's Worth," featuring Neil Young's sinister-sounding lead guitar, brought the group immediate fame and a following. Their first album, *Buffalo Springfield* (1967), had included "Clancy" and this biggie, but had not sold well; with the success of "For What It's Worth," the LP took off.

By the release of their second album (*Buffalo Springfield Again*) in late 1967, Palmer was gone, having been deported for a visa violation. He was replaced by Jim Fielder (later a member of Blood, Sweat & Tears). Young, who did not get along well with Stills, departed briefly, and Doug Hastings stepped in. Young soon returned, Hastings left, and the group's recording engineer—Jim Messina, a future member of Loggins & Messina—took over bass and vocal duties for Fielder.

By this point, the group began falling apart while recording their third album, as internal dissension and acrimonious exchanges grew. In order to finish the LP, a great deal of over-dubbing was necessary, since certain members did not want to be present with other members in the studio. By the end of 1968, Buffalo Springfield's final album, *Last Time Around*, was issued—posthumously.

**Buffalo
Springfield**

Stills joined ex-Byrd David Crosby and ex-Hollie Graham Nash in the formation of Crosby, Stills & Nash (later, of course, Young would also join the act). Young set up a solo career with his back-up band, Crazy Horse. Furay and Messina formed Poco, while Martin made a vain effort to keep the "Buffalo Springfield" name alive with three new members. This version of the group never recorded, and Dewey embarked on an unsuccessful solo career.

Easybeats

FRIDAY ON MY MIND

(Harry Vanda, George Young)
United Artists 50108
No. 16 *May 20, 1967*

The Easybeats

The Easybeats met and merged at a youth hostel in 1963 in Sydney, Australia. Guitarist George Young (b. Nov. 6, 1947, Glasgow, Scotland) joined forces with lead singer "Little" Stevie Wright (b. Dec. 20, 1948, Leeds, England); bassist Dick Diamonde (b. Dec. 28, 1947) and lead guitarist Harry Vanda (b. March 22, 1947), who had both moved to Australia from their native Holland; and drummer Gordon "Snowy" Fleet (b. Aug. 16, 1945, Liverpool), who had played with the Mojos, and who picked the "Easybeats" name.

By 1964, the Easybeats were a scruffy-haired band playing at a Sydney club called The Beatle Village. A talent scout named Mike Vaughn caught one of their shows, and recommended them to J. Albert & Son, the label that issued the first of the beat group's many 45s, "For My Woman." Nothing much happened until "She's So Fine," their next Australian release: it topped the homeland charts, and the follow-up, "Wedding Bells," went top 10. Yet George and the rest were not pleased with the results.

"That's when all the bullshit started," Young told Greg Shaw, editor of *Who Put the Bomp.* "With that track, we tried to be commercial. It paid off, but wasn't as big as we thought it could have been. We decided then that we wanted to get out of Australia." Before leaving for England, three more collectible singles were issued—"Sad And Lonely And Blue," "Make You Feel Alright (Woman)," and "Come And See Her."

Once on British shores, the Easybeats recorded an irresistably pulsating track with a Beatle-esque yet rough-edged feel. "Friday On My Mind" was a slice of working-class rock and roll, and remains a classic here-comes-the-weekend party platter. According to George, that was the beginning of the end—the band was pressured to come up with another "Friday," and a U.S. tour was hastily arranged. Snowy dropped out, to be replaced by Tony Cahill.

"By that time, the band was really stoned most of the time, and we had been at it for a fair while. When everybody else was getting into it, we were trying to get out of it. The general lethargy of the band was due to dope, plus there were contractual hassles popping up and we *still* weren't making any money. Then we found ourselves exclusively signed to more than one record company! To this day [late '70s], we're still involved in lawsuits."

After just a handful of fine stateside singles and two albums—*Friday on My Mind* (1967) and *Falling Off the Edge of the World* (1968)—the Easybeats called it quits in 1969. Harry

Vanda and George Young have since moved on to become Australia's top producers (AC/DC, Rose Tattoo, JOHN PAUL YOUNG), and have recorded under pseudonyms like Paintbox, Tramp, Moondance, the Band of Hope, Flash & The Pan, Grapefruit, and the Marcus Hook Roll Band. Young's two younger brothers are AC/DC's Angus and Malcolm Young.

Tony Cahill later joined the Australian quintet Python Lee Jackson (whose 1972 hit "In A Broken Dream" featured Rod Stewart guesting on lead vocals). Dick Diamonde reportedly retired to New South Wales in Australia. Snowy Fleet has taken over his family's construction company. Stevie Wright conquered a dreadful heroin problem; as he admitted to *Rolling Stone*, "[it] was devastating, going from the stardom of the Easybeats to sweeping floors."

labels like Capitol, ABC, and his own Little Eskimo label. Jerry has also produced, in Spector-like fashion, collectible disks for Clydie King, Ramona King, the Lornettes, Shango, Bobby Sheen (of Bob B. Soxx & The Bluejeans), Sugar 'n' Spice, Nino Tempo & April Stevens, and Bonnie & The Treasures.

Early in 1967, Riopelle, Murray MacLeod, and Smokey Roberds went into a studio as Parade. "Sunshine Girl," with its light, West Coast hippie feel, was a big success. The five high-quality follow-ups—"She's Got The Magic," "Frog Prince," "I Can See Love," "A.C.D.C.," and "Laughing Lady"—were not.

"I'm the guy in *One Trick Pony*," Riopelle lamented. "Oh, Paul Simon wasn't thinking about Jerry Riopelle when he made the movie, but he was thinking about a guy who has good songs, but never became famous. That's me."

Parade

SUNSHINE GIRL
(Jerry Riopelle, Murray MacLeod, Smokey Roberds)
A & M 841
No. 20 *May 27, 1967*

Jerry Riopelle was born almost a half-century ago in Detroit, and his family moved to Arizona shortly thereafter. He relocated to California more than 20 years ago, but he is Arizona's favorite pop artist—his obscure disks sell by the thousands there. "Other guys [like me] who didn't get that break have to quit the business and get into selling pharmaceuticals or something," Riopelle told Steve Clow of the *Los Angeles Herald*. "The best thing is that I get to do what I like to do, and that's write and play the music and make records. It's nice to go to Arizona and play the star."

Riopelle was the first and only producer hired by the legendary Phil Spector in the early '60s, when the "Wall of Sound" man was planning to develop a stable of in-house producers for his Philles label. Jerry played piano and sang back-up on sessions for the Righteous Brothers, the Ronettes, and Ike & Tina Turner. He produced "Things Are Changing," a song for the U.S. Government in the '60s (with Spector and Brian Wilson) that encouraged kids to stay in school.

Over the years, Jerry's songs have been recorded by Rita Coolidge, Kenny Loggins, and Meatloaf. He has been an A & R man for A & M Records, and has recorded nine LPs for

Whistling Jack Smith

I WAS KAISER BILL'S BATMAN
(Roger Greenaway, Roger Cook)
Deram 85005
No. 20 *June 3, 1967*

Whistling Jack Smith never existed. There had been a *Whispering* Jack Smith, though—a British recording artist who half-talked and half-sang his way through tunes because of a World War II injury. Not a soul who bought "I Was Kaiser Bill's Batman" suspected that Whistling Jack Smith was a total fabrication. Even knowing this would not have made much difference: the song and the artist had silly names, the tune had an infectious little melody, and the dingy disk was disturbingly different from anything on top 40 radio at that time.

A fog surrounds the actual conception of Jack the whistler. Was it the uncredited producer of the session, or the tune's conceivers—the songwriting team of Greenaway and Cook—who dreamed up the idea? Possibly the whole episode was a spur-of-the-moment studio fluke. We do know that the song features the Mike Sammes Singers, a then-popular TV group, plus some session musicians.

Once copies of "I Was Kaiser Bill's Batman" began flying off the shelves, a Jack Smith had to be located for making personal appearances. Billy Moeller (b. Feb. 2, 1946, Liverpool)—brother of Tommy Moeller, lead singer for Unit Four Plus Two—agreed to play the role of Jack Smith and tour behind the single. He had been recording for British Decca as Coby Wells, and his disks under that name had not exactly been burning holes in the charts.

When Whistling Jack's magic moment had passed, Billy Moeller returned to being Coby Wells and, later still, recorded under his God-given name. Poor fellow: even under three different pseudonyms, he was unable to place another disk on the charts in the U.S. or the U.K.

Jon & Robin & The In-Crowd
DO IT AGAIN A LITTLE BIT SLOWER
(Wayne Thompson)
Abnak 119
No. 18   *June 24, 1967*

Jon and Robin Abnor were a husband-and-wife team from Dallas. Sonny & Cher were fabulously popular at this time, and other duos were hopping on the folk-rock bandwagon. Jon & Robin's slightly suggestive hit single (pressed on yellow vinyl, an unusual practice back then) was produced by rockabilly legend Dale Hawkins of "Susie Q" fame, as was "Do It Again"'s follow-up, "Drums" (#100, 1967).

One other Jon & Robin 45 charted—"Dr. Jon (The Medicine Man)" (#87, 1968). Thereafter, Jon worked alone and with studio players as Jon & The In-Crowd, Jon Abnor, H. Rabon, Jon Howard, Jon Howard Abnor, and the Abnor Involvement. Wife Robin even had a solo try as (naturally) Robin. Most of these offerings eluded critical notice with the greatest of ease.

The Abnors reportedly owned Abnak Records, the label of a group called the Five Americans that racked up a number of pop hits—"I See The Light" (#26, 1966), "Evil Not Love" (#52, 1966), and "Western Union" (#5, 1967). Herein lay the source of the financial wherewithal that allowed Jon and Robin to prolong what otherwise might have been more truncated careers.

Fifth Estate
DING DONG! THE WITCH IS DEAD
(E. Y. Harburg, Harold Arlen)
Jubilee 5573
No. 11   *July 1, 1967*

Despite suspicions to the contrary, the Fifth Estate was actually a legitimate performing group. "We started about 1964," D. Bill Shute

told *Goldmine*'s Tom Bingham. "The English styles were in, and we looked like Manfred Mann, turtlenecks and haircuts down to here." And despite bios shipped by the Jubilee label claiming that "Ding Dong!" was the group's vinyl debut, the Fifth Estate was "on four different labels over the years. United Artists first, then the Veep label . . . We did the 'Hullaballoo' show on TV, and I guess it was 1965. Eventually we were on Kapp Records, then Red Bird was next, and Jubilee was last."

Well, that's five record companies. And unfortunately, other than a lone single bearing their name on Red Bird ("Love Is All A Game" b/w "Like I Love You"), no record collector has yet identified any of these pre-"Ding Dong!" disks.

"We had an organist—he was our lead singer, arranger, and everything else, a real whiz kid. Wayne ["Wads"] Wadhams graduated from Dartmouth and also had degrees from MIT and Harvard in English, nuclear physics, and everything. He wound up running the Orson Welles Cinema in Boston. Now I think he's got a recording studio there."

According to *Cashbox*, all the fellows lived in the same neighborhood in Springdale, Connecticut. Wads, they report, was one to have frequent cellar parties, and it was through this pleasing tradition that the group's members met. Their line-up at the time of their history-making moment was D. Bill Shute on mandolin, guitar, and fuzz guitar; Rick "Rik" Engler on vocals, kazoo, electric clarinet, violin, and bass; Furvus Evans on drums and maracas; Dick "Duck" Ferrar on vocals, guitar, string bass, and fuzz bass; and Wayne "Wads" Wadhams on piano, electric harpsichord, and fuzz organ.

"We did a tour with Gene Pitney in 1967," Shute recalled. "There were a bunch of other groups, too; the Happenings, THE MUSIC EXPLOSION, THE EASYBEATS. Anyway, that was a real taste of rock and roll stardom. I figured, 'I don't want to do *this* anymore!' That was enough of that."

Bill didn't have much of a choice anyway—he was drafted. And after a total of eight Jubilee 45s and a non-charting LP (*Ding Dong! The Witch is Dead*), the group broke up. On Bill's return, he married and settled into a life as a teacher. In the mid-'70s, Shute formed the Green Linnet record label with Lisa Null and Patrick Sky. Shute and Null have collaborated on two LPs: *The Feathered Maiden & Other Ballads* (1977) and *American Primitive* (1981).

"Wads" Wadhams currently lives in Boston. He teaches recording techniques at the Berklee College of Music, and does independent production work.

Every Mothers' Son
COME ON DOWN TO MY BOAT
(Wes Farrell, Jerry Goldstein)
MGM 13733
No. 6 *July 8, 1967*

For five years, Dennis (b. Nov. 22, 1948) and Larry Larden (b. Aug. 10, 1945) had been a two-guitar folk duo working clubs and pubs in New York's Greenwich Village. Much like fellow folkies the Lovin' Spoonful and the Mamas & The Papas, they went electric. It was early in 1967 when a mutual friend introduced the brothers to a New York University dental student, pianist Bruce Milner (b. May 9, 1943).

The threesome hit it off, and within a week, two theater majors, drummer Christopher Augustine (b. Apr. 25, 1941) and bassist Schuyler "Sky" Larsen (b. Feb. 19, 1947), were added. Chris had acted in New York's Shakespeare Festival and the American Playrights' Festival in Maine; since the age of 11, Sky had been making money in TV commercials. All the guys were New York-born and bred, and each of them looked as squeaky-clean as the boy next door.

After a month of working together, rehearsing and writing songs, the well-groomed group approached Peter Leeds. Leeds was impressed, signed on as their manager, and connected them with noted songwriter/producer Wes Farrell. Wes, who had written "Boys," "Come A Little Bit Closer," and "Hang on Sloopy," cut 12 sides on the band. Included at Wes' suggestion was a cover version of the Rare Breed's bubble-gummy "Come On Down To My Boat."

Industry legend has it that five major labels grappled to acquire the rights to the Son sounds. MGM won, and hastily issued the *Every Mothers' Son* album and "Come On Down To My Boat." Image-constructing ads—playing on the boys' natty neckties and closely-cropped hair—depicted Every Mothers' Son as alert, brave, cheerful, clean, courteous, friendly, healthy, helpful, kind, and loyal. Their "Boat" single cruised up the charts, and the future looked bright for this wholesome bunch.

But as so often happens, instant success created instant dissension within the group. Rather than follow Wes' paternal advice, the Larden boys decided to produce and record their own tunes by themselves. Three further 45s made *Billboard*'s Hot 100, but each one sold more poorly than its predecessor. By 1969, the group was relegated to playing small halls, high school hops, and senior proms. After one prom, Every Mothers' Son called it quits.

Dennis Larden continued to rock and roll. In addition to supplying back-up vocals for Keith Moon's *Two Sides of the Moon* (1975) album, Dennis, for much of the '70s, played guitar for Rick Nelson's Stone Canyon Band. Bruce Milner is now Dr. Milner, a dentist in Manhattan. Chris Augustine was spotted in the late '70s as a contestant on "The Dating Game."

Music Explosion
A LITTLE BIT OF SOUL
(John Carter, Ken Lewis)
Laurie 3380
No. 2 *July 8, 1967*

Volcanic, eruptive, explosive. Yes, the publicity puds at Laurie Records spared no superlatives in their claims for these music-making teens from Mansfield, Ohio. The Music Explosion was to be the next great thing to overwhelm the fickle rock and roll *haut monde*. They never were, of course, but before self-destructing at an unrecorded point in time, they did leave mankind with "A Little Bit Of Soul," a mammoth moment in the annals of vinyl popdom.

Don "Tudor" Atkins (guitar), Bob Avery (drums, harmonica), Jimmie "Jamie" Lyons (lead vocals), Rick Nesta (guitar), and Burton "Butch" Sahl (bass, keyboards) were Ohio Valley dreamers who had only been playing together for weeks when they happened onto an agreeable number written by John Carter and Ken Lewis, both members of the British group Ivy League. "A Little Bit Of Soul" and another side were cut and issued on the Attack label.

Somewhere in this story, Elliot Chiprut and the future fathers of bubblegum music, Jeff Katz and Jerry Kasenetz, put their two cents in. With production credits claimed by Elliot and the Kasenetz-Katz team, a revamped version of "A Little Bit Of Soul" appeared on the Laurie label. No hype needed—sales of the single were truly explosive. Of all the group's future disks, however, only their follow-up, "Sunshine Games" (#63, 1967), made a respectable chart showing.

After several years' worth of volatile singles that failed to detonate, Lyons formed the Jamie Lyons Group and issued a few unsuccessful 45s on the Laurie label. In 1973, Jamie bounced back with a one-off album and a new group, The Capitol City Rockers, but the Rockers fizzled fast. After the Music Explosion blew apart, Bob Avery stuck around with Kasenetz and Katz. Rewarding Avery for his loyalty, K & K seated Bob in the drummer's chair of one of their concocted groups, CRAZY ELEPHANT.

Bill Cosby
LITTLE OLE MAN (UPTIGHT— EVERYTHING'S ALRIGHT)
(Sylvia Moy, Stevie Wonder, Henry Cosby)
Warner Bros. 7072
No. 4   October 14, 1967

A phenomenon . . . Bill Cosby. What's left? He is the production seer and "acting" head of the house on one of TV's biggest blockbusters, the top-rated NBC sitcom "The Cosby Show." He is one of TV's most sought-after commercial pitchmen—he has plugged away for Coca-Cola, Ford, E.F. Hutton, Jell-O, Kodak, and Texas Instruments. He is also a pack-'em-in stand-up comedian, with a 1988 asking fee of $250,000 a night; a TV star with a history ("I

Spy," "The Bill Cosby Show," "The New Bill Cosby Show," and "Cos"); a successful author (*Fatherhood, Time Flies*); a movie star (*Uptown Saturday Night, California Suite, Hickey and Boggs, Leonard Part 6*); and a whole lot of fun.

Time Magazine has noted that solid-gold Mr. C. has dominated the media like no star since the days of Lucille Ball and Milton Berle. His earnings for 1987 were estimated at $57,000,000, making him at that point the highest-paid entertainer on the face of the earth. Perhaps no performer in history has or ever will be as successful as Bill Cosby, but in terms of top 40 success, Bill is but a one-hit wonder.

In terms of album sales, Cosby was the hottest comedian of the '60s: his first seven comedy albums, recorded from 1965 to 1968, were all million-sellers. Three of these LPs even went platinum—*I Started Out As A Child* (1965), *Wonderfulness* (1966), and *Bill Cosby Is A Very Funny Fellow, Right!* (1966). "Little Ole Man," a novelty number based on a Stevie Wonder tune, was his only single to crack the top 40. Cosby's funny-boned follow-ups, though less successful, still made the Hot 100 listings: "Hooray For The Salvation Army Band" (#71, 1967), "Funky North · Philly" (#91, 1968), "Grover Henson Feels Forgotten" (#70, 1970), and "Yes, Yes, Yes" (#46, 1976).

"When you're younger," Cosby told *Time*'s Dan Goodgame, "you want to be sure that by the time you're 80 years old, you can sit on the park bench and look back and say, 'Man, I did it all. I didn't miss a thing.'"

Hombres
LET IT OUT (LET IT ALL HANG OUT)
(Bill Cunningham)
Verve Forecast 5058
No. 12   November 18, 1967

Billy B. Cunningham (organ), Gary Wayne McEwen (guitar), and Johnny Will Hunter (drums) had a mountain more than a mite in common. They were all one-time students at Memphis High, they all had instruments, and they all shared a hankering to make music. As members of the touring edition of Ronny & The Daytonas, a Nashville studio group, the guys were en route to a gig in Houston when they conceived "Let It Out (Let It All Hang Out)."

"I had heard the phrase from someone that I

By this time, bassist Jerry Lee Masters from Little Rock, Arkansas, had joined the Hombres. Jerry Lee liked the sight of sweet young girls, water sports, and all those other Hombre activities. "Let It Out (Let It All Hang Out)," the band's first release and only chart-chumper, was a verbal collage of profound non-sense, featuring a lead vocal that sounded like a funked-up Dylan with a face full of marbles.

Nothing these rock and rollers created would ever replicate the silliness of their hit disk. Subsequent singles with provocative titles like "Am I High (Boy, Am I High!)," "Mau, Mau, Mau," and "Take My Overwhelming Love And Cram It Up Your Heart" met with resistance in record stores across the nation. Sales were miserable. A lone album, bearing a cover photo of the Hombres posing as *bandoleros* in a garbage dump, was released and quickly dropped from sight. Shortly after, the Hombres did likewise.

B.B.'s brother, incidentally, is Bill Cunningham, an original member of the Box Tops. B.B. and Jerry Lee are still involved in music. Gary has become a preacher, and lives outside Nashville. John Hunter died in 1976.

Robert Knight

EVERLASTING LOVE
(Buzz Cason, Mac Gayden)
Rising Sons 705
No. 13 *November 18, 1967*

Robert's (b. Apr. 24, 1945, Franklin, Tenn.) mother died giving birth to his stillborn twin brother. She had been a musician who played various woodwind instruments in local bands; Robert's father taught music at the Tennessee State University. Young Robert took trumpet lessons and sang as a soprano in the Franklin High School choir. When his voice broke, he teamed up with some friends—Pete Hollis, Neal Hopper, Richard Simmons, and Kenny Buttrey—and formed a vocal harmony group, the Paramounts.

On a vacation to New York City in the late '50s, Knight met Jimmy Breedlove, formerly the lead voice for the Cues. Jimmy reportedly introduced the group to Noel Ball, a producer at Dot Records and manager of Arthur Alexander and JOE HENDERSON. Dot issued at least three singles: one by the Paramounts, two as solo efforts by Robert. Nothing matched the musical needs of the nation, so the group dispersed.

The Hombres

was staying with at a boardinghouse," B.B. Cunningham recalled to *Goldmine*'s Stu Fink. "I didn't invent the phrase, it was just in the wind. What prompted us to put it with a tune was Dylan playing on the radio. We heard 'Subterranean Homesick Blues' [and] thought that he was really putting the kids on. And we said, 'If that sold records, then *we* could do something crazy, and really put [the kids] on.'"

When the Hombres shopped that song and several others around to the record companies, no one seemed too interested in recording the group until the band met producer Shelby Singleton. Singleton liked the Hombres' silly, country-boy/funky numbers, and lined up a recording session with producer Huey P. Meaux.

As a chemistry major, Knight attended Tennessee State University and sang on evenings with the Fairlanes (Daniel Boone and James Tait). In 1967, Mac Gayden, co-owner with Buzz Cason (a.k.a. GARRY MILES) of the Rising Sons label, heard the group giving their all at a Nashville night spot. Gayden offered to manage and record Knight as a solo act. "Everlasting Love," Robert's first release, clicked like nothing he would ever again record; it was an even bigger hit seven years later, for Carl Carlton (#6, 1974). Of a small pile of similar-sounding singles, only "Blessed Are The Lonely" (#97, 1968) and "Isn't It Lonely Together" (#97, 1968) placed on the Hot 100.

When last noted, Knight was a chemist involved in research. He occasionally performs, and releases a single or two every now and then. Gayden went on to become a member of Area Code 615, record three solo albums, and do Nashville session work for Hoyt Axton, J.J. Cale, Dave Davies, Kris Kristofferson, Dave Loggins, Tracy Nelson, and Pearls Before Swine. Cason formed the ELF label with Bobby Russell, wrote "Popsicle" (Jan & Dean) and the English lyrics to "Sukiyaki" (KYU SAKAMOTO), and produced the Crickets, Ronnie & The Daytonas, and Freddy Weller.

Miriam Makeba

PATA PATA
(Miriam Makeba, Jerry Ragavoy)
Reprise 0608
No. 12 *November 25, 1967*

Miriam Makeba (b. Zensi Makeba, Mar. 4, 1932, Johannesburg, South Africa) has had more than her fair share of trials and tribulations. In her 1988 autobiography, *Makeba: My Story*, she details her exile from South Africa (1960), several bouts with cancer, the death of a daughter, five marriages (among her husbands were HUGH MASEKELA and Stokely Carmichael), and 11 car crashes. She also describes being blackballed by the music industry following her 1968 marriage to black radical Stokely Carmichael.

Miriam's parents were of the Xhosa nation; she was born in Prospect Township. For eight years, she received a musical education through the Methodist-sponsored Kilmerton Training School in Pretoria. Miriam sang in school and church choirs, and toured in the late '50s with the 11-man Black Manhattan Brothers musical revue. A bit part in an American documentary, *Come Back Africa* (1959)—as a singer in a *shebeen*, an illegal club where blacks are served alcohol—brought Makeba international attention, even though she only sang two numbers in the movie. Concert engagements were soon lined up in Venice, London, and the U.S.

Steve Allen and Harry Belafonte befriended Miriam, becoming her mentors. Reviewing her performance at New York's Village Vanguard, *Newsweek* dubbed her "easily the most revolutionary talent to appear in any medium in the last decade." She recorded one successful album after another: *The World of Miriam Makeba* (1963), *The Voice of Africa* (1964), *An Evening with Belafonte/Makeba* (1965), *Miriam Makeba in Concert* (1967), and *Pata Pata* (1967). "Pata Pata" was issued as a single, and its success took many people by surprise.

"The song 'Pata Pata' was a turning point because it was a hit," Makeba told the *Chicago Tribune*. "I didn't understand why *that* one became so popular, because it's one of my most insignificant songs. And here I have songs that I think are very serious, and people remember 'Pata Pata.'"

The next year, Miriam followed up "Pata Pata" with "Malayisha" (#85, 1968). She married Stokely Carmichael, the controversial black-power activist, with disastrous consequences. "My marriage to Stokely didn't change my life—it just made my career disappear in [the U.S.] and England! I don't know why people did that to me. . . . I married him, and then all my contracts were canceled."

Miriam has never stopped singing her mixture of traditional and jazz-influenced pop, nor has she curtailed her political activities, which have included four appearances before the United Nations to testify against South Africa's racial policies. After a 20-year vinyl hiatus in the U.S., she released *Sangoma*, an album of sacred tribal songs, in 1988.

Victor Lundberg

AN OPEN LETTER TO MY
TEENAGE SON
(Victor Lundberg)
Liberty 55996
No. 10 *December 2, 1967*

At the time of his cultural impact, Victor Lundberg was the owner of a company that specialized in creating radio and TV ads. Hippies were growing their hair everywhere; flower power was in full bloom; there was talk of a generation gap. Who better to address this social situation but someone with the credibility of an ad man? Are you buying this? Someone did. Lundberg's "Open Letter To My Teenage Son" was a pin-headed narrative with advice and optimism and more advice. Some people obviously needed reassurance and snapped up what Lundberg was hawking—"Open Letter" became one of the fastest-selling spoken-word disks in recording history.

Victor was born in 1923 in Grand Rapids, Michigan. He created his own advertising company, worked for five years in the Psychological Warfare Department (aptly enough) during World War II, and became an announcer and newsman at various stations in

Grand Rapids, Tulsa, and Phoenix. After his "Open Letter To My Teenage Son" found a soft spot in the wallets and heads of mass America, Lundberg tried to package an entire LP's worth of ninny narratives that would address other important social topics. His marketing stratagem, however, had run its course.

Rose Garden
NEXT PLANE TO LONDON
(Kenny Gist, Jr.)
Atco 6510
No. 17   *December 30, 1967*

Rose Garden sprouted in Parkensburg, West Virginia. Diana Di Rose had been a fan of beat

poetry, the sounds of bongos, and the aroma of espresso. She performed at such New York night spots as the Bitter End and the Night Owl, and appeared on TV's "Hootenanny." Just how they all came together is not known, but by the end of 1966, Di Rose was part of a band named after her. Rose Garden consisted of Diana Di Rose, drummer Bruce Boudin (b. 1946), bassist/pianist William Fleming (b. 1949), guitarist James Groshong (b. 1947, Los Angeles), and lead guitarist Johnny Noreen (b. 1950, Los Angeles).

The following year, Di Rose and her Garden group ventured to L.A. to improve their lot and, if possible, get recorded. As luck would have it, they met Charlie Greene and Brian Stone, two hip and hungry hot-shot producers. Greene and Stone were doing studio work for BUFFALO SPRINGFIELD, DR. JOHN, the Daily Planet, the Rising Sons, and a whole horde of other '60s acts.

"Next Plane To London" was an innocent period piece from the pen of Kenny Gist, Jr., who grazed the top 40 in 1967 as Kenny O'Dell with a peace-and-love single entitled "Beautiful People." With seemingly little effort, "Next Plane" landed on the charts. An album and "Here Today," a Byrds-like follow-up, were quickly pressed. Neither sold well, but it didn't matter: Rose Garden's season had passed, and the group disbanded.

John Fred & His Playboy Band

JUDY IN DISGUISE (WITH GLASSES)
(John Fred, Andrew Bernard)
Paula 282
No. 1 *January 20, 1968*

John Fred Gourrier (b. May 8, 1941, Baton Rouge, La.) had been listening to Fats Domino, Smiley Lewis, and the Spiders since he was knee-high. He started his first band in 1956 at the age of 15; the idea was to work the weekend dances, make some money, and have fun. Three years later, Sam Montel spotted John and his Playboy pack and signed them to his Montel label. "We went down to Cosimo's [Recording Studio in New Orleans] and recorded 'Shirley' with Fats Domino's band," John told *One Hit*'s Steven Rosen. "That day, Fats was recording 'Whole Lotta Lovin'' and 'Little Coquette.' After he got through recording that, I just went right in with his band."

"Shirley" came out in February of 1959, and charted at number 82. After touring up North and appearing at one of Alan Freed's rock and roll shows at the Brooklyn Paramount Theatre, John—the son of Fred Gourrier, one-time third-baseman for the Detroit Tigers—decided to put his career on hold while he attended Southern Louisiana College on a basketball scholarship. When he graduated in 1964, John formed a new Playboy Band and cut a remake of bluesman John Lee Hooker's "Boogie Chillun" for the En-Joy label.

When "Boogie Chillun" began attracting some sales action, En-Joy chief Rocky Robin approached Stan Lewis at the Shreveport-based Jewel/Paula record complex about national distribution. Soon afterward, Fred and his Playboys moved over to Lewis' labels. "[Lewis] let me do pretty much what I wanted," Fred explained. "And I got to produce the band. Slowly, I learned about record producing. Andrew Bernard, our sax player, did most of the arrangements."

The members of the Playboy Band at the recording of "Judy In Disguise" were saxophonist Andrew Bernard (b. 1945, New Orleans), bassist Harold Cowart (b. June 4, 1944, Baton Rouge, La.), keyboardist Tommy "Dee" DeGeneres (b. Nov. 3, 1946, Baton Rouge), trumpeter Ronnie Goodson (b. Feb. 2, 1945, Miami), percussionist Joe Miceli (b. July 9, 1946, Baton Rouge), guitarist Jimmy O'Rourche (b. Mar. 14, 1947, Fall River, Mass.), and trumpeter Charlie "Spinn" Spinosa (b. Dec. 29, 1948, Baton Rouge).

"Judy In Disguise (With Glasses)" was the group's 16th single. "We were playing in Florida, and all the girls at that time had these big sunglasses. One of the guys was hustling this chick. She took off these glasses, and she could stop a clock. I said, 'That's it.' That's what gave me the idea." That, and the Beatles' "Lucy In The Sky With Diamonds."

Where did John Fred and Andrew Bernard, the song's writers, pick up "Judy"'s bizarre/psychedelic references to "lemonade pies" and "cantaloupe eyes"? "At the time, 'The Monkees' were on TV, and [the show was] presented by Yardley and Playtex," Fred recalled. "I was sitting there and writing words while the TV was on, and they said something like 'Cross your heart with a living bra.' I just wrote that down, too."

"Judy" was a weird one, but what a hit—it stayed perched atop the charts for two weeks straight. Though Fred and his Playboy Band tried to repeat the trick, only their immediate

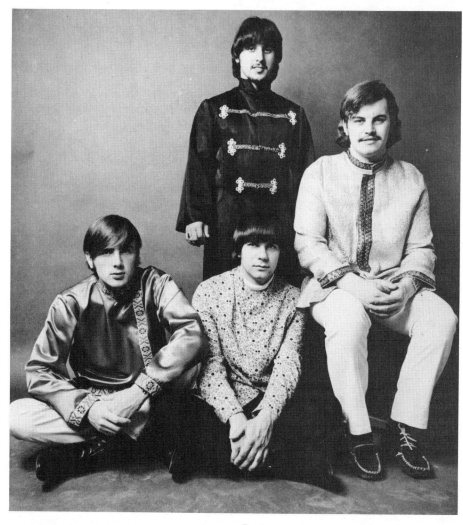

The Human Beinz

follow-up, "Hey, Hey Bunny" (#57, 1968), managed to make the national listings.

John Fred remained a full-time music-maker until 1976, when he became the vice president of Deep South Records. There, he wrote commercials and did some production work (one notable project: IRMA THOMAS' *Safe With You* album). Currently, he runs John Fred Music and the Sugarcane record label. He and his retooled Playboy Band still perform and tour throughout the South.

Human Beinz

NOBODY BUT ME
(Rudolph Isley, O'Kelly Isley)
Capitol 5990
No. 8   *February 3, 1968*

Although they left behind one of the more accessible psychedelic treasures from the '60s, they were not one of the decade's best— or best-known—bands. In fact, no one really seems to know just who the Human Beinz were.

Richard (guitar, lead vocals), "Ting" (guitar), Mel (bass), and Mike (drums) were a Cleveland bar band. They are probably the same unit that recorded covers of "The Times They Are A-Changin'," "Gloria," and "Pied Piper" for the tiny Gateway label; but they are probably not the same Human Bei*ngs* who recorded at about the same time for Impact and Warner Bros.

In 1968, the Human Beinz made two albums—*Nobody But You* and *Evolutions*— and cut three singles for Capitol. Only their retread of the Isley Brothers' 1962 tune "Nobody But You" went top 40; their cover version of Bobby "Blue" Bland's "Turn On Your Love Light" logged in at number 80 in 1968. After releasing an uninspired original entitled "Everytime Woman," the Human Beinz became a blurred footnote to pop history.

All of their Capitol sessions took place at the Cleveland Recording Company. John Hanson was there in the studio at the time, and offered his vague memories about the group in an exclusive interview.

"I couldn't tell you who they were, but I remember the session. The boys were after some kind of sound, and nobody there knew just how to help them get it. I remember they wanted to multi-track and use feedback, and nobody knew how to handle them. They did have that big hit, so all wasn't lost—right?"

Lemon Pipers
GREEN TAMBOURINE
(Paul Leka, Shelley Pinz)
Buddah 23
No. 1 *February 3, 1968*

They were almost history before they made it. Their 1967 single, "Turn Around, Take A Look," had stiffed badly. Had they not accepted bubblegummy Buddah Records' offer to record one more tune—of the label's choice—the Lemon Pipers (once known as Ivan & The Sabres) would now be remembered by very few people.

Shelley Pinz got the idea for "Green Tambourine" from a newspaper article about a British street musician who would play a number of instruments while seated in front of his receptacle of donations—a tambourine, filled with green. Producer/writer Paul Leka (later to work his winning ways with STEAM, Harry Chapin, The Left Banke, and REO Speedwagon) added the music to Ms. Pinz's piece, and before long, the boys at Buddah were excited about the song's hit potential. But first, someone had to persuade the Lemon Pipers to learn it and to get it down on vinyl.

"It was a strange meeting," Leka recalled to Fred Bronson in *The Billboard Book of Number One Hits*. "I played the song on an upright piano they had, and asked [the group] what they thought. They were more into psychedelic songs. They went into the other room, and came out and said they really didn't like the song. I said, 'I don't know if I should say this—you're being dropped from the label. Bob Reno

and Neil Bogart [then the president of Buddah] are determined to record this song. You're gonna be dropped if you don't record this.'"

The band—all raised in Oxford, Ohio, except Britisher William Albaugh—acquiesced. Albaugh (drums), William Bartlett (lead guitar), Ivan Browne (lead vocals, guitar), Reg G. Nave (keyboards, green tambourine, fog horn, toys), and Steve Walmsley (bass) entered the Cleveland Recording Studios, where they waxed "Green Tambourine," the *Green Tambourine* album, and a couple of unmemorable sides: "Rice Is Nice" (#46, 1968) and "Jelly Jungle (Of Orange Marmalade)" (#51, 1968).

Guitarist Bill Bartlett would reappear years later as the leader of RAM JAM.

Paul Mauriat
LOVE IS BLUE
(Andre Popp, Pierre Cour)
Philips 40495
No. 1 *February 10, 1968*

No one expected fireworks and bliss from the union of Paul Mauriat and an innocent item called "Love Is Blue." In 1967, the tune was selected to represent Luxembourg at the annual Eurovision Song Contest. Vicky Leandros sang the number at the festival, where it came in fourth; on record, even recorded in 19 languages, it sold only mildly. No instrumental had topped the American charts in more than five years, and no born-in-France single had ever reached number one on the pop charts. In short, no one expected Mauriat's mood music to pillage the charts, but the dulcet ditty did.

Born in 1925, Paul Mauriat grew up in a house full of music. When he was four years old, ma and pa taught him how to have his way with a piano. At the age of 10, when his family moved to Paris, he enrolled in the Conservatoire. And by his 17th year, Paul was leading an orchestra and touring Europe's concert halls. He soon found a nice niche arranging, conducting, and producing artists like Charles Aznavour and himself.

There is no indication that Paul conceived of "Love Is Blue" as anything more than just another track for his *Blooming Hits* album. The tune remained at the top of the charts for five weeks, as did the LP which featured the song. Two further singles, "Love In Every Room" (#60, 1968) and "Chitty Chitty Bang Bang" (#76, 1969) later appeared on *Billboard*'s Hot 100.

Gene & Debbe

Gene & Debbe

PLAYBOY
(Gene Thomas)
TRX 5002
No. 17   *April 13, 1968*

Gene Thomas was born on December 28, 1938, in Palestine, Texas. In his early 20s, he gathered a youthful C & W following with his self-penned rockaballads "Sometime" (#53, 1961) and "Baby's Gone" (#84, 1964). In 1967, while a staff songwriter at the Acuff-Rose music-publishing house, Gene met an aspiring country singer from Nashville named Debbe Neville. Gene had some new Sonny & Cher–type tunes that he thought could make Gene and a female sidekick into a lucrative pop act. Debbe agreed to give the songs a shot, and singer/songwriter Don Gant, before his days with THE NEON PHILHARMONIC, produced the sessions.

"Go With Me," their first folkie-flavored 45, charted at number 78 in 1967, and was followed by "Playboy." Gene & Debbe's future looked bright; they appeared on TV shows and made the nightclub rounds. Later in the year, their third single, "Lovin' Season," reached number 81 on the Hot 100, but only briefly. Nothing the duo recorded would ever sell as well as these disks. Gene returned to his staff position at Acuff-Rose, and Debbe disappeared into the wilds of anonymity.

Sweet Inspirations

SWEET INSPIRATION
(Dan Penn, Spooner Oldham)
Atlantic 2476
No. 18   *April 27, 1968*

It all began in Newark's New Hope Baptist Church, where Emily "Cissy" Houston, her nieces Dee Dee and Dionne Warwick, and the sisters Judy (a.k.a. Judy Clay) and Sylvia Guions (a.k.a. Sylvia Shemwell) became members of the Drinkard Singers. Before evolving into the Sweet Inspirations, the group recorded traditional gospel for RCA.

"Growing up, mine was a pretty narrow road," Cissy Houston—perhaps best known to younger pop fans as the mother of Whitney Houston—recalled to Gerri Hershey in *Nowhere to Run*. "Now I had been brought up strict, to think that all of it, rock and all, was

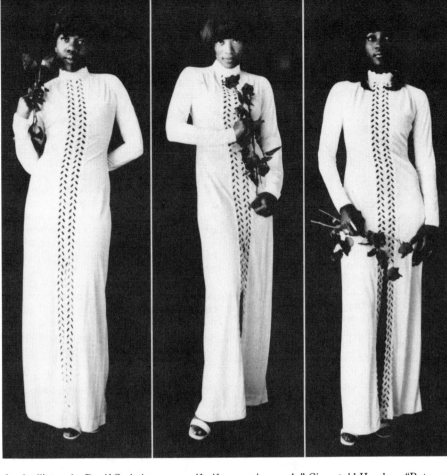

The Sweet
Inspirations

the devil's music. But if God gives you a gift, if he gives you a voice, well, I don't think He's gonna discriminate on how you best put it to use. But I didn't always feel this way. Not at all . . . I suffered a great trauma when I went over [to singing pop music]. But I had three children to raise."

Over the course of the '60s, after some personnel changes, the Drinkard crew became one of the finest—and most recorded—back-up vocal groups in the business. Little did they suspect as much when Cissy, Sylvia, Estelle Brown, and Myra Smith did their first secular studio work behind Ronnie Hawkins and a group later known as The Band. For six years, the girls labored behind the scenes, spicing and enticing the best performances out of acts such as WILLIAM BELL, Maxine Brown, Solomon Burke, Neil Diamond, Aretha Franklin, Wilson Pickett, and Dusty Springfield. It was Jerry Wexler at Atlantic Records who dubbed them "The Sweet Inspirations" and gave them the opportunity to record their own effort.

"A lot of girls got into doing that kind of session work," Cissy told Hershey. "But once we got it together in the Inspirations, well, nobody could touch us. Except maybe the Blossoms."

Elvis, beginning in 1968 and throughout his much-publicized comeback, constantly drew upon the Sweet Inspirations' vocal talents for his nationwide extravaganzas and Vegas shows. But as soloists—out front and on their own—the Sweets clicked on the top 40 with only one 45, a tune dashed off by Dan Penn and Spooner Oldham. A few other disks, appearing before and after their big moment, did stir up some chart action—"Why (Am I Treated So Bad)" (#57, 1967), "Let It Be Me" (#94, 1967), "To Love Somebody" (#74, 1968), and "Unchained Melody" (#73, 1968)—but Cissy and the others never achieved a sustained stardom.

Cissy left the group in 1970 to tour with Darlene Love and Dee Dee Warwick as backup singers for Dionne Warwick, and soon thereafter, tried her way with a solo career. "Be My Baby" (#92, 1971) has been her only Hot 100 entry to date. Estelle, Myrna, and

Sylvia have continued on as sessionists, recording several disappointing solo projects during the '70s. In 1981, Myrna resurfaced as co-writer of many of the songs on Carl Wilson's 1981 solo LP (*Carl Wilson*).

Blue Cheer
SUMMERTIME BLUES
(Eddie Cochran, Jerry Capehart)
Philips 40516
No. 14   *May 4, 1968*

The first truly American heavy-metal band, Blue Cheer was excessive in every way—with their hair length, the volume of their music, and their guitar solos. Their name came from a particular strain of LSD then in vogue. From behind their towering wall of Marshall amps, Blue Cheer, in the words of their manager, could "play so hard and heavy they [made] cottage cheese out of the air."

The *Sturm und Drang* started in Boston in 1967. Bassist Dick Peterson (b. 1948, Grand Forks, N. Dak.) was dissatisfied with the off-the-wall psychedelic music that his band, Group B, was playing. He wanted to do more stripped-down and heavier material, so he quit Group B. Dick located lead guitarist Bruce "Leigh" Stephens through a newspaper ad; several drummers came and went before Paul Whaley, a friend of Dick's and a member of a group called Oxford Circle, completed the thunderous trio.

After moving to San Francisco, the band was spotted by Abe "Voco" Kesh. "Voco was a DJ at KMPX, the first real FM underground station," Peterson told *Goldmine*'s Geoff O'Keefe. "Most blues people at the time were saying, 'Oh, man, this [Blue Cheer] is trash. These guys are so loud. Look at the dwarfs.' But Voco liked it. So we went into the studio and we did a tape of 'Summertime Blues,' 'Doctor Please,' and 'Out Of Focus.' We gave it to Voco and asked him to play it on his station. He did, and people went nuts! We were getting play every hour. We didn't even have a contract or an album or anything."

That state of affairs changed, and quickly. Philips Records signed Blue Cheer to a contract and issued their debut cut—the trio's take on Eddie Cochran's "Summertime Blues." Their debut album, *Vincebus Eruptum* (1968), hit number 11 on the top pop albums chart; their next three LPs—*Outsideinside* (1968), *New! Improved! Blue Cheer* (1969), and *The*

Original Human Being (1970)—did not sell quite as well. The group's career momentum stalled when a follow-up suitable for AM radio was not forthcoming.

Meanwhile, personnel problems began to develop. Peterson and Whaley fired their lead guitarist, briefly replacing him with Randy Holden. Holden soon departed, so guitarist Bruce Stephens and keyboardist Ralph Burns Kellogg, both formerly of Mint Tattoo, stepped in. That crucial follow-up, "Just A Little Bit" (#92, 1968), was finally pulled from Blue Cheer's second LP—but for many radio programmers, it was a case of too little, too late. This was Blue Cheer's last charting single. Soon Whaley was gone (replaced by Norman Mayell), and so was their trademark sound.

"Those [first] three albums were all done during tours, and we just burned ourselves out," Peterson admitted. "[By 1970] I was the only original member left . . . I was just fulfilling contracts. I was so frustrated with Blue Cheer and everything that was happening around it . . . I wanted to get away."

After the release of one more album (*Oh! Pleasant Hope*, 1971), minus still more members, Peterson shut down the band to become a baker. Paul Whaley was spotted in the mid-'80s making pizza in San Francisco. Bruce Stephens, who is now married to Peterson's wife and works as an electrician, recorded one solo LP (*Watch That First Step*) in 1982. Ralph Kellogg is a producer and owner of the Radio Tokyo Studios. Leigh Stephens, who currently runs a thoroughbred horse ranch in California, issued two solo albums, one LP as part of Silver Metre, and two albums (with the accompaniment of Bruce Stephens) as part of Pilot.

In 1979, and again in 1984, Peterson formed a new Blue Cheer band. Megaforce Records released an album, *The Beast is Back*, in 1985, but soon the group was extinct again. Dick has since joined Motown's Foxtrot.

Hugo Montenegro
THE GOOD, THE BAD AND THE UGLY
(Ennio Morricone)
RCA Victor 9423
No. 2   *June 1, 1968*

Hugo was born in 1925 and raised in New York City. He attended the city schools, and after a two-year stay in the Navy, graduated from Manhattan College. Montenegro was for some years the staff manager for André Kostelanetz, the conductor for Harry Belafonte sessions, and (starting in 1955) a purveyor of easy-listening music. None of Hugo's mellow recordings made the top pop albums chart until the release of *Original Music from "The Man from U.N.C.L.E."* in 1966.

Montenegro moved to Los Angeles to do film work, creating and conducting the scores for Otto Preminger's *Hurry Sundown* (1967) and *The Ambushers* (1968). The following year, he undertook what he thought would be his last project for RCA—*Music from "A Fistful of Dollars" & "For a Few Dollars More" & "The Good, the Bad and the Ugly."*

Hugo wanted the album to be different and hip. After studying a number of rock and roll disks, he brought electric guitars, a full set of drums, and an assortment of oddball instruments into the studio. On the title track to the final entry in Sergio Leone's "spaghetti Western" trilogy, Montenegro used an electric violin (the only one then in existence, played by Elliot Fisher), a piccolo trumpet (played by Manny Klein), an ocarina (played by Arthur Smith), and an electronic harmonica (played by Tommy Morgen). The whistler was Muzzy Marcellino, noted for his extensive blow job throughout John Wayne's *The High and the Mighty* (1954). The tune's distinctive grunting was actually Hugo himself, mumbling nonsensical syllables in Italian.

Hugo Montenegro died of emphysema on February 6, 1981, at the age of 55.

Four Jacks & A Jill

MASTER JACK
(Marks)
RCA 9473
No. 18 *June 8, 1968*

Here today, gone tomorrow—Four Jacks & A Jill was a fivesome that fit that cliché all too well. One hit, one other Hot 100 charting, two singles, and two albums, and these South Africans were never to be heard from again.

Their eerie "Master Jack" was a bizarre little item, and not just because of its folk-like, sucked-clean-and-dry instrumentation. This Jack fellow is apparently a teacher of some mysterious insights that lead singer Glenys Lynne thanks him for imparting. In the song, she repeatedly tells him, "It's a strange strange world we live in, Master Jack," and announces she is leaving him, probably never to return. Glenys sings all of this as if she has experienced ontological reality, has been transformed forever, and is not very happy about the whole matter.

Not content to rest on the despair created by their big moment, the unit that seems to have taken its name from a lackluster 1942 Ray Bolger flick created an ode to an equally wise old "Mister Nico" (#96, 1968). Nico's place of business is about to be torn down in the name of progress, and Glenys laments that no one cares. With Clive Harding (bass), Till Hanamann (guitar), Bruce Barks (guitar), and Tony Hughes (drums) providing a starkly shallow backdrop to this tale, "Mister Nico" sounds like the onset of an existential vacuum.

Formed in the heart of the British Invasion in 1964 as the Nevadas, the Jacks decided to freak out and grow their hair long. Once their new look was in place, the guys became the Zombies (no relation to the legendary English group). At one of their performances, they met their "Jill," Glenys Lynne. She with the angst-ridden voice convinced the fellows that only *she* should be the one with the long hair. The Four Jacks trimmed their locks and secured a recording contract, soon garnering a homeland hit with "Timothy."

On their post-"Jack" and post-"Nico" recordings, the group seems to have found philosophical grounding: all of a sudden, Four Jacks & A Jill sounded upbeat, the instruments sounded gayer, and their lyrics were less profound. While their popularity continued in South Africa, further success in the U.S. thoroughly eluded them.

Friend & Lover
REACH OUT OF THE DARKNESS
(Jim Post)
Verve Forecast 5069
No. 10   *June 22, 1968*

"**I** met Cathy in Edmonton, Alberta, at this state fair in the summer of '64," Jim Post (b. Oct. 28, 1939, Houston), the male half of Friend & Lover, recalled in an exclusive interview. "She was a dancer; I was with a folk group, the Rum Runners, on a Canadian tour. When we got there, I saw this wonderful woman jumping off a balcony and two other dancers catching her, and then she flipped five or six times across the stage."

Chicago-born Cathy Conn soon quit her acrobatic activities to marry Post. When she began pining for the stage shortly afterward, Jim started teaching her to be a singer. After much practice, some demo tapes, and a few discouraging gigs in awful clubs, the husband-and-wife act landed a manager and a recording contract as Friend & Lover. A Joe South production of "If Tomorrow" b/w "A Town Called Love" was issued by ABC-Paramount, but sales were minimal, so the label let Jim and Cathy slip away. They played a Playboy Club in Atlanta, toured with the Buckinghams, and even opened for Cream on their last U.S. tour.

"We went to MGM/Verve and saw Jerry Schoenbaum and said we wanted to sing for him. He said, 'I only take tapes, 'cause I don't want to be impressed by the way you look.' So I said, 'Good, turn around and look out the window.' We sang this song—probably only the fourth thing I had ever written—called 'Reach Out Of The Darkness.' He liked the idea."

"Reach Out" was inspired by Post's experience at a New York love-in. "People were throwing flowers; this was before cops knew that the kids were probably tripping on acid. 'Reach out of the darkness, and you might find a friend/Freak out in the darkness' . . . Wow, man! If you listen, you'll hear one of us singing 'freak out in the darkness' while the other is

singing 'reach out of the darkness.' They mixed it way down, but it's in there."

Despite the huge success of "Reach Out," Verve issued only two other Friend & Lover singles—"If Love Is In Your Heart" and "I Wanna Be Free"—plus an album. According to Post, the label "thought and acted like we were a one-record group; that's the way they treated us." Columbia Records offered the twosome $222,000 to sign with them, but Verve wouldn't release Jim and Cathy from their contract. Once they were free, though, they recorded a couple of 45s ("People Stand Back," "Hard Lovin' ") as Jim & Cathy for Cadet. Sales of the Cadet sides were next to nil; their career on a downslide, Jim and Cathy divorced.

Jim Post has gone on to record numerous albums for the Fantasy, Mountain Railroad, Flying Fish, and Freckle labels (the title of his Freckle effort: *The Crooner From Outer Space*). Since 1988, Post has been promoting *Galena Rose*, a one-man play which he wrote and produced. Reviews have been quite favorable.

Richard Harris
MacARTHUR PARK
(Jim Webb)
Dunhill 4134
No. 2   *June 22, 1968*

Richard Harris (b. Oct. 1, 1932, Limerick, Ireland) was educated at the Sacred Heart Jesuit College and trained in drama at the London Academy of Music and Art. He made his acting debut in 1956, and his first film appearance two years later in *Alive and Kicking* (1958). He acted in many notable flicks, including *The Guns of Navarone* (1961) and *Mutiny on the Bounty* (1962), but attained international notoriety with his role in *This Sporting Life* (1963). He received an acting award from the Cannes Festival for his performance, and was nominated for an Oscar. Four years later, Harris played King Arthur in the film version of *Camelot* (1967).

Do inquiring minds still want to know? It's been over 20 years since we first heard of this poor cake that was left out in the rain: "I don't think I can make it/'Cause it took so long to bake it/And I'll never have the recipe again, oh, no." Richard Harris' seven-minute singing sensation seemed so sincere and ever so impassioned. But *what* was this tune all about?

"The song is about a girlfriend of mine,"

songwriter Jimmy Webb told Joe Smith in *Off the Record.* "You associate a place with a person. You spend a lot of time there with that person, and when the relationship ends, you do a lot of thinking about that place. That's what 'MacArthur Park' is all about. I used to go there [to a park at the end of Wilshire Boulevard in Los Angeles] and have lunch. That's where the cake comes from. 'Sitting in the park on a bench eating cake.' The image is, the rain comes, and the whole thing is going, or melting, and then it's gone."

Okay, one of the pop world's perplexing mysteries has been solved, and right from the horse's mouth. Sometimes things *are* much simpler than they seem.

Harris, not primarily known for his vocal chops, did manage to sustain a recording career of sorts with more Webb creations like "The Yard Went On Forever" (#64, 1968), "Didn't We" (#63, 1969), and "My Boy" (#41, 1972). He also recited his way through best-selling spoken-word albums like *Jonathan Livingston Seagull* (1973) and *The Prophet by Kahlil Gibran* (1974). His post-popdom screen work includes *A Man Called Horse* (1970), *Cromwell* (1970), *Robin and Marian* (1976), *The Cassandra Crossing* (1977), *Gulliver's Travels* (1977), *Orca* (1977), and *Tarzan The Ape Man* (1981).

As for Jimmy Webb's little cake, the drenched dessert reappeared on the Hot 100 via renditions by Waylon Jennings (#93, 1969), The Four Tops (#38, 1971), and Donna Summer (#1, 1978).

People
I LOVE YOU
(Chris White)
Capitol 2078
No. 14   *June 22, 1968*

Success comes too late for some. Such was the case with the Zombies, the British group that originally wrote and recorded this powerful gem in 1965. By the time the group crashed the top 10 with "Time Of The Season," the Zombies were no more. Jeoff Levin—fresh out of the country-leaning Pine Valley Boys, a group that included David Nelson of later New Riders Of The Purple Sage renown—surrounded himself with Larry Norman, Gene Mason, Albert Ribisi, Robb Levin, and Denny Friedkin. The San Jose sextet cut a demo of the two-year-old Zombie flop, and in a wink,

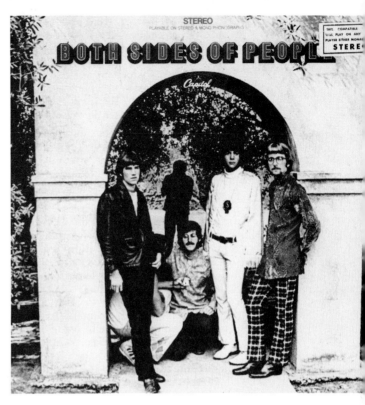

Capitol packed and shipped a finished version.

Any pop fan who had heard the Zombies creation, with all of its soul and polish, must have wondered how People's version could have outstripped the original in popularity. People never again made the top 40, or even the Hot 100. Capitol issued three more singles, Paramount released four, and in 1971—with the issuance of "Chant For Peace" on Polydor—People apparently called it quits.

Ironically, each of People's successive post-Capitol sides was an artistic improvement over its predecessor. By the time the group switched over to the Paramount label, the unit had developed a tight sound and moved beyond its previously limp arrangements. Not many people were listening, however, and People's third and last album, *There Are People and There Are People*, remains a sought-after collector's item.

Cliff Nobles & Co.
THE HORSE
(Jesse James)
Phil-L.A. 313
No. 2   *June 29, 1968*

No one—not the tiny record label, not Cliff, not even Cliff's mama—could have figured that this "Horse" thing was going to be a big hit. Heck, the tune was what's called in the recording profession a throwaway. Not that the recording was not done with the finest of care and enthusiasm, but "The Horse" was an instrumental intended as the flip side of a single. Poor Cliff—his one big moment, and he doesn't appear anywhere on this contagious little number!

Cliff was born in Mobile, Alabama, in 1944. From early on, he sang in the church choir, and before his move to Philadelphia in 1965, Cliff was already quite well-known in his hometown as a gospel singer. Within months of this move, Nobles was signed to Atlantic Records; he cut three singles, but each one fell on deaf ears.

For the next two years, Cliff made audition tapes for a producer named Jimmy Rogers. In the company of Benny Williams (bass), Bobby Tucker (lead guitar), and Tommy Soul (drums), Nobles hooked up with producer Jesse James and Phil-L.A. Records. The second release for the label, "Love Is All Right," was a tight, soulful item fleshed out with brass sounds from future members of MFSB. On the flip side was the filler—"The Horse"—which was nothing more than "Love Is All Right" with Cliff's vocal track scraped off. Cliff does not play an instrument, so in effect, Cliff was not even on what became his only top 40 moment. A Florida DJ played the wrong side of the record, and within a week, 10,000 copies of "The Horse" were sold in Tampa alone.

Two more instrumentals credited to "Cliff Nobles"— "Horse Fever" (#68, 1968) and "Switch It On" (#93, 1969)—followed, but Cliff's voice has yet to be heard again. After "The Horse" galloped up the pop listings, Rogers compiled some pre-"Horse" tracks as an album for Moonshot Records called *Pony the Horse*. Although Nobles sings on only three of the cuts (none of which show the man in his best light), record collectors to this day will pay more for this elusive album than for Cliff's own LP, entitled (naturally) *The Horse*.

Merrilee Rush & The Turnabouts

ANGEL OF THE MORNING
(Chip Taylor)
Bell 705
No. 7 *June 29, 1968*

"The day I wrote 'Angel,' I was fooling around with some chords for about three or four hours," Chip Taylor told Bob Shannon and John Javna in *Behind the Hits*. "But nothing came out. So I took a little break, and still nothing came out. Then all of a sudden, out of nowhere, came 'There'll be no strings to bind your hands, not if my love can't bind your heart.' I said, 'What the hell is that? That is beautiful' . . . Within ten minutes I'd written the whole song."

Chip is legendary for his oddball C & W solo albums; for compositions like "Wild Thing," "I Can't Let Go," and "Step Out Of Your Mind"; and for his part in the folk-rock duo Just Us. Taylor had penned "Angel Of The Morning" for Evie Sands, one of rock and roll's unsung singing sensations. "Angel," issued on the Cameo label, was going to make her a star. The record company, however, went bankrupt, and Evie's single died along with it.

Seattle-born Merrilee Rush had been taking piano lessons since she was knee-high. After ten years of classical training, the 13-year-old joined a local band called the Aztecs, then assembled the first of her bands, Merrilee & Her Men, a year later. ("She played piano and sang like wild," hometown DJ Pat O'Day wrote in the liner notes to her first solo album in 1968.) In 1962, Merrilee joined Tiny Tony & The Statics, recording for the Seafair/Bolo labels and playing clubs, hops, and dives.

Merilee was soon fronting a new group, the Turnabouts, which consisted of bassist Terry Craig, drummer Pete Sack, guitarist Carl Wilson, and saxophonist Neil Rush. After catching one of their performances, Paul Revere set up a managerial relationship with Merrilee and company; featured them on Raiders tours; had them booked as a semi-regular act on Dick Clark's "Happening '68" TV program; and secured a production deal for them with Tommy Cogbill and Chips Moman. Bell Records issued "Angel Of The Morning," and it became that million-seller Evie Sands would never see.

Despite two fine follow-ups—"That Kind Of Woman" (#76, 1968) and "Reach Out" (#79, 1968)—Merrilee was unable to consolidate a high-profile career. Recordings bearing her name surface sporadically; she returned to the Hot 100 in 1971 with "Save Me" (#54). In 1982, the resurrected Liberty label issued a long-overdue album.

As for the Turnabouts: Carl formed White Heart (later shortened to "Heart") with sisters Anne and Nancy Wilson. Pete became a real estate broker and currently resides in Tacoma, Washington. Neil lives in the Portland area and runs a floor-covering company; Terry lives and works in L.A. as a studio musician.

Tiny Tim
TIP TOE THRU' THE TULIPS WITH ME
(Al Dubin, Joe Burke)
Reprise 0679
No. 17 *June 29, 1968*

"**I**'m the only living artist, probably the only celebrity in the world, who actually is able to duplicate the sound of Byron G. Hardin. He was Thomas Edison's favorite singer in 1902," quoth the not-so-tiny but still very much Tiny Tim to *Record Collector's Monthly*. Tim is quite a character, then as now, with his unruly hair, prominent nose, loud clothes, ratty-looking shopping bag, ukulele, wavering falsetto—and that featherheaded song (initially popularized by Nick Lucas in 1929), "Tip Toe Thru' The Tulips With Me."

Tiny Tim seemed to sprout up fully formed from nowhere; his past is rather sketchy. As Herbert Khaury (b. Apr. 12, 1930, New York City), he used to perform in the '50s, but was booed quite often. Apparently, audiences failed to understand that "the spirits of the

Tiny Tim

The
Sixties

singers whose songs I do are living within me," as Tim explained to *Rolling Stone's* Jerry Hopkins.

In the mid-'60s, as Darry Dover and/or Larry Love, Tim played to receptive crowds in Greenwich Village coffee-and-bongo spots like the Fat Black Pussycat Cafe. "Laugh-In" and "The Tonight Show" brought him national exposure; he starred with Paul Butterfield, The Electric Flag, and BARRY McGUIRE in the film *You Are What You Eat* (1968). His televised wedding to his true love, "Miss Vicki" (Victoria May Budinger), took place in 1969 on "The Tonight Show," as 35,000,000 viewers watched in wonderment.

The immediate follow-up to Tim's "Tulip" tune was "Bring Back Those Rock-A-Bye Baby Days" (#95, 1968). "Horribly done," groaned Tim to *Record Collector's Monthly*. "Don't mean a thing that it made the Hot 100 . . . 'Hello, Hello' [Tiny's fourth single] was also horribly done. I'm an artist who needs a sketch, and needs time to complete his work. That song was first done in 1922, by Lee Morse . . . I did it in August of 1968 when I was in Las Vegas and when that horrible album *Concert in Fairyland* came out. It wasn't produced by Warner Bros., it was recorded six years before. The owners wanted $25,000 from Warner Bros. to withhold the release, and they refused to pay. It was old studio tracks with a canned audience, and it had 100,000 buyers. That's what killed me in the phonograph business."

Reprise, the Warner Bros. subsidiary, dropped Mr. Tim in 1971. Recordings have been issued thereafter, but only sporadically and on labels with limited distribution. Some of these, if you can find them, are quite interesting, such as: "I Saw Elvis Presley Tiptoeing Through the Tulips," "Am I Just Another Pretty Face?", "I'm Gonna Be a Country Queen," and "The Hicky On Your Neck." He has become more active of late, appearing on TV talk shows, "acting" in the gory slasher flick *Blood Harvest* (1986), working rock and roll revival shows, and touring with Alan C. Hill's Great American Circus.

"I think this is my 39th comeback," Tim quipped to the *Chicago Sun-Times'* Patricia Smith. "I've been trying to record for years. [In 1983] I did a cover on AC/DC's 'Highway To Hell.' It was just released [in 1989]. It started out kinda wobbly, but I sold 900 copies in the first week, and that's more than I've sold in 20 years. Who knows? Maybe my future is in heavy metal."

Shorty Long
HERE COMES THE JUDGE
(Billie Jean Brown, Suzanne DePasse, Frederick Long)
Soul 35044
No. 8 *July 6, 1968*

Shorty was born Frederick Earl Long in Birmingham, Alabama, on May 20, 1940. As a teenager, he was tutored by Alvin "Shine" Robinson and W.C. Handy—he could play piano, organ, drums, guitar, trumpet, harmonica. Before moving to Detroit in 1959, Shorty worked as a local DJ, toured for nearly two years with the Ink Spots, and played keyboards at a club called the Old Stable. Some now-collectible sides were issued on the Valley, Tri-Phil, Harvey, and Anna labels.

When Berry Gordy acquired the Tri-Phil/Harvey/Anna family of labels, he also picked up Shorty's contract. "Devil With The Blue Dress On," a self-penned piano boogie complete with a bluesy guitar break, was Shorty's first single for Motown organization and the debut disk for Gordy's Soul label. This "Devil" didn't chart, though years later it proved to be a monster hit for Mitch Ryder & The Detroit Wheels (#4, 1966). "Function At The Junction" (#97, 1966) and "Night Fo' Last" (#75, 1968) did stir up some action before Shorty scored with "Here Comes The Judge," a novelty tune based on a PIGMEAT MARKHAM comedy skit. (Pigmeat's version of "Here Comes The Judge" made him a one-hit wonder as well.)

After two unsuccessful follow-up 45s, Shorty Long and his friend Oscar Williams drowned on June 29, 1969, during a boating mishap on the Detroit River.

Hugh Masekela
GRAZING IN THE GRASS
(Philemon Hou)
Uni 55066
No. 1 *July 20, 1968*

Hugh Ramapolo Masekela was born in Wilbank, South Africa, on April 4, 1939, the son of a famous sculptor. Hugh's grandmother raised him until school age. He attended missionary schools, and learned how to play the piano by age seven. When he was 13, Hugh saw Kirk Douglas in *Young Man with a Horn* (1950), the film biography of Bix Beiderbecke. His future appeared to him with crystal clarity—within a year, he had his first trumpet.

Masekela played in the Huddleston Jazz Band, until the group's leader—a priest and anti-apartheid advocate, Father Trevor Huddleston—was deported. Hugh formed the Merry Makers of Springs. In 1958, he played in the orchestra for the road company of the opera *King Kong*, which starred MIRIAM MAKEBA (his wife from 1964 to 1966). Thereafter, he toured with the Jazz Epistles (reportedly the first black band to record a jazz album in South Africa), Dollar Brand, and Miriam Makeba.

In 1959, British orchestra leader John Dankworth arranged for Hugh to receive a scholarship to the Royal Academy of Music in London; the following year, Harry Belafonte lined up a four-year scholarship for Hugh at the Manhattan School of Music. In 1965, Masekela formed his own band and started recording on his own label, Chisa. A number of his instrumental albums, then leased to MCA's Uni label, sold quite well—*Hugh Masekela's Latest* (1967), *Hugh Masekela is Alive and Well at the Whisky* (1968), and *The Promise of a Future* (1968). In addition to topping the charts with "Grazing In the Grass," Hugh made the pop listings with "Up, Up And Away" (#71, 1968), "Puffin' On Down The Track" (#71, 1968), and "Riot" (#55, 1969). His duet with Herb Alpert, "Skokiaan," registered at number 87 on the R & B charts in 1978.

As for the tune by which Masekela is best remembered, "It was all very contrived," he told *Rolling Stone's* Gordon Fletcher. "It happened because I came along about the time Herb Alpert was making it big with his 'South American sound,' so MCA figured that they would make me into a black Herb Alpert. I did it but it wasn't what I wanted—I wanted the fullfillment of playing something that was *me*."

Less than a year later, Floyd Butler, Jessica Cleaves, Harry Elston, and Barbara Jean Love—the Friends of Distinction—did a vocal rendition of "Grazing In The Grass" that went top 10 on both the pop and R & B listings (#3/5, 1969).

Pigmeat Markham

HERE COMES THE JUDGE
(Billy Jean Brown, Suzanne DePasse, Frederick Long)
Chess 2049
No. 19   *July 27, 1968*

The late Dewey "Pigmeat" Markham (b. 1904, Durham, N.C.) began performing in Southern carnivals and medicine shows. He would dance and do a comedy bit with George Wilshire, his buddy and straight man of many years. In the late '20s, Markham and Wilshire came to New York City, making appearances at the Apollo and Alhambra Theatres.

For years, Pigmeat would appear "under cork," that is, he would perform with burnt cork applied to his face (a variation of blackface). After World War II, Markham and other vaudevillians ceased to employ this device. Many of Pig's plentiful fans were surprised to see that he was just as dark without the cork he had been using.

Before his death in 1981, Pigmeat traveled the world, and made numerous TV appearances on shows like "Laugh-In," "The Tonight Show," and "The Ed Sullivan Show."

Status Quo

PICTURES OF MATCHSTICK MEN
(Francis Michael Rossi)
Cadet Concept 7001
No. 12   *August 3, 1968*

For more than two decades now, Status Quo has been dishing out three-chord bone-crunching music, and there's no end in sight. Critics have consistently dismissed the band's trademark sound as lowbrow and monotonous, but Status Quo has acquired a legion of British fans who don't want them to ever stop playing, though the guys have tried. At the end of their 1984 European tour, and prior to their appearance at the Band Aid concert (1985), members declared that after more than 20 years it was, indeed, all over. But after many such announcements, Status Quo usually returns in their tried and true form to the British charts.

Despite the group's sole appearance on the U.S. top 40 with "Pictures Of Matchstick Men"—an early and atypically psychedelic pop platter—main man Mike Rossi and his rockers have racked up more than 40 U.K. hits (surpassing the Rolling Stones, the Beatles, and the Hollies), making them one of the most successful British groups in rock history. Half of these singles went top 10, and every Status Quo album issued in the U.K. since 1974 has made the British top 5.

Guitarist Francis Michael Rossi (b. Apr. 29, 1949, London), bassist Alan Lancaster (b. Feb.

7, 1949), and guitarist Alan Key met in their school orchestra in the spring of 1962. All were 12-year-olds with a desire to make some music, and for a while, they played together as a traditional jazz combo. Keyboardist Jess Jaworski replaced Key, drummer John Coghlan (b. Sept. 19, 1946) stepped in, and the group's sound began leaning toward rock and roll.

In 1965, the Spectres, as they were now known, started gigging around holiday camps outside London. Jaworski dropped out, and his spot behind the organ was filled by Roy Lynes. The Spectres signed to the Piccadilly label and issued three singles—"I (Who Have Nothing)," "Hurdy Gurdy Man," and "We Ain't Got Nothin' Yet." All of them sank without a trace, as did a single credited to Traffic Jam entitled (aptly enough) "Almost But Not Quite There."

By 1967, the group, now called Traffic Jam, was working mostly as a back-up band for Madeline Bell and a miscellanea of touring U.S. rock and rollers. Steve Winwood of Traffic reportedly complained about the similarity of the guys' new name to his own outfit's moniker. To avoid any possible legal problems, Rossi and Traffic Jam became Status Quo.

Guitarist Richard Parfitt (b. Richard Harrison, Oct. 12, 1948, Woking, Surrey) joined the group, and Status Quo recorded "Pictures Of Matchstick Men." Before that bashin'-boogie trademark had fully evolved, Lynes quit the band. Several similar-sounding follow-ups were cut and canned: "Ice In The Sun" (#70, 1968), "Technicolour Dreams," and "Black Veils Of Melancholy."

The group persisted on a pile-driving path through the '70s and '80s. Coghlan retired in 1982, and their line-up has shifted repeatedly over the years, with Rossi and Parfitt as the mainstays. At various times, keyboardist Andy Bown, bassist John Brown, ex-Original Mirrors guitarist Pete Kirchner, and ex-Climax Blues Band drummer Jeff Rich have been touring and/or recording members. Toward the end of the decade, Status Quo went through some label changes; releases are now more sporadic, and sometimes are not even issued in the States. The group name—and that head-banging brand of boogie—still exist.

Mason Williams

CLASSICAL GAS
(Hank Snowball)
Warner Bros. 7190
No. 2 *August 3, 1968*

At Oklahoma City University, Mason Williams (b. July 24, 1936, Abilene, Tex.) studied mathematics and music. After classes, he played guitar and sang in folk clubs, briefly joining up with the Wayfarers Trio. Following a stint in the Navy, Mason took up folksinging full-time. At a coffeehouse in L.A., he met the Limeliters' GLENN YARBROUGH, who introduced him to Tommy Smothers. Mason and Tommy became good friends, and eventually shared an apartment together.

Williams joined the Smothers Brothers' back-up band, penned tunes for the clean-cut but controversial duo, and even wrote some comedy material. Johnny Desmond, GALE GARNETT, the Kingston Trio, and Claudine Longet recorded some of his compositions. Esther and Abi Ofarim's cover of his "Cinderella Rockefeller" topped the British charts, and Longet's work on Mason's marvel in 10/4 time, "Wanderlove," was a sizeable seller in Singapore.

By the release of "Classical Gas"—which he described to *Goldmine* as "half flamenco, half Flatt & Scruggs, and half classical"—Williams was a writer for "The Smothers Brothers Comedy Hour," the highly-popular TV program. Before the brothers' boob-tube demise and Mason's departure from the show in 1969 for other creative endeavors, Williams won an Emmy for "Outstanding Writing Achievement for a Variety Show." "Classical Gas," his three-minute classic, garnered three Grammys: "Best Instrumental Arrangement," "Best Contemporary-Pop Performance," and "Best Instrumental Theme."

Over the next year, Warner Bros. did a rather brisk business of selling Williams' mongrel music. His first three LPs—*The Mason Williams Phonograph Record* (1968), *The Mason Williams Ear Show* (1968), and *Music by Mason Williams* (1969)—were all bestsellers. A few of his singles dotted the lowest reaches of the Hot 100—"Baroque-A-Nova" (#96, 1968), "Saturday Night At The World" (#99, 1969), and "Greensleeves" (#90, 1969).

Mason periodically pops up in the record racks on one label or another. In the meantime, he is certainly not idle. He has had, at last count, seven books published, including such tomes as *The Mason Williams Reading Matter* and *The Bus Book,* and he writes material for Glen Campbell, Petula Clark, Pat Paulsen, Andy Williams, and the brothers Smothers. For a period in the early '80s, he was the head writer for NBC's "Saturday Night Live."

The Amboy Dukes,
with Ted Nugent
(second from left)

Amboy Dukes

JOURNEY TO THE CENTER
OF THE MIND
(Ted Nugent, Steve Farmer)
Mainstream 684
No. 16 *August 24, 1968*

I started playing guitar when I was about six or seven years old," wrote Motor City Madman and chief Amboy Duke Ted Nugent in a self-penned piece for *Hit Parader*. "I got an acoustic guitar from my aunt, and was highly influenced by Elvis, Ricky Nelson, and James Brown songs that I'd heard on the radio. I took about two years of guitar lessons in Detroit at the Royal School of Music. Learned the basics

and got into boogie-woogie and honky-tonk. I did my first professional performance when I was 10, at the Detroit State Fair Grounds for the Polish Arts Festival. And I was a sensation."

Detroit-born Nugent also formed his first band at age 10, The Royal High Boys. "It was just me and a drummer named Tom Noel," Nugent told *DISCoveries'* Allan Vorda. "The band's name came from this shirt that all greasers wore. We wore it, too, 'cause we were cool. We ended up getting a bass player and that became the nucleus of the Lourds." The Lourds quickly attracted a local following, and even opened a sold-out show in Detroit with the Supremes and the Beau Brummels. (The band's only recorded tracks, three in number, are currently available on a compilation LP called either *Long Hot Summer* or *Friday at the Cafe A Go Go.*) But all that ended when Ted's father accepted a phone-company job in Chicago; the family moved there in 1965.

Once in Chicago, Nugent (lead guitar) formed a group with Greg Arama (bass), Steve Farmer (rhythm guitar), Dave Palmer (drums), and Andy Soloman (keyboards). As Ted explained to Vorda, the "Amboy Dukes" name came from a Detroit R & B band that had recently broken up. "I thought it was a cool name and when I moved to Chicago, I decided to use the name. Obviously, I learned much later there was a street gang in the '50s from Perth Amboy, New Jersey. And there was this famous novel about the gang called *The Amboy Dukes*, but I've never read it . . . That's how the original Detroit group got the name."

With graduation behind him, Ted moved his group to Detroit. There, they competed with a budding bunch of local talent like Bob Seger & The Last Heard, Tim Tam & The Turn-Ons, The Rationals, and The Wanted for a recording contract. Mainstream Records, wowed by Nugent's Hendrix-like guitar pyrotechics, signed the guys and issued their self-titled debut album in 1968. The LP largely eluded public attention, but their quickly-pressed second outing, *Journey to the Center of the Mind* (1968)—plus the 45 of the title cut—were successful enough to launch Ted's rock and roll career.

"When we put out *Journey to the Center of the Mind* in 1968, it had that pipe collection on the front cover and I didn't have the faintest idea what those pipes were all about! Everybody else was getting stoned and trying every drug known to mankind; I was meeting women and playing rock and roll. I didn't know anything about this cosmic inner probe. I thought 'Journey To The Center Of The Mind' meant look inside yourself, use your head and move forward in life."

How could the obviously drug-related connotations have escaped him? "I have never smoked a joint. I have never done a drug in my life. I've never had a cigarette in my mouth. I don't drink . . . I watched incredible musicians fumble, drool, and not be able to tune their instruments. It was easier to say no than to say, 'Hey, gosh, that's for me.' I've seen my fellow musicians die."

Nugent's indignant anti-drug stance shaped the short careers of his Dukes. John Drake was fired partly due to his inability to meet rehearsal schedules. Also removed was Steve Farmer, whom Nugent described as a brilliant

and creative thinker but who was "so high and so irresponsible you couldn't get from point A to point B with him." As for Greg Arama, "heroin took over and I had to get rid of him" (Greg is reportedly deceased). Rusty Day? "He insisted on doing LSD together as a band; after I fired him, he was machine-gunned to death because of a bad drug deal.

"There never really was a break-up of the Amboy Dukes. It just got to be such a revolving door mentally with the musicians. I also took a break in 1973. I was so upset internally. I felt like a babysitter! I also acted as a road manager—I used to book the band, I used to maintain all the equipment, I used to change the oil in the cars."

By album number four—*Survival of the Fittest—Live* (1971)—the band was billed as "Ted Nugent & The Amboy Dukes." The following year, the artist credit for their *Call of the Wild* album read simply "Ted Nugent." The Amboy Dukes officially disbanded in 1975, at which time Nugent signed as a solo artist with Epic Records.

According to Ted, John Drake is now a car salesman. Steve Farmer is a conservationist planting trees in Oregon. Robbie LaGrange is a realtor in San Diego, and Andy Soloman is "doing commericals in Philadelphia."

Barbara Acklin
LOVE MAKES A WOMAN
(Eugene Record, William Sanders, Carl Davis, Gerald Sims)
Brunswick 55379
No. 15   *August 31, 1968*

Barbara Acklin (b. Feb. 28, 1944, Chicago) came from a musical family. Her grandma was blues singer Asa Eskridge; her cousin was keyboardist/arranger Monk Higgins. Mom and Dad were attuned and hip, so they encouraged Barb to sing her soul out. By age 11, she was a featured vocalist in the choir of the New Zion Baptist Church. While still a student at Dunbar Vocational High, Acklin sang secular at night spots on Chicago's South Side. When Barbara graduated, Monk Higgins got her a job as a secretary with St. Lawrence Records, where he worked as a producer and recording artist. "When somebody would come in to record and they needed a background singer, I would run in the back and sing," Acklin told *Goldmine* R & B editor Bob Pruter. Monk recorded one single on her as "Barbara Allen," but it fizzled.

Higgins moved his base of operations to Chess Records, and Barbara followed. At Chess, she sang back-up for Fontella Bass, Etta James, MINNIE RIPERTON, and Koko Taylor. In 1966, Barbara obtained the job of secretary/receptionist for Carl Davis at Brunswick Records, and began writing songs on the side.

"I kept asking Carl to record [me]," recalled Acklin, "and he kept saying 'I will, I will, just keep on writing.' I wrote a tune with another person called 'Whispers,' and Jackie Wilson heard the tune and really liked it. He recorded it, and after it became a big hit for him, he told me, 'If there is anything I can do for you, let me know.' I said, 'You tell Carl I want to record!'"

Three weeks later, Barbara was in a recording studio. Her first two singles flopped, but a duet with Gene Chandler called "Show Me The Way To Go" (—/#30, 1968) did moderately with the R & B crowd. Then "Love Makes A Woman" appeared and soared into the top 40. A number of follow-up solo sides and duets with Chandler placed fairly well on *Billboard*'s R & B charts—but none of them could duplicate the success, or recapture the charm, of "Love Makes A Woman."

Disappointed by her lackluster chart showings, Acklin left Brunswick in 1973 and signed with Capitol Records. Over the next few years, three singles and an album—*A Place In The Sun* (1975)—were issued by Capitol. Of these 45s, "Raindrops" sold the best, but these would prove to be her last disks to date.

Later in the '70s, Acklin stepped out of the spotlight. "I went out on the road with Tyrone Davis as a back-up singer. Everybody thought I was nuts, but it was a way of staying in touch with the business without a deep involvement."

In 1979, Barbara parted company with Capitol and joined the Chi-Sound label the following year, but no records were released. In the '80s, Barbara Acklin was spotted in the role of road manager for Ike Turner's occasional "Tina" fill-in Holly Maxwell.

Jeannie C. Riley
HARPER VALLEY P.T.A.
(Tom T. Hall)
Plantation 3
No. 1 *September 21, 1968*

Barbara Acklin

Before writing that song about the small-town widow who would arouse local ire for her free-thinking ways, her short skirts, and sexy sways, TOM T. HALL was a traveling DJ and a $50-a-week songwriter. Hall has claimed that Miss Johnson, the heroine of "Harper Valley P.T.A.," was an actual woman whom he had seen as a schoolboy in Carter City, Kentucky. As for the tune's vocalist, Jeannie C. Riley, she was a secretary and a sometime demo singer. Within two weeks of its release, almost 2,000,000 copies of "Harper Valley P.T.A." had been sold, and much had changed for Tom T. and Ms. Riley.

Jeannie Carolyn Stephenson (b. Oct. 19, 1945, Anson, Tex.) grew up dreaming of being a big-time country singer. After graduating from high school and marrying Mickey Riley, her childhood sweetheart, Jeannie convinced her hubby to do what all aspiring country stars do—move to the center of the country-music action. Once in Nashville, Mickey found work in a filling station, while Jeannie struggled as a secretary at Jerry Chesnut's Passkey Music Company. In her spare time, she cut demos for the Wilburn Brothers, Johnny Paycheck, and the folks at Little Darlin' Records. She would call home often and tell here mama that someday this little girl would make it big.

Shelby Singleton, Jr., the maverick producer who had acquired Sun Records from the legendary Sam Phillips, was sitting on what he thought would be a sure hit. All he needed was a singer with the right appeal to pull off this tasty nugget about Southern hypocrisy. Then Singleton heard that voice—Jeannie C. Riley—on a demo she had made. On the night of July 26, 1968, after Ms. Riley had ripped though "Harper Valley" in just one take, she called her folks in Texas and told them that she had just cut a million-seller. Having heard this type of news before, her mother responded with skepticism.

But Jeannie was on the mark this time— sales of her single eventually reached 6,000,000. She became an overnight star, bought a purple Cadillac, polished up her image, and weeks later appeared in a mini-skirt and boots on "The Ed Sullivan Show." She made the rounds of TV talk shows, and won a Grammy in 1968 for "Best Female Country Vocal Performance." Other plaques were presented, photos taken, and concerts given. The *Harper Valley P.T.A.* LP, naturally, sold in massive quantities. A couple of "Sin City"-type tunes made the C & W listings in 1969 ("The Girl Most Likely," and "The Back Side Of Dallas"), and several of her follow-up disks made the Hot 100— "The Girl Most Likely To" (#55, 1969), "There Never Was A Time" (#77, 1969), "Oh, Singer" (#74, 1971), and "Good Enough To Be Your Wife" (#97, 1971).

All was not well, however. "I wanted to change the image," Ms. Riley told Bob Gilbert and Gary Theroux in *The Top Ten.* "I wanted to build a more wholesome image and convince people that I'm not like the heroine of 'Harper Valley P.T.A.'. I was just tellin' a story in those songs, but I soon found out people thought that's what I was really like."

Things began to unravel. She started drinking heavily, and her marriage to Mickey ended. The C & W hits slowed to a trickle in the mid-'70s, then stopped altogether in 1976. But by then, Jeannie was a born-again Christian, singing gospel songs. Mickey and Jeannie remarried in 1976.

Don Fardon
INDIAN RESERVATION
(John D. Loudermilk)
GNP Crescendo 405
No. 20 *October 5, 1968*

The Sorrows of Coventry, England—home of rugby and the Rolls Royce—were one of the best beat groups around in 1965. Their lead singer, Don Maughn, remembered his mother holding him in bomb shelters during the Nazi blitz; Maughn sang with pain even when singing of love. The Sorrows' "Take A Heart" grazed the British charts and was released in the U.S. on the Warner Bros. label. Despite the Sorrows' haunting and atmospheric sound, none of this futuristic unit's singles ever again charted in England. Early in 1967, the group came apart.

Miki Dallon, the group's manager, was also a songwriter, producer, record company executive, and sometime RCA recording artist. Miki had plans for the Sorrows' mournful 6'6" vocalist: he renamed Maughn "Don Fardon" and had him record cover versions of "The Letter" and "Indian Reservation," encasing the soulful lad in both bubblegum and easy-listening settings.

Despite a misconceived orchestral accompaniment, Don's reworking of John D. Loudermilk's 1963 lament for the Cherokee Indians, "Indian Reservation," touched home. Paul Revere & The Raiders would have a massive hit with the song two years later, but "Indian Reservation" was Fardon's only notable release in the U.S. He did have a British hit even before his stateside success, however: "Belfast Boy." Five years later, Fardon popped up on the Hot 100 with "Delta Queen" (#86, 1973).

Over the years, Don Fardon has continued his relationship with Miki Dallon and his Young Blood label. In 1974, Capitol released a brassy rendition of the Kinks' "Lola." Decca/MCA toyed with the idea of Don recording a prepubescent cover version of CRAZY ELEPHANT'S hit, "Gimme Gimme Good Lovin'." Both Don and his manager have recorded solo versions of the classic Sorrows single, "Take A Heart," but nothing much happened with either reworking. (The Sorrows' original rendition and their lone album, 1965's *Take A Heart*, are highly sought-after by American and European record collectors.) When last spotted, Fardon was singing bubblegum material, his vocal talents constricted by antiquated orchestral arrangements.

O'Kaysions

GIRL WATCHER
(Buck Trail, Wayne Pittman)
ABC 11094
No. 5   *October 5, 1968*

In 1954, at the tender age of eight, Donny Weaver (lead vocal, bass) started singing around the house. A decade later, a neighborhood guitar man named Jimmy Hennant (b. 1947) joined Donny in making joyful noise. Over the next few years, other O'Kaysions-to-be would join the duo to sing praises of the Lord: Bruce Joyner (drums), Wayne Pittman (guitar), Jim Spidel (sax), and Ronnie Turner (trumpet). As the Kays, they played gospel and, later, country music in the coastal areas of their home state, North Carolina.

By the spring of 1968, they were the secular-singing O'Kaysions, and they had recorded a leering lyric about ogling babes for the peewee Northstate label. Local DJs, appreciating that bird-watching was a popular pastime for their listeners, rode the number as if it had a satin saddle. Sales of the single outpaced the little label's ability to produce the merchandise fast enough, so ABC picked up distribution and gave the O'Kaysions their lone top 40 moment.

Despite a few further releases, featuring Donny Weaver's raspy voice, only the immediate follow-up to "Girl Watcher"—"Love Machine" (#76, 1968)—managed to chart. An album was casually tossed together; as Wayne Pittman admitted to the *Washington Times*, it was this careless attitude, plus the group's lack of direction, that brought an end to the O'Kaysions. "You had the hippie generation and acid rock, and music was going in crazy different ways. There was no one voice [within the band] saying 'this is the way we should go.'" The O'Kaysions broke up in 1968.

Wayne is currently fronting a new version of the O'Kaysions. They are working the highways, byways, and backwater bars of the Carolinas, where even now, worn-out copies of "Girl Watcher" can be found on jukeboxes.

Crazy World of Arthur Brown

FIRE
(Arthur Brown, Vincent Crane)
Atlantic 2556
No. 2   *October 19, 1968*

"Crazy world" may be a marked understatement when it comes to describing the realm which Arthur Brown inhabits even to this day.

Believe it or not, the genesis of "Fire" as well as Brown's pioneering rock theatrics (i.e. moving stage, outlandish costumes, hideously-painted face, and helmeted head ablaze) was Brown's deep involvement with . . . philosophy! "Ah, philosophy will never touch reality," Brown mused to *Blitz's* Allan Vorda. "It always describes it. It's an idea of what reality is. But reality isn't an idea."

Arthur Wilton was born on June 24, 1944, in Whitby, Yorkshire. He studied philosophy and law at both Reading University and Yorkshire University, and reportedly was a school-teacher when the Who's Pete Townshend offered him the chance to act out his deepest and darkest dreams. For years, Brown had been soaking up the sounds of Sinatra, Elvis, Delta blues, New Orleans jazz, Scottish folk tunes, and classical music. Brown and his band—

The O'Kaysions

keyboardist Vincent Crane and drummer Drachian Theaker—were indulging in their special brand of musical and visual lunacy at the underground UFO Pub when Townshend spotted the act. He persuaded his manager, the owner of Track Records, to record The Crazy World of Arthur Brown (in 1989, Townshend even included a cover version of "Fire" on his *Iron Man* album).

"Fire" was Brown and company's first release, and their only charting single here or abroad. Success came upon them too fast—constant touring, plus the ingestion of large amounts of mind-altering substances, took a hefty toll on the band. As Brown told the *Chicago Tribune*'s Dave Hoekstra, Crane was dosed with LSD at a party: "For a long number of years, he never came back. He talked in numbers for a day and a half. He had to return to England for mental attention." Drachian Theaker "used to kick his drums offstage during an act; he would run by hotels, pressing his vital parts against the windows! After that, we became unmanageable."

Yes, after that, the Crazy World blew apart. Crane and his tour replacement, Carl Palmer, formed Atomic Rooster; Palmer would later join Keith Emerson and Greg Lake in Emerson, Lake & Palmer. Theaker, after a stint with Arthur Lee's Love, worked as a percussionist with the Scottish Symphony Orchestra, and now tours Europe with a traveling band of Indian artists.

And Brown? Well, Arthur has been keeping busy with an unusual project or two. After three LPs of increasingly electronic excursions with a new outfit, Kingdom Come, Brown did studio work with Alan Parsons, appeared in the Who's *Tommy* (1975) flick, had some obscure solo albums issued in Europe on the Gold label, and spent some years recording and touring with the technologically-attuned Klaus Schulze. Not one to remain rooted in any one reality for too long, Brown lived in the late '70s in Burundi, Africa, where he reportedly taught music history and directed the Burundi National Orchestra. In the '80s, Arthur took guitar lessons from King Crimson's Robert Fripp, then moved to Austin, Texas, to form a keyboard-based band. When the latter activity proved unfulfilling, he formed a carpentry and painting concern with ex–Mothers of Invention drummer Jimmy Carl Black.

Did the flaky flavor of "Fire" typecast Art Brown as a nut and a novelty act? "Yeah, it was like that. They just thought I made fun records. Most of them still do. I look at it as being extremely lucky, however. Here I am, 20 years after I've had a hit, and I'm still in line to get a big record deal. In between, I've been making albums. I've got 15 out, and they vary between sheer electronic, industrial electronic, and electronic synthesizer."

The pending "big record deal" of which Brown speaks is said to possibly involve Jack Bruce, Peter Gabriel, Carl Palmer, Alan Parsons, and African juju man King Sunny Ade. Release is slated for 1990. Currently available via Blue Wave Records is a collaboration with Jimmy Carl Black entitled *Brown, Black, and Blues*. There is also an anti-nuclear Arthur Brown LP available on the Republic label, *Requiem*. "It's not something with a heavy message," Art explained to Fred Dellar in *Where Did You Go To, My Lovely?* "There's a conversation between an ant and a cockroach who meet after the world's blown up."

Jimi Hendrix
ALL ALONG THE WATCHTOWER
(Bob Dylan)
Reprise 0767
No. 20   *October 19, 1968*

James Marshall Hendrix's death on September 18, 1970, dealt a stunning blow to rock and roll fans the world over. An unusually innovative musician, he singlehandedly redefined the role of the electric guitar in rock music, inventing a sonic vocabulary still drawn upon by rock guitarists to this day. This psychedelic voodoo child and father of Heavy Metal was also a one-hit wonder.

More than a hundred LPs of his music have been issued; many of them were issued posthumously and consist of unauthorized live recordings, studio outtakes, and the like. Several of them have made *Billboard*'s top pop albums chart: *Are You Experienced* (1967), *Axis: Bold as Love* (1968), *Electric Ladyland* (1968), *Smash Hits* (1969), *Band of Gypsys* (1970), and *The Cry of Love* (1971). Yet despite Hendrix's superstar status, his success with top 40 audiences was limited to but one 45—and it is not, as many would guess, "Purple Haze" (#65, 1967).

Jimi's version of "All Along The Watchtower"—originally penned by one of his heroes, Bob Dylan—was a performance of which the guitarist was especially proud. With the Experience (Mitch Mitchell and Noel Red-

Jimi Hendrix

ding), Jimi made the Hot 100 with five other 45s: "Foxy Lady" (#67, 1968), "Up From The Skies" (#82, 1968), "Crosstown Traffic" (#52, 1968), "Freedom" (#59, 1971), and "Dolly Dagger" (#74, 1971).

Leapy Lee
LITTLE ARROWS
(Albert Hammond, Mike Hazelwood)
Decca 32380
No. 16   *December 7, 1968*

Even when he was a mere tyke, Leapy Lee could not keep from bounding, bouncing, frolicking, and making other bodily movements. He was born as Lee Graham to an apparently normal set of parents on July 2, 1942, in Eastbourne, Sussex, England. From early on, this was a frisky squirt with diverse interests. Before terminating his school career at the age of 15, Lee had already done some preliminary work toward becoming an actor and a rock star. Once out of an educational setting, however, money was an issue, and he worked a year or so in a factory.

Leapy's group, with a name now lost to time, became professional and played about the town. Leapy billed himself as an entertainment manager and searched out clients, worked as an antiques dealer, wrote songs, performed in plays such as *Sparrows Can't Sing* and *Johnnie the Priest*, and acted for a year in *Large As Life*. Not a bloke to sit on his laurels or even sit still, Lee even opened up a bingo hall in London's Shepherd's Bush.

While pursuing all these activities, Leapy also found time to make recordings for the Cadet and Decca labels. Before the Kinks' Ray Davies became internationally known for his songwriting abilities, Lee, noting Ray's talents with words, cut a version of Davies' "King Of the Whole Wide World." The disk bombed, much like every recorded effort Leapy ever issued save his good-timey "Little Arrows." This cutesy tune about Cupid and his missiles of love has not worn well, has probably irritated more listeners than it has tickled, and consequently, is rarely heard on oldies radio stations.

Lee persisted in expelling records, like a cover version of Christie's "Yellow River" and "Little Yellow Aeroplane," well into the '70s. Nothing ever again charted on the Hot 100, and it is not known with certainty just what line of business this antsy Lee is in at this time. One source, however, has claimed that Leapy

is still on the move and working the British circuit as a comedian.

René & René
LO MUCHO QUE TE QUIERO (THE MORE I LOVE YOU)
(René Ornelas, René Herrera)
White Whale 287
No. 14   *January 4, 1969*

At 14, René Victor Ornelas (b. Aug. 26, 1936, Laredo, Tex.) sang and played trumpet in his father's band, the Mike Ornelas Orchestra. But a few years later, rock and pop music would gain entry to his soul. In high school, two Renés and two Juans—René Ornelas, René Herrera (b. Nov. 1935, Laredo, Tex.), Juan Orfila, and Juan Garza-Gongora—formed a vocal quartet patterned after the Four Aces and the Four Lads, who were hot at the time.

"We toured all over and got to make some records for Deluxe and Dot," René Ornelas recalled in an exclusive interview. "It was hard back then being a Latin act. The things we had to do! We had hits in the Spanish community, and the top 40 stations took notice, but we couldn't come in the front door—it had to be through the back or the side door."

After 10 years together, the Quarter Notes broke up in 1962. The two Renés, however, stayed together and recorded as a duo for another decade. "We did a lot of records, made it to Dick Clark's Caravan of Stars, and toured with the Beach Boys and the Grass Roots. But we couldn't get away from our roots: we'd put a Latin song on one side and a pop-rock song on the other. We couldn't get away from it.

"Herrera quit in '72. For a while, I picked up a couple of guys to sing harmony with. I was the lead singer, always. I tried to keep on touring and recording, and I still used the 'René & René' name. As long as there were two of us and the sound was there, the people didn't care."

For a spell in the early '70s, René retired from performing. He wrote songs or did arrangements for Herb Alpert, Vikki Carr, Peter Nero, Trini Lopez, José Feliciano, and Lawrence Welk. He earned a teaching degree and tried to teach for a few years, but missed singing and was soon back in action. During the last few years, Mr. Ornelas has been performing under the monicker of René René. "That way they'll only expect one of us, right?"

If you look, they're out there—more than 30 albums with either the "René & René" or "René René" name. René Ornelas' most recent effort is *El Gallito Enamorado* (1989) for the JB label.

Derek

CINNAMON
(George Tobin, Johnny Cymbal)
Bang 558
No. 11 *January 11, 1969*

"Derek" was an alias briefly assumed by singer/songwriter JOHNNY CYMBAL. After his 1963 hit "Mr. Bass Man," Johnny recorded five years' worth of flopped 45s, so he needed a new, untarnished, and heavily hip name to represent his case to the American people. Yes, out of all the silly pseudonyms in the world, "Derek" was chosen.

"I had just written 'Mary In the Morning' [a top 40 hit for Al Martino]," Johnny explained in an exclusive interview. "It was probably the most successful song I've ever written. And I had this deal to produce Gene Pitney and some other acts. I did the vocals on 'Cinnamon,' but I thought, I can't go out on the road and produce these things at the same time. So my brother, who's really named Derek and who was part of my band at the time, went out as me—he did the road work. Hey, there were three different touring versions of the Crystals, and two different versions of the Drifters, so it seemed like a good idea to have two different Dereks."

"Cinnamon," a self-penned bubblegum tune, outsold even "Mr. Bass Man," but except for "Back Door Man" (#59, 1969), future releases under the Derek persona bombed.

Brooklyn Bridge

WORST THAT COULD HAPPEN
(Jim Webb)
Buddah 75
No. 3 *February 1, 1969*

Johnny Maestro (b. John Maestrangelo, May 7, 1939, New York City) shook the charts with the Crests on such golden oldies as "Sixteen Candles" (#2, 1959), "Six Nights A Week" (#28, 1959), "The Angels Listened In" (#22, 1959), "Step By Step" (#14, 1960), and "Trouble In Paradise" (#20, 1960). When internal dissension and a decline in popularity set in, Johnny was pruned from the Crests. Groomed as a teen idol, he had hits on his own with "Model Girl" (#20, 1961) and "What A Surprise" (#33, 1961), but by 1962, the times they were a-changin'.

Maestro tried to reform the Crests and cut more teen-dream disks. In the mid-'60s, when all else had failed, he joined what remained of the Del Satins: Les Cauchi (b. 1945) and Fred

Brooklyn Bridge

Ferrara (b. 1945). The Del Satins had never clicked on the national listings, but they did have a solid reputation on the East Coast, and they had backed up ERNIE MARESCA and Dion on a number of their chart-toppers.

One night in 1968, the Del Satins apppeared in a Battle of the Bands on Long Island. One of the contending acts was the Rhythm Method, a co-ed seven-member unit fronted by the husband-and-wife team of Tom Sullivan (b. 1946) and Carolyn Wood (b. 1947). After the contest was over, both groups exchanged words of praise, and later that night, discussed the possibility of merging into one big group.

By April 1968, the two had indeed become one—a conglomeration of 11 members. The line-up featured Maestro (lead vocals), Les Cauchi (vocals), Fred Ferrara (vocals), Tom Sullivan (sax), Carolyn Wood (organ), Artie Cantanzarita (drums), Shelly Davis (trumpet, piano), Mike Gregorio (vocals), Richie Macioce (guitar), Jimmy Rosica (bass), and Joe Ruvio (sax). When word got around that these musicians were considering forming so huge a performing entity, someone exclaimed, "That is going to be as easy to sell as the Brooklyn Bridge." All members agreed that there was the name for them.

Buddah Records caught the Brooklyn Bridge's act at the Cheetah, then the ultimate in hip Big Apple clubs. *Brooklyn Bridge* (1969), an album of pop and jazz-inflected numbers, was quickly produced (by Wes Farrell), packaged, and shipped. With the group's second single, a cover version of a Fifth Dimension tune called "Worst That Could Happen," the Bridge had found their groove. A second LP (*The Second Brooklyn Bridge*) was released in 1969, and a string of follow-up singles made the Hot 100: "Blessed Is The Rain" (#45, 1969) b/w "Welcome Me Love" (#48), "Your Husband—My Wife" (#46, 1969), and "You'll Never Walk Alone" (#51, 1969).

In the early '70s, the group shortened their name to Bridge, and by mid-decade, they had shrunken to a quintet. Maestro led a version of his pop-rock band through the '80s, and Bridge is still performing.

Virginia Pugh is one of the most successful female country singers of all time. Don't let her inclusion in this book fool you—Virginia Pugh, a.k.a. Tammy Wynette, has made *Billboard*'s C & W listings on more than 60 occasions; 20 of these singles reached the coveted number-one position. For three consecutive years, Tammy was named the Country Music Association's "Vocalist of the Year" (1968–1971). Her *Tammy's Greatest Hits* (1969) album and her lone crossover pop hit are considered, respectively, the best-selling album and best-selling single by a female in the entire history of country and western music!

"The First Lady of Country Music" was born in Itawamba County, Mississippi, on May 5, 1942. Her father died when she was a few months old; her mother moved to Birmingham, Alabama, to work in an aircraft factory, leaving little Virginia with her grandparents until the end of World War II. There, she fiddled with her pa's old instruments. She married at 17 and produced three little ones.

To add to her earnings as a Birmingham beautician, Virginia sang in local night spots, and from 1963 to 1964, was the featured vocalist on WBRC's early-morning TV program, "The Country Boy Eddie Show." After some appearances on Porter Wagoner's syndicated TV show, Virginia made the usual Nashville record-company rounds. Hickory, Kapp, and others turned her down; Epic's Billy Sherrill, however, thought he heard something special. With "Apartment No. 9" (—/—/#44, 1967), her very first record, Tammy Wynette, as she henceforth was to be known, proved Billy Sherrill oh so right.

Tammy has been married five times; her union with country legend George Jones (1968–1975) proved fruitful in the form of numerous duet hits, but the Tammy-George merger, like the three before it, ended in "D-I-V-O-R-C-E" (#63, 1968). This country queen has withstood some disastrous marriages, ill health, numerous home fires, threats on her life, and even a kidnapping. Her autobiography, *Stand By Your Man*, was made into a 1981 TV movie starring Annette O'Toole.

Tammy Wynette

STAND BY YOUR MAN
(Tammy Wynette, Billy Sherrill)
Epic 10398
No. 19 *February 1, 1969*

Arbors

THE LETTER
(Wayne Carson Thompson)
Date 1638
No. 20 *April 5, 1969*

Brothers Ed and Fred Farran from Grand Rapids, Michigan, crossed paths with Scott Herrick of East Lansing, Michigan, at the University of Michigan, where all three were students. Ed was studying zoology and biology, Fred, aeronautical and mathematical engineering, and Scott, industrial engineering. In their spare time, the guys discovered their mutual interest in singing and their vocal compatibility. Scott's twin brother Thomas dropped out of Michigan State to join the others as the Arbors, so named after Ann Arbor, the location of the University of Michigan campus.

In 1965, after the silky-smooth group had established a local reputation, Mercury Records showed an interest in signing them. "Anyone Here for Love" was their only release; it bombed, and the boys were let go. Despite their singing talents, their sound, by 1966, seemed antiquated and definitely un-British. Their appearance was all-too-wholesome and thus unhip. Yet the success of groups with similar images, such as the Association and the Vogues, won the act a final shot at stardom. Date, a Columbia Records subsidiary, released a small heap of 45s by the Arbors before their moment in the sun. Only their easy-listening but psychedelicized rendition of the Box Tops' chart-busting "The Letter" would receive national top 40 acceptance.

After their luke-warm career had cooled, the Arbors moved their base of operations to Chicago, where they set themselves up in the jingle business. For years, they were reportedly making in the six figures singing masterworks like "It's the real thing," "In the valley of the jolly, ho, ho, ho," and "You deserve a break today."

Bubble Puppy

HOT SMOKE & SASAFRASS
(Roy E. Cox, Jr., William Rodney Prince)
International Artists 128
No. 14 *April 12, 1969*

Bubble Puppy was a hot and heavy herd of good ole boys from Austin, Texas. Composed of Roy Cox (bass), Todd Potter (guitar), Rod Prince (guitar), and M. Taylor (drums), the psychedelic punksters (originally known as the New Seeds and, later, the Willowdale Handcar) were signed in 1968 to the tiny Texas-based International Artists label—home of the Lone Star State's decidedly dusted Thirteenth

Bubble Puppy

Floor Elevators. The members of Bubble Puppy (named after a phrase in Aldous Huxley's *Brave New World*) looked like Dixie-fried and drugged flower children in the photo on their only album, *Gathering Promises*. "Hot Smoke & Sasafrass" featured near-nonsensical hippy-dippy lyrics, but is also one of the finest disks ever to be created by a one-off act.

A year's worth of singles were issued, but not one disk packed the charge or the magic of that silly "Sasafrass" song. In 1970, the International Artists label folded, so Cox, Potter, Prince, and a new drummer, David Fore, signed on with the fine folks at ABC Records. As Demian, they recorded a self-titled album of heavenly heaviness and frilly folk that went largely unnoticed. The group disbanded after one Texas tour.

In 1986, all the original members of Bubble Puppy reunited to record a live version of "Hot Smoke & Sasafrass" for a European compilation LP. The following year, the group's long-awaited second album—*Wheels Go Round*—was released in Europe only, on the One Big Guitar label.

Crazy Elephant

GIMME GIMME GOOD LOVIN'
(Joey Levine, Ritchie Cordell)
Bell 763
No. 12 *May 3, 1969*

The story of Crazy Elephant appeared in a *Cashbox* article. According to *Cashbox*, a Welsh newspaper called *Mining News* had mentioned the hard-rock activities of a group of coal miners who would dig by day and play rock and roll by night. *Cashbox* also described how Neville Crisken, a London nightclub owner, read this human-interest item and rushed to Wales to check out this crew. Upon his arrival, Crisken descended " '18,372,065 feet beneath the surface' " and signed the blokes on the spot. When *Mining News* inquired if the group was any good, Crisken was quoted as saying, " 'Who cares? All the publicity about how I discovered them will guarantee their first album a million dollars in sales.' "

A fanciful tale indeed—especially since the *Cashbox* article was a complete fabrication. The story apparently was planted by publicity people: Crazy Elephant was actually a studio creation courtesy of veteran bubblegum-*meisters* Jerry Kasenetz and Jeff Katz.

Leading the studio group that actually laid down the sounds for "Gimme Gimme" was the former lead singer of the Cadillacs, Richard Spencer. The unit that toured as Crazy Elephant consisted of five New Yorkers: drummer Bob Avery (ex-MUSIC EXPLOSION), bassist Ronnie Bretone, Hal Hing (credited with "[doing] various things as the feeling moves him"), lead singer/organist Larry Afuer (a.k.a. Larry Lafuer), and someone named Jethro on flute, sax, guitar, bass, and percussion.

Edwin Hawkins Singers

OH HAPPY DAY
(Edwin R. Hawkins)
Pavilion 20001
No. 4 *May 31, 1969*

The Edwin Hawkins Singers were 42 strong and originally known as the Northern California State Youth Choir. They were formed in 1967 by Betty Watson and Edwin Hawkins (b. Aug. 1943, Oakland, Cal.) to represent their Berkeley church, the Ephresian Church of God In Christ, at a youth congress that summer in Washington, D.C.

In 1968, anticipating the next congress in Cleveland, the choir commissioned Century Record Productions to record one of their performances. A thousand copies of "Oh Happy Day" were pressed and sold to family and friends; one copy of the group's spirited vanity pressing fell into the hands of Tom Donahue, former owner of Autumn Records and future father of underground radio. "Big Daddy" Donahue began riding the record on his program on San Francisco's KSAN, and the response was incredible. Neil Bogart of Buddah Records flew in and acquired the national distribution rights, the State Youth Choir was renamed, and the sounds of God's gospel were on the nation's charts again.

The Edwin Hawkins Singers toured the States and abroad, appearing at churches and colleges, on TV, and in concert halls. Dorothy Morrison, the lead voice on "Oh Happy Day," left the group for a solo career within minutes of the tune's charting—in the coming years, several of her sides ("All God's Children Got Soul," "Spirit In The Sky," "Border Song") would appear on the Hot 100 and R & B listings. In 1970, the choir would revisit the top 10 as back-up singers on Melanie's "Lay Down (Candles In The Wind)" (#6). Three of the Hawkins crew's albums—*Let Us Go into the House of the Lord, Children (Get Together)*, and *I'd Like to Teach the World*—sold well, but the choir's success was fading rapidly.

By 1980, the core of the Hawkins Singers consisted mainly of family members: brothers Edwin (keyboards), Daniel (bass), and Walter (keyboards); sisters Carole, Freddie, and Lynette; cousin Shirley Miller; nephew Joe Smith (drums); and Walter's wife, Tremaine (lead singer).

The Edwin Hawkins Singers are still touring, and currently record for the Birthright label. Their most recent release is *Give Us Peace* (1987).

Mercy

LOVE (CAN MAKE YOU HAPPY)
(Jack Sigler, Jr.)
Sundi 6811
No. 2 *May 31, 1969*

Jack Sigler, Jr., was born in Tampa, Florida, in 1950. In high school, while playing in the school band, Jack decided to stuff the Sousa and form a rock and roll unit with some fellow bandmembers. In almost no time, the group,

Mercy, was gigging at local dances. In 1968, Jack went off to the University of Southern Florida. Mercy's line-up shifted a bit at this point, but soon settled down to include Sigler (guitar), Ronnie Caudell (guitar), Rodger Fuentes (drums), Buddy Goode (bass), Debbie Lewis (organ), Jamie Marvell (guitar), and Brenda McNish (piano).

George Roberts, a Hollywood producer, came to Tampa with Lou Chaney, Jr., to film *Fireball Jungle*. Jack's father was good friends with the movie mogul, and recommended that Roberts catch his son's act. The producer liked one Mercy number called "Love (Can Make You Happy)," so the tune was recorded and included in *Fireball Jungle*—only the film was never released.

Not overly discouraged, Mercy managed to place their gooey Steve Alaimo-Brad Shapiro production with Sundi, a small independent label. After months of airplay and some chart action in the Miami area, Warner Bros. stepped in and acquired the disk for national distribution.

"Love (Can Make You Happy)" proved to be an unrepeatable smash. Mercy's immediate follow-up was "Forever," a well-worn Buddy Killen number to which THE LITTLE DIPPERS owe their one-hit wonder status. Mercy managed to chart with their re-tread (#79, 1969),

but the platter would be their final nota-ble—only one more single is known to have been released. Jack, Jr.'s interest apparently turned elsewhere, and the "Mercy" name was shelved.

Neon Philharmonic

MORNING GIRL
(Tuppy Saussy)
Warner Bros. 7261
No. 17   *June 7, 1969*

The Neon Philharmonic was a two-man studio act. Tuppy Saussy, an arranger and conductor, had the words and music for what he called a "phonographic opera"; Don Gant had the voice. Both were based in Nashville, and both were well-versed in the ways of music-making.

While no one is certain of the chronological order, there are numerous scraps of biographi-cal detail on Don Gant. He had given pop sing-ing a try in the early '60s, and Colpix released some of his solo sides. Don was also a one-time member, with producer/singer/songwriter Norro Wilson, of an Everly Brothers-type duo. Nothing much happened with either of these ventures, but Don Gant kept on writing songs (he co-wrote "Cry Softly, Lonely One" with Roy Orbison), worked day jobs with the Acuff-Rose and Tree International music-publishing houses, and sang back-up for artists like John D. Loudermilk, Don Gibson, and Mickey Newbury.

Gant also produced recordings for artists like Bobby "Blue" Bland, Bobby Braddock, Jimmy Buffett, GENE & DEBBE, Lefty Frizzell, Ferlin Husky, the Newbeats, and Eddie Raven. He was director of ABC-Dunhill Records, and served as president of the Nashville chapter of the National Academy of Recording Arts & Sciences. At the time of his death in 1987, he was the head of Don Gant Enterprises and a board member of the Country Music Foundation.

"Morning Girl," recorded with a chamber-sized gathering of musicians from the Nashville Symphony Orchestra, was a surprise smash. The immediate follow-up, "No One Is Going To Hurt You," sank like a stone, but 1970's "Heighdy-Ho Princess" did score at number 94. Warner Bros. released two albums and five more singles, but the Neon Philharmonic's magic moment had passed.

To this day, a cult following surrounds this "group" of pop-rockers. Over the years, Donald and Tuppy have returned to the studio twice to revive their Neon project: the result has been two limited-release singles, "Annie Poor" (for the TRX label) and "So Glad You're A Woman" (for MCA).

Spiral Starecase
MORE TODAY THAN YESTERDAY
(Pat Upton)
Columbia 44741
No. 12   *June 14, 1969*

The Sacramento-based Spiral Starecase had been working the varnish off of their tootsies for half a decade before they received their first and only national notice. For years, they paid their dues in hometown liquor holes and tacky Reno/Tahoe lounges. When SONNY KNIGHT discovered the Spirals at a Las Vegas gig, they consisted of Pat Upton (lead vocals, guitar), Harvey Kaye (organ), Dick Lopes (sax), Vinny Parello (drums), and Bobby Raymond (bass).

Columbia Stereo

MORE TODAY THAN YESTERDAY SPIRAL STARECASE

PROUD MARY
FOR ONCE IN MY LIFE
SINCE I DON'T HAVE YOU
THIS GUY'S IN LOVE WITH YOU
OUR DAY WILL COME
THE THOUGHT OF LOVING YOU
JUDAS TO THE LOVE WE KNEW
SWEET LITTLE THING
BROKEN-HEARTED MAN
NO ONE FOR ME TO TURN TO
MORE TODAY THAN YESTERDAY

Sonny liked their stuff, and approached their manager about cutting some sides on the group for Columbia Records. Upton's brassy "More Today Than Yesterday," the Spiral Starecase's second single, was a shiny success. Two follow-ups charted—"No One For Me To Turn To" (#52, 1969) and "She's Ready" (#72, 1970)—and their future seemed bright.

Horns were hot at that point in pop history: Chicago (Transit Authority) was waiting in the wings, and Blood, Sweat & Tears was invading the top 10. Unfortunately, Spiral Starecase could not re-create their record's sophisticated brass arrangements in a live setting, since they didn't blow their own horns. Pop fans were sticklers for authenticity: a brassy band had to have brass, simple as that.

Abruptly, the end was at hand. Nothing further made of vinyl and stuffed in a sleeve by this band ever made the charts again.

Desmond Dekker & The Aces
ISRAELITES
(Desmond Dacris, Leslie Kong)
Uni 55129
No. 9   *June 28, 1969*

It was Bob Marley who convinced a young Jamaican named Desmond Dacris to approach Leslie Kong, owner of Beveley's Records. Marley and Dacris both worked in the same welding shop. Marley had his dreams of pop success and would soon achieve his own triumph, but it was Dacris (a.k.a. Desmond Dekker) who got there first—he became the first successful reggae artist in the U.S. and Europe. "Israelites," his personalized portrait of the Biblical Exodus saga, was Desmond's only charting in the States. Jamaica and England responded strongly to his rhythms, providing him with a string of popular singles in those regions.

Dekker (b. July 16, 1942) grew up in Kingston, Jamaica. In his teens, he worked the streets as an amateur performer. By 1962, knowledgeable natives were calling Desmond "King of the Blue Beat." From 1963 through 1969, he won the Golden Globe award as Jamaica's top vocalist. Starting with his initial release ("Honor Your Father And Mother"), his Kong singles repeatedly made the Jamaican listings. By 1967, English ears were beginning to take notice of Dekker's reggae rhythms— "007 (Shanty Town)" nearly made the top 10 over there. (A cover version of this tune ap-

peared on the seminal stateside reggae album *The Harder They Come*.)

Besides "Israelites" and "007," Desmond secured British chartings with "It Miek" (1969), "Pickney Gal" (1970), a rendition of Jimmy Cliff's "You Can Get It If You Really Want" (1970), and "Sing A Little Song" (1975). Unfortunately, Dekker's career slowed to a halt soon after Leslie Kong, his producer and mentor, died of a heart attack in 1970.

Stiff Records signed Dekker up at the height of the British rock-steady/ska revival in 1980. Two LPs followed: *Black and Dekker* (1980) and the Robert Palmer-produced *Compass Point* (1981).

Sonny Charles & The Checkmates, Ltd.
BLACK PEARL
(Phil Spector, Toni Wine, Irwin Levine)
A & M 1053
No. 13   *July 5, 1969*

Sonny Charles (lead vocals, keyboards), Marvin "Sweet Louie" Smith (drums), and Bobby Stevens (lead vocals) grew up together, played together, and attended the same Fort Wayne, Indiana high school. In 1958, they started performing together as the Checkmates, Inc., playing blues, rock, and light jazz. In the '60s, Bill Van Buskirk (bass) and Harvey Trees (guitar) were added, making the group multiracial. The guys were sidetracked for a few years for military service, but on their return, the group's persistence paid off with gigs throughout the Midwest and ultimately, Las Vegas.

While working the Pussycat A Go-Go, a late-night desert resort where the stars would stop by, the Checkmates were spotted by Nancy Wilson. She offered to manage the group, so a deal was struck the next morning; Wilson handled the Checkmates for several years. Under her direction, they appeared at swanky venues like Caesar's Palace, the Cocoanut Grove, and the Copa. In 1966, Wilson secured a recording contract for them with Capitol Records, but "Do The Walk," "Mastered In The Art Of Love," and a critically-acclaimed LP (*The Checkmates Live in Las Vegas*) failed to sell.

Meanwhile, the legendary Phil Spector, after a two-year hiatus, was ready to return to the studio. His deal with A & M called for him to produce some sides on the Checkmates. Their A & M debut, "Love Is All I Have To

Give" (#65, 1969)—penned by Stevens and Spector—almost clicked. Their second effort, "Black Pearl," is considered one of Spector's finest productions.

All, however, was not bliss. The billing on "Black Pearl"'s label read "Sonny Charles & The Checkmates, Ltd.," and Bobby Stevens, a founding member and co-lead singer, was not pleased. "Proud Mary" (#69, 1969)—credited to "The Checkmates, Ltd. featuring Sonny Charles" and also produced by Spector—and a hastily-assembled album, reportedly budgeted at $450,000, were released. As "Sweet Louie"

Smith told *Black Stars*, the album "didn't make us a dime." Further recording plans fizzled, and in 1970, the Checkmates split up.

The group has since re-formed, separated, re-formed, separated. . . . For a while, they had their own record label (Rustic), their own TV production company (Associated Video Artists), and their own L.A. night spot (The Club). Sonny Charles had a solo hit in 1983 on the Highrise label with "Put It In A Magazine" (#40).

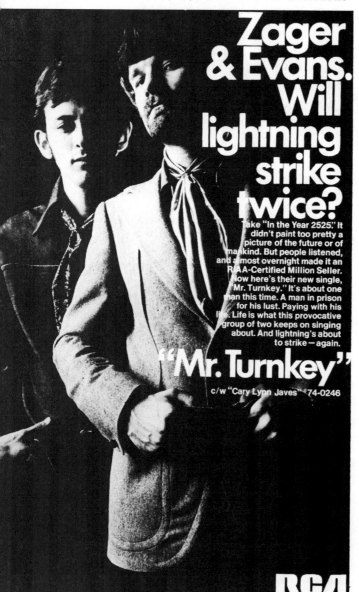

Zager & Evans
IN THE YEAR 2525
(EXORDIUM & TERMINUS)
(Rick Evans)
RCA 0174
No. 1 *July 12, 1969*

Denny Zager, born and raised in Wymore, Nebraska, was a member of the local Eccentrics when he chanced on Lincoln, Nebraska native Rick Evans in 1962. Denny stumbled onto Rick at a talent contest at Wesleyan University, and offered him the guitarist slot in his band. Rick accepted and joined the Eccentrics, but left in 1965 to form his own group of giggers, the DeVilles. As the '60s drew to a close, Denny and Rick, equally disenchanted with their respective group situations, formed a folkie duo.

Rick was eager to try out "In the Year 2525," a futuristic fable he had dashed off in 30 minutes. Since 1964, the darn thing had been collecting dust in his dresser drawer. Denny agreed to perform the tune, but clearly wasn't happy about it. "I didn't go nutty over the song," Zager confessed to Fred Bronson in *The Billboard Book of Number One Hits*. "It really wasn't the style I wanted to do." But wherever they sang the song, audiences seemed to like it.

Rick convinced Denny to travel to Odessa, Texas, where they taped the tune and pressed up a thousand copies on Truth Records to sell at concerts and hand out to local radio stations. Someone over at RCA heard the disk and signed Rick and Denny to a recording contract. "In The Year 2525" darted to the pinnacle of the pop listings, where it remained for six weeks, eventually selling more than 5,000,000 copies. Nothing the Nebraskans ever again recorded managed to muscle more than minimal attention.

"We tried everything to come up with that second hit, but it never happened," Zager lamented to Daniel Mills of the *Washington Times*. "A lot of groups climb their way up very slowly. They get a mediocre hit, then a little bigger hit, and then they get a super-big hit and just stay in the limelight. But we were misfortunate enough to have a monster right off the top. What do you do to top it?"

In the year 1970, Zager quit the duo. Denny now lives in Lincoln, where he makes string instruments, teaches music, and continues to perform country-type tunes in local clubs. Rick Evans lives in Arizona and works as a real estate broker, occasionally writing songs.

Winstons

COLOR HIM FATHER
(Richard Spencer)
Metromedia 117
No. 7 *July 19, 1969*

As a recording act, the Winstons began and ended in 1969. They are remembered for one song, their first disk and a Grammy winner for best R & B song, "Color Him Father."

The band was born in the late '60s in Washington, D.C. Richard Spencer was the leader, singer, songwriter, and tenor sax man. G.C. Coleman, their drummer, had been a Motown sessioneer and a member of the Marvelettes' touring band. Lead guitarist Quincy Mattison had been with Arthur Conley's band when the Otis Redding protegé was on the charts with "Sweet Soul Music." Rich, Quincy, and G.C. had all played with Otis Redding. Ray Maritano, the Winstons' alto saxophonist, had attended the Berklee College of Music and played in the U.S. Air Force Band. Keyboardist Phil Tolotta doubled on lead vocals, and bassist Sonny Peckrol completed the line-up.

The Impressions discovered the band, took them out on the road as their back-up players, and eventually gave them a solo spot on the tour. Spencer's ode to the ideal dad—protective, kind, and loving—came to the attention of the Atlanta-based Metromedia label. "Color Him Father" was the Winstons' first 45, and it struck a chord with both pop (#7) and R & B (#2) listeners. In just months, the Winstons faded from view, leaving in their wake only two more 45s—"Love Of The Common People" (#54, 1969) and "Birds Of A Feather"—plus a lone LP named after their hallowed hit.

Joe Jeffrey Group

MY PLEDGE OF LOVE
(Joseph Stafford Jr.)
Wand 11200
No. 14 *July 26, 1969*

Little can be pieced together about Joe Jeffrey and his flash flight into and out of fame. He was a Buffalo-based boy who had been playing the local bar circuit. Someone, possibly Jerry Meyers at Stone Gold Productions, took a liking to him and booked studio time at Cleveland's Audio Recording Studio and, later, at Chip Moman's American Sound Studio in Memphis. "My Pledge Of Love" seems to have been Joe's first recording.

Following "My Pledge Of Love" were three more singles—"Dreamin' Til Then" (1969), "Hey Hey Woman" (1969), and "My Baby Loves Lovin'" (1970)—plus an album, *My Pledge of Love*. Despite glowing liner notes on the latter supplied by DJ Sandy Beach, who favorably compared Joe's effort with the Beatles' *Sgt. Pepper*, Joe's moment had come and gone by the end of 1969.

Roy Clark

YESTERDAY, WHEN I WAS YOUNG
(Charles Aznavour, Herbert Kretzmer)
Dot 17446
No. 19 *August 2, 1969*

By the time he was 11, Roy Linwood Clark (b. April 15, 1933, Meherrin, Va.) was already a hell of a country picker. His family had moved to Washington, D.C., where his father was working as a computer programmer. Hester Clark had been a tobacco farmer by day, but played guitar five nights a week in a local country/bluegrass band. The house was always full of music: there was a ukulele, a mandolin, a banjo, and ma's piano. Before Roy's grammar school days were done, Hester Clark had taught his son everything he knew about stringed instruments; Roy started sitting in on some of his dad's gigs. In 1951 and 1952, Clark won two consecutive National Banjo Championships. The second win awarded him an appearance at the Grand Ole Opry.

Back in D.C., Clark tried out for the St. Louis Browns baseball club, won a string of boxing matches, and—in his spare time—played at local bars. Eventually, he was offered

Tony Joe White

after country hit, with more than 50 of his 45s scoring on the C & W charts.

Roy has made many TV stops on talk and variety shows. But perhaps he is best known for his long-running appearances as co-host (with Buck Owens) of country music's answer to "Laugh-In," "Hee Haw." He also guested as "Cousin Roy" and (in drag) as "Big Mama Halsey" on "The Beverly Hillbillies."

Clark performs over 250 shows a year; he was reportedly the highest-paid country concert star between 1969 and 1971. He also works the Las Vegas scene, and has occasionally hosted "The Tonight Show." In 1973, the Country Music Association named Roy Clark "Entertainer of the Year."

Charles Randolph Grean Sounde

QUENTIN'S THEME
(Robert W. Lorbert)
Ranwood 840
No. 13   *August 2, 1969*

Charles Grean was born in New York City on October 1, 1913. He studied as a music major for two years at Wesleyan University. For over a decade thereafter, Grean played bass with various orchestras and combos. In the early '40s, he free-lanced, and worked as a copyist for the Glenn Miller Orchestra. He then became an A & R man and music conductor with RCA and Dot Records. During the '60s, "Dark Shadows" was a cult TV show—a daytime vampirc soap. Grean's recording of the program's theme would be the only time he would stand near the spotlight of stardom.

Charles Randolph Grean is married to pop lark and multi-hit artist Betty Johnson. He continues to labor in the dark shadows, scoring the background music for soap operas, movies, and variety shows.

Tony Joe White

POLK SALAD ANNIE
(Tony Joe White)
Monument 1104
No. 8   *August 23, 1969*

Rock critics have dubbed Tony Joe White's funky country-blues style "swamp rock," but

a job as back-up guitarist for an up-and-coming country singer, Jimmy Dean. Roy appeared on some of Dean's ABC-TV spots, and then secured a similar slot with "The George Hamilton IV Show."

Clark's early recorded efforts were issued on the Four Star, Debbie, and Coral labels. After working as the lead guitarist for MARVIN RAINWATER and Wanda ("The Female Elvis") Jackson, Jackson's manager hooked Roy up with Capitol Records. The pairing was quite fruitful, producing C & W hits like "Tip Of My Fingers" (1963), "Through The Eyes Of Love" (1964), and "When The Wind Blows In Chicago" (1965).

Numerous country hits followed once Clark switched over to the Dot label in 1968. His flashy guitar and banjo licks adorned tunes that ranged in style from easy-listening to hardcore bluegrass; "Yesterday, When I Was Young" was representative of much of his material, and just happened to be that one single that crossed over to the top 40. He continues to rack up hit

"swamp soul" might be a more accurate description. White (b. July 23, 1943) was born and raised in Oak Grove, Louisiana, near the borders of Arkansas and Mississippi, in a community that he described to *Blues & Soul* as "[thriving] around one cotton gin and three stores." The youngest of seven, Tony Joe spent much of his youth picking cotton and listening to the rest of the family playing tunes.

"I didn't care much about music when I was growing up," White recalled to Irwin Stambler in *The Encyclopedia of Pop, Rock, and Soul.* "I heard it all the time. My daddy played every kind of instrument you could think of. But I was much more interested in baseball." All that changed in Tony Joe's late teens, by which point he was roaming the region playing in country-rock bands. "The first group I had was called Tony and the Mojos. We wore blue-speckled smoking jackets and played a lot of bars around home. Another band was called Tony & The Twilights."

Tony and his Twilights migrated to Texas in the mid-'60s, but then splintered. White stayed on in Corpus Christi, working the bars as a solo act. He soon took that obligatory trek to Nashville to make the rounds of the publishers and record companies. Combine Music signed him on as a songwriter, and one of his demo disks found its way to the offices of Monument Records. A variety of now-rare singles ("Georgia Pines," "Watching The Trains Go By," "Soul Francisco") were issued before Tony Joe hit paydirt with "Polk Salad Annie"; all of these sides, incidentally, were produced by BILLY SWAN.

White did make the Hot 100 on three other occasions, with "Roosevelt And Ira Lee" (#44, 1969), "Save Your Sugar For Me" (#94, 1970), and "I Get Off On It" (#79, 1980). In the early '80s, he picked up a minor following with watered-down country material for Columbia Records. "Mama Don't Let Your Babies Grow Up To Be Cowboys" (1980), "The Lady In My Life" (1983), and "We Belong Together" (1984) all made the C & W charts—an interesting development, considering Tony Joe's distaste for the genre. "I listen to most things as long as they've got guts and soul," he told *Blues & Soul.* "I just can't stand Cajun music at any price, same goes for country. Now, blues I like."

In addition to recording, White has written notable numbers for Brook Benton ("Rainy Night In Georgia"), Dusty Springfield ("Willie And Laurie Mae Jones"), and Elvis Presley ("Polk Salad Annie" and "I've Got A Thing About You Baby").

Youngbloods
GET TOGETHER
(Chester Powers)
RCA Victor 9752
No. 5   *September 6, 1969*

"**C**ome on people now/Smile on your brother/Everybody get together/Try and love one another, right now." Classic lines indeed. "Get Together" was jangling 12-string folk-rock, message music, and—as faithful fans will attest—the Youngbloods at their very best.

Jesse Colin Young (b. Perry Miller, Nov. 11, 1944, New York City) was a moderately successful folksinger with two LPs under his belt—*Soul of a City Boy* (1964) and *Youngblood* (1965)—when he met a fellow folkie and former bluegrass picker from Cambridge named Jerry Corbitt (b. Tifton, Ga.). When in town, Jesse would drop in on Jerry, and the two would jam for hours, exchanging harmonies.

Beginning in January 1965, the two began gigging on the Canadian circuit as a duo (eventually, as the Youngbloods, Young would play bass, and Corbitt would play lead guitar). Corbitt introduced Young to a bluegrass boy named Harmon Banana (b. Lowell Levinger, 1946, Cambridge, Mass.). "Banana" was handy with the banjo, mandolin, mandola, guitar, and bass; he had played in the Proper Bostoners and the Trolls, and knew of a fellow tenant in his building who could flesh out the band. Joe Bauer (b. Sept. 26, 1941, Memphis), an aspiring jazz drummer with experience playing in society dance bands, was at first quite unmoved by the offer to perform in a rock and roll outfit, but soon gave in.

Once the line-ups was set, Jesse Colin Young & The Youngbloods, as the group was then known, began building a solid reputation from their club dates. (Early demo sides recorded in 1965 were later issued by Mercury on the *Two Trips* album.) Their first gig had been at Gerde's Folk City in Greenwich Village; months later, they were the house band at the Cafe Au Go Go and had snagged a recording contract with RCA Records. Jesse, though, was not too satisfied with the label. "Nobody [at RCA] was really mean or anything; everybody was just kind of stupid," he explained to *Rolling Stone.* "They never knew what to make of us, and tried to set us up as a bubblegum act . . . they never knew what we were, and never knew how to merchandise us."

The arrangement did produce one solid item in "Grizzly Bear" (#52, 1967). Several classic

The Youngbloods

albums followed—*The Youngbloods* (1967; later retitled *Get Together*), *Earth Music* (1967), and *Elephant Mountain* (1969). When that paean to universal brotherhood, "Get Together," first appeared in the Summer of Love, it did not sell too well (#62, 1967). But two years later—after the National Council of Christians and Jews used the song as their theme song on radio spots—the track was re-released and cracked the top 40.

The Youngbloods recorded a few more albums, then split up. In an interview with *Crawdaddy*'s Peter Knobler, Jesse ascribed the legendary act's break-up to a conflict over one of his tunes, "Peace Song."

"I played ["Peace Song"] the night I wrote it, during the recording session for *Rock Festival* at the Fillmore, and the people just went crazy, they loved it! And the next night the guys played on it, and I didn't dig it. I thought [their playing] detracted from the power of the song . . . For the first time since the band had been together, I said, 'I want to do this alone.' Also, Joe [Bauer] said, 'That's not Youngblood music,

that's you; I don't want that on the Youngbloods album,' and it hurt."

According to Young, tensions within the Youngbloods came to a head a year later. "Banana came to me and said, 'Joe thinks that there's some musical value to the ["Peace Song"], some musical direction.' I said, 'Musical direction? Screw off!' . . . It made me think, what am I doing in this band?"

The group's final LPs were *Ride The Wind* (1971), *Good and Dusty* (1971), and *High on a Ridgetop* (1972). Corbitt, who had left the Youngbloods in 1971, became a producer (Charlie Daniels, Don McLean) and cut two LPs on his own (*Corbitt* and *Jerry Corbitt*). Bauer made one solo record (*Moonset*) and, with Banana, recorded as Banana & The Bunch (*Mid Mountain Range*) and Noggins (*Crab Tunes*). Jesse, the Youngblood with the highest profile, established the solo career he apparently always wanted. No hit singles so far (not even "Peace Song"), but albums like *Light Shine* (1974), *Songbird* (1975), and the live *On The Road* (1976) have sold well.

240

Electric Indian

KEEM-O-SABE
(Bernard Binnick, Bernice Borisoff)
United Artists 50563
No. 16 *September 27, 1969*

"**B**ernie Binnick [co-founder of Swan Records] had this idea for a sitar instrumental," Frank Virtue (formerly of THE VIRTUES) told Tony Cummings in *The Sound of Philadelphia.* "It was around the time all the kids were into that Indian stuff. So he got together a bunch of musicians, a lot of the guys who're in MFSB now, and they put down this sitar thing called 'Keem-O-Sabe.' It was like funky Indian music. They leased the tape to United Artists Records. It was a gimmick, but it was a stone smash."

This "group" recorded an album's worth of similarly inane instrumentals (*Keem-O-Sabe,* 1969) and even did an Indian-flavored cover version of "Land Of 1000 Dances" (#95, 1969) as a follow-up 45. But pop fans wearied quickly of Electric Indian's brand of auditory cotton candy.

Motherlode

WHEN I DIE
(William Smith, Steve Kennedy)
Buddah 131
No. 18 *October 11, 1969*

Motherlode was part of a short-lived, big-time burst in the Canadian rock scene. Nineteen sixty-nine was the year that the Guess Who opened the door for a "Canadian Invasion," and before the door closed, more than a dozen Northern acts ran up and down the U.S. charts: Edward Bear, Five Man Electrical Band, Lighthouse, the Poppy Family, the Stampeders, THE BELLS, OCEAN, and, of course, Motherlode—not to mention Gordon Lightfoot, Joni Mitchell, and Anne Murray.

Before Motherlode came together in London, Ontario, Steve Kennedy had been blowing barroom sax for almost a decade. In the mid-'60s, Kennedy and Dougie Riley had been members of the R & B–oriented Silhouettes and Eric Mercury & The Soul Searchers. When Kennedy (sax, harmonica) first hooked up with Kenny Marco (guitar), Wayne

Motherlode

"Stoney" Stone (drums), and William "Smitty" Smith (keyboards), Motherlode was a top 40 cover band working at the Image Club. Dougie brought the group to the attention of Mort Ross at Revolution Records, and Motherlode was soon asked to create some original material for the label.

As soon as Buddah Records boss Neil Bogart heard Motherlode's first Revolution single, "When I Die," he issued the tune on his stateside label. The situation looked bright as the soulful single cut its way up the charts. But business hassles developed, and before the year was even over, Motherlode was no more. Their debut album sold fairly well, but the follow-up single, "Memories Of A Broken Heart," did poorly.

In 1971, Kennedy, Marco, and Stone formed a new group, Dr. Music, and issued several unsuccessful singles. In 1973, "Smitty" Smith asssembled a new Motherlode and recorded an LP for Buddah, *Tuffed Out*. The album died without notice.

Over the years, Ken Marco has recorded with the King Biscuit Boy Band and Crowbar; he has also worked sessions for David Clayton-Thomas, Genya Ravan, and the Ozark Mountain Daredevils. "Smitty" Smith has played on albums by Blood, Sweat & Tears, Bob Dylan, RICHIE HAVENS, The James Gang, Billy Joel, DAVE LOGGINS, Robert Palmer, and the Pointer Sisters.

Cuff Links

TRACY
(Lee Pockriss, Paul Vance)
Decca 32533
No. 9   *October 25, 1969*

"I had two different singles in the top 10 at the same time under two different group names and nobody seemed to notice," Ron Dante, lead singer for the Archies and multi-tracked voice of the Cuff Links, told *DISCoveries*' Gary Theroux. "I couldn't believe it, 'cause my voice sounded the same. The same week that 'Tracy' entered the top 10, 'Sugar Sugar' was the number-one record in the country. I even had a third record out as the Pearly Gate ["Free," 1969]. It was yet another of my ghost groups."

Ron Dante was born Carmine Granito, on Staten Island, New York, on August 22, 1945. When he was 11 years old, he fell out of a tree, and learned how to play the guitar as he recuperated. A year later, he was fronting the Per-

suaders, a junior-high band made up of fellow classmates. By 1963, Carmine was working as a "runner" for an accounting firm, and he would drop by 1619 Broadway (the famed Brill Building) to knock on doors in hopes of selling off some of his songs.

Don Kirshner hired Carmine as a staff songwriter for Kirshner's Aldon Music and renamed him "Ron Dante." When Tony Orlando, Kirshner's top demo-maker, left to pursue a solo career, Ron was called in to fill the void. In that capacity, he cut background tracks for Neil Diamond, Jay & The Americans, Andy Kim, and The McCoys. He also did demos for songs that would eventually be recorded by the Animals, Ronnie Dove, Gene Pitney, and the Vogues.

In 1965, one of Dante's demos was recorded by THE DETERGENTS—"Leader Of The Laundromat," a parody of the Shangri-Las' "Leader Of The Pack," was a smash. Four years later, Ron sang lead on the Archies' "Sugar Sugar" (#1, 1969). At that time, he was struggling to establish a solo career, but decided to do some singing, songwriting, and producing for the cartoon group. "I did the singing for the Archies, yes, but I didn't want to become a star from that. I just wanted to earn some money to pay some rent. When those records first hit the charts, I just hid."

As for the Cuff Links, "Tracy" was a song that a friend handed to Dante. Ron agreed to record it, so he overdubbed his vocal tracks to sound like a group of singers. He refused to tour behind it because he was "in a ghost-group phase." But he did consent to doing just one album (*Tracy*, 1969). "When the royalty check came in, Paul Vance called me up and said, 'Well, are you ready for the next album?' I said, 'What next album? I told you I was going to do just one LP and that's it. Now where's my money?'"

Ron did get his money and Vance did get a second Cuff Links album, but not with Dante's involvement. Called in to substitute was Rupert Holmes, the arranger on the "group's" first LP and later quite a successful singer/songwriter in his own right.

Ron Dante has never stopped, or even slowed down. In addition to doing jingles (for Coca-Cola, Coppertone, Dr. Pepper, Pepsi, Kentucky Fried Chicken, and Lifesavers), he has worked as a record producer (Irene Cara, Cher, Lady Flash, Barry Manilow), as a producer of plays (*Duet for One, Whose Life Is It, Anyway?*), and as co-producer of the Fats Waller revue *Ain't Misbehavin'*. Dante has had solo recordings issued by Almont, Music Voice, Musicor, Columbia, Dot, Mercury, Kirshner, Scepter, Bell, RCA Victor, Handshake . . . whew! As a continuation of his ghosting activities, Ron has recorded as Bo Cooper, Dante's Inferno, Ronnie & The Dirtriders, C.G. Rose, and the Webspinners. Ron Dante was also, for a brief time, the publisher of the *Paris Review*—reportedly, he acquired the literary journal from George Plimpton by beating him in a billiards match.

Garland Green
JEALOUS KIND OF FELLA
(Josephine Armstead, Garland Green, Maurice Dollison, Rudolph Browner)
Uni 55143
No. 20   *November 1, 1969*

Garland Green, the tenth in a brood of eleven, was born on June 24, 1942, in Dunleath, Mississippi. When he was 16, he moved to Chicago to attend Englewood High, and later worked at the Argo Corn Starch plant. Garland had been singing and swinging since his early years in the Mississippi Delta region. While performing at a community recreation center, he was discovered by one of Chicago's barbecue kings, Argia B. Collins. Argia, who had a mess of barbecue houses and marketed Mambo Bar-B-Que Sauce, sponsored Garland, sending him to the Chicago Conservatory of Music.

While attending the Conservatory, Green worked the black club scene on the South Side. One night while he was singing in Chicago's Sutherland Lounge, Melvin Collins and Josie Jo Armstead—the husband-and-wife owners of the Gamma/Giant labels—happened to be in the audience. "I really liked Garland's voice," Armstead, a one-time Ikette, explained to *Soul Survivor*'s Robert Pruter. "There was that pleading quality that I knew that women would just love. I was with Melvin and I told him, 'I believe I can get a hit on him.'"

"Jealous Kind Of Fella" was a telephone talkie tune: Garland calls his girl and apologizes for the jealous rage that caused him to "hit that guy last night." Droves of females snapped up the record. About a third as many went for his follow-up, which mined the same vein—"Don't Think That I'm A Violent Guy" (—/#42, 1970). Though none of his successive singles made the Hot 100, eight of them (nine if you count the re-release of 1974's "Let

The Good Times Roll" in 1975) charted on the *Billboard* R & B listings, right up through 1983.

Smith
BABY IT'S YOU
(Bacharach, David, Williams)
Dunhill 4206
No. 5   *November 1, 1969*

Gayle McCormick had been screaming bluesy rock since her high school days in St. Louis. Fronting a unit called the Chevels, Gayle waxed a few singles in 1966 for the Musicland U.S.A. label. With a limp concept of hip in mind, they changed their name to Gayle McCormick & The Klassmen. "Without You" and "Mr. Loveman" both came and passed without much public fanfare. At about the same time, a band called the Smiths came to town touring behind a Columbia single, "Now I Taste The Tears." Most of the Smiths' members had departed, and the remaining players needed replacements. Gayle and one of the Klassmen, Steve Cummings, joined Jerry Carter and Rich Cliburn to form Smith.

Right from the start, the heart and soul of the revamped Smith was McCormick. She was only 20 years old that day in 1969 when Del Shannon and Brian Hyland stopped in to wet their whistles at the Rag Doll, a bar in the San Fernando Valley. Smith had only been together a month or so, but Shannon loved what he heard. He immediately offered to manage and produce the group, and they quickly consented.

Del brought Smith back to his house, where he had a roomful of recording equipment. Reportedly, not one of the group had heard the original Shirelles version of "Baby It's You" (which the Beatles covered), and that was just the way Shannon wanted it. Del showed them the outlines of the song and worked with them until he got the sound just right. With demo in hand, he hawked the tape to Steve Barri at Dunhill, who agreed to give Smith a shot at success only if Shannon would cut some sides for the label.

The tale gets foggy from this point on. Del and Smith came to a disagreement about something, and Steve Barri and Joel Sill wound up producing Smith's hard-rockin' remake of "Baby It's You." By the time the disk was out, most of Smith had apparently flown the coop; only Gayle and Jerry remained. "Take A Look

Recorded by THE FLYING MACHINE on Congress Records

SMILE A LITTLE SMILE FOR ME

Words and Music by TONY MACAULAY & GEOFF STEPHENS

JANUARY MUSIC CORP.
A Subsidiary of
A. SCHROEDER MUSIC CORPORATION
25 West 56th Street, New York, N. Y. 10019

Sole
Selling
Agents
CIMINO PUBLICATIONS INCORPORATED
400 Maple Avenue   Westbury, L.I., N.Y. 11590

PRICE
$1.50
IN U. S. A.

The Flying Machine

a hot band called The King Bees. They had a contract with RCA and several biting rhythm rockers in release. Crowds loved them, and their sound, rock and roll with an R & B edge, was ahead of its time. The problem was, no one was buying their records.

Kootch had grown up with a skinny depressive kid named James Taylor. As the Bees bit the dust, Kootch, O'Brien, and Taylor went into the studios and cut some sides for producers Al Gorgoni and Chip "Wild Thing" Taylor. One single credited to "The Flying Machine" ("Rainy Day Man") was issued on Rainy Day Records in the summer of 1967. Nothing much happened, and James Taylor flew to England to see if he could interest the Beatles' Apple label into recording "Carolina In My Mind" and some of his other folky material.

This short-lived unit is the group that many people think recorded "Smile A Little Smile For Me." They didn't. After "Smile" was a huge hit, Gorgoni, Chip Taylor, and others repackaged these early James Taylor recordings with the "Flying Machine" name prominently featured on the album cover, hoping to trick record buyers into thinking that this was the second album by the "Smile" group. For the most part, the ruse worked.

The Liberators from Rugby, England, had been playing together since 1964. Reg Calvert, the manager of the Fortunes, stumbled upon the Liberators, hooked them up with British Decca, dressed them up in pink sport coats, and renamed them Pinkerton's Assorted Colours. In their motherland, Barrie Bernard (bass), Dave Holland (drums), Samuel Kempe (vocals, autoharp), Tom Long (guitar), and Anthony Newman (guitar) had a huge hit with their first release, "Mirror, Mirror." Their follow-ups did poorly, and by the late '60s, the Pinkertons needed a change. Many record collectors believe that *this* was the Flying Machine that recorded "Smile A Little Smile For Me." Wrong again.

Songwriter/producer Tony Macauley had written "Smile A Little Smile For Me" with Geoff Stephens. Experienced music men that they were, Tony and Geoff just knew they had a hit on their hands. Using studio musicians, and possibly the lead vocal of Macauley himself, a recording was quickly made. "Smile" was never a chart wonder in England, but for what seemed like an eternity in the U.S., the tune was played on top 40 stations.

When "Smile" exploded on the stateside landscape, a touring version of The Flying Machine was needed, so the remaining pieces

Around," a fairly tough follow-up, sold well (#43, 1970), but the group was down to just Gayle by then. After the second album, the group's name was dropped altogether. Gayle McCormick carried on for a while with releases on the MCA and Fantasy labels.

Flying Machine

SMILE A LITTLE SMILE FOR ME
(Tony Macauley, Geoff Stephens)
Congress 6000
No. 5 *November 22, 1969*

In the winter of 1966, Danny "Kootch" Kortchmar and Joel O'Brien were members of

of the Pinkertons—Anthony Newman, Samuel Kempe, Stuart Colman, Steve Jones, and Paul Wilkinson—were invited to fill the bill. "Baby Make It Soon" (#87, 1970) was the pseudo-group's follow-up.

Shortly afterward, and miles outside the proverbial spotlight, The Flying Machine crashed and burned on the isle of perishable pop platters. Surviving the crash was Dave Holland, who reappeared in the '80s playing drums in Shakin' Steven's band.

Steam

NA NA HEY HEY
KISS HIM GOODBYE
(Gary DeCarlo, Dale Frashuer, Paul Leka)
Fontana 1667
No. 1 *December 6, 1969*

Steam came from Bridgeport, Connecticut. As the Chateaus, Gary DeCarlo (drums), Dale Frashuer, and Paul Leka (piano) recorded some failed 45s in the early '60s for Coral and Warner Bros. As time moved on, they separated but kept in touch. Paul became a tunesmith with Circle Five Productions. In 1968, Leka met Shelley Pinz; the couple wrote and produced THE LEMON PIPERS' "Green Tambourine" plus other Pipers numbers.

The following year, Leka was working at Mercury Records. Gary DeCarlo, his old Chateau buddy, had convinced the label's A & R man, Bob Reno, to let DeCarlo record some solo sides. With Paul producing, four numbers were quickly canned. Reno liked the tracks,

and thought that each would do well issued as an "A" side. To fill up the "B" side of the first single, Paul and Gary were sent back into the Mercury Sound Studios to cut a throwaway flip side. Dale Frashuer stopped by the studios that night and suggested using a 1961 ballad from the trio's Chateau days called "Kiss Him Goodbye." "I said we should put a chorus to it," Leka told Fred Bronson in *The Billboard Book of Number One Hits*. "I started writing while I was sitting at the piano going 'na, na, na, na, na, na, na, na'. . . Everything was 'na na' when you didn't have a lyric."

To the great surprise of all involved, the powers-that-be at the label decided to release "Na Na"—"an embarassing record . . . an insult," in Leka's opinion—as the "A" side on Fontana, a Mercury subsidiary. Since no one wanted credit for creating the tune, a name for this nonexistent group had to be concocted. Steam—now there's a name that sounds nebulous. Gary's solo singles, which Leka and Reno had preferred to "Na Na," were eventually issued as by Garrett Scott, but not one even charted. Steam's "Na Na," however, sold more than a million copies, and is currrently the unofficial anthem for the Chicago White Sox.

Paul assembled a Steam band to tour in support of the studio creation: Jay Babins (guitar), Ray Corries (drums), Mike Daniels (bass), Hank Schorz (keyboards), Bill Steer (vocals), and Tom Zuke (guitar) were all from the Bridgeport area. When an album was needed, Gary was approached, but refused to return to the studios. Before Steam went the way of all water vapor, more singles appeared, but only one made the charts—"I've Gotta Make You Love Me" (#46, 1970).

The
··

Seventies

Crow

EVIL WOMAN DON'T YOU PLAY
YOUR GAMES WITH ME
(Larry Weigand, Dick Weigand,
Dave Wagner)
Amaret 112
No. 19 *January 10, 1970*

Before their precarious perching on the charts, Crow was South 40, a Twin Cities bar band known for playing hard-edged R & B. One album, *Live at the Someplace Else*, was issued locally and in limited numbers on the Metrobeat label. South 40's big break came when they won first prize in a Minneapolis talent contest in early 1968—a recording session with Columbia Records.

After listening to their demos, Columbia passed on the group. One of the contest judges had been Bob Monaco, co-owner with Bill Traut of the Chicago-based Dunwich/Amaret labels. Monaco felt the bird band had something special to offer rock and roll listeners; Traut didn't. Nearly a year passed before Traut caved in to his partner's insistence.

In the spring of 1969, Dave Wagner (vocals), Kink Middlemist (organ), and brothers Dick (guitar) and Larry Weigand (bass), were flown to Chicago to record a number of tracks, including what was to become their lone hit, "Evil Woman Don't You Play Your Games With Me." Traut objected to the group's original drummer, and replaced him with Denny "Ludwig" Craswell, a former member of THE CAST-AWAYS. The line-up was now complete. A first single, "Time To Make A Turn," was issued and quickly sank into oblivion. Someone suggested issuing "Evil Woman" as the next release, but seasoned with overdubbed horns.

The band balked at the idea, but the label

Crow

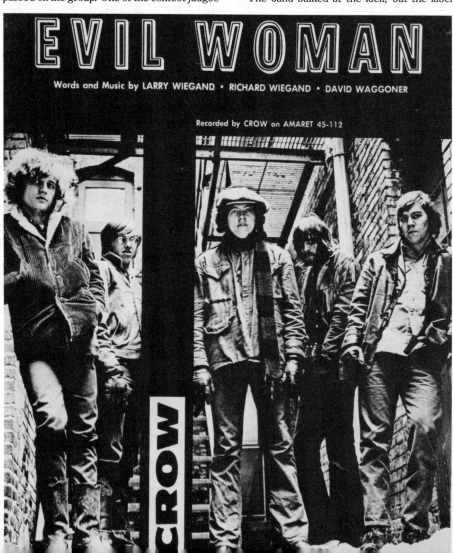

Shocking Blue

lads went ahead and did the deed anyway. "Evil Woman" became a national notable, but until their demise, Crow disliked the horrible horns and refused to duplicate the sound in their live performances. Two follow-ups charted, "Cottage Cheese" (#56, 1970) and "Don't Try To Lay No Boogie Woogie On The King Of Rock & Roll" (#52, 1970). Reportedly, Wagner wanted the group to do more gospel and torch songs, but Craswell and the rest of the Crow men wanted to rock, and hard. After the release of several unsuccessful singles which alternated between the two styles, Crow unceremoniously flew apart.

Dave Wagner recorded a poor-selling solo album for Amaret Records; Denny Craswell returned to Minneapolis, where he now owns a recording studio with former band-mate Bob Folschow of the Castaways.

Shocking Blue

VENUS
(Robby van Leeuwen)
Colossus 108
No. 1 *February 7, 1970*

Dark-haired, brown-eyed, and lovely lead singer Mariska Veres (b. 1949) is the daughter of Lajos Veres, internationally-known gypsy violinist. "I really enjoy myself when I'm per-

forming," she once told *Hit Parader*. "I love to smile. And I am very happy when people smile back at me." As a little girl, the half-Hungarian/half-German Mariska accompanied her father on the piano. She later played in garage bands.

Shocking Blue was a Dutch group founded by lead guitarist/sitarist Robby van Leeuwen (b. 1944). Robby had been a member of the Motions, one of Holland's leading beat groups. In 1969, he lured drummer Cor van der Beek, bassist Klaasie van der Wal, and lead singer Fred de Wilde away from their band (Hu & The Hilltops) to form Shocking Blue. Pink Elephant Records signed the group and issued their first disk, "Lucy Brown Is Back In Town," which went to number 21 on the Dutch top 40.

While attending a party given to honor Golden Earring's first chart-topping homeland single, van Leeuwen spotted Mariska, then singing with the Bumble Bees, the evening's entertainment. That night, legend has it, Fred de Wilde was asked to leave Shocking Blue, and Mariska was asked to join. The group's next single, "Send Me A Postcard Darling," charted in Holland.

When "Venus," their third single, was clocking in at number three on the Dutch listings, American record producer Jerry Ross was there to sign Shocking Blue—plus the George Baker Selection and THE TEE SET—to a U.S. distribution deal via his Colossus label. Considering the odds, it's incredible that all three Dutch acts charted in the States with their debut disks. Baker's "Little Green Bag" (#21, 1970) and "Paloma Blancia" (#26, 1975) both went top 40, as did the Tee Set's "Ma Belle Amie" (#5, 1970).

Despite her charms, Ms. Veres and her band hit the American airwaves with only two more singles, "Mighty Joe" (#43, 1970) and "Long And Lonesome Road" (#75, 1970), the former a global million-seller. Ross continued to issue Shocking Blue sides in the States, although 45s like "Never Marry A Railroad Man" usually did better overseas. The group's lone stateside LP, *The Shocking Blue* (1970), sold a respectable number of copies. In 1974, Shocking Blue disbanded, apparently due to quarrels over van Leeuwen's inability to craft another "Venus."

In the mid-'70s, Robbie resurfaced with a folk- and jazz-inflected unit called Galaxy Inc. He also produced some solo sides on Ms. Veres. Neither projects garnered much notice. In 1984, Shocking Blue did reunite for two shows in a Back-to-the-'60s festival. Two years later, the strains of "Venus" were once again permeating the nation's airwaves—a cover version by Bananarama (#1, 1986) went all the way to the top of the charts.

Eddie Holman
HEY THERE LONELY GIRL
(Earl Shuman, Leon Carr)
ABC 11240
No. 2 *February 21, 1970*

With more than 20 years of recording history behind him, Eddie Holman is still best remembered for his soulful, falsettoed/sex-changed recycling of Ruby & The Romantics' big-time smoothie from 1963, "Hey There Lonely Boy."

Eddie was maneuvered toward a musical career not long after the third day in June, 1946, when he was born in Norfolk, Virginia. He was trained in the ways of sounds at the Victoria School of Music and Art in New York City, and later attended Cheyney State College in Philadelphia. While in Philly in 1965, Eddie connected with Parkway Records and won himself his first Hot 100 hit with "This Can't Be True" (#57, 1966). One more Parkway single, "Am I A Loser" (—/#17, 1966), rode onto the R & B listings before the label collapsed.

After a brief stay with Bell, Eddie hit his stride with ABC Records and arranger/producer Peter DeAngelis. Pete dressed Eddie's high-pitched voicings in the sticky-sweet

strings of the Philadelphia Symphony Orchestra. The first DeAngelis-Holman collaboration, "I Love You" (—/#30, 1969), was a fruitful one, but their second creation, "Hey There Lonely Girl," went almost to the pinnacle of popularity.

"[Peter] recommended I do the song," Holman told *Goldmine*'s Stu Fink. "I really didn't want to do it. The only reason I did is because my wife asked me to—and that's a very good reason."

"Don't Stop Now" (#48, 1970) b/w a take on the Skyliners' sorrowful "Since I Don't Have You" (#48) was a double-sided success; years later, Eddie's voice would once again grace the pop charts with "This Will Be A Night To Remember" (#90, 1977). In 1975, Holman's smash was re-released and soared to the top 10 in England. Eddie was still going strong through the '80s with recordings on the GSF, Silver Bird, Salsoul, and Agape labels.

Tee Set
MA BELLE AMIE
(Hans Van Eijck, Peter Tetteroo)
Colossus 107
No. 5 *March 14, 1970*

The Tee Set hailed from Delft, a tiny town in the Netherlands best known for its blue-and-white earthenware. When American pop producer Jerry Ross met these Dutch darlings, the Tee Set consisted of Pete Tetteroo (vocals), Dill Bennink (guitar, flute, banjo), Joop Blom (drums), Franklin Madjid (bass), and "Heavy" Hans Van Eijck (keyboards). Weeks earlier, Ross had stumbled onto Holland's SHOCKING BLUE, and in anticipation of a "Dutch Invasion," he signed up the Tee Set, the George Baker Selection, and a host of other Dutch acts. While Shocking Blue, the Tee Set, and the George Baker Selection did score some stateside success, other Dutch acts never dented a chart. By the end of 1970, the Dutch Invasion was essentially over.

The Tee Set had first assembled in 1966; their debut disk, "Early In The Morning," was a homeland hit. Many of their singles sold well in Denmark, Luxembourg, and other European rock regions. "Heavy" Hans, who had studied piano and composition at the Royal Conservatory, wrote tunes that were covered by the Spencer Davis Group and Germany's legendary Rattles. Lead singer Tetteroo recorded solo material concurrently with the group's platters; "Red Red Wine" was a winner in Holland. A handful of U.S. follow-ups to "Ma Belle Amie" appeared, including the tasty "She Likes Weeds"—the last song the Tee Set ever recorded.

Jaggerz

THE RAPPER
(Donnie Iris)
Kama Sutra 502
No. 2 *March 21, 1970*

The Jaggerz were a hard-workin' Pittsburgh bar band formed in the mid '60s. At the moment of their flash flight to fame, the Jaggerz were keyboardist/trumpeter Thom Davis (b. Duquesne, Penn.), guitarist/bassist Benny Faiella (b. Beaver Falls, Penn.), drummer/bassist Billy Maybray, drummer Jim Pugliano, trombonist/bassist Jimmy Ross (b. Aliquippa, Penn.), and lead singer/guitarist Dominic Ierace (b. Ellwood City, Penn.). Their individual roots dated back to the pre-Beatle years and bands with names like the Silvertones, the Starliners, and Donnie & The Donnells.

Joe Rock, manager of Jimmy Beaumont and the Skyliners, discovered the Jaggerz in a saloon one night. The story goes that without much effort, he convinced Kenny Gamble and Leon Huff, later kingpins in the creation of the "Philadephia Sound," to record the guys for the Gamble label. The resulting 1969 album (*Introducing the Jaggerz*) and several singles (notably "Baby I Love You," with Maybray singing lead) stiffed. Rock next approached Kama Sutra, brandishing one of Dominic's songs in particular. True, "The Rapper" has not aged with its colors flying, and is not a heavily-requested oldie, but at the time, "The Rapper" was a stone-cold smash.

Later sides like "I Call My Baby Candy" (#75, 1970) and "What A Bummer" (#88, 1970) did not do as well. Five years later, Wooden Nickel Records gave what remained of the Jaggerz another go-round in the studios, but the results were worse than could be expected.

Dominic Ierace, the group's voice and main tunesmith, changed his name to Donnie Iris. For a while, Iris was a member of WILD CHERRY. His subsequent solo career produced a string of Hot 100 hits from 1980–1985 and several LPs on MCA. Jimmy Ross is now a member of eternally touring Skyliners.

Edison Lighthouse

LOVE GROWS (WHERE MY ROSEMARY GOES)
(Tony Macaulay, Barry Mason)
Bell 858
No. 5 *March 28, 1970*

Just when it appeared that the bubblegum balloon had finally burst . . . just when the Ohio Express, 1910 Fruitgum Company, and all those other Kasenetz & Katz session creations had lost all their flavor and gone totally limp . . . along came Tony Burrows.

Tony, born and bred in England's West Country area, started out with the Kestrels, a Bristol-based beat group. Roger Cook and Roger Greenaway, the prolific pop tunesmiths who scored their own top 40 hit as DAVID & JONATHAN, were fellow members. When the Kestrels broke up in the mid-'60s, Burrows recorded with the Ivy League. As a member of the psychedelic Flowerpot Men, along with Perry Ford and Neil Landon (who later joined Noel Redding's Fat Mattress), Burrows had a British hit in 1967 with "Let's Go To San Francisco."

Flowerpot follow-ups failed to sufficiently freak people. With seven years of barrooms and ballrooms behind him, Tony called it quits and returned to what promised to be a sedate life with his wife and two children. But writer/producer Tony Macauley needed a session singer to bring to life a bubblegummy tune

Edison Lighthouse

251

called "Love Grows (Where My Rosemary Goes)," so he approached Burrows.

Once "Love Grows" and the "Edison Lighthouse" name were on the charts, Macauley faced the same problem that had historically plagued every packager of studio groups: finding a band that would tour under the monicker on the label. After auditioning 35 or more acts, Macauley settled on guitarist Ray Dorsey (b. Feb. 22, 1949, Berkshire), guitarist Stuart Edwards (b. May 18, 1949, Kent), bassist David Taylor (b. Oct. 7, 1950, High Wycombe) and drummer George Weyman (b. May 18, 1949, Kent). Together, these musicians had been appearing as the Greenfield Hammer. A few more Edison Lighthouse 45s were issued, but after the mild success of "It's Up To You Petula" (#72, 1971), the "Edison Lighthouse" name was retired; Dorey and the rest of his crew reverted to being Greenfield.

For Tony Burrows, Edison Lighthouse was only the beginning of a fruitful career as the lead singer for studio groups. He worked with the Brotherhood of Man ("United We Stand"), WHITE PLAINS ("My Baby Loves Lovin'"), and THE PIPKINS ("Gimme Dat Ding") for their 1970 hits. Macauley was so impressed with Burrows' vocal abilities that he signed him to a solo contract with Bell Records. Two years' worth of 45s issued under Tony's own name did so poorly that in 1974, Burrows returned to working sessions. As a member of THE FIRST CLASS, yet another pseudo-group of studio players, Burrows mounted the charts for a final time when the Beach Boys-esque "Beach Baby" nearly topped the pop charts.

The seemingly tireless Tony Burrows continues to do session work for artists like Elton John, Alan Price, Chris Spedding, and KIKI DEE.

Frijid Pink
THE HOUSE OF THE RISING SUN
(Alan Price)
Parrot 341
No. 7 *April 4, 1970*

Frijid Pink

When Motor City pop music is discussed, Berry Gordy's Motown empire springs to mind quicker than a hungry hound after a cheese-and-sausage pizza. "Detroit" might conjure thoughts of Bob Seger, self-proclaimed "Motor City Madman" Ted Nugent, John Sinclair's MC5, and Iggy Pop's psychedelic Stooges. Somewhat of the latter ilk—though neither as gifted nor as well-known—was Frijid Pink (when the band members were asked what the name meant, they replied "cold excellence"). Frijid Pink's hopped-up and fuzzified cover version of the Animals' 1964 hit was their briefly magical moment in pop music.

Organized in Detroit in the late '60s, the band initially consisted of lead screamer Kelly Green and high school buddies Gary Ray Thompson (lead guitar) and Thomas Beaudry (bass). Drummer Richard Stevens and keyboardist Larry Zelanka were recruited from a pool of local talent. All too soon, these Pink men were under contract with Parrot and ravaging the charts with their third single. "Sing A Song For Freedom" (#55, 1971) and "Heartbreak Hotel" (#72, 1971) followed their smash, but the next three 45s sold poorly. Whether the band might have developed into a top-flight act is unknown, for in 1972 most of the group's original core members departed.

In 1972, with Stevens and Zelanka remaining, Pink reorganized, signed with MGM's Lion subsidiary, and issued the *Earth Omen* album and two singles, all to little avail. In 1975, with only Stevens present, another reorganization generated a final but pedestrian package for Fantasy, *All Pink Inside*.

Norman Greenbaum

SPIRIT IN THE SKY
(Norman Greenbaum, Erik Jacobsen)
Reprise 0885
No. 3 *April 18, 1970*

While still in high school, Norman Greenbaum (b. Nov. 20, 1942, Malden, Mass.) picked up a guitar and started playing and singing folk songs. As a college student at Boston University, Norm worked the city's bongo parlors and java joints. In 1966, after years of this scene, Norm put together what surely must be one of the first psychedelic jug bands. Greenbaum, Jack Carrington, Evan Engber, and Bonnie Zee Wallach—collectively known as Dr. West's Medicine Show & Junk Band—would rub,

whack, or blow on such objects as a washtub, whiskey jug, Taiwan finger piano, Tibetan temple block, and their favorite, a 1949 Buick bumper bracket.

The Dr. West stage show featured the group shaking about with faces painted and bodies clad in multicolored garments, while projectors doused them with splotches of psychedelic color, man. Go Go Records caught the Dr. West act, and invited the gang to lay down oddball tunes like "Bullets LaVerne," "How Lew Sin Ate," "Gondoliers, Shakespeares, Playboys, and Bums," and "The Eggplant That Ate Chicago" (#52, 1966). Months later, the band split up.

Greenbaum moved to the City of Angels, and after some aborted efforts to reconstruct a jug band, he went solo. Norm was discovered by Erik Jacobsen while playing at the Troubador; Jacobsen was then producing the Lovin' Spoonful and Sopwith Camel. The quasi-religious "Spirit In The Sky" was one of several Greenbaum-Jacobsen efforts. Warner Bros. issued "Spirit" and an LP full of similarly neonutty sounds. The success of the single surprised everyone, including Norman, who did not have a touring band ready to take advantage of the disk's popularity. With his subsequent releases—"Canned Ham" (#46, 1970), "I.F. Fox," and "California Earthquake" (#93, 1971)—Greenbaum lost his momentum for good.

"I sat back, and I said, 'Well, I'm not a rock and roller," Greenbaum told *Creem*'s Ed Ward. "I got money—f*** it. And I went into the dairy business." Norman and his wife marketed their Velvet Acres Goat Milk in health-food stores in Berkeley and Marin County; he also recorded several acoustic and country-bent LPs for Reprise. He excitedly planned to tour in support of these latter efforts, but divorce proceedings soon left him in a funk. According to Jacobsen, Greenbaum's wife got the farm, and when last spotted, Norman was "living in a reconditioned chicken coop."

Michael Parks

LONG LONESOME HIGHWAY
(James Hendricks)
MGM 14104
No. 20 *April 18, 1970*

With an eye to the success of *Easy Rider*, NBC constructed a TV series about a youth, his motorcycle, and the search for the meaning

The Seventies

253

of life. Each week for a year, America watched stone-faced, alienated Jim Bronson as he moved about meeting faces and places and doin' his thing, man. While the series was warm, Mike had MGM Records issue his "Long Lonesome Highway." When the series left the scene, so did Mike's singing career.

Born on April 4, 1938, in Corona, California, Michael's real life was much like that of Jim Bronson. As a teen, he left home and took up odd jobs trying to get a fix on his place in the universe and a spot on the mammoth movie screen. During the '60s, he guested as off-beat characters on TV shows like "The Asphalt Jungle," "Bus Stop," and "The Detectives." In 1966, Mike played the nudie role of Adam in John Huston's *The Bible*. Other movie roles followed: *The Happening* (1967), *The Private Files of J. Edgar Hoover* (1977), and *The Evictors* (1979). In 1980, he did some episodes for a TV pilot called "Reward." The program was to be about an alienated cop. But alienation was no longer hip, and the series was shelved.

Marmalade
REFLECTIONS OF MY LIFE
(W. Campbell, T. McAleese)
London 20058
No. 10   *May 9, 1970*

Marmalade was formed in 1961 when two aspiring guitarists, Junior Wullie Campbell (b. July 24, 1946, Glasgow, Scotland) and Pat Fairley (b. Apr. 14, 1946, Glasgow), met in Glasgow. Pat and Junior recruited vocalist Dean Ford (b. May 31, 1947, Airdrie, Scotland), bassist Graham Knight (b. Dec. 8, 1946, Glasgow), and soon-to-depart drummer Raymond Duffy. Before Marmalade's sight and sound jelled, the unit was named the Gaylords. They quickly became quite popular in Scotland, and were voted the country's top group from 1964 to 1966.

Duffy left, and Alan Whitehead (b. July 24, 1947, Owestry, England) was whacking the skins by the time the group decided to move to London. Once settled there, they redubbed themselves Marmalade for a show-stopping appearance at the 1967 Windsor Jazz Festival. After a successful Thursday-night residency at the Marquee Club—where the Yardbirds, the Animals, and the Rolling Stones first earned their reputations—England's CBS label signed the group to a recording contract.

From 1968 through 1976, Marmalade could do little wrong with British fans. Almost a dozen of their singles became U.K. hits, and more than half of these reached the number-one slot (a cover of the Beatles' "Ob-La-Di, Ob-La-Da" sold a million copies). Ten albums were released, yet the moody "Reflections Of My Life" was the band's only excursion into the hallowed halls of stateside hitdom. Before Marmalade's success soured, "Rainbow" (#51, 1970) and "Falling Apart At The Seams" (#49, 1976) caused minor U.S. chart disturbances.

As of the mid-'80s, an edition of Marmalade was still actively working the London bars. A solid self-titled LP appeared in the U.S. on G & P Records in 1982, produced by Junior Campbell. By this point, Graham Knight was the only original member present. Junior had left the fold in 1972 to attend the Royal Academy of Music and to record with Fishbaugh Fishbaugh Zorn. He went on to cut a few solo albums and to score in England with two singles, "Sweet Illusion" and "Hallelujah Freedom." Dean Ford exited in 1974, did sessions for the Alan Parsons Project, and recorded an unsuccessful solo album; reportedly, he now works as a house painter in L.A.

Ides Of March
VEHICLE
(Jim Peterik)
Warner Bros. 7378
No. 2   *May 23, 1970*

Jim Peterik (lead vocals, guitar) was only 13 when he and some fellow high school students from Berwyn, Illinois, formed the Shondells. Peterik, Bob Bergland (guitar, sax, piano), Mike Borch (drums), and Larry Millas (bass, vocals) played Beatles tunes and recorded a one-off single for the Epitome label, "Like It Or Lump It." Paul Sampson, the owner of The Cellar—a converted warehouse known for featuring the Shadows of Knight, Saturday's Children, the Little Boy Blues, H.P. Lovecraft, and other garage bands—liked the spunky Shondell sound enough to let the guys play there as regulars. The catch was, they had to appear as Batman & The Boy Wonders.

"We did it," Peterik told *Chicago Sound* researcher Jeff Lind, "but when we showed up to play, we took the stage dressed liked everybody else in the audience. Sampson had to make up some kind of excuse for us, saying that our capes and masks were at the cleaners! It was our first experience with rock and roll hype."

Displeased with the Batman concept, the Shondells renamed themeselves the Ides of March, after the day of Julius Caesar's assassination. (All the guys were still in high school, studying Shakespeare's play.) They signed with Parrot Records for "You Wouldn't Listen" (#42, 1966), but because their labelmates were acts like Tom Jones, Them, and the Zombies, most listeners thought these infectious Ides were British. "We had to wear these really strange wigs and put on English accents whenever we were in public," Peterik complained. "Roller Coaster" (#92, 1966) did all right, but three other 45s for Parrot failed to connect. Recast as a horn band—with Ray Herr (vocals, keyboards), John Larson (horns), and Chuck Somar (horns)—the Ides switched to Warner Bros; "Vehicle" was their second single.

"The idea for the song," Peterik explained, "came from the stereotype [of the] dirty old man, cruising the streets in his black sedan and enticing little girls by offering them candy. Also, my mother showed me this anti-drug pamphlet that depicted the drug pusher as a 'friendly stranger.' So, I put those things together and came up with 'Vehicle.' "

"Superman" (#64, 1970), basically a remodeled "Vehicle," was a solid follow-up, but the Ides were being pegged as a horn band or jazz-rockers. Peterik and Herr were at odds over the band's musical direction, and the guys were now college students. The following year, another sound change was made with the folk-flavored "L.A. Goodbye" (#73, 1971). When further 45s flopped, the group moved to RCA for several albums and singles. They played their last set before screaming teens in a high school gymnasium one November night in 1973.

Bergland became an accountant. Borch joined a group called M.S. Funk. Herr appeared in various local acts, such as the Orphanage, Scott & Stevens, and Showboat. Larry Millas and John Somar got together in 1974 with Tom Dooley of the Cryan' Shames to form the Ides/Shames Reunion. Thereafter, Millas became an engineer and part-owner of Chicago's Tanglewood Studios.

Peterik had some solo work issued by Epic. His Chi-Rhythm band later evolved into one of the Midwest's biggest name acts. As Survivor, the Peterik band has charted repeatedly throughout the '80s—with soundtrack hits like "Eye Of The Tiger" (#1, 1982) for *Rocky III*, "The Moment Of Truth" (#63, 1984) for *The Karate Kid*, and "Burning Heart" (#2, 1986) for *Rocky IV*.

White Plains
MY BABY LOVES LOVIN'
(Roger Cook, Roger Greenaway)
Deram 85058
No. 13 *June 27, 1970*

White Plains was a one-off grouping of British sessioneers assembled by producers Roger Cook and Roger Greenaway. Recording as DAVID & JONATHAN, Cook and Greenaway had secured their own niche as a one-hit wonder act with "Michelle" (#18, 1966). More importantly, the two Rogers were a formidable songwriting duo throughout the '60s and '70s, penning hits for artists like CAROL DOUGLAS, EDISON LIGHTHOUSE, the English Congregation, the Fortunes, the Hollies, the New Seekers, THE PIPKINS, and WHISTLING JACK SMITH.

Fronting White Plains was Tony Burrows, a one-time member of the British hitmakers Ivy League and the Flowerpot Men. Earlier in 1970, Burrows had fronted two pseudogroups, the Brotherhood of Man and Edison Lighthouse, and would move on to contribute to two similarly studio-bound units—the Pipkins ("Gimme Dat Ding") and FIRST CLASS ("Beach Baby").

White Plains' immediate follow-up to "My Baby Loves Lovin" was "Lovin' My Baby," which charted at number 82 in 1970. Nothing further issued in the U.S. even so much as hinted at hitdom, though British record-buyers were much more receptive—nearly half a dozen more pop puffs by White Plains left their marks on the U.K. charts.

Blues Image
RIDE CAPTAIN RIDE
(Frank Konte, Carlos Pinera)
Atco 6746
No. 4 *July 11, 1970*

They were high school friends, all born and raised in Tampa, Florida—percussionist Manuel Bertematti (b. 1946), drummer Joe Lala, and lead singer/guitarist Mike Pinera (b. Sept.

Blues Image

29, 1948). Beginning in the mid-'60s, they performed together at local functions. It wasn't, however, until after they graduated, and after Joey had worked for a while as a barber, that the threesome met bassist Malcolm Jones (b. Cardiff, Wales) and the idea of a Latin-like blues band became a reality. Malcolm was a pro, had spent ten years in bands in Wales, and was now settled in the States as the DJ for an underground radio program called "The London Scene."

They toured about the East Coast, and even touched down in Europe, presenting their evolving blues blend. For a while, they ran a psychedelic hangout in Tampa called Dino's. Keyboardist Frank "Skip" Konte (b. Canyon City, Okla.)—Alaskan-raised philosophy dropout, and one-time welder and sign-painter—joined early in 1968. By year's end, the group was based in New York City, where they ran a club in a converted bowling alley called The Image. Besides offering their own performances, the Blues Image booked acts like the Mothers of Invention, the Lovin' Spoonful, and Cream.

Reps from Atlantic Records spotted the troupe at the Whiskey-A-Go-Go in 1968. A first album, *Blues Image*, was issued in 1969; it was quickly followed by *Open* (1970). *Open* featured what would become the group's singular single of significance, "Ride Captain Ride." But with success came dissension: Pinera left to join Iron Butterfly, so singer Dennis Correll and guitarist Kent Henry were brought in. Before the name was shelved, one more LP—*Red, White and Blues Image* (1971)—was patched together.

In the early '70s, Pinera and Bertematti recorded with the New Cactus Band. Thereafter, Mike recorded with Ramatram, his own Thee Image, and in the early '80s, with Alice Cooper. Jones moved to England, where he did studio work with Pink Floyd's Syd Barrett and the Soft Machine's Kevin Ayers. Konte has since recorded with Brooklyn Dreams, Cold Blood, and Three Dog Night. Lala has hardly been out of the studio limelight, having played with artists like the Bee Gees, Jackson Browne, Harry Chapin, John Cougar Mellencamp, Crosby, Stills, Nash & Young, Rick Derringer, and others.

Five Stairsteps

O-O-H CHILD
(Stan Vincent)
Buddah 165
No. 8 *July 18, 1970*

Clarence Burke, Sr., a Chicago policeman, had been stabbed and shot twice in the line of duty, and considered himself fortunate to be alive. He was the father of five when the idea struck him. Mrs. Burke had been lining her offspring up on the couch and teaching them to sing along with TV commercials and pop records. Stepping back to view them, she remarked, "They look just like stairsteps." In 1965, when the quality of the harmonizing had improved, Papa entered his brood in a contest at the famed Regal Theatre. They sang, they danced, and they walked off with first prize.

While shopping in a neighborhood grocery, Papa boasted about his kids to Fred Cash, a guy he knew from way back. What he didn't know was that Cash was now a member of the Impressions. Cash offered to set up an audition for the Five Stairsteps with his boss, Curtis Mayfield. Curtis liked what he heard, and before long, the group—guitarist Clarence, Jr. (b. May 25, 1949), guitarist James (b. Sept. 19, 1950), guitarist/drummer Dennis (b. 1952), bassist Kenny (b. Sept. 28, 1953), and Alohe "Lannie" (b. 1948), the group's eldest and the only female—was an overnight success.

"You Waited Too Long" (#94/16, 1966), the flip side of their first release for Windy C, did well with R & B listeners, like nearly every disk right up until their double-sided monster masterpiece, "O-o-h Child" b/w "Dear Prudence." Up until this point, they billed themselves as "America's First Family of Soul." Thereafter, things changed.

Mr. and Mrs. Burke eventually had 11 children. The group's line-up fluctuated constantly. Little Cubie (b. 1966) was added: he would make sounds, prance, and wet his pants. Pop even slapped the bass and sang lead. But more threatening to the group's credibility were their unsuccessful forays into pop and rock, which created internal conflicts about musical direction.

The family group splintered in the early '70s. In 1976, some members regrouped for an album, *Second Resurrection*, and a few singles for George Harrison's Dark Horse label. "From Us To You" (—/#10) did quite well on *Billboard*'s R & B listings, but the revised edition was short-lived.

In 1980, Clarence, Dennis, James, and Kenny returned as The Invisible Man's Band with "All Night Long" (#45/9). Kenny (now spelled "Keni") left to forge a promising solo career: to date, he has had some mild R & B chartings: "Let Somebody Love You" (—/#66, 1981) and "Risin' To the Top" (—/#63, 1983).

Pipkins

GIMME DAT DING
(Albert Hammond, Mike Hazelwood)
Capitol 2819
No. 9 *July 18, 1970*

The Pipkins were a one-off grouping of British sessioneers, assembled by producer John Burgess. During the '60s, John had helped create hit disks for Freddie & The Dreamers, Manfred Mann, Peter & Gordon, and Adam Faith. Soon after "Gimme Dat Ding," Burgess would assemble yet another studio group, the English Congregation.

Handling lead vocals for the Pipkins was Tony Burrows, a onetime member of two British groups, the Ivy League and the Flowerpot Men. Burrows pops up quite frequently singing with studio units. Earlier in 1970, Burrows had appeared on "Love Grows (Where My Rosemary Goes)" by EDISON LIGHTHOUSE, "United We Stand" by the Brotherhood of Man, and on "My Baby Loves Lovin'" by WHITE PLAINS. Post-Pipkins, he would apply his vocal wares to "Beach Baby," a 1974 hit for FIRST CLASS.

"Gimme Dat Ding" was an Albert Hammond and Mike Hazelwood composition commissioned for a British TV show for children, *Oliver and the Underworld*. While "Yakety Yak" and further singles by the Pipkins failed to chart, such was not the case for Albert Hammond. Albert had scored in 1968 as a member of the Magic Lanterns ("Shame Shame") and would have later pop success with "It Never Rains in Southern California" (#5, 1972) and "I'm A Train" (#31, 1974).

Miguel Rios

A SONG OF JOY
(HIMNO A LA ALEGRIA)
(Orbe-W. De Los Rios)
A & M 1193
No. 14   *July 18, 1970*

Family and friends say that Miguel (b. 1944, Granada, Spain) started singing when he was six. Two years later, he was a member of his school choir. Once his school days were behind him, he formed a rock group that worked the local bars. A record man with the Hispavox label let the lad cut a commemorative number, with composer/conductor Waldo De Los Rios' Orchestra, for the bicentennial of Beethoven's birth. De Los Rios and someone named Orbe had concocted a mammoth production of the last movement of Beethoven's Ninth Symphony, complete with a huge chorus and a host of instruments.

After Ludwig's immortal melody worked its way through the world's pop charts, Miguel's popularity was mostly limited to his homeland. But the following year, Waldo returned to *Billboard*'s listings with his own pop treatment, "Mozart's Symphony No. 40 in G Minor K 550, First Movement" (#67, 1971). His album, *Sinfonias* (1971), also sold well.

Waldo De Los Rios died on March 28, 1977.

Miguel Rios

Pacific Gas & Electric

ARE YOU READY?
(Charlie Allen, John Hill)
Columbia 45158
No. 14   *August 1, 1970*

Not well known, they were a long-haired experiment in tolerance and love. That's how Frank Cook, the band's drummer, has described Pacific Gas & Electric. "We think of PG & E as not just a music group, but a brotherhood," Cook explained in the liner notes on the group's first album. "We've found that if there is a bad karma going down between any members of the group, the music does not fall together." Eventually, the inevitable "bad karma" was the band's downfall.

Formed early in 1968, at the peak of the San Francisco peace + love phenomenon, the band consisted of Charlie Allen (lead vocals), Brent Block (bass), Tom Marshall (guitar), Glenn Schwartz (guitar), and Canned Heat alumnus Frank Cook (drums). "A Jew, a Christian, a black, a greaser, and a WASP" was Cook's description. "Five more different and divergent personalities could not be conceived of."

In 1969, Bright Orange Records issued an album of their blues- and gospel-influenced rock sounds, *Get It On*. Months later, Columbia Records took great notice of the thunderous applause the act received for their four performances at the optimistically-titled First Annual Miami Pop Festival. The event was a success in generating revenues, good vibes, and a Columbia contract for PG & E. It would, however, be the last such three-day affair (December 28-30, 1968) in the state.

A truncated-for-radio version of "Are You Ready?" from the brotherhood's second Columbia LP (*Are You Ready?*) proved to be a winner. While a few other 45s—"Father Come On Home" (#93, 1970), "Thank God For You Baby" (#97, 1972)—gathered some interest, and a fourth LP (*PG & E*, 1971) sold fairly well, all was not well within the fold. Guns were drawn and shots fired after a gig at the Cat's Eye, a reported redneck room in Raleigh, North Carolina. The band's lead guitarist swore off drugs, found God, and unwittingly had the group barred from Canada when he confessed to his former drug habit. Various personnel changes resulted and "bad karma" was now pervasive. After their final effort, *The Best of PG & E*, Pacific Gas & Electric, in the words of one record-company rep, "went the way of all rock and roll flesh."

Charlie did resurrect the band's name for a one-off album (*Pacific Gas and Electric, Starring Charlie Allen*) on Dunhill in 1973. No other original brothers were in attendance.

Alive And Kicking

TIGHTER, TIGHTER
(Tommy James, Bob King)
Roulette 7078
No. 7   *August 8, 1970*

"**I** should have recorded that—it was my song," claimed Tommy James, the undisputed bubblegum king, in an exclusive interview. "But, I'll tell ya, I decided that I had taken it as far as I could take it. I was a burn-out. Matter of fact, I played Montgomery, Alabama, and that's when it happened—I conked out on stage. I just wasn't interested in doing anything anymore."

Alive and Kicking was a late-'60s Big Apple-based band fronted by two vocalists, Pepe Cardona and Sandy Toder. They accrued a solid reputation as a happening band by playing clubs like the Bitter End and the Electric Circus. Pepe, Sandy, and the rest—Vito Albano (drums), John Parisio (guitar), Bruce Sudano (organ), and Thomas "Woody" Wilson (bass)— soon came to the attention of their producer and mentor, Tommy James.

"He came to see us at this Hullaballoo club in Brooklyn," Pepe recalled in an exclusive interview. "Man, he loved us, and decided to give us this song, 'Crystal Blue Persuasion.' That was nice, but then he changed his mind, saying, 'Don't worry, I'll write something else for you guys, 'cause I want this one.' It was disappointing, 'cause we had worked it up, the vocals and all, then 'No, I'll write you another one.'"

After a lay-off from the Shondells of some months, Tommy and writing partner Bob King went into the studios to tape some Tommy James solo sides. Tommy wanted out of the teenybopper image of Tommy James & The Shondells, yet his own singles, which began appearing in 1970, did not sound too dissimilar from his Tommy James & The Shondells 45s.

Tommy wrote and produced "Tighter, Tighter," with an arrangement by Jimmy Wisner (of KOKOMO), for Alive and Kicking. James' career would experience something of a second coming with the charting of "Draggin' The Line" (#4, 1971), "I'm Comin' Home" (#40, 1971), and "Nothing To Hide" (#41, 1971), but Alive and Kicking died after the

release of one self-titled LP and two flawed, Tommy James-less 45s, "Just Let It Come" (#69, 1970) and "Good Lovin' Back Home."

Why couldn't the group have James write some more tunes for them? "Well, we were real cocky," Pepe explained. "We thought that 'Tighter, Tighter' was too bubblegum. We were really long-haired and doing all original material, and we wanted to go into more heavy rock. Tommy felt we ought to come out with something along the lines of 'Tighter.' We didn't want to do it, so then Tommy didn't want to record us anymore.

"We did three singles and that one LP and broke up just after that last single. They didn't even put our names on the back of the album; it was terrible. We finally had to break up just to get away from Morris Levy [owner of the Roulette label].

"I lost track of Sandy. For a long time after, she was trying to make it on her own—she did a little off-Broadway and a play, but I lost contact. In 1976, I re-formed the group with Vito Albano and Woody Wilson. We're still doin' it, five nights a week in the New York area. Basically, we do covers [of current hits], but we each have our own projects. I have this remake of 'Tighter, Tighter' that I'd like to get released."

John Parisio has recently resurfaced in the Lynch Boys Band; Bruce Sudano, who married Donna Summer, has had some solo sides issued in the '80s by Millenium and has experienced some success with his trio, Brooklyn Dreams.

Eric Burdon & War

SPILL THE WINE
(Howard Scott, Morris Dickerson, Harold Brown, Charles Miller, Lonnie Jordan, Sylvester Allen, Lee Oscar Levitin)
MGM 14118
No. 3   *August 22, 1970*

As lead singer of the Animals, Eric Burdon (b. May 11, 1941, Walker-on-Tyne, England) had helped create some of the finest R & B–based British Invasion records. After a string of hits like "House Of The Rising Sun," "Don't Let Me Be Misunderstood," "It's My Life," and "We Gotta Get Out Of This Place," Eric discovered LSD and led his New Animals through a psychedelic love-and-peace phase. Gentler and softer singles followed: "San Francisco

Nights," "Monterey," "Anything." In 1968, Burdon announced that the album *Love Is* would be the group's final record, and soon dropped out of sight.

Meanwhile, an early incarnation of War— a group called either the Creators, the Romeos, or Senior Soul—was cutting unsuccessful sides. When Eric ran into them in L.A. in 1969, the band, redubbed Night Shift, consisted of percussionist Sylvester "Papa Dee" Allen (b. July 19, 1931), drummer Harold Brown (b. Mar. 17, 1946), bassist B.B. Dickerson (b. Aug. 3, 1949), keyboardist Lonnie Jordan (b. Nov. 21, 1948), saxophonist Charles Miller (b. June 2, 1939), and guitarist Howard Scott (b. Mar. 15, 1946).

"We were playing in North Hollywood with Deacon Jones, the football-player-turned-singer," Harold Brown recalled to *Rolling Stone*. "One night we were sitting around wait-

ing for the star to arrive. He never did show up, but Eric Burdon and [harmonica virtuoso] Lee Oskar [b. Mar. 24, 1948, Denmark], a musician from Copenhagen, did. Lee got up there and we started doing this shuffle, it must have lasted about 40 or 45 minutes . . . When it was over, everybody's mind was blown."

The next day, Eric invited Night Shift over to his manager Jerry Goldstein's pad in Benedict Canyon. Burdon offered the guys co-billing if they would work for him as his back-up band. They agreed; Goldstein and his partner, Steve Gold, renamed the band War.

"We started doing road shows with Eric— and I mean road shows in the real sense of the word. We took seven band members plus our road manager, and a trailer on the back of a '66 Ford station wagon that was knocking before we even left California. We did that for two years."

Eric Burdon & War

Eric Burdon & War crafted a soulful mix of Latin, funk, and jazz. Success finally materialized with "Spill The Wine" and its follow-up, "They Can't Take Away Our Music" (#50, 1971). Their collaboration generated two best-selling albums, *Eric Burdon Declares War* (1970) and *The Black Man's Burdon* (1970), but problems with the MGM label beset the group.

"Right to this day [1973], I haven't seen any kind of statements or money from MGM," Brown complained. "Steve [Gold] decided that he wasn't going to let MGM have us, especially since they already had Eric all tied up. So we became the first group in the history of the record business to get a gold record who wasn't signed to a record company."

During a 1971 European tour with the group, an exhausted Burdon departed. Steve Gold negotiated a contract for War with United Artists, and later that year, they released *War*. Burdon moved on to pursue a low-keyed solo career, while War scored on the charts with 45s like "Slippin' Into Darkness," (#16, 1972), "The World Is A Ghetto (#17, 1973), "Cisco Kid" (#2, 1973), "Low Rider" (#1, 1975), and "Why Can't We Be Friends?" (#6, 1975).

In 1976, MCA Records issued *Love Is All Around*, a collection of Burdon & War outtakes and leftovers.

Robin McNamara

LAY A LITTLE LOVIN' ON ME
(Jeff Barry, Robin McNamara, Jim Cretecos)
Steed 724
No. 11 *August 22, 1970*

Not much is known about this Robin fellow. He was one of the original cast members of *Hair*, and one of the longest-lasting members, too. We don't know when or where he was born, what he did before becoming a hairy guy, or what he has done since. But while he was a hairy guy, he met songwriting legend Jeff Barry, who was starting up a new record label and in need of talent. Together, they grooved and groomed nearly a dozen tunes. "Lay A Little Lovin' On Me" was one of those creations. A lot of the brothers and sisters bought that record, and it almost smoked its way into the Establishment's top 10.

"Got To Believe In Love" (#80, 1970)—a follow-up recorded with the cast of *Hair*—sold only a few copies, and Rob and Steed Records rode off into the sunset.

Assembled Multitude

OVERTURE FROM TOMMY (A ROCK OPERA)
(Pete Townshend)
Atlantic 2737
No. 16 *August 29, 1970*

Thomas Coleman Sellers (bass, keyboards) was born and raised in Wayne, Pennsylvania. Back in Wayne 39 years later, on March 9, 1988, he died in a freak fire in his parents' home. Tom's career saw him labor as an arranger, producer, songwriter, singer, and musician.

In the mid-'60s, Tom became involved with ex-Spokesman John Madara's production company as a songwriter. Madara matched Sellers up with Daryl Hall, Jim Helmer, and Tim Moore. They all recorded together as Gulliver. Madara placed an album of these playable and now-rare tracks with Elektra. Nothing much happened, and by year's end, the group was no more.

The Assembled Multitude was a studio conception. Sellers rounded up some of what would later become MFSB and slapped together some orchestrated reworkings of a theme from the Who's *Tommy* album, Crosby, Stills, Nash & Young's "Woodstock" (#79, 1970), and a medley of jewels from "Jesus Christ Superstar" (#95, 1971).

When the Assembled concept had worn itself out, Tom dismantled the Multitude and returned to the studios to produce sessions for Eric Anderson, Chubby Checker, Millington, Essra Mohawk, SILVER, and others.

During the mid-'70s, Sellers worked in New York City for Radio Band of America, composing and arranging radio and TV commercials. Just prior to his death, he had formed his own production company.

Mungo Jerry

IN THE SUMMERTIME
(Ray Dorset)
Janus 125
No. 3 *September 12, 1970*

Ray Dorset (vocals, guitar, casaba, feet) was born March 21, 1946, in Ashton, England. For years, Ray played any kind of music that might put food on his table. In 1968, "Mungo" Dorset was a member of a starving London-based

Mungo Jerry

soon added to the roll call. A magazine plea for a manager garnered the group sometime-producer Barry Murray. After Mungo Jerry successfully opened for Traffic and the Grateful Dead at London's Hollywood Music Festival, Murray was able to secure a contract for the group with England's Dawn label. "In The Summertime" was their debut disk, and the first of what would total a towering 10 top 40 45s in their homeland. In England, they were a pop phenomenon; pundits talked of "Mungo-mania" and publicity hand-outs labeled them "The New Beatles."

"What we're about," Dorset said to a *Circus* interviewer, "is everybody getting up and jumping about. We just want everybody to be happy." Yet Americans soon wearied of jumping up and dancing. Singles and albums chock-full of cheerfully cheesy Mungo shuffles appeared well into the '70s, but nothing sold worth a darn. Eventually, a despondent Dorset dissolved the band.

Ernie

RUBBER DUCKIE
(Jeffery Moss)
Columbia 45207
No. 16 *September 26, 1970*

Since childhood, Jim Henson (b. Sept. 24, 1936, Greenville, Miss.) had been fascinated by puppets. With glee, he followed the adventures of Edgar Bergen and Charlie McCarthy as well as the "Kukla, Fran & Ollie" characters. While a senior in high school, he had a TV program on a local Maryland station. In college, Jim and his future wife, Jane Nebel, presented a series called "Sam and Friends" over WRC-TV in Washington.

In the late '50s and early '60s, Jim and his Muppets (a combination of *m*arionettes and *puppets*) made TV commercials and appeared on "The Perry Como Show," "The Ed Sullivan Show," and "The Tonight Show." Beginning in 1967, Jim became affiliated with the Children's Television Workshop. By the fall of 1969, the company was ready to unveil "Sesame Street," a groundbreaking program destined to become what Alex McNeil, author of *Total Television*, has called "the most important children's show in the history of television." Central to this success were Jim's Muppets—Big Bird, Cookie Monster, Bert, Ernie, Grover, and Oscar the Grouch.

In addition to teaching children the alphabet

progressive-pop band called Camino Real. Their future looked bleak, when out of the blue, things took a turn for the worse. The band's bass player walked off, and Dorset sacked the drummer—but replacements couldn't be found in time for a gig at Oxford University.

Ray and his diminished Camino cluster, bass-less and drum-less, nonetheless put on a fine show. Dorset, piano man Colin Earl (b. May 6, 1942, Hampton Court, England), and a washboard player named Jo Rush explored the terrain of their new musical turf as The Good Earth Rock & Roll Band. Before he left the group, Rush turned them on to the sounds of Leadbelly, Willie Dixon, and Britain's banjo-beating skiffle king, Lonnie Donegan.

A "goodtime"/jug band/country-blues sound was coming together. Banjo-picking and jug-blowing Paul King (b. Jan. 8, 1948, Dagenham, England) and the bass-bashing Mike Cole were

and numbers, Jim presented beguilingly informative skits and songs. One of these told of the joyous relationship between a mite Muppet and his "Rubber Duckie." Jim Henson is the voice of the innocent and mischievous Ernie, the song's star. Over the years, a number of spin-off albums have been issued. Only one other Muppet, however, has earned the distinction of placing a tune on the nation's top 40 charts—Kermit the Frog, with "Rainbow Connection" (#25, 1979).

Jim Henson passed away on May 16, 1990, from pneumonia. He was 53 years old.

Free

ALL RIGHT NOW
(Paul Rodgers, Andy Fraser)
A & M 1206
No. 4   *October 17, 1970*

Guitarist Paul "Koss" Kossoff (b. Sept. 14, 1950, London) and drummer Simon Kirke (b. July 28, 1948, Shropshire, England) were unhappy playing in a band called Black Cat Bones. When they happened to catch a glimpse of lead singer Paul Rodgers (b. Dec. 14, 1949, Middlesbrough, England) fronting Brown Sugar, they knew he would fit into a new band they were hoping to create. A mutual friend introduced the three to 15-year-old Andy Fraser (b. Aug. 7, 1952, London), then playing bass in John Mayall's Bluesbreakers. Andy was not keen on the jazzy direction that Mayall was moving toward, and agreed to drop by and jam with the other three.

"We were just a bunch of kids who loved rock and roll and the blues," said Kirke to *Circus'* Andy Secher. "When we got together, the oldest of us was 20, and while that might have been the reason we had a great deal of inner turmoil, it also helped us sacrifice just about everything for that music."

The British blues institution Alexis Korner gave the guys the name "Free" and walked them into Island Records and a contract. The band's first two LPs—*Tons of Sobs* (1968) and *Free* (1969)—passed by both U.K. and U.S. audiences without much notice. Album three, *Fire and Water* (1970), contained something just too fine to be ignored by anyone, even by those who only listened to top 40 radio. "All Right Now" had a pulsating, electric sound, packed with blues power and rock excitement. Rodgers was gritty, the riff was contagious, and Kossoff's guitar was hot.

"There was a purity to what we were doing that was very special," Kirke explained. "We weren't that concerned with making hit records, and we weren't jaded by the industry— we just wanted to keep everything as simple as possible."

Highway (1971), their next LP, offered "Stealer" (#52, 1971) as a single. The boys would never make the stateside pop/rock 45 listings again, though British fans would later rechart the group name with takes on "My Brother Jake," "Little Bit Of Love," and "Wishing Well."

Free ran its course. Their label packaged a live set *(Free Live*, 1971). Rodgers went off and formed Peace; Kossoff formed Toby. Both efforts were short-lived. Kossoff then rejoined Kirke to record an instrumental LP with Tetsu Yamauchi and John "Rabbit" Bundrick called *Kossoff Kirke Tetsu and Rabbit* (1971).

The original band members reunited for one explosive occasion and a resulting album, *Free at Last* (1972). Fraser departed, then Rodgers dropped out. Rabbit and Tetsu functioned as

Free

replacements for the band's last effort, *Heartbreaker* (1973). Rodgers and Kirke formed Bad Company and carried on for another decade or more. Fraser joined the Sharks and later fronted his own Andy Fraser Group; Rabbit recorded with Pete Townshend and toured with the Who; Tetsu joined Rod Stewart's Faces.

Paul Kossoff, possibly the group's most talented individual and certainly one of rock's most distinctive guitarists, formed Back Street Crawler, but died on March 19, 1976, of a drug-induced heart attack.

R. Dean Taylor

INDIANA WANTS ME
(R. Dean Taylor)
Rare Earth 5013
No. 5 *November 11, 1970*

Born in 1939 in Toronto, little Dean set his sights on becoming a country singer. Rock and roll didn't officially exist yet, but when it did, Dean was ready. In 1960, under the influence of Jerry Lee Lewis, Taylor recorded a rough tune entitled "At The High School Dance." A Canadian label, Parry Records, released the rocker and at least two follow-up singles. The kid must have been ripe and on to something, because in 1964 Mala Records in the U.S. decided to pick up his second single, the two-year-old "It's A Long Way To St. Louis," for release.

Between 1965 and 1973, Taylor occasionally released singles on Motown's VIP and Rare Earth labels. From Motown's point of view, Dean was present primarily to co-write hit songs like "Love Child" and "I'm Living On Shame" for the Supremes, as well as "I'll Turn To Stone" and "You Keep Turning Away" for the Temptations. Taylor has claimed that he was "shafted" by the label when songs that he wrote were listed on the label as the creations of others. He also worked as part of the Clan and the Corporation production teams. These gatherings, comprising Taylor, Jeffery Bowen, Marc Gordon, Hal Davis, Freddie Perren, Deke Richards, and Frank Wilson, were called in to fill the void at Motown when the Holland-Dozier-Holland songwriting team and production company walked out on the label.

With all the pressure to keep the Hitsville production line rolling, not much attention was apparently given to the production work-up Dean was preparing for some of his self-penned tunes. One of these, "Indiana Wants Me," was the tale of a critter on the lam for murdering a fellow who says something foul about the critter's lady. Dean followed this vacuous ode with three more mournful situations that each charted the lower reaches of the Hot 100. The last one, "Taos New Mexico" (#83, 1972), is about a poor thief serving time in the Big House, feeling sorry for himself.

Shortly after this last release, Taylor separated from the Motown empire to set up Jane Records, and issued one single, "Bonnie." No one is known to have actually heard this record, or to know what it is about. A few years later, another 45 surfaced on the Farr label, only to vanish without a trace. Apparently, Dean had served his time in the spotlight, and neither Indiana nor any of the other 49 states wanted him any longer.

One Hundred Proof Aged In Soul

SOMEBODY'S BEEN SLEEPING
(Greg Perry, General Johnson, Angelo Bond)
Hot Wax 7004
No. 8 *November 14, 1970*

Clyde Wilson was born in Walhall, South Carolina, on Christmas morning, 1945. By 1954, he and his family were living in Detroit. Clyde, along with Wilbert Jackson, were signed by Harvey Fuqua to his HPC label as the Two Friends. Fuqua, former lead singer of the Moonglows, would later give the Spinners the opportunity to record their debut disk, and would also be the main force behind New Birth, Sylvester, and the Nite-Liters. Unfortunately for Clyde and Wilbert, Fuqua's magic did not work well for them: "Just Too Much To Hope For" was a flop.

Years later, Don Davis invited Clyde to record for his Wheelsville/Groovesville/Groove City labels. Davis suggested that Clyde become "Steve Mancha." Clyde acquiesced, and shortly after, the Mancha man made the R & B charts with "I Don't Wanna Lose You" (—/#34, 1966) and "Don't Make Me A Story Teller" (—/#34, 1967).

When Clyde's contract ran out, the Motor City souls at Holland-Dozier-Holland's newly-established Hot Wax/Invictus complex enticed Clyde to join a Four Tops-ish unit to be called 100 Proof Aged In Soul. The original line-up included Clyde, Eddie Holiday, and Joe Stubbs (brother of the Four Tops' Levi Stubbs, and a veteran of THE FALCONS and THE CONTOURS). Before disagreements and mutiny set in, the Aged in Soul singers recorded "Too Many Cooks (Spoil The Soup)" (#94/28, 1969) but hit the big time with "Somebody's Been Sleeping." Two other raunchy recordings clicked: "One Man's Leftovers (Is Another Man's Feast)" (#96/37, 1971) and "Driveway" (—/#33, 1971).

It was just as "Sleeping" topped out that the original group folded. Clyde reformed the group with guitarist Ron Byowski, percussionist Dave Case, drummer Darnell Hagen, and bassist Don Hatcher. "90 Day Freeze" (—/#34, 1971) and "Everything Good Is Bad" (#45/15, 1972) sold quite well, but successive 45s failed to chart. In 1973, the group's name was shelved, and Steve Mancha returned to being Clyde Wilson, a gospel singer and producer for Heavy Faith Records.

Bobby Bloom

MONTEGO BAY
(Jeff Barry, Bobby Bloom)
L & R/MGM 157
No. 8 *November 28, 1970*

Shortly after Bobby Bloom's career had blossomed and seemingly withered, he was killed by a spray of bullets in an accidental shooting. His essentially behind-the-scenes 15-year career began in 1961, when he had two unsuccessful but now quite collectible singles with his group, the Imaginations, released for the Music Makers label. His craft germinated in the mid-'60s when—in various affiliations with John Linde, Peter Andreoli, Vinnie Poncia, Jr., and the legendary Jeff Barry—he wrote tunes, produced records, and worked as a sessions singer. Bloom filled in for THE MUSIC EXPLOSION's lead vocalist on one of their last recordings, "Where Are We Going." Bloom was also the voice for Captain Groovy and His Bubblegum Army on their lone and quite forgettable number, "The Bubblegum March."

On several occasions, Bobby had tried to establish himself as a solo act; in 1967, he recorded some blue-eyed soul for Kama Sutra. The only single released, "Love Don't Let Me Down," stiffed, as did the 1969 White Whale release, "All I Wanna Do Is Dance."

In 1970, bubblegum producers Joey Levine and Artie Resnick formed L & R Records. Bloom's first release for the novice label was

Bobby Bloom

the culmination of his efforts—"Montego Bay" finally made Bobby Bloom a household word. The Staple Singers' cover version of "Heavy Makes You Happy," a tune he co-authored with Jeff Barry, made the Hot 100 in February 1971. Two more Bloom singles and a couple of sides from the 1967 Kama Sutra sessions also charted on the Hot 100 before Bobby's sudden death on February 28, 1974.

Presidents

5-10-15-20 (25-30 YEARS OF LOVE)
(Tony Boyd, Archie Powell)
Sussex 207
No. 11 *December 26, 1970*

None of their former labels, nor usually knowledgeable industry heads, could tell us much about the Presidents. While they did sell some records, they received scant coverage in the media. So here is what little could be gleaned: Tony Boyd, Archie Powell, and Billy Shorter were from Washington (others insist that they were from Philadelphia). Before their limited success on Sussex, they had recorded for Hollywood (1968) and Deluxe (1969–1970, with

"Gold Walk," "Which Way," and "Lover's Psalm"). Possibly, they are the same Presidents that recorded for Warner Bros. in 1961 and sang "Pots & Pans" for Mercury the following year.

Only four 45s are known to have been issued by the group while on Sussex: "For You" (—/#45, 1970), "Triangle Of Love (Hey Diddle Diddle)" (—/#5, 1971), "The Sweetest Thing This Side of Heaven" (—/#30, 1971), and their hit, "5-10-15-20." Mysteriously, Archie, Bill, and Tony reappeared on a Columbia charting—"On And Off (Part 1)" (—/#41, 1972)—as Anacostia. Presumably, the Presidents no longer exist, though as Anacostia, they did continue to have numerous disks issued by Columbia (1972–1975), MCA (1977), Tabu (1978–1979), and possibly Roulette (1984).

Ray Price
FOR THE GOOD TIMES
(Kris Kristofferson)
Columbia 45178
No. 11 *January 2, 1971*

Ray Nobel Price (b. Jan. 12, 1926, Perryville, Tex.) grew up on a farm, served in the Marines, and attended the North Texas Agricultural College in Abilene with plans to become a veterinary surgeon. Ray, however, had been moonlighting—singing under the guise of "The Cherokee Cowboy" at school events—and beginning in 1948, he appeared on the "Hillbilly Circus" radio show on KRBC. The response was better than he had hoped, so the next year, he joined KRLD's "Big D Jamboree" in Dallas. School days were done.

The program received some network coverage, and soon Price was recording for Bullet, singing on the Grand Ole Opry, and hanging around with the country legend Hank Williams. Their styles were similar, and often, when Williams was under the weather and unable to perform, Ray would fill in. Months before Hank's death, Price earned his first country charting with "Talk To Your Heart" (—/—/#3, 1952), followed by "Don't Let The Stars Get In Your Eyes" (—/—/#4, 1952). Upon Hank's death, members of Williams' Drifting Cowboys became Price's band, the Cherokee Cowboys.

For years, Ray successfully worked the honky-tonk genre. His country songs are in some cases even well-known to pop/rock fans:

"Release Me" (—/—/#6, 1954), "If You Don't Somebody Else Will" (—/—/#8, 1954), "Crazy Arms" (#67/—/1, 1956), "My Shoes Keep Walking Back To Me" (#63/—/1, 1957), "City Lights" (#71/—/1, 1958), "Heartaches By The Number" (—/—/#2, 1959), "Under Your Spell Again" (—/—/#5, 1959), and "Make The World Go Away" (—/—/#2, 1963). In all, more than 100 of his 45s have made *Billboard*'s C & W listings, and Ray is still going strong.

But 1967 marked a major turning point for Price, pundits claim. The more perceptive detected his future leanings as early as 1964, in "Burning Memories" (—/—/#2, 1964). Ray abandoned his Texas stylings, scrapping the fiddle, the steel guitar, and all the other instrumental touches that rural folk considered "authentic" country. Great numbers of violins—whole symphonies, it seemed—were added, as Ray overhauled his repertory.

"For The Good Times" is a fine example of Ray's MOR phase. Eventually, he or his staunch public tired of this easy-listening syrup, so Price recorded gospel for the Myrrh label before semi-retiring to his Golden Cross Ranch in Texas. He recorded a duet album with Willie Nelson, acted in Clint Eastwood's *Honkytonk Man* (1982), and recently returned on record, full-circle, to his honky-tonkin' ways. Ray and his Cherokee Cowboys—a band that at times has included Johnny Bush, Buddy Emmons, Willie Nelson, Roger Miller, and Johnny Paycheck—are now back playing that authentic country music.

Lynn Anderson
ROSE GARDEN
(Joe South)
Columbia 45252
No. 3 *February 13, 1971*

Nineteen sixty-six was a big year for Lynn. She was named the California Horse Show Queen at the state fair and was offered a contract with Chart Records. A good dozen country chartings would result from the latter.

Lynn was born the daughter of country singer Liz Anderson, on September 26, 1947, in Grand Forks, North Dakota. By the mid-'60s, Liz was having C & W top 10 hits like "I'm A Lonesome Fugitive," and little Lynn was showing signs of following in Ma's line of endeavor. None of mother's waxings, however, would approach the magnitude of Lynn's cover of Joe South's "(I Never Promised You A) Rose Garden." Even the *Rose Garden* album has sold over a million copies.

Lynn cut the South tune shortly after marrying songwriter-producer Glen Sutton and moving to Sutton's base of operations, Columbia Records. From the sales of "Garden" sprouted a Grammy plus the Country Music Association's "Female Vocalist of the Year" award.

"["Rose Garden"] was perfectly timed," Ms. Anderson explained to Joe Edwards of the Associated Press. "We were just coming out of the Vietnam years, and a lot of people were trying to recover. The song's message was that you can make something out of nothing. You [can] take it and go ahead."

Five more of Lynn's singles made the Hot 100, and several more charted on the C & W listings. In the mid-'70s, Sutton and Anderson divorced. In 1978, Lynn married Louisiana oil man Harold Stream III and retired from performing to concentrate on horse riding. Four years later, that marriage over, Lynn Anderson was back in the music-business saddle again. "I am the Annette Funicello of country music," she declared. "Music is in my blood and bones—I ain't done yet."

Wadsworth Mansion
SWEET MARY
(Steve Jablecki)
Sussex 209
No. 7   *February 27, 1971*

Here lies what must be considered the archetypal one-hit wonder act. These period-appropriate but grubby-looking boys seem to have no recorded history. The bubblegummy "Sweet Mary" appears to be their very first recording. Two other 45s ("Michigan Harry Slaught" and "Nine On The Line") and an LP (*Wadsworth Mansion*, 1971) of similar sounds were issued, went nowhere, and the band all but disappeared. No revivals, no lineage—nothing turns up.

All of their known music was recorded in late 1970 at Hollywood Sound Recorders. Producing were Jim Calvert and Norm Marzano. Wadsworth's line-up, per their minimal liner notes, consisted of the Jablecki brothers, Mike (drums, percussion, vocals) and Steve (keyboards, lead vocals, guitar, percussion), plus Wayne Gagnon (lead guitar, handclap, cowbell) and John Poole (bass, vocals, percussion).

Janis Joplin
ME AND BOBBY MCGEE
(Kris Kristofferson)
Columbia 45314
No. 1   *March 20, 1971*

She was found in a room at Hollywood's Landmark Hotel, on October 4, 1970, with puncture marks in her arm. Her death was ruled an accidental heroin overdose. She was the premier white blues singer of the '60s, a gutsy but vulnerable tough-mama icon from Texas, an overnight sensation, and yes, literally a one-hit wonder.

While every album that featured Ms. Joplin—*Big Brother & the Holding Company*

Janis Joplin

(1967), *Cheap Thrills* (1968), *I Got Dem Ol' Kozmic Blues Again Mama!* (1969), *Pearl* (1971), *Joplin in Concert* (1972), *Janis Joplin's Greatest Hits* (1973), *Janis* (1975), and *Farewell Song* (1982)—sold well enough to grant her superstar status, only the posthumous release of "Me And Bobby McGee" (penned by her ex-lover, Kris Kristofferson) managed to make the nation's hit parade. Four other 45s did make the Hot 100, though: "Kozmic Blues" (#42, 1969), "Cry Baby" (#42, 1971), "Get It While You Can" (#78, 1971), and "Down On Me" (#91, 1975).

Sammi Smith

HELP ME MAKE IT THROUGH THE NIGHT

(Kris Kristofferson)
Mega 0015
No. 8 *March 27, 1971*

"**I**'ve been singin' as far back as I can remember, and there's always been music around me," saucy-voiced Sammi Smith (b. Aug. 5, 1943, Orange, Cal.) recalled in an exclusive interview. "While other kids were out doin' stuff, I'd be staying home, singin' or listenin' to records by Dinah Washington and Louis Prima and Keely Smith—not country music. I got into country proper a long time later. When I was 12, I started doin' pop standards with the big bands, but I also sang with some rock bands."

While Sammi was fronting a country unit in 1967 in Oklahoma, bassist Marshall Grant—half of Johnny Cash's back-up band, the Tennessee Two—spotted her and convinced Sammi to take the Greyhound to Nashville. There, Johnny Cash hooked her up with his label, Columbia. Some moderately successful singles were issued, like "So Long Charlie Brown, Don't Look For Me Around" (—/—/ #69, 1968).

Two years later, Columbia terminated their contract with Ms. Smith. "What happened next was, I was playing the Alley in Nashville, and the chairman of the board of Mega [Records] kept harassin' me—sayin' that he wanted to have me be the first artist with this new label. Finally, I did go ahead and sign with 'em. The label, I found out later, was actually formed as a tax write-off, and I wasn't supposed to have a hit record!

"Trouble for them was that once my album [*He's Everything*, retitled *Help Me Make It Through The Night*] came out [in 1971], DJs were playin' 'Help Me Make It Through The Night' and there was no stoppin' it. They *had* to issue it as a single." More than 2,000,000 copies have been sold since. The song was awarded a Grammy and was named the Country Music Association's "Single of the Year" (1971). "Help Me" was also used on the soundtrack of John Huston's flick *Fat City* (1972).

While Ms. Smith has made the pop listings on only one other occasion, with "I've Got To Have You" (#77/—/13, 1972), she has been continuously popular on the C & W charts with songs like "Then You Walked In" (—/—/#10, 1971) and "Today I Started Loving You Again" (—/—/#9, 1975). She has had nearly 40 charting C & W singles.

"There are those who sell a million records and as quickly as it happens, it's gone—I was one of those," Sammi noted. "But I knew I was gonna always sing whether it was for $10 a night or in the big time. I've forfeited makin' the top 10 'cause I've always felt I would only do songs I wanted to do."

Brewer & Shipley

ONE TOKE OVER THE LINE

(Mike Brewer, Tom Shipley)
Kama Sutra 516
No. 10 *April 10, 1971*

They were talented, but when they are remembered at all, it is for that one song.

"People are always asking, 'Geez, what was the meaning of it? Was it a drug song?'" Mike Brewer said in an exclusive interview. "I always look 'em in the eye and ask 'em, 'Come on, have you ever been one toke over the line; done one hit too many?' Yeah, it's about any drugs, or anything that you push too far. A toke seemed apropos at the time. And at that time, I'd had one too many hamburgers, one too many Holiday Inns, one too many nights on the road: toots, tokes, everything."

Both Mike Brewer (b. 1944, Oklahoma City, Okla.) and Tom Shipley (b. 1942, Mineral Ridge, Oh.) had a folk-music history, five or more years apiece, preceding their union in 1966. Each had worked the coffeehouse circuit and the college stops on his respective turf. After Tom graduated from Baldwin Wallace College in Berea, Ohio, he and his new bride moved to California, then Toronto, and even lived in a tent on a Hopi Indian reservation before settling in L.A. In the City of Angels,

Brewer & Shipley

Shipley worked as a duo with Tom Mastin and signed a songwriting contract with Good Sam Music, an affiliate of A & M Records. Mastin grew tired, and disappeared.

Luckily for Brewer and for Shipley, their paths crossed one smoggy L. A. night. Immediately, they began writing together and recording demos for Good Sam Music. In 1968, A & M issued their incomplete tracks as an album (*Down in L.A.*) without their permission, so the duo actively sought out a firm recording contract. Kama Sutra obliged. "One Toke Over The Line"—featuring Mark Naftalin on keyboards and Jerry Garcia on pedal steel guitar—was the opening cut from their second Kama Sutra LP, *Tarkio* (1971).

"The song came about by chance, in a dressing room, one night," Brewer recalled. "We'd had one too many and just broke into song. We were just kiddin' around, not tryin' to write a song or anything. Neil Bogart [founder of Buddah and later Casablanca Records] heard us do the number as an encore, at a show. He said it was a natural and had to be our next single."

Over the next couple of years, a few more countrified albums appeared, and two more singles—"Tarkio Road" (#55, 1971) and "Shake Off The Demons (#98, 1972)—won positions on the Hot 100. Mike, Tom, and their families lived on a farm outside of Kansas City. Into the '80s they continued to tour, to eat hamburgers, and to stay at Holiday Inns.

Michael Brewer's 1983 release, *Beauty Lies*, received favorable reviews.

Bells
STAY AWHILE
(Ken Tobias)
Polydor 15016
No. 7 *May 1, 1971*

The bells started ringing when folksinger Jacki Ralph (b. Surrey, England) first met vocalist Cliff Edwards (b. Montreal) in 1965 at a ski resort in Montreal. Jacki was performing there, and Cliff was a skier with an interest in forming a rock and roll band. Edwards had noticed local drummer Doug Gravelle (b. Montreal) playing at a bar; Doug liked the idea of joining Cliff and Jacki in a group, and Cliff rounded up a few others. For five years, they worked the Montreal club scene as the Five Bells. In 1968, Polydor signed them to a recording contract—a few singles were moderately successful on a local level.

By 1970, the success of groups like the Guess Who and MOTHERLODE laid the foundation for a "Canadian Invasion"; more and more Canadian groups were tempted to try their luck in the States. Guitarist Charlie Clarke, bassist Mike Waye, and keyboardist Denny Will joined the Bells. (Annie Edwards, an interim member and Cliff's wife, left the group to have a child.) Polydor issued a debut album and began a publicity campaign in the U.S., where the band started to tour.

"Fly Little White Dove Fly" (#95, 1971) made an impressive showing, yet the slinky, sexy "Stay Awhile" was a much bigger hit. The follow-up, "I Love You Lady Dawn" (#64, 1971), did fairly well. But over the course of the year, dissension set in, and by the end of 1971, Denny Will and Jacki Ralph were gone. They were replaced by keyboardist FRANK MILLS (later of "Music Box Dancer" fame) and singer Jackie Edwards, Cliff's sister.

A second album and more singles were issued in the States—all to no avail.

Buoys
TIMOTHY
(Rupert Holmes)
Scepter 12275
No. 17 *May 1, 1971*

Cannibalism! Surely a song about the bodily consumption of a poor fellow named Timothy would not be tolerated on the top reaches of *Billboard*'s Hot 100. A call to Rupert Holmes—the tune's creator, and previously a writer/arranger for artists like the Drifters, the Platters, and Gene Pitney— seemed in order.

"The Buoys were from Wilkes-Barre, Pennsylvania, and were so named to conjure images of cleanliness, you know, like Lifebuoy soap. Michael Wright, a junior engineer at Scepter Recording Studios, discovered them. Mike and I were buddies, so he came to me for advice. He really liked the group and wanted to record them, but he told me that Scepter didn't take the group seriously. I said, 'I think you should record a song that will get banned— that way, you can take the Buoys to another

The Buoys

label and say "This is the band that everyone is talking about." Mike asked me if I could write something that would get the group banned.

"I wasn't going to write about drugs, and everything that could be said on the air about sex had been said already. At the time, I was working on an arrangement of '16 Tons' for Andy Kim, and in this kind of 'Proud Mary' guitar groove. In the other room there was this TV on. The show was 'The Galloping Gourmet.' I started singing the lyrics: 'Some people say a man is made out of mud/A coal man is made out of muscle and blood/Muscle and blood and skin and bones.' I thought, 'God, that sounds like a recipe.' I said, 'Yeah, muscle and blood and skin and bones: bake in a moderate oven for three hours. That's it! Cannibalism and mining.

"I just turned out this story song about three boys who were trapped in a mine. And when they're pulled out, there's only two of them left. They don't know what happened to the third one, but they know that they're not hungry anymore!"

The Buoys—Fran Brozena (keyboards), Chris Hanlon (guitar), Gerry Hludzik (a.k.a. Joe Jerry, bass), Billy Kelly (lead vocals), and Carl Siracuse (drums)—gathered in the studio. Rupert played piano on the track. Bill Kelly sang lead. Scepter issued the disk and no one noticed, not even the label, for 14 months. A part-time promo man at the company finally took it into his own hands to drum up interest in the disk, particularly on college stations—in short order, gatherings of the "Timothy For Lunch Bunch" were being reported in university tabloids.

The Buoys followed their top 40 hit with other tall tales of death and whatnot. There was "Give Up Your Guns" (#84, 1971), about a Tex/Mex showdown, followed by "Bloodknot," about some reform-school ritual. Both were written by Rupert, who likewise penned most of the tunes for the Buoys' 1971 *Portfolio* LP. Two further singles were issued by Polydor ("Don't Try To Run" and "Liza's Last Ride"), but Holmes wrote neither of these numbers.

Rupert Holmes continued writing, producing, and arranging. He also launched a solo career that eventually led to chart success—with singles like "Escape (The Piña Colada Song)" (#1, 1979) and "Him" (#6, 1980), and the *Partners in Crime* (1980) album. In 1980, Billy Kelly and Gerry Hludzik resurfaced as Dakota with a self-titled LP on Columbia Records.

Ocean
PUT YOUR HAND IN THE HAND
(Gene MacLellan)
Kama Sutra 519
No. 2 *May 1, 1971*

Ocean was, like, a hippie band, or something. According to Greg Brown, the band's keyboardist and vocalist, he and this dude, lead guitarist Dave Tamblyn, came together as a weekend group in the summer of 1970, the year of the birth of *Jesus Christ Superstar*. Greg brought in clear-voiced Janice Morgan, who would sing up-front on Ocean's only top 40 hit; his booking agent, meanwhile, was on the lookout for other guys to gig with. "Primarily, we were searching for a bunch of people that we would like," Greg told Ritchie Yorke in *Axes, Chops, and Hot Licks*. "Ocean is more of a people thing than anything else."

Jeff Jones and Chuck Slater were located to fill in on bass and drums, respectively. Canadian Arc Records signed Ocean to a contract, put them in a studio, and told them to, like, do their stuff. Never to be known for their song-creating abilities, the group decided to cover singer-songwriter Gene MacLellan's "Put Your Hand In The Hand." (Months before, Anne Murray had sold a million copies of her cover version of MacLellan's "Snowbird.")

With the success of Norman Greenbaum's confused "Spirit In The Sky" and George Harrison's "My Sweet Lord," it looked to Greg like the world was ready for religious pop-rock songs. "I wouldn't say that we feel strongly about the religious angle of the song," Greg explained to Yorke. "We were concerned that it might give the group a gospel image."

Unfortunately for the group, that is just what the record did. Top 40 radio will take to a spiritually-inclined tune every now and then, but not even when Jesus was a superstar and great numbers were under a Godspell could an act sing the praises record after record and get away with it. Three follow-up singles, all ecological or religious in theme, did chart in the lower reaches of the Hot 100. Thereafter, Ocean remained a Canadian happening.

When last heard from, the brothers and sisters, except for Slater (who committed suicide sometime in the '80s), were living together on a farm in Markham, about 30 miles outside of Toronto. The main building is, like, a 100-year-old log cabin, man.

Richie Havens

Daddy Dewdrop

CHICK-A-BOOM (DON'T YA
JES' LOVE IT)
(Janis Lee Guinn, Linda Martin)
Sunflower 105
No. 9 *May 8, 1971*

The original Daddy Dewdrop was Dick
Monda. Publicity handouts from Dick's long-
deceased record label would have us believe
that he was born in Cleveland in 1952. Reportedly, at the ripe age of 19, Dewdrop turned to
music, and was hired as a songwriter and producer for a CBS cartoon series, *Sabrina & the
Groovy Ghoulies*. The publicity releases fail to
mention Monda's previously unsuccessful waxings for Verve and Moonglow.

"Chick-a-boom, Chick-a-boom/Don't ya jes'
love it"—it was fluff, all right, but catchy to the
ear, for a spin or two. As performed by the
Groovy Ghoulies on the Saturday-morning cartoon show, this novelty number began attracting much notice. In an effort to beat out the
Ghoulie "group"'s release of the tune for RCA,
Dick Monda assembled a studioful of sessioneers, whom he called the Torrance
Cookers (Larry "Boom Boom" Brown, Tom
"The Hen" Hensley, Bill "Ma Brutha" Perry,
and Steve "Atom Bomb" Rillera). They ran
through not only "Chick-A-Boom" but many
other noxious numbers like "John Jacob Jingle
Heimer Smith" and "Abracadabra Alakazam."

More public-pleasing pablum appeared under the "Daddy Dewdrop" name, but fared
poorly. In the late '70s, another Daddy Dewdrop surfaced with more 45s, but none of these
efforts—not even "Nanu Nanu (I Wanna Get
Funky Wich You)"—received much of a
response.

Richie Havens

HERE COMES THE SUN
(George Harrison)
Stormy Forest 656
No. 16 *May 22, 1971*

Richie Havens (b. Jan. 21, 1941, Brooklyn) was
born into a large, musical family, and grew up
in the Bedford-Stuyvesant section of Brooklyn. "Kids who didn't have jobs or who didn't
finish school ended up singing together," Havens told *Frets*' Mark Humphreys. "That's
what I was doing when I was 13. In the '50s,

everyone did that to stay out of trouble. There was nothing else to do.

"When I first started playing the guitar, it wasn't for myself; it was because I sang with *a cappella* groups. I had a girlfriend who had two younger brothers, 11 and 13. They had a little group, and they were dynamic. I used to do rehearsals with these kids, and a friend loaned me a guitar. This was the time of the hootenannies in Greenwich Village, so I took the kids over there. They killed everybody . . . I wasn't really into jumping up on anybody's stage and singing by myself. But once I started fooling around with the guitar, it was fun. And I started doing hootenannies [about 1960]." To support himself, Richie drew portraits, and also worked for a florist and Western Union.

Havens developed a distinctive style, which has been preserved for all time in the *Woodstock* (1970) film footage: eyes shut, a sawing, thrashing guitar attack, and the unorthodox use of his thumb in chord fingering. Albert Grossman, Dylan's manager, discovered Richie at the Cafe Wha? in the Village. Richie subsequently issued a few LPs on the Douglas label before switching to Verve-Folkways, and later, Stormy Forest, for the creation of his most noted work. He appeared at the Newport Folk Festival (1966), then the Monterey Pop Festival (1967), the Isle of Wight Pop Festival (1968), and finally, the Woodstock Festival (1969).

"I opened the [Woodstock] Festival," Havens told *Goldmine*'s Bob Grossweiner. "I was supposed to be fifth. I said, 'What am I doing here? No, no, not me, not first!' I had to go on stage because there was no one else to go on first—the concert was already two-and-a-half hours late. Everyone was at the Holiday Inn seven miles away and couldn't get to the stage because the one back road they thought they could take was completely blocked.

"My impression was that there were over a million people there. It was a completely unique experience. No one expected it. 'Freedom' [Havens' peak performance, featured in the film] was written right there on the stage; it had never been sung before! It was spontaneous . . . I was alone on stage for two-and-a-half hours before any of the other performers came."

Havens never became a successful singles artist, but his large collection of LPs sold well throughout the '70s—albums such as *Richard P. Havens, 1983* (1969), *Alarm Clock* (1971), and *Richie Havens On Stage* (1972). Currently living in New York City, Richie continues to perform and record, and is also a sculptor.

Tin Tin
TOAST AND MARMALADE FOR TEA
(Steve Groves)
Atco 6794
No. 20 *May 29, 1971*

Tin Tin consisted of two Steves, surnamed Groves (guitar, bass, mellotron) and Kipner (keyboards, bass). In the late '60s, both blokes walked out on group affiliations in their native Australia to form what was intended to be a successful songwriting partnership. After cranking out a number of tunes, the Steves recorded some demos and moved to London.

With a stack of psychedelicized Beatles-like records cut and canned, the Down Under dudes approached fellow Australian Maurice Gibb of the Bee Gees. Gibb liked their stuff, particularly an item called "Toast And Marmalade For Tea." For some long-forgotten reason, the guys named themselves after Tin Tin, a Belgian cartoon character. Atco Records released the disk, and a sizeable chunk of the Western world concurred with Maurice's thumbs-up assessment. "Marmalade," produced by Gibb, oozed onto the charts. The follow-up, "Is That The Way" (#59, 1971)—also produced by Gibb—struggled with the lower reaches of the Hot 100, but "Talkin' Turkey" and other singles stiffed.

By the close of 1973, each Tin had gone his own way. Groves found security in obscurity. Kipner resurfaced in the late '70s with an album and some singles for Elektra and RSO. Kipner has also done session work for George Benson and ex-Hollie Allan Clarke. A number of his tunes have charted as recorded by other acts—in 1984, Chicago clicked with his "Hard Habit To Break" (#3), and Olivia Newton-John had success with his "Physical" (#1, 1981) and "Twist Of Fate" (#5, 1984).

Beginning of the End
FUNKY NASSAU—PART 1
(Ralph Munnings, Tyrone Fitzgerald)
Alston 4595
No. 15 *July 17, 1971*

The Beginning of the End was one of the few Caribbean acts at the time that managed to tickle America's fancy. Essentially, the band was a brothers act—Rafael Munnings (vocal and organ), Frank Munnings (drums), and

LeRoy Munnings (guitar)—augmented by Fred Henfield (bass) and the Funky Nassau Horns: Ralph Munnings (tenor sax), Nevill Sampson (trumpet), and Kenneth Lane (tenor sax). They cut some tracks in Miami for the fledgling Alston label. The very first release was their big one, "Funky Nassau." Rafael sang from his stuffings, the beat swirled, the brass blasted, and in a three-month period, America bought a bargeful of the Munnings' "junkanoo" sound.

The brothers hung in there long enough to lay down some sunny album tracks and a few singles with names like "Come Down Baby" and "Monkey Tamarino." But their monster moment was indeed the beginning of the end. According to *Goldmine*'s Robert Pruter, one executive at the Alston label quipped: "They had one helluva lot of talent—problem was, they just didn't trust Americans."

By 1974, Henry Stone's Alston label had been folded into TK Productions, and the Beginning of the End was history.

Cymarron

RINGS
(Eddie Reeves, Alex Harvey)
Entrance 7500
No. 17 *August 7, 1971*

Producer Chips Moman had something of an open-door policy at his American Recording Studios in Memphis. One promising day in 1969, Rick Yancey (b. 1948) walked through that door. Yancey, who was born and raised in Memphis, had drifted in and out of music and likewise Memphis State University. That morn, Rick approached Moman with some self-penned songs. "Chips listened, didn't like the songs, and hired me," Yancey joked on the liner notes to Cymarron's lone album. For a year, Rick hung around the studios, working on recording sessions and trying to write that smash hit.

Looking for some action, Sherrill Parks (b. 1948, Jackson, Tenn.), a guitarist and sax player from Tennessee, dropped by the studios. Rick and Sherill hit it off, and soon talked of constructing a group to cut some hit records. Rick suggested the addition of Richard Mainegra (b. 1948, New Orleans) to the group that was to be named after a local TV Western series, "Cymarron Strip." Richard had co-written some songs cut by Gary Puckett and Skeeter Davis, had recorded with the Phyve,

and had made some unsuccessful solo singles for Scepter Records.

Cymarron's sound resembled the mellow folkie emissions of Crosby, Stills, Nash & Young and America. Moman, agreeing that the blend of their voices was quite good, gave the group a pile of tunes to practice, and arranged for some top session musicians to flesh out Cymarron's acoustic instrumentation. Sweet and bouncy, "Rings" scaled the pop listings and nearly creased the top 10. Nothing more, however, charted. At least three more singles were issued before the fellows decided to branch off into other endeavors.

Later in the decade, Rich Mainegra made appearances on albums by Doug Kershaw and Billy Burnette.

Tom Clay

WHAT THE WORLD NEEDS NOW IS LOVE/ABRAHAM, MARTIN AND JOHN
(H. David, B. Bacharach/D. Holley)
Mowest 5002
No. 8 *August 14, 1971*

Tom Clay was a substitute DJ, with a three-week assigment at L.A.'s KGBS. Using his own funds, he created a narrative collage which combined snatches of speeches by John Kennedy, Robert Kennedy, and Martin Luther King with sound effects and recordings of little children attempting to define terms like "bigotry," "prejudice," and "segregation." Gene Page arranged the period piece, and the Blackberries (Oma Drake, Jessie Smith, and Clydie King) supplied the vocal backdrop. Clay spun the disk on his radio program.

Motown mastermind Berry Gordy, Jr., heard the DJ's sociopolitical statement, and soon issued a shaved version on Gordy's Mowest label. The timing was right, and Clay found himself with a national audience. Followups such as "Whatever Happened To," a rambling reminiscence about sugar sandwiches wolfed when young, sold little.

Jean Knight

MR. BIG STUFF
(Joe Broussard, Ralph Williams, Carrol Washington)
Stax 0088
No. 2 *August 14, 1971*

Jean Knight was born in New Orleans, on January 26, 1943. During the early '60s, she sang on weekends in small clubs. By 1970, she had hooked up with Wardell Quezerque, a noted New Orleans arranger and producer who had started out as a trumpet man in Dave Bartholomew's band. (Wardell had fronted bands like the Sultans and the Royal Dukes of Rhythm; DR. JOHN had even played piano for him at one point.) Jean Knight worked for Quezerque as a back-up singer on his sessions.

Quezerque had made arrangements with Tommy Couch and Wolf Stevenson of Malaco Productions to record some sides at their studio in Jackson, Mississippi. He brought Jean, King Floyd, and a number of other acts down to Jackson for a one-off Saturday afternoon session. Knight taped "Mr. Big Stuff," and King Floyd did his "Groove Me." Both waxings would eventually rocket to the top of the R & B charts.

Initially, no one was interested in leasing the sides from Quezerque. Couch and Stevenson resolved the situation by forming Chimneyville Records—so named after the nickname given Jackson following its destruction in the Civil War—to release the King Floyd track. Once "Groove Me" became a huge pop hit (#6, 1971), a number of labels began bidding for Wardell's other Saturday-afternoon sides, Knight's "Mr. Big Stuff" included.

"Big Stuff," picked up by the Stax label, was a smooth shaker and, once released, a big moneymaker. Why not work that groove again? The follow-up, "You Think You're Hot Stuff" (#57, 1971), did well, but the next two singles for Stax flopped, then Stax folded. Without a label, Jean continued gigging on weekends locally and attended nursing school.

In 1981, Jean's recording career was revived when a song she had waxed for Isaac Bolden's Soulin' label—"You Got The Papers (But I Got The Man)" (—/#56, 1981)—was picked up for national release by Cotillion and nicked the R & B charts. Her tasty cover of Rockin' Sidney's Zydeco zinger "My Toot Toot" (#50, 1985) was promising; quite probably, we've yet to see the end of Jean's soulful sounds.

Undisputed Truth

SMILING FACES SOMETIMES
(Norman Whitfield, Barrett Strong)
Gordy 7108
No. 3 *September 4, 1971*

Joe Harris, the only constant member of this ever-evolving group, was born and raised in Detroit. "I came out of the Brewster Projects, along with Martha & The Vandellas, Diana Ross, and Mary Wilson," Harris told *Blues & Soul's* Denise Hall and Tony Cummings. "In high school, I was involved with Little Joe & The Moroccos. We had been competing against the Spinners in a series of talent shows and finally we were the ones to win."

A 1957 release entitled "Bubblegum" on the Bumblebee label bombed, and the group disbanded. After some college, Harris and Richard Street (later a member of the Monitors and the Temptations) formed the Peps and had a series of unsuccessful disks issued on Thelma and D-Town. Joe left for the Ohio Players, and was their lead vocalist for a year in the late '60s. "I co-wrote and produced most of their first album for Capitol, but found myself hooked up with a bogus production deal." After a short stay in Canada with the Stone Soul Children, Harris returned to Detroit and met Norman Whitfield, a top-flight producer-writer for Motown and later, head of Whitfield Records.

Whitfield (then on a hot streak with million-selling productions on Marvin Gaye, Edwin Starr, and the Temptations) wanted to put together a new act to feature his abilities. Undisputed Truth was Joe Harris plus the Delicates—Billie Rae Calvin and Brenda Joyce Evans, who had been singing back-up sessions for the Four Tops and the Supremes.

"Smiling Faces Sometimes" was a sure hit. To the dismay of the Temptations, Whitfield pulled it off the Temps' *The Sky's the Limit* LP and gave it to the Undisputed Truth for their second single. While a cover of "Papa Was A Rolling Stone" (#63, 1972) and several other increasingly funkified Undisputed Truth 45s cracked the pop and R & B listings, "Faces" proved to be the group's only top 40 showing.

After the marginal success of "Law Of The Land" (—/#40, 1973) from the LP of the same name, Billie and Brenda left the group. The Magictones (Tyrone Berkley, Tyrone Douglas, Virginia McDonald, and Calvin Stevens), a Motor City bar band, was brought in to back Harris as the "new, higher-than-high, cosmic 'Truth.'" This reworked group's sound was more rock-oriented, and obviously influenced by JIMI HENDRIX and Sly Stone. Truth also took on an overtly theatrical image: silver faces, flashing sequins, and towering white afros.

Before the apparent demise of Truth in the late '70s, Harris and Whitfield fired the entire line-up and shelved the freaky fashions. Among the members of the last incarnation were Melvin Stuart, Marcy Thomas, Hershel "Happiness" Kennedy, and Chaka Khan's sister, Taka Boom, who has had several R & B hits during the '80s.

Mac & Katie Kissoon

CHIRPY CHIRPY CHEEP CHEEP
(Harold Stott)
ABC 11306
No. 20 *October 2, 1971*

Jerry "Mac" Kissoon and his younger sister Kathleen were born in Port of Spain, Trinidad. The Kissoon family moved to England in the late '50s. Mac did some solo singing and eventually joined a couple of West Indian youths, Lance Ring and Pauline Sibbles, in the Marionettes. After Katie joined the group, a number of singles were issued in Europe by Pye. In 1965, while still a member of the group, Katie, recording as Peanuts, covered the Bonnie & The Treasures classic "Home Of The Brave." That same year, the siblings also recorded a few girl-group sides with the Rag Dolls. None

of these charted in England or the States.

Years later, freed of all solo and group alignments, Mac and Katie finally scored in the U.S. with their bubblegum number, "Chirpy Chirpy Cheep Cheep." While years of follow-ups charted on the Continent, the Kissoons returned to oblivion in the States. "Sugar Candy Kisses," "Don't Do It Baby," and other cute pop-soul numbers became big U.K. sellers in the mid-'70s.

Katie is still a pop performer. She has toured and recorded with Van Morrison and Roger Waters, and has made 45s for the Jive label.

Denise LaSalle

TRAPPED BY A THING CALLED LOVE
(Denise LaSalle)
Westbound 182
No. 13 *October 30, 1971*

Born in LeFlore County, Mississippi, on July 16, 1939, Denise Craig had early childhood ambitions of becoming a fiction writer. At age 15, after moving to Chicago to live with her brother, Denise was delighted when *TAM*, a magazine of black culture, bought one of her

Denise LaSalle

The Bitch Is Bad!

stories. Only rejection slips followed, but Ms. Craig (who changed her name to "LaSalle" in order to sound French) was not one to be defeated easily.

Denise turned to songwriting, and in 1968, she started recording for Billy "The Kid" Emerson's Tarpon label. Neither "A Love Reputation" nor its follow-up, "Count Down," charted. In 1969, she set up her own production company, signed artists, wrote tunes for them, and recorded them in Willie Mitchell's Memphis studio. That same year, she also met her husband-to-be, Bill "Super Wolf" Jones, then a DJ on Memphis' WDXI.

While she was hitless herself, Denise produced R & B hits like Bill Coday's "Get Your Lie Straight" and the Sequins' "Hey Romeo." Magazine editors had turned down her writing, but now Little Milton, Ann Peebles, and others were seeking her out and recording her tunes. Encouraged by her behind-the-scenes success, Denise walked into a recording studio to lay down some tracks with her voice up front. "Heartbreaker Of The Year," released on her own Crajon label, did not chart, but Westbound Records signed her, and one of the tracks from her first session secured her a place in rock and soul history.

"Trapped By A Thing Called Love" caught a large audience, hit number one on the R & B charts, and gave Denise the hellfire-loving image she has to this day. A sassy, gritty singer, Denise told a *Blues & Soul* reporter that she likes her music "mean, down-home, and funky." The flip side of "Trapped" was the suggestively-titled "The Deeper I Go The Better It Gets." Trailing that ditty by a year was "A Man Sized Job" (#55, 1972), on which Denise informs her former lover that he "left his job half done" and that she's now with a younger dude. Her next release continued the theme: in "What It Takes To Get A Good Woman," she sings that "You can't start out a loverman and wind up being a sleeper."

Denise has said that despite her racy innuendos, she is ladylike and a feminist of sorts.

"Maybe it isn't the kind of stereotype of femininity that women have been tagged with. And maybe it isn't that sweet delicate, fragile, gentle image of womanhood that a lot of people still envision. But it's a new side of women—it portrays a strength that has never been portrayed before. Women aren't just housewives any longer . . . they are out there fighting and standing up for their rights. That's the kind of woman that Millie [Jackson] and I are portraying—the woman of today who won't be no doormat."

Free Movement

I'VE FOUND SOMEONE OF MY OWN
(Frank K. Robinson)
Decca 32818
No. 5 *November 13, 1971*

History doesn't reveal just how they came together, nor just how and why they fell apart so rapidly. All we know is that they were six kids from all across the country who met in Los Angeles in 1970. Only Josephine Brown and Godoy Colbert had any musical background. Godoy, the oldest, had sung professionally in the Afro Blues Quintet, the Pilgrim Travelers, and the Pharaohs; Josephine had received training from her gospel-singing father and had been a member of the Five Bells of Joy. The others in Free Movement were Cheryl Conley, Jennifer Gates, and the Jefferson brothers, Adrian and Claude.

After rehearsing for a few months, Free Movement made a demo and shopped it around town. Decca Records liked what they heard and quickly issued "I've Found Someone Of My Own" as a single. Six months later, when the pop/soul single charted, the group had already changed their allegiance, having signed with Columbia Records. An album and two more singles were released. "The Harder I Try (The Bluer I Get)" (#50, 1972) did so-so, and then—silence.

Freddie Hart

EASY LOVING
(Freddie Hart)
Capitol 3115
No. 17 *November 20, 1971*

Freddie Hart: what a man, what a life. No way could it have been easy.

Born one of 15 children in Lockapoka, Alabama, on December 21, 1933, Freddie ran away from home when seven years of age. To survive, he picked cotton, washed dishes, layed pipeline, worked in sawmills, steel mills, and on oil rigs. At age 14, Freddie passed himself off as being of proper age, and enlisted in the Marines, where he saw action on Iwo Jima, Okinawa, and Guam. On completing his tour of duty, Freddie, always a physical-fitness advocate and possessor of a black belt in karate, became a self-defense instructor at the Los Angeles Police Academy.

Barely 20, Hart met C & W honky-tonk legend Lefty Frizzell. Lefty took the kid under his wing, put him in his band, let him sing some songs, and walked him into Capitol Records in 1953. It would be six years before Hart would have his first major C & W hit with "The Wall" and another decade before nearly the whole world would hear of Freddie and his "Easy Loving." The self-penned tune eventually sold more than a million copies and garnered the Country Music Association's "Song of the Year" award for both 1971 and 1972.

"Pretty Sex, that's what I like to put across in my songs," Freddie told *Country Music*'s Joan Dew. "'Easy lovin', so sexy lookin'' . . . that one line says it all. I almost took it out of the song."

While Hart never again managed to cross over onto the pop/rock charts, he continued for much of the '70s to claim top-five C & W positions with recordings that included "My Hang-Up Is You," "Got The All Overs For You," "If You Can't Feel It, It Ain't There," and "Hang On In There Girl." In addition to recording as a solo artist, Hart has been composing tunes for more than 30 years, some of which have been successfully waxed by other country performers. His "Loose Talk" has been covered more than 50 times.

Freddie Hart is reportedly a very wealthy man. He owns a trucking company, raises fruit and cattle, and runs a school for handicapped children. While his popularity in country circles has declined of late, Freddie still records honest, honky-tonkin' material for the small Brylen label.

Les Crane
DESIDERATA
(Max Ehrmann, Fred Werner)
Warner 7520
No. 8   *December 4, 1971*

Not much is known about where he came from or even where he went to, but TV talk-show host Les Crane annoyed plenty of people in the mid-'60s with his sandpapery communication style. ABC had set up Crane's program to compete against NBC's "Tonight Show." The attempt, like similar efforts today, was short-lived—Crane's show nose-dived into oblivion within months. Six years later, the sometime DJ had a top 10 hit with a reading of Max Ehrmann's 1906 poem, "Go Placidly Amid The Noise And Haste."

The groundwork had been laid a year earlier. In 1970, ex-Nice drummer Brian Davidson's group Every Which Way had utilized Ehrmann's words for a song on their only album; that same year, King Crimson, thinking the poem was an ancient document, had also used it, in an ad for their *Lizard* album.

The Crane dubbing did garner a Grammy for

The Hillside Singers

"Best Spoken Word Recording" of 1971, but, to no one's surprise, Les never charted again.

Jonathan Edwards

SUNSHINE
(Jonathan Edwards)
Capricorn 8021
No. 4 *January 15, 1972*

Jonathan Edwards was born on July 28, 1946, somewhere in Minnesota. His father worked for the FBI, and at the age of six, Jon and the family moved with the old man to Virginia. In the pre-Beatles '60s, Jon formed a bluegrass band called the Rivermen. Over the years the name, the personnel, and the overall sound of the group changed: they were the St. James Doorknob, then Headstone Circus, and finally, the heavy and blues-influenced Sugar Creek (Edwards, Gary Gans, and the McKinney brothers, Malcolm and Tod).

Peter Casperson heard Sugar Creek's top-quality sounds at a one-nighter and approached the guys about becoming their guiding light and manager. The group agreed, and Casperson set the band up with Metromedia Records. Sugar Creek's self-titled album was a musical winner, but fared poorly sales-wise, so the band split up.

Jonathan signed on as a singer-songwriter with Phil Walden's Capricorn label. "Sunshine," a hastily-composed tune from his first solo album, connected with pop listeners. The single and the album sold in healthy quantities, but nothing further charted.

Edwards has moved in a more bluegrass-inflected direction, but still records and tours for a loyal following. His most recent album, *The Natural Thing*, appeared on MCA/Curb in 1989.

Hillside Singers

I'D LIKE TO TEACH THE WORLD TO SING (IN PERFECT HARMONY)
(William Backer, Billy Davis, Roger Cook, Roger Greenaway)
Metromedia 231
No. 13 *January 15, 1972*

He's a collection of moments in pop music history, a personable man with stories and snapshots. At what now seems like the dawn of rock and roll, Al Ham was functioning and in top form—long before producers were given a second glance, label credits, or much else (like money). He was a bass player and arranger for Tex Beneke, Artie Shaw, and Glenn Miller.

As a producer with Columbia Records, he worked throughout the '50s for acts like Tony Bennett, Rosemary Clooney, RAY CONNIFF, Percy Faith, Erroll Garner, the Kirby Stone Four, Johnny Mathis, and Mitch Miller (on his "Sing Along with Mitch" albums). He also produced the original cast recordings for *My Fair Lady*, *Gypsy*, *West Side Story*, and *Bells Are Ringing*. In the intervening years, Ham has scored films like *Harlow* (1965) and *Stop the World, I Want to Get Off* (1966); arranged and composed commercials for Breck, Gillette, and McDonald's; and handpicked and groomed a number of vocal units, the most successful of these being the Hillside Singers.

"I was the arranger and producer and they were my group," Ham recalled in an exclusive interview. "I formed them explicitly for the purpose of making that record. In fact, it was our idea—Jack Wiedinman was the president of Metromedia—to do this cover version of a Coca-Cola jingle. We got the permission from the ad agency, BBDO, to record it." The New Seekers muscled in on the Hillside Singers' action with their own version of the jingle (#7, 1972) and eventually outsold—and out-charted—Ham's Hillsiders.

The Hillside Singers comprised Ham's daughter Lori, his wife Mary Mayo, Ron and Rick Shaw, and a group called the Good Life (Frank, Bill, Laura, and Joelle Marino). Ham assembled the unit, worked up an arrangement, and made the record. The disk took off, and the Hillside Singers recorded two LPs before the downslide began.

"It was bad timing, or bad luck, but by the time we had that hit, they wanted to kill the [Metromedia] label, if you can imagine that. We went through the motions with our albums and our touring, but by the time the last LP was out, the label was defunct." The Hillside Singers are still active—"it's been pretty much an ongoing thing, all these years, but obviously it's not been as active as we'd like it."

Mary Mayo, once a New York nightclub singer and Capitol recording artist, has since died. Ron Shaw, a later member (with Don Williams) of the Pozo Seco Singers, has since gone on to much C & W fame, charting nearly ten times. His most notable country winner was "Save The Last Dance For Me" (—/—/ #36, 1978).

Apollo 100 featuring Tom Parker

JOY
(J.S. Bach)
Mega 0050
No. 6 *February 26, 1972*

Tommy Parker (b. Newcastle-on-Tyne, England) was playing the piano at age six. By his teens, he was successfully performing at local jazz clubs. In the '60s, he did some production or session work with the Animals, Jimmy James & The Vagabonds, and the Mark Leeman Trio.

Apollo 100 was Tom's idea. The so-called group comprised Clem Cattini, Vic Flick, Z. Jenkins, Jim Lawless, and Brian Odgers, among others. Their "Joy" was an adaptation of Bach's "Jesu, Joy of Man's Desiring." While Parker had a hundred such instrumentals up his sleeve, the public took a lean liking to his version of "Mendelssohn's 4th (2nd Movement)" (#94, 1972), and passed on all subsequent Apollo flights.

Once the Apollo concept was scrapped, Parker joined the Doggerel Bank as a keyboardist for their two mid-'70s albums on the Charisma label. Tom has also done some production work for Marc Ellington, Gerry Rafferty, Chris White, and STATUS QUO.

Climax

PRECIOUS AND FEW
(Walter Nims)
Carousel 30055
No. 3 *February 26, 1972*

The Cleveland-based Outsiders were well within the nation's charts for one solid '60s year. "Time Won't Let Me" (#5, 1966), "Girl In Love" (#21, 1966), "Help Me Girl" (#37, 1966), and their remake of the Isley Brothers' "Respectable" (#15, 1966)—what Baby Boomer can forget them? Lead singer Sonny Geraci (b. 1947, Cleveland) and his Outsiders seemed to have the scene sewed up. They toured constantly, and three of their four LPs sold well—*Time Won't Let Me* (1966), *The Outsiders Album 2* (1966), and *Happening 'Live'* (1967).

Immediately after the original group's dissolution in 1967, Sonny moved to Los Angeles with Walter Nims (guitar), a late addition to the Outsiders line-up. After some failed late-'60s sides as Climax for Patti Platters ("Composite Of Unrelated Birthdays" and "Love Will Find a Way"), Paramount ("You've Gotta Try"), and Bell ("Rainbow Rides Are Free"), Sonny and Walter—plus a crew that would eventually include Robert Nelson (drums), Virgil Weber (keyboards), and Steven York (bass, harmonica)—were spotted by Fifth Dimensions manager Marc Gordon and singer Al Wilson.

Gordon and Wilson signed Climax to their Carousel label (later renamed Rocky Road). The group's debut, "Hard Rock Group," flopped, but the follow-up, "Precious And Few," did what no other Climax cut would ever do—it went top 10. Numerous poorly-distributed disks were tried (and trampled) over the next several years. "Life And Breath" (#52, 1972) and their one LP (*Climax*, 1972) were the only successes.

Tired of performing in Cleveland bars, Sonny married in 1982 and became a father, a born-again Christian, and a salesman of siding and replacement windows. "One day I realized something," Geraci told *Rolling Stone* in 1986. "I'm a salesman. I'm a district manager, I oversee other salesmen. I make good money. And I'm still entertaining when I go to people's houses." More recently, Sonny has found a new personal manager, re-formed and modified an Outsiders/Climax group, and is now musically active on a part-time basis.

In his post-Climax career, Steve York has become a top-notch session bassist, having recorded with Joan Armatrading, Graham Bond, THE CRAZY WORLD OF ARTHUR BROWN, DR. JOHN, Marianne Faithfull, Manfred Mann, Charlie Musselwhite, and others.

T. Rex

BANG A GONG (GET IT ON)
(Marc Bolan)
Reprise 1032
No. 10 *March 4, 1972*

Marc Bolan never did pick up a following in the States like he did in England. Most American rock fans have little idea of just how big a star this seminal glam-rocker was in the U.K. At the height of Bolan's powers (1971-1974), his T-Rex concerts could generate a level of hysteria not seen since Beatlemania. Before Bolan's death in 1977, he had sold 37,000,000 records—surpassing the combined sales in

England of all product issued by JIMI HENDRIX and the Who.

"The people in the business think I've had a cold spell since 'Bang A Gong,' whereas in reality I've been selling loads of records all over the world," Bolan explained in 1974 to *Rock*'s Alan Betrock. "But if you're not hot in their country, they think you've had it. I admit that I should've approached America differently after 'Bang A Gong' was a hit here. I should have come over and followed it up, but we were just so busy all over the rest of the world, we didn't have time."

Guitarist Marc Bolan (b. Mark Feld, July 30, 1947, London) attended the same primary school as British pop singer Helen Shapiro and Procol Harum's Keith Reid. At 15, he was a male model. His early rock career had him signed with British Decca for a few solo singles as Toby Tyler, Marc Bowland, and finally, as Marc Bolan. Briefly, in 1967, he was a member of the proto-glam-rock group John's Children.

In 1968, drawing on percussionist Steve Peregrine-Took (b. July 28, 1949, London), his own considerable imagination, and imagery from J.R.R. Tolkien's *The Hobbit*, Bolan assembled Tyrannosaurus Rex. Starting with their debut album, *My People Were Fair and Had Sky in Their Hair But Now They're Content to Wear Stars on Their Brows*, the duo played acoustic instruments and dressed in flower-power threads, beads, and headbands. Bolan's mystical lyrics spoke of unicorns, gnomes, impish forest folk, and fairies.

Gradually, Bolan added more electric sounds to his recordings; *Unicorn* (1970), a half-acoustic and half-electric set, produced the act's first major hit, "Ride A White Swan" (#76, 1971). By LP number five (*A Beard of Stars*, 1971), Took had taken leave. His replacement was Mickey Finn, a former rocker from Hapash & The Coloured Coat. Also added were bassist Steve Currie (b. May 21, 1947, Grimsby) and drummer Bill Legend (b. Bill Fifield, May 6, 1944, Essex). Subtracted were a number of letters from the group's name: they became simply "T. Rex."

"The [British] press have never been off my back, ever," Bolan complained. "With a few exceptions I've never had a good review for anything." Not that it mattered: T. Rex racked up 11 singles on the British top 10 from 1970 to 1973, including four number-one disks.

While T. Rex only made the U.S. Hot 100 on one other occasion, with "Telegram Sam" (#67, 1972), the act gathered a growing stateside following and had two best-selling

T. Rex, with Steve Took and Marc Bolan

albums—*Electric Warrior* (1971), which featured "Bang A Gong," and *The Slider* (1972). *Tyrannosaurus Rex (A Beginning)* (1972) and *Tranx* (1973) also did well.

Bolan perished in a car crash in England on September 17, 1977. Peregrine-Took and Currie died in 1980 and 1981, respectively.

Chakachas

JUNGLE FEVER
(William Albimoor)
Polydor 15030
No. 8   *March 25, 1972*

Fiction is often stranger than truth: a case in point is the story of the Chakachas. Fiction has it that these guys were led by a mysterious Gaston Boogaerts, who would paint raw chickens and other assorted livestock. Gaston and the group, including a conga-beating beauty named Kary, supposedly appeared in an Italian movie, introduced the Twist to much of the Continent, and had a European hit called "Eso Es El Amor" back in 1958. What a strange little story.

In truth, the musicians were six Belgian studio players, married and middle-aged. They cut "Jungle Fever" and some other sides, then walked off into the sunset. Polydor Records issued "Jungle Fever," and to the surprise of many, it took off. To tour behind the record (always a problem when studio groups have hits), the label located a New York Latino group called Bario to pose as the Chakachas. Chee Chee Navarro, Felix Tollinchi, Eddie Perez, Paul Alicia, Eddie Babato, and Frankie Malabe did record some further albums and singles as the Chakachas, but nothing ever budged from the basement. Eventually, Chee Chee and the guys reassumed their original name.

Malo
SUAVECITO
(Richard Bean, Abel Zarate, Pablo Tellez)
Warner Bros. 7559
No. 18   *May 6, 1972*

Malo was a Latin-rock group from San Francisco fronted by Carlos Santana's brother, Jorge. Formed in the early '70s, this short-lived conglomerate included vets from a number of top-notch Bay Area rock and Latin acts. Guitarist Jorge Santana (b. June 13, 1954, Jalisco, Mexico), guitarist Pablo Tellez (b. July 2, 1951, Granada, Nicaragua) and lead singer Arcelio Garcia, Jr. (b. May 7, 1946, Manati, Puerto Rico) were former members of the Malibus. Trumpeter/trombonist/flutist/saxophonist Roy Murray, drummer Richard Spremich (b. July 2, 1951, San Francisco, Cal.) and guitarist Abel Zarate (b. Dec. 2, 1952, Manila, Philippines) had been in a unit called Naked Lunch. Trumpeter Luis Gasca (b. Mar. 23, 1940, Houston) and keyboardist Richard Kermode (b. Oct. 5, 1946, Lovell, Wyo.) had worked together in Janis Joplin's Kozmic Blues Band (Gasca had also played with Count Basie, Woody Herman, and Mongo Santamaria). Percussionist Raul Rekow (b. June 10, 1944, San Francisco) had been with Soul Sacrifice, and percussionist Leo Rosales (b. San Francisco) had performed with the Escovedo Brothers and Soul Sauce.

Shortly after pulling their numbers together, Malo (Spanish for "bad") met with David Rubinson, one of the area's name producers and managers. Rubinson—who shaped the sounds of ELVIN BISHOP, the Chambers Brothers, and Moby Grape—arranged for the group to be signed to Warner Bros. "Suavecito," from the unit's self-titled first album, would be their lone chart entry. Each of Malo's four albums sold well, their debut LP best of all.

For reasons now lost in time, Malo splintered in 1974. Richard Kermode toured and recorded with Betty Davis. Luis Gasca went

on to play with George Duke, Mother Earth, and Van Morrison, also cutting solo sides for Fantasy Records. Kermode, Gasca, Raul Rebow, and Pablo Tellez provided support for Carlos Santana. Jorge Santana had a few solo disks issued, and has appeared as a guest artist with the Fania All-Stars.

Commander Cody & His Lost Planet Airmen
HOT ROD LINCOLN
(Charles Ryan, W.S. Stevenson)
Paramount 0146
No. 9   *June 3, 1972*

Piano-plunking Commander Cody—George Frayne IV (b. July 19, 1944, Boise, Id.)—was raised in Brooklyn and on Long Island. His interests were serious indeed: art, painting, and sculpture. At the University of Michigan in Ann Arbor, George sidelined in such bands as the Amblers, Lorenzo Lightfoot, and the Fantastic Surfing Beavers. But it was while seeking out some Strohs at an Ann Arbor bar that Frayne conceived what would become the Lost Planet Airmen's trademark sound.

"This was 1966," the Commander told *Sound Trax* writer Martin Porter, "and they had this stack of Buck Owens records on sale. I had never heard anything by him . . . I picked up one of the records, the one with 'Act Naturally' and also this number 'Tiger By The Tail.' And I got turned on by that . . . [here was] stuff that nobody had ever heard before. And it even had a 'yahoo!' in there somewhere. That's what northern hippies always like about country music—that 'yahoo!', that knee-slappin'."

The first version of Commander Cody & His Lost Planet Airmen was formed in 1966. (The Commander's name derived from "Commando Cody," a '40s radio serial, and the band's name came from a line in Coleridge's "The Ancient Mariner.") Ultimately, a regrouped and seemingly ever-changing organization fronted by Frayne and lead guitarist/vocalist Bill Kirchen (b. Jan. 29, 1948, Ann Arbor, Mich.) was firmly planted in San Francisco. Their best-known line-up was of this period, and included "Buffalo" Bruce Barlow (b. Dec. 3, 1948, Oxnard, Cal.) on bass, Bobby Black on pedal steel, Lance Dickerson (b. Oct. 15, 1948, Livonia, Mich.) on drums, Billy C. Farlow (b. Decatur, Ala.) on harmonica and vocals, Andy Stein (b. Aug. 31, 1948, New York City) on fiddle and

Commander Cody
& His Lost
Planet Airmen

sax, and John Tichy (b. St. Louis) on guitar and vocals.

The band quickly developed a substantial reputation among partyin' people of all persuasions, playing a hodgepodge of Texas swing, boogie-woogie, and rockabilly. They became known as the first hippie country band—genuine synthesizers of flagrant flower-power and country-roots music. They would sing everything from truck-driver tunes and corny country ballads played tongue-in-cheek to jump numbers from the '40s.

"When it hit, we weren't ready for it," the Commander recalled. "We were on the road at the time and they called us and said that they thought 'Hot Rod Lincoln' [a cover version of a 1960 novelty hit for country artists Johnny Bond and Charlie Ryan] was gonna be a hit. I said, 'What?' And, you know, what you gotta do next is come up with something of equal quality right away. We went right back into the studio and re-did 'Beat Me Daddy Eight To The Bar' [#81, 1972] to follow it up. It should have been a good follow-up, but for some reason it wasn't."

While only making marginal inroads with two further 45s—a remake of Tex Williams' 1947 hit "Smoke! Smoke! Smoke! (That Cigarette)" (#94, 1973) and a cover of the Jesse Stone shouter "Don't Let Go" (#56, 1975)—Cody and his Airmen did sell plenty of LPs: *Lost in the Ozone* (1971), *Hot Licks, Cold Steel and Trucker's Favorites* (1972), *Country Casanova* (1973), and on through the mid-'70s. All was to end, however, when the band broke up in 1976.

The Commander had a few solo efforts issued in the late '70s by Arista (*Rock 'n' Roll Again* and *Flying Dreams*), a 1980 LP for Line/Peter Pan (*Lose it Tonight*), and has since continued with a spin-off band, the Moonlighters, (which also included Barlow and Kirchen).

The Royal Scots Dragoon Guards

Royal Scots Dragoon Guards
AMAZING GRACE
(John Newton)
RCA Victor 12304
No. 11 *July 1, 1972*

After 300 years of togetherness, the Royal Scots Greys Band dissolved in July 1971. Shortly after, though, members of the Greys joined the Prince of Wales Dragoon Guards, the 3rd Carabineers. Together, this new formation became the Royal Scots Dragoon Guards, a bagpipes-and-drums military band. Within months of this new alliance, they made a series of recordings; John Newton's 1779 classic, "Amazing Grace," was one of more than 30 tunes that were taped. When the album, *Farewell to the Greys*, received some BBC late-night airplay and a positive response, RCA issued the timeless tune as a single.

Record sales were truly phenomenal—at its peak, the Royal Scots record was selling 70,000 copies a day. Pipe Major Tony Crease and company became the first group to ever sell a million copies of a record with the bagpipe as the predominant instrument. More accurately, 20 pipes were piping, and 10 drums were drumming; eventually, 7,000,000 copies were spinning. With that kind of success, "The Day Is Done"—the Guards' follow-up 45—couldn't help but be a royal disappointment.

Mouth & MacNeal
HOW DO YOU DO
(Henry van Hoof, Hans van Hemert)
Philips 40715
No. 8 *July 22, 1972*

The Mouth (Willem Duyn)—so named because he was always running off with it—and Maggie MacNeal (Sjoukje Van't Spijker) teamed up in 1971 after both artists' solo releases bombed. Mouth happened to hear a tape of Maggie's at the Phonogram Studios in Amsterdam. He approached producer Hans van Hermert about arranging a meeting with MacNeal. Frustrated with her failed single, MacNeal agreed to a coupling with the gravel-throated Duyn. "Hey Love You," their first release, did well regionally. "How Do You Do," their second single, sold incredibly well internationally. Eventual sales in the U.S. alone exceeded a million copies.

Commander Cody & His Lost Planet Airmen's most recent effort, *Let's Rock*, was released in 1986. For a while, both Barlow and Dickerson were members of Roger McGuinn's Thunderbyrd.

Buffalo Bruce had a pair of LPs issued in the '70s (*Lovin' in the Valley of the Moon* and *Desert Horizon*) and has done session work for Bette Midler, Steve Miller, and DAVID SOUL. Dickerson has played with Hoyt Axton, David Bromberg, the New Riders of the Purple Sage, Link Wray, and others. Farlow has had some obscure solo singles issued. Andy Stein was involved in the National Lampoon films and had a jazzy LP (*Goin' Places*) issued in 1987 on the Stomp Off label.

Willem Duyn was born in 1942, in Haarlem, Netherlands. For years, he worked as a construction worker, and played drums on evenings and weekends in a jazz combo, the Holland Quartet. Willem joined the more pop-oriented Jay-Jays in 1968. Not content, he moved on to spinning records at a radio station, opening up his own nightclub, and, in 1970, fronting a beat group, Speedway. The latter configuration achieved some success, and Duyn was becoming known as something of a Dutch Joe Cocker. After the group splintered, he cut some solo sides. Mouth's cover of the Shangri-Las' "Remember (Walkin' In The Sand)" failed to generate sales.

Maggie MacNeal was born in 1951, also in the Dutch city of Haarlem. When 18, Maggie studied classical singing for three years before quitting school to join up with a pop group. A local DJ liked her stuff and arranged an audition with the Philips label. Her first release, a cover of "I Heard It Through The Grapevine," flopped.

It was at this point that Mouth and MacNeal came together for their mini-moment on the American airwaves. Never again were they able to interest stateside ears to buy their solo or duet recordings—four singles and two albums were issued in the U.S.—though in the Netherlands, their popularity continued. In 1974, they represented Holland in the Eurovision Song Contest.

Godspell

DAY BY DAY
(John-Michael Teblak, Stephen Schwartz)
Bell 45210
No. 13 *July 29, 1972*

It was designed to be a two-act rock musical based upon the Gospel according to St. Matthew. *Godspell's* original conceiver, and later the author of the like-titled book, was one John-Michael Teblak, a Carnegie Tech student who created the work as a requirement for his master's program. Music and new lyrics were furnished by Stephen Schwartz (b. Mar. 6, 1948, New York City). Stephen was a recent Juilliard graduate and co-author, with Leonard Bernstein, of the English text for Bernstein's *Mass. Godspell* debuted at the Carnegie-Mellon Institute in Pittsburgh; its Big Apple opening took place at the Cherry Lane Theatre on May 17, 1971 (the better-remembered *Jesus*

Christ Superstar opened a few months later).

Original cast members, decked out in colorful clown costumes and facial make-up, included Lamar Alford, Peggy Gordon (co-writer with Jay Hamburger of "By My Side"), David Haskell (as John the Baptist and Judas), Joanne Jonas, Robin Lamont (lead vocalist on "Day By Day"), Sonia Manzano, Gilmer McCormick, Jeffrey Mylett, Stephen Nathan (as Jesus), and Herb Simon.

Despite the musical's near-blasphemous touches (like the portrayal of Jesus as having a clown's red nose and wearing a Superman T-shirt with striped overalls), most critics were liberal in their praise. Five singles from the cast recording were issued, but none were noticed save the rousing "Day By Day." The original soundtrack album sold well.

After 2,124 performances, *Godspell* was temporarily tucked away. It was revived in 1976 and ran for over 500 performances on Broadway at the Broadhurst Theatre. A filmed adaptation, directed by David Greene, appeared in 1973.

Derek & The Dominos

LAYLA
(Eric Clapton, James Beck Gordon)
Atco 6809
No. 10 *August 5, 1972*

"This business devours so much of your time. You don't know if you're doing the right thing or the wrong thing—or even who you are!" Having said this (according to Irwin Stambler's *Encyclopedia of Pop, Rock, & Soul*), Eric Clapton and the rest of Cream—Jack Bruce and Ginger Baker—split up in mid-1968. The strain of playing loud and long night after night had taken its toll: Clapton needed to recuperate, and sought the lower profile offered by Blind Faith and an equally short-lived group, Derek & The Dominos.

The Dominos were Jim Gordon (b. 1945, Los Angeles) on drums and (on "Layla") piano, Carl Radle (b. 1942, Oklahoma) on bass, and Bobby Whitlock (b. 1948, Memphis) on keyboards and vocals. All of them had worked with Leon Russell and Delaney & Bonnie, and they backed Clapton on his first solo album (*Eric Clapton*, 1970). Eric and the Dominos gathered in the fall of 1970 at Atlantic's Criteria Studios in Miami. No one knew it, but only one studio album—*Layla and Other Assorted Love*

Derek & The Dominos, with Eric Clapton (far right)

Songs (1970)—would result from these sessions.

The Allman Brothers' Duane Allman (b. Nov. 20, 1946, Nashville) became a major contributor to the album and something of a pseudo-member, later making limited personal appearances with the band. Producer Tom Dowd had told Duane of the impending sessions; work was already underway when he arrived. "Eric knew me, man, greeted me like an old friend," Allman told Irwin Stambler. "He said, 'Come on, you got to play on this record'—so I did. We'd sit down and plan it out, work out our different parts . . . Everybody contributed. Most of it was cut live, no overdubbing—and it was all done in ten days."

Their label was only to issue three singles. A Phil Spector-produced version of "Tell The Truth" (a hopped-up variation on the album version) missed the charts entirely. "Bell Bottom Blues" made the lowest reaches of the Hot 100 (#91, 1971). And a truncated version of "Layla"—inspired by Clapton's unrequited love for Patti Harrison, George Harrison's wife—only managed to make number 51 in 1971.

"Layla" is often considered the pinnacle of Clapton's musical achievement, and is a much-requested (and much-performed) part of his live set even today. The tune features soaring slide guitar from Duane Allman—Clapton even reported at one time that Allman plays all the electric guitars on the track—and a piano section composed by Jim Gordon. In 1972, the song was reissued, this time in its entirety—all seven minutes and ten seconds of it.

The Dominos' follow-up LP was aborted, although tracks from the sessions appear on Clapton's *Crossroads* compilation. The group received a critical drubbing during its tour in 1972; a half-hearted live LP for RSO, *Derek & The Dominos In Concert*, appeared in 1973. The Dominos had fallen apart by this point, and Clapton had gone into hiding. He did some session work and appeared at 1971's *Concert for Bangladesh*, but was otherwise out of public view. Clapton had acquired a serious heroin habit—due to a deep depression from the sudden death of Duane Allman, and from what he perceived as a lack of public acceptance for Derek & The Dominos.

Argent

HOLD YOUR HEAD UP
(Rod Argent, Chris White)
Epic 10852
No. 5 *August 26, 1972*

Although vast sums of money were offered, Rod Argent and his fellow Zombies refused to reunite for even one show. Surely, Rod and Paul Atkinson, Colin Blunstone, Hugh Grundy, and Chris White would want to have a second shot at stardom. Since the Zombies' break-up, PEOPLE had unearthed "I Love You" (#14, 1968), an obscure "B" side. And both "Time Of The Season" (#3, 1969) and the *Odessey [sic] and Oracle* (1969) album were suddenly stateside smashes.

But alas, such was not to be. Once the pressure for a Zombies reunion had abated, Rod Argent (b. June 14, 1945, St. Albans, England) set to work launching a self-named group. The unit's first album, *Argent*, appeared in 1970, and featured Argent, lead singer/guitarist Russ Ballard (b. Oct. 31, 1947, Waltham Cross, England), bassist Jim Rodford (b. July 7, 1945, St. Albans), and drummer Bob Henrit (b. May 2, 1945, Broxbourine). Ballard and

Henrit were both ex-members of the Unit 4 Plus 2 and Adam Faith's back-up band, the Roulettes.

Neither *Argent* nor *Ring of Hands* (1970) sold in sizeable amounts, though Three Dog Night did all right with "Liar" (#7, 1971), a cut from the first album. The band toured America, with stops at both Fillmores, the Whisky-A-Go-Go, the Kinetic Playground, and the Boston Tea Party. The audience response was favorable and growing.

With the issuance of *All Together Now* (1972) and its lead single, "Hold Your Head Up," Argent had found a niche, though they seemed to notice not. "Tragedy," the group's follow-up cut, was similarly dense and hook-ridden and should have charted; it did in England. Months later, a much more self-indulgent *In Deep* (1973) was released.

A year later, Ballard left the fold to start his solo career. Russ has since written for FRIDA, ACE FREHLEY, and Rainbow. He also penned "You Can Do Magic" for America (#8, 1982), and had his own solo success with "On The Rebound" (#8, 1980) and "Voices." His replacements in Argent were guitarist John Grimaldi (b. May 25, 1955) and guitarist John Verity (b. May 2, 1944). A double-live set,

Argent

Encore—Live in Concert (1975), was issued while the band attempted their regrouping. Two more LPs followed—*Circus* (1975) and *Counterpoint* (1975)—but these were marred by Rod's pseudo-classical pretenses. When Grimaldi left the group in 1976, Rod folded his band up.

Verity, Rodford, and Herit remained together as Phoenix for two unsuccessful LPs. Verity has fronted a band named after himself; Rodford has since joined the Kinks; Henrit joined G.B. Blues & Company, and is now involved in musical-instrument retailing. Argent had his first musical, *Masquerade*, staged at London's Young Vic Theatre. He has worked sessions (Colin Blunstone, the Hollies, CHRIS REA, Andrew Lloyd Webber, the Who), had two jazz-oriented LPs issued (*Moving Home*, 1978; *Ghosts*, 1982), and has recently lent his name to a chain of keyboard shops. In 1985, Rod briefly reformed a group under his own name for a charity appearance.

Sailcat
MOTORCYCLE MAMA
(John Wyker)
Elektra 45782
No. 12   *August 26, 1972*

Sailcat was never a group per se. They were more of a happening that, well, happened to find one good soft-shoe song. Their lone self-titled album indicates that "officially" Sailcat comprised two guitar pickers named Court Pickett and John Wyker. They had been hanging around the Muscle Shoals, Alabama, recording scene, and had picked up some influential friends, like Clayton Ivey (bass), Chuck Leavell of the Allman Brothers (keyboards), and Pete Carr (guitar)—a producer, songwriter, and later one-half of LeBLANC & CARR. All of these sessioneers and two others played on the tracks. And all of the aforementioned (with the exception of Leavell) contributed to writing Sailcat's tunes.

"Motorcycle Mama" was a fluke hit from Sailcat's debut LP. When a follow-up was needed, all returned to the Widget Studios to cut something called "Baby Ruth." Sales were slow, to say the least. Their swan song, "She Showed Me," came next. In light of the disk's poor showing, the "Sailcat" name was shelved, and the loosely-knit aggregation directed their energies elsewhere.

In 1973, Courtland Pickett had a solo album issued by Elektra.

Daniel Boone
BEAUTIFUL SUNDAY
(D. Boone, R. McQueen)
Mercury 73281
No. 15   *September 16, 1972*

Like many other young lads, Peter Stirling was given piano lessons. At age 13, while laid up with an illness, the Britisher took to strumming a guitar; three years later, he was playing in the Beachcombers. In 1963, just as the known world was being overtaken by Beatlemania, Peter was a member of a pop group named the Bruisers, who had a medium-sized hit in England with "Blue Girl." The group was not part of the British Invasion, and after a few more singles on Parlophone, the Bruisers disbanded.

In 1965, Stirling began his career as a session musician with songwriter Les Reed, and reportedly played on many Tom Jones sessions (including the one that produced "It's Not Unusual"). The Merseybeats and Kathy Kirby were among the first artists to record Peter's early songwriting efforts. Larry Page—producer of the Troggs and founder of Page One and Penny Farthing Records—took a demo Stirling had created on "Daddy Don't You Walk So Fast," sweetened the thing with strings, credited the track to "Daniel Boone," and released it on his Penny Farthing label. The recording made the top 20 in the U.K., but Wayne Newton's cover rendition stole some of Stirling's glory by making the top 10 stateside.

Peter's moment, however, was at hand. The very next release was the infectious and bouncy "Beautiful Sunday." The world could not get enough of this tune; but the world also did not take kindly to any future recordings Peter ever made, either as Daniel Boone or as Peter Lee Stirling. By July 1972, Pete's high point had sold a million copies worldwide. Two years later, producer Page re-released the recording, and sales continued. Two more years passed, and "Beautiful Sunday" was picked up as the theme song for a popular Japanese TV program. Another million copies were sold, and the tune remained number one on the Japanese charts for four months—reportedly becoming one of the top-selling records in Japanese pop history.

Hot Butter

POPCORN
(Gershon Kingsley)
Musicor 1458
No. 9 *October 21, 1972*

Hot Butter was Stan Free, a session keyboardist and Moog synthesizer player. As a
Moog man, Stan had provided behind-the-
scenes synth sounds to rock, pop, and semi-
classical works. Over the years, he had sound-
seasoned recordings by John Denver, ARLO
GUTHRIE, and even Arthur Fiedler's Boston
Pops. Not counting a few forgettable solo sides
for the Amy label in the mid-'60s, Stan's catchy
"Popcorn" was his first front-line outing. Although the instrumental was momentarily appealing, in a humbly hummable way, its allure
diminished with each hearing.

In an attempt to forestall the inevitable satiation with Stan's quirky sounds, Steve Jerome,
Bill Jerome, and Danny Jordan (formerly with
THE DETERGENTS) at MTL Productions had
Stan "Moog-ize" former hits with distinctive
melodies. "Tequila," "Percolator," "Pipeline,"
and "Apache" were all issued as singles, but not
a one found a receptive audience.

Arlo Guthrie

THE CITY OF NEW ORLEANS
(Steve Goodman)
Reprise 1103
No. 18 *October 28, 1972*

For a brief period in the late '60s, Arlo Guthrie
was America's favorite folkie. Many fondly recall the classic lines—"You can get anything
you want/At Alice's Rest-au-rant"—from
"Alice's Restaurant," the rambling 18-minute
saga about his arrest for littering in Stock-
bridge, Massachusetts, on Thanksgiving Day
of 1965. Not only did that offense render Arlo
ineligible for the draft, but it also launched his
career. "Alice's Restaurant" became the core
of his same-titled 1967 debut LP, and served
two years later as the flaky foundation for Arthur Penn's film of the same name.

Arlo (b. July 10, 1947, Coney Island, N.Y.)
was born the eldest son of folk legend Woody
Guthrie and his wife, Marjorie. People like
Bob Dylan, Ramblin' Jack Elliott, Cisco
Houston, and Pete Seeger were always drop-
ping by and playing music together. When he

Arlo Guthrie

was three, Arlo danced and blew his harmonica
for Leadbelly. A few years later, his mom, a
former Martha Graham dancer, taught him the
workings of the guitar. He attended private
schools and, for a while, a college in Billings,
Montana.

In mid-'65, Arlo started working the East
Coast coffeehouse circuit. He toured Japan
with Judy Collins, and on his return in 1967, he
presented the initial work-up on "Alice's Re-
sturant" at the WNYC Folk Song Festival. After his first album, a number of highly-praised
LPs followed: *Arlo* (1968), *Running Down the
Road* (1969), *Washington County* (1970), and
Hobo's Lullabye (1972). Some of Guthrie's most
popular numbers included "Coming Into Los
Angeles," a song about dope-smuggling that
Guthrie performed at Woodstock; the deli-
ciously vicious anti-Nixon number, "Presiden-
tial Rag"; an Arab-Israeli political commen-
tary, "Children of Abraham" . . . and that
Steve Goodman train tune, "The City Of New
Orleans."

Arlo is still active on the music scene. During the '70s, he toured and recorded with Pete Seeger. He frequently performs for causes like the anti-nuclear and ecological movements. But Guthrie rarely sings of Alice and the restaurant these days. As he told an interviewer in the late '70s: "Alice, it's just too long. I forgot it about four or five years ago. I'm trying to learn it again, but . . . I got the first part down, the garbage down. I'm just workin' on the trash part now."

Danny O'Keefe

GOOD TIME CHARLIE'S GOT THE BLUES

(Danny O'Keefe)
Signpost 70006
No. 9 *November 4, 1972*

Danny O'Keefe, who wrote many portrait pieces that others would popularize, is primarily remembered for his lone, lazy lingering in top 40-land. "Good Time Charlie's Got The Blues" was no party platter, but a poignant vignette of an abandoned Charlie, his pills, and his pain. "It was about a good friend of mine," O'Keefe told *Rolling Stone*'s Judith Sims. "He's a very mellow, beautiful friend who was going through heart attacks and it was rough [back in 1968]. It was a rough period for me, too."

Danny grew up in the small town of Wenatchee, Washington. Papa was a lawyer, an insurance adjustor, and, by Dan's pre-teen years, a dying man. "My grandmother put me into a military school in St. Paul. That was for the first two years of high school." About the time of his dad's death, O'Keefe began writing poetry and hanging out in the area's coffee houses. After a short stay at the University of Minnesota, he returned to his hometown to attend Wenatchee Valley College. "In the winter when I was 20, I stayed there being lonely and crazy, starting to take drugs and playing guitar. I did it for a release, not seriously trying to do anything except to get some of the stuff inside out."

In the mid-'60s, O'Keefe was seriously injured in a motorcycle accident that involved extensive surgery and years of recovery. During this time, O'Keefe was encouraged to continue writing. By 1966, he had some songs and a band, later labeled the Bandits. A musical buddy introduced them to Jerry Dennson, who had recorded IAN WHITCOMB, the Sonics, and

early sides on Paul Revere & The Raiders. (Dennson also discovered the Kingsmen of "Louie Louie" fame.) A few O'Keefe singles (like "That Old Sweet Song") and a Bandits 45 ("Little Sally Walker") were issued on Dennson's Jerden label, but no great wealth and popularity were to follow. As Calliope, the Bandits band had singles issued on a variety of labels (Epic, Jet Set, Shamley) and an LP (*Steamed*, 1968) on Buddah, but again, nothing quite clicked.

Charlie Greene and Brian Stone—who supervised the careers of BUFFALO SPRINGFIELD, BOB LIND, and Sonny & Cher—spied O'Keefe palling around with a group called Daily Flash, and managed to convince Atlantic Records' Ahmet Ertegun to record him as a singer-songwriter solo act. "Good Time Charlie" was included on Danny's debut album; the tune was recorded on four or five occasions before everything was deemed just right.

A few follow-ups nearly cracked the Hot 100 ("The Road," "Angels Spread Your Wings") and two LPs sold well—*O'Keefe* (1972) and *Breezy Stories* (1973). But Danny never managed to solidify a mass audience for his story songs. Jackson Browne, Judy Collins, Waylon Jennings, B.W. STEVENSON, and even Elvis have recorded his material.

Most recently, Danny O'Keefe had an album (*The Day to Day*, 1984) and single ("Along For The Ride") issued by Coldwater Records. In 1985, he was a member of the Seattle Helps The Hungry configuration that issued "Give Just A Little" as a 45 on the DJ label.

Chi Coltrane

THUNDER AND LIGHTNING

(Chi Coltrane)
Columbia 45640
No. 17 *November 18, 1972*

Born in Racine, Wisconsin, on November 16, 1948, Chi began her classical piano studies at the tender age of seven. She sang in her church choir, and at the age of 12 gave her first public keyboard performance. By high school graduation, Chi was singing in the bars and hot spots of the Badger State. She attended Salter School of Music in L.A. for two years, and led the first of her bands. Shortly after, she moved to the Windy City and formed the Chicago Coltrane.

While working the club scene, Chi caught

the attention of talent scouts for Columbia Records. Contracts were signed, arrangements were made, and songs were recorded. But with the exception of her lone tuffy, "Thunder And Lightning," Chi's self-titled debut disk featured only humdrum hoofers. The LP did place on *Billboard*'s top pop albums chart, and "Thunder" rumbled the airwaves, but lightning did not strike twice for Chi. Follow-up 45s like "Go Like Elijah," "You Were My Friend," and "Who Ever Told You" sank from sight with nary a spin.

Delegates
CONVENTION '72
(Nick Cenci, Nick Casel)
Mainstream 5525
No. 8 *November 18, 1972*

"The Delegates were myself and two other principals," Tampa DJ Bob DeCarlo (b. Jan. 9, 1941, New York City) explained in an exclusive interview. "One was Nick Cenci. The name might ring a bell with some because a long time ago, he was involved in a record distributorship in Pittsburgh called Co & Ce. He also had a label [bearing the same name] and handled Lou Christie and, early on, the Vogues. The other guy was his partner, Nick Kousaleous [a.k.a. Nick Casel]. They would handle Motown and some other labels in the tri-state area.

"We played golf together, all three of us. And we'd been kicking this idea around for a long time. It seemed no one had done a break-in record [wherein a narrative is intercut with excerpts from then-current hits] in a long, long time, and here was this convention. So, we decided to do it. I brought over a bunch of singles from KQU, where I worked, and we sat in my kitchen and wrote it.

"Cenci set out to sell it. He must have visited all the offices he could. Buddah, Motown—no one wanted to press it. Then Mainstream, the jazz label, comes up and says 'Sure, let's do it.' It was a shock, like 'Really, you will?' Cenci had 10,000 copies pressed, and it started to take off in Parkersburg, West Virginia.

"I worked at KQU, one of the big pop stations and an ABC affiliate, at the time. They thought it smacked of payola if they played the tune, so they didn't . . . But it made the top 10, and without any airplay, on WLS in Chicago, another affiliate. And we got no play in New York. But wherever it was played, it sold well. It was a cute record."

When "Convention '72" hit big, Mainstream issued a now-rare but low-grade album that included Nick Casel lisping his way through "My Way." The label called for a follow-up LP, but DeCarlo's station forbade him to be involved with the project, and recording funds were in short supply anyway. An obscure follow-up single, "Richard M. Nixon—Face The Issues, Pt. 1 & 2," appeared under the "Delegates" name, but DeCarlo has denied any knowledge of its existence. Almost as quickly as they appeared, the Delegates vanished into pop oblivion.

Brighter Side of Darkness

LOVE JONES
(Randolph Murph, Clarence Johnson,
Ralph Eskridge)
20th Century 2002
No. 16 *February 3, 1973*

Ralph Eskridge, Randolph Murph, and Larry Washington met at Calumet High on Chicago's South Side in 1971. Anna Preston, a one-time entertainer and mother of a houseful of music-makers, became their manager, music director and body-and-soul shaper. She added 12-year-old Darryl Lamont to the group to give them a touch of Jackson Five/teen-appealing bubble-gum soul.

After the group had played a few talent contests and successful gigs, producer Clarence Johnson cut a demo on the trio and rushed it over to 20th Century's new president, Russ Regan. Russ liked what he heard, and "Love Jones" became the group's first record. "Jones," a slang expression for addiction, was a string-infested talkie thing that surprised many folks when it mounted the upper reaches of *Billboard*'s pop charts.

Overnight, the teens were a full-grown success, but only momentarily. En route to a "Soul Train" appearance, a dispute of some sort took place, and the record company fired three-quarters of the group; only Lamont remained. The group had already recorded an album's worth of material; after its release, and three more singles, 20th Century dropped them.

Both parties wrangled in court over who—management and the record company, or the fired parties—owned the rights to the "Brighter Side of Darkness" name. The courts eventually ruled in favor of the former.

Clarence Johnson hired Jesse Harvey, Nate Pringle, and Arthur Scales to fill in the vocal void behind Lamont. A one-off single for his Starve label was issued, but on release, it sank from sight. Later that year, 20th Century decided to pick up on some Johnson-produced sides by the new Brighter Side (Harvey, Pringle, Scales, and newcomer Tyrone Stewart). For whatever reason, 20th Century renamed the group the Imaginations; two albums and a batch of singles were shipped, but nothing ever charted.

In the late '70s, Darryl Lamont and Randolph Murph re-formed Brighter Side of Darkness. Apparently, the rightful owners of the group's faded moniker no longer cared whether anybody used the name or not. The Magic Touch label released one final single, "He Made You Mine," in 1978.

Timmy Thomas

WHY CAN'T WE LIVE TOGETHER
(Timmy Thomas)
Glades 1703
No. 3 *February 10, 1973*

"I was born in Evansville, Indiana, on the 13th of November, 1944," Timmy Thomas told *Blues & Soul*. "By the time I was 10 I was playing organ at my father's church. I always had a good ear for music. I was one of 12 kids and most of them were into music, but I guess I pushed a little harder."

Timmy formed his first band in high school. In 1962, he won a scholarship to attend the Stan Kenton Jazz Clinic. There he studied with CANNONBALL ADDERLEY, Donald Byrd, and Woody Herman. "When I got a scholarship to attend Lane College in Jackson, Tennessee, I started messing with a lot of the dudes who were into a soul thing. I started getting session work with Stax, and I played on a lot of Stax/Volt Records. I played with the MAR-KEYS, filling in when Booker T. took leave."

Thomas also worked as a house musician for Bobby Russell's and Quinton Claunch's Gold-wax label. Timmy's keyboards accompanied James Carr, Percey Milem, Spencer Wiggins, and O.V. Wright. Impressed with his abilities, Russell and Claunch let Thomas, with the aid of Willie Mitchell's band, record two solo singles—"Have Some Boogaloo" and "Whole Lotta Shakin' Goin' On." Neither gathered much notice.

When Goldwax shut its doors, Tim returned to college to complete his musical studies. In 1970, he moved to Miami, took a teaching position with Florida Memorial College, and opened a lounge in the beach area. Thomas would often provide entertainment at his bar. One tune in particular was getting quite a reaction. Once all the wrinkles were ironed out, Thomas walked "Why Can't We Live To-gether" into Henry Stone's offices at TK Records.

"Why Can't We" has got to be one of the most memorable of all hits from the '70s—and one of the simplest. With its cheesy organ, a rhythm box ticking out a metronome beat, and Timmy sincerely sobbin' about peace, love, and the brotherhood of man, the disk was effective and sold several million copies. The follow-up,

"People Are Changin'" (#75, 1973), did well; in all, 13 of his singles made the R & B listings from 1973 to 1984, with "Gotta Give A Little Love (Ten Years After)" (#80/29, 1980) also scoring on the Hot 100.

Until TK went under in 1980, Tim provided back-up services for K.C. & The Sunshine Band, Betty Wright, and others. Thomas still runs his lounge and records for Gold Mountain Records.

Hurricane Smith

OH, BABE, WHAT WOULD YOU SAY?
(Hurricane Smith)
Capitol 3383
No. 3 *February 17, 1972*

Born in northern England in 1923, reportedly to a family of gypsies, little Norman Smith began messing with instruments as diverse as the drums, piano, vibes, trombone, and stand-up bass. As a young adult, he held down gigs as a jazz trumpeter for years. With the offer of an eventual apprenticeship as a recording engineer, Norman went to work as a "gofer" in 1955 at EMI's legendary Abbey Road studios. One of his first shots at being a full-fledged engineer came with the FRANK IFIELD session that produced "I Remember You" (#5, 1962).

Norman was present as the engineer on June 6, 1962, when the Beatles auditioned for George Martin. "I couldn't believe what louts they looked with their funny hair cuts —they didn't impress me at all," Smith said in Brian Southall's *Abbey Road.* Impressed or not, Smith engineered nearly all the Beatles sessions through *Rubber Soul* and *Revolver.* In the late '60s, Norman was given the chance to produce Pink Floyd, a bizarre new group named after Georgia bluesmen Pink Anderson and Floyd Council. From Pink Floyd's earliest singles—such as "Arnold Layne," the tale of an undergarment-stealing transvestite—through many of their albums, it was Norman Smith who attempted to manage the occasionally chaotic Pink Floyd sessions.

Smith had always secretly wanted to be a pop star. He had written something called "Don't Let It Die," and one day when things were not going too well at a Floyd session and all the band members had left for a break, Norman taped the song. When noted producer Mickie Most overheard the recording session, he encouraged Norman to release the disk

himself rather than approach John Lennon with the song, as Smith had intended.

Naming himself after the title character in a 1952 Yvonne de Carlo flick, Hurricane, at age 49, had his first British hit with "Don't Let It Die" in June 1971. His follow-up, the charming "Oh, Babe, What Would You Say?", made Hurricane a genuine pop star—at least for a moment or so.

"The melody [was] happy and simple," he told *Rolling Stone*'s Pete Gambaccini. "It was the producer in me that designed the lyric to recapture almost the era I grew up in. It's almost a true story of my life. I would go to a ballroom, but I was so shy I couldn't even ask someone to dance. I'd walk home imagining a romance when I'd never even reached first base. 'Oh, Babe' was about those fantasies."

By the time the follow-up—"Who Was It?" (#49, 1973)—and at least one more single were released, Norman had retired his "Hurricane" character and was breeding racehorses in Surrey, England. He has, however, popped up blowing trumpet on various pop projects, like the first Teardrop Explodes album in 1980. He works as a free-lance producer, and recently did production work on Wings alumnus Denny Laine's albums.

King Harvest

DANCIN' IN THE MOONLIGHT
(Ronald Altback)
Perception 515
No. 13 *February 24, 1973*

The members of King Harvest came from diverse musical backgrounds. Tony Cahill (bass) had played with the Easybeats, done some session work with R & B shouter Willie Mabon, and, with David Montgomery (drums), had played on Python Lee Jackson's *In A Broken Dream* (1970). Davy "Doc" Robinson (keyboards, trombone) had recorded with Boffalongo. Ron Altback (keyboards), the band's prime writer, had a heavy leaning toward the Beach Boys, ballads, and jazzy musical structures. Completing the line-up were Sherman Kelly (keyboards), Rod Novack (sax), and Ed Tuleja (guitar).

Terry Phillips' Perception label had been unsuccessful in the realm of hit-making. When Phillips heard of the sounds that Altback and his Big Apple-based band were creating, he quickly offered them a recording contract.

King Harvest

"Dancin' In The Moonlight," a Boffalongo track revamped with jiggly keyboards and tight vocal harmony, appeared as the group's debut single. To the dismay of the more hard-rockin' faction within the group, "Dancin'" cracked the charts. Harvest was promptly pegged as a "lite" group, a purveyor of pop puffery.

"A Little Bit of Magic" (#91, 1973) and later releases sold poorly, and members came and went. In 1976, with the aid of Beach Boys Mike Love and Carl Wilson, a reconstructed band—featuring Altback, Novak, Robinson, and Tuleja—was signed to A & M. Their lone self-titled album died shortly after birth.

Ed Tuleja did some session work on Dennis Wilson's 1977 solo album. Ron Altback and Doc Robinson joined Mike Love in the creation of his Celebration band, which did the soundtrack to the film *Almost Summer* (1978).

Deodato
ALSO SPRACH ZARATHUSTRA
(Richard Strauss)
CTI 12
No. 2 *March 31, 1973*

Deodato was born Eumire Almeida on June 21, 1942, in Rio de Janeiro, Brazil. Deo is a self-taught musician who can work his way with the keyboard, bass, or guitar. He made his professional debut in Brazil accompanying Astrud Gilberto and won honors for a composition, "Spirit Of Summer," at a Rio song festival.

In 1967, Deo started making connnections with musicians and producers in the U.S. By 1970, he was involved in studio work with Roberta Flack, Bette Midler, Wes Montgomery, and Frank Sinatra. Three years later, Deo was in the spotlight with his funky instrumental rendition of Richard Strauss' "Also Sprach Zarathustra," a.k.a. the theme from *2001: A Space Odyssey*. His scoring abilities were thereafter made use of for TV programs, specials, and movies.

Deodato has recorded numerous albums for CTI, MCA, and Warner Bros., and produced Kool & The Gang from 1979 to 1982. He carries on to this day with his distinctively disco-fied music.

Loudon Wainwright III
DEAD SKUNK
(Loudon Wainwright III)
Columbia 45726
No. 16 *March 31, 1973*

"I'd like it if people knew about a lot of other songs, instead of, 'Oh, yeah, that's the guy that wrote 'Dead Skunk,' '" remarked Loudon Wainwright to *DISCoveries'* Rush Evans. "But on the other hand, it created some opportunities for me and gave me some exposure, and it was kind of fun . . . I feel pretty good about it."

Loudon (b. Sept. 5, 1945, Durham, N.C.) was born into a noted lineage. He is a direct descendant of Peter Stuyvesant, the renowned Dutch sovereign and first governor of New Amsterdam (New York). His grandfather was an insurance magnate, and his father (Loudon Wainwright II) was a journalist for *Life* Magazine. Loudon III attended a private school in Middlebrook, Delaware—the very same Episcopalian boarding school that was the setting for the film *Dead Poets Society* (1989). When he was 16, he made his folksinging debut at the Coffee Gallery in San Francisco's North Beach.

Loud had attended the Carnegie Mellon Institute in Pittsburgh with the intention of becoming an actor. The romance of the open road hit, however, and Loud was soon hitchhiking across the land. He was in San Francisco in 1967 for the Summer of Love. It was after this experience and upon his return to the East— and assorted gigs in Greenwich Village houses like the Gaslight—that Wainwright, like his father before him, put words to paper.

In 1970, Atlantic Records signed him in the hopes that he would turn out to be "the next Dylan." Critical response was enthusiastic; two starkly bitter albums were issued by the label, followed by three more accessible works for Columbia. The first of these Columbia LPs (*Album III*) included Loud with a countrified back-up band and *that song*. "I wrote 'Dead Skunk' in 15 minutes as an answer to those who kept saying I was too intellectual," he told *Crawdaddy's* Rob Patterson. A dozen more Loudon Wainwright III LPs have been issued, two of which sold reasonably well—*Unrequited* (1975) and *T Shirt* (1976).

Over the years, Loudon has taken periodic pot-shots at the music business. There was "The Grammy Game," which recounts a dream Loud had about winning the cherished statue, complete with the standing ovation and the mumbled, humbling speech: "I'd like to thank my producer and Jesus Christ." Most recently, there was "T.S.D.H.A.V.," a cut on Loud's *Therapy* (1989). The lines go: "This song don't have a video/Use your imagination/Forget about the radio/They won't play it on the station."

"I have some bitterness about the Biz," he told *DISCoveries*, "but who doesn't? . . . I consider myself very lucky to be doing something that I really like to do."

Loudon has also found an outlet playing various roles on TV ("M.A.S.H.," as Captain Spaulding), the stage (*Pump Boys and Dinettes*), and the silver screen (*The Slugger's Wife*, 1985; *Jackknife*, 1988).

Vicki Lawrence
THE NIGHT THE LIGHTS WENT OUT IN GEORGIA
(Bobby Russell)
Bell 45303
No. 1 *April 7, 1973*

Vicki Lawrence, to most anyone with a soft heart for TV comedy, is known for her appearances on "The Carol Burnett Show" and her own short-lived spin-off series, "Mama's Family." Legend has it that a young Vicki was

Deodato

pestered by her mother to write to Carol Burnett; she told the comedy star just how much she resembled her, and just how much it would mean to her little heart if they could meet, even if just for a moment. Burnett's secretary supposedly spotted this plea among the hordes of fan mail and brought it to Carol's attention. And, yes, a meeting was arranged and consummated. Different tale-tellers describe the actual meeting in various ways, but the gist is that at that moment, Vicki was discovered.

Miss Lawrence, born on March 26, 1949, in Inglewood, California, had been preparing for show business nearly all of her days. As a child, she had studied ballet and tap dancing and had taken lessons on the piano and guitar. In college, she performed with various folk groups, and three years prior to meeting with Miss Burnett, Vicki joined a singing group, the Young Americans. A journalist reviewing a concert by the group mentioned Lawrence's resemblance to Burnett. Vicki sent the clipping to Burnett, and reportedly was quite surprised to receive a return phone call from her,

suggesting that Vicki audition for a role in Carol's upcoming TV series.

Vicki became a regular member of the cast. In 1969, while filming an episode, she met songwriter ("Honey," "Little Green Apples") and husband-to-be Bobby Russell. A few years later, when Russell had a fact-based, murder-out-of-passion song turned down by Cher, he looked to his wife to record the number. She did so, and the results were pleasant enough, but no one in his or her right mind expected "The Night The Lights Went Out In Georgia" to sell as well as it eventually did. Two more Lawrence disks, "He Did It With Me" (#75, 1973) and "The Other Woman" (#81, 1975), made the Hot 100, but Vicki never again waxed anything that approached the contagious popularity of her murderous ode.

In 1976, Vicki Lawrence closed the door on her pop-music career. None of her recordings are currently in print, but almost every day, somewhere on the planet Earth, Vicki's likeness can be spotted in syndicated reruns of "The Carol Burnett Show" and "Mama's Family."

Lou Reed

Lou Reed

WALK ON THE WILD SIDE
(Lou Reed)
RCA 0887
No. 16 *April 28, 1973*

"The apostle of rock nihilism" or "the king of decadence," as he has been dubbed, will readily acknowledge that he hasn't had a hit single since "Walk On The Wild Side," his 1973 ode to the gender-bending Andy Warhol crowd. "I haven't even tried to duplicate it," Lou Reed told *Revolution*'s Roy Trakin. How a controversial cut such as "Wild Side"—with its reference to "giving head"—ever snuck past the nation's censors, is not known.

Reed has been in the public eye quite a bit recently. His appearance at the 1986 Amnesty International concert, the Greenspan compilation LP, and TV commercials for Honda and American Express card, have all increased his visibility among young rock fans. His most recent album, *New York* (1989), like a fair number of his earlier works, has received critical praise, and may yet yield that second big hit. Reed also collaborated with John Cale in 1990 to compose and perform *Songs For Drella*, a musical tribute to Andy Warhol.

He was born Louis Firbank on March 2, 1943, to an upper-middle-class family in Long Island, New York. By age 14, Lou was opting for a life of rebellion and rock and roll. He played guitar in garage bands with names like the Jades, Pasha & The Prophets, the Shades, and the Eldorados. He attended Syracuse University but dropped out; dabbled in journalism and acting; and worked for a number of years as a staff songwriter and ghost artist for Pickwick Records. As such, Lou wrote hot rod and surfing songs, recorded as the Beach Nuts, and almost had a local hit as the Primitives with "The Ostrich."

In 1964, Reed teamed up with John Cale and Sterling Morrison, and came under the guiding hand of multi-media artist Andy Warhol. With the addition the following year of Maureen Tucker, they became the Velvet Underground, stark minstrels of urban decay, drugs, and the perverse. During the reign of flower power and LSD-stoked utopianism, the Velvets were proto-punks, crafting music that depicted the sleazy underbelly of the Beat Generation and the evolving counterculture. Their albums sold only marginally at first and their time was short, but the influence of their sound and attitude on today's rock music was profound.

Jud Strunk

With the release of the group's *Loaded* in 1970, Lou called it quits, dropping out of music and working at his father's accounting firm in Long Island. The following year, Reed returned to the scene with the release of *Lou Reed*, the first of now nearly 20 albums, all of which have charted on *Billboard*'s top pop albums listings. Each album, fans will attest, has its distinctive direction and style, and each is peopled by a predictable assortment of bizarre characters: the speed freak, the trashy biker, the killer, and, yes, the elder rock statesman.

Jud Strunk

DAISY A DAY
(Jud Strunk)
MGM 14463
No. 14 *May 19, 1973*

On one of his last eclectic albums, Jud referred to himself as "a semi-reformed, tequila-crazed gypsy." He was born Justin Strunk, Jr., on June

11, 1936, in Jameston, New York; he died in a plane crash on October 15, 1981. People were just getting to know and appreciate who this story-telling, banjo-picking, folkie-cum-country man was.

He was raised in Farmington, Maine. While in second grade, he won first prize at a community hall talent contest playing spoons and tap dancing. In his teen years, he would recite poetry in nearby clubs and sing. For a while, he toured as a "one-man show" for the U.S. armed forces. Not many noticed, but he appeared in the off-Broadway production of *Beautiful Dreamer.*

In the '70s, Jud moved west to California, where he would do his personalized entertaining on local TV programs. For a couple of years (1972–1973), he was a regular on "Laugh-In." His records, when you could find them, were always a little different. He'd sing of amnesia, describe Howard Hughes' permanent plot on this planet, read patriotic poetry, or recite verse about an old man's undying love for his long-departed wife. Some of his stuff made minor motions onto the pop and country listings—"Next Door Neighbor's Kid" (—/—/ #86, 1973), "My Country" (#59, 1974), "The Biggest Parakeets In Town (#50, 1975), and "Pamela Brown" (—/—/#88, 1976). But only "Daisy A Day" was a box-office smash.

Skylark

WILDFLOWER
(D. Richardson, D. Edwards)
Capitol 3511
No. 9 *May 26, 1973*

Skylark was a fleeting fling for Bonnie Jean Cook, David Foster, and their fluctuating fraternity. Bonnie Jean and David had been members of Ronnie Hawkins' Hawks before they hatched a scheme to start their own band in the early '70s. Based in Vancouver, Canada, Cook (lead vocals) and Foster (keyboards) rounded up some hometown help from Donny Gerrard (lead vocals), Carl Greaves (percussion), Duris Maxwell (drums), Norman McPherson (guitar), and Steven Pugsley (bass).

After six months of rehearsals, Capitol of Canada took an interest in the group. Little did the label know that the band's days were numbered. By the time Skylark's self-titled LP was released, Greaves, McPherson, and Pugsley were ex-members. After the group's first 45

flopped, Windsor's CKLW took a protracted airtime interest in a tender track called "Wildflower."

Reportedly, internal tensions resulted from the swelling success of "Wildflower." Follow-up 45s failed to fly, and by the time their second and last album was recorded, the only Skylarks remaining were Donny Gerrard and the Fosters (David had married Bonnie Jean Cook by this time).

In addition to doing session work with Eric Carmen, Donovan, and Yvonne Elliman, Donny Gerrard had a solo hit in 1976 with his Greedy release, "Words (Are Impossible)" (#87). Duris Maxwell resurfaced in the '70s as a member of Doucette, and in the '80s drummed for the Powder Blues Band. David Foster has been a member of groups like Airplay, Attitudes, Fools Gold, Highway, and later, the Average White Band. Foster has also racked up an incredible list of session credits, having played keyboards for Patti Austin, George Benson, Kim Carnes, Chicago, Earth, Wind & Fire, Hall & Oates, Michael Jackson, Gladys Knight, Little Feat, Lynyrd Skynyrd, the Pointer Sisters, and both George Harrison and Ringo Starr—to name but a few.

Focus

HOCUS POCUS
(Thijs van Leer, Jan Akkerman)
Sire 704
No. 9 *June 2, 1973*

They were a Dutch group whose goal was to perform a fusion of rock, jazz, and even the classics. Drummer Hans Cleuver, bassist Martin Dresden, plus classically-trained founder/ frontman Thijs van Leer (b. Mar. 31, 1948, Amsterdam) on organ and flute, banded together in 1969. Focus developed a strong local reputation; they soon added guitarist extraordinaire Jan Akkerman (b. Dec. 24, 1946, Amsterdam) and worked as the pit band for the Dutch production of *Hair.* In 1971, Polydor issued *In and Out of Focus,* an LP of their music-merging meanderings. Two years later, after Focus' touring and charting success in England and in the States, Sire Records would reissue the album.

By the time of the recording sessions for *Moving Waves* (1973), Cleuver and Dresden were gone. Their replacements were bassist/ singer Cyril Havermans and drummer Pierre Van der Linden (b. Feb. 19, 1946), who had played with Akkerman in one of his former groups.

If Focus is recalled at all by top 40 listeners, it is for that near-novelty number, "Hocus Pocus," with its yodels, yelps, and manic guitar runs. But there was more to the band than just this song, or so believed the devotees of Focus' progressive sounds who liked to flow with the group's long, stylized improvisations. It was this following that snapped up offerings like *Focus 3* (1973), *Live at the Rainbow* (1973), *Hamburger Concerto* (1974), *Dutch Masters* (1975), *Mother Focus* (1975), and *Ship of Memories* (1977).

Havermans left the fold in 1971, and was replaced by bassist Bert Ruiter (b. Nov. 26, 1946). Van Der Linden departed in 1973; his replacement was former Stone the Crows drummer Colin Allen, who himself was replaced but two years later by David Kemper.

Havermans had his own LP (*Cyril*) issued in 1973 by MGM. Numerous solo efforts were issued by van Leer during the '70s—*Introspection* (1972), *O My Love* (1975), *Nice to Have Met You* (1978). Akkerman, who left Focus in 1976, has gone on to create a fairly successful and critically-acclaimed solo career, with albums like *Profile* (1973), *Tabernakel* (1974), and *Jan Akkerman* (1978).

Focus' last recorded work seems to have been the much-anticipated *Focus Con Proby* (1978), which involved the addition of vocal sensation P.J. Proby and Akkerman's fill-in, Phillip Catherine.

Sylvia
PILLOW TALK
(Sylvia Robinson, Michael Burton)
Vibration 521
No. 3 *June 9, 1973*

While Sylvia did share a huge hit as half of MICKEY & SYLVIA, her solo singles would be issued for nearly a quarter of a century before Syl managed to crack the pop and R & B charts on her own.

Born Sylvia Vanderpool on March 29, 1935, in Washington, D.C., she was discovered at a function at Washington Irving High in 1950. Sylvia was but 14 when she recorded hot numbers like "Chocolate Candy Blues" opposite the trumpet of Hot Lips Page. More bluesy sides appeared on Savoy, Jubilee, and Cat, as by Little Sylvia. In 1954, she teamed up with McHouston "Mickey" Baker, her guitar

teacher and New York sessioneer supreme. With their sixth duet, "Love Is Strange," the duo captured the imaginations of rock and rollers worldwide. Follow-ups inexplicably failed to generate a similar response, and in 1959, Mickey & Sylvia split. While the two assayed a number of reunions and many recordings during the '60s, only "Baby You're So Fine" (#52, 1961) b/w "Lovedrops" (#97), released on their Willow label, managed to gain any chart action.

In 1964, Syvia married Joe Robinson. The couple have since established the All Platinum Studios and numerous labels like Horoscope, Stang, Turbo, Vibration, and Sugar Hill. Over the years, Sylvia has produced recordings for Linda Jones, the Moments, SHIRLEY & CO., the

Sugarhill Gang, the Whatnauts, and Lonnie Youngblood. Her hit compositions include "Love On A Two-Way Street," "Sexy Mama," and "Shame, Shame, Shame," a tune she wrote for her friend Shirley Goodman, the lead vocalist for Shirley & Co.

After years of recordings as Sylvia Vanderpool, Little Sylvia, and Sylvia Robbins (for Sue and Jubilee in the early '60s), Ms. Robinson finally cracked the charts on her own, as Sylvia, with the breathy and self-penned "Pillow Talk." "I thought it'd be right for Al Green," Sylvia told *Blues & Soul*'s Tony Cummings. "I cut the song and put my voice on it to show Willie Mitchell [Al Green's producer] how it might be good for Al. But they turned it down, so we decided to release my version."

Other than a duet each with the Moments and Ralph Pagan—and the initial follow-up to "Pillow Talk," "Didn't I" (#70, 1973)—subsequent Sylvia sides have not found niches on the pop/rock airwaves. Nearly a dozen of her singles, however, have placed on the R & B charts. She continues to have records issued sporadically to this day.

Clint Holmes
PLAYGROUND IN MY MIND
(Lee Pockriss, Paul Vance)
Epic 10891
No. 2   *June 16, 1973*

"In a sense, 'Playground' hurt me," Clint Holmes told Bob Gilbert and Gary Theroux in *The Top Ten*. "It branded me as a novelty singer . . . We recorded another song in the similar vein, which I did not want to do. It was called 'Shiddle-ee-Dee' and the very title tells you what the song was like—a bomb."

Born in Bournemouth, England, on May 9, 1946, Clint was raised in Farnham, New York. Holmes showed an interest in music while quite young, and his mother, a former British opera singer, encouraged him and acted as his first vocal coach. While in high school, Clint had his own pop band, and majored in music at Fredonia College. After a stay in the service as part of the Army Chorus, Clint began playing nightclubs in Bermuda and the Bahamas. One night, the successful songwriting team of Paul Vance and Lee Pockriss happened onto his stage act. After Clint's performance, they approached him with some tunes they hoped he might record—in particular, "Playground In My Mind."

Clint was not ecstatic about recording the ditty, but agreed to give it a shot. Upon the issuance of the disk, certain regions of the country took an immediate liking to "Playground," but it was nearly a year before the nation began buying up skids full of Clint's "Playground." Lightning need not always strike twice, however, and all of Clint's future singles on Epic Records stiffed—as did his years and years of releases on the Buddah, Atco, and Private Stock labels. Nothing, but nothing Clint recorded seemed to ever recapture the pulse of pop America.

Clint Holmes is still carrying the torch of hope and making the nightclub circuit. "I'm trying to create a new image, which is why I don't do that song in my act anymore. 'Playground' was an excellently-made record, but it could have been almost anybody singing it; therefore, it was not a career-making record. It didn't bear the stamp of Clint Holmes. I think that's why, even today, a lot of people remember the song but not the fellow who sang it."

New York City
I'M DOIN' FINE NOW
(Thom Bell, Sherman Marshall)
Chelsea 0113
No. 17   *June 23, 1973*

John Brown, Claude Johnson, Tim McQueen, and Eddie Schell were high school buddies with a history of singing that goes way back. John had chirped with the Five Satins (1957–1960) and the Cadillacs, also filling in for the Moonglows. Just prior to N.Y.C.'s big moment, John and the others recorded a lone single for Buddah Records as "Triboro Exchange," after the bridge linking three of New York City's boroughs. The record did little, but Chelsea Records man Wes Farrell liked the group just the same. He convinced the fellows to change their name to the more memorable "New York City"; they acquiesced.

Farrell persuaded Philly magic man Thom Bell to cook up some instrumental tracks for the chaps to lay some vocals on. With four in the can, Thom sent for New York City. "The session was so easy, so relaxed," lead vocalist Tom McQueen reported to *Blues & Soul*'s Tony Cummings. "Everybody just mellowed out down there and when we finished we knew we had a hit." "I'm Doin' Fine Now" was one of the tracks, and it did real fine. McQueen's self-penned "Make Me Twice The Man" (#93,

1973) and "Quick, Fast, In A Hurry" (#79, 1974) did all right, but nothing further charted.

Trivia buffs, take note: the back-up band that toured with New York City was called the Big Apple Band; two of its members were Nile Rodgers and Bernard Edwards, future founders of Chic.

Dr. John
RIGHT PLACE, WRONG TIME
(Mac Rebennack)
Atco 6914
No. 9 *June 30, 1973*

Malcolm "Mac" John Rebennack, Jr. (b. Nov. 21, 1940, New Orleans) grew up in a world full of music. "There was this white baby grand Kimball piano in our house," Mac recalled in an exclusive interview. "My sister, who was, like, 10 years older, would have musicians over rehearsing. My uncle John could play, and the family was near always gettin' together for these jam sessions. Then there was my aunt named Odetta who used to play the boogie-woogie piano; I learned some from her as a little kid.

"I also had some friends that used to work around my father's [appliance] store, like Al Johnson. He taught me how to play another kinda boogie. I took guitar lessons formally. I studied maybe two, three years under studio cats like Walter ["Papoose"] Nelson, Ralph Montell, and Paul and Al Bowman. I think that's what got me accidentally working as a studio cat. Now with the piano, I learned more from watchin' people like Professor Longhair and HUEY "PIANO" SMITH."

By the mid-'50s, Mac was doing sessions for Ace, Edd, Ric, and Specialty, among other New Orleans labels. He toured in the back-up bands for Jerry Byrne, Professor Longhair, Joe Tex, and for his second cousin, FRANKIE FORD. He also began producing and arranging sessions for other recording acts. In 1962, Mac moved to the West Coast and studio activity with SONNY Bono, H.B. Barnum, and Phil Spector. His work with Spector included some of the legendary "wall-of-sound" sessions.

"I liked that they were using a lot of New Orleans cats and that they'd combine some funk with their sound. But when I first saw this deal of using five piano players and six guitarists—even though they added echo and stuff to get a new sound—I was under the

Dr. John

impression they was paddin' the payroll. I didn't realize they was doin' this 'cause it was *the sound* they dug."

While working a Sonny Bono session, Mac got the chance to book for himself some otherwise unused studio time. With the help of producer Harold Battiste, Jessie Hill, and others, Rebennack came up with a heady musical concoction and a voodoo persona that he called "Dr. John Creaux, The Night Tripper." Bono heard the tracks and sold Atco on issuing the *Gris Gris* album in 1968 as a one-off deal. The music was a mix of Creole chants and West Coast psychedelia; the visuals were equally offbeat. Mac's Night Tripper was a self-proclaimed "Grand Zombie," complete with witch-doctor robes, weirdly feathered head-dresses, and—later airbrushed from the cover photo—a finely-rolled marijuana joint.

Two more similarly-styled LPs—*Babylon* (1969) and *Remedies* (1970)—followed before the good doctor, aided by Mick Jagger and Eric Clapton, recorded *The Sun, The Moon & Herbs* (1971). The next year's *Gumbo*—a more straightforward affair and a salute of sorts to his New Orleans roots—sold even better. Gradually, the Grand Zombie was accruing a following; all he needed was a hit single to consolidate his base. With "Right Place, Wrong Time"—a funky track cut with the Meters/Neville Brothers as accompanists—Dr. John found it.

"After we did the *Right Place* album [1973], they more or less demanded that I do something real commercial. We tried to do a couple of tracks commercial for 'em, but we really wanted to do something fresh that no one else was doin'. So we got into experimentin', so they weren't knocked out with it when it wasn't super-commercial."

The Doctor went on to make a number of largely one-off albums for Columbia (like *Triumvirate*, a 1973 collaboration with Mike Bloomfield and John Hammond), United Artists, DJM, Horizon, and Street Wise. He appeared at the Band's 1976 farewell concert (filmed as *The Last Waltz*) and recorded two albums of solo piano music for the Demon (1982) and Clean Cuts (1988) labels.

Mac Rebennack was involved in a serious car crash late in 1988. Ribs were broken, but the Doctor is now back on the road—and back on the record racks with *In A Sentimental Mood* (1989). No longer is he clad in robes, hoodoo make-up, and glittery whatnot. It's tweed suits, or tuxedos and top hats, but the sounds remain as fresh as ever.

Stories

BROTHER LOUIE
(Errol Brown, Anthony Wilson)
Kama Sutra 577
No. 1 *August 25, 1973*

Lead singer Ian Lloyd (b. Ian Buonconciglio, 1947, Seattle) and keyboardist Michael Brown (b. Apr. 25, 1949, Brooklyn) were introduced by their fathers, two old friends who had worked together for years as session violinists. Ian had been singing for years and had attracted local notice recording as Ian London. Michael had played with his group the Left Banke: their success included "Baroque rock"

items like "Walk Away Renee" (#5, 1966) and "Pretty Ballerina" (#15, 1967).

The two seemed to click once they met, and agreed to set about forming a Beatlesque band. They recruited New Yorkers Steve Love (guitar) and Bryan Madey (drums) and located an interested record company in Kama Sutra. A self-titled album and a single—"I'm Coming Home" (#42, 1972)—followed. Success was immediate, and quite probably a surprise to all involved. The second LP, *About Us* (1973), likewise did well, but primarily because of the inclusion of an afterthought, "Brother Louie." This tune about a black girl and her white boyfriend had been a British hit for Hot Chocolate in 1973. Once issued as Stories' second single, the group's whole world changed.

"All of a sudden," Lloyd explained to *Triad*'s Russel Wiener, "we had a big hit with a song that did not represent *our* music and the direction we were trying to go in. I didn't think it would affect me *that* much, but it did. Consequently, I decided that I had to remove myself from that, so that I could come back and show what I really can do."

Lloyd did remain with Stories for one more album—*Traveling Underground* (1973)—but Brown left immediately. Bassist Kenny Aaronson (b. Apr. 14, 1952, Brooklyn) and keyboardist Ken Bichel (b. 1945, Detroit) stepped in to fill the void. This new group made the Hot 100 with "Mammy Blue" (#50, 1973) and "If It Feels Good, Do It" (#88, 1974). Before their short story ended, Madey moved on, and was replaced by Rick Ranno, of later Starz fame.

Lloyd has since recorded some sorely-overlooked solo albums and has done studio work for Foreigner, Fotomaker, and Peter Frampton. Brown next formed the Beckies, yet another Beatles-like band. Love reappeared in the early '80s in Landscape. Madley, after a two-LP stay with the Earl Slick Band, reportedly now plays for Peggy Lee. And Aaronson has been quite busy, first as the frontman for Dust, then as co-founder (with Carmine Appice's brother Vinnie) of Axis. Bichel has since worked sessions for Hall & Oates, Billy Squier, Leslie West, and Rick Derringer.

B.W. Stevenson

MY MARIA
(B.W. Stevenson, Daniel Moore)
RCA Victor 0030
No. 9 *September 29, 1973*

His visual trademark was a stovepipe hat and that expansive amount of hair, beard, and belly. He was shy, afflicted with stage fright, but quite a drinker. He also had a formidable voice that was rarely heard "unpackaged." Jan Reid, author of *The Improbable Rise of Redneck Rock*, considered him in a league with Texan "outlaws" (long-haired country-music rebels) like Waylon Jennings and Willie Nelson. Reid even dedicated a chapter in his book to this chap, dubbing him "The Voice."

Louis C. Stevenson was born in Dallas, on October 5, 1949. In his teen years, he worked in bar bands; the most locally notable was called Us. He attended North Texas State in Denton on a voice scholarship, transferring to Cooke County Junior College. He joined the Air Force, and not too long afterwards, played the clubs in Austin.

Reid, who spent an evening at Stevenson's spread with multiple six-packs, reported that "The Voice" was a singular talent capable of singing "understated, gut-wrenching, backwoods blues." Yet few listeners ever heard that side of the big man: RCA signed him early in his career, called him B.W. (short for "Buckwheat"), and positioned him, against his wishes, as a pop-country singer.

In mid-'73, B.W. almost had his breakthrough hit with "Shambala" (#66, 1973). But he was beat to the punch by Three Dog Night's hugely successful cover of the tune, so RCA needed another disk to issue. Fortunately, Stevenson and songwriter Daniel Moore had just worked up a similar-sounding number called "My Maria." It was catchy, and finally the company had their hit, plus a successful LP, *My Maria* (1973).

Other albums and singles were tried, but B.W.'s limited fame faded. He was only 38 when he died on April 28, 1988.

Byron MacGregor

AMERICANS
(Gordon Sinclair)
Westbound 222
No. 4 *February 9, 1974*

Byron was the news director of CKLW radio in Detroit when his brief rub with national notice paid off. MacGregor had heard a winning editorial broadcast on Canadian radio by Gordon Sinclair about those mighty but maligned minions to the south, "The Americans," and decided to read the opinion piece himself over the air. Listener response was overwhelming—the station was swamped with calls. Not much coaxing was needed to get the newsman into the recording studios of Armen Boladian's Detroit-based Westbound Records. The disk became an instant but one-off smash.

Tom T. Hall
I LOVE
(Tom T. Hall)
Mercury 73436
No. 12 *March 2, 1974*

He's been called "the Nashville Storyteller" and "the Mark Twain of Country Music." Tom T. Hall's songs are vignettes of intriguing characters and offbeat situations. Tom has written of a visit with a dying also-ran girlfriend ("Second Hand Flowers"), of the aftereffects of a mining disaster on a small community ("Trip To Hyden"), and of the would-be star who pathetically insists that his next record will be his big one ("Homecoming").

One need not be a die-hard country fan to have heard many of Tom T's tunes. JEANNIE C. RILEY's "Harper Valley P. T. A." (#1/—/1, 1968) is a landmark Hall hit. You might have caught Dave Dudley's performance of the anti-war anthem "What Are We Fighting For" (—/—/#4, 1966), or Hall's own voice on "Old Dogs, Children, And Watermelon Wine" (—/—/#1, 1973) and "The Year That Clayton Delaney Died" (#42/—/1, 1971).

Tom T. Hall (b. May 25, 1936, Olive Hill, Kent.) was born in a log cabin, and into poverty. His daddy, the Reverend Virgil L. Hall, was a lay preacher, a worker in a brick factory, and the owner of a battered old Martin guitar. Tom took an interest in the instrument and repaired it. The year after his mom died, when he was 14, Tom quit school to work in a graveyard, a funeral home, and later, a clothing factory.

Within two years, Hall had himself a band of bluegrass pickers called the Kentucky Travelers. They played local dates, and made radio appearances on WMOR in Morehead, Kentucky. When the band broke up, Hall remained at the station as a DJ for five years before joining the army. On his return to civilian life in 1961, he moved around, filling various DJ slots. Tom would work in the evenings with a band called the Technicians, all the while sketching out songs based on the characters he observed.

In 1963, Jimmy Newman recorded Hall's "DJ For A Day" (—/—/#9, 1964); the following year, Dave Duddley cut his "Mad" (—/—/#6, 1964). Tom moved to Nashville in 1964 to work as a staff writer, and soon other country artists were approaching him for hits: Bobby Bare, Roy Drusky, Flatt & Scruggs, Burl Ives, STONEWALL JACKSON, and George Jones. With the phenomenal success of "Harper Valley P. T. A.," Hall was offered a recording contract with Mercury Records. And despite the lone top 40 charting of "I Love," Tom T. has seldom been more than a month or so away from a country smash. Nearly 60 of his singles have made the C & W listings, including "Ballad Of Forty Dollars" (—/—/#4, 1969), "Me And Jesus" (#98/—/8, 1972), "That Song Is Driving Me Crazy" (#63/—/2, 1974), and "I Like Beer" (—/—/#4, 1975).

When Hall's career cooled in the late '70s, he took some time off to do book reviews for the *Nashville Tennessean* and write books—*How I Write Songs . . . Why You Can*, *The Storyteller's Nashville*, *The Laughing Man of Woodmont Coves*, and *Acts of Life*. He also hosted the syndicated "Pop Goes the Country" TV variety show.

Terry Jacks
SEASONS IN THE SUN
(Jacques Brel, Rod McKuen)
Bell 45432
No. 1 *March 2, 1974*

Terry Jacks was born in Winnipeg, Manitoba, Canada. As a child, he won an art contest and planned to be an architect someday. When Buddy Holly died, Jacks was moved to buy a $13 guitar, and joined a rock and roll band soon afterward. "I was the worst in the group," Terry admitted to Ritchie York in *Axes, Chops, and Hot Licks*. "So I decided to write some songs in the hopes that they'd keep me. The only trouble was, they expected me to sing them, too." As the Chessmen, the band waxed a number of locally successful singles.

When the Chessmen made an appearance on Canadian TV's "Music Hop," Terry met Susan Pesklevits, a folkie from Vancouver who was making her national debut. The two soon pooled their resources, becoming man and wife and forming a quartet, the Poppy Family. The idea was that Sue would sing and Terry would work behind the scenes—writing, arranging, and producing.

Terry Jacks

When "Which Way You Goin' Billy?"—the "B" side of the Poppy Family's third single—hit big all over North America (#2, 1970), Jacks was caught off-guard. " 'Billy' was cut for only $125. It was done as cheaply as possible. It was simple music, simple lyrics." When the follow-up, "That's Where I Went Wrong" (#29, 1970), charted, Terry called it quits. "I went fishing for two or three months. I couldn't take it anymore. The pressure was incredible." Terry and Sue split up as well: "We'd been together 24 hours a day for almost four years, and it was just too much—telling her what to wear, what to sing, how to sing."

During the Poppy Family's brief travels, Jacks had met and befriended Al Jardine of the Beach Boys. In late 1972, Jardine called Terry to L.A. to produce a Beach Boys session. Jacks suggested they record a tune by Belgian poet-composer Jacques Brel originally entitled "Le Moribond (The Dying Man)." The tune—a sure hit, thought Terry—was taped and completed. When the Beach Boys nixed the idea of releasing the track, Jacks returned to Canada and, with Link Wray, recorded his own version of what was to be called "Seasons In The Sun." Terry received permission to rewrite the reflective tale's final verse in order to lighten up the song.

Four seasons came and went before Terry decided to form Goldfish Records to release his mournful masterwork. The initial response was staggering: "Seasons" became the biggest-selling single in Canadian history. Despite Jacks' limited touring in support of the disk, worldwide record sales eventually totaled 11,500,000 copies. A few more follow-up 45s were issued—"If You Go Away" (#68, 1974) and "Rock 'N' Roll (I Gave You The Best Years Of My Life)" (#97, 1974)—but then Terry seemed to drop out of sight entirely.

Currently, Jacks lives on a large estate in Vancouver. His Goldfish label sporadically releases records, including singles by his ex-wife, Susan Jacks. However, Terry is through with being a performer. "I play 'Old Mac-Donald' on my guitar for my daughter, but that's about it," he told *Goldmine*'s Randy Ray and Mark Kearney. "Hey, I'm 44, I've done music for 20 years. I'm fed up with it."

David Essex

ROCK ON
(David Essex)
Columbia 45940
No. 5 *March 9, 1974*

His given name was David Cook (b. July 23, 1947), and he grew up in the Plaistow district of London's tough East End. Early on, he picked up some drumsticks and formed a beat band called the Everons. The archetypal blokes with the big cigars and shiny cars pulled the lad aside, said he'd go far, that he'd be made into a star.

"It sounded like quite a good idea to me," Essex told *Creem*'s Richard Cromelin. "So I went off with them. They were all in Rolls Royces, and I had like lived in a council house—the workhouse—when I was a kid. I had nothing, so I thought, 'Well, they must know what they're doing.' They'd come up with a song and I'd sing it, and it'd come out and not do a thing."

Essex had 10 disks issued prior to his Grammy nomination for "Rock On." All were, as he described them, ill-conceived. David might not have even had the opportunity to cut his most remembered record were it not for *Daily Express* theater columnist Derek Bowman, his manager. In the late '60s, at Derek's behest, David began taking voice and dance lessons, and tried out for some parts in plays. "There I was, off on the stage. I didn't know anything about it. I'd never seen a play. I don't really enjoy it, especially those rehearsals. It was all a bit of a fluke."

But theater did save his floundering musical career. He played the lead in *The Fantasticks*, and in 1971, he earned rave reviews as Jesus in the London production of *Godspell*. The following year, he starred as rags-to-riches '50s rocker Jim MacLaine in the film *That'll Be the Day* (which also featured Ringo Starr, Billy Fury, and Adam Faith). At the request of producer David Putnam, David wrote "Rock On" for the flick's freeze-frame ending.

"I think 'Rock On' has an atmosphere—it's not just people playing, it's not just somebody singing . . . 'Rock On' was basically '50s lyrics, and a '70s sound. If we'd just done a straight rock and roll 'Rock On,' I don't think it really would have meant much."

Dave went on to inspire teenybopper hysteria in his homeland. While only his immediate follow-up—"Lamplight" (#71, 1974)—made the listings in the States, 20 further offerings charted in England. He continued his stage and film work throughout. Essex appeared with Ringo, Dave Edmunds, and EDD BYRNES in *Stardust* (1975), and in the late '70s, played the part of Che Guevara in the London production of *Evita*. He starred with Beau Bridges in *Silver Dream Racer* (1980), and in the mid-'80s, he portrayed Fletcher Christian in his own film project, *Mutiny*.

Cliff DeYoung

MY SWEET LADY
(John Denver)
MCA 40156
No.17 *March 23, 1974*

Cliff DeYoung was the lead vocalist with Clear Light, an early L.A. folk-rock band. In addition to DeYoung, the mid-'60s unit comprised Doug Lubahn (bass), Mike Ney (drums), Ralph Schuckett (keyboards), Bob Seal (guitar), and Dallas Taylor (drums). They impressed Paul Rothchild, the big cheese at Elektra Records who went on to produce the Doors. And for two years, Clear Light dazzled the Sunset Strip scene with their psychedelicized/folkie repertory. Rothchild ordered up one critically-acclaimed debut—and departure—album, plus a lone single, "Black Rose." Nothing charted, and the band folded.

Lubahn is still very much alive and active. He went on to do session work for the Doors, Dreams, John Phillips, and Billy Squier; in the '80s, he was a member of the group Riff Raff. Taylor, in addition to being a member of Crosby, Stills, Nash & Young and of Stills' Manassas outfit, has recorded with Buddy Guy, Sammy Hagar, Graham Nash, and Stephen Stills. Most prolific of the Clear Light crew has been Ralph Schuckett: his keyboard services have been used by David Blue, James Cotton, the Four Tops, Hall & Oates, and Carole King, to name a few. As for Cliff DeYoung, he became an actor.

DeYoung was born in Los Angeles, on February 12, 1946. He attended the California State College and later, Illinois State University. Shortly after Cliff's fling with Clear Light, Hollywood beckoned. In addition to his TV work in the short-lived "Sunshine" series (1975), the "Centennial" (1978) mini-series, and the *King* and *Robert Kennedy and His Times* made-for-TV flicks, Cliff has appeared in films like *Harry and Tonto* (1974), *Blue Collar* (1978), *The Hunger* (1983), *Protocol* (1984),

Mocedades

F/X (1985), and *Glory* (1989). DeYoung's return to the disk world in 1974 was confined to a solo album and a year's worth of singles—among them, his "Sunshine" spin-off, "My Sweet Lady."

Mocedades
ERES TU (TOUCH THE WIND)
(Juan Carlos Calderon)
Tara 100
No. 9 *March 23, 1974*

The Amezaga sisters—Amaya (b. Feb. 18, 1947) and Izaskum (b. Apr. 17, 1950)—are the voice of Mocedades. They were born and raised in Bilbao, Spain, as were guitarist Roberto Amezaga (b. Apr. 21, 1948), bassist Javier Barrenechea (Dec. 16, 1946), and keyboardist Carlos Uribarri (b. Oct. 10, 1944). Guitarist José Urien was born in Madrid, on January 7, 1949. Together they are, and have been for many years, the sweet-sounding Mocedades.

Their initial North American release, "Eres Tu," caught pop fans by surprise. The sound was delicate, folk-flavored, and mysterious. Mocedades' follow-up 45, "Dime Señor," went nowhere. While their debut disk has been their only major success, the group still has a sizeable following with its predominantly Spanish-speaking audience.

Sister Janet Mead
THE LORD'S PRAYER
(Arr. by Arnold Strals)
A & M 1491
No. 4 *April 13, 1974*

Miss Mead was born in 1938 in Adelaide, Australia. At 17, she became a member of the Sisters of Mercy Convent. During the '70s, when youth-oriented masses were common, Sister Mead and a unit she called her Rock Band provided music for a weekly rock mass at the Adelaide Cathedral. Her music also began attracting attention via her weekly radio progam.

In 1973, Sister Janet was asked to make some recordings that would be distributed only to churches and schools. Australia's Festival Records became interested, and they decided to use her version of Donovan's "Brother Sun, Sister Moon" for her first record. The "B" side was reserved for a modern-age rendition of the prayer that Jesus taught his disciples nearly two millennia ago.

Sister Janet Mead

Within months, 2,000,000 copies of "The Lord's Prayer"—which featured an earthy bass line, ominous fuzz-tone, plushly uplifting strings, and an ethereal lead vocal—were sold. Sister Mead donated all of her royalties to charity. She continued recording for Festival Records, and at least one further single was issued in the U.S. —"Take My Hand."

MFSB & The Three Degrees
TSOP (THE SOUND OF PHILADELPHIA)
(Kenny Gamble, Leon Huff)
Philadelphia International 3540
No. 1 *April 20, 1974*

To those in the know, like Philly arranger Bobby Martin, MFSB stood for "Mother F***in' Son of a B****." But if you asked any one of the group's members what the initials stood for, he or she would look you straight in the eye and reply, "Mothers, Fathers, Sisters, Brothers." Cute.

For years, this 30-plus crew of session musicians, the house band at Philadelphia's Sigma Sound Studios, were crack accompanists. In the guiding hands of Kenny Gamble and Leon Huff, the founders of the Philadephia International label, MFSB created and embodied "The Sound of Philadelphia." Some helium-headed

pundits have posited that what the Motown Sound had been to the '60s, the Sound of Philadelphia was to the '70s. A bit of an over-statement, but Gamble, Huff, and MFSB did indeed crank out an assembly line of hits.

On virtually every disk recorded in the late '60s and '70s by Archie Bell & The Drells, Jerry Butler, the Intruders, Herald Melvin & The Blue Notes, the O'Jays, Billy Paul, Bunny Sigler, and the Three Degress, odds are that the back-up band present is MFSB. Prior to the release of their own charter, an assorted crew of Mothers-to-be created "The Horse" as CLIFF NOBLES & CO., "Keem-O-Sabe" as THE ELECTRIC INDIAN, "United (Part 1)" as the Music Makers, "Overture From Tommy (A Rock Opera)" as THE ASSEMBLED MULTITUDE, an instrumental version of Sly & The Family Stone's "Family Affair" as the Family, and a number of obscurities as the Locomotions and the Men From Uncle.

At the time of "TSOP," MFSB included Ronnie Baker (bass), Roland Chambers (guitar), Bobby Eli (bass), Kenny Gamble (piano), Norman Harris (guitar), Ron Kersey (guitar), Vince Montana (vibes), Lenny Pakula (organ), Larry Washington (percussion), Earl Young (drums), Zach Zachery (sax), and Don Renaldo (conductor, contractor for the horns, reeds, and strings). The Three Degress co-credited on the disk—singers Sheila Ferguson, Valerie Holiday, and Fayette Pinkney—had their own hit at the end of 1974 with "When Will I See You Again."

"A practice that jocks were into [some years back] was finding a little-known or forgotten record with a special quality and using it as a theme song," Don Cornelius, creator of "Soul Train," explained to Bob Gilbert and Gary Theroux in *The Top Ten.* "Whenever I did a [radio] show, I would open and close with my personal theme, which was 'Hot Potatoes' by King Curtis." When Cornelius premiered "Soul Train" on TV, an instrumental theme was needed, but arrangements to use Curtis' tune fell through.

"People in music were just starting to hear about the show when I happened to run into Kenny Gamble in New York. We really hit it off, and I mentioned that I wanted to do a special song for the show." Months later, Cornelius had his new theme—but not for long. The immediate popularity of the number compelled Gamble and Huff to back out of the deal with "Soul Train" and offer the disk to the record-buying masses.

A nice little pile of follow-up 45s placed well on the R & B listings, particularly "Love Is

The Message" (#85/42, 1974) and (minus the Three Degrees) "Sexy" (#42/2, 1975). Several of MFSB's LPs also sold in large quantities.

Mike Oldfield

TUBULAR BELLS
(Mike Oldfield)
Virgin 55100
No. 7 *May 11, 1974*

"**I** suppose the first things I liked were by the Beatles, really," Mike told *Guitar Player's* Stefan Grossman and Tom Mulhern. "After that, I started liking Bert Jansch and John Renbourn, when I was 10 or 11. [About then] I started playing on a 6-string acoustic guitar that my father gave me." By all reports, Mike (b. May 15, 1953, Reading, England) was a precocious kid. By age 14, he and his sister Sally were Sallyangie, a recording act; their *Children of the Sun* (1968) album sold only moderately. Oldfield fronted a unit called Bearfoot before joining ex-Soft Machine founder Kevin Ayers' band, the Whole Wide World, as a bass player. The teenager remained with Ayers for three albums and accompanying tours.

"[Thereafter] I did occasional jobs. I was adapting the play *Hair* for six months or so, and I played a couple of gigs with Alex Harvey. Then I was introduced to composer David Bedford and Richard Branson [who were just starting Virgin Records], who spent about a year making up their minds about whether to take 'Tubular Bells.'" For some time, Mike had been staying in a flat in Tottenham, feverishly working up his "Bells" idea on a friend's borrowed tape recorder. He approached five record companies with the resultant demo, and met with five rejections.

Once Virgin was up and running, Mike was generously allowed a year's time in the Manor Studios in Oxfordshire. There, he singlehandedly taped some 80 tracks using 28 different instruments. He expanded the layers of sound exponentially, dubbing and over-overdubbing hundreds of times. The result was the Grammy-winning ("Best Instrumental Composition") "Tubular Bells," a singular 49-minute fusion of riffs and fragments from rock, folk, and classical themes. These musical elements had been melded to form a musical collage that, some claim, anticipated the meditative sounds of New Age music.

In a talk with Karl Dallas of *New Musical Express*, Mike descibed the creation of his 1973 effort in relation to his life at the time: "There was one point where I suppose you'd say that I had a nervous breakdown . . . I just went mad for a few weeks. I was incredibly frightened all the time, about being alive, and the only thing that gave me any comfort was playing the guitar. I had to invent a mood that was totally opposite to what I was feeling."

Both the *Tubular Bells* (1973) album and an edited version of the single, the Virgin label's first outings, were runaway best-sellers. That year, Oldfield's opus was used as the theme for *The Exorcist* (1973). While none of his later 45s placed on the U.S. charts, the reclusive Oldfield continues to create music—reportedly, in darkened, late-night, solitary studios. His more popular albums include *Hergest Ridge* (1974), *Ommadawn* (1975), *QE2* (1981), and *Five Miles Out* (1982).

Mike Oldfield

Marvin Hamlisch

THE ENTERTAINER
(Scott Joplin)
MCA 40174
No. 3 *May 18, 1974*

From the time of his first encounter with the instrument, Marvin (b. June 2, 1944, New York City) was a marvel with the piano. By his seventh year, he had become the youngest student ever admitted to the Juilliard School of Music. In 1963, while working at a summer camp, Hamlisch met Liza Minnelli and her mother, Judy Garland, who performed one of his first creations at the London Palladium. Lesley Gore soon recorded his "Sunshine, Lollipops And Roses" (#13, 1965) and "California Nights" (#16, 1967).

A chance meeting with movie producer Sam Spiegel at a Broadway party opened the big door to cinematic success. Sam liked the kid's compositions, and hired him to create the theme music for *The Swimmer* (1968). Marvin moved to Hollywood and was asked to compose scores for *The April Fools* (1969), *Take the Money and Run* (1969), *Bananas* (1971), *Kotch* (1971), *Save the Tiger* (1973), *The Spy Who Came In from the Cold* (1977), and *Starting Over* (1979).

In 1974, Marvin won an unprecedented three Academy Awards: one for "The Way We Were" (with co-writers Alan and Marilyn Bergman), another for the score to *The Way We Were* (1973), and another for his adaptation of ragtime master Scott Joplin's music for *The Sting* (1973). Two years later, his score for the Broadway show *A Chorus Line* won Hamlisch a Tony Award.

William DeVaughn

BE THANKFUL FOR WHAT YOU'VE GOT
(William DeVaughn)
Roxbury 0236
No. 4 *June 29, 1974*

Once upon a time, there was this record operation in Philadelphia called Omega Sound. Omega had an unusual method of working: they would seek out talent, then charge the artist to be recorded. William DeVaughn was a songwriting guitarist from Washington, D.C., who had a hankering to be a singing star. Will noted Omega's ad in a music publication and sent the company a demo of some tunes he had hammered out. "They said they'd record me if I paid for a session," DeVaughn explained to *Blues & Soul*'s Tony Cummings. "That would cost me $1,400. I went home and managed to raise $900. We were able to scrape by on that, and I went down to Sigma Studios."

As producer Alan Felder recalled to Cummings, "We did the session real quick, with the guys feeling it as they went along. It wasn't mixed properly; the whole thing was done quickly and cheap." Weeks later, Roxbury Records picked up "Be Thankful For What You've Got," and it sold in huge amounts: before the record gasped its last, nearly 2,000,000 copies had flown off the shelves. But DeVaughn lost interest in the music business shortly after his big hit—he became a Jehovah's Witness.

"By the time the record was number one, [William] was going door-to-door in Washington, handing out pamphlets," the single's producer, John Davis, told *Blues & Soul*. "That's why the album, which was recorded after, was all religious. William didn't feel he could put the two things together. He'd come into a club to do a gig, and instead, he'd tell people, 'You're crazy, you shouldn't be in here, you shouldn't be drinking, you shouldn't be chasing women!'"

DeVaughn's follow-up, "Blood Is Thicker Than Water" (#43, 1974), nearly floated into the top 40. One other single is known to exist; soon William returned to the void.

Dave Loggins

Paper Lace

Dave Loggins
PLEASE COME TO BOSTON
(Dave Loggins)
Epic 11115
No. 5 *August 10, 1974*

Dave was born on November 10, 1947, in Mountain City, Tennessee, the son of a country fiddler and a cousin to Kenny Loggins. Like mockingbirds and moonshine, music was everywhere. After sowing some oats and a short stay at East Tennessee State University, Dave trekked to New York City in search of a music career. MCA Music signed the lad to create tunes for them, but nothing much happened.

In 1972, the Vanguard label took an interest in Loggins' musings and dished out a disappointing debut LP, *Personal Belongings*. In a Denver coffeehouse, a member of Three Dog Night heard Dave's "Pieces Of April." As covered by the Dog band, Loggins, the writer, had a top 20 hit. Epic Records stepped in and ordered a helping of Dave's acoustic numbers. The plaintive "Please Come To Boston" was culled from his *Apprentice (in a Musical Workshop)*, the only Loggins LP still in print. While Dave's disks continued to be issued well into the '80s, his "not really rock/not wholly country" style has left him with a very small audience.

Paper Lace
THE NIGHT CHICAGO DIED
(Mitch Murray, Peter Callander)
Mercury 73492
No. 1 *August 17, 1974*

Paper Lace rewrote a piece of history in 1974 when they sang about a showdown between Al Capone's goons and Chicago's men in blue. These boys with bubblegummy voices maintained that 100 officers died one mythical night in a big gun battle on Chicago's East Side. By evening's end, the forces of truth and justice triumph by either killing or arresting all the vermin, and the Windy City lives happily ever after.

Formed in Nottingham, England—known for its lace, hence the band's name—Paper Lace started up in 1969 with lead singer/drummer Phil Wright (b. Apr. 9, 1948, Nottingham) and bassist Cliff Fish (b. Aug. 13, 1949, Derbyshire). Within the next few years, lead guitarist Michael Vaughn (b. July 27, 1950, Sheffield) and guitarist Chris Morris (b. Nov. 1, 1954) joined. For a while, they were the house band at a club called Tiffany's in Rochdale. Several TV appearances garnered the group the attention of the production/songwriting team of Mitch Murray and Peter Callander. By this point, a third guitarist, Carlo

• • • • • • • • • • • • • •

Santanna (b. June 29, 1947, Rome), had joined the group.

Murray and Callander auditioned the unit, liked what they heard, signed them to their Bus Stop label, and gave the fellows a tender teenybop tune, "Billy, Don't Be A Hero." "Billy" became a number-one British hit but, to the group's dismay, Bo Donaldson & The Heywoods—a Cincinnati septet—covered the song in 1974 and took it to the top of the charts in the U.S. Paper Lace's thunder was not stolen, however, with "The Night Chicago Died," another Murray-Callander creation. A third Murray-Callander piece, "The Black-Eyed Boys" (#41, 1974)—an ode to a gang of super-bad motorcyclists who come to town to make rock and roll—made the Hot 100.

Someone whispered in the group's collective ear that they might make a better deal with some other record company, the guys reportedly walked out on their contract, and little has been heard of them since. Supposedly, there was a fourth single, "The Himalayan Lullabye"—and Paper Lace did show up for a duet billing with the Northingham Forest on a fairly successful British hit called "We've Got The Whole World In Our Hands"—but for most teenybop pop-watchers, Paper Lace died one night in 1974.

Johnny Bristol

HANG ON IN THERE BABY
(Johnny Bristol)
MGM 14715
No. 8   *October 5, 1974*

"**I** got into showbiz by accident, pure accident," Bristol told *Blues & Soul*'s Tony Cummings. "I'd joined the Air Force in the '50s. I was born in Morgantown, North Carolina, but was stationed near Detroit. In the force I met a guy named Jackey Beavers. We found we both dug singing and formed a duo, called ourselves Johnny and Jackey."

The two servicemen did a couple of local shows and were spotted by Gwen Gordy (the sister of Motown mogul Berry Gordy and the wife of Harvey Fuqua, leader of the Moonglows). Gwen signed the guys on to her Tri-Phil label and issued a slew of regional winners. Johnny would later recycle two of these—"Someday We'll Be Together" and "Do You See My Love (For You Growing)"—for the Supremes (#1, 1969) and Junior Walker (#32, 1970), respectively.

By 1960, as their military duty was ending, the doo-wopping duo separated. Jackey returned to Georgia, where he has since had a number of poor-selling sides issued on Mainstream, Sound Stage 7, Warner Bros., and others. As for Bristol: "After I starved a little, I got involved with the Motown situation. I knew Lamont Dozier—he was Lamont Anthony for a while, when he was with Harvey [Fuqua]—and he helped me get in there."

At Motown, Bristol was Fuqua's assistant. For six years, the pair wrote and produced some of the finest Motown moments: "Ain't No Mountain High Enough," "My Whole World Ended," "Twenty-Five Miles," "Pucker Up, Buttercup," and "Yester-Me, Yester-You, Yesterday."

In 1973, Johnny moved to Columbia Records. There, as an in-house producer, he worked with Buddy Miles, O.C. Smith, and Boz Scaggs, among others. But it was a shot at a singing career that he wanted. Columbia turned down his request to cut some sides himself. MGM, meanwhile, agreed to let the music vet have his chance.

"Hang On In There Baby" was to be the first single to bear his name as lead singer. "When I heard the final thing, I flipped! You see, after I'd finished putting down the vocal tracks, H.B. Barnum and I had spent a lot of time 'sweetening'—getting the strings and the girl chorus integrated into the sensuous feeling I wanted. I just broke up when I caught the final mix . . . sometimes you can tell a new recording's a hit . . . with 'Hang On In There Baby,' I could taste it."

Johnny has had some mighty R & B chart-movers and a couple of best-selling albums. But unfortunately, the excitement generated by "Hang On" has yet to be duplicated for more mainstream pop/rock listeners.

In the mid-'70s, Bristol turned to producing and writing for Tom Jones, Johnny Mathis, and Tavares.

First Class

BEACH BABY
(Carter, Shakespeare)
UK 49022
No. 4   *October 5, 1974*

Tony Burrows, John Carter, Del John, and Chas Mills were First Class, the one-shot assemblage of British studio musicians behind the Beach Boys-esque "Beach Baby." Instrumental accompaniment on the tune was supplied by Clive Barrett (keyboards), Spencer James (guitar), Eddie Richards (drums), and Robin Shaw (bass).

First Class was the brainchild of producer/songwriter John Carter. During the early '60s, John, long-time buddy Ken Lewis, and future Yardbird Jimmy Page were members of Carter-Lewis & The Southerners. The group had a minor British charting with "Your Mama's Out Of Town" before they turned into the Ivy League. The Ivy League, while successful in England, never notched a hit in the States, and eventually evolved into a psychedelic group called the the Flowerpot Men.

Fronting First Class was Tony Burrows, a one-time member with Carter in the Ivy League and the Flowerpot Men. Burrows had a history of singing with studio groups: he appeared on hits by EDISON LIGHTHOUSE, the Brotherhood of Man, WHITE PLAINS, and THE PIPKINS. Before his descent into the abyss of anonymity, Chas Mills participated in session work for Long John Baldry, Alan Price, and Al Stewart; he was briefly a member, with Burrows, of the Goodies.

First Class did chart on the Hot 100 with their next two singles, "Dreams Are Ten A Penny" (#83, 1974) and "Funny How Love Can Be" (#74, 1975). Nothing thereafter was noticed, and in 1976 the pseudo-group was dismantled. John Carter went on to form a less successful studio unit, Ice.

Reunion

LIFE IS A ROCK (BUT THE RADIO ROLLED ME)
(Norman Dolph, Paul DiFranco, Joey Levine)
RCA Victor 7559
No. 8   *November 16, 1974*

"There's a Reunion philosophy," Paul DiFranco, the group's co-writer and co-producer, revealed to *Rolling Stone*'s Ian Dove. "We're in the business to make happy, funny records, and I think right now it's important for the music to stay happy. The country is going to dive economically and people are going to need this kind of record."

The construction of "Life Is A Rock" was placed under the production abilities of bubblegum veteran Joey Levine, who co-penned "Chewy, Chewy," "Gimme, Gimme," "Yummy, Yummy, Yummy," "Mercy," "Down At Lulu's,"

and "Quick Joey Small." Levine was (with Kris and Artie Resnick) one-third of the Third Rail, and was reportedly involved in a number of sessions for the 1910 Fruitgum Band, the Ohio Express, and the Kasenenetz-Katz Singing Orchestra Circus.

"Life Is A Rock" lay on the shelf for two years. DiFranco and his co-writer, Norman Dolph, apparently had little success as Reunion with 45s like "Smile" and "Just Say Goodbye," so they approached Joey about working up a bubblegum bit on "Life Is A Rock." (While Joey produced the song, there is some dispute about whether he actually sang it.) "The machine-gun vocal delivery," DiFranco explained, "is a result of no rehearsing whatsoever; the key was to read the lines rapidly and not to memorize them at all. Just take a deep breath and let it go."

Follow-ups to the group's biggie included "Disco-Tekin'" and "They Don't Make 'Em Like That Anymore"—but Reunion's moment had passed.

Billy Swan

I CAN HELP
(Billy Swan)
Monument 8621
No. 1   *November 23, 1974*

Billy (b. May 12, 1944, Cape Girardeau, Mo.) grew up listening to his uncle play the saxophone. At 14, he learned to master the drums, later teaching himself organ, piano, and guitar. By 1959, Swan had a band called Mirt Mirley & The Rhythm Steppers; their "Lover Please" single, a Swan song, bombed ignobly. "Bill Black took it to Clyde McPhatter," Swan told *Rolling Stone*'s Chet Flippo, "who didn't like it but went ahead and cut it." Clyde's recording of "Lover Please" (#7, 1962) became a huge pop hit. It also earned Billy a nice chunk of change—"I figured show business was the easiest thing in the world."

Swan moved to Memphis, and later to Nashville, doing whatever he could to make it in this "easy" biz. He chauffeured for Webb Pierce, and lived in a hearse for awhile. While staying with Travis Smith, Elvis' uncle, Billy tended the gate at Graceland. In Nashville, he worked as a recording assistant at the Columbia Records Studio. Initially, he was a janitor, but by 1966, Billy was signed to Monument Records as a recording artist and producer. Over the next few years, Swan would produce TONY JOE

WHITE's first three albums and White's hit single, "Polk Salad Annie" (#8, 1969).

Eight years of solo efforts had yielded no chart action for Billy on either the pop or country listings. While waiting for that big hit, Swan wrote songs for Bill Black's Combo, worked as a road manager for country acts like Mel Tillis, and played guitar in Kris Kristofferson's band. For a time, Billy was even a member of Kinky Friedman's Texas Jewboys band. Finally, it happened.

In 1974, Kristofferson bought Swan a compact RMI organ as a wedding gift. "My wife had one of these little electric drummers, so I was just sitting at the organ and . . . started playin' chords, and pretty soon the words came out. I did it in two takes and didn't even overdub the vocals—just stood up and played the organ and sang." The song was "I Can Help." And while Billy has yet to have another pop hit, 15 of his 45s have chalked up positions on *Billboard*'s C & W chart.

In 1986, Swan, ex-Eagle Randy Meisner, and ex-Bread members James Griffin and Rob Royer formed a band called Black Tie. *When the Night Falls*, their debut album, was issued by Bench Records.

Jim Weatherly
THE NEED TO BE
(Jim Weatherly)
Buddah 420
No. 11   *November 23, 1974*

James Dexter Weatherly (b. Mar. 14, 1943, Pontotoc, Miss.) was an All American quarterback for Ole Miss. Jim chose songwriting over pro football, the story goes. Jim Nabors hired him to tour with him; RAY PRICE recorded about 50 of his tunes; LYNN ANDERSON, Brenda Lee, BOB LUMAN, and Gladys Knight & The Pips (to name but a few) also etched some of his creations in vinyl. Knight, in particular, has been quite successful with her renditions of Weatherly's "Midnight Train To Georgia" (#1, 1973), "Neither One Of Us (Wants To Be The First To Say Goodbye)" (#2, 1973), and "Best Thing That Ever Happened To Me" (#3, 1974).

As a performer, Weatherly cut his teeth on some obscure sides in 1965 for 20th Century Records. After a layoff, he returned in the early '70s with a contract to RCA. Nothing seemed to jell until those Pips platters peaked, at which point Jim moved over to Buddah Rec-

ords, Gladys Knight's post-Motown home. While only his "Need To Be" collected a following of easy listening fans, Jim did manage to stir up some C & W interest in the mid- to late '70s. He has had half a dozen country hits to date, including "I'll Still Love You" (#87/—/9, 1975) and "All That Keeps Me Going" (—/—/#27, 1977).

Kiki Dee Band
I'VE GOT THE MUSIC IN ME
(Bias Boshell)
Rocket 40293
No. 12   *November 30, 1974*

Freddie Matthews was a British textile worker. Every night, he would come home to his modest dwellings in Bradford, Yorkshire, and find his daughter Pauline (b. Mar. 6, 1947) singing the daylights out of some Top of the Pops tune. Freddie did what most proud papas do—he entered his little 10-year-old in a talent contest, which she won. Pauline continued with her schooling, and worked in a neighborhood drugstore. In her teens, while working days in her sister's beauty shop, she began singing with local dance bands.

"The determination to sing has always been with me," Dee told Mick Patrick, editor of *That Will Never Happen Again*, "since I first found that I had a voice. At 16, I knew that my voice was the only thing that could get me free—get me away from the environment that I was born in." Her reputation grew. Someone suggested that she make a demo and send it to record companies. One found its way to songwriter Mitch Murray, later to be known for such sterling staples as "I'm Telling You Now," "How Do You Do It," and "The Ballad Of Bonnie And Clyde."

At Murray's insistence, Fontana signed Pauline, now known as Kiki Dee, to a contract in 1964. Over the next five years, numerous singles and an LP—*I'm Kiki Dee* (1968)—were issued. Murray produced the latter, as well as many of her singles, but nothing charted in her homeland. In the late '60s, Liberty and World Pacific issued some of these sides in the States. Despite Kiki's soulful similarities to Dusty Springfield, all of them went without notice.

In 1969, Kiki became the first and only British white female signed to the Tamla/Motown label. *Great Expectations* and a few 45s were shipped, but sales were well below expectations. Apparently, the label's attention was elsewhere, for the releases were of uniformly high quality. Disillusioned and frustrated with the business, Kiki headed for Africa and Australia, where for the next few years, she worked the cabaret circuit.

Upon her return, John Reed, the former head of the Motown label in England, got in touch with her. Reed, who was now Elton John's manager, introduced the two. Elton knew of Dee and offered to sign her to his newly-established Rocket label. "I've Got The Music In Me," her third release for Rocket Records, brought Pauline Matthews pop success, brief though it was. (The single credits "The Kiki Dee Band," actually a studio group; for touring purposes, the band included keyboardist Bias Boshell, bassist Phil Curtis, guitarist Jo Partridge, and drummer Roger Pope.)

A few other 45s cracked the Hot 100— "How Glad I Am" (#74, 1975) and "Once A Fool" (#82, 1976). "Don't Go Breaking My Heart" (#1, 1976), a one-off duet with Elton, brought the two to the top of the pop charts in both England and the U.S.

Several of Kiki's albums sold well, but Dee left the Rocket label in the late '70s. In 1981, *Perfect Timing* appeared on the Ariola label.

Carl Douglas
KUNG FU FIGHTING
(Carl Douglas)
20th Century 2140
No. 1 *December 7, 1974*

Kiki Dee

Carl was born in Jamaica, raised in California, and attended college in London. He had intended to become an engineer and work in his family business. Friends, however, heard him sing and encouraged him to stop in at London's Two I's Coffee Bar on Old Compton Street. At lunch hour, the java joint offered an open mike to any takers. After a few performances, Carl was asked to front the all-white Big Stampede.

Beginning in 1964, Big Stampede waxed soul singles for Strike, Okeh, United Artists, and Columbia. "Crazy Feeling" almost did something; "Nobody Cries" sounded like a chart-stalker. Various names were assumed and discarded, different styles were tried— but nothing clicked. Carl toured Europe with a band called Explosion, and for a while was a member of the British band Gonzales.

Biddu, who would chart in 1975 with the theme to the *Summer of '42*, was an Indian-born producer in need of a singer for a London session. A friend of his, New York songwriter Larry Weiss, had a new tune he needed to have recorded. (Weiss had previously hit paydirt in 1967 with "Mr. Dream Merchant" for Jerry Butler, and would strike again in 1975 by penning "Rhinestone Cowboy" for Glen Campbell.) Biddu, having worked with Douglas on the theme song for the Richard Roundtree flick *Embassy* (1972), presented Carl with Weiss' number, "I Want To Give You My Everything."

Once Douglas had recorded the song, a flip side was needed, and Carl offered one of his own compositions—"Kung Fu Fighting." "Fu" was intended as little more than filler: reportedly, only 10 minutes of studio time were used in creating this lightweight number. But the commercial timing was right—fu flicks were everywhere, and David Carradine and Bruce Lee were cult figures. Once the record company loosed its promotional arsenal on the "B" side, Carl had his huge hit. "Fu" even became the first 45 from England to top *Billboard*'s R & B charts. Before his disappearance, Carl managed to milk the kung fu theme for one more single, "Dance The Kung Fu" (#48, 1975).

Carol Douglas
DOCTOR'S ORDERS
(Roger Cook, Roger Greenaway,
Geoff Stephens)
Midland International 10113
No. 11 *February 8, 1975*

Since her teen years, Carol Douglas (b. Apr. 4, 1948, Brooklyn) had been making commercials and playing small roles on TV; she also performed on the silver screen. She appeared in the off-Broadway production of *Moon on a Rainbow* with James Earl Jones and Cicely Tyson. During the early '70s, Carol also worked the revival circuit as a member of the Chantels. In 1974, she began her solo singing career and a four-album association with producer Ed O'Loughlin.

"Doctor's Orders," Douglas' disco dinger, was culled from her debut LP. The tune was written by songwriting pros Roger Cook, Roger Greenaway, and Geoff Stephens. Geoff had dashed off hits for Wayne Newton and THE FLYING MACHINE, and was both creator and lead singer of THE NEW VAUDEVILLE BAND's "Winchester Cathedral." Cook and Greenaway had recorded as DAVID & JONATHAN, and were the writers behind successful 45s by EDISON LIGHTHOUSE, the English Congregation, WHISPERING JACK SMITH, and WHITE PLAINS.

Follow-ups have continued to appear for Carol Douglas into the '80s, but only "A Hurricane Is Coming Tonight" (#81, 1975) managed to chart. Carol still lives in New York City, is the mother of three, and currently records for 20th Century Records.

Polly Brown
UP IN A PUFF OF SMOKE
(Gerry Shury, Phillip Swern)
GTO 1002
No. 16 *March 15, 1975*

In 1970, producer and tunesmith John MacLeod, who had dreamed up some hit disks for the Foundations and THE FLYING MACHINE, wrote what he believed to be a sure-fire hit. To realize it just as he heard it in his head, he fabricated a group consisting of blue-eyed soul singer Polly Brown and five guys. MacLeod coached them in rehearsal, placed them in the studio, and, for unknown reasons, called them Pickettywitch. "That Same Old Feeling" (#67, 1970) went top 10 in England and charted modestly in the States. After two more homeland hits and a fallow two years, Pickettywitch was parked and junked.

For a brief spell in 1974, Polly was singing in blackface as Sarah Leone with a British reggae romper named Tony Jackson. Billed as Sweet Dreams, Brown and Jackson charted in both the U.S. (#68, 1974) and England with "Honey Honey." By year's end, the duo was done, and Gerry Shury and Phillip Swern were entrusted with writing material for Polly to record as a solo act. "Up In A Puff Of Smoke," with Brown doing her best Diana Ross impersonation, was her initial waxing. It clicked in the States, but flopped in England. All other vinyl ventures by the white chick named Brown who sang black failed to ignite record-buyers' interest.

Sweet Sensation
SAD SWEET DREAMER
(D.E.S. Parton)
Pye 71002
No. 14 *March 22, 1975*

Sweet Sensation was a soft-soul band from Manchester, England. They were a struggling pub unit working the local circuit when, in 1974, they happened upon a 15-year-old tenor named Marcel King. "I used to work in this delicatessen, but they fired me for messing about," King told *Blues & Soul*. "I was always singing when the customers were in. This guy that worked there with me introduced me to Leroy [Smith] and he took me to where the group was rehearsing. When I started singing, they all fell out laughing. They said it was because I was so ugly! After that, I hung around with them all the time, and I just sort of joined."

Prior to the addition of little King, Sweet Sensation consisted of Junior Daye (vocals), Roy Flowers (drums), Barry Jackson (bass), Vincent James (vocals), St. Clair Palmer (vocals), Gary Shaughnessey (guitar), and Leroy Smith (keyboards). With Marcel now on board, young girls screamed, shouted, and threw kisses whenever "Ugly" and the boys hit the stage. Taking note of this ruckus, Decca Records made some demos, but nothing came of them. Pye Records signed them and issued "Snow Fire," but still no action.

Next up was the soulful and pretty "Sad Sweet Dreamer," which topped the charts in England. Sweet Sensation's follow-up, "Purely By Coincidence," did nearly as well, but only in their homeland. The group recorded a self-titled album and possibly a single or two more.

In 1989, the group's name returned to the top 40. This Sweet Sensation, also from the U.K., is an entirely new outfit—all three are female.

Shirley & Company
SHAME, SHAME, SHAME
(Sylvia Robinson)
Vibration 532
No. 12   March 29, 1975

Shirley Goodman (b. June 19, 1936, New Orleans) was working as a switchboard operator at Playboy Records in L.A. With access to a WATS line, she would call her old pal Sylvia regularly to chat—the two had met when they were both touring the country with their respective R & B acts, MICKEY & SYLVIA and Shirley & Lee. During one of these exchanges, Sylvia asked Shirley to come on down and take a shot at recording a Sylvia composition called "Shame, Shame, Shame."

The "Company" portion of this entry's name—and the male vocalist on this disco-driven ditty—is Jesus Alvarez (b. Dec. 28, 1951, Havana), an aspiring singing sensation and Cuban refugee. Originally, the legendary Hank Ballard was supposed to sing along with Shirley Goodman, but for some reason, Hank couldn't make it. Jesus had written some tunes and created some demos for Sylvia Robinson (of SYLVIA fame) and her All Platinum/Sugar Hill/Stang/Vibration stable of labels. Nothing was released, but a couple of labelmates did take an interest in Jesus; the Moments recorded a few of his songs.

Shirley (Goodman) & Lee was a short-lived R & B duo that started when Eddie Mesner at Aladdin/Philo Records teamed Shirley up with Leonard Lee in 1953. "I'm Gone" (—/#2, 1953) launched the act nicknamed "Sweethearts of the Blues" and best remembered today for 1956's "Let The Good Times Roll."

"Mesner thought that this was a cute little thing, to make people think that we were sweethearts," Goodman told *Blues & Soul*'s Norbert Hess, "because with all the records that we recorded, it was like a story. From 'I'm Gone' we did 'Shirley Come Back To Me,' then we did 'Lee's Dream' and 'The Proposal'—it was like a story, like one day I was leaving and the next I was back."

Shirley and Lee parted in 1963. She moved to L.A., but Lee stayed in New Orleans, reportedly completing college and working for the government. He died of a heart attack on October 26, 1976. They only reunited once over the years—for Richard Nader's Rock 'n' Roll Revival in New York, in 1972.

Shirley Goodman, meanwhile, cut some solo 45s and a few team efforts issued as by Shirley & Alfred (with Brenton Wood), Shirley & Jessie (with Jessie Hill), and Shirley & Shep (with songwriter Maurice Rodgers). She sang back-up for Jackie DeShannon, Sonny & Cher, DR. JOHN, and the Rolling Stones (on *Exile on Main Street*). In the '70s, Shirley became a PBX operator, a Girl Friday, and a switchboard operator before hooking up with Sylvia for her top 40 moment.

Following "Shame," the *Shame, Shame, Shame* LP (1975), and a few minor-league R & B hits, Shirley Goodman once again drifted away. Today, she lives in New Orleans just a few blocks from her birthplace, and confines her singing to spirituals. "I've written a few hymns and I'd really be interested in recording them," she recently told *Goldmine*'s Almost Slim. "Gospel is what's in my heart now."

Minnie Riperton
LOVING YOU
(Minnie Riperton, Richard Rudolph)
Epic 50057
No. 1   April 5, 1975

"My mother graduated from Rust College in Mississippi," Ms. Riperton told *Goldmine*'s Robert Pruter. "She was an English major and she couldn't find a job when she moved from the South to the North; so guess who ended up scrubbing somebody's floors? She studied voice and sang, and my sisters, everybody in my family studied music, piano, or something."

Minnie (b. Nov. 8, 1947) was born on the poor side of Chicago, the youngest of eight. When she was 10, her mother signed her up at the Lincoln Center. "When I started [singing], my voice teacher, Marion Jeffery, taught me about breathing, we just learned about breathing for months and months. Then we got into songs. They were classical, mostly. We did a show tune every now and then, but it was operas and operettas mostly. I studied until I was 16, but I got swayed off my path once I got a little rock and roll dangling in front of my eyes."

Representatives for the Gems, a success-seeking Chess group, spotted her performing in the Hyde Park High School *a cappella* choir. One of the Gems was leaving the group, and a replacement was needed. Minnie joined, but was soon forced to make a major decision. "My teacher wanted to put me in the Junior Lyric Opera, but I was offered to go on tours and things [with the Gems] and God, I couldn't pass that up." Unfortunately, not many record-buyers took a shine to any of those girlie-group Gems disks, nor did many people snap up Riperton's initial solo flight, "Lonely Girl" (issued as by Andrea Davis).

Numerous critics have considered the output that followed as Riperton's artistic peak. With Sidney Barnes, Mitch Aliotta, and an ever-changing configuration of studio characters, Minnie recorded six albums (the best-known: 1968's *Rotary Connection* and *Aladdin*) and several singles as part of the Rotary Connection. The Rotary Connection concept, born of Marshall Chess' intention to update the Chess label, was to create something unheard of before and since—psychedelic soul. The group would roll out revamped versions of "Lady Jane," "Soul Man," or "The Weight."

The Connection came apart in 1970. Minnie moved to Gainesville, Florida, to raise her family and to retire. It was Stevie Wonder who coaxed her back, first with the offer of a position in his Wonderlove group, and later with the offer of a solo contract with Epic. Wonder produced *Perfect Angel* (1974), from which a third and most soaring single, "Loving You," was pulled. Despite Minnie's vocal talents (including a five-octave range) and choice material, only one other 45 made the pop listings— "Inside My Love" (#76, 1975). Her LPs, however, continued to sell—*Adventures in Paradise* (1975), *Stay in Love* (1977), *Minnie* (1979), and *Love Lives Forever* (1980). She also had a string of successes on the R & B listings.

Minnie Riperton died of cancer at Cedar-Sinai Medical Center in L.A., on July 12, 1979. She was 31; the disease had first been diagnosed in 1976. The night before her death,

Stevie Wonder visited Minnie. Reportedly, she said, "The person I was waiting for has arrived, and everything will be all right now."

Phoebe Snow

POETRY MAN
(Phoebe Snow Laub)
Shelter 40353
No. 5 *April 12, 1975*

"**A**n undeniable virtuoso" (*Musician*), "one of the most versatile" (*Creem*), "one of the most gifted voices of our generation" (*Rolling Stone*)—these are just a few of the critical accolades that have been bestowed on vocal stylist Phoebe Snow. Raised in Teaneck, New Jersey, Phoebe Laub (b. July 17, 1952, New York City) played piano and guitar as a child and teenager. Friends of her mother—folk players like Woody Guthrie, Cisco Houston, Leadbelly, and Pete Seeger—used to drop by regularly. Her musical endeavors took a serious turn in the late '60s. She was very shy—"to the point of being mortified to have to look at people," she once confessed to *downbeat*—but nonetheless, she began performing folk, pop, jazz, and bluesy numbers in Greenwich Village nightclubs.

In 1972, while working a hootenanny at the Bitter End, Phoebe was spotted by a rep for Leon Russell's Shelter label. Two years passed before the release of her self-titled debut album on Shelter, but once it came out, the response was immediate and overwhelming. *Phoebe Snow* (1974) made the top 10 on *Billboard*'s top pop albums chart, and went gold. It also generated what would become her only hit to date—"Poetry Man."

By the time Columbia released her second album (*Second Childhood*, 1976) two years later, life had become complicated. There were record-company lawsuits when Phoebe left Shelter; tense family relations; a separation and ultimately, divorce; and, most crippling, the birth of a severely brain-damaged daughter, Valerie, in late 1975.

"Once I woke up to the realities of the situation, I knew my world was shattered," Ms. Snow told Edward Kiersh in *Where Are You Now Bo Diddley?* "It was rock-bottom time. I just gave up on myself, emotionally and professionally."

For a while, new LPS were issued on a regular basis: *It Looks Like Snow* (1976), *Never*

Letting Go (1977), and *Against The Grain* (1978). The albums were well-crafted and sold well, but not quite as well as her initial output; critical favor also began to slip. Phoebe was also finding herself typecast by the style of her first LP.

"I was taking a backseat to whoever was producing my albums," Snow admitted to *Illinois Entertainer*'s Joan Tortorici Ruppert. "I never said, 'Hey, this is what I want to do,' and everybody started thinking I was a jazz singer. And it's obvious when I do live shows that I'm not just a jazz singer. I like to rock out."

"Rock is something I've always wanted to do and no one would have ever believed it," she told the *Chicago Tribune*'s Chris Helm. "Everybody said, 'You're this, because your first record happened that way.' I really didn't know who I was [then], so I let everybody else intimidate me and tell me who I was musically."

Other than a one-off LP for Mirage (*Rock Away*, 1981), Phoebe kept a low profile throughout the '80s. She did jingles for beer, phone, and greeting-card companies to support herself. In 1989, she came forward and told the music press that she just wanted to rock and roll. That year's release on Elektra, *Something Real*, marked her professional comeback.

Sammy Johns

CHEVY VAN
(Sammy Johns)
GRC 2046
No. 5 *May 3, 1975*

Little Sammy was big on Elvis, and at the impressionable age of 10, he got a hold of his first guitar and started shakin' and strummin'. Later, someone noted the teenager's twitches and music-like sounds, and placed him in a group of fellow Charlotte, North Carolina, youths that wanted to make rock and roll. The Devilles, as they were known, cut several singles for the Dixie label and had something of a local hit with their tune "Makin' Tracks." Sam aged 10 years with the Devilles before he opted for a change and embarked on a folk-like solo career.

A bigwig from the newly-forged General Recording Corporation happened to catch a Sammy Johns performance, signed him to the label, and installed him in Atlanta's Sound Pit Studio with session pros like Jim Gordon, Buddy Emmons, Jim Horn, and James Burton.

Phoebe Snow

Larry Knechtel, one-time member of Duane Eddy's Rebels and the keyboardist for Bread at the time, produced this 1973 session. Released were two singles that went nowhere fast; the third, "Early Morning Love" (#68, 1974), was a teasing male fantasy with a folkie feel and countrified pedal-steel guitar underpinnings.

The follow-up to "Early Morning Love," "Chevy Van," gave vent to a more galvanic male fantasy. "Chevy Van" tells of a sweet young thing, oh so innocent, who shyly asks you to please make love to her. You obediently oblige her request and take her in your big, fully-rigged machine to a tiny town far away from it all, whereupon the virginal goddess walks off in bare feet. Now here was a tune that Sammy clearly could not top!

The next single, "Rag Doll" (#52, 1975), was a chaste and sad ode. Sammy, it seemed, had spent his creative juices. In 1977, he switched to Warner Bros., and more recently made some recordings for Real World Rec-

Ace

ords. But never again would his name or his fantasies grace the *Billboard* charts.

Hollywood was not unmoved by Sammy Johns' "Chevy Van" premise: within months of the recording's penetration of the top 10, an inane movie called *The Van* (1976), featuring Danny DeVito and some nymphets, was quickly tossed together. Sammy was asked to concoct a soundtrack album that would flesh out the concept, but both the film and the album were a bust.

Ace

HOW LONG
(Paul Carrack)
Anchor 21000
No. 3 *May 31, 1975*

A quarter of a century ago, a beat group called the Action were a hip and happening part of the swinging London scene. Alan "Bam" King (b. Sept. 18, 1946, London) had been a member of that fading memory. Over the years, Action went through a number of transformations. During the flower-power era, they were the

bottom-heavy Mighty Baby. Remnants of that unit evolved into Clat Thyger, then Ace Flash & The Dynamos. When guitarists Phil Harris (b. July 18, 1948, London) and "Bam" King from the latter grouping merged with keyboardist Paul Carrack (b. Apr. 22, 1951, Sheffield) and bassist Terry "Tex" Comer (b. Feb. 23, 1949, Burnley, Lancashire) from Warm Dust, Ace Flash became simply Ace. With the addition of drummer John Woodhead, Ace eventually developed a reputation as a top-notch London pub-rock outfit.

After a year on the pub circuit, Ace was picked to be the opening act for a planned Hawkwind tour. John Anthony—who had done production work for Genesis, Van Der Graaf Generator, and Lindisfarne—happened to catch one of the band's performances, and offered the guys a chance to record some sides. At about this time, Woodhead departed to join the Sutherland Brothers & Quiver. He was replaced by Fran Byrne (b. Mar. 17, 1948, Dublin), formerly of Rockhouse and Bees Make Honey.

Carrack, who was angered by Woodhead's ill-timed departure, wrote "How Long" and dedicated it to the drummer. Surprisingly, this smoothie became Ace's lone top 40 hit. For *No Strings*, Ace's third and final album, Byrne was banished and Woodhead was allowed to return to the fold. Unable to consolidate their initial success, the band with the rootsy history ceased operations in 1977.

For an album in 1977 and a few good miles, Byrne, Comer, and Carrack served as a large part of Frankie Miller's back-up band. In the early '80s, Byrne and King became ingredients in the little-noted Juice On The Loose. Most visible and remunerative have been the recent rumblings of Paul Carrack. After his prized 1978 stay with Mel Collins' Retainers, Carrack joined Roxy Music for two years and two albums (*Manifesto, Flesh and Blood*). Session work for the Undertones and John Hiatt followed. For a blink, Carrack was a member of Squeeze (singing on "Tempted"), Carlene Carter's band, and NICK LOWE's Noise to Go. In the '80s, Paul has had a few major hits as a soloist, and several as the voice of Mike + The Mechanics.

Jessi Colter

I'M NOT LISA
(Jessi Colter)
Capitol 4009
No. 4 *June 21, 1975*

Jessi was born Miriam Johnson on May 25, 1947, in Phoenix, Arizona. Daddy was a race-car builder, and Mama played piano. By the age of 11, Miriam was an accomplished church pianist and accordion player. Just five years later, while performing in a Phoenix club, Miss Johnson met guitar icon Duane Eddy; they married shortly thereafter. They toured the world, with Duane delivering twangy sounds all around. Duane's producer, Lee Hazlewood, taped some tracks on Eddy's wife, releasing the sides as by Miriam Eddy on the Jamie and RCA labels. Nothing much became of her records, and by tour's end in 1968, the couple's split was official.

At one of her recording sessions, Miriam met former Buddy Holly accompanist and C & W "outlaw" Waylon Jennings. The attraction grew, and in 1969, Miriam Johnson became Miriam Jennings. To make a new start, she changed her name to "Jessi Colter" after her great-great-grandfather, who had been a buddy of Jesse James. In the following years, Jessi sold solid country sides, had C & W duets with her hubby, and wrote successful tunes for

Eddie Arnold, Anita Carter, Don Gibson, Patsy Sledd, and Dottie West.

In 1974, Jessi switched to Capitol Records and released *I'm Jessi Colter*, produced by Waylon. Her anguished "I'm Not Lisa" earned two Grammy nominations and secured a mammoth but momentary pop/rock audience. The follow-up, "What's Happened To Blue Eyes" b/w "You Ain't Never Been Loved (Like I'm Gonna Love You)" (#57, 1975), was a Hot 100 hit, but these would be Colter's last crossovers. Two years later, Jessi made an appearance on the colossally successful and genre-shaping *Outlaws* album, which also featured Waylon, Willie Nelson, and Tompall Glaser.

Major Harris

LOVE WON'T LET ME WAIT
(Bobbie Eli, Vinnie Barrett)
Atlantic 3248
No. 5 *June 21, 1975*

Major Harris

Love Won't Let Me Wait

As Recorded By Major Harris   On Atlantic Records

Harris was born in Richmond, Virginia, on February 9, 1947. His grandparents were vaudevillians, his father was a professional guitarist, and his mother was leader of the church choir. During the late '50s, Major claims that he was a member of Frankie Lymon's Teenagers. In the early '60s, he joined THE JARMELS. Both acts had peaked, but Harris says that he recorded with the latter group and later cut some solo singles for the Jarmels' label, Laurie Records. Later in the decade, Major was called upon to front the Philly Groove act Nat Turner's Rebellion, which resulted in a few unsuccessful 45s. Yet one more group was to play a part in Major's musical career: between 1971 and 1974, Harris was a member of the Delfonics, and with his assistance, the group had their last pop chartings, "Tell Me This Is A Dream" (#86, 1972) and "I Don't Want To Make You Wait" (#91, 1973).

Freedom at last from the confines of groupdom came in 1974, when Major passed an audition as a solo act for W.M.O.T. Productions. He made an album for Atlantic Records, and while his first single, "Each Day I Wake Up," flopped, "Love Won't Let Me Wait" fared much better. Several other smooth-talkin' singles did well on the R & B charts. Some say Major hired personal bodyguards to protect him and keep the ladies at a safe distance. Two years later, even these R & B hits stopped (presumably, the guards were dismissed). Harris is currently appearing as a member of the reconstituted Delfonics.

Roger Whittaker

THE LAST FAREWELL
(R.A. Webster, R. Whittaker)
RCA 50030
No. 19   *June 21, 1975*

Roger's father was a grocer from Staffordshire, England. In 1929, on the advice of a doctor, he moved to East Africa, where Roger was born. As a child, Roger took to playing mandolin, guitar, and singing in his school choir. Two years of military service in the Kenya Regiment turned young "Whittie" into a performer. "Stuck in the bush camps for months on end meant we had to make our own entertainment," Whittaker explained to Sharon Tracy in *Who's Who in Popular Music in Britain.* "Before I knew it, I was standing on a makeshift stage, guitar in hand, having enor-

mous fun developing into a second Elvis."

On his return from the wilds, he attended the University of Capetown in South Africa and the University of Bangor, Wales, where he acquired a Bachelor of Science degree. Before closing the books on his interests in zoology and biochemistry, Whittaker got the chance to record some disks. Despite some chart successes on the Continent, Roger remained an unknown in the U.K. until the end of the '60s and the release of his self-penned "Durham Town (I'm Leavin')." Five more of his easy-listening 45s found their way onto the British pop listings in the '70s. The last of these, aptly titled "The Last Farewell," was to be his only introduction to the American top 40.

Roger, who currently lives in Essex, England, continues to tour for his devoted following. His many middle-of-the-road LPs still sell fairly well, thanks to those late-night-TV mail-order commercials.

Pilot

MAGIC
(David Paton, Bill Lyall)
EMI 3992
No. 5   *July 12, 1975*

In the early '70s, keyboardist Bill Lyall (b. Mar. 26, 1953, Edinburgh, Scotland) was the head engineer at Edinburgh's Craighall Recording Studio. It was there that he met bassist Dave Paton (b. Oct. 29, 1951, Edinburgh) and drummer Stuart Tosh (b. Sept. 26, 1951, Aberdeen), two frequent sessioneers. The three decided to form a rock and roll group, and derived the unit's name from the initial letters of each surname (*P*aton, *L*yall, *T*osh). No one noticed at the time that there was already a recording act named Pilot. No matter—that BLUE CHEER spin-off crashed after a lone album.

Early in 1974, the threesome created some demos and took them around in search of a record deal. Attracted by their Hollies-like harmonies and *Sgt. Pepper* styling, EMI took a bite and ushered the guys into the Abbey Road studios in London. Alan Parsons, the studio's long-time engineer, was given the task of producing Pilot's first product. The Beatle-esque "Magic" and the follow-up, "Just A Smile" (#90, 1975), were both pulled from the band's self-titled LP. These disks charted extremely well in the U.K., as did two other 45s. Overall, the group seemed to fare better in England than in the States: "January," their third U.S. single, was number one over there but only reached number 87 (in 1976) over here.

Before Pilot bailed out, guitarist Ian Bairnson (b. Aug. 3, 1953, Shetland Isles, Scotland) was added to the group's line-up. By their third album, *Morin Heights* (1976), Pilot was a fairly accomplished outfit. An unsuccessful fourth LP, *Two's A Crowd*, appeared in the States on Arista in 1977, but by this point—and for the remainder of the '70s and part of the '80s— Pilot (minus Lyall) was absorbed into the Alan Parsons Project. Each ex-Pilot person did session work: most notable is Tosh's late-'70s studio stint with 10cc. Lyall, meanwhile, had a solo album (*Solo Casting*) released on EMI in 1976, became a member of the short-lived Runner, and guested on ALI THOMSON's first two albums.

Van McCoy

THE HUSTLE
(Van McCoy)
Avco 4653
No. 1 *July 26, 1975*

He died young—of a bad heart, they say. Like Bobby Darin, whose fate was similar, Van started early and maintained a pace fueled with an unusual drive and motivation.

While a sophomore, pianist Van McCoy (b. Jan. 6, 1944, Washington, D.C.) got some of the singers in the Dunbar High glee club to join him in forming a Frankie Lymon & The Teenagers–style group called the Starlighters. Like their mentors, they sang "Why Do Fools Fall In Love" and "I'm Not A Teenage Delinquent," and even had letter sweaters made up with huge "S"'s on them. Although they bombed at their high school talent contest, they eventually became good enough to literally impersonate Frankie Lymon & The Teenagers at John Brown's Farm, a club near Harpers Ferry, West Virginia. Before breaking up, the band waxed three singles for the End label and briefly replaced one member with Marvin Gaye.

McCoy went on to release some fine solo material that caught the attention of Florence Greenberg at Scepter/Wand Records. Greenberg hired McCoy as an all-around studio hand, A & R man, songwriter, and assistant to producer Luther Dixon. In this capacity, Van

would soon contribute to the success of Chuck Jackson, the Shirelles, and Dionne Warwick.

Van became a part-owner, with Larry Maxwell, of Maxx Records, and began producing disks for Gladys Knight & The Pips. Subsequent production/writing credits included the Drifters, Aretha Franklin, Jay & The Americans, the Marvelettes, IRMA THOMAS, Bobby Vinton, and Jackie Wilson. During this period, Columbia attempted to make a solo singer out of Van. His own offerings were disappointing, considering the brilliance of his work for other artists. Nothing with his name on it sold, not even singles he recorded as the Sound City Symphony.

"It was all exhausting . . . I needed more time," McCoy told *Blues & Soul*'s Tony Cummings. "The whole thing was so hectic, like I was working seven days a week." Under doctor's orders, Van took a short rest. Then he was back, writing, arranging, and producing.

"When I wrote 'The Hustle' I'd never even been to a disco to see the dance. What happened was that David Todd, who's one of the top DJs in the New York discos, came to me and told me about this new dance. I got a couple of girls to do the Hustle for me in the office so I could get the rhythm right, and I wrote the tune. Pretty hard to believe, huh?

"It's tough to have to follow a record like 'The Hustle.' It sold 10,000,000 copies and was a complete accident—how do you top it? It changed my life." It also won a Grammy as "Best Pop Instrumental" of 1975, and was to become (according to the *New York Times*) "the biggest dance record of the '70s." Van had a point: what may be the best-selling disco disk of all time *was* going to be a tough act to follow.

Van quickly dispatched LPs like *Disco Baby* (1975), *From Disco to Love* (1975), and *The Disco Kid* (1975), plus a few more dance singles that made the Hot 100—"Change With The Times" (#46, 1975), "Night Walk" (#96, 1976), and "Party" (#69, 1976). But by the decade's end, he was ready for a change. "Disco has played an important role in the development of my career," he told *Billboard*. "But I am seeking greater versatility. I do not want to be forever locked into the image of the 'disco kid.'"

Before his death in Englewood, New Jersey, on July 6, 1979, Van McCoy did manage to make musical moves in other directions. He wrote the scores for Cicely Tyson's made-for-TV movie *A Woman Called Moses* (1978) and Mae West's *Sextet* (1978).

Bazuka

Bazuka

DYNOMITE—PART 1
(Tony Camillo)
A & M 1666
No. 10 *August 2, 1975*

Bazuka was a studio disco group assembled by producer Tony Camillo. Prior to creating this short-lived hit, Tony had worked with the Persuasions and Gladys Knight & The Pips. "Love Explosion," Bazuka's follow-up to "Dynomite," just barely made the R & B listings (—/#92, 1975), but "Police Woman," "(C'est) Le Rock," and a string of other dance-floor riffers stiffed.

In the mid-'70s, Camillo teamed up with Bob Marcucci (of Frankie Avalon and Fabian fame) to form Camillo/Marcucci Productions.

Gwen McCrae

ROCKIN' CHAIR
(C. Reid, W. Clarke)
Cat 1996
No. 9 *August 2, 1975*

Gwen was born in Pensacola, Florida, on December 21, 1943. Reportedly, in 1969, she met a soused sailor named George McCrae. Gwen at first resisted his charms and told the so-and-so to get lost. A few weeks later, Gwen and George were married, and shortly thereafter, became a recording act for Henry Stone's TK label. Their debut, the country warhorse "Three Hearts In A Triangle," died a dreadful death.

George, who had a history of crooning with locals like the Jivin' Jets and an outfit called the Atsugi Express, was then handed a tight-tailored junkanoo jumper entitled "Rock Your Baby." The tune had been written specifically for Gwen, but George's spouse turned it down flat. Little did Gwen know that the number would go on to sell millions, help launch the discomania of the mid-'70s, and become the very hub of her hubby's series of hits. Some writers have written that George's meteoric rise to pop stardom hastened the demise of the couple's marriage.

After the success of "Rock Your Baby," Gwen was less reluctant when offered the similar-sounding "Rockin' Chair," her lone pop crossover hit to date. Over the years, a number of her soul singles have modestly mounted the R & B listings. Before George's death from cancer on January 24, 1986, George and Gwen secured a minor R & B hit with their final 45 as a duo—"Winners Together Or Losers Apart" (—/#44, 1976).

Amazing Rhythm Aces
THIRD RATE ROMANCE
(Howard Russell Smith)
ABC 12078
No. 14 *September 13, 1975*

Howard Russell Smith (lead vocals, guitar, harmonica) and Butch McDade (drums) grew up in and around Lafayette, Tennessee. Beginning in the early '70s, the two played together in a succession of bands. They met Jeff Davis (bass) and Danny Kennedy (guitar) in 1972 and formed a foursome to work bashes and bars in Alabama and East Tennessee. When the offer came for Davis and McDade to join Jesse Winchester's touring band, they accepted and began calling themselves the Rhythm Aces. The "Amazing" tag was added in 1974 when the two accompanists left Winchester to form— along with Smith, Barry "Byrd" Burton (guitar, steel guitar, dobro, mandolin), and Billy Earheart III (keyboards)—a group that would play all kinds of music: old-timey, bluegrass, R & B, country, gospel, whatever.

The Amazing Rhythm Aces were brought into a studio in Memphis by Knox Phillips, the eldest son of Sun Records legend Sam Phillips. James Hooker (piano), who played on the group's first session, joined the line-up. The Aces' *Stacked Deck* (1975)—from which "Third Rate Romance" was drawn—and their next three LPs were all recorded at Sam Phillips' Recording Studios. The Amazing Rhythm Aces had only two more Hot 100 hits— "Amazing Grace (Used To Be Her Favorite Song)" (#72, 1976) and "The End Is Not In Sight" (#42, 1976)—but single after single made the country charts. "The End Is Not In Sight" even won a Grammy for "Best Country Vocal Performance" of 1976.

All six of their LPs sold well, but management problems began to plague the band. Their penultimate album, *Amazing Rhythm Aces* (1979), first appeared on ABC, but was soon withdrawn and reshipped on Columbia when their contract changed hands. Another label switch followed: their final LP, *How the*

Hell Do You Spell Rhythm (1980), was issued by Warner Bros.

Russell Smith has become a solo artist with Capitol Records. A few of his singles, like "Three Piece Suit" (—/—/#53, 1988) and "Betty Jean" (—/—/#49, 1988), have had success with the C & W crowd. Russ has also had country artists like George Jones, Mel McDaniels, and Conway Twitty record some of his tunes.

In 1986, Bill Earheart joined Hank Williams, Jr.'s back-up unit, the Bama Band. A number of Bama Band 45s have clicked, most recently "Real Old-Fashioned Broken Heart" (—/—/#69, 1989).

Morris Albert
FEELINGS
(Morris Albert)
RCA 10279
No. 6 *October 25, 1975*

Legend has it that one sunny day, when Morris was a mere lad of five in Brazil, he snuck up on the family keyboard and plucked out "I Wish You Love" entirely by ear. Well, Mom and all the other kinfolk encouraged him to be a musician. At 14, he had his own band, the Thunders. They played covers of the current tunes at parties and dances. Two years later, Albert became a solo act and began making a reputation for himself at the local night spots. After graduating high school, he came to the U.S. to attend Columbia University as a phonology major, but soon returned to his native Brazil to pursue a career in music. In 1975, Morris Albert had his international moment in the sun with one of his own creations, "Feelings."

For nearly eight months, this lounge-lizard classic remained on the Hot 100. At first, it sounded harmless enough—a touch of Bread, a pinch of Fleetwoods-like harmonizing, and that ethereal melody. Soon, millions of people were singing "whoa, whoa, whoa" along with Morris. The *Feelings* album flew off the shelves, and Albert became a pop sensation— until, thanks to airplay ad nauseam, radio listeners grew weary of his sentiments. Morris' follow-up, "Sweet Loving Man" (#93, 1976), was no chart-buster.

In 1985, a Federal District Court in Manhattan found that more than 80 percent of "Feelings" had been plagiarized from "Pour Toi," a 1956 composition by French composer Louis Gaste. A settlement of $500,000 was awarded

Morris Albert

to Mr. Gaste. Currently, Morris is living and performing in Sao Paulo, Brazil. Word is that he is on the lookout for a smash sequel to his hit, perhaps to be entitled "Feelings Revisited"—or better yet, "Feelings II."

Pete Wingfield

EIGHTEEN WITH A BULLET
(Pete Wingfield)
Island 026
No. 15 *November 29, 1975*

Pete was born in England in 1948. From early on, he was mesmerized by American black music. Wingfield was educated at Sussex University, where he wrote R & B articles for British mags and published his own fanzine called "Soul Beat." He played keyboards in

bands like the Cossacks, Pete's Disciples, and Jellybread. The latter group (named after a Booker T. & The MGs instrumental)—consisting of Wingfield, bassist John Best, guitarist Paul Butler, and drummer Chris Waters—crafted Bobby "Blue" Bland/Percy Mayfield–influenced R & B on two albums for the Blue Horizon label. When Jellybread crumbled, Pete joined the Keef Hartley Band for the 1972 session that produced the *Seventy Second Brave* album.

Pete formed the fine and funky Olympic Runners in 1974 with producer and Blue Horizon Records chief Mike Vernon on harmonica and percussion, DeLisle Harper on bass, Joe Jammer on guitar, and Glen LeFleur on drums. For the remainder of the decade, Wingfield and company churned out a pile of pumped-up 45s and LPs. While the band never cracked the pop charts, they did have a string of R & B hits from 1974 to 1976 with insistent titles like "Do It Over" b/w "Put Your Money Where Your Mouth Is," "Grab It," "Drag It Over Here," and "Party Time Is Here To Stay."

In 1975, Pete got an offer from Island Records to step out from the shadows and do a solo platter. For his debut disk, he picked a nostalgic little number with double-entendre lyrics called "Eighteen With A Bullet" that he had written two years earlier. Strangely enough, on November 11, his first single hit number 18 on the Hot 100 chart—with a bullet.

Nothing Wingfield waxed afterwards caused even a ripple, so he returned to the shadows. Over the years, he has toured as a back-up pianist and singer for Maggie Bell, the Everly Brothers, and Van Morrison. Pete has also recorded with Bloodstone, the Hollies, B.B. King, Freddie King, Lightnin' Slim, Memphis Slim, IAN MATTHEWS, NAZARETH, Al Stewart, and Jimmy Witherspoon.

Leon Haywood

I WANT'A DO SOMETHING FREAKY TO YOU
(Leon Haywood)
20th Century 2065
No. 15 *December 13, 1975*

"**I** was born [Feb. 11, 1942] and raised in Houston, Texas, and I grew up listening to people like Muddy Waters, Jimmy Reed, and Roy Brown," Leon Haywood told *Blues &*

Soul's Denise Hall. "My parents got me a piano when I was about three. I didn't care nothin' about singing in those days. When I was about 14, I played with a professional group. I can't recall their name, but we played a lot of local gigs."

For a while, Leon accompanied Guitar Slim (of "The Things That I Used To Do" fame) and Clarence Greene. He moved to L.A. and worked in car washes until he managed to hook up with saxophonist Big Jay McNeeley. In 1962, the honkin' horn man arranged for Leon to record his first disk, an instrumental for Swingin' called "Without A Love." "It did pretty well, sold about 100,000. Anyway, I didn't make no money out of it."

Leon joined Sam Cooke's band as a keyboardist. Months later, super-soul-singing Sam was dead. "You're All For Yourself" and "The Truth About Money," Leon's solo efforts, were issued by Fantasy. "The truth about money," Haywood quipped, "was there wasn't any."

Magnificent Montague, a wheeler-dealer DJ in L.A., got Haywood his next contract and his first chart ride, but reportedly at quite a price. "She's With Her Other Love" (#92, 1965) made the airwaves and the listings all right, but since Imperial made the deal directly with Montague, he received all the royalties and Haywood never got a cent. To add insult to injury, the label spelled his name "Leon Hayward."

Before finally finding his niche and working it raw, Leon cut some more sides set up by Montague. "One of the guys [Charles "Packy" Axton of THE MAR-KEYS] who played on a lot of the Stax things was in L.A., and Montague got him together with me and a bunch of the other musicians and cut a record that had that 'Memphis Sound.'" The instrumental, "Hole In The Wall" (#43, 1965), was credited to "The Packers." Haywood also did sessions with Dyke & The Blazers and recorded with Kenny Gamble's and Thom Bell's Romeos.

Finally, in 1974—after many singles for Decca, Capitol, and Atlantic (not to mention some earlier sides for Fat Fish, Galaxy, and his own Eve-Jim)—Leon struck gold at 20th Century Records. In addition to hitting the big time with his sexually suggestive "I Want'a Do Something Freaky To You," Haywood has made the R & B chart more than 20 times.

"The success hasn't really changed me," Haywood told *Blues & Soul*'s John Abbey. "The biggest change for me will be financial. For the first time, my bank manager really loves me!"

Wing & A Prayer Fife and Drum Corps
BABY FACE
Wing & Prayer 103
(Benny Davis, Harry Akst)
No. 14   *March 6, 1976*

The Wing & A Prayer Fife and Drum Corps was nothing more than a temporary studio venture. Stephen Scheaffer and Harold Wheeler had just set up a label with a national distribution network supplied by the Warner Communications conglomerate. Disco was the rage; Steve and Harry had a smart idea, and rounded up a heap of Big Apple sessioneers. The twosome's scheme was to take stiff standards and, with the assistance of David Horowitz, violate them with that insistent disco beat.

Seven such songs were cut: "The Charleston," "Eleanor Rigby," and, yes, "Baby Face." Perched atop the repetitious churning were the voices of Vivian Cherry, Arlene Martell, Helene Miles, and Linda November. The fife blowers were Lew Delgatto, Louis Manni, and Gerald Nielwood. On sticks and skins were Roy Markowitz and Andrew Smith.

"Baby Face" became an instant sensation with disco devotees. Nothing further charted, but before Steve and Harry's Wing & A Prayer crashed, *Babyface Strikes Back*, another LP of pulsating oldies, was dispensed.

Cledus Maggard & The Citizen's Band
THE WHITE KNIGHT
(Jay Huguely)
Mercury 73751
No. 19   *March 13, 1976*

Now, Cledus can't be that boy's real name, you say? You're right as night ain't day. See, Cled is really Jay Huguely (b. Quicksand, Kent.), a one-time Shakespearean actor turned ad-man. Yup, Cledus Maggard was just an idea gone loco.

One day while working at an ad agency in Greenville, South Carolina, Jay got this joltin' notion to do a novelty number around the then-hot CB (citizen's band radio) craze. Jay got some jingle men to give him a hand, and poof! There it was, "The White Knight." Some

• • • • • • • • • • • • • • •
The Seventies

copies were pressed and circulated. "I figured the agency would be giving these away as Christmas presents for the next 20 years," Huguely told Jeannie Sakol in *The Wonderful World of Country Music.* Mercury Records got wind of the effort, and decided to distribute the disk worldwide.

For the remainder of the decade, Mercury kept shipping Cledus' comedic, country corn pone. "Kentucky Moonrunner" (#85/—/42, 1976), "Virgil And The $300 Vacation" (—/—/#73, 1976), and "The Farmer" (—/—/#82) managed to tickle some funny bones.

Nazareth

LOVE HURTS
(Boudleaux Bryant)
A & M 1671
No. 8   *March 13, 1976*

Pete Agnew (bass), Dan McCafferty (lead vocals), and Darrel Sweet (drums) were all born in Scotland. They played in various local bands and met during the '60s as members of the Shadettes, a junior version of Cliff Richards' Shadows. When fellow Scot Manny Charlton (guitar) joined the guys in 1969, they changed

their name to Nazareth, after the first line of the Band's "The Weight" ("I pulled into Nazareth . . ."). In 1971, the band moved to London and secured a record deal.

"Our recording career started off strangely," Agnes told *International Musician*'s Ed Nash. "We were just knocking about playing 'covers.' And when we did our first album, it was a case of leaving our full-time jobs and being told to get in the studio . . . We hadn't really made up our mind about what we wanted to be musically, either. We were torn between being a heavy rock band or playing the more subtle kind of stuff we enjoyed listening to. We never actually *listened* to hard rock—we just enjoyed playing it."

Nazareth has been pounding away in a semi-heavy metal vein ever since. While only the remake of the Everly Brothers classic "Love Hurts" and "Holiday" (#87, 1980) made the U.S. charts, a solid dozen tracks made the British listings. Their popularity has always been greater in Europe than in the States, though nearly every LP released domestically through the early '80s made the top pop albums chart. The Nazareth specialty seems to be pile-driving cover versions of subdued folkie fare like Tim Rose's "Morning Dew," Joni Mitchell's "This Flight Tonight," Bob Dylan's "The Ballad Of Hollis Brown" (which they

Nazareth

worked into a nine-minute metallic frenzy), and, of course, "Love Hurts."

While their releases are fewer in number, Nazareth apparently is still seeking an ever-larger following. Guitarist Zal Cleminson (b. May 4, 1949, Glasgow, Scotland), formerly of the cultish Sensational Alex Harvey Band, was also a Naz man from 1978 to 1980; in 1982, guitarist Billy Rankin and ex-Spirit keyboardist John Locke were added to the group's membership. Nazareth's most recent LP, a self-titled item for A & M, appeared in January 1989.

Larry Groce
JUNK FOOD JUNKIE
(Larry Groce)
Warner Bros. 8165
No. 9 *March 20, 1976*

Lots of chunky souls recall this silly bit about cheatin' in the middle of the night with those Ho-Ho's, Twinkies, and Ding Dongs. But where did this junk-food junkie come from? Prior to his fleeting success, Larry (guitar, mandolin) plus his sidekicks—Berke McKelvey (bass) and the Currence brothers, Jimmie (banjo, fiddle) and Loren (guitar, fiddle, mandolin)—were working the backwoods bar circuit for quite a spell. Groce had recorded four LPs of folkie things on tiny labels like Peaceable and Daybreak, albums that were so poorly distributed that even Larry may not be aware of them.

Larry Groce was born in Dallas on April 22, 1948. Attending W. H. Adamson High School at the same time as Larry were future music-makers Michael Murphy, Ray Wylie Hubbard, and B. W. STEVENSON. With school behind him, Lar and guitar moved about the states—St. Louis, New York, Los Angeles—singing folk music and rhyming tales. (Walt Disney's Vista label issued his "Winnie The Pooh For President" as a single.) Early in the '70s, Groce went to work for the National Endowment for the Arts' program to send artists into the public schools. Larry was sent to West Virginia, where the kids' wild imaginations aided him in coming up with his one and only hit. Recorded before a live audience at McCabe's in Santa Monica, "Junk Food Junkie" touched a repressed nerve.

As the *Junk Food Junkie* album reveals, Groce and his cohorts were capable of creating some pleasing rural sounds, but the label ap-

John Sebastian

parently felt the record-buying public wanted more novelty numbers. Warner Bros. issued follow-up singles with titles like "Big White House In Indiana," "The Bumper Sticker Song," and "Turn On Your TV," all to little avail.

Larry Groce still resides in a farmhouse outside of Philippi, West Virginia. We hear that he still sings some, and writes a mite, too.

John Sebastian
WELCOME BACK
(John Sebastian)
Reprise 1349
No. 1 *May 8, 1976*

They said 'Write the theme song,' John Sebastian (b. Mar. 17, 1944, New York City) told *Rolling Stone*'s Patrick Snyder. "I said, 'What's the title?' and they said, 'Kotter,' and I said, 'Gimme a chance!' So I read the original treatment and wrote 'Welcome Back,' and the next week, they made that the show's title. Then, a few weeks later, some network guy had a flash of brilliance—'If we call it "Welcome Back," it'll sound like a nostalgia show. So we should call it "Welcome Back, Kotter." ' I wrote it in 15 minutes. Generally, they're hits if you write them fast."

Sebastian ought to know—he was the principal songwriter and de facto leader of the Lovin' Spoonful. In their haymaking days, the Spoonful created a string of '60s chestnuts: "Do You Believe In Magic?", "You Didn't Have To Be So Nice," "Daydream," "Summer In The City," "Nashville Cats." Their sound was magical, but their success soon evaporated. "I'm glad the group broke up when it did," Sebastian told Bruce Pollock in *When the Music Mattered*, "because the alternative is sort of playing in cheesier and cheesier entertainment parks as a lot of famous groups going down the tubes do. So, instead of cashing in on the downfall and taking the slow road, we just pulled the plunger."

John was off on a solo career that got an early boost at the Woodstock festival. He was not scheduled to appear, and his tie-dyed, dazed-hippie routine was the result of a healthy dose of LSD. The crowd response was enthusiastic, though Sebastian remains "sorry that the highest visibility performance I've ever given was one where I was smashed beyond belief."

In the recording world, Sebastian was headed for an even bigger bummer. MGM apparently wanted his initial solo product issued as a Lovin' Spoonful record. Sebastian balked, and signed with Reprise, who agreed to issue the same material under his own name. Eventually, the disk in question—*John B. Sebastian* (1970)—was released on both labels at the same time! To make matters worse, MGM, in what John claims was either an act of vindictiveness or an effort to cash in on his Woodstock appearance, released a half-finished, poorly-recorded live LP (*John Sebastian Live*, 1970) boldly bearing his name.

Disenchanted, John moved into a tent outside an apartment complex run by his friend, Cyrus Faryar. The place was called Chicken Flats, and Sebastian remained there for two years. "I did a crazy year of cocaine and then I said, 'Oh my God, I'm not funny anymore . . . It was about 1974 when I really said to myself, 'Okay, you're going to have some slim years as far as recording goes, so you better go where you can work.'"

After three albums for Reprise, John hit the East Coast college circuit, where he often performs to this day. "Welcome Back," unfortunately, was his sole hit; nothing further has been issued. Of late, one of the '60s most talented songwriters has been engaged in work for a Canadian animation firm, writing

tunes for children's TV shows and supplying the music for a musical based on E.B. White's *Charlotte's Web*. John also wrote the music to the NBC-TV production of *The Jerk II* (1984).

Elvin Bishop
FOOLED AROUND AND FELL IN LOVE
(Elvin Bishop)
Capricorn 0252
No. 3 *May 22, 1976*

For "Pigboy Crabshaw," the alter ego of blues guitarist Elvin Bishop, there was a recording layoff of more than a decade prior to his recent return to vinyl. "For 99 percent of the people," Bishop explained to *Guitar World*'s Bill Milkowski, "if you don't have a record, you're not on the radio . . . you don't exist. For some reason, I never felt much pressure to make a record. I lead a pretty full life. Got a real nice home, nice wife, nice kid, got a catfish lake five miles down the road."

As for the Pigboy persona often flogged by critics, Bishop told *Relix*'s Clark Peterson: "What's wrong with being a good old fella? I didn't see a TV until I was 12. I was born and raised on a farm outside Tulsa, and I'd seen a lot more chickens and pigs than people."

Despite his hayseed image, Elvin (b. Oct. 21, 1942, Tulsa, Okla.) was a bright kid. It was while studying physics at the University of Chicago on a National Merit Scholarship that he fell under the mesmerizing sway of the blues. "There must've been 40 blues clubs that were just hoppin' every night, all over the South Side and the West Side," Bishop recalled to Milkowski. "Needless to say, I got swept up by the scene."

Elvin hooked up with a young harmonica-player named Paul Butterfield. The two worked parties as a duo, backing up blues greats like Magic Sam, Junior Wells, and Hound Dog Taylor. In 1965, Bishop and Butterfield formed a blues band that became quite popular in Chicago. The Butterfield Blues Band, featuring the lead-guitar work of Mike Bloomfield, succeeded in bringing the authentic blues (by white kids, no less) to middle-class rock and folk fans. For three classic albums—*The Paul Butterfield Blues Band* (1965), *East-West* (1966), and *The Resurrection of Pigboy Crabshaw* (1968)—the band purveyed its unique brand of electric blues. When Bloomfield left after the second album, Bishop moved into the lead-guitar chair.

Elvin Bishop

In the late '60s, Bishop left Butterfield, moved to the Bay area, and led his own group. A few LPs were issued on the Epic, Fillmore, and Capricorn labels. Two singles—"Travelin' Shoes" (#61, 1974) and "Sure Feels Good" (#83, 1975)—as well as two albums—*Let it Flow* (1974) and *Juke Joint Jump* (1975)—did well. But it was not until 1976 that Bishop won the major portion of his audience. "Fooled Around And Fell In Love," featuring vocals by future Starship singer Mickey Thomas, sold beyond all expectations.

"I wrote that song four or five years earlier," Bishop told *Creem*'s Tom Dupree, "and I never was able to sing it well enough, and there was nobody singing in my group who could do it to my satisfaction until Mickey tried it. It was just a throw-in on the last album. We needed a little bit more time filled."

A few more hit singles and albums followed, but by 1980, Elvin was nowhere in sight. He resurfaced in 1989 with *Big Fun* on Alligator Records, ably assisted by DR. JOHN.

Pratt & McClain
HAPPY DAYS
(Norman Gimbel, Charles Fox)
Reprise 1351
No. 5 *June 5, 1976*

They started early and were persistent in their pursuit, but talent is also of some importance. Three months on the charts and they were history. Viewers of "Happy Days" would endure their voices for a much longer time, however.

Truett Pratt (b. San Antonio, Tex.) sang as a youngster in the choir. But in high school, it was a rock band that grabbed his interest. Jerry McClain's (b. Pasadena, Cal.) daddy was a man of the cloth, so it's no surprise to learn that Jerry also started out singing for the Lord.

In the mid-'60s, Jerry met up with Michael Omartian. Michael would one day do production work for folks like Cher, Christopher

331

Cross, Dion, Richie Furay, Jermaine Jackson, Tom Johnston, Rod Stewart, Donna Summer, and ROGER VOUDOURIS. Together, Jerry and Mike formed the American Scene and recorded a single or two for Dot Records. In 1970, Omartian went off to make those hit records for others (and a few failed solo efforts to boot). Before leaving, he introduced Jerry to Truett. These two were part of a group called Brotherlove, did studio back-up work, and made TV and radio commercials.

As Pratt & McClain, Truett and Jerry made an LP and some 45s for ABC/Dunhill, but it wasn't until Michael Omartian and Steve Barri signed the act to Warner Bros. that their ship came in. They were chosen to record a tune that would replace the theme song for the "Happy Days" TV show. Once Bill Haley's "Rock Around The Clock" had been pulled as the series' theme in favor of the marketable Pratt & McClain substitute, the brass ring was theirs.

Follow-ups were few and flops all, save Pratt & McClain's remake of Mitch Ryder's "Devil With The Blue Dress On" (#71, 1976). Their second and last known LP, *Pratt & McClain Featuring "Happy Days,"* appeared in 1976.

Brass Construction
MOVIN'
(Randy Muller, Wade Williamston)
United Artists 775
No. 14 *June 26, 1976*

"**O**ur roots go back to the Gershwin Junior High in Brooklyn," the Guyana-born Randy Muller (keyboards, flute, percussion, vocals) told *Blues & Soul*'s John Abbey. "My original roots were South American music, but as soon as I got to the States in 1963, I started being exposed to R & B, jazz, rock and roll, everything. In 1967, I formed a quartet in school—me, Wade Williamston [bass], Larry Payton [drums, vocals], and Jessie Ward, Jr. [sax, vocals]—and we played a few school dances, youth clubs, things like that."

Two years later, Morris Price (trumpets, vocals) and Wayne Parris (trumpets, vocals) were added, and the growing group became the Dynamic Soul. Sandy Billups (vocals, conga), Michael "Mickey" Grudge (sax, vocals), and Joseph Arthur Wong (guitar) joined up in the early '70s, and the Brass Construction line-up was complete.

With the aid of Jeff Lane, their manager and the producer for B.T. Express (a group that frequently worked with Muller and Brass Construction), a unique sound was forged. "Two Timin' Woman," Brass Construction's debut single on Lane's Dock label, failed to sell, largely due to a lack of distribution. Follow-up tapes cut at the Ultra-Sonic and Groove Sound Studios, however, found their way into the hands of the people at United Artists. Brass Construction's self-titled album was a big seller, and featured an unusual mixture of strings, horns, and fuzz guitar.

"Until ["Movin'"] hit, we had a regular gig at a disco in New York, the Adonis," Muller recalled. "Then, all of a sudden we were stars!" While "Ha Cha Cha (Funktion)" (#51, 1977) was the only other disk to cross over to the pop/rock listings, Brass Construction did go on to rack up well over a dozen R & B hits and sell an impressive quantity of albums.

While no Brass Construction tracks have dusted the listings since the mid-'80s, Randy Muller has continued as a producer for B.T. Express, Iris, Garnet Mimms, Motivation, Mark Raddice, Skyy, and the Spider's Webb.

Starland Vocal Band

AFTERNOON DELIGHT
(Bill Danoff)
Windsong 10588
No. 1 *July 10, 1976*

Lead singer Kathy "Taffy" Danoff of the Starland Vocal Band explained to *Rolling Stone* just how "Afternoon Delight" was conceived. "[My husband] Bill wrote it after having lunch at Clyde's in Washington, D.C. It seems Clyde's has a menu called 'Afternoon Delight' with stuff like spiced shrimp and hot Brie with almonds. So Bill ate it . . . [then] explained to me what an 'Afternoon Delight' *should* be."

Oh sure, it was naughty, but nice. Conservative AM radio stations played it and consumers bought it up by the million. The group was awarded Grammys for "Best Arrangement for Vocals (Duos, Group or Chorus)" and "Best New Artists of the Year." Their *Starland Vocal Band* (1976) album sold well, and later 45s charted modestly—"California Day" (#66, 1976), "Hail! Hail! Rock And Roll" (#71, 1977), and "Loving You With My Eyes" (#71, 1980).

These Mamas & The Papas clones were given a six-week CBS summer replacement TV show—a major shot at stardom. "Major mistake" is how keyboardist/guitarist Jon Carroll (b. Mar. 1, 1957, Washington, D.C.) characterized the move. "To make a long story short, it was a bad show and we knew it early on." The show did feature, as a comedy regular, one David Letterman. The Starland Vocal Band remained together through 1980, issuing predictable musical product; their efforts came and went with little fanfare.

Taffy (b. Kathleen Nivert, Oct. 24, 1944, Washington, D.C.) and co-lead singer Bill Danoff (b. May 7, 1946, Springfield, Mass.) had been working the D.C. music scene for some years before their meteoric rise. During the late '60s, Bill was the light and sound man at the Cellar Door. It was there that he met Chad Mitchell Trio member John Denver. Danoff slipped Denver some of his songs, and a friendship grew. Later, Bill and Taffy wrote "Take Me Home, Country Roads," a colossal hit for John. Years later, after the Danoffs recorded failed efforts as both Fat City (*Reincarnation*, 1969; *Welcome to Fat City*, 1971) and as Bill and Taffy (*Pass it On*; *Aces*), Denver returned the favor by signing the duo to his Windsong label. "Afternoon Delight" was the first single for Windsong.

Jon Carroll has continued to write songs. In 1982, he was particularly successful when Linda Ronstadt had a hit with his "Get Closer" (#32, 1982). Jon and the Starland Vocal Band's fourth member, singer Margot Chapman (b. Sept. 7, 1957, Honolulu) have since married. Bill and Taffy have since separated, though they have reappeared as Fat City during the late '80s in Washington, D.C.

Thin Lizzy

THE BOYS ARE BACK IN TOWN
(Phil Lynott)
Mercury 73786
No. 12 *July 24, 1976*

Thin Lizzy was known for its well-crafted lyrics, hard-rock riffs, raised fists, and anger. "The aggression is what I love," said Phil Lynott, the charismatic frontman and bass anchor of Thin Lizzy, in an exclusive interview conducted shortly before his death in 1986. "I get that feeling whenever I hit the stage. I'm sure I'd be locked up for doin' something if I didn't have rock and roll. It quiets me and we quiet the kids. I love that black leather, it feels so lovely on the skin . . . The power pose is to show I'm black, black Irish. The fist is the black power salute. I have to do it—I don't know, I hit the stage and I'm in another world."

The only constants in the group's decade-plus history were lead singer/bassist Lynott (b. Aug. 20, 1951, Dublin) and drummer Brian Downey (b. Jan. 27, 1951, Dublin). "We go back to being school kids together, and had this thing called the Black Eagles," Lynott explained. "We'd cover the hit records, do some soul hits, and Elvis things, too." Phil and Brian separated briefly: Phil joined Garry Moore in Skid Row, and Brian played with Sugar Shack.

In 1969, Lynott and Downey formed Orphanage with guitarist Eric Bell (b. Sept. 3, 1947, Belfast), a one-time member of the legendary Them. Orphanage scored a hit in Ireland with their single "Morning Dew." Word of these Irish rowdies reached Decca Records in 1970, whereupon one of the label's A & R men scouted the group out and signed them up. Thin Lizzy's first (and self-titled) album appeared in 1971, and by the next year, the band had moved to London to launch a successful worldwide career.

After their third album, Eric Bell dropped out and returned to Ireland. A number of fine musicians drifted in and out of the band over the years: John Cann, Andy Gee, Scott Gorman, Gary Moore, Mark Nauseef, Brian Robertson, John Sykes, Midge Ure, Darren Whaton, and Snowy White. In 1976, Thin Lizzy broke through in both the U.S. and England with the *Jailbreak* album, which yielded "The Boys Are Back In Town." From that point on, the group racked up 16 hits in the U.K., including top 10 smashes like "Waiting For An Alibi" and "Killers On The Loose." In the States, nine Thin Lizzy albums made the listings, but only "Cowboy Song" (#77, 1976), their immediate follow-up to "The Boys Are Back In Town," managed to make the Hot 100.

In 1978, Phil recorded *Solo in Soho*, his first solo album, and fronted Greedy Bastards with Garry Moore, Jimmy Bain, and Gary Horton. He continued to work both with Thin Lizzy and

on his own throughout the '80s, until the band broke up in 1983. On January 4, 1986, Phil Lynott died of heart failure and pneumonia, complications from a drug overdose.

Keith Carradine

I'M EASY
(Keith Carradine)
ABC 12117
No. 17   *August 7, 1976*

Keith, son of John Carradine and half brother of David Carradine, was born in San Mateo, California, on August 8, 1949. He studied drama at Colorado State University and starred in *Hair* (1969–1970) at the Baltimore Theatre. Keith has appeared in films like *McCabe and Mrs. Miller* (1971), *Welcome to L.A.* (1977), *The Duellists* (1977), *Pretty Baby* (1978), *The Long Riders* (1980), *Southern Comfort* (1981), and *The Moderns* (1988). In Robert Altman's *Nashville* (1975), Carradine, in the role of a corrupt rock star, sings "I'm Easy," which won an Academy Award for "Best Song." Well into the '80s, Keith continued his attempts to bore his way back into the pop charts, but all of his efforts to date have been fruitless.

Vicki Sue Robinson

TURN THE BEAT AROUND
(Pete and Gerald Jackson)
RCA 10562
No. 10   *August 14, 1976*

"I've paid my dues," Ms. Robinson told *Soul's* Duane Folke. "I come from a very mixed background: my father, who is black, was an actor, and my mother, who is white, was a folksinger. She sang with famous folksingers like Woody Guthrie and Pete Seeger. When I was eight, I sang at the Philadelphia Folk Festival with my mother—I had to stand on a crate to reach the microphone."

Vicki (b. 1955, Philadelphia) grew up in Harlem, studying acting and dancing at New York's Neighborhood Playhouse. At 16, she appeared in the original Broadway production of *Hair*. She acted in Scott Fagan's rock musical *Soon* and played Mimi Farina in a production of *Long Time Coming, Long Time Gone.* She portrayed a frizzy-haired hippie in the Lloyd

Bridges flick *To Find A Man* (1972), and had a bit part in Robert Mitchum's *Going Home* (1971).

Robert Stigwood noticed Vicki and landed a part for her in the original Broadway production of *Jesus Christ Superstar*. This led to a trip to Japan to model, sing commercials, perform with the Sadistic Mica Band, and record an album with Itsuru Shimoda. On her return to the Big Apple, Vicki worked as a waitress, a salesperson, and for *Ms.* magazine.

She next formed a rock band with Wendy Simmons, and was discovered by Walter Schwartz, who in turn made arrangements for RCA to record Vicki. The disco-fied "Turn The Beat Around" was the first single from Robinson's debut LP, *Never Gonna Let You Go*; she was only 21 when her big hit bounced onto the charts. "Daylight" (#63, 1976) and "Hold Tight" (#67, 1977) cracked the Hot 100, but "Turn The Beat Around" remains the pinnacle of Vicki Sue Robinson's pop success.

Wild Cherry

PLAY THAT FUNKY MUSIC
(Robert Parissi)
Epic 50225
No. 1 *September 18, 1976*

Guitarist/lead singer Rob Parissi (b. Steubenville, Ohio) was laid up in a hospital in 1970. His bandmates came by to pay him a visit and drop off a box of get-well goodies. "As they were getting ready to leave," Parissi recalled to Bob Gilbert and Gary Theroux in *The Top Ten*, "one said, 'Hey, we don't have a name for our band.' So I held up this box of cough drops, as a joke, and said, 'You can call it this,' and pointed to the words 'wild cherry.' They liked it, and I hated it. I said, 'Are you serious?'"

In 1972, Terry Knight, manager of Grand Funk Railroad and head of the Brown Bag record label, heard the newly-dubbed Wild Cherry and had the guys cut some singles. A few years later, Jeff Barry thought he heard something special, and produced "Voodoo Woman," an obscure 45 for A & M. None of these numbers gained much notice.

The original Wild Cherries scattered. Parissi sold all of his equipment and became a manager of some Bonanza steakhouses. Our tale could have ended here, but the gnawing itch for pop success got the best of Rob. He reformed Wild Cherry with musicians from the Steubenville, Ohio, area: keyboardist Mark

Vicki Sue Robinson

Avsec, guitarist Bryan Bassett, drummer Ronald Beitle, and bassist Allen Wentz.

While playing Pittsburgh discos, Parisssi and his new Cherries made a discovery that would lead to their monster moment in top 40-land. "We played too much rock, I guess," Rob explained, "because people came up to us and said, 'Play that funky music.' In the dressing room, I told the guys that we had to find a rock and roll way to play this disco stuff. Our drummer said, 'Well, I guess it's like they say, you gotta play that funky music, white boy.' I said, 'That's a great idea.'"

Once Parissi had crafted a number around the phrase, the band went into a studio to record "Play That Funky Music" and a cover version of the Commodores' 1974 hit, "I Feel Sanctified." The latter was meant to be the "A" side. Fortunately, Mike Belkin and Carl Maduri at Sweet City, a Pittsburgh-based production company, suggested that "Funky Music" should be the unit's first single for Epic Records.

"Funky" sold more than 2,000,000 copies and won the group two Grammy nominations, for "Best New Vocal Group" and "Best R & B

Wild Cherry

Performance by a Group or Duo." A number of Hot 100 heavies followed: "Baby Don't You Know" (#43, 1977), "Hot To Trot" (#95, 1977), "Hold On" (#61, 1977), and "I Love My Music" (#69, 1978). Wild Cherry's first three LPs—*Wild Cherry* (1977), *Electrified Funk* (1977), and *I Love My Music* (1978)—were healthy sellers as well.

"After that, we started to overproduce our records," Parissi admitted, "and that's probably why we never had another major hit. A lot of that was my fault, striving to sound different. We cut our [fourth and] last album in February 1979, and then just kind of fell apart."

Rob Parissi currently lives in Mingo Junction, Ohio, and works as a morning DJ at a station in Wheeling, West Virginia. "My bags are packed," he told David Mills of the *Washington Times*. "All I need is material. I'd like to get just enough hits—two or three—to build a catalog and be visible for a while—to know that I was there long enough for people to remember who the hell I was."

Silver

WHAM-BAM (SHANG-A-LANG)
(Rick Giles)
Arista 0189
No. 16   *October 2, 1976*

Singer/guitarist John Batdorf was entranced with the sounds of country-rock from the moment of its birth. In the late '60s, Batdorf met up with Mark Rodney. Both were situated in L.A., and both were fans of Crosby, Stills & Nash. For five years, starting in 1971, the Atlantic, Asylum, and Arista labels issued unsuccessful singles and albums featuring the duo's acoustic music. Rodney, apparently discouraged by the critical and commercial drubbing, dropped out of sight.

Batdorf bounced back in 1976. John had met keyboardist Brent Mydland at an Eric Andersen recording session, and the two agreed to join forces. Guitarist Greg Collier, bassist Tom Leadon, and drummer Harry Stinson were added to form Silver, a country-rock outfit. Tom Sellers, who had produced the final Batdorf & Rodney album, was brought in for Silver's first and only album; Sellers had produced hits for THE ELECTRIC INDIAN and THE ASSEMBLED MULTITUDE.

"Wham-Bam," an atypically pop-oriented number from the band, clicked, unlike Silver's two subsequent singles. By year's end, Batdorf and company were finished. Stinson went on to play with the Shot In The Dark band and to do session work for Jay Ferguson, Peter Frampton, Juice Newton, and the Pointer Sisters. Mydland, for several albums and several years, has been with the Grateful Dead.

Walter Murphy

A FIFTH OF BEETHOVEN
(Arr. by Walter Murphy)
Private Stock 45073
No. 1 *October 9, 1976*

Walter was born in New York City in 1952. At the age of four, he was taking piano lessons from Rosa Rio, an organist for radio soap operas. By the time he entered the Manhattan School of Music, Murphy was quite proficient on the keyboards, and was writing arrangements for Doc Severinsen's "Tonight Show" orchestra. With graduation, Walter entered the world of advertising, writing jingles for Lady Arrow, Korvette's, Revlon, Woolworth's, and Viasa Airlines. After a spell concocting B-grade movie scores for made-for-TV flicks like *The Savage Bees* (1976) and *The Night They Took Miss Beautiful* (1977), Murphy approached Major Records with disco-fied Christmas tunes. A few singles like "Disco Bells" were issued.

Early in 1976, Murphy acted on what he described to Bob Gilbert and Gary Theroux in *The Top Ten* as a "crazy idea to take symphonic music and combine it with contemporary rhythm." The idea was not totally new: Tom Parker's APOLLO 100 had hit paydirt in 1972 with "Joy," a pseudo-rock rendition of Bach's "Jesu, Joy Of Man's Desiring." With Walt playing nearly every instrument, a demo tape of some disco-styled classical works was made. Murphy shopped his wares around until Larry Uttal at Private Stock Records took an interest. An album's worth of the stuff was cooked up. The bouncy Beethoven number was released as a single, and Walter Murphy had his one moment in the sun. Similar treatments of Gershwin and Rimsky-Korsakov met with much less enthusiasm.

When last observed, Walter Murphy was with MCA Records. His take on the "Theme From E.T. (The Extra Terrestrial)" charted at number 47 on *Billboard*'s Hot 100 in 1982.

Rick Dees & His Cast of Idiots

DISCO DUCK (PART 1)
(Rick Dees)
RSO 857
No. 1 *October 16, 1976*

Rigdon Osmond Dees III has made money for years as a "personality" DJ—and as Rick Dees, he has done the same as the man behind a string of nutty novelty numbers.

Rick attended North Carolina University, where he specialized in radio and TV studies. His first spot on the dial was WBGB, in his hometown of Winston-Salem, North Carolina. As the "move-'em-out" morning man on WMPS in Memphis, Mr. Dees devised an array of wacky promotions. Reportedly, he holds some sort of world record for whipping up the largest fruitcake (3,000 lbs.), the world's largest jelly doughnut (300 lbs.), and the world's largest lollipop (150 lbs.).

"I was working out in a gym in Memphis when disco was coming out," Dees explained to Fred Bronson in *The Billboard Book of Number One Hits*, "and I also worked in a club called Chesterfield's, telling jokes and spinning records. The more I played the songs, the more I knew it might be time for a disco parody. One of the guys who worked out in the gym did a great duck voice, and I remembered a song called 'The Duck' [by JACKIE LEE] back in the '60s, so I said, how about a 'Disco Duck'?"

Dees went home, tossed the idea around for an afternoon, and that was it. Three months later, he walked the idea into Fretone Records, a small label owned by Estelle Axton, founder of the once-mighty Stax organization. "Actually, they thought I was an idiot," Dees told Bob Shannon and John Javna in *Behind the Hits*. "I went into the studio with a bunch of song ideas, all of them warped. First, I hit them with my song about Elvis exploding, 'He Ate Too Many Jelly Doughnuts.' And later, 'Disco Duck.'" First out of the stall was an item called "The National Wet Off." It bombed, but that darn "Disco Duck" didn't: once it became popular throughout the South, RSO acquired the track for national release.

Everywhere one went, that quacker could be heard—except in Memphis, where rival stations refused to play the disk and where Rick's own WMPS forbade Dees from spinning it. "I talked about it on my morning radio show," Dees told Bronson, "and the station manager came in and said, 'We think that's a conflict of interest—you're fired.'"

WHBQ-AM, his former station's chief competitor, swiftly hired Rick away. Dees later transferred to KHJ in L.A. and has since moved to KIIS-FM, the top radio station in the City of Angels. Rick has hosted TV's "Solid Gold," and currently appears on a syndicated

Top 30 countdown radio program for the United Stations.

As for follow-ups, it's a wonder, but Rick Dees still finds the time to issue amusing musings like "Dis-Gorilla" (#56, 1977), "Big Foot" (1978), "Barely White," and "Eat My Shorts" (#75, 1984) b/w "Get Nekked."

Barry DeVorzon & Perry Botkin, Jr.
NADIA'S THEME (THE YOUNG AND THE RESTLESS)
(Barry DeVorzon, Perry Botkin, Jr.)
A & M 1865
No. 8 *December 12, 1976*

There is quite a history to this eerie melodic movement called "Nadia's Theme." DeVorzon and Botkin originally conceived this instrumental number for a film, *Bless the Beasts and Children* (1972). It was titled "Cotton's Dream" and was featured on the movie's soundtrack, then basically forgotten. A staffer involved in the production of a new TV daytime soap, "The Young and the Restless," then acquired the rights to the Barry and Perry piece. Renamed in honor of the tube tearjerker, the work wondrously went on to become the most recognized theme in all of soapdom.

During the 1976 Olympics, ABC-TV used the soap theme during playbacks of the gymnastic feats of Romania's 14-year-old Nadia Comeneci. The response was such that A & M Records issued the number as a single. Two competing albums appeared in 1976— A & M's *Nadia's Theme (The Young and the Restless)* and Arista's *Nadia's Theme (The Young and the Restless)*—and both of them sold well. Another DeVorzon-Botkin instrumental, "Bless The Beasts And Children" (#82, 1977), followed before Barry and Perry quietly returned to their former behind-the-scenes music careers.

Barry had been involved in the music biz for quite a while before his big moment. RCA Victor (1957–1959) and Columbia Records (1959–1961) issued some of his teen-idol sides. With Botkin arranging, DeVorzon and two others, as Barry & The Tamerlanes, created a momentary stir on the pop charts with their debut single, "I Wonder What She's Doing Tonight" (#21, 1963). Reportedly, Barry managed and eventually married singer-songwriter Shelby Flint. In 1960, Perry was a member with Gil Garfield and rockabilly legend Ray Campiof in the McCoy Boys, and cut one 45, "Our Man In Havana."

Over the many intervening years, DeVorzon and Botkin have each worked as an arranger, producer, and writer for Valiant, Warner Bros., and A & M.

In 1983, a California jury awarded Barry $241,000 in damages against A & M because the label had failed to credit DeVorzon as the co-writer of "Nadia's Theme" on first pressings of the single.

David Dundas
JEANS ON
(David Dundas, Roger Greenaway)
Chrysalis 2094
No. 17 *January 29, 1977*

David Dundas is an aristocrat, born in the mid-'40s in Oxford, England, the son of the Marquess of Zetland. Although he sang with a skiffle band during high school, it was acting that captured his adolescent attention. He spent three years in drama school, swept stages, bummed around France, and wound up in bed with Judy Geeson. Figuratively speaking, that is: an intimate scene with Geeson in the Deborah Kerr–David Niven flick *Prudence and the Pill* (1968) was the peak of David's acting career.

Before mothballing this phase of his existence, Dundas joined the Royal Shakespeare Company for a few performances. "I was really a committed actor," Davy told *Melody Maker*. "I used to be quite good, but I gradually became worse. Mentally, it's a precipitous way of living, and though I did some plays and television things, they got worse until I decided I wanted to get into music."

David turned to the world of advertising and jingle-writing. "Jeans On" was, in effect, one long commercial for Brutus Jeans; the jingle on which the tune was based, and the ad itself, were conceived by Dundas. To flesh out the ditty, a jingle-juggling comrade, producer, and songwriter, Roger Greenaway (of DAVID & JONATHAN), was brought in.

"I like doing jingles because if you get a good one, it's a sort of musical theatre, like a mini-film," Dundas explained. "The ultimate [now] is to get good songs and a good band together . . . [T]his isn't going to be a one-off thing."

David Soul

DON'T GIVE UP ON US
(Tony Macauley)
Private Stock 45129
No. 1   *April 16, 1977*

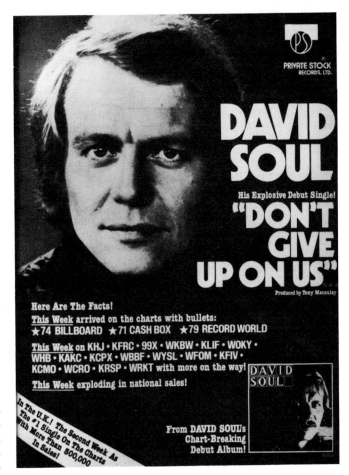

Born on August 28, 1943, the son of a Lutheran minister and diplomatic advisor to the U.S. State Department, Davey Solberg moved about this spaceship Earth quite a lot when he was small. In the magic '60s, Dave dropped out of college to become a folksinger. He apparently developed a sizeable reputation, since he soon landed work as the opening act for the Byrds and the Doors. He was also aware that you needed a gimmick to be noticed at all in the world of music. To this end, Dave sent a photo of himself in a ski mask to the William Morris Agency. They took the bait, and so did Merv Griffin, who eagerly had David and ski mask perform as "The Covered Man" on his TV program a good 20 times. MGM Records released some singles, but none of them charted.

Dave removed his covering and a casting director, noting his fair-haired ruggedness, offered him a slot on the "Here Come the Brides" TV series. A brief stay with the "Owen Marshall, Counselor at Law" series followed before Soul signed on with Paul Michael Glaser to star in his biggest small-screen success, "Starsky and Hutch." Playing hip bachelor/detective Ken Hutchinson on this teen-centered cops-and-robbers show, David Soul became visible and popular.

Again, he tried to hawk his vocal wares. Private Stock Records provided the medium and the songwriter, British tunesmith Tony Macaulay, who created and produced all of Dave's U.S. chart entries.

With most listeners unaware of Soul's musical history, "Don't Give Up On Us" seemed a surprisingly smooth and well-rendered pop effort. "Going In With My Eyes Open" (#54, 1977) and "Silver Lady" (#52, 1977) were solid follow-ups, and did extremely well in England. About the time Detective Ken was asked to turn in his badge, Dave also shut down his recording activities. No one has yet confirmed rumors that Soul has been seen performing with a certain ski mask at semi-seedy coffee-houses as "The Covered Man." David did, however, go on to appear in two more TV series ("Casablanca" and "The Yellow Rose"), and his likeness has been seen in TV movies such as *Salem's Lot, Rage,* and *World War III.*

William Bell

TRYIN' TO LOVE TWO
(William Bell, Paul Mitchell)
Mercury 73839
No. 10   *April 30, 1977*

He was born William Yarborough on July 16, 1939, in Memphis, Tennessee, just a few blocks from where Stax Studios would eventually set up shop. William attended Booker T. Washington High and was a member of the Central Baptist Choir. While still in school, he formed the Del Rios with Harrison Austin (tenor), David Brown (bass), and Melvin Jones (baritone). They won second prize in a talent contest and signed a recording contract with Les Bihari's Meteor Records. "Alone On A Rainy Night" was shipped, but quickly sank from sight, so the Del Rios disbanded. As a solo artist, Bell worked for two years at the

Plantation Inn before joining Phineas Newborn's band in the late '50s as a vocalist.

"I was studying to be a doctor, but during the summer of 1961 I went to New York with Phineas on a job and I started writing a few songs," Bell told *Goldmine*'s Almost Slim. "When I got back to Memphis, Chips Moman, who was a local songwriter/producer, asked me if I wanted to do a session for a new label called Stax. I had nothing to lose."

Four songs were recorded that day; the country-soul classic "You Don't Miss Your Water" (#95, 1962) became a heavy Southern hit, and the largest chart-mover in Stax's brief history. The response convinced Bell to bury his medical ambitions. Before Bell rocked the pop and R & B listings with his "Tryin' To Love Two," he had a slew of gritty Stax singles grease the pop and R & B charts in the late '60s: "Share What You Got" (—/#27, 1966), "Never Like This Before" (—/#29, 1966), "Everybody Loves A Winner" (#95/18, 1967), "A Tribute To A King" (#86/16, 1968), "I Forgot To Be Your Lover" (#45/10, 1969), and "My Whole World Is Falling Down" (—/#39, 1969).

William Bell has also had success singing duets with Janice Bullock, Mitty Collier, Mavis Staples, Carla Thomas, and Judy Clay. Bell wrote the bluesy "Born Under A Bad Sign," Albert King's signature tune, and he was the one who introduced Booker T. Jones, his church's organist, to the funky fold at Stax.

Currently, Bell and his manager operate the Peachtree and Wilbe record labels, as well as the Bel-Wyn Management company.

Bill Conti

GONNA FLY NOW
(THEME FROM "ROCKY")
(Bill Conti, Carol Connors, Ayn Robbins)
United Artists 940
No. 1 *July 2, 1977*

William Conti was born in 1940 in Providence, Rhode Island. Bill's father was an accomplished pianist, and piano lessons had been a must for the boy from the time he turned seven. He ultimately majored in piano and composition at Louisiana State University, and earned a master's degree at Juilliard.

In the mid-'60s, Conti moved to Rome, where he directed the Italian version of *Hair* and wrote the music to *The Garden of the Finzi-Continis* (1971), winner of an Oscar as

"Best Foreign Language Film." In 1972, Bill returned to the U.S. to score *Harry and Tonto* (1972) and Sylvester Stallone's mythical tale about a down-and-out boxer who triumphs against heavy odds: *Rocky* (1976). The soundtrack went to number 4 on *Billboard*'s top pop albums chart. Conti has since scored *An Unmarried Woman* (1978) and *For Your Eyes Only* (1981); he also wrote the theme for the "Dynasty" TV series (#52, 1982).

As Annette Kleinbard—her real name—Carol Connors, the co-lyricist for "Gonna Fly Now," was a member of THE TEDDY BEARS. After the Bears broke up, Connors recorded a handful of collectible singles, and co-wrote the Rip Chords' "Hey Little Cobra." She also wrote "Don't Ask To Stay Until Tomorrow" for *Looking for Mr. Goodbar* (1978) and "With You I'm Born Again" (#4, 1980) for Billy Preston & Syreeta. Carol has composed movie themes for *Falling In Love* (1980), *Sophie's Choice* (1982), *Rocky III* (1983), and *Mr. Mom* (1983).

Alan O'Day

UNDERCOVER ANGEL
(Alan O'Day)
Pacific 001
No. 1 *July 9, 1977*

"There was a local hit on the radio called 'He Did Me Wrong, But He Did Me Right' by Patti Dahlstrom," Alan O'Day told Fred Bronson in *The Billboard Book of Number One Hits*. "In that song, she used the word 'undercover.' I thought it was a neat idea. I've always loved things about angels, too, so the words came together." O'Day's own "Undercover Angel," a hypnagogic, spacey tune with sexual undertones, shot to the top of the charts.

Alan was born in Hollywood on October 3, 1940. As a tot, he'd stare out the window at all the glitz and tap his tiny xylophone until Ma and Pa turned the boy loose on a piano. Spike Jones was his favorite—that is, until he saw *Blackboard Jungle* (1955). Thereafter, while attending Coachella Valley Union High School, O'Day played in rock and roll bands with names like the Imperials, the Renees, and the Shoves.

A break of sorts happened when Alan got a job for $1.50 an hour at a nearby recording studio. There he met one Sidney Goldstein, who liked the kind of tunes that Alan was knocking out and signed him on as a writer for his Viva Music publishing firm. O'Day eventually wrote tunes for Cher, Dobie Gray, and Bobby Sherman, and had several of his numbers recorded by Helen Reddy ("Angie Baby") and the Righteous Brothers ("Rock And Roll Heaven").

In 1977, Ed Silvers, the president of Warner Bros. Music, gave Alan the chance to record some of his songs—Warner had recently purchased Viva, and was launching a new label for its own staff songwriters. Alan O'Day was the first to record for Pacific Records, and "Undercover Angel" was the first thing he etched in vinyl.

America ate up "Undercover Angel," but no second helping was called for. Alan O'Day left via the back door, never again to move a nation.

Hot

ANGEL IN YOUR ARMS
(Terry Woodford, Clayton Ivey, Tom Brasfield)
Big Tree 16085
No. 6 *July 16, 1977*

"The whole thing was an accident," Gwen Owens told Leonard Pitts, Jr. of *Soul* magazine. "None of it was planned at all. We *accidentally* happened to be from three ethnic backgrounds [Gwen is black, Cathy Carson is white, and Juanita Curiel is Mexican], we *accidentally* happened to choose the material we chose on our album, which *accidentally* happened to be commercial."

Cathy (b. Oct. 7, 1953) and Gwen (b. June 19, 1953) met in the early '70s in Los Angeles while auditioning for Wolfman Jack's "Shock & Rock" tour. They won the slot and became Sugar & Spice (not to be confused with the '60s recording act of the same name). By 1976, they were making appearances on BILL COSBY's show, which brought them to the attention of the folks at Big Tree Records. Juanita (b. Feb. 25, 1953) was added to the group, and Sugar & Spice became Hot. An album was cut in Muscle Shoals, Alabama, with "Angel In Your Arms" issued as their debut single. "Angel," with its catchy chorus, catty but coy lyrics, and slick pop styling, clicked with both pop/rock (#6) and R & B (#29) listeners. For a week of Sundays, Hot was hot. But then even the sun, they say, is cooling at a frightening pace. . . .

Over the next two years, a pile of 45s and three LPs were released. "The Right Feeling At The Wrong Time" (#65, 1977) and "You

Brought The Woman Out of Me" (#71, 1977) made respectable showings, but nothing further made it to the niches of *Billboard*'s charts.

Peter McCann

DO YOU WANNA MAKE LOVE
(Peter McCann)
20th Century Fox 2335
No. 5 *August 6, 1977*

Peter McCann, a Connecticut native, sang in barbershop quartets and liked Cole Porter plus other tunesmiths from the '30s and '40s. In 1971, while attending Fairview University on a glee club scholarship, Pete hooked up with the critically-underrated, folk-rockin' Repairs. The group was produced by Andrew Loog Old-

Alan O'Day

ham, and recorded two highly sought-after LPs for the Motown subsidiaries Rare Earth and Mowest. Despite the high quality of their sound and material, neither album sold well enough to justify the group's continued existence.

In 1973, after the Repairs had proved unsalvageable, McCann joined the staff of ABC Music Publishers. Nothing much happened until Pete suggestively applied his voice to his self-penned (and banned in Bismarck, North Dakota) "Do You Wanna Make Love." Meanwhile, Jennifer Warnes, a former actress and lead player in the L.A. production of *Hair*, had a top 10 hit with a McCann composition, "Right Time Of The Night" (#7, 1977). For a brief period, each of McCann's songs shared positions on the *Billboard* pop listings.

Warnes' "Right Time" proved to be the start of a sizeable string of hits, the most prominent of which was "Up Where We Belong" (#1, 1982), her duet with Joe Cocker. McCann has yet to re-chart.

Meri Wilson

TELEPHONE MAN
(Meri Wilson)
GRT 127
No. 18 *August 20, 1977*

Born in Japan and raised in Marietta, Georgia, Meri Wilson played piano and flute from childhood. Following a spell at Indiana University as a music major, Meri began singing and playing in supper clubs and night spots, and worked as a jingle singer in Dallas in the mid-'70s. "Telephone Man," a novelty number, was her first pop recording; "Midnight In Memphis" and other successive singles, like "Peter The Meter Reader," failed to re-ignite popular interest in her career.

Ram Jam

BLACK BETTY
(Huddie Ledbetter)
Epic 50357
No. 18 *September 3, 1977*

Ram Jam's main man, guitarist Bill Bartlett (b. 1949) complained to *Illinois Entertainer*'s Don Case that civil-rights groups like NAACP and CORE were calling for a boycott of "Black Betty." "[They say that] 'Black Betty' is considered an insult to black womanhood, but that's a lot of hogwash. Leadbelly [Huddie Ledbetter] was black, and he wrote all of the lyrics. No blacks that I've talked to find the song offensive."

Despite the protest against what some considered objectionable lyrics, "Black Betty" became a top 40 hit. Nonetheless, as Bartlett noted, "just over 40 percent of all rock stations [would] not play it due to the boycott."

Ten years earlier, Bartlett had been the lead guitarist with THE LEMON PIPERS, known the globe over for their bubblegummy and allegedly drug-drenched "Green Tambourine." "Well, I must admit I still hate that song as much now as I did then," Bill told Case. "But the idea of playing in such a band no longer bothers me—after all, Joe Walsh was with the Ohio Express at the same time."

After the Lemon trip turned sour, Bill went into semi-retirement, and passed the time by soaking up the sounds of Albert Ammons, James Burton, Cliff Gallop, and Leadbelly. One of the tunes he happened across was Leadbelly's "Black Betty." Bill cut a demo of the song and left his Ohio farm for New York City. Through a series of coincidences, Bartlett met those bubblegum boys from Buddah Records, Jerry Kasnetz and Jeff Katz. Jerry and Jeff immediately spotted the hit potential of the old Leadbelly tune.

For their brief duration, Ram Jam was composed of Bartlett, bassist Howie Arthur Blauvelt (an ex-member of an early Billy Joel unit, the Hassles), drummer Pete Charles, and lead singer Myke Scavone, a fellow that Bill met hitchhiking on the New Jersey turnpike. Two LPs—*Ram Jam* (1974) and *Portrait of an Artist as a Young Ram* (1975)—were released, and only two additional 45s—"Keep Your Hands On The Wheel" and "Pretty Poison"—were issued.

Floaters

FLOAT ON
(Marvin Willis, Arnold Ingram, James Mitchell, Jr.)
ABC 12284
No. 2 *September 17, 1977*

Fame did not float in gently for this act; it ran fleet of foot. In an instant the Floaters were big-time; in another they weren't.

Charles Clark (first tenor), Larry Cunningham (second tenor), and brothers Paul (baritone) and Ralph Mitchell (lead) were born and raised in Detroit. As the pre-teen Junior Floaters, they danced and lip-synched their way through local gigs until, 13 years later, they were discovered by Arnold "Brimstone" Ingram, James Mitchell, Jr., and Marvin Willis of the Detroit Emeralds. Brim, Jim, and Marvin arranged for the Floaters to open for the Emeralds tour, and hooked them up with ABC Records. Once ABC signed the group up, Ingram, Mitchell, and Willis wrote, produced, and arranged the tunes for the Floaters' debut album. "Float On," extracted from that first album, sold astonishingly well, but no subsequent product could match that feat.

"It was a refreshingly different sound, at the time," Cunningham told *Blues & Soul*. "And because 'Float On' was our first record, it became a burden—one that we still haven't gotten off our backs. Now, don't get me wrong—without it, we'd be nowhere today. And hundreds of groups would give their lives for such a record! I think the mistake we made afterwards, though, was to try to better 'Float On.' And it can't be done."

The group has remained afloat. "As long as we can keep a good stage show together w can continue to work," Cunningham told *Black Star*'s Frederick Douglas Murphy, "whether we have another hit record or not."

Sanford/Townsend Band
SMOKE FROM A DISTANT FIRE
(Sanford, Townsend, Stewart)
Warner Bros. 8370
No. 9   *September 17, 1977*

Aspiring songwriters Eddie Sanford (keyboards, vocals) and Johnny Townsend (lead vocals, keyboards) met in L.A. in the mid-'70s and decided to form a band. John was an old pro, having played in the mid-'60s psychedelic group Dead Sea Fruits. He had also done session work, most notably with Loggins & Messina and Steve Harley & Cockney Rebel. With seasoned studio players like Otis Hale (guitar, woodwinds), Roger Johnson (guitar), Jim Varley (bass), and Jerry Rightmer (drums), the Sanford/Townsend Band was complete.

Expectations were high. For their first LP, the two writers had a bag full of tunes, Jerry Wexler and Barry Beckett as producers, and access to the famed Muscle Shoals recording studio.

"Smoke From A Distant Fire," the catchy opening track on their debut album, was a very '70s-sounding moment. Two other less-inspired LPs—*Duoglide* (1977) and *Nail Me to the Wall* (1979), minus both Wexler and Beckett—followed, as did several singles. Nothing gathered much notice, and the band folded in late 1979. Sanford has since worked as a back-up for Michael McDonald; Townsend was a charter member in Cher's short-lived hard-rock experiment, Black Rose, and later did studio work for Lauren Wood.

Debby Boone
YOU LIGHT UP MY LIFE
(Joe Brooks)
Warner Bros. 8455
No. 1   *October 15, 1977*

Like it or not, "You Light Up My Life," composed by Joe Brooks—a one-time $500,000-a-year advertising man—spent more time at number one than any song since Guy Mitchell's

Debbie Boone

343

1956 hit "Singing The Blues." It garnered a Grammy Award for "Song of the Year," one for Debby as "Best New Artist of the Year," and an Academy Award for "Best Original Song" of 1977. "Light" eventually sold more than 5,000,000 copies worldwide, making it the biggest-selling record of the year and the biggest-selling single in Warner Bros. history.

Born to Pat and Shirley Boone in Hackensack, New Jersey, on September 26, 1956, Debby was surrounded from birth by the sounds of music. During her teen years, Debby and her three sisters toured state fairs, theaters, and revivals with Ma and Pa. The Boones—Cherry, Lindy, Laury, and Debby—cut some white-soul singles for Motown and later for Warner Bros./Curb, but none of these efforts sold well, so each of the clan moved on to other interests. Debby still wanted to pursue music. Mike Curb—producer, anti-drug crusader, and future lieutenant governor of California—obliged, offering her the title song of a low-budget Columbia Picture.

Despite the moderate success of her follow-ups, "California" (#50, 1978) and "God Knows" (#74, 1978), Debby Boone has yet to find another "Light" in her life. She resurfaced in 1990 as Maria in a Broadway stage revival of *The Sound of Music*.

Ronnie McDowell

THE KING IS GONE
(Ronnie McDowell, Lee Morgan)
Scorpion 135
No. 13 *October 22, 1977*

Ronnie McDowell's unique talent in the world of top 40 pop is that he is—or was—an Elvis impersonator, and one of the best of the bunch. Ronnie told *Country Music*'s Kip Kirby that following a particular session, Presley producer Felton Jarvis told him, "Lord, son, I only wish Elvis had been able to sing that good." McDowell's uncanny ability to reproduce the hip-shaking sounds of the legendary one brought him overnight success, screaming hordes, a healthy hit, and a stigma.

He was born in Fountain Head, Tennessee, 30 miles outside of Nashville. While in the Navy in 1968, Ronnie started writing songs and singing "sound-alikes" in public; his Elvis medley always brought the house down. On his return to civilian life, McDowell headed to Nashville in hopes of peddling his songs and finding his fortune. Roy Drusky, Jean Shep-

pard, Billy Walker, and others would record his tunes, but Ronnie continued working as a commercial sign painter.

In the mid-'70s, McDowell wrangled a job as a clean-up boy at the Chart and Scorpion labels. He cut a sound-alike record of Roy Orbison's "Only the Lonely" in 1976, but the disk stiffed.

When Elvis died, Ronnie and a friend, Lee Morgan, quickly penned a homage to the King. At first, no one was interested in doing a tribute single, so McDowell bankrolled a recording session himself and shopped the acetate around to Nashville radio stations. Within hours, phone lines were lighting up; within weeks, Ronnie was appearing at L.A.'s Palomino Club and on "American Bandstand," "Midnight Special," and "Solid Gold."

"It was frightening," McDowell recalled to *Country Music*'s Kip Kirby. "People were coming to my concerts in droves, but they were really comin' to see Elvis. They'd scream, holler, reach out and try to touch me. Sometimes I couldn't hear a note I was singin'." A few more ersatz-Elvis platters made the country listings, but Ronnie soon wearied of the gimmick. "I was losing my identity. I wanted to sound like myself, like Ronnie McDowell, but everyone else wanted to hear another Elvis. I felt like I was beatin' a dead horse. I knew I had to get away from it or it would destroy my career."

Ronnie has successfully broken free of what he has called "the Elvis thing," and gone on to major C & W success. More than 30 of his singles have made the country listings, with no letup in sight. And while he occasionally reaches into his sound-alike tool kit—as he did for the short-lived "Elvis" TV series in 1989—McDowell feels that he is finally his own man.

Paul Nicholas

HEAVEN ON THE SEVENTH FLOOR
(Dominic Bugatti, Frank Musker)
RSO 878
No. 6 *November 26, 1977*

A performer of stage, screen, and vinyl, Paul Nicholas (b. Paul Beuselinck, Dec. 3, 1945, Peterborough, England) launched his show-biz career at the age of 16—pounding piano with wild man Screaming Lord Sutch & The Savages. In 1967 he landed the role of Claude in the London cast of *Hair*, which he followed with the title role in *Jesus Christ Superstar*

(1972) and a brief stay in the cast of *Grease*.

Nineteen seventy-five was a big year: Nicholas appeared with ANN-MARGRET in *Tommy*, with ROGER DALTREY in *Lisztomania*, and with EDD BYRNES and Adam Faith in *Stardust*. RSO Records offered to record some sides; the resulting "Reggae Like It Used To Be," "Dancing With The Captain," and "Grandma's Party" were smash singles in England. Only "Heaven On The Seventh Floor," however, found its way onto the stateside radio waves. A few more 45s were issued, but nothing further garnered any airplay.

Before Paul Nicholas' disappearance from the world of high visibility, he starred in *Nutcracker* (1982), *The World Is Full of Married Men* (1979), and as Billy Shears' brother in *Sgt. Pepper's Lonely Hearts Club Band* (1978).

High Inergy

YOU CAN'T TURN ME OFF (IN THE MIDDLE OF TURNING ME ON)
(P. Sawyer, M. McLeod)
Gordy 7155
No. 12 *December 24, 1977*

High Inergy

Linda Howard, Michelle Martin, and the Mitchell sisters, Barbara and Vernessa, were Pasadena, California born and raised. Fresh out of Blair High School, the quartet entered Pasadena's federally-funded Bicentennial Performing Arts Program. During one afternoon rehearsal, word reached the teen queens that Gwen Gordy, the sister of Motown mainman Berry Gordy, had caught a glimpse of their act, and that she wanted them to stop by her Beverly Hills mansion to audition. Gwen (who a decade earlier had shaped the surging Supremes) was immensely impressed with High Inergy, a packed act that one magazine would dub "The Miss American Teenagers of Soul." Gordy and a sidekick, Gwendolyn Joyce Fuller, became the girls' managers, molders, and mothers. Together, they groomed the girls with tried-and-true tips on hair care, makeup, poise, and all the do's and don't's of stage appeal.

The suggestively-titled "You Can't Turn Me Off (In The Middle Of Turning Me On)" was High Inergy's debut disk, and their only major moment on the pop charts. "Love Is All You Need" (#89, 1978) and "He's A Pretender" (#82, 1983) danced at the bottom of the Hot 100, and more than a half-dozen disks did likewise on the R & B listings from 1978 to 1983.

In 1978, High Inergy became a trio when Vernessa left the group. After four albums and an appearance on Motown's 25th Anniversary TV special in 1983, High Inergy called it quits. Shortly thereafter, Barbara Mitchell signed a solo contract with Capitol Records.

Randy Newman

SHORT PEOPLE
(Randy Newman)
Warner Bros. 8492
No. 2 *January 28, 1978*

"'Short People' was the worst kind of hit anyone could have," Randy Newman (b. Nov. 28, 1943, Los Angeles) told Joe Smith in *Off the Record*. "It was like having [SHEB WOOLEY'S] 'Purple People Eater.' I'd try to watch a ball game and the band would play the song and the announcers would make jokes about it. It was too noisy. I prefer quiet money."

As a recording artist, Newman is a cult figure; as a writer, he has achieved more sub-

Randy Newman

songs at 16, and I took them to a publisher [Metric Music, then a subdivision of Liberty Records] and they signed me up. I did that for about eight years before I recorded myself in '67 or '68."

The reaction to Newman's first album, a self-titled effort for Warner Bros., was what one might call underwhelming. His second LP—*12 Songs* (1970)—brought a little more notice; it contained "Mama Told Me Not To Come," a major hit for Three Dog Night. Commenting on the tune, Newman told *Rolling Stone*: "I was never crazy about that song. I didn't want to record it. The origin of the song is just about a fool at a party, that's all. I didn't think it would be a hit."

Album number three—*Randy Newman/ Live* (1971)—was the first to reach the top pop albums chart. To this day, Randy continues to issue critically-acclaimed records; his best-selling LPs include *Sail Away* (1972), *Good Old Boys* (1974), *Little Criminals* (1977), *Trouble in Paradise* (1983), and *Land of Dreams* (1988). He has also, in the family tradition, written evocative film scores for movies like *Ragtime* (1981), *The Natural* (1984), and *Parenthood* (1989).

Santa Esmeralda
DON'T LET ME BE MISUNDERSTOOD
(Bennie Benjamin, Sol Marcus, Gloria Caldwell)
Casablanca 902
No. 15 *February 18, 1978*

Leroy Gomez was born and raised in Cape Cod, and became proficient on the sax, guitar, and flute at an early age. Nineteen seventy-three was his year: Elton John made use of Leroy's sax sound on *Goodbye Yellow Brick Road*, and Gomez toured with Tavares. He had moved to Paris and started working the cabaret scene when Nicolas Skorsky and Jean-Manuel de Scarano of Fauves-Ruma Productions approached him about performing as lead vocalist for a proposed studio group to be called Santa Esmeralda.

Four tunes were recorded. Don Ray, who had assisted in arranging and mixing a hit for Cerrone and would do the same for Love & Kisses, did the disco arrangements on two Gomez originals and on two British Invasion classics, "Gloria" (Them) and "Don't Let Me Be Misunderstood" (the Animals). Gomez's vocals were soulful, and even the pulsating

stantial (and more enduring) success. His early songs were recorded by a number of artists, including Ray Charles, Joe Cocker, Judy Collins, Art Garfunkel, Harry Nilsson, Peggy Lee, the Animals' Alan Price, Linda Ronstadt, NINA SIMONE, Ringo Starr, Barbra Streisand, and Three Dog Night.

"My music has a high irritation factor," Randy told *Rolling Stone*'s Timothy White. "I've always tried to say something. Eccentric lyrics about eccentric people. Often it was a joke. But I would plead guilty on the grounds that I prefer eccentricity to the bland."

"I started taking piano lessons when I was six or seven," Newman recalled to *Keyboard*'s Gil Podolinsky. "At 11 or 12, I got into studying theory, harmony, and counterpoint. I wanted to be a film composer, because I was influenced by what my uncles [Lionel, Emil, and the late Alfred Newman] were doing. So I studied with Mario Castelnuovo-Tedesco for about four years, and then went to UCLA and studied with George Tremble—a good man; I should go back to him, too. I started writing

background was much more appealing than the usual disco drone. "Don't Let Me Be Misunderstood" was issued as a 45, and an album of the same name also shipped. Both the single and the LP fared well on the charts—even rock fans enjoyed that hypnotic beat.

"House Of The Rising Sun," another Animals hit, was the choice for a follow-up single. Unfortunately, neither Don Ray nor Leroy Gomez were involved in the project. Jimmy Goings was brought in to do lead vocals. "House" (#78, 1978) was a Hot 100 item, and the *House of the Rising Sun* (1978) album sold well. Once Gomez was gone, so was the chart activity. Three more LPs were released before Casablanca shelved the "Santa Esmeralda" name.

Dan Hill
SOMETIMES WHEN WE TOUCH
(Dan Hill, Barry Mann)
20th Century 2355
No. 3   *March 4, 1978*

It was Dan Hill's pairing with American songwriting vet BARRY MANN that resulted in Hill's hit performance of "Sometimes When We Touch." Both worked for the same music company. It was the publisher's president who suggested that the two give it a try. "When we wrote it," Hill told *Vibes*, "we thought of the way people need to reach out to each other to touch each other, and of the way we punish ourselves and the people we love when we hold back—when we don't touch."

Daniel Hill, Jr. (b. June 3, 1954, Toronto) was born of American parents who had fled to Canada during the McCarthy era. Dan's father is black and is currently the head of the Ontario Human Rights Commission. His mother is white. Both are sociologists with PhDs. "I was raised in an extremely competitive environment, in Dom Mills, an upper-middle-class suburb of Toronto," Hill told *Circus* writer Daisann McLane. "My father would scrutinize my report card. If it wasn't up to expectations—no hockey."

After a rebellious pre-teen period during which he admits to being something of a troublemaker, Dan found poetry and also discovered Frank Sinatra, Ella Fitzgerald, and Sarah Vaughan.

When 18, Hill took his guitar and hit the road. His pop warned him, he recalled to *Circus*, that "You can't make a living selling

your feelings. But I knew if I wasn't gonna be a songwriter, I was gonna be a failure." After his share of coffeehouses, bars, and rejected demos, Hill did manage to secure a Canadian recording contract. By the time he hit stateside stardom, Dan had already achieved status as a homegrown Canadian hero with successful singles, platinum LPs, and several Juno Awards.

Following "Sometimes When We Touch" were several Hot 100 singles—"All I See Is Your Face" (#41, 1978), "Let The Song Last Forever" (#91, 1978), "Never Thought" (#43, 1988)—plus albums like *Longer Fuse* (1977), *Hold On* (1978), and *Frozen in the Night* (1978). Hill currently records for Columbia Records; his most recent release, as of the close of the '80s, was *Real Love*.

Samantha Sang
EMOTION
(Barry Gibb, Robin Gibb)
Private Stock 45178
No. 3   *March 18, 1978*

"One thing I always have to make clear to people who only know me from . . . my association with Barry [Gibb] and his brothers—*I am not a Bee Gee girl*," Ms. Sang declared to *Vibe*'s Kit Lachatte. "I have been a performer

for most of my life. My parents were performers. I love working with the Bee Gees. I love singing their songs. But what they have always wanted for me was that I was a success. And that means being able to stand on my own feet."

Australian Samantha Sang was already an experienced vocalist—having sung on the radio as eight-year-old "Cheryl Gray" and having performed with her warbling parents—when she met Barry Gibb at the age of 16. He suggested that she record some material he had been concocting. Samantha recorded Gibb's "Don't Let It Happen Again," but it flopped. A single or two was issued in the States that same year, but thenceforth, until "Emotion," citizens of this land heard no other musical offerings from Sang.

With the Bee Gees on top of the charts with their Caucasian disco gyrations, Sam approached Barry about lending her another number. Within an hour's time, Gibb brothers Robin and Barry shaped up a smoothie with more than a morsel of Bee Gee mystery magic encased therein. On "Emotion," Samantha's and Barry's vocals blended together so well that it was impossible to tell at any given instant just who was breathing and panting those passionate words. With Gibb at her side, Sammi sounded like a virile Bee-Gee-ette.

"You Keep Me Dancing" (#56, 1978) and "In The Midnight Hour" (#88, 1979) did not have Barry's participation, nor did any of Sang's successive singles. The *Emotion* LP sold well, but never again would Sammi crash the charts.

LeBlanc & Carr

FALLING
(Lenny LeBlanc, Eddie Struzick)
Big Tree 16100
No. 13   *April 1, 1978*

By the time they met in 1968, Floridians Lenny LeBlanc (b. June 17, 1951) and Pete Carr (b. Apr. 22, 1950) were both accomplished musicians. Carr had been a member of Hourglass with Paul Hornsby and Duane and Gregg Allman. When the Glass shattered, Carr (guitar, bass) and LeBlanc (guitar) trekked to Cincinnati in search of session work. Pete subsequently moved to Muscle Shoals, Alabama, where he became a guitarist with the Muscle Shoals Sound Rhythm Section; he wound up producing and performing on the SAILCAT sessions that resulted in "Mo-

torcycle Mama." Lenny likewise relocated to Muscle Shoals following the disbanding of his recording act, Whalefeathers.

By 1976, each had solo albums issued by Big Tree, but listener response was less than enthusiastic. The following year, the old friends joined forces for their lone top 40 hit. *Midnight Light* produced three back-to-back charting singles: "Something About You" (#48, 1977), "Falling," and "Midnight Light" (#92, 1978). However, all was not well. The duo had a falling out, the exact nature of which is not known. In support of their hits, the LeBlanc-Carr Band toured, but minus Pete Carr. No follow-up LP was ever issued.

Lenny LeBlanc placed two solo singles on *Billboard*'s Hot 100—"Hound Dog Man (Play It Again)" (#58, 1977) and "Somebody Send My Baby Home" (#55, 1981)—and has worked recording sessions for Dobie Gray, DELBERT McCLINTON, Roy Orbison, and Swamp Dogg. In 1979, Pete and two former members of the LeBlanc-Carr Band, Thom Flora and Steve Nathan, recorded as Boatz for Capricorn Records. Carr remained incredibly busy as a studio musician, playing on albums by Jim Capaldi, Kim Carnes, Joe Cocker, Art Garfunkel, Millie Jackson, Paul Kossoff, Wilson Pickett, Johnny Rivers, Boz Scaggs, Bob Seger, Paul Simon, Cat Stevens, Rod Stewart, and Travis Wammack, among others.

Patti Smith Group

BECAUSE THE NIGHT
(Patti Smith, Bruce Springsteen)
Arista 0318
No. 13   *June 24, 1978*

Her interest in rock and roll began when she first heard Little Richard's "The Girl Can't Help It." Well, by the mid-'70s Patti Smith *really* couldn't help it: she was bashing out guitar feedback, copping Keith Richards stances, and screaming out raw poetry laced with surreal images. Shocked a lot of people, did this skinny, pouting punk with her erratic and most unlady-like moves.

Patti Lee Smith was born in Chicago on December 30, 1946, was raised in Pitman, South Jersey, and grew up "shy, sickly and creepy lookin'," per her self-penned press bio. She took an early interest in the Bible, prayer, art, and literature—in particular, the works of William Burroughs and French poet Arthur Rimbaud. In the '60s, she attended Glassboro

State College in New Jersey. With savings earned while working in a New Jersey factory, Patti and her sister Linda tripped to Paris, where Smith studied art and worked the roadways as a musician with a street troupe of poets, singers, and fire-eaters. Back in New York, she attended Brooklyn Art College and befriended photographer Robert Mapplethorpe, who took her in for a stay in his Chelsea Hotel apartment.

The next several years were productive. Patti co-wrote a book of plays (*Mad Dog Blues*); performed with Sam Shepard in *Cowboy Mouth*, a one-act play she co-wrote with the renowned playwright and actor; had her first book of poetry (*Seventh Heaven*) published; and wrote articles and reviews for *Creem* and *Rock*. Her poetry readings at St. Mark's Church in lower Manhattan began attracting a sizeable following. On February 10, 1971, Pat invited Lenny Kaye to accompany her readings on his electric guitar; by 1973, keyboardist Richard Sohl had been added, and the Patti Smith Group was born. This avantgarde aggregation recorded "Piss Factory" b/w "Hey Joe," a one-off, limited-release 45 (1,600 copies) for Mer Records.

Bassist/guitarist Ivan Kral and drummer Jay Dee Daugherty soon climbed aboard. An engagement at New York's CBGB caught the attention of Arista Records head Clive Davis, who signed the Patti Smith Group in 1975. *Horses* (1975), the band's debut album—produced by former Velvet Underground member John Cale—sold well beyond expectations. *Radio Ethiopia* (1976) followed, but no tracks were issued as singles.

On January 23, 1977, Smith suffered a near-fatal accident when she fell off a stage in Tampa, Florida and broke her neck. After a year's recuperation, Patti and her group returned with *Easter* (1978) and "Because the Night," a single written with Bruce Springsteen. In 1979, after the *Waves* LP and two further 45s—"Frederick" (#90, 1979) and "So You Wanna Be A Rock 'n' Roll Star"—the Patti Smith Group quietly dissolved.

Sohl and Daugherty pursued solo projects. Kral formed his own group, the Eastern Bloc, while Kaye helped produce Suzanne Vega's *Suzanne Vega* (1985) and *Solitude Standing* (1987) albums. Patti married Fred "Sonic" Smith, founder of the militant MC5 and the Sonic Rendezvous.

In 1986, Patti started work on a comeback album. Three years later, a full nine years after her retirement, her *Dream of Life* album appeared. The sound was strikingly calm and

The Patti Smith Group

peaceful, compared to her previous work; critics differed in their assessments. "People Have The Power," the only single extracted, did not chart.

"I view my absence from the business as a sabbatical—a nine-year study period of positive inner strengthening," Smith told *The Music Express*. "I've been using my time in a very disciplined way, writing my first novel and a bunch of short stories—being a good mother, wife, and concerned citizen."

Eruption

I CAN'T STAND THE RAIN
(Donald Bryant, Ann Peebles, Bernard Miller)
Ariola 7686
No. 18　*July 8, 1978*

"**W**hat we really want to develop is a *real* kind of British soul music," explained Lintel in an interview with *Blues & Soul*. "[We] could be the Beatles of soul music!" Ah, but that was not to be. After Eruption's debut single, Lintel became a pop memory. A few more disks, and the whole Eruption experience sputtered to a halt.

For a brief period, however, Lintel (lead vocals), Miss Precious Wilson (lead vocals), Eric Kingsley (drums), Horatio McKay (keyboards), and the Petrineau brothers, Gregory (guitar) and Morgan (guitar), were England's Eruption, a bottom-heavy funk/dance unit. They were Jamaica-born and London-based and bred. Early in 1976, after three months of rehearsals, the band's manager entered them in the RCA-sponsored "Soul Search"— Eruption grabbed top honors.

One of "Soul Search" 's judges, Philly record producer Billy Jackson, approached the budding band to cut some sides for RCA's Ariola subsidiary. Eruption's factory-fresh debut "Funky Love" failed to chart, but "One Way Ticket" and "I Can't Stand The Rain" (a cover version of Ann Peebles' 1973 hit) were smashes in England. Only the latter disk made the U.S. pop listings.

About this time, someone must have whispered "solo career, solo career" in Miss Precious Wilson's ears, for in a wink, she was gone. So ends our tale of fickle fame. Eruption ceased to emit, and aside from the limited success of "I'll Be Your Friend" (—/#40, 1986), Precious Wilson still hopes to hit the big time.

Steve Martin

KING TUT
(Steve Martin)
Warner Bros. 8577
No. 17　*August 12, 1978*

A former "wild and crazy" stand-up comedian and current maestro of comic invention on the big screen, Steve Martin has earned accolades from audiences and critics alike.

These days, he's primarily an actor and screenwriter. The list of his cinema credits is long: *The Jerk* (1979), *Pennies from Heaven* (1981), *Dead Men Don't Wear Plaid* (1982), *The Man with Two Brains* (1983), *The Lonely Guy* (1984), *All of Me* (1984), *Roxanne* (1987), *Trains and Boats and Planes* (1988), *The Three Amigos* (1988), *Dirty Rotten Scoundrels* (1989), and *Parenthood* (1989).

When not thus occupied, Steve has also made comedy records like *Let's Get Small* (1977), *A Wild and Crazy Guy* (1978), *Comedy Is Not Pretty* (1979), and *The Steve Martin Brothers* (1981). Rarely has the Martin man been found in the 45 RPM format. Among the latter efforts are "Grandmother's Song" (#72, 1977); "King Tut," given a full-production treatment on an early "Saturday Night Live" show; and the sadistic "Cruel Shoes" (#91, 1979). All of these are worth a listen.

Toby Beau

MY ANGEL BABY
(Danny McKenna, Balde Silva)
RCA 11250
No. 13　*August 12, 1978*

Balde Silva and the guys were just a happy Texas bar band until star-maker Sean Delaney came to town. Sean—who had a few notches on the rod as a producer for Kiss and the force behind the heavy-metal Starz—offered to transform Balde and company into big-time celebrities. He whisked the group off to the Big Apple, instructed them to create original material, and then shipped them to England to record their eponymous debut album. RCA issued the *Toby Beau* LP and the syrupy "Angel Baby" as the first 45. The catchy, countrified number clicked, and image-makers at Aucoin Management were off and running. First Balde and the boys were packaged as young Texas toughs; later, they were cutey-

pies with cactus in their teeth. While "Then You Can Tell Me Goodbye" (#57, 1979) and "If I Were You" (#70, 1980) made the Hot 100, Toby Beau never managed to come up with anything potent, and never shook their staid, tumbleweed persona.

Balde Silva (vocals, guitar, harmonica), Danny McKenna (guitar), Ron Rose (guitar, banjo, mandolin), Rob Young (drums), and "Zip" Zipper (bass) had been classmates, all born and raised in the Rio Grande Valley. The band formed in 1975 and was named after a shrimpboat that one of them had spotted on the Gulf of Mexico.

McKenna quit during the band's first recording session. By the time of their third LP in 1980, only Balde remained.

Walter Egan

MAGNET AND STEEL
(Walter Egan)
Columbia 10719
No. 8 *August 26, 1978*

Walter Egan (b. July 12, 1948, Jamaica, N.Y.) grew up in Forest Hills, New York, though he is usually thought of as being a genuine Cal-State soft-rocker. In the early '60s, Walt fronted the Malibooz, a surf band, one of the very few surf bands to catch a wave off the coast of the Empire State. Things were looking promising for Walt (guitar, bass, vocals), Dennis "Ace" Lopez (bass), Chris "Golden Rule" Murray (vocals), Tom "Sparkle Plenty" Scrap (drums), and John "Z" Zambetti (guitar, vocals). They played at the New York World's Fair in 1964 and issued "Goin' To Malibu," an impossible-to-find single.

During the psychedelic era, Walt and his band became Sageworth. With Annie McLoone as a co-lead singer in the band, Sageworth edged toward country-rock; Gram Parsons and Emmylou Harris even recorded some of Egan's songs. Reportedly, it was Harris who encouraged Walt to give up the East Coast for those Golden State waves he had been singing about years back.

Once situated in L.A., Egan joined a group called the Wheels. A scout for Columbia Records caught their act, and singled out Walter for a solo recording contract. Lindsey Buckingham and Stevie Nicks were brought in to support and co-produce Egan's *Fundamental Roll* (1977) album, which yielded "Only The Lucky" (#82, 1977). Buckingham also produced a second release, *Not Shy* (1978), from which "Magnet And Steel" was culled. The similarity of Egan's sound to that of Fleetwood Mac, plus the presence of Buckingham and Nicks on his recordings, led to Walter being unjustly pegged as a Fleetwood Mac clone.

Walter Egan

The Seventies

Two more charts items—"Hot Summer Nights" (#55, 1978) and "Fool Moon Fire" (#46, 1983)—followed, as did three more LPs. Both Randy Meisner ("Hearts On Fire," 1981) and Night ("Hot Summer Nights," 1979) had success with remakes of Egan songs.

In 1981, Walter combined the old and the new Malibooz to cut some exciting surf sounds for Rhino Records. With boss sounds like "The Fluorescent Hearse," "The Lonely Surfer," and a remake by the original band of "Goin' To Malibu," *Malibooz Rules* is worth a look-see.

Chris Rea

FOOL (IF YOU THINK IT'S OVER)
(Chris Rea)
United Artists 1198
No. 12 *September 16, 1978*

"**M**iscast is probably the best way of puttin' it," Chris Rea remarked to *Circus'* David Fricke. "But I can see how it happened. There's a bootleg going around Middlesbrough [England] now of the full eight-minute version of 'Benny Santini' and it sounds more like Springsteen's 'Jungleland.' But Gus [Dudgeon] took only the hooks of the song and nothing else."

"The English Springsteen," as Chris Rea (b. 1951, Middlesbrough, England) has often been labeled by the British press, was probably quite happy to have a hit recording in America. "Fool (If You Think It's Over)," a tune he wrote for his sister, came from his debut LP, *Whatever Happened to Benny Santini?*, produced by Gus Dudgeon. However, Chris was not pleased with this over-orchestrated and, in his view, misconceived album (although it did eventually sell 1,000,000 copies in the U.S.). A few years later, Columbia Records allowed Rea a free hand in their Chipping Norton Studios in Oxfordshire, England. Chris referred to the resulting album, *Tennis* (1980), as "my first album—one that sets the record straight." Neither the LP nor any of the singles pulled from it have sold well.

In the five years preceding his one-hit wonder status, Chris worked as a construction laborer, a salesman of vibrating chairs, and a musician on the pub and concert circuit fronting Magdelene, later called the Beautiful Losers. David Coverdale of Whitesnake was once a member of the Beautiful Losers, designated by *Melody Maker* as the "best new band of the year." Magnet Records soon signed a recording contract for Rea's solo services. The

"miscast" *Benny Santini*, his best-selling American album, was the initial result.

In the '80s, Chris has continued to record, with substantial success in his homeland. "Whatever Happened to Benny Santini?" (#71, 1978) was issued in the States as his follow-up to "Fool." Two of his later singles cracked the Hot 100: "Diamonds" (#44, 1979) and "Loving You" (#88, 1982).

John Paul Young

LOVE IS IN THE AIR
(Harry Vanda, George Young)
Scotti Brothers 402
No. 7 *October 14, 1978*

J. Paul was born in Glasgow, Scotland, in 1953, and his family moved to Australia when he was a tot. Left to his own devices, he played around with the family accordion and later tinkered with the piano. But music was not to be his primary occupation, so it seemed. He served a five-year apprenticeship as a sheet-metal worker, and toward the end of this workout, John began playing music on weekends in local watering holes.

Producer Simon Napier-Bell—who had ventured into recording studios with acts like the Yardbirds and Marc Bolan (of T. REX fame)—had a sure-shot hit song in his hands called "Pasadena," and needed a vocalist. Reportedly, Napier-Bell spotted Young doing one of his weekend gigs and offered to record him. John Paul accepted, and though the tune did zip in the States, it made the British top 10. Other disks placed on the Aussie charts, and Young won a slot in the Australian production of *Jesus Christ Superstar*.

A few years prior to his big moment with a composition by Harry Vanda and George Young (Vanda and Young had been members of THE EASYBEATS), John Paul had a moderate stateside success with "Yesterday's Hero" (#42, 1975). To date, only one other John Paul Young single has made the Hot 100 listings: "Lost In Your Love" (#55, 1979).

Nick Gilder

HOT CHILD IN THE CITY
(Nick Gilder, James McCulloch)
Chrysalis 2226
No. 1 *October 28, 1978*

In 1961, Nick Gilder (b. Nov. 7, 1951, London) moved with his family to Vancouver, Canada. Nicky soon started singing with a group called Throm Hortis. They won a talent contest, worked in some clubs and high schools, and attracted the attention of several record labels.

In 1971, Jim McCulloch, lead guitarist with Rasputin, asked Gilder to join his own group. As Sweeney Todd (after the mythical barber who slashed his patrons' throats), they performed throughout Vancouver with high visibility, i.e. with garish make-up, hideous clothes, flashpots, and a smoke machine. By 1976, some Sweeney Todd 45s for London Records, in particular the Gilder-McCulloch song "Roxy Roller" (#90, 1976), had begun to receive major attention.

At this point, Nick and Jim abandoned Sweeney Todd (which reportedly included Bryan Adams) and moved to L.A.; Gilder signed a contract with Chrysalis Records, and the twosome collaborated on Nick's solo projects. "Hot Child In The City" really clicked— 2,000,000 copies were eventually sold. Speaking of "Hot Child," Gilder told *Rolling Stone*: "I've seen a lot of young girls, 15 and 16, walking down Hollywood Boulevard with their pimps. Their home environment drove them to distraction so they ran away . . . It hurts to see that so I tried writing from the perspective of a lecher—in the guise of an innocent pop song."

"Here Comes The Night" (#44, 1978) and "Rock Me" (#57, 1979) as well as Nick's second and third albums—*City Lights* (1978) and *Frequency* (1979)—have sold well. His most recent effort was a self-titled 1985 album for RCA.

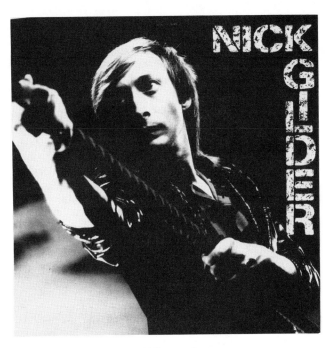

tainly looked like it. "Nightlife" was a Grammy nominee for "Best Song of the Year." Her follow-up, "Body Heat" (#86, 1979), was less successful. Further recordings were issued by A.V.I. and Second Wave to nary a smidgen of success.

"Since I turned to guitar one Sunday, music has been the most important thing in my life," Alicia told Bret Primack of *Grooves*. "There are people I love and care about, but music is the moving force . . . I live it, and I am dedicated to it."

Alicia Bridges

I LOVE THE NIGHTLIFE
(DISCO 'ROUND)
(Alicia Bridges, Susan Hutcheson)
Polydor 14483
No. 5 *December 23, 1978*

Alicia is not saying how old she is, but we do know that she was born and raised in Lawndale, North Carolina. After working in a bank and pushin' goods at Sears, Roebuck, Bridges began her singing career in Zachary Ridge, a heavy rock band that played accompaniment for strippers in burlesque houses.

The disco staple "I Love The Nightlife" was not Alicia's first or last recording, but it cer-

Ace Frehley

NEW YORK GROOVE
(Russ Ballard)
Casablanca 941
No. 13 *February 3, 1979*

When Paul "Ace" Frehley (b. Apr. 27, 1951, Bronx) walked away from Kiss, they still were one of the hottest and most influential rock and roll bands in the world. Nearly all of their albums had gone double platinum, and their concerts were sell-outs. Their memorabilia— posters, T-shirts, necklaces, keychains, belt buckles, concert books, buttons, and all the rest—was still raking in m-i-l-l-i-o-n-s.

"At the end of my stay with Kiss, even playing live had become something of a drag,"

Frehley confessed to *Hit Parader*'s Winston Cummings. "The fun had gone out of it for me. I realize now that it was my health that was making me feel that way, because once I got my life straightened out, the only thing I wanted to do was get in front of people and play."

Ace left the band in 1983, and spent the next four years battling a drug habit. He bounced back with three hard-rocking, fairly-well-reviewed LPs on Atlantic/Megaforce—*Frehley's Comet, Live + 1,* and *Second Sighting*—and commands a cultish following of aging metal-heads and Kiss fans.

Frehley started playing guitar at 13. "Once I played an electric guitar I was hooked," Frehley told *Guitar Player.* Ace played in high school and local groups. To make a living, "I drove a cab, and I worked in an upholstery place. I was a mailman, an art student—you name it, I did it."

Peter Criss, Paul Stanley, and Gene Simmons had already formed Kiss (then called Rainbow) when Ace was enlisted in 1972. "They advertised in the *Village Voice.* At the time I was unhappy with the group I was with, and I just thought I would try an audition. We worked out pretty good, and they said, 'We can't give you a definite answer today' . . . They called me back and said, 'Come back and jam with us again.'"

"Look, I don't expect this band [Frehley's Comet] to ever be as big as Kiss was," Frehley told *Hit Parader.* "That was a once in a lifetime experience which is still very near and dear to me. But I'm happy as I've ever been."

Cheryl Lynn
GOT TO BE REAL
(Cheryl Lynn, David Paich, David Foster)
Columbia 10808
No. 12 *February 17, 1979*

Cheryl Lynn is a big woman, but critics have also noted that she is hugely talented.

"You know what is projected on television," Ms. Lynn told *Black Star*'s Gerrie E. Summers. "We never saw the large-sized woman until a few years ago. Now we have the Jennifer Holidays and Nell Carters—we have more of the Cheryl Lynns."

Delbert Langston believed in her. He was her manager and boyfriend, and arranged for Cheryl to audition for "The Gong Show."

"I guess Delbert got tired of me singing in

church and thought I could do more. He begged me to audition and I argued because I was kind of shy. I didn't like being in front of people because I was inhibited. I've never liked being in front of the guys because I didn't want them snickering."

Cheryl (b. Mar. 11, 1957, Los Angeles) met Delbert Langston at Washington High in L.A. Del was forming a group called Happy, Free, and Easy, and needed a girl's voice—he found one in Cheryl Lynn (a.k.a. Lydia Smith). They remained together for a few years, doing gigs whenever and wherever. Finally, in 1976, Langston set Cheryl up with auditions for "The Gong Show" and for the national touring company of *The Wiz.* She was accepted for both, and while waiting for the "Gong" episode to air, Lynn subbed for three months as the Wicked Witch of the West.

"[When the show aired], I got a call from Chuck Barris' production company," Lynn told *Soul*'s Leonard Pitts, Jr. "He says, 'You're gonna be a star overnight. We've never gotten a response like this for anybody on "The Gong Show."'"

Producer Bob Johnston brought her to the attention of the powers at Columbia Records. Once they viewed the 90-second "Gong" spot, she was signed to the label. Her self-titled debut album and single, "Got To Be Real," were instant successes. Over the years, she has followed through with "Star Love" (#62, 1979), "Shake It Up Tonight" (#70, 1981), and "Encore" (#69, 1984). Her string of R & B hits is impressive: 16 singles on the listings through 1988, including a duet with Luther Vandross.

Ian Matthews
SHAKE IT
(Terence Boylan)
Mushroom 7039
No. 13 *February 17, 1979*

He has told *Rolling Stone* that he's known primarily as a rebel. Outside of his faithful cult following, however, singer-songwriter Ian Matthews is known mostly for his smooth work with the Fairport Convention and his namesake band, Matthews Southern Comfort. Both of his former groups were at the peak of their creative and pop powers when Ian left them.

He was born Ian McDonald in Lincolnshire, England, in June 1946. He began attracting notice playing guitar and singing with a teenaged rhythm & blues band called the Rebels. "The Drifters, the Coasters, that's what I latched onto," Matthews told *Rolling Stone*'s Byron Laursen. "I must have sounded so *dumb*." Next, Matthews tried playing surf music in a Deram recording act called the Pyramid. One single was issued, "Summer Of Last Year."

In 1967, Ian was asked to join the original Fairport Convention (for three albums). "I've never really been a folkie," he explained to *Guitar Player*. "When I joined Fairport Convention, they weren't a folk band, not by any stretch of the imagination. They were doing their own interpretations of mainly American material; they'd do songs by the Byrds and Tim Hardin. That's the nearest we came to folk music." All was to change, however, when Sandy Denny was admitted into the fold, and the group's direction veered toward Celtic allusions and medieval English balladry. "That was when I really became disillusioned with the band."

Ian left in 1969 to form his own group, Matthews Southern Comfort, with Carl Barnwell (guitar), Ray Duffy (drums), Mark Griffins (guitar), Gordon Huntley (pedal-steel guitar), and Andy Leigh (bass). Three country-folkrockin' LPs followed; with the success of a take on Joni Mitchell's "Woodstock" (#23, 1971), Ian was gone, though two other singles from Matthews Southern Comfort's *Later That Same Year* album made the Hot 100: "Mare, Take Me Home" (#96, 1971) and a cover of Neil Young's "Tell Me Why" (#98, 1971). Huntley and the rest carried on as Southern Comfort for three more LPs before disbanding in 1972.

It's been almost 20 years since his departure from the Southern Comfort band, and for most of the time Ian has carried on as a soloist with a loyal following. There have been occasional one-off projects with groups like Plainsong (*In Search of Amelia Earhart*), the Hi-Fi's, and the Mallards. Critics have praised Matthews for his tasteful and folk-tinged interpretations of songs by Jackson Browne, Carole King, RANDY NEWMAN, Tom Waits, and Neil Young. A few of these solo efforts sold well: *Tigers Will Survive* (1972), *Valley Hi* (1973) (produced by ex-Monkee Mike Nesmith), and *Stealin' Home* (1978). Only one of the many singles taken from these albums has been a top 40 hit: producer/singer/songwriter Terence Boylan's "Shake It." In reference to his big moment, Ian said to *Rolling Stone* that "I don't think I did anything different. I guess it's my

reward. After all, I've been doing exactly what I want for 14 or 15 years."

Ian Matthews is currently an A & R director at the Windham Hill label. His most recent solo excursion, *Walking a Changing Line: The Songs of Jules Shear*, was issued in the spring of 1988.

Bobby Caldwell
WHAT YOU WON'T DO FOR LOVE
(Caldwell, Kettner)
Clouds 11
No. 9   *February 24, 1979*

Bobby Caldwell has inhabited two distinct musical worlds. Those who have written about him usually praise one side of him and totally ignore the other. Rock and rollers, after all, don't usually mess with songs that sound like they could have been on the *Saturday Night Fever* soundtrack. How is it possible, then, for Bobby Caldwell to make hard-rock records with Johnny Winter and Rick Derringer one day, and sing well-baked disco ballads the next?

Born in Manhattan on August 15, 1951, Bobby pulled together his first group, the Rooftops, during his teens, and they frequently made side money at parties and rock and roll hops. At 19, his new group, Katmandu, recorded an album for Mainstream Records. The LP didn't sell well, but it did catch the attention of Little Richard, who hired the band to be an opening act for his Las Vegas appearances. Caldwell left the group months later and joined up with Johnny Winter's band.

After a live album with Winter, Bobby joined ex-Iron Butterfly bassist Lee Dorman for an album with Dorman's Captain Beyond. He moved on to ex-McCoy Rick Derringer's band for the *All-American Boy* (1971) album, then played alongside ex-Yardbird Keith Relf in the short-lived Armaggedon. One highly-collectible album later, Bob vanished, but not for long. He reappeared on later albums by Derringer, Winter, and Captain Beyond, also making scads of TV commercials and recording tracks for Walt Disney's "New Mickey Mouse Club."

After 20 years in the shadows, Bob stepped out with a solo release on Clouds Records. Could this be the same Bobby Caldwell? With its lazy feel and smooth veneer, "What You Won't Do For Love" sounded like something a tipsy George Benson might have recorded. The ballad fared well, even though it surprised listeners who were more familiar with the hard-rockin' Caldwell. Two follow-ups, both in a similar vein—"Coming Down From My Love" (#42, 1980) and "All Of My Love" (#77, 1982)—made the Hot 100, and a few more singles placed on the R & B listings.

"I think that my album [1978's *Bobby Caldwell*, which featured "What You Won't Do For Love"] is nice," Bobby told *Soul*. "You can listen to it over and over again, but I know there is nothing there that really sticks its foot up your ass."

Caldwell switched recently to MCA Records, where he continues to work the terrain created by his lone top 40 hit. Bobby has also become known for his songwriting abilities— Roy Ayers, Peabo Bryson, Natalie Cole, Roberta Flack, CHERYL LYNN, and Dionne Warwick have all recorded his compositions.

Bell & James

LIVIN' IT UP (FRIDAY NIGHT)
(LeRoy Bell, Casey James)
A & M 2069
No. 15   *April 21, 1979*

Florida native LeRoy Bell and Casey James from Portland, Oregon, met in a Philly-based band called Special Blend. Their band bombed and broke up, but Bell & James stayed together and formed a songwriting team.

LeRoy's uncle was none other than Thom Bell, the producer/arranger/tunesmith for Gamble & Huff and their renowned "Sound of Philadelphia." Once Special Blend had dried up, Bell (drums, guitar) & James (guitar, bass, keyboards, synthesizers) were hired by uncle Bell's Mighty Three Music company to write songs and create demos. Elton John, L.T.D., MFSB, Maxine Nightingale, the O'Jays, Freda Payne, Gladys Knight & The Pips, and the Pockets all recorded some Bell & James tunes. A sprinkling of their disco ditties appeared in the Jonathan Winters flick *The Fish that Saved Pittsburgh* (1979).

At about this time, executives at A & M Records heard one of their demos, and offered the duo a recording contract. Instant success was theirs: "Livin' It Up," Bell & James' debut disk, went solid gold. Weeks later, Elton John repeated the feat with his rendering of their "Mama Can't Buy Me Love." A few more weeks, and their popularity was on the wane. Before the onset of their obscurity, three more

45s graced the middle reaches of the R & B chart through 1980.

Amii Stewart

KNOCK ON WOOD
(Eddie Floyd, Steve Cropper)
Ariola 7736
No. 1   *April 21, 1979*

"**I**'ve never bought a disco record in my life," Amii Stewart told *Record Mirror*'s Paul Sexton. "And I don't want to buy one. When I go home and close the door I don't want my brains to be blown out." A peculiar comment indeed, considering that Amii's "Knock On Wood," her one and only international chart-topper, was one of the hottest disco disks of 1979.

Amy Stewart was born in 1956 in Washington, D.C., the daughter of a top-secret Pentagon man. As a child, she was given music and dance lessons. She attended Howard University, but left to work with the D.C. Repertory Dance Company, where she studied ballet and modern dance. In 1975, she joined the Miami cast of *Bubbling Brown Sugar* and, soon after, the Broadway cast. Amii also appeared in *The Return of the Pink Panther* (1975), *King Kong* (1976), and *The Greatest* (1977).

Stewart's big break occurred in 1977, when one of her old dance instructors, bringing *Bubbling Brown Sugar* to London, picked Amii to not only join him as assistant director but also play Ella, one of the lead roles. The part offered Amii the opportunity to show off her vocal abilities on "I Got It Bad" and the title tune. Sitting in the audience one brisk September night was songwriter/producer Barry Leng, who was looking for a female to cut a demo on a tune that he and his associate Simon May had written. Amii agreed to give the song a whirl. The demo turned out so well that Leng and May walked the tape into the offices of Hansa Productions. "You Really Touched My Heart" was released, and sold fairly well in Europe.

Peter Meisel, Hansa's part-owner and controller, suggested that Amii cover one of his '60s favorites, Eddie Floyd's "Knock On Wood," for her next single. Disco or not, Stewart initially seemed to like the idea. "Pete went in and did the track," Stewart told *Blues & Soul*, "and when I heard it, I just flipped out! In fact, I asked him what I was supposed to sing since the track sounded so good just as it was."

The disk was a genuine knockout with both pop (#1) and R & B (#6) audiences worldwide. An altered, appended, and equally disco-fied cover of the Doors' classic "Light My Fire/137 Disco Heaven" (#69/36, 1979) followed, and sold fairly well. A year later, Amii duetted with JOHNNY BRISTOL on a reworking of Mary Wells'/ the Temptations' "My Guy/My Girl" (#63/76, 1980), which was a moderate success.

When last spotted in 1984, Amii had a top 10 platter in the U.K. with "Friends." The track "is totally different from anything I've ever done, thank God," Stewart told *Record Mirror*. "You can't spend your life singing songs like 'Knock On Wood.'"

Frank Mills

MUSIC BOX DANCER
(Frank Mills)
Polydor 14517
No. 3 *May 5, 1979*

"**M**aybe 'Music Box Dancer' will be it, but I don't think so, because I'm not going to quit," Mills told *Music Scene* magazine. "I would rather think that my 'Moon River' isn't too far around the corner."

Frank Mills was born in 1943 in Toronto. For years, he studied piano, theory, composition, and arranging. After leaving Montreal's McGill Conservatory of Music, Mills sold industrial gases and real estate, eventually joining THE BELLS. They recorded a few of his tunes, but by 1972, Frank felt he wanted to go it alone and do his stuff his way. A first-off single, "Love Me, Love Me Love" (#46, 1972), made the U.S. pop listings; follow-ups like a cover of Rick Nelson's "Poor Little Fool" charted in his homeland.

By 1974, Frank was without a label. For a long time, he had been stifling his aspirations to create easy-listening mood music for the older, more sedate crowd. He publicly praised the MOR orchestral strains of Bert Kaempfert and particularly James Last, and proposed creating soothing sounds of this nature. When all the record labels turned him down, Mills paid out of his pocket to have an album of these Muzak-like smoothies made. Years later, someone noticed with a tingle the pleasing piano puffery of the "Music Box Dancer" album track. In the midst of the disco phenomenon, Polydor boldly reissued "Music Box Dancer" and that five-year-old album to an enthusiastic response.

Frank Mills still plays music for an audience he has described as "the totally forgotten." Late in 1987, Capitol Records issued his *Transitions* album.

Instant Funk

I GOT MY MIND MADE UP
(YOU CAN GET IT GIRL)
(Kim Miller, Scotty Miller, Raymond Earl)
Salsoul 2078
No. 20 *May 12, 1979*

Raymond Earl (bass) and the Miller brothers, Kim (guitar) and Scotty (drums), met in the mid-'60s in their hometown of Trenton, New Jersey. They formed the Music Machine (not to be confused with the similarly-titled one-hit wonder act) and shopped their sounds around for three years before an up-and-coming vocal group named the TNJs hired them as a back-up band. The Newark label issued a few promising sides by the TNJs in the late '60s, but nothing monumental happened, so Ray and the brothers moved their base of operations to Philadelphia in 1971.

A chance meeting with Bunny Sigler led to both a job as Sigler's back-up band and a recording contract with Gamble & Huff's TSOP. Sigler had the guys assume the "Instant Funk" monicker and encouraged them to flesh out their sound with the addition of Dennis Richardson (piano) and Charles Willams (percussion). Some funkified 45s and an album, *Get Down with the Philly Jump*, were issued in the mid-'70s, all to little avail; Bunny and the band departed from the label.

While with TSOP, Instant Funk was also a studio band for Archie Bell & The Drells, Evelyn "Champagne" King, the O'Jays, and Sigler. After Bunny connected the group with Salsoul Records, they continued working sessions for the likes of Double Exposure, Loleatta Holloway, the Love Committee, and the Salsoul Orchestra. For their first album on the Salsoul label, George Bell (second guitar), James Carmichael (lead vocals, percussion), Larry Davis (trumpet), Johnny Onderline (sax), and ex-Ritchie Family member Eric Huff (trombone) were added to the group. The *Instant Funk* (1979) album was released, and the opening cut, "I Got My Mind Made Up," was issued as a single. "Got My Mind" got the nation funkin' again. The 45 held down the R & B chart's number-one slot for three weeks. The LP even made the top pop albums chart.

Instant Funk

Eight other follow-up singles charted on the R & B listings through 1983, but nothing further found favor with the nation's pop fans.

Randy Vanwarmer

JUST WHEN I NEEDED YOU MOST
(Randy Vanwarmer)
Bearsville 0334
No. 4 *June 16, 1979*

Randall Vanwarmer was born on March 30, 1955, in Indian Hills, Colorado—a town with a gas station, a post office, a trading post, and 2,000 souls. Randy's folks were Fundamentalists and disallowed many activities, including listening to rock and pop music. When Randy was 12, his dad died in a car crash; his mother moved the family to a fishing village near Cornwall, in the south of England. While attending St. Austell College, Randy took to playing the guitar and began making demo tapes. Familial restrictions apparently were lifted, because Vanwarmer soon began singing songs in secular clubs and night spots.

In 1979, Randy moved to Woodstock, New York, and signed with the Bearsville label. "Just When I Needed You Most" was delicate, easily digestible, and a huge hit. After "Whatever You Decide" (#80, 1970) and "Suzi" (#55, 1981), Vanwarmer's career seems to have cooled. Few critics noted the appearance, late in 1988, of Randy's warm release on 16th Avenue Records, *I Am*.

Rex Smith

YOU TAKE MY BREATH AWAY
(Bobby Hart, Stephen Lawrence)
Columbia 10908
No. 10 *June 23, 1979*

Rex Smith was born on September 19, 1956, in Jacksonville, Florida. After a series of moves, Rex's family settled in Atlanta. He played in bands (as did his older brother, Michael Lee Smith of Starz) and got involved in amateur theater productions.

In the mid-'70s, Smith moved to the Big Apple to give up rock music and become an actor. Before these dreams firmed up, David Krebs and Steve Leber, a couple of hot-shot music managers, convinced Rex to front a hard-rock combo comprising Lou Van Dora (guitar), Lars Hansen (guitar), Mike Ratti (drums), and Orville Davis, formerly of the Capricorn recording act Hydra. Krebs and Leber called the boys Rex. Two albums' worth of raunchies were issued by Columbia Records, but sales were nil, despite the photos of would-be teen heartthrob Smith on the LP covers.

In 1979, Rex landed the lead in *Sooner or Later*, a made-for-TV movie about a rock star who lusts for a pre-teen fan. "You Take My Breath Away," from the soundtrack, was shipped as Rex's first solo side. The album and the single clicked, but aside from "Everlasting Love" (#32, 1981), a one-off duet with Rachel Sweet, Rex's chart-topping days were over.

For a season (1981–1982), Rex was a co-host, with Marilyn McCoo, of TV's "Solid Gold," then appeared in a short-lived series, "Street Hawk." Smith performed in, and sang the title tune to, *Headin' for Broadway* (1980), and also starred in the Broadway and East Coast productions of *Grease*. With Linda Ronstadt and Kevin Kline, he worked in both the Broadway and film renditions of *The Pirates of Penzance* (1983).

Anita Ward
RING MY BELL
(Frederick Knight)
Juana 3422
No. 1   *June 30, 1979*

Anita Ward (b. Dec. 20, 1957, Memphis) was always interested in music. While attending Rush College in Holly Springs, Mississippi, she sang in their *A Cappella* Choir and with the Rush Singers, who appeared on an album with Metropolitan Opera star Leontyne Price.

While Anita worked days as a substitute elementary-school teacher, her manager sent photos, bio sheets, and demo tapes out to record companies. Frederick Knight, president of Juana Records, agreed to record some tunes with Ms. Ward.

Fred had a tune in his head that he had hoped to place with 11-year-old Stacy Lattisaw. "It was then a teenybopper type of song, about kids talking on the telephone," Knight told Bob Gilbert and Gary Theroux in *The Top Ten*. "Ring My Bell" had to be rewritten, but once Freddie did so, and once Anita moved her way

Rex Smith

MᶜFADDEN & WHITEHEAD

Ain't no stoppin' them now.

Gene McFadden and John Whitehead started behind the scenes in Philadelphia. Writing hits like "Back Stabbers" for the O'Jays, "Bad Luck" and "Wake Up Everybody" for Harold Melvin & the Blue Notes, and "The More I Get, the More I Want" for Teddy Pendergrass. Also, they've helped build careers with their production skills. Like with Melba Moore's smash hit "You Stepped Into My Life." And they've also written and produced for people like The Jacksons and Lou Rawls.

But now McFadden and Whitehead have finally stepped into the spotlight themselves. With a debut album that shows that's just where they belong. It's called "McFadden & Whitehead." And it features their first hit single, "Ain't No Stoppin' Us Now"—a song that's quickly becoming an anthem. It's already exploding on both R&B and Top 40 stations across the country.

You see there's no stopping McFadden and Whitehead. And when you hear their music, you won't exactly be standing still yourself.

On Philadelphia International Records and Tapes.
Distributed by CBS Records.

Produced by John Whitehead, Gene McFadden and Jerry Cohen.

McFadden & Whitehead

AIN'T NO STOPPIN' US NOW
(Gene McFadden, John Whitehead, Jerry Cohen)
Philadelphia International 3681
No. 13   *July 21, 1979*

They met in a North Philly ghetto, when their primary interest in life was playing in the sandbox and flying on the swings. While in high school in the '60s, Gene McFadden (b. 1948, Philadelphia), John Whitehead (b. 1948, Philadelphia), and Alan Beatty formed the Epsilons. Legend has it that one morn, while Gene was standing on a street corner holding some Otis Redding records, Otis' bandleader noticed and asked him if he would like to meet the "Southern Soul King." That evening, the Epsilons got to sing for Redding, who asked the boys to join his Revue. Gene, John, and Alan remained in the entourage for a year before tiring of the one-nighter grind.

"We told Otis that we [were real tired and] wanted to go home," Whitehead told *Blues & Soul*'s John Abbey. "Otis said he wanted us to stay because he had a song he wanted us to record—but we were adamant and we just said we were too tired so he would have to get somebody else. So he did! He brought in Arthur Conley and they cut that song, 'Sweet Soul Music.' The worst thing was that we *didn't* end up going home and we sang the backgrounds for Arthur."

Only weeks later, Otis was dead. Gene and John returned home. Al Beatty left the group. With their new member, James Knight, and a new group name, Talk of the Town, McFadden and Whitehead approached Kenny Gamble and Leon Huff, then heads of the newly-established Philadelphia International label. After a few Talk of the Town singles flopped, John was relegated to the position of chief mail boy. Gene was unemployed.

One night in desperation, while sitting at a kitchen table in a Philly project, they wrote "Back Stabbers." "I told Gene to come to work with me 'cause we were gonna show that song to Huff," John told *Soul*'s J. Randy Taraborrelli. "So we were standing at the elevator door in front of Huff's office. I knew he'd have to go to the bathroom. When he did come out, he went to the soda machine and I followed him all the way, reading the lyrics." By the time Whitehead got to the chorus, Huff was sold on the song's potential. The rest, as they say, is history. "Back Stabbers" became the O'Jays' first

through the suggestive romp—which featured Knight playing a synthesized drum—the record became a stone-cold smash, topping both *Billboard*'s pop and R & B charts.

"'Ring My Bell' was almost an accident," Ms. Ward recalled to *Cashbox*. "When we went into the studio we had no intention whatsoever of cutting a disco number. We were down to our last number in the studio, and we realized that we needed something uptempo." Anita was not even enthusiastic about her gigantic hit. "I am not really a disco queen," she told *Blues & Soul*. "You see, I'm basically just a naive, shy little church girl. I don't smoke and I don't drink." Ward had never even been to a disco when her bell-ringer was reverberating off the walls of countless dance halls.

Ward's first album, *Songs of Love* (1979), was a huge seller. Before year's end, one more single and another, tamer LP were issued. Only the single, "Don't Drop My Love" (#87, 1979), sparked even mild interest. It is quite possible that Anita made no further recordings.

R & B chart-topper and Philadelphia International's first gold single.

McFadden and Whitehead went on to write and/or produce some of the biggest chart-movers, playing a seminal role in the development of the "Philadelphia Sound." Archie Bell, the Intruders, Harold Melvin & The Blue Notes, Melba Moore, Teddy Pendergrass, Lou Rawls—all recorded tunes by the duo.

"I guess that after 22 gold records, 2 platinum albums, and 2 Grammy nominations, we simply felt we wanted to do something for ourselves," Whitehead told Abbey. Seeking to gain some of the public acclaim that they had been dispensing to others, McFadden and Whitehead walked into the studios as recording artists; "Ain't No Stoppin' Us Now" was their debut disk. Nary a thing stood in their way—"Ain't No Stoppin'" scaled the pop charts and hit number one on the R & B listings, eventually selling 2,000,000 copies. The *McFadden & Whitehead* album went gold.

Unfortunately, only McFadden & Whitehead's "I Heard It In A Love Song" (—/#23, 1980) came anywhere near to being as popular, although "I've Been Pushed Aside" (—/#73, 1980) and "One More Time" (—/#58, 1982) were solid efforts. After serving some time in jail for tax evasion, John Whitehead returned to the R & B charts as a solo act with "I Need Money Bad" (—/#50, 1988).

David Naughton

MAKIN' IT
(Dino Fekaris, Freddie Perren)
RSO 916
No. 5   *July 21, 1979*

Dave Naughton is primarily an actor and a dancer, and only a sometime singer. Born on February 13, 1951, and raised in Hartford, Connecticut, he received a degree in English literature from the University of Pennsylvania and studied acting at the London Academy of Music and Dramatic Arts.

Naughton's big break came in the late '70s, when he sang and danced in a series of minimusical Dr. Pepper commercials. The spots caught the attention of the casting director for an upcoming TV series, "Makin' It," to be based on the film *Saturday Night Fever* (1977). Dave had the honor of playing the John Travolta role. To beef up the connection with the movie, the producers used Bee Gees music, gave John's sister Ellen Travolta a small part, and

brought in the film's producer, Robert Stigwood, for "technical" input. Two months later, ABC pulled the plug on the series.

The tune "Makin' It" was not only used as the theme for the short-lived TV series, but was also called into action for the flick *Meatballs* (1979). Despite the massive response to Naughton's single, only a few more efforts were issued before Dave turned his full attention to being an actor. Naughton has since had roles in two other TV series, "At Ease" and "My Sister Sam," and starred in the films *An American Werewolf in London* (1983), *Hot Dog . . . The Movie* (1984), and *Kidnapped* (1987).

Patrick Hernandez

BORN TO BE ALIVE
(Patrick Hernandez, Herve Tholance)
Columbia 10986
No. 16   *September 28, 1979*

Pat's Spanish dad had been a big-band guitar player; his Austrian/Italian mom had been a singer. With that kind of background, it would seem nearly impossible for the young man (b. 1949, Guadeloupe, France) not to have developed at the least a fleeting interest in music.

From 1963 through 1966, Hernandez attended school in England, where the pervasive audio backdrop consisted largely of Beatles sounds. Patrick, like most others, took notice. He later moved to Paris and decided to give singing a try. After more than a decade of getting by on the bar circuit with a succession of rock bands, Hernandez got the chance to tape some songs, in particular a vibrant, dancy thing that he and Herve Tholance had written called "Born To Be Alive."

The response was awesome. The disk topped or nearly topped music charts in Australia, Brazil, Canada, Mexico, and a number of countries in Europe.

Nothing Patrick has had released in the States since has made the Hot 100.

Nick Lowe

CRUEL TO BE KIND
(Robert Ian Gomm, Nick Lowe)
Columbia 11018
No. 12   *September 29, 1979*

He's one talented lad, this Nick Lowe. He's worked with top-notch groups, written great

Nick Lowe

performed on the soundtrack to David Bowie's *Ziggy Stardust* (1983, filmed in 1973), masquerading as the Electricians. Brinsley Schwarz labored for half a decade, creating critically-lauded but commercially unsuccessful albums that featured a number of Lowe compositions.

The Schwarz boys split up in March 1975. After cutting sardonic glam-rock sides as the Disco Brothers ("Let's Go To The Disco") and the Tartan Horde ("Bay City Rollers We Love You"), Lowe began playing what would become his most winning role—that of producer. Over the years, he has produced recordings for his wife (and Johnny Cash's step-daughter) Carlene Carter, Paul Carrack (formerly of ACE and later of Mike + the Mechanics), Huey Lewis' Clover, Elvis Costello (every album up through 1981's *Trust*), the Damned, Dave Edmunds, the Fabulous Thunderbirds, Dr. Feelgood, John Hiatt, Michael Jupp, the Kursaal Flyers, Graham Parker & The Rumour, the Pretenders ("Stop Your Sobbing"), and Wreckless Eric. He was present for the famed "Live Stiff"/Stiff Records packaged tour of 1977. And for a while—with Billy Bremner, Dave Edmunds, and Terry Williams—Lowe was a member of the short-lived but incredibly promising Rockpile.

All the while, Nick recorded solo singles, sporadically issuing LPs and EPs. Only "I Love The Sound Of Breaking Glass" (from his first album, 1978's *Pure Pop for Now People*) and "Cruel To Be Kind" (a remake of one of his early "B" sides) made any major dents in the British charts, and only the latter would do likewise in the States. His "I Knew The Bride (When She Used To Rock And Roll)" (#77, 1986), credited to Nick Lowe & His Cowboy Outfit and produced by Huey Lewis, marked his return to *Billboard*'s Hot 100.

Lowe seems to be as busy as ever these days; his most recent album release was *Party of One* (1990).

songs, and recorded treasured tracks. But as of this date, it's his producing skills that have earned him his major success.

Like scads of other music appreciators, bassist/guitarist Nick (b. Mar. 24, 1949, Woodchurch, Suffolk, England) grew up listening to Elvis and dreaming of making ethereal rock and roll. The son of a Royal Air Force officer, he learned guitar and organized a few bands with his school chum, guitarist Brinsley Schwarz. They were the Sounds 4 Plus 1, Three's a Crowd, and—with the addition of keyboardist Bob Andrews, keyboardist Barry Landerman, and drummer Pete Whales in 1965—the Kippington Lodge. The band made some inroads and in the following year recorded five failed singles for Parlophone. Pete and Barry dropped out in 1969, drummer Billy Rankin was added, and the group renamed itself after their lead guitarist—Brinsley Schwarz.

Brinsley Schwarz acquired a riotous reputation and became the centerpiece of the blooming British pub-rock scene. They briefly appeared in DAVID ESSEX's *Stardust* (1974) and

Sniff 'n' The Tears
DRIVER'S SEAT
(Paul Roberts)
Atlantic 3604
No. 15 *September 29, 1979*

Sniff 'n' The Tears was the realization of a British rocker named Paul Roberts. Paul wrote and shaped all of the "group"'s songs, sang lead, played guitar, created the album covers, and—when not otherwise occupied—

painted. His reputation in Europe is more for his artwork than for his musical abilities: exhibitions of his paintings have been held in Amsterdam, London, Milan, and Paris.

The predecessor of this peculiarly-named act was put together by Roberts in 1974. He eventually dismantled the band, but some demo tapes had been made that found their way to drummer Luigi Salvoni. Roberts, meanwhile, had left for France to concentrate on painting for three years. Upon Paul's return, Luigi convinced him to put aside his palette and give rock and roll another spin.

Chiswick Records was interested in the venture. Luigi rounded up bassist Chris Birkin, guitarist Mick Dyche, keyboardist Alan Fealdman, and guitarist Loz Netto —the first official Sniff 'n' the Tears line-up. *Fickle Heart* (1979) and "Driver's Seat" (released domestically on Atlantic) followed, and both fared well. Reviewing *Fickle Heart*, *Billboard* compared the band to Dire Straits and proclaimed their debut album as heralding "a new age of music that will hold up long after the last dance has ended."

By the time *The Game's Up* (1980) appeared, only Roberts, Dyche, and guitar genie Loz Netto remained. Roberts and an entirely new "group" recorded *Love Action* in 1981. The latter remains Sniff's last stateside recording. Both albums are intriguing, well-crafted works well worth a listen.

Ian Gomm

HOLD ON
(Ian Gomm)
Stiff/Epic 50747
No. 18   *October 27, 1979*

For four of the band's five years, Ian Gomm (b. Mar. 17, 1947, Ealing, England) was a member of Brinsley Schwarz with Bob Andrews, NICK LOWE, Billy Rankin, and Brinsley Schwarz himself. "The Brinsleys were intimate, alright," Gomm told *Trouser Press*' Dave Schulps. "They not only worked together but lived communally in the same house, families and all. Ugh, it was awful—three wives in the one kitchen. It had nothing to do with the music, nothing to do with the group. Everybody's personal life just became jumbled together. Maybe if we'd split into separate flats we might still be together today. That, plus our never being able to break through commercially, finished the group."

Gomm left the group, depressed, and lazed around. In the meantime, Andrews and Schwarz achieved some success backing Graham Parker in the Rumour; Lowe went on to establish himself as a producer.

In the mid-'70s, Gomm revived himself. Hanging out at the 16-track Foel Studios in Wales, Ian learned the technical side of recording from Buzzcocks and Stranglers producer Martin Rushent. Ian produced some sides for the Stranglers and the bagpipe-blowing Second Battalion of the Scots Guard. In his off-time, he compiled some solo demos.

"I took them around and got rejected by everyone," Gomm lamented. "It's the old story, but even worse. I'd go into the offices and they'd say, 'Face it, Ian, not only are the tunes awful, but you can't even sing. Why bother? Get a day job.' I began to think they might be right." Only months before the release of *Gomm with the Wind* (1979) and "Hold On"— one of those "awful tunes"—Ian's mom took him aside and told him to stop all of this rock-and-roll nonsense and get a real job.

Intermittent singles have been shipped and two further albums have been offered, but Gomm has yet to re-establish a foothold on the charts.

M

POP MUSIC
(Robin Scott)
Sire 49033
No. 1 *November 3, 1979*

M is Robin Scott, a former art school student and folksinger from England. Hard to believe, you say? Once you have heard his hit single, it is difficult to imagine that Scott ever did anything other than commune with computers and noise-making techno-toys.

Press releases claim he grew up like a regular lad in London, managed a couple of groups, wrote a few songs (for Johnny Halliday and others), and even set up a small-time record label: Do It Records. Before collapsing, his Do It label would discover Adam Ant.

In 1978, Rob moved to Paris, where he conceived of his bizarre, electro-novelty number. (He picked "M" as a pseudonym from the signs around Paris for the Metro.) "I was looking to make a fusion of various styles which somehow would summarize the last 25 years of pop music," Scott told Fred Bronson in *The Billboard Book of Number One Hits*. "Whereas rock and roll had created a generation gap, disco was bringing people together on an enormous scale. That's why I really wanted to make a simple, bland statement, which was 'All we're talking about basically [is] pop music.'"

Three different versions of "Pop Muzik" were shaped and taped. There was an R & B rendition; a funky burner à la James Brown; and the punchy, three-minute opus that we all have come to know. His hit-containing debut LP, *New York-London-Paris-Munich* (1979), sold well in the States. While M's three immediate follow-ups charted in the U.K., none of these unique but markedly less appealing 45s made the *Billboard* listings.

Robin has collaborated on a pair of albums with actor Ryuichi Sakamoto (he appeared in 1983's *Merry Christmas, Mr. Lawrence*) and the keyboardist of the Yellow Magic Orchestra. In 1985, Scott recorded an album in London entitled *The Kiss of Life*.

France Joli

COME TO ME
(Tony Green)
Prelude 8001
No. 15 *November 17, 1979*

France Joli (b. 1963, Montreal) hit the ground running. As a tot, she took drama, dance, and voice lessons; at age four, she was performing professionally. By 11, France was so busy doing local radio and TV spots that her parents let her drop out of school to pursue her career.

Two years later, Joli sought out Canadian recording artist/teen idol Tony Green. After one of his sets, she followed a bunch of excited teenyboppers backstage. "They went backstage to get Tony's autograph," she told *Cashbox*. "I went backstage to audition."

As Tony Green recalled to *Cashbox*, "She showed up with a couple of Barbra Streisand albums and had the nerve to sing a duet with the record." Apparently, Tony was impressed: he eventually became France's manager, wrote some songs for her (including her lone hit), produced her first recordings, and got the girl her first recording contract.

"Come To Me" was the 16-year-old's virgin vinyl voyage, and it charted fairly well on both *Billboard*'s pop and R & B (#36) listings. Despite the rapid fire of subsequent releases, however, Joli retains one of the lowest profiles in all of one-hitdom.

"I'm starting young and have a lot of time," Ms. Joli explained to *Variety*'s Andy Nulman. "If I fail, I have a lot of time to make it up. And if I don't make it now, I have more of a chance to make it later."

J.D. Souther

YOU'RE ONLY LONELY
(John David Souther)
Columbia 11079
No. 7 *December 15, 1979*

John David Souther was born in Detroit but raised amid the tumbleweeds in Amarillo, Texas. In the late '60s, J.D. became fast friends with a fellow Motor City man named Glenn Frey. Both had independently trekked to L.A. to pick and sing. As the Longbranch Pennywhistle, the duo recorded an album for Amos Records in 1970. In attendance on that session were James Burton, Ry Cooder, Larry Knechtel, and Doug Kershaw.

Soon after, Frey wandered off to become a founding member of the Eagles. J.D., meanwhile, dashed off tunes, a number of which were recorded by sometime girlfriend Linda Ronstadt and Bonnie Raitt. In 1972, Asylum, Linda's label, took an interest in J.D. and re-

J.D. Souther

leased a self-titled album. Critics liked the disk, and commented that the boy showed promise.

In 1974, David Geffen, Asylum's main man, applied his negotiating abilities to creating a country-rock supergroup along the lines of Crosby, Stills & Nash. Richie Furay had helped form Poco and had played with BUFFALO SPRINGFIELD. Chris Hillman had been in the Byrds, the Flying Burrito Brothers, and Stephen Stills' Manassas. The Souther-Hillman-Furay Band's self-titled album was a big seller, as was Furay's fluffy "Fallin' In Love" (#27, 1974). But the whole was less than the sum of its parts, and after a disappointing second album, the group called it quits in 1976.

Over the years, J.D. has continued to record coolly-received albums. The Orbison-esque title tune from his third LP, *You're Only Lonely*, was a monster mover, but follow-ups have failed to sustain the Texan's career. The Eagles, however, have had hits with versions of his "Best Of My Love," "New Kid In Town," and "Heartache Tonight." As a session singer, Souther has backed up KARLA BONOFF, Jackson Browne, Christopher Cross, Joni Mitchell, and RANDY NEWMAN, to name but a few. "Her Town Too," a duet with James Taylor, hit all the right notes and heights (#11, 1981). Souther also made acting appearances on the "Thirtysomething" TV series during the 1989–1990 season.

The

Eighties

Steve Forbert

ROMEO'S TUNE
(Steve Forbert)
Nemperor 7525
No. 11   *February 23, 1980*

When White's Auto Parts Store in Meridian, Mississippi, went out of business in 1976, Steve Forbert (b. 1955), their warehouseman and truck driver, found himself out of a job. With Dylan dreams dancing in his head, Steve hopped a train for Greenwich Village, singing and strumming his guitar on street corners and in the echoey confines of Grand Central Station. After a bit more practice, Steve began working the folk haunts and opening for New Wavers like the Talking Heads and John Cale.

Danny Fields, the Ramones' manager, soon arranged for the talent police at Nemperor Records to give a listen to "the new Dylan in town." Critical acclaim greeted Forbert's first LP, *Alive on Arrival* (1978). "Romeo's Tune"

came from Steve's second album, *Jackrabbit Slim* (1979). Sales on the "Romeo" number surprised nearly everyone who had an inkling of who or what Steve was trying to be. Two more LPs were issued to a shrinking following, and in 1982, the big boys at Nemperor Records showed the lad from Meridian the back door.

Steve Forbert bounced back in 1988. While fronting the legendary Crickets at a Buddy Holly tribute in New York City, he was spotted by Garry Tallent, who recommended him to the powers at Geffen Records. Later in the year, Tallent, a member of Bruce Springsteen's E Street Band, produced Forbert's first release for the new label, *Streets of this Town* (1988).

Charlie Dore

PILOT OF THE AIRWAVES
(Charlie Dore)
Island 49166
No. 13   *May 3, 1980*

Charlie Dore was born and raised in London. She went to drama school, acted in a repertory company in Newcastle, and even did a brief stint on the TV series "Rainbow." With a voice like Emmylou Harris, she burst onto the British pop scene in 1977 with a band called Prairie Oyster. One of the seven drummers who made his way through the group's line-up was Pick Withers, later of Dire Straits. Charlie's Oysters played city-bred country music at a time when England was embroiled in the punk-rock assault, so the group's gigs were few and far between.

Prairie personnel kept wandering in and out of the band—by the time scouts from Island Records had opted to record the act, Prairie Oyster had perished. Nevertheless, the label signed Charlie, and assigned Bruce Welch of the Shadows and Alan Tarney of the Tarney-Spencer Band to produce Dore's disk. Part of the *Where to Now?* (1979) album was recorded in Nashville, with ex-Cricket Sonny Curtis among the stellar session crew.

"Pilot Of The Airwaves," Charlie's tribute to DJs, was her first 45 and so far, the only track of hers to make the pop charts. "Fear Of Flying," the follow-up single, crashed ignobly. The next year, Charlie changed labels and musical direction: *Listen!* (1981), her Chrysalis debut, was easy-listening music.

Steve Forbert

Lipps, Inc.
FUNKYTOWN
(Steven Greenberg)
Casablanca 2233
No. 1 *May 31, 1980*

Lipps, Inc. (pronounced "lip-synch") was the brainchild of Minneapolis native Steven Greenberg. Decades before the idea struck, little Stevie began coaxing sounds out of a multitude of instruments. By age 15, he was pounding drums in the Diplomats and later, the Storm Center. Five years later, with feverish dreams of stardom, Steve tripped to L.A. with a box of demos. No one paid much attention, and a dejected Greenberg caught a Greyhound home. Over the next eight years, he worked for a traveling party service, tried to set up an entertainment-production company, and sang as part of a duo (with Sandy Atlas) in brass-rail bars and dives.

After tiring of that scene, Steve resolved to make another major move on fame and fortune. With designs on integrating disco and R & B, Steve created a tune called "Rock It." A demo with him on nearly all the instruments was quickly cut, pressed, and promoted all over town. Minneapolis' KFMX rode the number, and Steve reapproached the music moguls in L.A. This time, Casablanca commissioned an album. Tinseltown sessioners were rounded up, and Steve recruited Cynthia Johnson to front his project. Cynthia had played sax since she was eight, had been 1976's Miss Black Minnesota, and, when discovered by Greenberg, was a police department secretary singing on weekends with a group called Flyte Tyme. (Flyte Tyme would later evolve into that punchy Prince satellite, The Time.)

"Funkytown" was one of but four tracks on Lipps, Inc.'s debut album, *Mouth to Mouth* (1980). After "Rock It," the first single, stiffed, the danceable "Funkytown" was issued. No one, not even Greenberg, expected this anachronistic disco ditty to sell 2,000,000 copies and become a huge pop and R & B (#2) hit. For a follow-up, a remastered version of "Rock It" (#64, 1980) was issued, and stirred a little interest on its second time out. Three more R & B chart entries appeared, but "Rock It" was the last sighting of Lipps, Inc. on the pop listings.

In 1983, after three albums and a handful of failed singles, Johnson left Greenberg's unit to raise a daughter. Margaret Cox and Melanie Rosales have since taken her place.

Gary Numan
CARS
(Gary Numan)
Atco 7211
No. 9 *June 7, 1980*

Some souls claim that Gary Numan (b. Gary Anthony James Webb, Mar. 8, 1958, Hammersmith, England) is an innovative and exciting figure on the techno-pop landscape. Then there are those listeners who consider this mascara-faced alien to be nothing more than a Kraftwerk-influenced, David Bowie clone.

Right from the start, Gary dreamed up his own tunes. "I had to write my own songs," he told *Hit Parade*'s Janel Bladow. "I couldn't play anybody else's." He joined his first band in 1977 when he was 19—per his report, they threw him out on his ear. Soon after, he auditioned and was accepted as a member of the Lasers; within a year, Numan was in charge, and renamed them the Tubeway Army.

The Tubeway Army issued a couple of punk-styled singles ("That's Not It" and "Bombers") on the Beggar's Banquet label before Gary was struck by inspiration. While the group was recording their *Tubeway Army* (1978) album, Gary started fiddling about with some studio synthesizers. The resulting sounds—icily soulless, robotic noises—seemed to him to be a perfect match for the lyrics of alienation, despair, and desolation that he was crafting. The rest of the group, except for bassist Paul Gardiner, disagreed with this musical direction and walked out, later forming the Station Bombers. To complete the LP, drummer Jess Lidyard, Gary's uncle, was enlisted in the revamped Tubeways.

"Are Friends Electric"—credited to the Tubeway Army, and extracted from the group's second album, *Replicas* (1979)—was a big British hit. The Tubeway Army monicker was tossed aside. "Cars"—from Numan's *The Pleasure Principle* (1980) LP—was Gary's only appearance on the U.S. charts, but went to number one in the U.K. By the end of 1985, Gary had racked up 15 British hits. He and his strange-looking sidemen toured the States complete with smoke machines, throbbing fluorescent lights, frigid demeanors, and deadpan vocals. Americans were not all that interested—two albums later, with *Telekon* (1980) and *Dance* (1981), Gary's career on these shores began to vaporize.

"I've got a very big fear of being a has-been," Numan admitted to *Trouser Press*' Jim Green.

Gary Numan

Eddie Cochran, Gene Vincent, and Elvis were often over at the house when Rocky (b. Jonathan Burnette, June 12, 1953, Memphis) was small, so music was all around when he was growing up. Jon was even nicknamed after his relatives' favorite musical style. Despite the family tradition, Burnette attended college with dreams of being a football player, and studied theater, cinematography, and the Bible. He had written some tunes when a teen, and worked briefly for the Acuff-Rose music-publishing outfit, but it was not until the '70s and the completion of his education that Rocky sought to record his songs.

After a failed affair with Curb Records, Rocky traded songwriting credits for studio time to cut "Clowns From Outer Space." The flip side was "Tired Of Toein' The Line." EMI issued the 45 in Europe, and later, it met with success in the U.S. The album featuring the track, *The Son of Rock 'n' Roll* (1980), sold well, and the future looked bright.

Nothing to date—and a number of sides have been issued by EMI, Goods, and KYD— has managed to regain a chart footing for this self-proclaimed son of rock and roll.

"I'm getting out of it before I get too involved to get out of it. I have to face not being famous anymore."

In 1981, Gary Numan announced his retirement. Yet albums have continued to be released, including compilations, some live sets, and a few new Numan waxings.

Rocky Burnette

TIRED OF TOEIN' THE LINE
(Rocky Burnette, Ron Coleman)
EMI-America 8043
No. 8 *July 26, 1980*

His nephew is Billy Burnette, one of the most recent additions to the Fleetwood Mac line-up. And his father and his uncle were, respectively, Johnny and Dorsey Burnette, co-pioneers in the development of rockabilly music. Johnny and Dorsey plus Paul Burlison were Memphis' Rock 'n' Roll Trio, a unit that from 1953 to 1957 crafted classic rockabilly singles like "Tear It Up," "Train Kept A-Rollin'," "Hush Hush," and "Lonesome Train."

S.O.S. Band

TAKE YOUR TIME (DO IT RIGHT) PART 1
(Harold Clayton, Sigidi Abdullah)
Tabu 5522
No. 3 *August 16, 1980*

It all began in 1977, in a bar in Atlanta. Jason "T. C." Bryant (keyboards, synthesizers, lead vocals), Billy R. Ellis (saxophone) (who had played with Billy Preston, Otis Redding, and NINA SIMONE), James Earl Jones III (drums), and Mary Davis (lead vocals, keyboards) were the house band at a jumpin' night spot called Lamar's Regal Room. Milton Lamar took an interest in the outfit, and in short order became their manager. The group played top 40 tunes, ballads, and jazzy jams, and alternately called themselves Santamonica or the Sounds of Santa Monica.

Local publicist Bunnie Jackson Ransom hooked the band up with Clarence Avant, president of Tabu Records. By this point, Santamonica had expanded to include Willie "Sonny" Killebrew (saxophone, flute) (who had worked with Millie Jackson, Gladys Knight, Johnny Taylor, and the Ohio Players), John Alexander "Skin" Simpson III (bass, keyboards), and Bruno Speight (guitar). Avant signed the act and changed their name to "The S.O.S. Band," the acronym variously interpreted as standing for the Sounds of Success, the Sound of the South, or Satisfaction on Stage.

"Take Your Time (Do It Right)," the S.O.S. Band's funk-flavored premier platter, was a huge hit and a number-one R & B record, eventually selling 2,000,000 copies. The *S.O.S.* (1980) album was a healthy seller, and went gold, as did *On The Rise* (1983) and *Sands of Time* (1986). In all, 17 of their 45s have placed on the R & B listings through 1987. Yet in spite of all this success, "Take Your Time" remains the group's only foray into top 40-land.

Jerome "J.T." Thomas (drums) replaced James Earl Jones III in 1981; the same year, Abdul Raoof (trumpet, flugelhorn, congas) was added. In 1987, Ms. Davis left the fold for a solo career; ex-Reach vocalist Pennye Ford filled her shoes. Ford is the daughter of Gene Redd, Sr., James Brown's long-time producer.

Fred Knoblock

WHY NOT ME
(F. Knoblock, C. Whitsett)
Scotti Brothers 518
No. 18 *August 23, 1980*

J. Fred Knoblock was born and raised in Jackson, Mississippi. He first gained notice in the mid-'70s playing in a rock unit called Let's Eat. For six years, Let's Eat labored. Shortly after country acts began recording some of his tunes, Fred managed to convince the folks at the Scotti Brothers label that he had the makings of a country-rock star. "Why Not Me" was a successful effort—yet while Knoblock continued to appear on the C & W charts, staging a follow-up on the pop listings was another matter entirely. "Let Me Love" was neglected by pop programmers, but Fred did score with "Killin' Time" (#28, 1981), a one-shot collaboration with TV star Susan Anton.

In the mid-'80s, Fred teamed up with Thom Schuyler, Jr., and Paul Overstreet. As Schuyler, Knoblock & Overstreet (a.k.a. SKO), they started their string of country hits with "You Can't Stop Love" (—/—/#9, 1986), "Baby Got A New Baby" (—/—/#1, 1987), and "American Me" (—/—/#16, 1987). Overstreet left the fold, and Craig Bickhardt joined. The group's new name? Schuyler, Knoblock & Bickhardt, naturally. This aggregation continues to make the country listings to this day.

Ali Thomson

TAKE A LITTLE RHYTHM
(Ali Thomson)
A & M 2243
No. 15 *August 23, 1980*

While little Ali (b. 1959, Glasgow, Scotland) was struggling to learn his multiplication tables, his big brother Dougie was blasting his bass in the Alan Bown Set. After this group's break-up in the early '70s, Dougie joined his fellow Bown buddy John Helliwell in Supertramp. Encouraged by Dougie's example, brother Ali started singing and playing piano in local bands. In the mid-'70s, he moved to London, took a job with Mountain Records, and tried his hand at composing. Gary Wright crashed the stateside top 10 charts in 1976 with his cover of Thomson's "Dream Weaver." Wright would return to hitdom in 1982 with yet another Thomson tune, "Really Wanna Know You."

Ali moved to California to join his brother, who set up an audition for him with A & M Records. "Take A Little Rhythm," a mellow McCartneyesque number, was featured on Ali's debut album. Scads of souls thought the record was yet another puffball from ex-Beatle Paul. "Little Rhythm" sold big. Another track, "Live Every Minute" (#42, 1980), made the Hot 100, another album appeared, and not a whisper has been heard from Ali Thomson since.

Benny Mardones

INTO THE NIGHT
(Benny Mardones, Robert Tepper)
Polydor 2091
No. 11 *September 6, 1980*

Benny was raised in a small factory community of 1,200. "I never took a voice lesson because I've always wanted to stay as raw and real as I can," he told a *Billboard* interviewer. "And besides, in Savage, Maryland, the only records people have are police records." By age 11, Mardones was imitating Elvis at county fairs and sock hops. In his teens, he left Savage to work the South fronting different bar bands.

By the mid-'70s, Benny was working in New York as a songwriter. Private Stock Records took an interest and issued his first LP, *Thank God For Girls* (1977). Although the album fea-

tured guitarist Mick Ronson and Humble Pie drummer Jerry Shirley, it stiffed. The label soon folded, but by then, Polydor had signed Mardones up.

Both "Into The Night" and the LP featuring it—*Never Run, Never Hide* (1980)—were, according to Benny, a lot of fun to record. "But that was where the fun stopped," Mardones revealed to interviewer Barry Alfonso for a Curb Records hand-out. "I was starting to slide into a world of drugs and fast living and just being crazy. Everything lost perspective for me, and I was very disheartened by the record company [Polydor]. I worked real hard, but when *Never Run, Never Hide* didn't sell, it broke my heart.

"In '82 and '83, I was in a self-destructive mode, flying back and forth coast-to-coast like it was a big party. Then it finally ended. I woke up one morning in '85, and I'd lost everything.

"Back around 1973, I met Elvis backstage and he autographed a photo for me. Well, when I was broke after my first success with 'Into The Night,' that Elvis photo and a bed were about all I had left. I didn't have food in my refrigerator; everything from diamonds to equipment was sold and gone. They were shutting my phone off the next day—I was penniless. Somebody offered me $2,500 for that Elvis photo, and I said, 'No . . . if I die tomorrow, at least they'll find me with this.' That was the day my life turned around."

Benny moved in with a friend in Syracuse and kicked his dependency on drink and drugs. He worked what gigs he could find, cutting a couple of independent LPs—*Unauthorized* (1985) and *American Dreams* (1988)—and awaiting his rediscovery. In 1989, a Phoenix DJ began playing "Into The Night" as if it were a new ballad. Other area stations picked up on the song, and soon Polydor reissued the dusty disk. It made the top 40 charts, making Mardones the only '80s artist to have a hit twice with the same record.

Larry Graham
ONE IN A MILLION YOU
(Sam Dees)
Warner Bros. 49221
No. 9 *September 20, 1980*

Before his teen years, Larry Graham (b. Aug. 14, 1946, Beaumont, Tex.) had taken tap dance lessons, learned to play the piano, guitar, harmonica, and drums, and fronted his own vocal

Benny Mardones

group. His father was a guitarist and his mother was Dell Graham, a lounge singer. By the time he was 10 years old, little Larry was playing bass, accompanying his mother at nightclubs in San Francisco. They would play standards like "Ebb Tide" and "Time After Time"—audiences loved it.

One night, Larry was forced to play with a "thumpin' and pluckin'" style on the bass to fill in for a missing drummer. Sylvester "Sly" Stewart, a local DJ, overheard Graham and asked him to join his Family Stone. Larry accepted and stayed with Sly for six years.

Shortly after his departure, Graham restructured Patryce "Chocolate" Banks' Hot Chocolate band into a hot soul outfit, Graham Central Station. Five funky albums and more than a dozen R & B hits later, Larry dismantled the Station and started singing in a much mellower, lounge-lizard style. "One In A Million You" was a million-seller, a number-one record on the R & B listings; his subsequent croonings, including a duet with Aretha Franklin, have graced those charts seven times since.

"Actually," Graham told *Black Star*'s Lisa Collins, "the singing that I'm doing was the style of singing I was doing before I joined up with Sly and went off into that funk bag. It just took me a little while to get back around to where it all started."

Johnny Lee
LOOKIN' FOR LOVE
(Wanda Mallette, Patti Ryan, Bob Morrison)
Full Moon 47004
No. 5 *September 20, 1980*

Johnny Lee Ham (b. July 3, 1946, Texas City, Tex.) was raised on a dairy farm in Alta Loma, in East Texas. While milking the cows, Johnny Lee would listen to rock and roll—"I thought country music was too twangy then," he told *Country Style*. In the early '60s, he and some of the guys at Sante Fe High formed Johnny Lee & The Road Runners. After his school days were done, Lee became a bosun's mate on a Navy cruiser that toured Vietnam; four years later, home safe and sound, he began bumming around California, undecided about his life's vocation.

Having decided to pursue the field of music, Johnny Lee met country star Mickey Gilley, one of his heroes. As Johnny recounted to *Country Style*: "I said 'Mickey, do you remem-ber me? I was on the Larry Kane TV show in Galveston with you.' Well, that was an outright lie, of course, but Mickey was busy, you know, and he wanted to be nice, so he said, 'Uh . . . yeah, yeah, I think I do remember you, but I can't remember what you did on the show.' "

Lee laid it on thick, then asked Gilley if he could sit in with his band. The audience response was encouraging, and after a few more appearances at Gilley gigs, Mickey asked Johnny to join his outfit full-time. When Mickey opened his legendary Gilley's Club (billed as "The World's Largest Honky Tonk") in Texas in 1971, Johnny Lee worked there as an opening act. Nine years later, when the cameras were there to record the goings-on for John Travolta's *Urban Cowboy* (1980) flick, Lee was still Mickey's right-hand man.

Johnny Lee Ham had already charted with a few C & W notables, like his remakes of Bing Crosby's "Red Sails In The Sunset" (—/—/#22, 1976) and Rick Nelson's "Garden Party" (renamed "Country Party,"—/—/#15, 1977). But it was "Lookin' For Love," a cut from off the *Urban Cowboy* soundtrack, that clicked big. Lee also met his wife-to-be in the film, Charlene Tipton ("Lucy Ewing" on TV's "Dallas").

Ham's been on a roll with country listeners ever since. Three cuts from his *Lookin' For Love* (1980) LP—"One In A Million" (—/—/#1, 1980), "Pickin' Up Strangers" (—/—/#3, 1981), and "Prisoner Of Hope" (—/—/#3, 1981)—were C & W winners, and "Bet Your Heart On Me" (#54/—/1) made the pop charts as well.

Johnny Lee's marriage to Charlene ended in divorce, but his disks remained active on the C & W airwaves through 1986. Gilley's is gone, but Ham opened up his own club nearby—Johnny Lee's. Alas, all that is past. "I lost everything except my talent," Lee recently told Joe Edwards of the Associated Press. "I never saw a dime."

Lee's autobiography, *Lookin' For Love*, was published by Diamond Books in 1989.

Devo
WHIP IT
(Mark Mothersbaugh, Jerry Casale)
Warner Bros. 49550
No. 14 *November 15, 1980*

It's still difficult to tell whether this bizarre quintet from Akron, Ohio, was serious or just plain mentally disturbed. Devo popularized emotion-less "singing," jerky hypnotic sounds, identical looks, flowerpot hats and toilet-seat collars, yellow jumpsuits, paper eye-wear, and contorted theories about the de-evolution of mankind. Were these guys for real? *The New Music Express*, a British magazine, surmised that these characters see themselves as "mirror-image representatives to the proletariat of the vegetable kingdom—song and dance men miming the plight of the human race in the modern world."

The Devo story dates back to the '70s and Akron, Ohio, a town that bassist Jerry Cazale described to *Grooves'* Charley Crespo as "industrial grey, hideous—culturally, a black hole." Jerry found a soulmate in keyboardist/

Roger Daltrey

guitarist Mark Mothersbaugh. "I met Mark at Kent State University. We were visual artists. Mark and I were doing more or less what we wanted visually, using a lot of printing techniques. We entered into music kind of from the angle of doing something *new*, from the beginning realizing that we didn't want to be musicians. We wanted to *use* instruments."

Soon there were five of them—added were Jerry's brother Bob Casale on keyboards and guitar, plus Mark's brother Bob Mothersbaugh on lead guitar and Alan Myers on drums. During the mid-'70s, their outlandish get-up and tonguc-in-cheek musical approach began accruing a sizeable following; they played in Cleveland and at New York's CBGB, then relocated to L.A. Iggy Pop spotted Devo's act and brought them to the attention of the proper authorities, David Bowie and Brian Eno (Eno produced the group's debut album). Two swell-selling singles were issued on Devo's own Booji Boy label, including a strangely syncopated version of the Rolling Stones' "Satisfaction." Warner Bros. signed the band in the hopes of capturing a mainstream audience for Devo's quirky music.

Despite the S & M connotations of "Whip It," Devo received massive airplay and the single went gold. Two other 45s—"Working In The Coal Mine" (#43, 1981), a herky-jerky remake of the Lee Dorsey classic, and "Theme From Doctor Detroit" (#59, 1983)—followed. All seven of their albums have sold well, particularly *Freedom of Choice* (1980) and *New Traditionalists* (1981).

Nothing much has been seen of Devo since the mid-'80s; it is currently unknown if these robotic music-makers have de-volved further than even they had intended. No need for concern, though: as Jerry told *Trouser Press* in a more candid moment, "De-evolution is basically an extended joke that was as valid an explanation of anything as the Bible is."

Roger Daltrey
WITHOUT YOUR LOVE
(Billy Nicholas)
Polydor 2121
No. 20 *November 29, 1980*

Roger (b. Mar. 1, 1944, London) grew up in a working-class neighborhood of London's Shepherd's Bush. At 12 years of age, Roger began making music on guitars he had constructed himself. Three years later, he was expelled from the Action County Grammar School. "I was a school rebel," Daltrey explained to Dave Marsh in *Before I Get Old*. "Whatever they said do, I didn't do. I was totally anti-everything. I was a right bastard, a right hard nut . . . Rock and roll was the only thing I wanted to get into."

With Reg Bowen on rhythm guitar, Daltrey formed a band, the Detours. He worked days in a sheet-metal shop, and weekends and nights the group played weddings, bar mitzvahs, and company gatherings. For two years, he envisioned himself as a guitarist, but then shelved the instrument to become the group's lead singer. About this time, John Entwistle and Pete Townsend, former members of the rival Scorpions, were invited to join the Detours. Before long, the band evolved into the Who, one of the biggest rock acts of all time.

By 1973, Roger, like the other Who men, was looking to step outside the confines of the band and try some solo projects. *Daltrey* (1973), his well-received solo debut, was produced by Adam Faith and featured songs by a then-unknown Leo Sayer. Leo's "Giving It All Away" (#83, 1973) gave Daltrey his first and biggest British hit. Once outside the blaring sounds of the Who, Roger toyed with ballads and softer songs. "Without Your Love" was his fifth Hot 100 entry but remains his only top 40 moment. Nearly all of his LPs have sold well, especially *Ride a Rock Horse* (1975), *One of the Boys* (1977), *McVicar* (1980), *Best Bits* (1982), and *Parting Should Be Painless* (1984). As an actor, Daltrey has appeared in *Tommy* (1975), *Lisztomania* (1975), *The Legacy* (1979), and *McVicar* (1980).

Korgis

EVERYBODY'S GOT TO LEARN SOMETIME
(James Warren)
Asylum 47055
No. 18   December 27, 1980

Before there were the Korgis, there was Stackridge (originally the psychedelic Stackridge Lemon). Jimmy Warren and Andy Davis were members of this eccentric British configuration, which recorded mutant melodies and loony lyrics about characters like Marzo Plod, Percy the Penguin, and Dore the Female Explorer. Stackridge was a colorful art-rock ensemble with an esoteric reputation and a cult following to match. Fans would bring

dustbin lids, rhubarb stalks, and a variety of unmentionables to the group's participatory concerts. Finally, in the late '70s, Warren, Davis, a manic man named Mutter Slater, and the others called it quits.

But before normalcy could grab hold of Warren and Davis, the twosome made demos of their off-beat tunes at a friend's house with the support of the Short-Wave Band (possibly comprising Stuart Gordon and Phil Harrison). After hearing material like "Young 'n' Russian," "Dirty Postcards," and "Mount Everest Sings The Blues," the Asylum label issued a now-rare *Korgis* (1979) album.

The following year, *Dumb Waiters* (1980), yet another package of palatable but peculiar pop product, appeared. Asylum shipped "Everybody's Got To Learn Sometime," one of the act's more conventional numbers. No additional disks by the duo have been released.

Delbert McClinton

GIVING IT UP FOR YOUR LOVE
(Jerry Williams)
Capitol 4948
No. 8   February 21, 1981

Playboy* once described Delbert McClinton as "the best white R & B rock and roller in the world." For more than 30 years, Del has been playing foot-stompin' blues for the boys in the bars. McClinton has also been around some rock greats and participated in creating some of popdom's most treasured tracks, including BRUCE CHANNEL's "Hey! Baby," on which he played harmonica.

"I spent a lot of nights in beer joints," Delbert told *Grooves'* Janel Bladow. "It's what I know. I love women and I love it when they run out on you. It inspires me. 'Damn, I thought I had it by the balls, I had this woman—now, I see she's gone.' Women ought to leave more often."

Delbert McClinton (keyboards, harmonica, vocals) was born in Lubbock, Texas, on November 4, 1940, and raised in Fort Worth. The son of a railroad man and a beautician, Del bought himself a $3.50 F-hole Kay guitar in his teens and performed for the first time at the Big "V" Jamboree in 1957. While driving a truck, he worked with his brother in a weekend band they called the Mellow Fellows. "There were four guitars, no bass, a sax, and a drummer," Del told Randy McNutty. "None of us could play."

The Eighties

Delbert McClinton

Gradually, the Mellow Fellows sharpened up and evolved into the Losers, the Bright Side, the Acme Music Company, and finally the Straitjackets—the house band at Jack's Place, a rowdy roadhouse outside Ft. Worth. There, Del and and the fellows backed all the blues legends that came to town: Bobby "Blue" Bland, Buster Brown, Lightnin' Hopkins, Howlin' Wolf, B.B. King, Joe Tex, Big Joe Turner, T-Bone Walker, Sonny Boy Williamson, and McClinton's idol, Jimmy Reed. Reed's wailing harp on "Honest I Do" had encouraged Del to pick up the harmonica in the first place.

Starting in 1960, McClinton and his Straitjackets recorded singles—under names like Mac Clinton and Del McClinton—for various labels owned by Major Bill Smith. McClinton also did some session work for the Major, backing Paul & Paul and Bruce Channel. It was while touring England with Channel that Del met John Lennon at the Castle Club in New Brighton. John, as the tale goes, asked McClinton how he got those sounds out of his harmonica. Results of the encounter were to appear as Lennon's harmonica break on "Love Me Do."

Upon his return, McClinton cut a great number of sides with Ronnie Kelly as the Ron-Dels, but only one made the pop charts—"If You Really Want Me To I'll Go" (#97, 1965). Tiring of the bar dates and failed 45s, Del moved to Los Angeles in 1970 and hooked up with hometown buddy Glen Clark. As Delbert & Glen, the duo recorded two country/soul LPs, *Delbert and Glen* (1972) and *Subject to Change* (1973); one track, "I Received a Letter" (#90, 1972), was a mild success.

The twosome parted company, and Del returned to Ft. Worth, where a local promotion man brought him to the attention of ABC Records. *Victim of Life's Circumstances* (1975), *Genuine Cowhide* (1976), and *Love Rustler* (1977) featured a critically-lauded blend of country, blues, and R & B. Then came two albums for Capricorn—*Second Wind* (1978) and *Keeper of the Flame* (1979)—and two more for Capitol, *The Jealous Kind* (1980) and *Plain' from the Heart* (1981). The former included Del's lone top 40 hit, "Givin' It Up For Your Love"; the latter featured "Shotgun Rider" (#70, 1981).

The 1989 release of *Live from Austin* on Alligator Records marked Delbert's return to the music business, after an eight-year lay-off. His most recent LP is *I'm With You* (1990).

Tierra

TOGETHER
(Leon Huff, Kenny Gamble)
Broadway 5702
No. 18   *February 21, 1981*

Tierra is a Latino band born and based in the barrios of East Los Angeles. The group's founders and core components are Rudy (guitar, vocals) and Steve Salas (lead vocals, trombone, timbales), music vets with a combined history of more than 50 years in the biz.

The brothers started when knee-high. "We were two kids imitating Mexican trios and singing in Spanish before we could even speak Spanish," Steve told Damon Webb in the *L.A. Supplement*. Under the care of Eddie Davis (producer of Cannibal & The Headhunters and THE PREMIERS), they recorded a number of singles as the Salas Brothers in the early '60s. In 1964, they joined an instrumental combo variously called the Jaguars and the Percussions. As the house band at L.A.'s El Monte Legion Stadium, the Salases had the opportunity to provide back-up services for the Coasters, the Olympics, and the Righteous Brothers.

In the late '60s, the brothers formed Six Pak, later to be renamed Maya. The group consisted of Max Carduno, ex-Jaguar Anthony Carroll, and three former members of Thee [*sic*] Midnighters: Jim Espinoza, Danny Lamont, and George Salazar. A Six Pak single was issued by the Gordo label. In 1970, the Salases' producer started working with a Latin-rock band called El Chicano, and as auxiliary members, Rudy and Steve appeared on a number of their disks. Reportedly, Steve sang lead on El Chicano's "Brown Eyed Girl" (#45, 1972).

Tierra, phase one, was created by the Salas brothers in 1972. In addition to Kenny Roman (drums), Dave Torres (keyboards), and Rudy Villa (sax), the group included Conrad Lozano (bass), later a member of Los Lobos. Before the group split, the *Tierra* (1974) album for 20th Century and a single for the Tody label were released.

Phase two began in the late '70s. After a salsa-orientated LP for Salsoul, the Salas brothers and the revamped Tierra—Andre Baeza (percussion), Steve Falomir (bass), Joey

Guerra (keyboards), Phil Madayag (drums), and Bobby Navarrete (reeds)—developed a jazzy/R & B/Latin-tinged sound and switched over to Neil Bogart's Boardwalk label. The boys from the barrios finally hit paydirt with "Together," a remake of the Intruders' 1967 R & B hit.

A few more albums and singles were shipped, including "Memories" (#62, 1981) and "La La Means I Love You" (#72, 1981), the latter a cover version of the Delfonics dusty. With Bogart's death, the Boardwalk label has ceased to exist. Tierra is still active, and currently records for the Satellite label.

Yarbrough & Peoples

DON'T STOP THE MUSIC
(Alisa Peoples, Lonnie Simmons,
Jonas Ellis)
Mercury 76085
No. 19   *April 11, 1981*

They first met when she was four and he was six. Calvin Yarbrough and Alisa Peoples shared the same piano teacher. Since Cal and Al lived in the same area of Dallas, their parents sent them to a neighborhood church, where they became soloists in the choir.

For years, Alisa and Calvin went their separate ways, attending different hometown colleges. Afterward, Peoples joined the 9-to-5 world; Yarbrough played in bars around town with units like Grand Theft. Charlie, Robert, and Ronnie Wilson—later known as the Gap Band—happened to catch a Grand Theft performance, and offered Cal a back-up vocal spot on a Leon Russell tour they were set to work. When the tour was over, Calvin returned to Grand Theft and local engagements. In 1977, Alisa showed up at a gig and sang a song or two with the band. The result was good-time, danceable music magic.

The Gap Band was burning up the R & B listings, and Yarbrough had them give a listen to the act. The Wilson brothers in turn recommended Yarbrough & Peoples to their manager and producer, Lonnie Simmons. After two years of delays, Yarbrough & Peoples' debut album, *The Two of Us* (1981), was issued to critical acclaim and healthy sales. "Don't Stop The Music," a pop hit and a number-one R & B item, was only the beginning: eight more singles made the R & B listings, including "Don't Waste Your Time" (#48/1, 1984) and "I Wouldn't Lie" (#93/6, 1986). And at this time,

◆◆◆◆◆◆◆◆

The Eighties

there is no indication that Y & P have seen their best days pass.

In the early '80s, Calvin and Alisa solidified their relationship with quietly-exchanged wedding vows.

Terri Gibbs

SOMEBODY'S KNOCKIN'
(Ed Penny, Jerry Gillespie)
MCA 41309
No. 13 *April 25, 1981*

Terri (b. June 15, 1954, Grovetown, Ga.), who has been blind since birth, first started playing with her parents' piano when she was three. In her teens, she played the keyboards regularly in church and school, winning talent contests and performing locally. From 1973 to 1975, she was a member of the Sound Dimension, but left that group to form her own unit for an extended gig at Augusta's Steak and Ale Restaurant. Gibbs plugged away there for five years, doing 50 songs five nights a week, three sets a night.

All the while, Terri made and distributed demo tapes, hoping someone would take notice. Jim Foglesong, president of MCA's Nashville operation, kept an eye on Terri for most of her stay at the Ale house. On the liner notes to her first album, *Somebody's Knockin'* (1981), Foglesong wrote: "It wasn't until earlier this year . . . when [independent producer] Ed Penny played some things and told me of his belief in Terri's talent, that it seemed to make sense for us to sign her to MCA, with Ed as her producer."

A masterful move, hindsight would surely say: the timing was perfect. Penny and Jerry Gillespie supplied Gibbs with an alluring country-blues number, "Somebody's Knockin'," and before long, *Music City News*, *Record World*, and the Country Music Association were all over Terri, showering her with awards and nominations for her debut effort.

Aside from one pop follow-up, "Rich Man" (#89, 1981), Terri has been most visible on the country listings. She has rocked out with "Baby I'm Gone" (—/—/#33, 1983) and "Tell Mama" (—/—/#65, 1983), stalled with "Somedays It Rains All Night Long" (—/—/#45, 1982), and tried to knock off her major moment with "Ashes To Ashes" (—/—/#19, 1982). Yet none of these disks ever connected with pop listeners more effectively than "Somebody's Knockin'."

Lee Ritenour

IS IT YOU
(Lee Ritenour, Eric Tagg, Bill Champlin)
Elektra 47124
No. 15 *June 27, 1981*

"**C**aptain Fingers," as Ritenour is known to friends and fans, is a top-of-the-line session artist, arranger, composer, and fusion-funkin' guitar virtuoso. Claims about his prolificness vary wildly. At the more imaginative end of the spectrum, pro-Rit forces affirm that "Fingers" has appeared on over 3,000 albums. More conservative estimates place the number at closer to 200. Regardless of which is the proper count, Lee has graced recordings by a host of pop artists, including George Benson, Stanley Clarke, Natalie Cole, George Duke, Aretha Franklin, Herbie Hancock, Peggy Lee, Kenny Loggins, Johnny Mathis, Diana Ross, Carly Simon, Paul Simon, Barbra Streisand, and Steely Dan.

Lee (b. Jan. 11, 1952, Palos Verdes, Cal.) first picked up the guitar at the age of eight. He progressed swiftly on the instrument: by age 12, he was playing with a 19-piece orchestra. A year later, Rit laid down some guitar lines on a yet-unreleased John Phillips solo album. He attended the University of Southern California and studied with Joe Pass, Howard Roberts, and classical guitarist Christopher Parkening. In 1975, he settled into the L.A. session scene.

Ritenour's picking can be heard on the soundtracks to such flicks as *Saturday Night Fever* (1977), *The Champ* (1979), and *An Officer and a Gentleman* (1982). Nearly half of his 16 albums have placed on *Billboard*'s top pop albums chart. "Is It You" and "Cross My Heart" (#69, 1982), both featuring vocals by Eric Tagg, are Lee's lone crossover pop successes.

Joey Scarbury

THEME FROM "GREATEST AMERICAN HERO"
(BELIEVE IT OR NOT)
(Mike Post, Stephen Geyer)
Elektra 47147
No. 2 *August 15, 1981*

Little Joey first won acclaim from his peers with his Elvis impersonation at a kindergarten show-and-tell session. His parents knew the tyke had something, and they would constantly enroll Joey in talent contests. Joey (b. June 7, 1955) was raised in Thousand Oaks, California, and discovered by singer-songwiter Jim Webb's father. Webb Senior walked into the furniture store where Mrs. Scarbury was working, and heard Mom praising Joey's singing abilities.

Jim Webb brought the 14-year-old into a recording studio in 1968 to cut a track on his tune "She Never Smiles Anymore." The record bombed, but Joey was now a professional. Over the years, Scarbury recorded for the Reena, Dunhill, Lionel, Bell, Big Tree, Playboy, and Columbia labels. He had one minor Hot 100 item, "Mixed Up Guy" (#73, 1971), but that was all. Everyone agreed that the kid had talent, so how come no hit records?

To support himself, Joey did back-up vocals for Loretta Lynn and sang on various recording projects run by producer Mike Post. Mike enlisted him to sing the theme to an upcoming ABC-TV series, "The Greatest American Hero." The series about a bumbling superhero carried on for two years, but Joey Scarbury's visibility in the record industry did not last quite as long. The follow-up single, "When She Dances" (#49, 1981), would be Scarbury's last chart showing.

After his separation from Elektra, Joey recorded a single or two for RCA. Nothing much happened, and currently, Joey occasionally plays second base for the Thousand Oaks softball league.

John Schneider

IT'S NOW OR NEVER
(Aaron Schroeder, Wally Gold)
Scotti Brothers 02105
No. 14   *August 15, 1981*

Born on April 8, 1954, in Mt. Kisco, New York, John came to the nation's attention as young Bo Duke on TV's "The Dukes of Hazzard." After practicing night and day, recording an obscure children's album in 1977, and spending three years crunchin' cars and watchin' girls on the show, John geared up for a career as a pop singer with country leanings. "It's Now Or Never," a remake of Elvis' operatic plea, was a monster moment, but smaller and smaller numbers bought his later offerings. "Still" (#69, 1981), "Dreamin'" (#45, 1982), and "In The Driver's Seat" (#72, 1982)

still found their way into plenty of teenage girls' bedrooms.

No longer a Duke or a pop crooner, John has continued his acting career, and has even branched out into directing and screenwriting. He sings straight country these days, and quite successfully, too—17 of his singles have made the C & W listings.

Royal Philharmonic Orchestra

HOOKED ON CLASSICS
[Various classical composers]
RCA Victor 12304
No. 10   *January 30, 1982*

The Royal Philharmonic Orchestra (RPO), like the London Philharmonic (LPO) before it, was formed by Sir Thomas Beecham (b. 1879, St. Helens, Lancashire, England), in 1947. Under his baton, the RPO became associated with the annual Glyndebourne opera season in Sussex. Sir Beecham became known for his advocacy of new and unusual music. His greatest achievement in this capacity was popularizing the then-little-known works of Frederick Delius.

Under the leadership of Louis Clark, the RPO has continued to experiment with its repertoire, performing pieces that are generally associated with the pop or jazz realms. Clark has done arrangements for the Electric Light Orchestra, and his crew has recorded with Deep Purple, Glen Campbell, and B.B. King and the Crusaders.

"Hooked On Classics," a disco-fied medley of classical themes, has been the RPO's only Hot 100 spot to date. Three similar LPs have sold quite well—*Hooked on Classics* (1982), *Hooked on Classics II (Can't Stop the Classics)* (1982), and *Hooked on Classics III (Journey through the Classics)* (1983). The RPO's concept also kicked off 45s like "Hooked On Big Bands" (#61, 1982) and "Hooked On Swing" (#31, 1982).

Buckner & Garcia

PAC-MAN FEVER
(Jerry Buckner, Gary Garcia)
Columbia 02673
No. 9   *March 27, 1982*

While diligently researching the subject one night in a local bar, Jerry Buckner (keyboards, vocals) and Gary Garcia (vocals) came up with the idea of writing a tune about their favorite video game. They sketched out their "Pac-Man Fever" concept to their manager, Arnie Geller. Upon further reflection, however, Jerry and Gary decided to nix the number, but Geller urged the duo to go ahead with it.

Arnie had the right instincts. Once "Pac-Man Fever" was issued on the garage-sized BGO label, the response was phenomenal. Columbia Records acquired the rights to national distribution, and the pair was promptly dispatched to research more video-game material. Novelty items like "Hyper-Space," "Ode To A Centipede," "Goin' Berserk," and "Foggy's Lament" were conceived, cut, and issued on Buckner & Garcia's debut album, *Pac-Man Fever* (1982). Follow-up efforts such as "Do The Donkey Kong" and "E.T. (I Love You)" failed to chart.

The Atlanta-based pair has since returned to producing and writing. Jerry and Gary were responsible for Steve Carlisle's TV theme "WKRP In Cincinnati" and Edgel Groves' "Footprints In The Sand." Recording as Willis "The Guard" & Vigorish, the twosome made the pop listings with the seasonal single "Merry Christmas In The NFL" (#82, 1980).

Bob & Doug McKenzie
TAKE OFF
(Kerry Crawford, Jonathan Goldsmith, Mark Giacommeli, Rick Moranis, Dave Thomas)
Mercury 76134
No. 16 *March 27, 1982*

Okay, so they were a couple of loveable hosers and bozo losers, eh? Still, these burpin', beer-swiggin' McKenzies in flannel shirts and toques parlayed their let's-poke-fun-at-the-Canadians routine from TV's "SCTV" comedy series into a hit single, a top-selling album (*Great White North*), a one-off book, and a full-length movie which they co-wrote and co-directed, *Strange Brew* (1983).

In real life, Bob and Doug McKenzie were Canadians Dave Thomas and Rick Moranis, respectively. Dave acquired an M.A. degree, then worked as a Canadian Broadcasting Company scriptwriter. He also appeared in Toronto stage shows as half of a comedy team with "SCTV"'s Catherine O'Hara. Rick, who went to grade school with Rush's Geddy Lee (the vocalist featured on "Take Off"), earned $3 an hour as a teenager writing gags and glib jibs for tongue-tied Toronto DJs. Four years later, he hosted his own all-night program, also doing stand-up comedy at local clubs and cabarets.

Dave—whose brother is Ian Thomas of "Painted Ladies" (#34, 1974) fame—has re-

cently been working in his own Canadian syndicated series, "The Dave Thomas Show." But Rick has moved on to become quite the hot item in Hollywood. In 1989 alone, he appeared in three major releases: *Ghostbusters II*, *Parenthood*, and *Honey, I Shrunk the Kids*. His earlier film appearances include *Ghostbusters* (1984), *Streets Of Fire* (1984), *The Wild Life* (1984), *Brewster's Millions* (1985), *Little Shop of Horrors* (1986), and *Spaceballs* (1987).

Bertie Higgins

KEY LARGO
(Bertie Higgins, Sonny Limbo)
Kat Family 02524
No. 8 *April 17, 1982*

In the early, pre-Beatles '60s, drummer Bertie (b. 1946, Tarpon Springs, Fla.) had a hometown band called the Romans. Besides Bert, there was guitarist Bob Clever, singer Lane Langfort, bassist Joe Pappalardi, and guitarist Ronnie Schwartz. With the help of Tommy Roe and his producer Felton Jarvis, the band toured the world and crafted some fine rock and roll.

"Felton discovered [the Romans] in Florida," Tommy Roe explained in an exclusive interview. "He really liked them and wanted to produce them. I was working in England a lot then, and we thought a good way to get them some recognition was to change their name slightly [to the Roemans] and have them tour with me. Felton would record them with me and as a separate act. They became quite popular in the States and had several singles on ABC, but they never did catch on nationally."

In 1968, the Roemans played the last of their one-nighters. Once the glory and the royalty checks were gone, Bertie returned to Tarpon Springs. He took to playing guitar, writing songs, and checking out old movies. Bert met Beverly Seaberg, and the two fell in love.

"I lived with [Bev] a long time," Higgins told Bob Shannon and John Javna in *Behind the Hits*. "We used to watch old movies on the weekends, and to us, the Bogart and Bacall romance was a phenomenal one." When the couple split up, Higgins was hurt. Inspired by the Bogie-Bacall flick *Key Largo* (1948), he penned what would be his only top 40 hit "as a plea for her return. And she did."

Bertie and Beverly are still together, perhaps sharing "Just Another Day In Paradise" (#46, 1982).

Le Roux

NOBODY SAID IT WAS EASY
(LOOKIN' FOR THE LIGHTS)
(Tony Haselden)
RCA Victor 13059
No. 18 *April 17, 1982*

They took their named from the Cajun/French term for the gravy base used to make gumbo, that Southern favorite. Jeff Pollard, the group's leader, pointed out to *Cashbox* the aptness of the monicker for a unit that could play "a little bit of this and a touch of everything." On their first two albums, the band was actually called Louisiana's Le Roux.

Pollard (lead vocals, guitar), Bobby Campo (trumpet, flugelhorn, flute, congas), Tony Haselden (guitar), Leon Medica (bass), David Peters (drums), and Rod Roddy (keyboards) met while working sessions at the Studio In The Country in Bogalusa, Louisiana. In this capacity, they accompanied Clarence "Gatemouth" Brown, Clifton Chenier, and the Nitty Gritty Dirt Band, among others.

"We had a lot of things that we wanted to do," Pollard explained. "Everybody wanted to express themselves musically. Backing up someone else is good because it keeps your chops in shape, but if you don't get the opportunity to get out and play what you want to play, that can stifle what you do."

Once the boys had a couple of albums' worth of their own material ready, William McEuen, the Dirt Band's manager, offered to represent them. Capitol Records issued three LPs: *Louisiana's Le Roux* (1978), *Keep the Fire Burning* (1979), and *Up* (1980). Each one sold moderately well, as did "New Orleans Ladies" (#59, 1978), but the group was still groping for that chart-topper. Two years later, Le Roux signed with RCA and scored big with the moody "Nobody Said It Was Easy" from the *Last Safe Place* (1982) album.

Despite Hot 100 listings with "The Last Safe Place on Earth" (#77, 1982) and "Carrie's Gone" (#81, 1983), nothing further has cracked the top 40. Following their fleeting encounter with success, Le Roux experienced a major shake-up in their internal workings; both Bob Campo and the group's lead voice, Jeff Pollard, left the unit. Replacements included guitarist Jim Odom and lead singer Fergie Frederiksen. Fergie, however, has since been spotted in Toto's evolving line-up. To date, only one other album—*So Fired Up* (1983)—has been issued by RCA.

The
Eighties

Greg Guidry

GOIN' DOWN
(Greg Guidry)
Columbia 02691
No. 17 *May 1, 1982*

"I want to be a viable artist, one with lots of hits, but one who can sell LPs, too—mass acceptance is what I'm definitely going for," Greg Guidry told *Circus*' Charley Crespo in 1982.

Greg was born in 1950, in St. Louis, Missouri. By kindergarten, he was singing in the family's gospel group at church and at local functions. In his teenage years, Greg took piano lessons, wrote touching tunes, and played with local rock bands. His big break came in 1981, when he sang back-up on the Allman Brothers' final album, *Brothers of the Road*. Gradually, acts such as the Climax Blues Band, Robbie Dupree, and England Dan & John Ford Coley recorded Greg's songs.

Over the Line (1982) was Guidry's debut album. His lone looper, "Goin' Down," did quite well for a novice. However, the follow-up 45, "Into My Love" (#92, 1982), went largely unnoticed. Not much has been heard or seen of this singing songsmith since.

Vangelis

CHARIOTS OF FIRE—TITLES
(Vangelis)
Polydor 2189
No. 1 *May 8, 1982*

A quarter of a century ago, Evangelos "Vangelis" Papathanassiou (b. June 15, 1947, Velos, Greece), Demis Rousso, and Lucas Suderas

Greg Guidry

formed Aphrodite's Child, a Greek rock band. All of them came from musical families, and had undergone extensive training. Vangelis—who had studied art and classical music in college—played vibraphone, organ, flute, and an array of native Greek instruments. The trio did variations on British and American pop/rock hits, but it was years before their homeland became interested in such ruminations.

In 1968, while attempting to move to London in search of a more receptive audience, Aphrodite's Child was discovered by Pierre Sberre, a producer at Philips Records. One of the group's first recorded efforts, "Rain And Tears" (a Vangelis adaptation of a 17th-century German song by Johann Pachelbel) charted worldwide, selling more than a million copies. "It's Five O'Clock" and "Spring, Summer, Winter And Fall" were equally popular. Greece and the U.S., however, never warmed up to the group. Following the issuance of *666*, their double-disk concept album in 1972, Aphrodite's Child split up.

Lucas disappeared; Demis went on to a successful international career as a big popster, a ballad singer who managed to secure a large following with the ladies. Vangelis moved to London, where he built a state-of-the-art synthesizer studio near Marble Arch, and scored the soundtrack for Frederick Rossiff's *L'Apocalypse des Animaux* (1974). In June of the same year, Van was asked to join Yes, as a replacement for keyboard wiz Rick Wakeman. He declined, but struck up a friendship with Jon Anderson, Yes' lead vocalist. In 1980, once Jon had quit the group, the two collaborated as Jon & Vangelis. This act cut singles like "I Hear You Now" (#58, 1980) and "I'll Find My Way Home" (#51, 1982), also recording *Short Stories* (1980), *The Friends of Mr. Cairo* (1981), and *Private Collection* (1983).

Since the release of his first solo projects in 1975, more than 20 Vangelis LPs have appeared. None have been as successful as the the soundtrack album he created for *Chariots of Fire* (1982). The catchy music heard under the film's opening titles was issued as a single. *Chariots* won an Oscar as the "Best Picture"; Vangelis won an Oscar for composing the "Best Original Score." Apparently, Van was not expecting the honor to be bestowed on him, for when friends called during the Academy Awards program to congratulate him, he was in bed, fast asleep. Further film projects have included *Blade Runner* (1982), *Missing* (1982), *Bounty* (1984), and *Mask* (1985). In 1985, Mr. Papathanassiou wrote the score for the Royal Ballet's version of *Frankenstein*.

Charlene

I'VE NEVER BEEN TO ME
(Ron Miller, Ken Hirsch)
Motown 1611
No. 3 *May 22, 1982*

Charlene D'Angelo was born on June 1, 1950, in Hollywood. In 1976, the Motown moguls happened upon this angelic miss and arranged for her to work with their short-lived Prodigal subsidiary and the Ron Miller–Ken Hirsch writing team. Tunes were hatched and patched, and before long, an album of smooth, country-flavored Charlene songs was gathering dust in radio stations and cut-out bins across the land. As a countrypolitan singer, D'Angelo was not considered the real thing by C & W purists; she was also neither a rock moll nor a soul singer. Easy-listening music might be the most apt description of her specialty.

After three Hot 100 singles on Prodigal, "I've Never Been To Me" (#97, 1977) appeared and fared as poorly as its predecessors. Charlene dropped out of the music business. Then, five years later, Scott Shannon, a Tampa DJ, reintroduced the disk to the airwaves. To meet the swelling demand for the single, the Motown brass re-signed Charlene and hustled her into the studio to re-record "I've Never Been To Me." (In order to underscore the tune's feminist sentiments, a metaphysical spoken segment was added to the middle of the song.) The record became a smash success.

Months late, "Used To Be" (#46, 1982), a duet with Stevie Wonder, was issued, but nothing further has been heard from Charlene since.

Dazz Band

LET IT WHIP
(Reggie Andrews, Leon "Ndugu" Chancler)
Motown 1609
No. 5 *July 17, 1982*

Nearly 20 years ago, alto saxophonist Bobby Harris started playing with a jazz combo in his hometown of Cleveland. By the early '70s, he was appearing around town in a hot four-piece jazz-fusion band, Bell Telephunk. When not with his Bell bunch, Bob would often hang out and jam with the house musicians at the Kinsman Grill. Eventually, the two groups merged into one dance band called Kinsman Dazz

The Eighties

("dazz" being short for "danceable jazz"). Some demos were made; 20th Century Fox signed up the group and shipped about a half-dozen singles. "I Might As Well Forget About Loving You" (—/#46, 1979) and "Catchin' Up On Love" (—/#33, 1980) sold promisingly with R & B listeners.

Motown offered the group a contract. They accepted, shortening their name and reworking their line-up to include Steve Cox (keyboards), Pierre DeMudd (trumpet, flugelhorn, vocals), Eric Fearman (guitar), Sennie "Skip" Martin III (trumpet, vocals), Kenny Pettus (percussion, vocals), Isaac Wiley, Jr. (drums), and Michael Wiley (bass).

"Let It Whip," a number-one R & B hit, was the first single pulled from the Dazz Band's *Keep It Live* (1982), their third album. "Joystick" (#61, 1984) and "Let It All Blow" (#84, 1984) were also pop-chart winners. While "Whip" remains Dazz's only top 40 intrusion,

Harris' outfit continues to rack up funky R & B hits to this day, 16 of them so far.

In 1988, after a short stay with Geffen Records, Harris and his funksters shortened their name again, to simply "Dazz." They currently record for RCA. Fearman, Martin, and Wiley, Jr., are gone; lead singer Jerry Bell, keyboardist Keith Harrison, and guitarist Marlon McClain have been added to the roster.

Soft Cell
TAINTED LOVE
(Ed Cobb)
Sire 49855
No. 8 *July 17, 1982*

"**W**e thought if we were really lucky, we'd scrape into the top 75 in Britain," Marc

The Dazz Band

Almond—the lipsticked, mascaraed, and ear-ringed half of Soft Cell—quipped to *Rolling Stone's* Steve Ponds. "We didn't think *anything* would happen over here [in the U.S.]."

Almond (b. 1957, Southport, England) and multi-instrumentalist David Ball met in 1979 at Leeds Art College. "I used the art school facilities for doing performances, writing songs, and making films," Marc explained to *Creem's* Chris Salewicz. "One day I heard a lot of noise coming from the sound room. I checked it out and found Dave working away in there. He wanted a vocal side to what he was doing. So basically our Fine Arts courses consisted of forming Soft Cell."

Both knew what they were after: "People were using electronics in unfeeling, robotic ways," Almond told Ponds. "But Dave got these rich, warm, moody sounds. Exciting and slightly dirty sounds." Their first gig was a Christmas party at a local nitery. Months later, the duo found a guiding light and manager in a former bricklayer named Stevo. This 19-year-old ran Some Bizarre, a small label distributed by Phonogram. "Memorabilia," Soft Cell's first single, sold fairly well. But the follow-up—a throbbing techno-pop remake of Gloria Jones' little-known '60s soul classic, "Tainted Love"—really shook things up. Not only was it a number-one hit in England, but it stayed on *Billboard's* Hot 100 chart for nearly a year!

Hughie Feather, a friend and designer, built a white padded cell with pink and blue neon bars for the fellows to perform in. All of England's "New Romantics" loved Soft Cell's musical approach. Eight more singles charted in the U.K., but not one of them did anything domestically. However, *Non-Stop Erotic Cabaret* (1982), *Non-Stop Ecstatic Dancing* (1982), and *The Art of Falling Apart* (1983) were respectable sellers in the U.S.

By 1984, Almond had grown weary of the Soft Cell concept, and went off to record a slew of successful projects. Ball, meanwhile, issued a solo album, *In Strict Tempo* (1983). Reportedly, Soft Cell's demise had to do with different needs: Marc wanted to tour, but Dave liked staying at home and experimenting with sounds.

Karla Bonoff

PERSONALLY
(Paul Kelly)
Columbia 02805
No. 19 *August 7, 1982*

Karla Bonoff

Karla, who was born on December 27, 1952, and raised in L.A., was inundated with music lessons when she was growing up. First it was piano, then violin, clarinet, and finally, in the thick of her teen years, guitar. When 16, Karla and sister Lisa formed a twosome to pick 'n' sing at the Troubadour's Monday-night hoot-enannies. In 1969, Bonoff met Linda Ronstadt's bass player, Kenny Edwards. Kenny was between jobs with Linda, and approached Karla about forming an acoustic group with him, session singer Andrew Gold, and songwriter Wendy Waldman. As Bryndle, they recorded a yet-unreleased album. Only one highly sought-after single, "Woke Up This Morning," was issued in 1972. After playing the folkie circuit for a bit, Bryndle broke up, and Bonoff returned to the Troubadour hoots.

Kenny Edwards had introduced Karla to Linda Ronstadt. On her 1976 *Hasten Down the Wind* album, Ronstadt recorded three of Bonoff's moody musings: "Someone To Lay Down Beside Me," "If He's Ever Near," and "Lose Again." Columbia Records decided to give Karla a spin, and a critically-acclaimed debut disk was issued late in 1977. Over the years, more LPs and a stash of singles have been released; "Personally" was pulled from her *Wild Heart of the Young* (1982) album. Lynn Anderson, Nicolette Larson, and Bonnie Raitt have also recorded Bonoff's tunes. "I Can't Hold On" (#76, 1978), "Baby Don't Go" (#69, 1980), and "Please Be The One" (#63, 1982) were Karla's additional Hot 100 items.

Sylvia

NOBODY
(Kye Fleming, Dennis W. Morgan)
RCA 13223
No. 15 *November 20, 1982*

As a teen, Sylvia Kirby Allen (b. 1957, Kokomo, Ind.) gained some notoriety doing pen-
cil sketches of the country stars that would
happen by Indiana's Little Nashville Opry concert hall. By high school graduation, Syl was
sure that she, too, wanted to be a country
queen. In 1975, with an *a capella* tape in her
hand, Sylvia headed for Nashville and
stardom—but like the perennial horde of
other aspiring Lorretta Lynns and Dolly Par-
tons that flock to Music City each year, Sylvia
had to settle for a less glamorous clerical job.

Fortunately for Ms. Allen, her boss was Tom
Collins, who was then producing Charlie Pride
and Barbara Mandrell. Sylvia persuaded Collins to let her make demo tapes and sing back-
up for Mandrell, Ronnie Milsap, and Dave &
Sugar. Finally, in the summer of 1979, RCA
signed her up as a solo artist. "You Don't Miss
A Thing," her debut disk, made the C & W

charts, as did a hefty heap of follow-up singles.
While "Nobody" is the Hoosier's only pop/rock
hit, Sylvia has had continued success as a
country singer.

Toni Basil

MICKEY
(Nicky Chinn, Mike Chapman)
Chrysalis 2638
No. 1 *December 11, 1982*

"What do you say about a woman who is prac-
tically the most influential choreographer of
popular music?" asked Bette Midler of
Dancemagazine's Kevin Grubb. "This is someone who found street dancing before anyone
knew what it was and successfully commer-
cialized it. She taught David Byrne how to
move. Anthony Tudor wrote her fan letters.
She pretty much discovered DEVO. She's
helped provide Bowie with an identity. Her
style has been ripped off by so many other
choreographers . . . It's about time she got
her due."

Toni was born Antonia Basilotta in 1950, in
Philadelphia. The family moved around quite a
bit: her dad was big-band leader Louis Basil,
and her mother was an acrobatic dancer. When
the relatives got together, there was often
quite a commotion in the house.

"It was an amalgamation of acrobatics and
comedy," Basil explained to *Dancemagazine*.
"They would jump through hoops with their
names on them and my mother and my uncle
would do a tap/boxing dance where she beat
him up . . . I also had an aunt . . . [who would]
put her leg around her neck and hop around like
a contortionist, or lie on a table while my two
uncles grabbed her legs and spun her around in
circles. Really! That's my roots."

She moved to L.A. to become a dentist, but
after completing her studies at Laughton Dental School, Toni turned to the world of dancing.
She started by doing choreography for seminal
TV shows like "Hullaballoo" and "Shindig."
Once in the industry, Toni met Brian Jones of
the Rolling Stones, Peter Fonda, and Dennis
Hopper. She was at Hopper's when *Easy Rider*
(1969) was conceived, and found herself playing a "spaced-out chick" in the flick. Her later
movie appearances include *The Cool Ones*
(1970), *Five Easy Pieces* (1970), *The Last
Movie* (1971), *Greaser's Palace* (1972), *Mother,
Jugs and Speed* (1976), *Hey Good Looking*
(1982), and *Slaughterhouse Rock* (1988). As a

TONI BASIL

Musical Youth

choreographer, she worked on the famed *T.A.M.I. Show* (1964), Elvis' *Viva Las Vegas* (1964) and *Girl Happy* (1965), the Monkees' *Head* (1968), and Bette Midler's *The Rose* (1979). She has also devised dance moves for ground-breaking tours and videos by such acts as David Bowie, Devo, Melissa Manchester, George Michael, Bette Midler, the Pointer Sisters, Linda Ronstadt, David Lee Roth, the Talking Heads, and Tina Turner.

In the early '70s, Toni became involved with South L.A.'s street-dancing scene and formed the Lockers (a.k.a. The Campbell Lock Dancers), a dance troupe. Moonwalkers and break-dancers are what we might call them now, but Toni and her team were way ahead of their time. Before breaking up in 1975, the Lockers opened for Sly Stone and Frank Sinatra, also appearing repeatedly on "Saturday Night Live."

As for her musical moment, "Mickey" was not Basil's first foray into popdom. Her recording history dates back to 1966 and two singles for A & M, "Breakaway" and "I'm 28." "Mickey"—originally titled "Kitty" and unsuccessfully recorded by a group called Smile—

was cut in 1980 as a pre-MTV music video, but Chrysalis passed on the record and its cheerleader concept until the overseas success of "Mickey" prompted the label to reconsider. The single eventually sold 2,000,000 copies.

To date, Toni has had only two other pop platters released—"Shoppin' From A To Z" (#77, 1983) and "Over My Head" (#81, 1984). Her debut album, *Word of Mouth* (1982), went gold, but after her second album—*Toni Basil* (1984)—failed to generate much in the way of revenue, Chrysalis Records let her go. Early in 1988, she signed with Island Records.

Musical Youth
PASS THE DUTCHIE
(Jackie Mitoo, Lloyd Ferguson, Fitzroy Simpson)
MCA 52149
No. 10 *February 26, 1983*

Freddie Waite had been the lead vocalist in the Techniques, a successful Jamaican reggae band. He moved his family to Birmingham, England, in the late '70s. Having spotted talent in a friend's offspring, Freddie encouraged the father to let him give the boys music lessons. Kevin and Michael Grant (then ages 9 and 11, respectively) were schoolmates of Waite's own two sons, Patrick (age 12) and Junior (age 13). Before the year was out, Waite had them all whipped up into a fairly decent band.

For the next few years, Kevin (guitar), Michael (keyboards), Junior (drums), and Pat (bass) made local appearances as the Cultural Music Workshop Youth. Freddie sang lead with the group (since he was a small fellow, nobody seemed to notice the age discrepancy). A homemade single ("Political" b/w "Generals") was recorded and shopped around; one of the copies found its way to John Peel, a big-time DJ on the BBC. Peel, impressed with the group's unique blend of reggae and pop, repeatedly played the disk on his show.

Charlie Ayre, an A & R man with MCA Records, suggested that Freddie replace himself with someone more age-appropriate. After the addition of 14-year-old Dennis Seaton and six months of rehearsals, MCA was ready to release Musical Youth's *Youth of Today* (1982) LP and what would become one of the best-selling singles in British pop history. "Pass The Dutchie" was an old reggae hit that had been updated by the Mighty Diamonds as "Pass The Kutchie." But since a kutchie is a marijuana jar and the musicians were all underage, the explicit drug references were toned down with the reinsertion of the word "dutchie" (a stewpot).

Irene Cara, Michael Jackson, Donna Summer, and Jody Watley guested on the group's second album, *Different Style!* (1983). Musical Youth's popularity and record sales remained high in the U.K. through the mid-'80s. "She's Trouble" (#65, 1984) made the U.S. pop charts, and two 45s appeared on the R & B listings, but none of their subsequent offerings have met with tremendous success.

"I hope the band will go a long way," Michael Grant told *Rock & Soul*. "People that think we're puppets or a one-hit wonder are wrong."

Frida
I KNOW THERE'S SOMETHING GOING ON
(Russ Ballard)
Atlantic 89984
No. 13 *March 26, 1983*

She was born Anni-Frid Lyngstad on November 15, 1945, in the little iron-export town of Narvik, Norway. At the age of 10, Frida made her first stage appearance in a talent contest, and a few years later she was fronting a local dance band. In 1967, she moved to Stockholm, became a local celebrity on a TV program called "Hyland's Corner," and met rock-and-roller—and husband-to-be—Benny Andersen. Up to this point, Frida had been a singer in what she described as a "traditional" mold, influenced by the likes of Ella Fitzgerald and Peggy Lee. "Benny was responsible for molding my musical taste towards more 'today' sounds," she told *Billboard* in 1979.

Benny had already seen success as frontman of the Hep Stars and as half of the duo Bjorn & Benny, with Bjorn Ulvaeus. Sides by each of these acts were issued in the States, but to only minimal notice. It was not until Benny, Frida, Bjorn, and Bjorn's wife Agnetha Faltskog became Abba that the entire world responded with overwhelming acceptance. In each year of its existence, the group reportedly earned more for the Swedish economy than the entire Volvo car-and-truck operation.

After numerous awards, hit singles, and LP chartings, Abba quietly retired. Frida and Benny were divorced in 1982. The following year, with Phil Collins producing, Frida recorded what would be the first of two albums, *Something Going On* (1982); *Shine* would follow in 1984. "I Know There's Something Going On," featuring Collins' pounding drums, remains Frida's only solo hit to date.

"I'd become stuck in a part working with Abba," she explained to *Record*'s Mark Mehler. "Benny and Bjorn do all the writing, you sing the way they want you to. Now I'm using my voice in a new, tougher way. I'm singing out. I'm not so afraid of giving it a little more from down here."

Dexy's Midnight Runners
COME ON EILEEN
(Kevin Rowland, Jim Paterson, Kevin Adams)
Mercury 76189
No. 1 *April 23, 1983*

In England, they were stars for three years. They had ten hits in their homeland; four of these went top 10. Only three LPs were issued while Dexy's Midnight Runners were the rage, but with each album a new image was utilized,

and a new group was needed to accompany the volatile Kevin Rowland.

Dexy's Midnight Runners were a Birmingham-based band. Lead singer/guitarist Rowland (b. Aug. 17, 1953, Wolverhampton) was the brains behind the operation. He and Al Archer had initially started in the music world as New Wavers in Lucy & The Lovers and another group called the Killjoys. The latter issued one single on Raw Records, "Johnny Won't Get To Heaven," in 1977. Then it was over, and the two were off to plan phase one of Dexy's Midnight Runners, a name they apparently derived from "dexedrine," a widely-used amphetamine.

At this point, the Runners were a soul band dedicated to the sounds of American acts like Sam & Dave and James Brown. They had a "look" that can best be described as straight out of Martin Scorsese's *Mean Streets*. They were tough, and their horn-filled music definitely ran counter to popular trends. Parlophone Records issued *Searching for the Young Soul Rebels* (1980) and three singles; their R & B–drenched sound sold well.

All the band members then left—except for Rowland and trombonist Jimmy Patterson—due to disagreements over the group's musical direction and which songs to issue as singles. A new Runners line-up—Billy Adams (guitar), Mickey Billingsham (keyboards), Brian Maurice (alto sax), Seb Shelton (drums), Paul Speare (tenor sax), and Steve Wynne (bass)—created *Too-Rye-Ay* (1983), and the chart-topping "Come On Eileen." In dungarees and street-urchin garb, this revamped unit added an Irish-folk tinge to their hard-edged soul style via a fiddle section. "The Celtic Soul Brothers" (#86, 1983) was a moderate mover of a follow-up.

Predictably, by the the third LP, *Don't Stand Me Down* (1985), there was another shift in the group's sound, and everyone left save Mr. Rowland. Dexy's new image was described by Ira Robbins in the *Trouser Press Record Guide* as "conservative pinstripes," and the music itself deemed "a torpid snore."

Kevin resurfaced three years later. His solo LP *The Wanderer* and its accompanying singles charted neither here nor in England.

After the Fire

DER KOMMISSAR

Epic 03559
(R. Ponger, Falco)
No. 5 *April 30, 1983*

Apparently, After the Fire is now little more than scattered ashes. Nothing has been heard from the foursome from East London and Essex since *ATF* (1982), the stateside album that featured a solitary hit single, "Der Kommissar."

Before the Fire flickered out, they consisted of a Mr. Memory Banks (synthesizer), Pete King (drums), Andy Piercy (lead vocals, bass), and John Russell (guitar). They all met in the post-punk late '70s. An EP issued on Rapid, their garage label, caught the attention of the big-money wielders at British CBS. The ATF sound was lacking in extended solos, flash, and pomposity, but CBS liked the group's respect for traditional Anglo-rock, their Beatles-like energy, and the splashes of Yes, Genesis, and 10cc that colored their music. This was a band that corporate types could appreciate, and maybe market.

Three fairly well-received LPs were issued in England from 1979 to 1982 before the CBS label's American affiliate saw fit to release *ATF*, a compilation of the more "commercial" sides from the British album releases. "Der Kommissar" was an English-language version of a song by German artist Falco; the single, the album, and a follow-up 45, "Dancing In The Shadows" (#85, 1983), all sold well. Reportedly, After the Fire disbanded shortly thereafter.

Thomas Dolby

SHE BLINDED ME WITH SCIENCE

(T. Dolby, J. Kerr)
Capitol 5204
No. 5 *May 14, 1983*

"**I** think it's the most meaningless song I've ever written," Thomas Dolby, the techno-pop geek behind "She Blinded Me With Science," told *Creem*'s Michael Goldberg. "It's about a sort of fuddy-duddy old scientist who gets obsessed with his lab assistant. When I made that song, it was with the thought in my head that . . . people were finding my music too demanding and that maybe I should let loose and make a record that was basically nonsense like everything else on the charts. And it's just a sad reflection on the state of things that it was that successful."

He was born Thomas Morgan Dolby Robertson, in Cairo, Egypt, on October 14, 1958. Papa was an archeologist, so little Tom's travels to and from obscure terrain were constant. He was in and out of boarding schools and piano lessons. When he could, he would tinker with ham radios and electronics, and soon developed interests in film production, meteorology, and computer programming. He dropped out of formal schooling to putter with a four-track tape player, and he took his homemade sytheszier to the streets of Paris, where he played Dylan tunes and passed the hat.

With his homemade PA system, Tom began traveling with several New Wave acts, mixing for the Fall, the Members, the Passions, and the U.K. Subs. In short order, Dolby become known to his peers as something of an electronics whiz. He recorded with the Thompson Twins, SW9, and Low Noise; joined Bruce Woolley & The Camera Club, producing their *English Garden* (1979) LP; and toured with Lene Lovich, writing and producing her European mini-hit, "New Toy."

After recording a few singles for Armageddon and Happy Birthday Records, Dolby formed his own EMI-distributed Venice In Peril label, issuing his first album—*The Golden Age of Wireless* (1982)—plus two British hit singles, "Europa And The Pirate Twins" and "Windpower." During this time, he also guested with his keyboards on LP projects by Joan Armatrading, Def Leppard, Andy Partridge's Fallout Club, Foreigner, and M. With the release of his "most meaningless song," Dolby was in public demand, and began performing as a one-man music-making entity— complete with computers, keyboards, tape machines, and video slides.

Thomas' *Blinded by Science* (1983), *The Golden Age of Wireless* (1983), and *The Flat Earth* (1984) albums all sold well, as did "Europa And The Pirate Twins" (#67, 1983) and "Hyperactive" (#62, 1984). Dolby continued to work sessions for the likes of Adele Bertel, Malcolm McLean, Joni Mitchell, Prefab Sprout, and Whodini. He appeared at the 1985 Grammy Awards ceremony with Herbie Hancock and Stevie Wonder; played keyboards for David Bowie's "Live Aid" performance; and created the movie scores for *Gothic* (1986) and *Howard the Duck* (1986). Recording as Dolby's Cube, he and funkmaster George Clinton have cut a few singles together.

Dolby's fourth album, *Aliens Ate My Buick* (1988)—and "Airhead," his first 45 in four years—appeared in 1988. The LP featured the unlikely musical aid of Ed Asner and Robin Leach. When last spotted, Thomas was engaged in the act of marrying "Dynasty" star Kathleen Beller.

Kajagoogoo
TOO SHY
EMI-America 8161
(Limahl, Nick Beggs, Kajagoogoo)
No. 5 *July 9, 1983*

At the start of the '80s, Kajagoogoo started a trend in England called Googoomania. Thank goodness for the waters that divide us: by the time these weird-lookin' pretty boys made it to the States, their number-one GooGoo was preparing to be gonegone.

In 1980, four guys from Leighton Buzzard, England—Steve Askew (guitar), Nick Beggs (bass), Stuart Croxford Neale (keyboards, synthesizers), and Jez Strode (drums)—formed Art Nouveau, renamed two years later the Handstands. They played Steely Dan and other off-beat fare in clubs and cabarets. Limahl (real name: Chris Hamill) placed an ad in *Melody Maker* describing himself as "good-looking, talented . . . and looking for four guys with the same qualifications." The Handstands responded, and before long, everyone agreed that some kind of musical magic was happening. A chance encounter with Duran Duran keyboardist Nick Rhodes led to a meeting with the folks at EMI, and soon Rhodes and Duran producer Colin Thurston were walking Kajagoogoo into a recording studio.

As for their bizarre name, Nick Beggs told Debbie Geller of *Record*: "It's like something a child would say. When people say it, they can't quite pronounce it but once they know it, they can never forget it."

Kajagoogoo

"Too Shy" was the first single pulled from Kajagoogoo's debut album, *White Feathers* (1983). A half-dozen singles would eventually chart in Britain. But in 1983, just as extensive plans had been made to spread Googoomania to the land of the free and the home of the brave, Limahl left the band to go solo.

Both Kaja (the "googoo" portion of their monicker was dropped with Limahl's departure) and Limahl have continued their respective careers. Stateside, neither has managed to reconstruct a winning arrangement of sights and sounds.

Taco
PUTTIN' ON THE RITZ
(Irving Berlin)
RCA Victor 13574
No. 4 *September 3, 1983*

Taco Ockerse (b. 1955, Jakarta, Indonesia) was born of Dutch parents. His grandfather was a professional pianist and artist in Indonesia. After settling in Hamburg, little Taco studied body movement, dance, and theater, and was acting in musicals by the mid-'70s. In

1979, he played Chino in a German remake of *West Side Story*. The following year, Mr. T.—in tails and talcum—was working night spots with his own group, Taco's Bizz. A portion of his act involved updating nostalgic numbers like the Irving Berlin evergreen "Puttin' On The Ritz."

Late in 1981, with the aid of arranger/multi-instrumentalist Werner Lang, Taco cut "Puttin' On The Ritz" and other reworked oldies for his debut LP, *Taco After Eight* (1983). Nearly a year passed before Taco's tune was tasted by the German public. "I tried everything [including acting out the song as part of a computer music program at a department store] to get it going," Taco told *Cashbox*. Finally, Germany, Austria, Yugoslavia, and a number of other countries took a transitory liking to Taco's take on Berlin's timeless tune.

To date, "Cheek To Cheek" and similar auditory excavations have fared poorly.

Frank Stallone
FAR FROM OVER
(Frank Stallone, Vince DiCola)
RSO 815023
No. 10 *October 1, 1983*

Frank Stallone, as his name would suggest, is the younger brother of Sylvester Stallone. The Philadelphia kid began dashing off lyrics when a mere lad of 14. After high school, Stallone moved to New York City to share an apartment with his brother, an aspiring actor. Years of odd jobs (like selling shirts in Bloomingdale's) and singing stints in seedy clubs followed before Frank's group, Valentine, got a shot at recording an album's worth of material. The debut disk sold poorly, and Valentine split up.

Frank continued with his vocalizing, and garnered a big break singing *a cappella* in Sly's first *Rocky* flick (1976). "Case Of You" (#67, 1980), a single on the Scotti Brothers label, was Frank's first chart dent. Perspiration and persistence paid off three years later when Stallone's "Far From Over"—an extraction from the soundtrack of *Staying Alive* (1983), Sly's athletic sequel to *Saturday Night Fever*—was issued as a single.

"No one gave me anything, I had to submit the songs like everybody else," Stallone insisted to *Cashbox*. "Just tell people to listen to [my stuff], to give me a fair chance—just give it a good listen and don't judge me by my brother. We're two different people."

Big Country

IN A BIG COUNTRY
(Big Country)
Mercury 814467
No. 17 *December 3, 1983*

"**B**ig Country is not punk, New Wave, heavy metal, progressive, or pop," Stuart Adamson, the group's lead singer/guitarist and frontman, remarked to *Creem*. Some critics heard traces of Celtic folk tunes in Big Country's music, and many pop pundits put the group in a class with the Alarm and U2. And on an auditory landscape of synthesizer washes and electronic rhythm machines, the bagpipe-like droning of Big Country's twin lead guitars defiantly stood out.

Adamson (b. Apr. 11, 1958, Manchester, England) was raised in Dunfermline, Scotland, and schooled in Scottish folk music. "There would always be folks around on Friday and Saturday night, after the pubs had shut," he told *Record*'s Adrian Thrills. "There would be guys up there playing guitars, bagpipes, accordions, and fiddles, so some of the things I write go right back to then."

He began writing songs when he was 12. From 1977 to 1981, Stuart played in a punk group with Eddie Jobson called the Skids. Virgin Records issued five albums, and nine of the Skids' singles charted in England (none of these were released in the U.S.). When the group split up, Jobson went on to form the Armoury Show, and Adamson returned home to Scotland.

Dunfermline—the burial place of seven Scottish kings—is also where the British Navy docks its nuclear submarines. Guitarist Bruce Watson (b. Mar. 11, 1961, Ontario, Canada) was scrubbing out those subs when he met Stuart. Both were ready to form a band, but it had to be something different. Together, Stuart and Bruce developed a distinctive twin-guitar sound beneath a community pool hall. When they felt ready, they took Big Country out on the road in support of Alice Cooper. Disappointed with the response, they disbanded, and the two returned to the basement for further practice.

Chris Briggs—an A & R man with the British Phonogram label who had worked with ABC, Def Leppard, and Dire Straits—knew of Adamson from his Skids days and invited him and Watson to London to record some demos. Briggs hooked the twosome up with drummer Mark Brzezicji (b. June 21, 1957, London) and bassist Tony Butler (b. Feb. 13, 1957, London). The four had met earlier: Mark and Tony had played with Simon Townsend's On The Air, an act that had once opened for the Skids. When Briggs located them, Mark was doing TV jingle sessions, and Butler had briefly played bass for the Pretenders.

"Something just clicked," Adamson recalled to *Rolling Stone*'s James Henske. "It was magic right from the start." Briggs signed the group on the spot, and ushered Big Country into a studio with producer Chris Thomas. The resulting album was *Harvest Home* (1982), a disappointing effort which nonetheless attracted critical attention. Producer Steve Lillywhite was brought in, and with the second LP, *The Crossing* (1983), everything jelled. The album went gold in the U.S., and featured "In A Big Country" and "Fields Of Fire" (#52, 1984).

Big Country had an extended run of British and European hits. *Wonderland* (1984), *Steeltown* (1984), and *The Seer* (1986) followed, but except for "Wonderland" (#86, 1984), no other Big Country sides ever again appeared on the American pop listings.

Peter Schilling

MAJOR TOM (COMING HOME)
(Peter Schilling, David Lodge)
Elektra 69811
No. 14 *December 24, 1983*

Some have called him a shameless Bowie impersonator, a charge based on the thematic similarity of "Major Tom" to Bowie's 1973 hit, "Space Oddity." "It's definitely not from Bowie, except the title, and the figure of Major Tom," Schilling declared to *Melody Maker*'s Paul Rider. "I was inspired to write the song by a film in 1968 called *Danger on the Moon*, with Gregory Peck [1969's *Marooned*?]."

Schilling (b. Jan. 28, 1956, Stuttgart, Germany) grew up listening to the Beatles and the Stones. He took up playing folk guitar, served in the army, and upon his return, worked for some music publishers and WEA Records. Some of his tunes were recorded by others; a few singles bearing his own name were shipped. In 1981, Peter became friends with a guitarist and the co-writer of many of his tunes, Armin Sabol. Schilling's debut LP, *Error in the System* (1983)—featuring his much-panned but entertaining hit—was first issued in Germany, and did not appear in the U.S. until nearly a year later.

Peter still continues to record, and has shown his skills at pessimism and electric protest with such items as "The Noah Play" and "Silent Night." The latter is worth a holiday listen. "I hate that Christmas song," Schilling told *Illinois Entertainer*'s Jeff Tamarkin. "I'm glad that my version got some negative reaction from some Christians because I want to say to them that it's not a holy night and a silent night; everything is not well."

Jump 'n The Saddle Band

THE CURLY SHUFFLE
(Peter Quinn)
Atlantic 89718
No. 15 *January 21, 1984*

"There hadn't been a novelty hit like 'The Curly Shuffle' for ten years," Saddle Band man T.C. Furlong said in an exclusive interview. "You know why it was a hit, even though it started on a basement label with no distribution? It was genuine. It was a tribute to Curly and the Three Stooges, and we meant it."

T.C. (steel guitar, electric guitar) and Pete Quinn (lead vocals, harmonica) formed a country bar band in 1974 with Jack Burchall and Don Bains. For three years they were Rio Grande, until Bains and Burchall quit and took the name with them. T.C. and Pete added Barney

Schwartz (guitar) and Ann Schwartz (bass), changed their repertoire slightly, and began calling themselves the Jump 'n The Saddle Band. The line-up fluctuated: Vince Dee (drums, vocals), Don Sternberg (fiddle, guitar), and Tom "Shoes" Trinka (sax) joined up, then Sternberg departed. He was briefly replaced by Dan Parks (fiddle, guitar), who then left to work with Dickie Betts and Mel Tillis.

"We came up with this 'Curly Shuffle' song. Pete just brought it in to a rehearsal—we knew it was good. So we recorded it and put it out as a single [the first for both the band and Chicago's Acme Recording Studio] and it was literally passed around from radio station to radio station.

"Atlantic had heard what a hot item the single was. They picked up its distribution and signed the band and asked us to make an album. It was all over, one, two, three. We did the *Jump 'n The Saddle Band* [1984] LP and one more single.

"We walked into a production meeting with the president of Atlantic Records and the head of A & R. 'Curly Shuffle' is on the charts, but they don't even know the name of the band. They were introducing us around as the Curly Shuffle Boys. So the president sits down with us and says, 'What have we got here? The Three Stooges? Fine. You guys are the creative geniuses—come up with a Marx Brothers song.'

"We told 'em we did 'Curly' as a homage; it

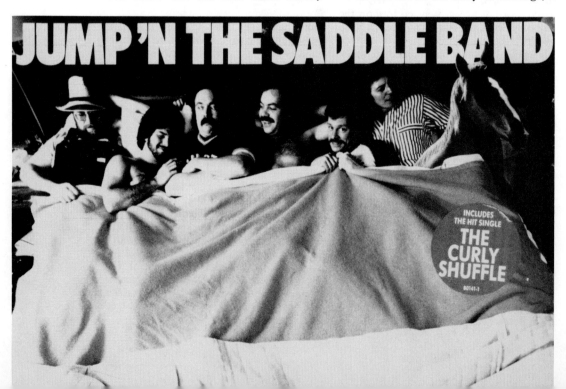

would be impossible to manufacture another one. So he says, 'Here's what you're gonna do: you're gonna do Benny Bell's "Shaving Cream."' So we did record 'Shaving Cream' big-band style, but Atlantic hated it and wouldn't issue it. I don't think they liked our last verse. The last line of each verse goes, 'I stepped in a big pile of . . . shaving cream, shaving cream.' Well, we changed the last verse to 'Atlantic wanted us to record a hit/We sent them a big pile of . . . shaving cream, shaving cream.' They had no sense of humor. We alienated the company, but at that point, we didn't give a . . . shaving cream.

"They put out 'It Should Have Been Me' from the album, and that was it for the band. We're still active and on the circuit—no records and no more tapes, though."

Shannon

LET THE MUSIC PLAY
(Chris Barbosa, Ed Chisholm)
Mirage 99810
No. 8 *February 25, 1984*

When success struck her like a bolt of lightning, Shannon Greene (b. 1958, Washington, D.C.) was a Brooklynite and a student at York University. She was majoring in accounting with a minor in music, and had taken years of formal voice and dance lessons. A few of her music professors insisted that she give music-making a serious try. Emergency Records believed in her, too, and in the fall of 1983 they released her debut disk, an extended play of a spunky little tune called "Let The Music Play."

"I always knew that it was possible," she told *Billboard*, "but I didn't know if I wanted to do it so soon." Mirage, a subsidiary of Atlantic Records, acquired her contract and the rights to "Let The Music Play." It was a huge hit, a catchy pulsating thing, surely just the first outing for a major new artist. "Give Me Tonight" (#46, 1984) and "Do You Wanna Get Away" (#49, 1985) were her sole Hot 100 hits, but numerous Shannon 45s have charted on *Billboard*'s R & B listings: "My Heart's Divided" (—/#48, 1984), "Stronger Together" (—/#26, 1985), "Urgent" (—/#68, 1985), and "Prove Me Right" (—/#82, 1986).

Only her debut album—*Let the Music Play* (1984)—struck pay dirt, however, and despite the issuance of fine funky numbers, Ms. Greene has yet to return to the nation's top 40.

Nena

99 LUFTBALLONS
(Joem Fahrenkrog-Peterson, Carlo Karges)
Epic 04108
No. 2 *March 3, 1984*

In 1980, lead singer Gabriela Susanne "Nena" Kerner (b. Hagen, W. Germany), drummer Rolf Brendel, and keyboardist Uwe Fahren-krog-Peterson were members of a fairly successful band called Stripes. Their self-titled CBS LP was selling decently in West Germany when the three Blondie protegés decided to split for the bright Berlin bar scene. With the addition in 1982 of bassist Jurgen Demel and guitarist Carlo Karges, both ex-members of a band called Odessa, Stripes became the nouveau Nena. Months of rehearsals and banging around Berlin passed before the band was invited into a recording studio. An innocent-sounding tune, "Nur Getraumt," was extracted from their first Nena album; both the LP and the 45 did quite well.

"99 Luftballons," a pseudo–nuclear-protest song, was the next Nena number issued. A disk jockey at L.A.'s KROQ-FM took a liking to the tune and ran it so often that the group's label decided to release the song in the U.S. Despite the 45's chart-topping success and healthy sales of *99 Luftballons* (1984), Nena's later releases have slipped by without even mini-notices in the States.

KC

GIVE IT UP

(Harry Casey, Deborah Carter)
Meca 1001
No. 18   *March 17, 1984*

In 1978, the times were a-changin' again, and the musical tastes that moved the nation's feet on the disco dance floor were shifting, too. Also present was some friction between the T.K. label and the two founders of KC & The Sunshine Band—Harry Wayne Casey (KC) and Rick Finch, popularizers of that funky, up-beat party music called the "Sunshine Sound" or "Miami Sound." KC and Finch claimed that the T.K. label was being lax in promoting their current output.

Despite the chart-topping success of the group's "Please Don't Go," KC, Finch, and the Sunshine name moved over to Epic Records early in 1980. Over the next few years, two LPs—*The Painter* (1981) and *All in a Night's Work* (1982)—plus a spray of singles were issued. Nothing charted in the States, and the two Sunshine boys separated. Casey issued *Space Cadet* (1982), his first solo album, though he had already made the Hot 100 duetting with Teri DeSario on "Yes, I'm Ready" (#2, 1980) and "Dancin' In The Streets" (#66, 1980).

In January 1982, Harry Casey was seriously injured in a head-on car crash. All feeling was lost on one side of his body as the result of nerve damage, and he spent over a year recuperating and learning to walk again.

Meanwhile, "Give It Up," an extract from *All in a Night's Work*, rose to the number-one slot in England. When Epic refused to issue the single in the U.S., Casey negotiated an end to his contract and formed his own Meca label. "Give It Up" was quickly released in the United States as a KC solo. It did quite well, but to this date, it remains the only solo effort by the former dance king to make the listings.

KC has referred to his music simply as "the happy sound." Its roots, he has freely admitted, are to be found in a form of Bahamian pop

music called junkanoo, which he first heard at Clarence "Blowfly" Reid's wedding in January 1973. "[The Junkanoo Rhythm Band] played all these percussion instruments," K.C. told *Circus*. "They were pounding steel drums and gut-covered instruments and clanging cow-bells and blowing whistles. The vibrations were just unbelievable." Within months of Reid's wedding, Rick Finch and KC had forged their Westernized work-up of that Bahamian pop style. Starting with "Get Down Tonight," nearly everything the two recorded from 1975 to 1980 made the pop charts.

"Weird Al" Yankovic

EAT IT

(Michael Jackson, Al Yankovic)
Rock 'n' Roll 04374
No. 12   *April 14, 1984*

Al Yankovic was a childhood accordion player. By high school, however, he wanted to answer the call of the big beat. "I really wanted to get into rock and roll," Weird Al told *Illinois Entertainer*'s Jeff Mintz, "but I was having a hard time convincing my friends to let me join their band. Accordion just wasn't considered part of that rock and roll sound. So I just started doing off-the-wall things with the accordion. Every time I'd sit down to write a straight-ahead rock song or a serious ballad, I'd have it come out a little warped."

By Al's 15th year, someone had turned him on to "The Dr. Demento Show," a radio outlet for pop music's most bizarre recordings. "I sent Dr. Demento a couple of songs [a parody of Queen's "Another One Bites The Dust" entitled "Another One Rides The Bus" and a take-off on "You Don't Bring Me Flowers" called "You Don't Take Showers"] on a really cheap little cassette tape I recorded in my friend's bedroom," he told Mintz. "To my amazement, the Doctor played it on the radio."

A few years later, as an architecture student at California Polytechnic State University, Al got the notion to poke some fun at the Knack's monster hit "My Sharona," renamed "My Bologna." "It was recorded in the bathroom across the hall from my campus radio station," Al told Bob Shannon and John Javna in *Behind the Hits*. "I was recording it strictly for airplay on 'The Dr. Demento Show.'" When the Knack made a concert stop at his college, Al got backstage and played the group his tape. The guys thought the parody was great and introduced Mr. Yankovic to the V.P. at their label. "Capitol Records heard the song and decided to put it out as a single . . . They put out the original bathroom recording."

After graduation from college, Yank was ready to unleash scads of equally inspired wacko wonders. There were a bunch of food-for-thought parodies: "Spameater" ("Maneater"), "Avocado" ("Desperado"), and, of course, Al's biggest send-up—his reworking of Michael Jackson's "Beat It."

"[In 1983] we approached Michael Jackson and gave him the first chorus that we'd written and asked him what he'd think of us doing this song. He was very open to it, so I wrote out the entire song and sent it to him and he gave us his final approval. He was really nice about the whole thing."

Weird Al's silliness has mocked TONI BASIL's "Mickey" ("Ricky," #63, 1983), the Police's "King Of Pain" ("King Of Suede," #62, 1984), Greg Kihn's "Jeopardy" ("I Lost On Jeopardy,"

#81, 1984), and Madonna's "Like A Virgin" ("Like A Surgeon," #47, 1985). All of these off-the-wall send-ups were produced by Rick Derringer, who also played the manic guitar break on "Eat It." Yancovic's first film appearance was in *UHF* in 1989.

Tracey Ullman
THEY DON'T KNOW
(Kristy MacColl)
MCA 52347
No. 8 *April 28, 1984*

Tracey Ullman (b. May 25, 1959) was born in the London suburb of Hackbridge. Her father died when she was six. "We had it hard," Ullman explained to the *Chicago Sun Times'* Ernest Tucker. "But we did everything for a laugh." Her mother encouraged her to sing, to

dance, to mimic. She attended the Italia Conti School for four years, but claims she was expelled. Soon after, she was appearing on British TV and performing in productions of *Grease* and *The Rocky Horror Picture Show*. In 1981, at the tender age of 21, she received the London Theatre Critics Award for her performance in the improvisational play, *Four in a Million*. This led to the BBC series "Three of a Kind," which established her as a TV star in Britain.

In rapid succession, Tracey appeared in Paul McCartney's *Give My Regards to Broad Street* (1984); played the part of Alice Park, the beat bohemian, in the Meryl Streep flick *Plenty* (1985); and recorded *You Broke My Heart in 17 Places* (1984), her first pop effort. Three singles from that '60s-sounding LP made the British charts. Thus far, only Tracey's retooling of IRMA THOMAS' "Breakaway" (#70, 1984) has managed to join "They Don't Know" on *Billboard*'s stateside Hot 100.

"I made that [album] as a lark, really," Ullman told *Spin*'s Glenn O'Brien. "I can't hold a note or hold a tune and it was good fun. But it was a joke that became successful. It was the old Midas touch. I was doing everything. When I go into a record store, I always look for it in the bargain bin."

In the meantime, Ullman made her U.S. TV series debut in "The Tracey Ullman Show" on the Fox Network in April 1987. Critics haved cheered, and the industry itself has decorated the vehicle with five Emmy nominations. She also appeared with Kevin Kline in the comedy *I Love You To Death* (1990).

Ollie & Jerry

BREAKIN' . . . THERE'S NO STOPPING US
(Ollie Brown, Jerry Knight)
Polydor 821708
No. 9 *August 4, 1984*

They met seemingly countless times on tours and at recording sessions. Both Ollie Brown (drums, vocals) and Jerry Knight (guitar, vocals) were born and raised in Detroit, and both eventually found themselves caught up in the Ray Parker, Jr., success story. They played for a while in Parker's Raydio, and Jerry even sang lead on the group's chart-shakin' debut, "Jack And Jill" (#8, 1978).

In the early '80s, Jerry repeatedly made the R & B charts as a solo act. His tunes were successfully recorded by such acts as Atlantic Starr, Philip Bailey, George Duke, and the Whispers. Ollie, meanwhile, worked and produced sessions, most notably for Patti Austin, Klique, and the Rolling Stones.

In 1983, Brown was conferring with Polydor's Russ Regan when the offer was made to work up material for the breakdancing flick, *Breakin'* (1984). "They asked me to get started on this fast," Ollie told *Billboard*'s Steve Ivory. "The movie had already been shot and they showed me the footage. The first thing one of the dancers said was 'They can't stop us.' I introduced that line to Jerry, and he went crazy with it."

Ollie & Jerry's "Breakin' . . . There's No Stopping Us" was the first single issued from Polydor's platinum-selling *Breakin'* soundtrack (1984). "Actually, we were writing that song about us," Knight admitted to *Billboard*. "The music business is full of hardships. It may be the title track of the movie, but we can relate to it."

In an attempt to do it once again, Ollie & Jerry scored some tracks for *Breakin' 2: Electric Boogaloo* (1984). Their title tune took off, as did the film's soundtrack album.

Scandal featuring Patty Smyth

THE WARRIOR
(Holly Knight, Nick Gilder)
Columbia 04424
No. 7 *September 22, 1984*

Zack and Patty met in 1982. They argued.

Guitarist Zack Smith (b. Westport, Conn.) had played with Dee Murray and Davey Johnston, Elton John's sidemen. In 1982, Zack had a Big Apple–based band called Scandal, a unit which would eventually consist of bassist Ivan Elias, keyboardist Benji King, and drummer Frankie LaRocka. But something was missing, and that something, Zack surmised, was the presence of a female. After they auditioned 80 or more promising presences, someone suggested Patty Smyth. The audition took so long to set up and was so poorly planned that Zack and Patty's first meeting turned into a heated argument.

Patty (b. June 26, 1957, New York City) was a hard-as-nails rocker who had grown up in Greenwich Village. Her mother was a club manager. "Backstage was my home," Smyth

**Patty Smyth
of Scandal**

told *Creem.* "I was a little kid hanging around while JOHN SEBASTIAN, Dylan, and THE BLUES MAGOOS went out to have their say."

Once the yelling subsided, Patty passed her audition, and the female-fronted Scandal was ready for the world. They toured with Hall & Oates, John Cougar Mellencamp, and the Kinks, and cut the five-tune *Scandal* (1983) EP for Columbia. The group's first two singles— "Goodbye To You" (#65, 1982) and "Love's Got A Line On You" (#59, 1983)—came from what was to become the largest selling mini-album in Columbia Records history. *The Warrior* (1984), the unit's first and only full-length LP, was a huge success, as was the title track (#7,

1984). The two immediate follow-ups— "Hands Tied" (#41, 1984) and "Beat Of A Heart" (#41, 1985)—just missed the nation's top 40 hit parade.

Meanwhile, all was not well within the hell-raisin', hard-rockin' group. Zack disappeared, saying he wanted to write and produce. Patty married punk rocker Richard Hell, had a child, and seemed to wave bye-bye to the world of rock and roll.

After three years, the label shipped *Never Enough* (1987), Patty's debut solo effort, plus a stack of 45s. The waxings presented a mellower woman and met with mixed reviews.

"You can't keep doing the same things when

you get married and have a family," Smyth told Dennis Hunt of the *Los Angeles Times*. "You have to slow down. You have to be responsible. You can be crazy if you only have yourself to worry about. I can't be that way anymore."

Dennis DeYoung
DESERT MOON
(Dennis DeYoung)
A & M 2666
No. 10   *November 11, 1984*

It began as one of those seldom-fulfilled, teen-dream long shots in 1963 in Roseland, Illinois. "John Panozzo [drums] and his brother Chuck [bass] lived across the street from me," said Dennis DeYoung (keyboards, vocals) to *Chicago Soundz's* Joe Ziemba. "We'd always hung around together and played whatever gigs we could get—it was a big deal when we got to do a college dance." They were called the Trade-winds. In 1968, once the threesome was attending Chicago State University and had added fellow student Johnny "J. C." Curulewski on lead guitar, they were simply TW4.

By 1970, Jim "J. Y." Young (guitar) was added, a demo record was cut for RCA's Brian Christian, and Bill Traut—a major force in the forging of '60s Chicago groups like the American Breed, H. P. Lovecraft, and the Shadows of Knight—offered to sign TW4 to his Wooden Nickel label. But first they would have to change their name to something a bit more hip,

like "Styx." (According to Greek mythology, Styx is the river that dead souls are ferried across to reach Hades.)

In rapid succession, Wooden Nickel issued *Styx I* (1972) and *Styx II* (1973). Both albums met a luke-warm response, but the latter LP did include what would become the first of 13 top 40 hits. Following "Lady" (#6, 1975), Styx—with DeYoung as lead singer—switched to A & M and clicked with such pop-radio memorables as "Come Sail Away" (#8, 1978), "Babe" (#1, 1979), "The Best Of Times" (#3, 1979), and "Mr. Roboto" (#3, 1983). Styx toured to sold-out concerts and scored big with albums like *The Grand Illusion* (1977), *Pieces of Eight* (1978), *Cornerstone* (1979), *Paradise Theatre* (1981), and *Kilroy Was Here* (1983). Of their 14 LPs, 27,000,000 copies were sold in all: 4 went triple platinum, 2 double platinum, and 1 gold.

"After *Kilroy*, we decided to do a live album and then to take some time off," DeYoung, the group's primary songwriter, told Joe Ziemba. "After 14 albums in 12 years, it was time to pursue other things . . . time for a period of growth." J.Y. Young, Tommy Shaw (b. Montgomery, Ala.; Curulewski's replacement as of 1976), and DeYoung have since pursued solo careers, the latter two with some success. In addition to his "Desert Moon" and the LP from which it was pulled—*Desert Moon* (1984)—DeYoung has appeared on the Hot 100 with "Don't Wait For Heroes" (#83, 1984), "Call Me" (#54, 1986), and "This Is The Time" (#93, 1986), the latter from *The Karate Kid Part II* (1986).

Artist Index

Song Index

The Runners-Up: More One-Hit Wonders

The following artists had only one top 40 hit, but that record peaked at position #21–40 on the pop charts.

Adams, Johnny
Afternoon Delight
Alexander, Arthur
Allan, Davie, & The Arrows
Allen, Deborah
Allen, Steve
Allison, Gene
Aquatones
Arms, Russell
Ashton, Gardner & Dyke
Avant-Garde

Backus, Jim, and Friend
Balance
Balloon Farm
Banks, Darrell
Barbour, Keith
Barnum, H. B.
Barry & The Tamerlanes
Barry, Joe
Bartley, Chris
Bell, Benny
Bell, Madeline
Bell, Vincent
Bellus, Tony
Belvin, Jessie
Black Oak Arkansas
Black, Cilla
Blanchard, Jack, & Misty Morgan
Bloodrock
Blue Haze
Blue Jays
Bond, Johnny
Boney M
Bram Tchaikovsky

Braun, Bob
Briley, Martin
Brood, Herman
Brown's Tunetoppers, Al
Brown, Boots, & His Blockbusters
Brown, Buster
Brown, Chuck, & The Soul Searchers
Brown, Nappy
Brown, Roy
Brown, Shirley
Brubeck Quartet, Dave
Bryant Combo, Ray
Buchanan Brothers
Buggles
Bull & The Matadors
Bullet
Burnette, Dorsey
Busch, Lou, & His Orchestra
Busters

Cain, Tane
Cale, J. J.
Campbell, Jo Ann
Cannibal & The Headhunters
Capaldi, Jim
Carefrees
Cargill, Henson
Cash, Rosanne
Cashman & West
Castleman, Boomer
Cat Mother & The All Night News Boys
Cate Brothers
Cavaliere, Felix
C. Company featuring Terry Nelson
Celebration featuring Mike Love
Cerrone
Change
Chanson
Charles, Sonny

Haircut One Hundred
Hall, Jimmy
Halos
Hamilton, Bobby
Harris, Betty
Harris, Eddie
Harris, Emmylou
Harris, Sam
Hawkins, Ronnie
Hawley, Deane
Heatherton, Joey
Hefti, Neal
Hendricks, Bobby
Henhouse Five Plus Two
Hesitations
Hill, Bunker
Hill, Jessie
Holland, Amy
Holland, Eddie
Holliday, Jennifer
Horne, Jimmy "Bo"
Hotlegs
Houston, David
Hughes, Fred
Hugo & Luigi Chorus
Humphrey, Paul, & His Cool Aid Chemists

Icicle Works
Illusion
Independents
Innocence
Intrigues
Iron Butterfly
Iron Horse
Irwin, Big Dee

Jackson, J. J.
Jamies
Jaye, Jerry
J. B.'s
Jefferson
Jive Bombers
Jo Jo Gunne
Jo, Sami
JoBoxers
John & Ernest
Johnson, Tom
Jones Girls
Jones, Etta
Jones, Linda
Junior
Just Us

Kasenetz-Katz Singing Orchestra Circus
Kermit
Kilgore, Theola
Kimberly, Adrian
King, Freddie
King, Peggy
Kingsmen
Knight, Frederick
Koffman Quartette, Moe
Kraftwerk

Ladd, Cheryl
Lady Flash
Lai, Francis, & His Orchestra
Laid Back
Lane, Mickey Lee
Larsen/Feiten Band
Lasley, David
Last, James
Lauren, Rod
Laurie Sisters
Lawrence, Eddie
Leaves
Lee, Laura
Lindisfarne
Little Joe & The Thrillers
Little Joey & The Flips
Little Milton
Lost Generation
Loudermilk, John D.
Love
Love & Kisses
Lynn, Gloria

Mabley, Moms
Magic Lanterns
Maharis, George
Majors
Mandrell, Barbara
Mann, Carl
Marchan, Bobby
Mark IV
Martin, Moon
Martin, Trade
Marvelows
Mashmakhan
Mathews, Toby, and Co.
Matthews Southern Comfort
Mayer, Nathaniel, & The Fabulous Twilights
McAnally, Mac
McClain, Alton, & Destiny
McDevitt Skiffle Group, Chas.

McFadden, Bob, & Dor
McGuinn, Clark & Hillman
McLean, Phil
Mello-Tones
Miles, John
Mills, Garry
Mojo Men
Montgomery, Melba
Moore, Bobby, & The Rhythm Aces
Moore, Jackie
Moroder, Giorgio
Mott the Hoople
Mountain
Moving Pictures
Mozart Quintet, Mickey
Myles, Billy

Nash, Graham
Natural Four
Neighborhood
Nero, Peter
Nesmith, Michael, & The
    First National Band
New England
Newbury, Michael
Newman, Jimmy
Nielsen/Pearson
Nite-Liters
Niteflyte
Nitzsche, Jack
Noguez, Jacky, & His Musette Orchestra
North, Freddie
Nova, Aldo
Nu Tornados
Nugent, Ted

Oak
O'Banion, John
O'Dell, Kenny
Odyssey
Original Caste
Orrall, Robert Ellis, with Carlene Carter
Osmond, Little Jimmy
Owens, Buck
Owens, Donnie
Oxo

Pastel Six
Pastels
Patton, Robbie
Patti & The Emblems
Pavone, Rita

Pearl, Leslie
Peebles, Ann
Pendergrass, Teddy
Peppermint Rainbow
Perkins, Tony
Peters, Bernadette
Pets
Phillips, John
Pink Lady
Pixies Three
Point Blank
Prelude
Pride, Charlie
Prism
Proby, P. J.
Pruett, Jeanne

Q
Quaker City Boys

Rainbow
Rambeau, Eddie
Ramrods
Randolph, Boots
Ray, Diane
Ray, James
Redding, Gene
Redeye
Re-Flex
Reid, Clarence
Revels
Reynolds, Lawrence
Rinky Dinks
Road Apples
Robert & Johnny
Rochelle & The Candles
Rockets
Rogers, Timmie "Oh Yeah"
Romeo Void
Roxy Music
Rubettes
Rubicon
Rugbys
Rush
Rushen, Patrice
Ryan, Charlie, & The
    Timberline Riders

Saga
Sager, Carole Bayer
Saint-Marie, Buffy
Salvo, Sammy

San Remo Golden Strings
Sandpebbles
Santos, Larry
Schwartz, Eddie
Scorpions
Sea, Johnny
Seeds
Sellars, Marilyn
Seymour, Phil
Shaw, Tommy
Shells
Sheppard, T. G.
Sherrys
Shirley Trio, Don
Sigler, Bunny
Silver Condor
Silvetti
Simmons, Patrick
Sinclair, Gordon
Singing Dogs
Six Teens
Skyy
Slave
Smith, Frankie
Smith, Jimmy
Smith, Ray
Smith, Verdelle
Smokie
Sneaker
Sopwith Camel
Soul Children
Sounds of Sunshine
Souther, Hillman, Furay Band
Sovine, Red
Spider
Spirit
Spokesmen
Spyro Gyra
Stallion
Stampley, Joe
Starcher, Buddy
Stargard
Starlets
Starr, Randy
Starz
Stein, Lou
Steinman, Jim
Stephenson, Van
Stereos
Stites, Gary
Stone Four, Kirby
Stonebolt

Stookey, Paul
Storm, Billy
Street People
Strong, Barrett
Style Council
Sugarhill Gang
Sunshine Company
Sweathog
Swinging Blue Jeans
Switch
Sylvers, Foster

Talk Talk
Tanega, Norma
Taylor, Bobby, & The Vancouvers
Techniques
Teegarden & Van Winkle
Tempos
Temptations
Ten Years After
Think
Thomas, Ian
Thompson, Kay
Thunderclap Newman
Todd, Nick
Tom Tom Club
Toney, Jr., Oscar
Tony & Joe
Tucker, Tanya
Turbans
Tuxedo Junction
Twisted Sister
Tycoon

Underground Sunshine
Unit Four Plus Two
Upchurch Combo, Phil
Uriah Heep
Utopia

Valenti, John
Valentino, Mark
Valjean
Vanderberg
Vapors
Vaughan, Frankie
Velvets
Venus, Vik
Viscounts
Volumes
Voudouris, Roger

Waikikis
Wailers
Wakelin, Johnny, & The Kinshasa Band
Wammack, Travis
Wanderly, Walter
Ward, Dale
Washington, Baby
Wednesday
Wilcox, Harlow, & The Oakies
Williams, Don
Wilson, Brian
Wilton Place Street Band

Winchester, Jessie
Wind
Wood, Lauren
Wright, Dale

Yellow Balloon

Zadora, Pia
Zager Band, Michael
Zahnd, Ricky, & His Blue Jeaners
Zappa, Frank
Zevon, Warren

About The Author

Wayne Jancik is a psychotherapist in private practice in Chicago. He received a Masters degree in Social Work from Loyola University and a Masters in Social Science from the University of Chicago. His record collection is one of the largest in the country—130,000 albums and singles. Mr. Jancik has written on pop music for *DISCoveries, Goldmine, Sh-Boom, RPM, Record Review, Triad,* the *Illinois Entertainer,* and the *Chicago Daily News.*